AF574509

VINCENT

VAN GOGH

Konecky & Konecky
156 Fifth Ave.
New York, NY 10010

All photographs from the archives of Edita S.A. and Office Du Livre

The authors wish to acknowledge their debt to Marc Edo Tralbaut's *Van Gogh, le Mal aimé*, in the preparation of this work.

ISBN: 1-56852-111-1

Manufactured in France

VINCENT

VAN GOGH

Concept, design and iconography:
Julia, Sophie & Mikaël Ferloni

Editorial direction:
Michel Ferloni & Dominque Spiess

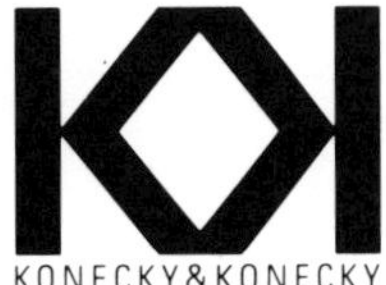
KONECKY&KONECKY

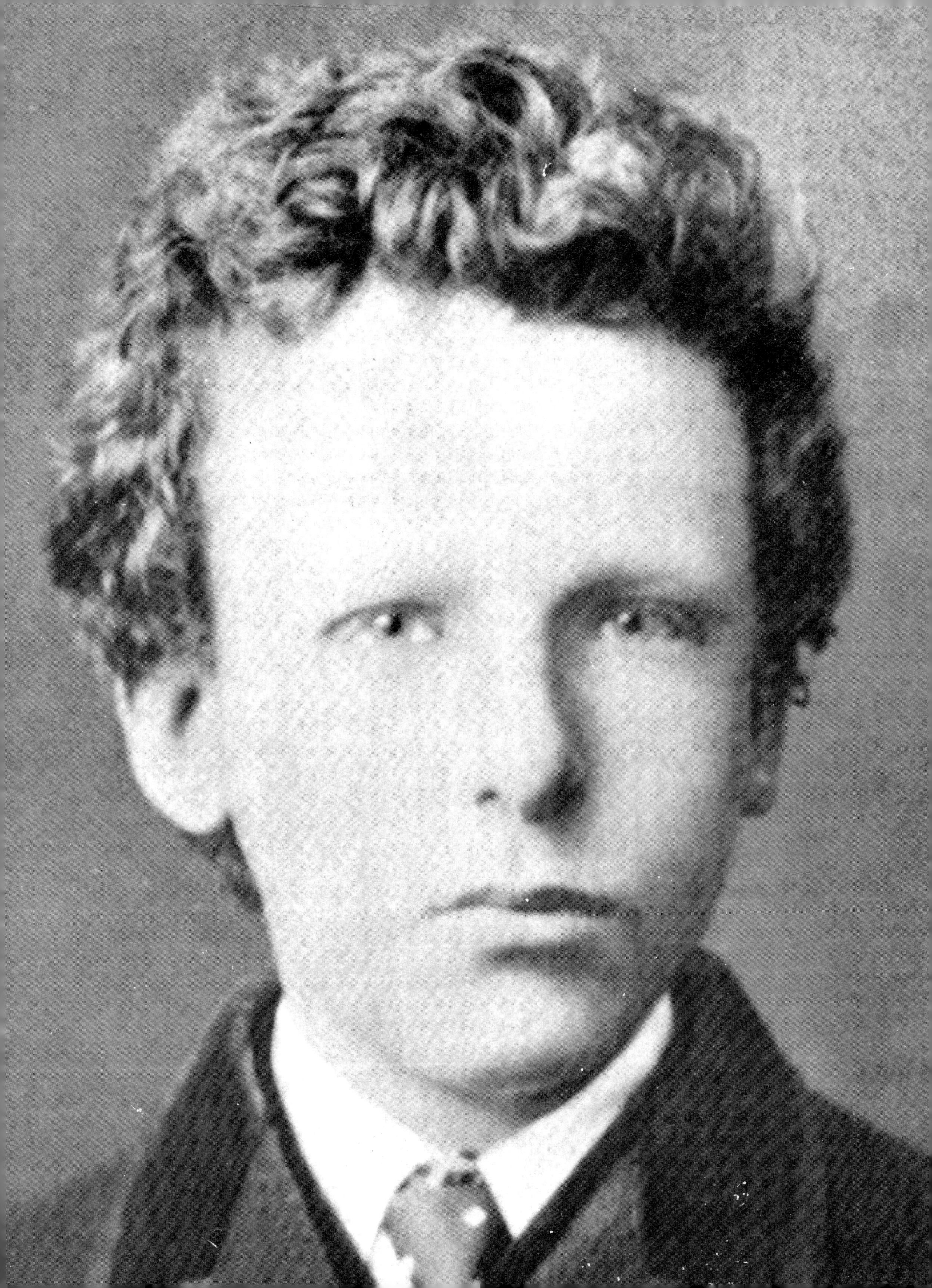

VINCENT, THE CHILD OF SORROW 1853 - 1869

Pastor van Gogh had six sons, of whom the eldest, Hendrik-Vincent, was a bookseller, then an artist. The second, Johannes, be came a Vice-Admiral of the Dutch Navy. The third son, Willem-Daniel, was a government tax inspector. The fourth, Vincent, became a pic ture dealer, the fifth, Theodorus, a pastor, and the sixth, Cornelius-Marinus, was also a picture dealer.

Of these six boys, only Theodorus, the father of Vincent, follow ed his father's example. One of the uncles of the painter, Vincent, who made his career in the art world, had a great influence over his young nephews Vincent- William and Theo.

In 1851, Theodorus married Anne-Cornelia Carbentus. Very artistic, Anne-Cornelia drew and painted in watercolour, mostly plants and flowers. The couple settled in Zundvert, a small village some twenty miles north of Anvers. Eleven months after their marriage, on the 30th March 1852, Vincent-William was born, but unhappily, did not survive.

One year later, day for day, the 30th March 1853, Theodorus van Gogh, still suffering from his loss, called at the town hall in order to register another birth, that of a male child, who was also to be called Vincent- William, and who arrived on the same date as the first.

To understand the personality of the second Vincent, account should be taken of these extraordinary circumstances and the shadow that they could have thrown over the upbringing of a child.

To find the name Vincent van Gogh on a tombstone must have given the child a sudden shock.He discovered that another Vincent had preceded him, and that his position was one of a replacement.

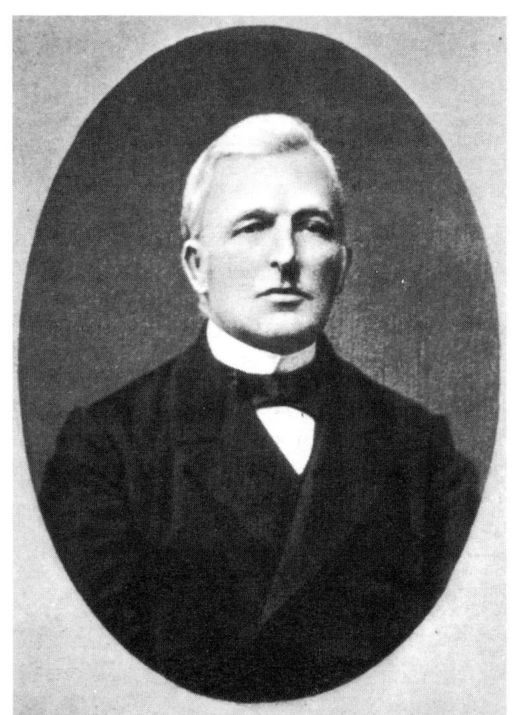

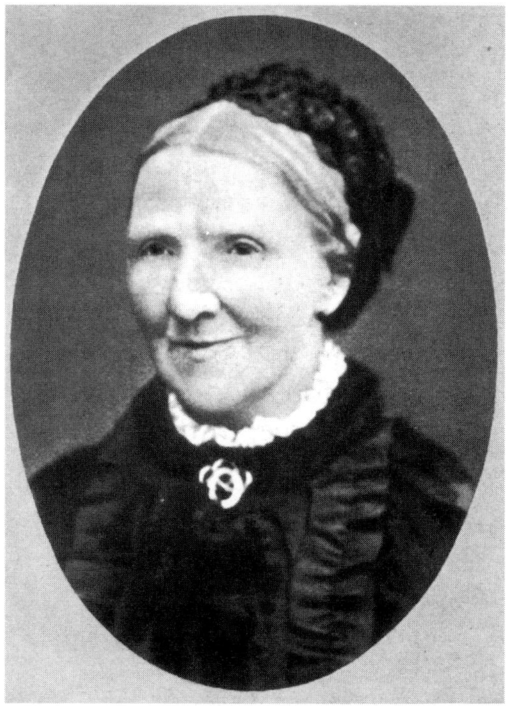

Vincent's parents

On that day, it became obvious to him that the second Vincent van Gogh only existed as a result of the first. As much as to say that he did not exist at all, save as a shadow of another.

Vincent was sent to school in his native village.

"There was something strange about him. He did not behave like a child, and was different from the others. What's more, he behaved badly and was often punished. He was very freckled. His hair was as red as fire. He looked like his mother. He did not stay long at school," said Widow S. Aertsen-Honcoop.

This woman, who worked for a year and a half as a servant to the van Gogh family, was well-placed to see what went on in the family. She found Vincent the least likable of the children, and that he showed little promise. To these memories, it is possible to add that of J. Franken, son of the carpenter who occasionally worked for the van Goghs. He recalled that Vincent would often come to the old craftsman's workshop to work there. He did such good work that the carpenter always spoke of him with praise. When Franken junior worked at the parsonage, Vincent was an onlooker. The Franken boy's information is important, for he certifies that he had seen Vincent not only drawing with a black crayon, but also with colours. From time to time, he even heard the pastor speak of the special attraction his son had for drawing. That the father was pleased by the precocious abilities of his son is not surprising, and one day he even framed a drawing that

Vincent had made at the age of eleven.

In any case, it is certain that Vincent when very young took a lively pleasure in drawing.

His sister Elizabeth recalled that Vincent, then still very young, was given some putty by a painter working at the parsonage, with which he very carefully modelled a small elephant. Johanna van Gogh-Bonger, his sister-in- law, adds to the story the following: when he saw that he had attracted the attention of his parents, he immediately de stroyed what he had done, on the grounds that they attached too much importance to it. Another time, Vincent, who was then about eight years old, astonished his mother by a drawing of a cat climbing in a leafless apple tree, in the winter surroundings of a garden.

The desire to draw

Throughout his life, Vincent was drawn to paint the country side.

At an age when most children hide behind their mothers' skirts, the little Vincent would go off by himself in the garden or the woods, the meadows and fields, to look at the many aspects of nature. A flower bud, or the mysterious movements of a beetle showed him the miracles of creation. It happened that he would stare for hours at whatever moved in the sky or on the land.

The flowers that Vincent painted at Nuenen, to express his sorrow after the death of his father, were executed with the patient, informed precision of a botanist. As for the birds' nests that he showed at Nuenen, they may be described as a naturalist's achievement above all.

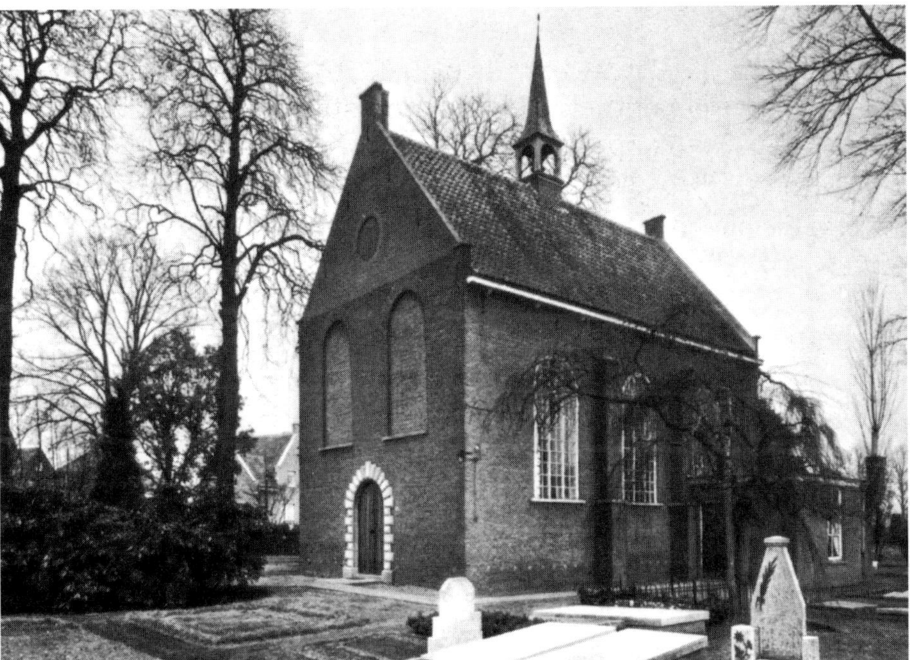

The small church in Zundert where Vincent's brother Vincent-William was buried in 1852

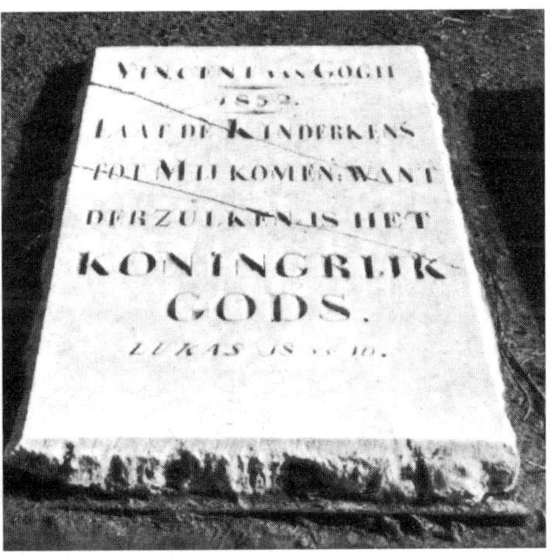

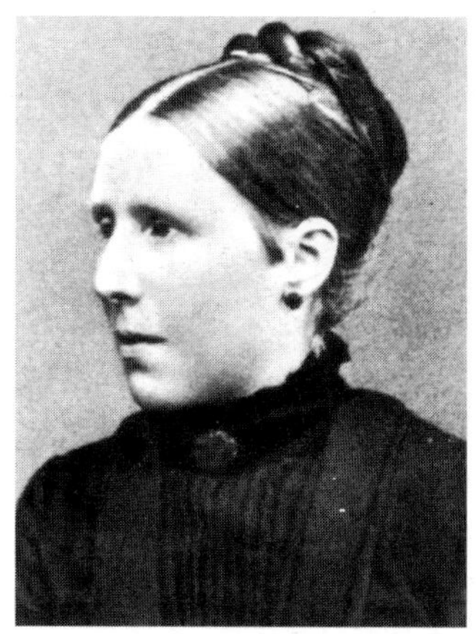

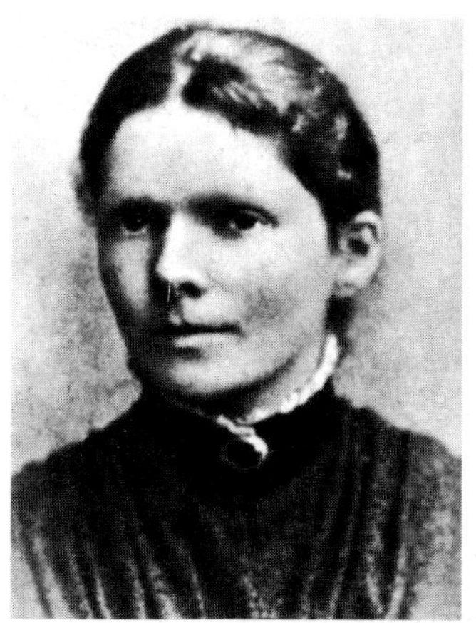

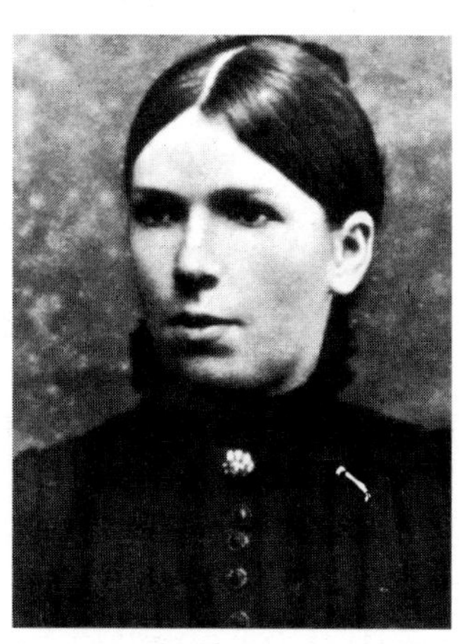

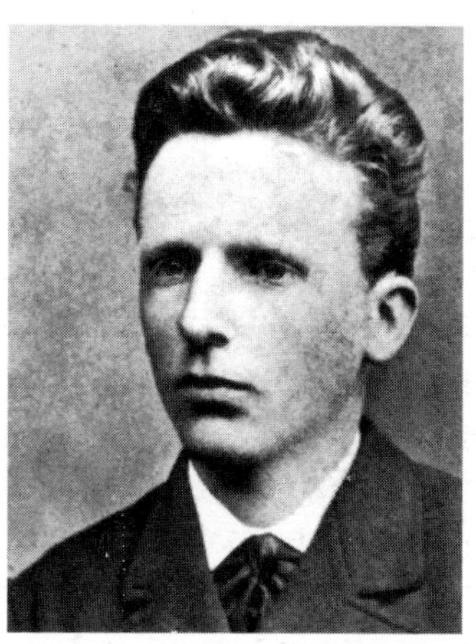

Vincent's brothers and sisters: (above left) Anne-Corneille, (above right) Elisabeth-Huberte (below left) Guillaumette Jacoba, (below right) Corneille-Vincent

It should also be said that during the course of his solitary walks at Zundert, Vincent propped up nests threatened by the wind, just as he saved caterpillars lost on the road.

Stuffed animals also found an echo in his art. They make their appearance in two canvases and a drawing, those of a kingfisher, a green parrot and an owl.

The two years he spent in Paris took place largely under the influence of flowers. The number of still lifes of flowers dating from that period is very considerable. In most cases, emphasis is laid on the beauty of the colours, but also a barely concealed intention to lay bare the botanical details, as a result of old habits, can be detected. Vincent even painted a flowerpot filled with nothing but herbs. On this subject, it is noticeable that purely aesthetic qualities go hand in hand with a remarkable naturalistic observation. Considering his powers of representation, he could have successfully illustrated a botany textbook.

At Arles, Vincent saw again the fruit trees he had always known: pear trees, apple trees, cherry trees; but the sunny climate of the South gave them particulary luminous colours. His discovery of the South brought him novel elements, a refreshment of his artistic vision and a deepening of his naturalistic feelings, to which we owe that superb flowering branch in a glass which, despite its small size, is the work of a great genius.

The revelation of what he called his "Provençal Japan" put him in contact with a vegetation that he did not know: olives, almonds and cypresses. In particular, the masterful *Almond Branch* will be recalled, which could only be the work of an artist devoted to nature from birth.

As for the celebrated sunflowers, Vincent observed them in all their aspects, from their glory to their fading, with their stems curved, or humbly drooping towards the earth.

On October 1st, 1864, Vincent, then eleven, took leave of his family, at least temporarily, for the first time. The pastor and his wife were convinced that their son could learn nothing more at the state school under the care of a schoolmaster who was too often drunk. They had another preoccupation: they wanted to prevent their son from being coarsened by contact with the village children, who were in general stubborn and vulgar. A practical solution came to hand: they sent him to a boarding school run by a Protestant, Jean Provily, at Zevenbergen, some 25 miles from Zundert.

Vincent stayed there two years, up until August 31, 1866. We know little about his time at Tilburg, at the Hannick Institute, where he continued the studies that he may have interrupted at the age of 15.

The house where Vincent was born

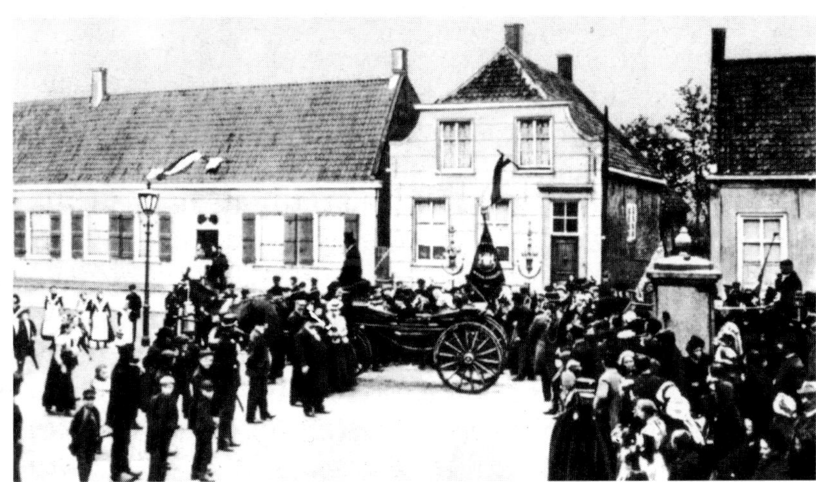

TRADE OR THE MINISTRY : THE CHOICE OF A CAREER 1869 - 1880

Vincent, having finished his schooling, was now faced with choosing a career. In 1869, on the recommendation of his Uncle Cent, Vincent became the youngest employee of the Dutch branch of Goupil & Cie, art dealers, which was situated at the Hague, a few hundred yards from the Mauristhuis with its notable collection of masterpieces.

He was also able to converse frequently with well-known artists who flocked to Goupil; these meetings contributed to the education of the apprentice thirsty for advice.

In his desire to keep himself informed and to extend his knowledge, Vincent went regularly to museums and exhibitions, studying the paintings and drawings that interested him. His letters reveal that his search after information led him to Amsterdam, Brussels, London and Paris when he was barely 19 years old.

Three small books for Betsy

At the Hague, Vincent also became friendly with the H. G. Tersteegs and their children. Tersteeg was his superior at Goupil & Cie, and had an apartment on the premises. Vincent was present for the birth of their first child, Elisabeth, who was born in 1869. They became attached to one another. He made some 40 sketches for her, bound together in three small books. These drawings possess a certain interest for a study of the development of the artist. They reveal, firstly, that naturalistic feeling mentioned in the previous chapter. It is very apparent in 30 of the sketches showing plants and animals, while several other sketches have a direct connection with nature. *An old woman knitting at the window* prefigures one of the subjects which, some years later, was to become especially dear to Vincent. He was to treat this theme then with less simplicity.

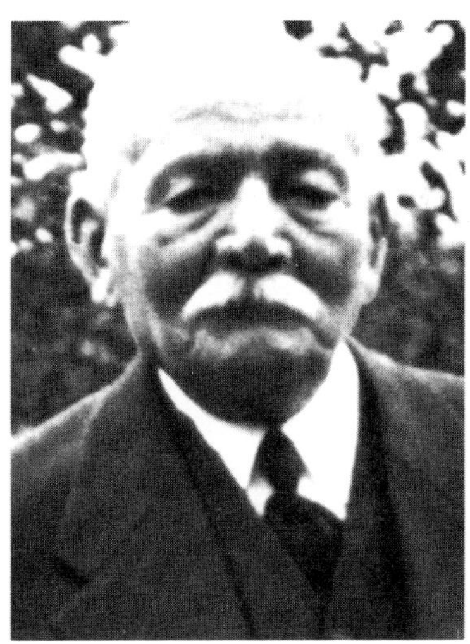

Henry Hoppenbrouwers, childhood friend of Vincent's

Uncle Cent

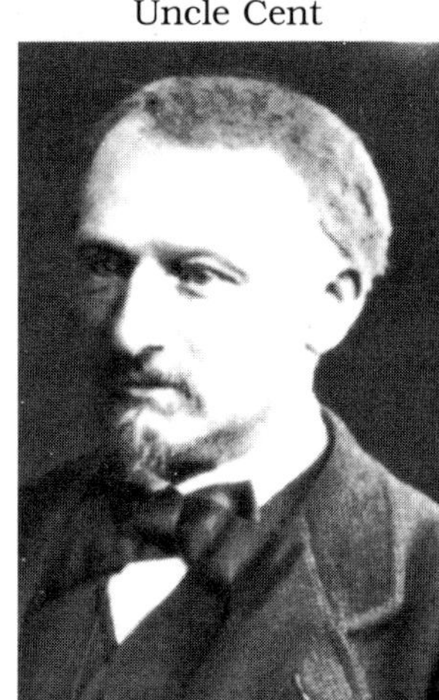

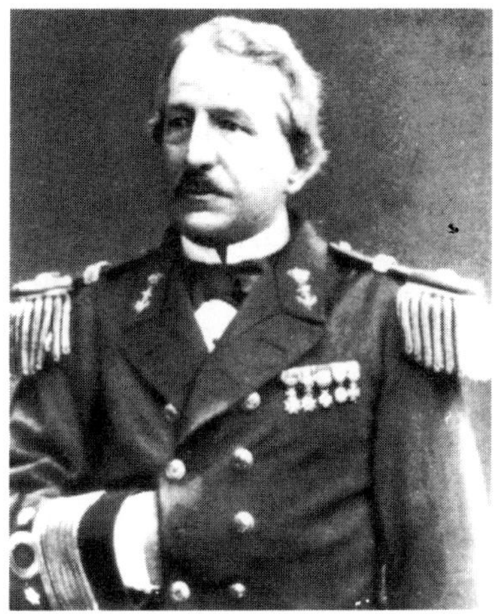

Uncle Jan, elder brother of Vincent's father

Two sketches show passing vehicles and, in one of them, a diligence is found. It can be imagined that the tired horse, shown on the right, has just been changed; a groom is taking it to a nearby stable. Was this a souvenir of Zundvert, where Vincent regularly watched the coaches changing horses, just beside his house? Much later, at Arles, Vincent was still interested in coaches. The horses were changed be side the famous Night Café, very near the "Yellow House" and the Tarascon viaduct, at the entrance to the town. Just before he died, he again painted a charming landscape, seen from the house of his friend Doctor Gachet, with, on the road below, a carriage drawn by a horse going in the direction of the village of Auvers-sur-Oise.

In another sketch, Vincent drew a church with a pointed tower. This subject reappeared frequently: one of the first drawings he was to make at Etten, after he had opted for a career as an artist, was of his father's church, not to mention the numerous village churches he was to paint and draw nearly everywhere, in the Drenthe, at Zweeloo, Neunen, Anvers, Saint-Rémy-de-Provence and Auvers-sur-Oise. Another drawing, showing a farm building, recalls the drawing that Vincent made when he was 11 for his father's 42nd birthday.

We may also observe, and this is not without interest, that Vincent had drawn a wagtail in its nest, which at once leads us to think of the great interest he showed in birds' nests during his Nuenen period.

This brief catalogue demonstrates that already there were certain constants in his choice of subjects. This would become clearer when Vincent finally gave himself up to painting. Despite their rudimentary nature, these drawings allow certain characteristics of

Vincent's style to appear which are to be found in his later work, both painted and drawn. One thing is striking: we feel throughout, the search for the maximum clarity in lineal expression. Nearly all the time, Vincent made efforts to clearly depict the outlines of the people or the objects he set down. In only a few cases, he adopted a light-shade effect, and the shadings seen in the drawing made for his father are as alike as drops of water to those in many other drawings made throughout his artistic career. Thus we recognise the importance of these drawings made for Betsy Tersteeg.

On January 1,1873, Theo was in turn employed by Goupil & Cie, at their Brussels branch. Now Vincent could speak to his brother in his letters of their common job and of painting and drawing.

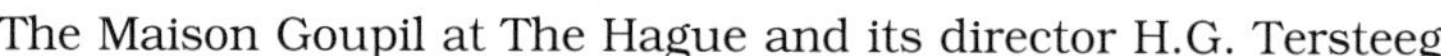

The Maison Goupil at The Hague and its director H.G. Tersteeg

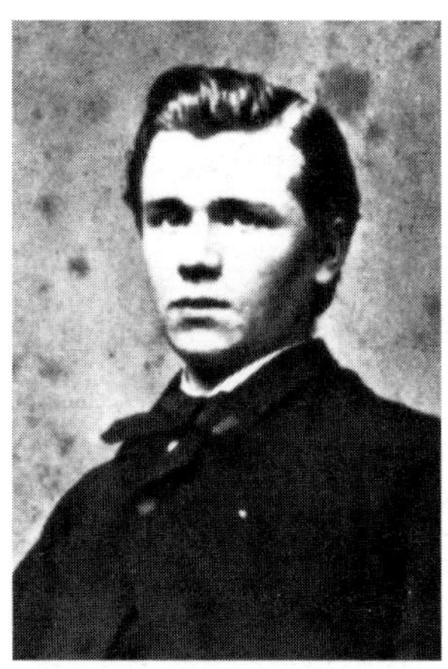

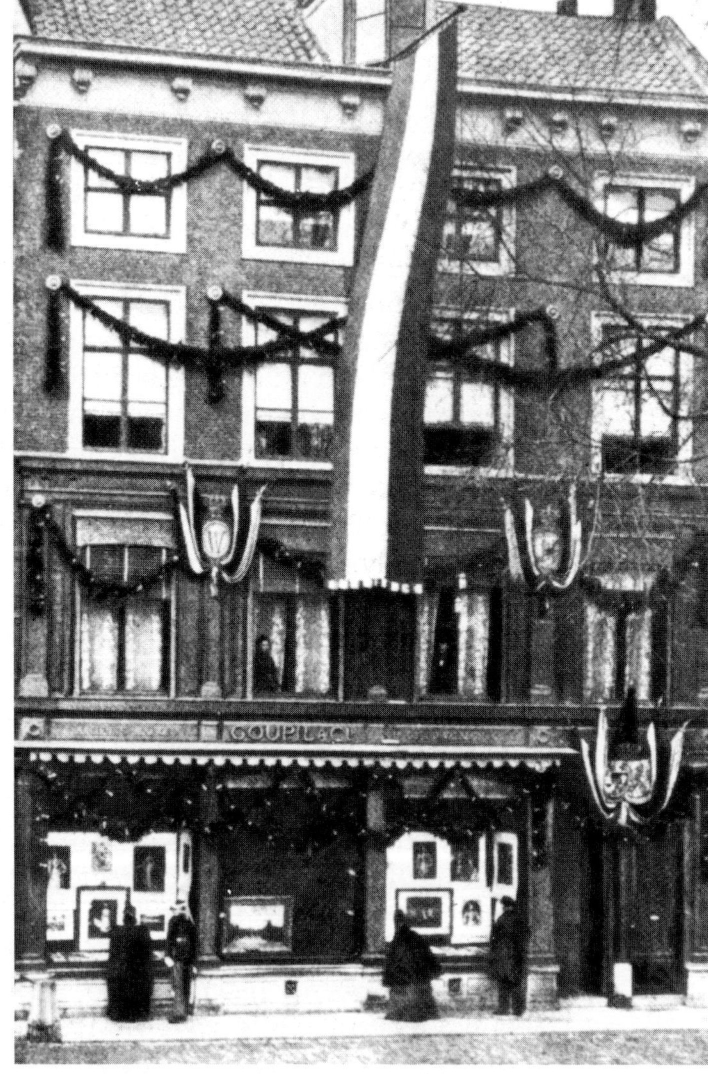

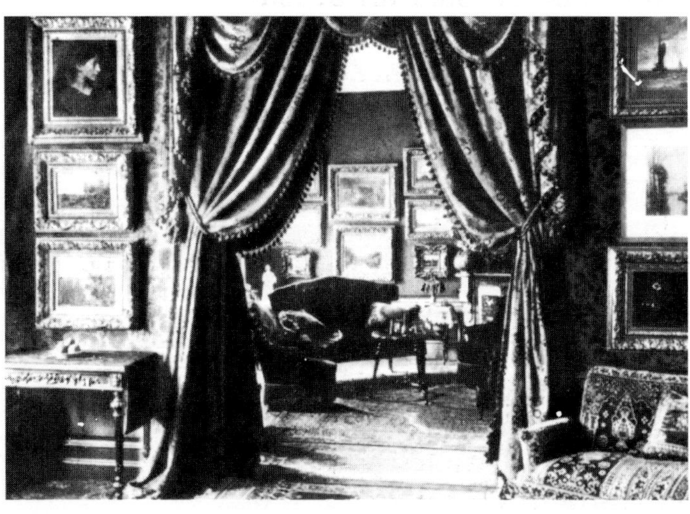

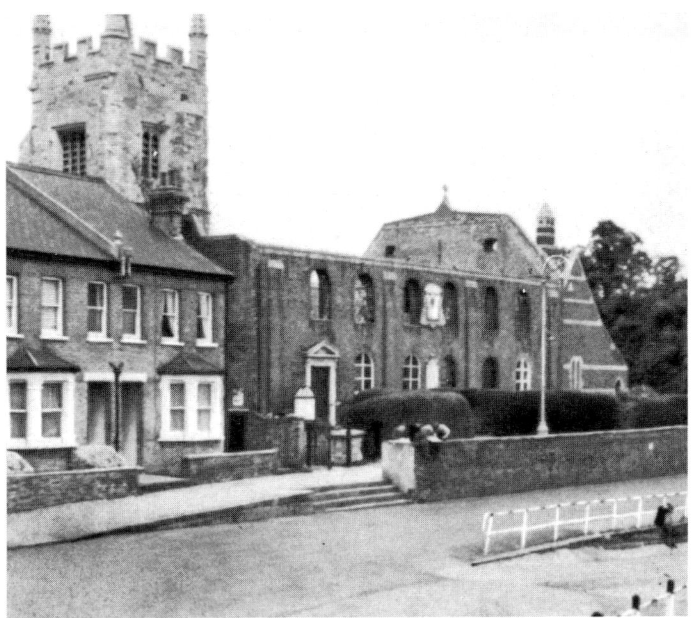

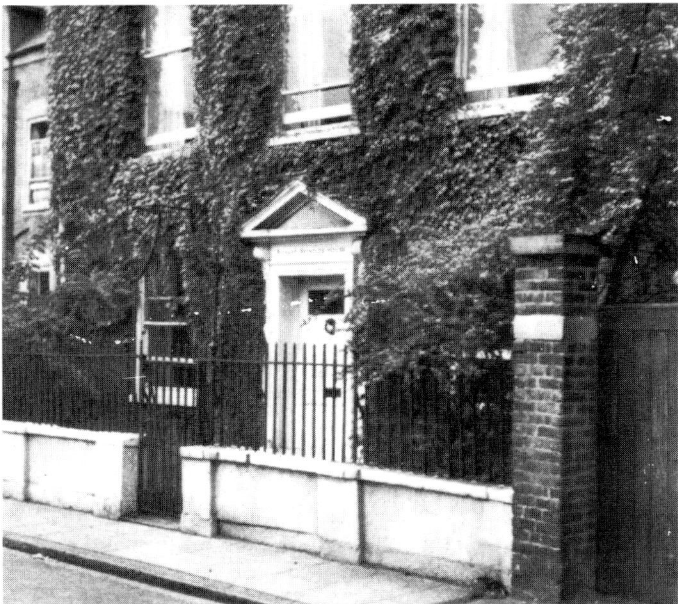

Church of the Tamise located nearby the house of Pastor Jones

Rejected love

In June 1873, Vincent was transferred to the London branch of Goupil & Cie, then to the headquarters in Paris, and then once more back to London; he lived successively in Ramsgate and Isleworth in England, and at Dordrecht and Amsterdam in Holland.

At Goupil & Cie, whether in Paris or the Hague, Vincent gave entire satisfaction. He was serious, zealous, replied patiently in an informed fashion to the wishes, the demands and often even the caprices of a sometimes difficult clientele. He was aware that these concessions were part of the job he had undertaken, and docilely conformed. The company, evenings and Sundays, of the daughter of his landlady, the charming Ursula, to whom he devoted an ardent love, certainly stimulated his application. He hoped to rapidly better his situation at Goupil in order to eventually marry. Vincent was enjoying the happiest months of his life.

Alas, Ursula did not love him. His rejected love took from Vincent all his enjoyment of life, and his look lost its gaiety. He left for a holiday in Holland, with his parents, who found difficulty in recognising their boy. He had become thin, taciturn, sombre, a man unable to recover from the terrible blow that had befallen him.

The Goupil executives sent him to the picture gallery section in Paris. This work did not interest him. Very early each morning, before going to Goupil, and each evening after work, he would read the Bible with his friend Harry Gladwell, an ex-employee of Goupil & Cie of Paris. Vincent resigned from the firm on April 1, 1876.

The influence of the Bible

In abandoning the art trade, Vincent made a clean break with his past, without, however, having a definite plan for his future.

He carefully read the English newspapers, hoping to find an engagement, preferably for a job in teaching.

This resulted in his finding a post in the then small village of Isleworth, near the Thames.

Vincent taught French; one of his pupils started German with him. He also taught arithmetic, grammar, heard lessons and, outside classroom hours, looked after the young boys. But he soon had to find other employment, since he could not depend on his salary being paid

On July 1, 1876, Vincent was engaged as curate by the Rev. Jones, a Methodist parson who also lived in Isleworth. Vincent thus changed from the world of art to that of the church. One Sunday, the Rev. Jones gave Vincent permission to preach. Vincent spoke in public for the first time, and from a pulpit in the House of God. Full of joy, he straightaway gave the news to Theo, and enclosed in his letter the English text of his sermon. *Because this sermon is the first of many,* he crowed, full of feverish enthusiasm.

Vincent sometimes left Isleworth at four in the morning to go to the poorest quarter of London, Whitechapel, as well as other places. Ceaselessly confronted by human misery in all its forms, Vincent was confirmed in his intention to live, without hesitation, for the service of others.

However, for reasons that remain unclear, Vincent's family decided that he should not return to Isleworth. *Many reasons make it better that I should stay in Holland,* he wrote briefly to his brother Theo.

Directly after New Year 1877, Vincent found a job in a bookshop, Blussé & van Brahm at Dordrecht.

In 1914, 24 years after the death of Vincent, Görlitz, a teacher who shared his room, published some recollections of his one-time friend. "He was an odd man," he recalled, "with an appearance that was equally so. He was strongly built, with completely straight red hair which stood up on his head, and a rather unhandsome face with freckles; his expression changed totally when he was seized by enthusiasm, which happened quite often. At table, he prayed for a long time, ate like a hermit, not eating any meat, nor taking any sauce. Very often, he would not lunch, saying that he did not want to live in opulence.

"When, exceptionally, he took part in conversation, he gave his impressions of London. His expression was usually dark, thoughtful, deeply serious, melancholy; but, when he laughed, it was loudly and heartily, and his whole face cleared."

Thus the portrait, painted by a contemporary, of Vincent at 24.

In the bookshop, Vincent showed not the slightest interest in the job his employer confided to him. Instead of doing what was expected of him, he was nearly always translating the Bible in four columns in French, German, and English, with the Dutch added. Braat also came across him making pen drawings which he thought were worth nothing. Braat, who was a nice man, came to the conclusion that Vincent's zeal for his job left much to be desired. He tried to discover the reason for this lack of interest, and heard from Vincent himself : *I want to become a pastor, like my father!*

Braat, with the best will in the world, tried to warn him against such a dangerous choice: "Don't you think it sad that after so many years of toil, your father has not gone further than Etten and Leur ? " Vincent became heated in front of his employer for the first time, and replied : *My father is in his right place : a true pastor!*

Vincent did not complain to his parents, but informed of their son's unhappiness, they decided to send him to Amsterdam. On May 9, 1877, he prepared for the entrance examinations for University faculty of theology.

The 30 long letters sent to Theo between May 1877 and May 1878 allow us to realise the impossibility of Vincent's submitting to his studies. They also show his manifest passion for drawing.

On June 12, 1877 he wrote : *Instinctively, while I write I make a little drawing from time to time, like the one I sent you the other day.*

For example, this morning, it was Elijah in the desert, with a stor-

Pastor Stricker and his wife. He was the father of Kee Vos-Stricker and the uncle of Vincent by marriage.

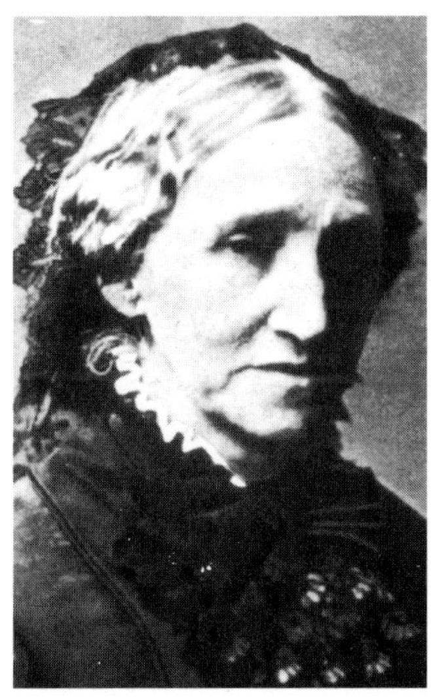

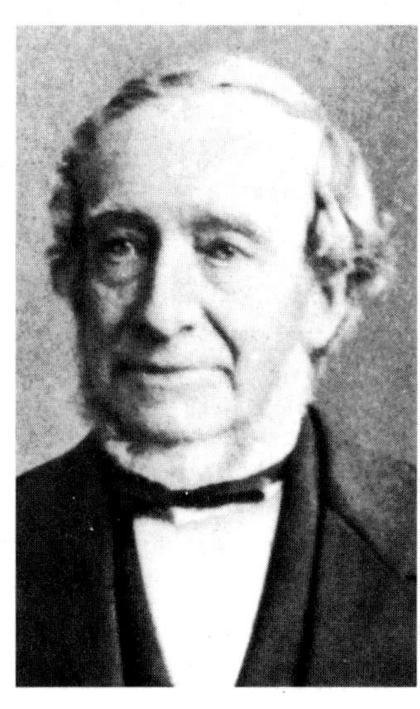

my sky, and in the foreground, some thorn bushes. Nothing extraordinary, but it came to me so distinctly, so clearly in my head. I think that at these moments, I can speak with enthusiasm on the subject.

Vincent gave up his theological studies in order to devote himself to missionary work, but it is possible to think that he also subconsciously left the door open to his artistic aspirations which, as will be seen later, were not in contradiction with his desire to be of ser vice to mankind.

To paint : an overwhelming urge

It might be said that a suppressed ambition - to paint ! - rose inexorably to the surface without his being aware of it. References to works of art become more numerous in his correspondence. A fierce combat took place in the depths of his being between what he was doing and what he wanted to do.

Everything was to start all over again ! Nevertheless, Vincent did not give up his ideals, the impulse to serve others did not leave him. He intended to forego an education founded on latin, greek and math; he felt that the Gospels alone would suffice for him to come to the aid of his neighbour.

His father, Pastor van Gogh, knew of the existence of a training school for Evangelical studies at Laeken, near Brussels. Vincent went there on 25 August 1878. At that time, there were only three pupils.

But there was to be another check after three months. His interest in painting manifested itself once again. In November 1878, he wrote to Theo : *Here is the scribble in question, the Colliery. I am tempted to draw rough sketches of very many things, of everything that I meet in my way, but it is better not to do so, because perhaps it will turn me away from my proper work.*

In January 1879, he was appointed Preacher for six months, at Wames in the Borinage. After a bad cxplosion in the local mine, and during a miners' strike, Vincent took care of the hurt and the ill. He lived in a poor worker's hovel where he lacked everything.

At the end of July, he was dismissed by his superiors, who thought that he sacrificed himself too much for others and was too negligent of himself.

In August 1879, Vincent removed to Cuesmes, where he remained until August 1880. He continued to preach on his own account. He spent his days in visiting the sick, and at nights, gave lessons to his landlord's children. Perhaps he could be considered as a forerunner of the worker-priests.

His soul, sanctified by passionate meditation and daily charity, was to expand into an aesthetic conscience without precedence in the history of art. From his childhood, Vincent was unable to resist the urge that pushed him to scribble on scraps of paper. In London, he sat

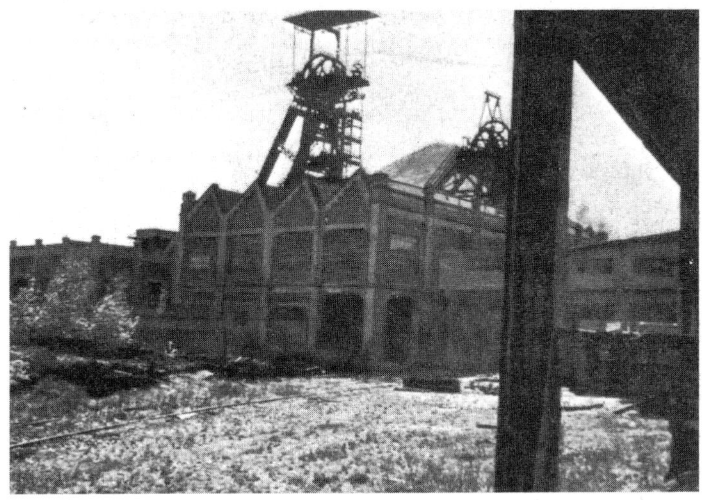

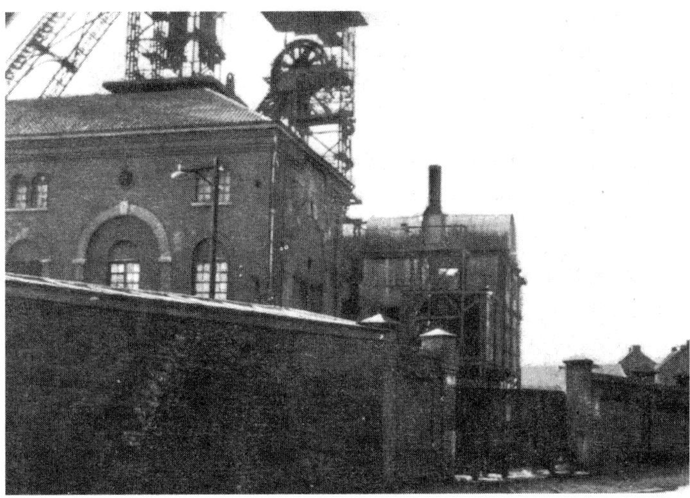

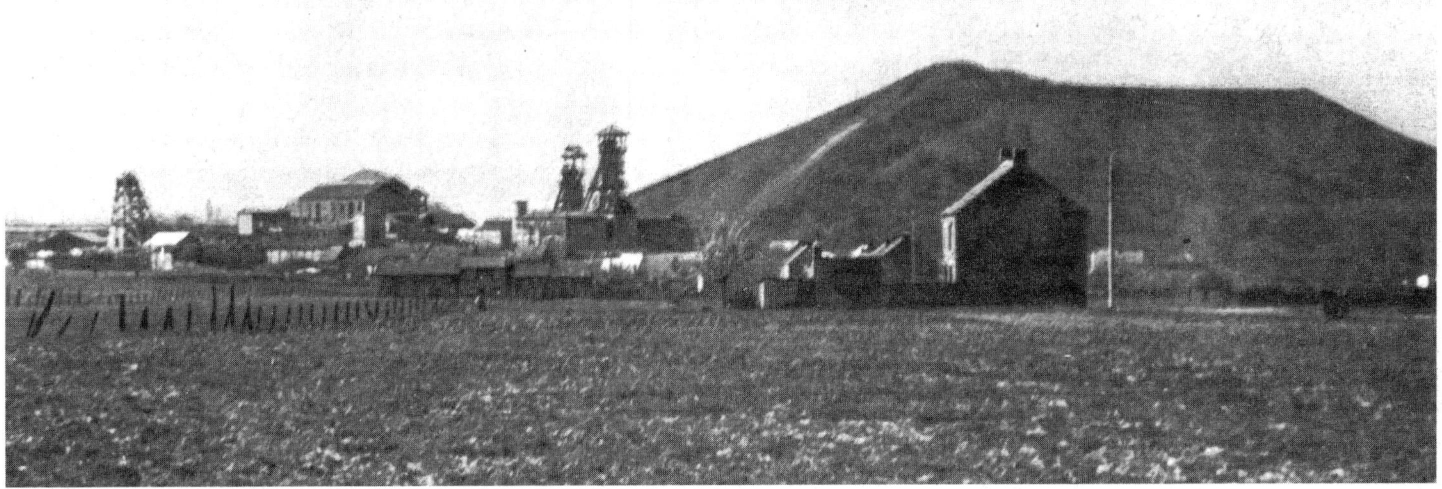

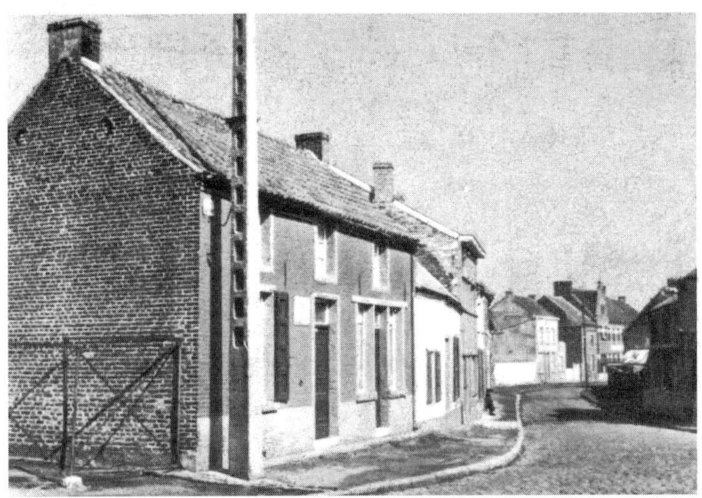

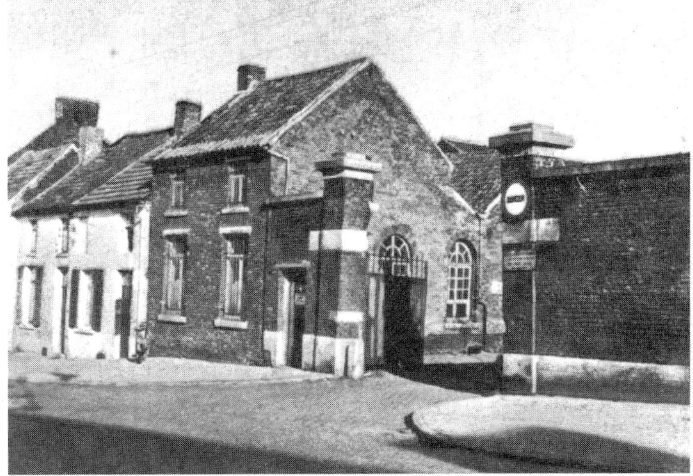

Mines and miners' houses in the Borinage

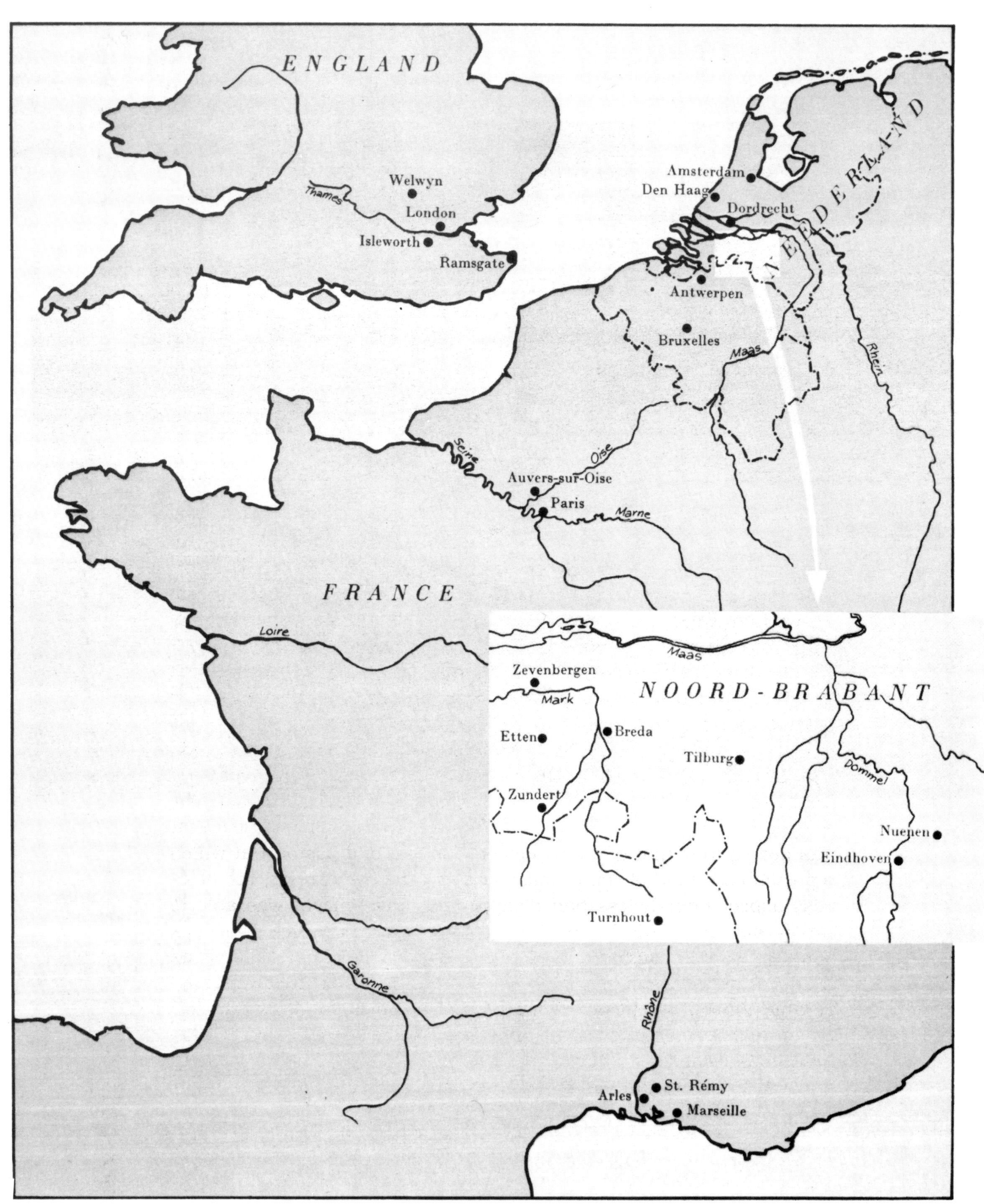
ENGLAND
Welwyn
Thames
London
Isleworth
Ramsgate
Amsterdam
Den Haag
Dordrecht
Antwerpen
Bruxelles
Maas
Rhein
Seine
Oise
Auvers-sur-Oise
Paris
Marne
FRANCE
Loire
Garonne
Rhône
St. Rémy
Arles
Marseille
Maas
Zevenbergen
NOORD-BRABANT
Mark
Etten
Breda
Tilburg
Dommel
Zundert
Nuenen
Eindhoven
Turnhout

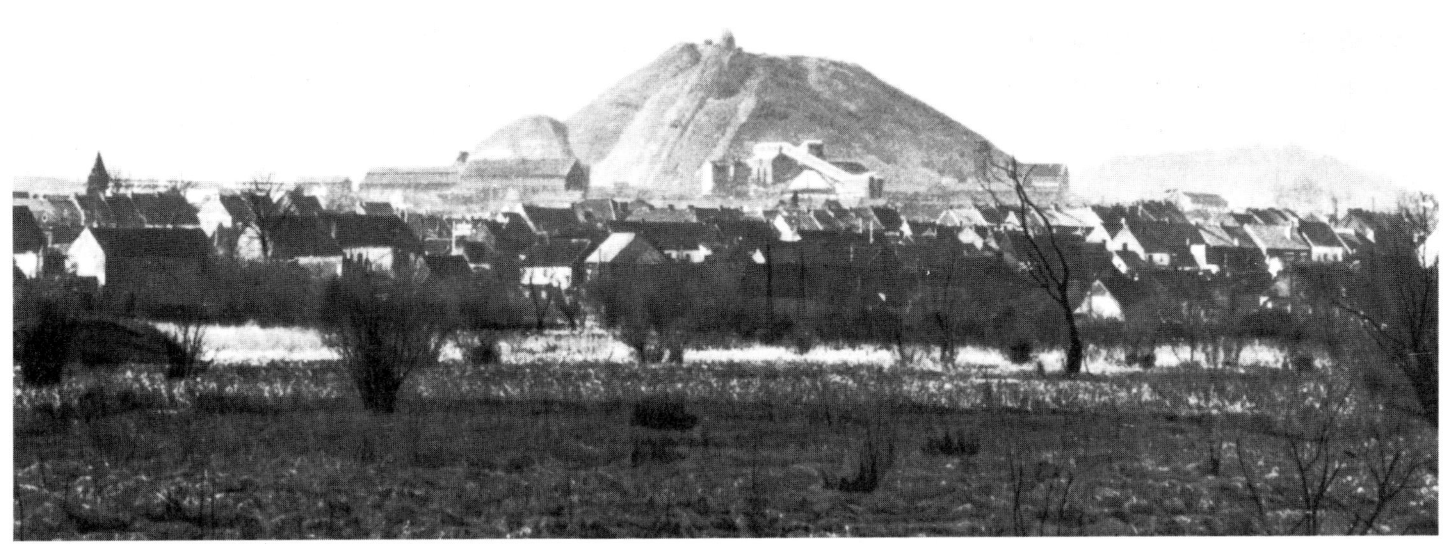

Landscape in the Borinage

down many times on the banks of the Thames to draw the river. At Ramsgate, staying with Mr Stokes, he sketched the shore as seen from his window. In the Borinage, during his leisure periods, he made large maps of Palestine (his father ordered four copies at 10 florins apiece). He also drew the miners' clothes and tools. So, it is not surprising then that Vincent had suddenly found, during one of the darkest periods of his life, the strength to start yet again another career.

A feeling of freedom lights up this confidence he made to Theo : *I said to myself : I'll pick up my pencil again, I will start drawing, and from that very moment, everything changed for me.* At last, he had discovered his true vocation, too long suppressed; a new life started that was not entirely that of an art dealer, nor that of a pastor, but which represented a kind of compromise between the two careers; the business aspect nonetheless had disappeared, and Vincent was able to satisfy his ideals and his desire to serve the human race. Vincent's aim, to "serve" mankind, underwent no change, only the means changed, and art took the place of religion. It is true to say that art became Vincent's religion. One day he set down this key phrase : *I want to give the poor brotherly greetings. When I sign Vincent, it is as though I become intimate with them.*

At 27, he began his life as an artist.

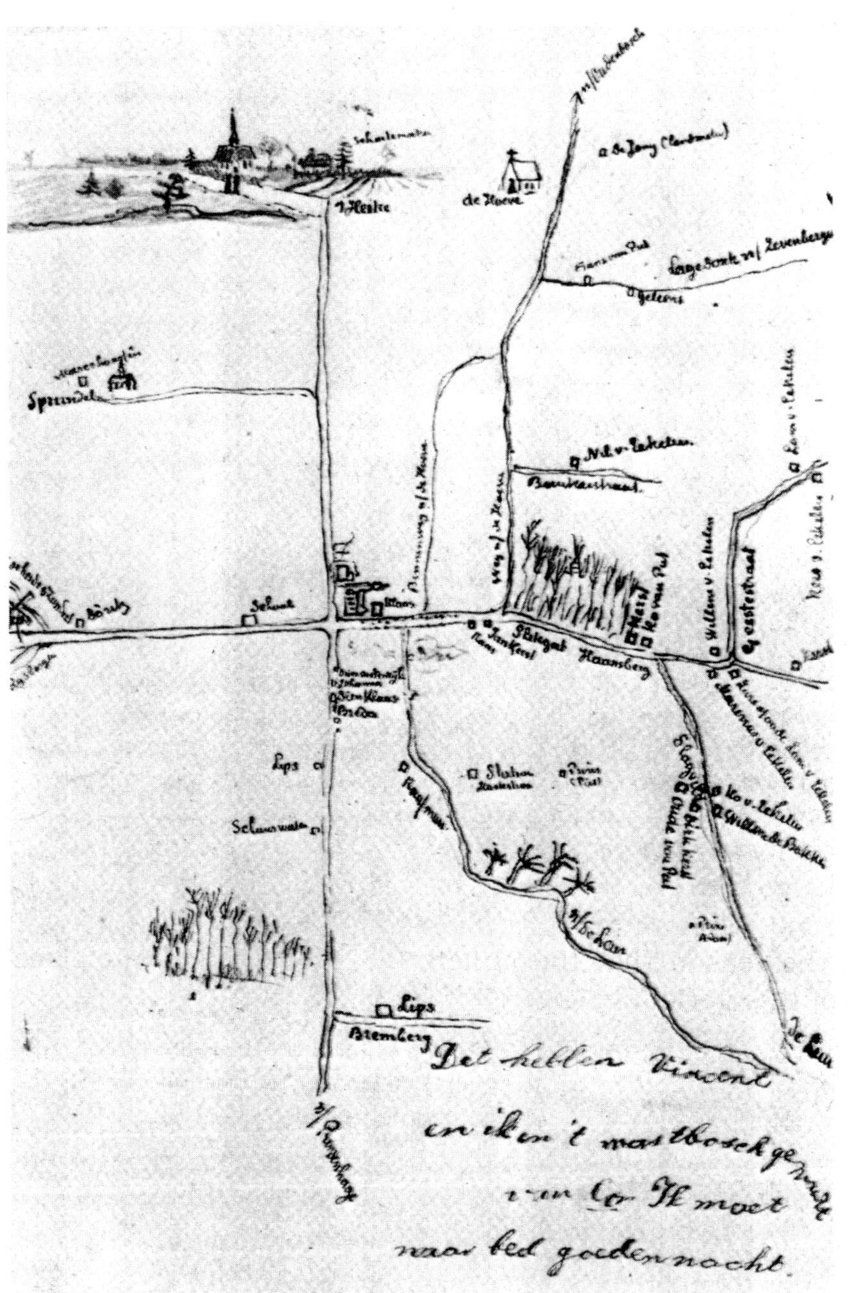

Map of Etten and its environs drawn by Vincent and his brother

APPRENTICESHIP TO THE ARTISTIC LIFE 1880 - 1882

Artistic creation struck him like a thunderclap. Vincent was unable to continue in the lifestyle that he had pursued up until then. His manner of clothing itself was to change according to his present situation. He bought two pairs of trousers and two bargain velvet jackets; he completed his wardrobe with various other clothes and a pair of shoes. His appearance underwent a sea change, without his, however, looking like an ordinary person.

In his letters to Theo, Vincent regularly lists the subjects he has undertaken. He interested himself exclusively, as might be expected, in outcasts, whose intolerable misery he intended to help. His burgeoning inspiration found an individual source in the Borinage ; this is the reason that the miners take a preponderant place in his works of this period.

In October 1880, he left the Borinage and stayed in Brussels. He went often to the studio of the Dutch painter van Rappard, and started a friendship with him that was to last more than five years. For Vincent not only was this a happy time, but also an extremely productive period. Invited by Vincent's parents, van Rappard made in his company numerous excursions in the surroundings of Etten. While van Rappard painted, Vincent made pen drawings of the market gardens. This common effort represented for Vincent the realisation of an ideal that he dreamed of throughout the greater part of his artistic career.

In practically all the drawings made at Etten, the vibrant emotional and human strengths surpass by far the ease and the perfection of the execution. Technique was not as yet up to the feelings expressed.

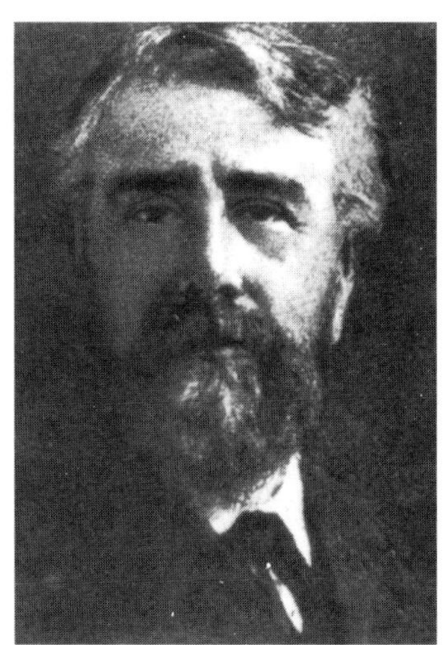

Antoine Mauve.

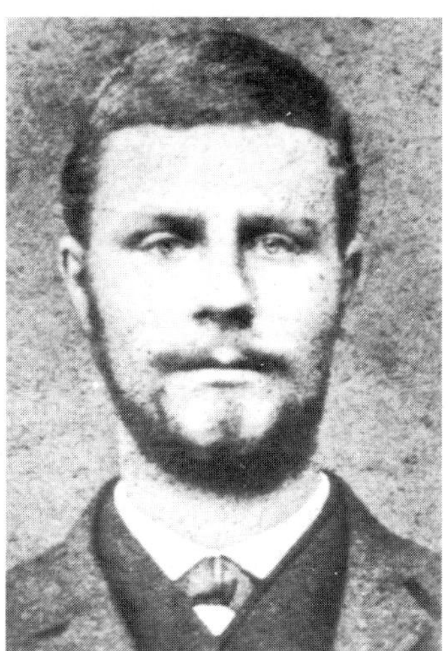

Anthon G. A. van Rappard.

Much later, in November-December 1888 at Arles, Vincent fin ished a marvellous landscape that may be considered one of the most beautiful that he ever made ; *the Promenade at Arles* or *Memory of an Etten Garden.*

As a faithful disciple of Millet, Courbet and Charles de Groux, Vincent was a realist ; he drew and painted what he saw around him. In other words, he did not call on imagination, like Gauguin, who composed, in the true meaning of the word.

Influenced by Gauguin, Vincent changed his style, and tried in his turn to detach himself from nature, at least to a certain extent. *Promenade at Arles* is a most instructive example : he composed, with neither models nor objects before his eyes, imagining a landscape that at one and the same time was a recollection of Etten in Holland and a picture of Arles, in France.

During the summer, he fell in love with his cousin Kee, but she rejected his advances. Vincent suffered another setback in love.

Moving into Mauve's

In November 1881, leaving for the Hague, he moved into Mauve's house the first month he was there. Mauve was a typical painter of the Hague School.

It was in the simplicity of his first studio (he later moved to the attic of the house next door) that the artist made the first painted and drawn studies of what would later be known as the Hague period.

The 22 months that Vincent passed in the town had a major influence on his artistic development. In fact, the some 200 drawings he made, without taking into account those he destroyed himself or which are lost, all show his preoccupation with strong drawing with the crayon as well as with the brush.

Thanks to the good advice of Mauve, Vincent made rapid progress; he realised this himself and in many passages in his letters from the beginning of 1882 are found echoes of his satisfaction : *I am more and more taken up by drawing, like a sailor for the sea,* he wrote. The apprenticeship proved difficult. Nevertheless, Vincent congratulated himself *on having pushed on without stopping with figure drawing,* instead of landscapes which bogged him down. But he had difficulty in finding models and persuading them to come to his studio. He tried techniques new to him : pen, chalks, charcoal, watercolour.

Mauve has put me in the way of a new means of expression, watercolour. I am developing it, I mess with the colours and take them off, that is to say, I try, and I make experiments. Because it is needful to make useless efforts. Because in the making of a watercolour there is something devilish. Because there is some good in every vigorous movement. I soon launched out on several small and one large watercolour.... It goes without saying that it does not come easy the first time.

Mauve warned me that I would spoil a good dozen drawings before being able to use the brush. Anyway, there is a better future at the end. As a result, I work with all the calm I am able to and am not put off by my mistakes.

Register from the Academy with Vincent's name right below that of van Rysselberghe

8488	Van Gogh, Vincent Guillaume, fils de Théodore et d'Anne Cornélie Carbentus né le 30 mars 1853, à Zundert et Wernhout (Pays-Bas) domicilié à Bruxelles, boulevard du midi, 72.	15 7. 1880.	1880-1881.	Dessin d'après l'antique : torse et fragments	22
8489	Vanrysselberghe, Théophile, fils de Jean Baptiste et de Mélanie Rommens, né le 23 novembre 1862,	15 7.	1880-1881	Dessin - nature Peinture - id	25 18

A glance at the watercolour of a woman of Scheveningen shows that already a striking dexterity is apparent, acquired in a very short time. Nevertheless, it is true that other paintings made at the same time do not display an identical progress.

The pleasant relations that obtained between master and student at first did not last for long. Concerning what happened to disturb this harmony, we have only Vincent's account to go on, and we know his fiery and obstinate character.

One of the grounds for disagreement was that Mauve insisted on drawings from plaster models. But Vincent detested drawing these, and even though he had several casts of feet and hands, he obstin ately refused to use them as models. In April, he broke with Mauve.

Where Vincent lived in Brussels

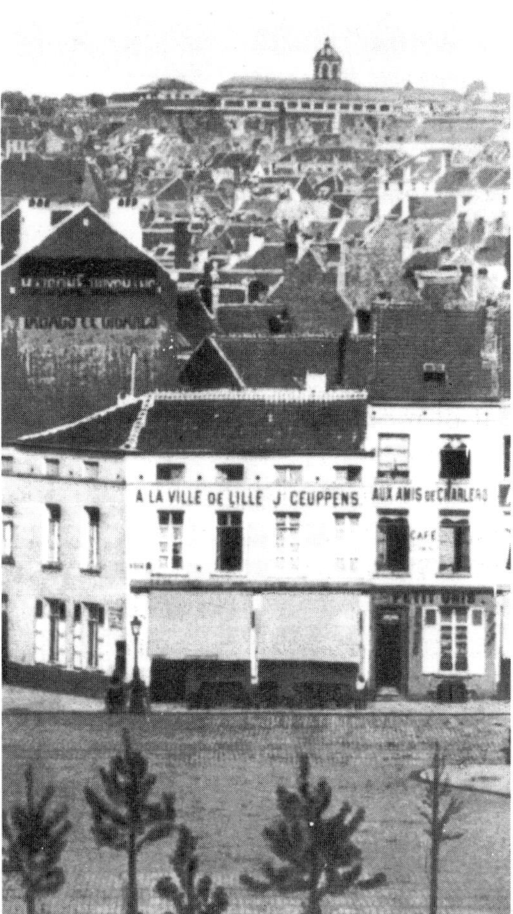

A HOME WITH SIEN
1882 - 1883

In January 1882, Vincent took in a pregnant woman who had been abandoned by the father of her future child. After having employed her as a model, he worked in her company all the winter, sharing his food with her, sheltering her from cold and hunger.

It seems to me, he said, *that any man worthy of the name would have done the same in a similar case. I thought it so natural, so normal, that I thought I could keep it to myself. At first, she did not know how to pose, but she finished by learning ; if I have made any progress, it's because I have a good model to draw.... She has no money, but she has helped me to make some by my work. I would have thought that people would have understood me without asking me for explanations.*

She was registered under the name of Clasina Maria Hoornik, but Vincent always called her Sien, a diminutive of her proper name. Born at the Hague February 22, 1850, she was 32 when she met Vincent, who thought of marrying her.

A parson's son living openly with a prostitute - it can be imagined to what extent the honourable family of churchmen and art dealers were scandalised, as were all their friends.

At one moment, Theo found himself obliged to warn Vincent that his family thought of having him shut up at Geel, in the Anvers district, where for centuries there had been a lunatic asylum. This news visibly worried him but did not make him change his intentions. He intended to listen only to his conscience.

Sien posed all the time for him, and Vincent made constant progress. Despite their occasionally crude aspect, some of the drawings made in these circumstances already show an emotional quality that would develop further in the years to come. It was Sien who posed for

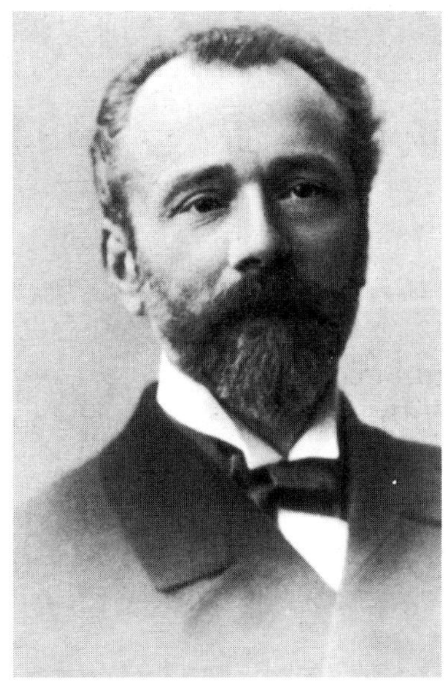

H. G. Tersteeg

Sorrow and *The Great Lady*, women shown to us in all their ugly nudity, without any fleshly charm. On the contrary, they shock us with their poor bodies, which bear witness to the trials lived through during their unhappy and obscure days.

These drawings, even though they are sufficient to demon strate the burgeoning power of expression, are not the only signs that nullify the statements of Tersteeg, his old superior at Goupil & Cie, who was more determined to make money than to support a beginner, and who denigrated the drawings of his ex-colleague. Tersteeg, in fact, saw Vincent as a pretentious and obstinate good-for- nothing. Yet dozens of his works, among them a number of sketches of old people in homcs, showed a firm hand and a penetrating eye. These are truly *people's heads.*

On 7 June 1882, Vincent was admitted to the municipal hospital of the Hague, where he stayed 23 days.

What I feared when I wrote you my last letter has happened, he wrote to Theo. *I was really ill, fever and nervous prostration kept me in bed for three days. Lasting headaches, and just to add to it all, tooth ache on and off.* Further on, he wrote : *Meanwhile, I am sometimes the prey of depression : it's the case at the moment, and then I drown.*

Hardly had Vincent left the hospital at the Hague when at the Leyden maternity ward, on July 2, 1882, Sien gave birth to a boy who was named Willem. Vincent quickly transformed the large flat he had just rented into a single room studio with a small kitchen and a bedroom in the attic.

The arrival of the baby fulfilled the dream of his life. *A studio where there are a cradle and a child's chair. A studio where nothing stagnates, but everything pushes forward, incites, stimulates work. My home is clean, bright, light and happy; I have most of the necessary furniture, bedding, and painting materials I require. That has cost what it has cost, but ... the money has enabled me to found a new studio which cannot yet do without your help, but from which will come more and more drawings.... It seems to me that my studio is stylish, with its grey-brown wallpaper, the scrubbed floorboards, and muslin hung on rods in front of the window; everything shines with cleanliness. There are studies on the wall, then an easel each side, and a large work table in white wood... near the window looking out onto the factory and the meadow which you know from the drawing, an iron cot with a green coverlet. I cannot look at the cradle without feeling emotional, for a man is overwhelmed by strong and deep feeling when he is seated beside the woman he loves, by the cradle where his child lies.*

One day, Tersteeg made an appearance in the studio.

Entering, he saw Sien and the children, and wrinkled up his nose as at a foul smell. He asked : "What is the meaning of that woman and child ? Is she your model, or something else ? Where did you get the idea to live with a woman and children into the bargain ? Isn't it as stupid as to go round town in a private carriage ? Are you a bit daft? You must be sick body and soul."

Vincent paid not the slightest attention to the stupid remarks of a complacent middle-class man, who went on : "You draw, but it will come to nothing."

Such a remark unfortunately meant that the head of the house of Goupil & Cie thought his work unsaleable.

Public hospital in the Hague where Vincent was cared for in 1882

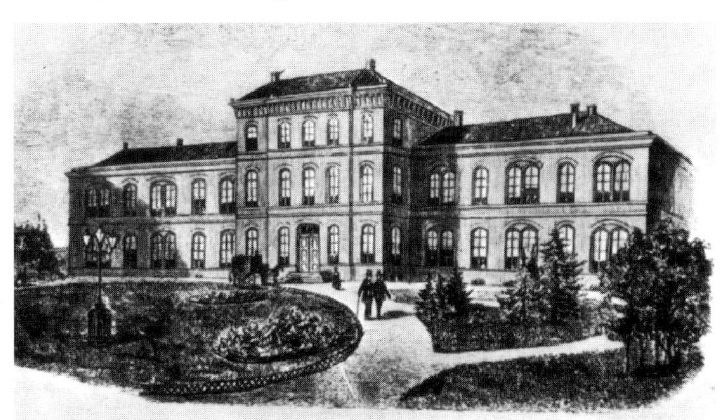

At that moment, (as in many other situations) Vincent's person ality, equally made up of tenderness and toughness, asserted itself. This strong man, decided on lifting himself from the ruck, was determined to make his own way, cost what it might. He would not let himself be discouraged. He worked tirelessly and piled up drawings always full of expression. He finished by garnering the fruit of his efforts and, after having spent himself for months in this rage for work, in August he suddenly turned towards colour and brushes. His first canvases showed, certainly, that he was still struggling with the medium, but they nonetheless surprise by their unexpected qualities. *The Beach at Sheveningen, The Lying Cow,* and *Woods of the Hague with Girl in White,* to limit ourselves to these three examples, are uncontestable proof that Vincent could have made a fortune, if he had not been obstinately determined to produce pioneering work, and if he had allowed himself to turn out by the square foot seascapes and landscapes in this style. He would also have been honoured by the Hague School, instead of having his innovations irritate certain influential masters who belonged to it.

In September 1883, Vincent realised that he had never felt any love for Sien, and that only a sincere pity had possessed him when they met. He decided to leave her and go to the Drenthe.

After Rappard's visit, I would like to go to the Drenthe. So much so, that I have already found out whether it is possible, yes or no, to send all my things there.

Life was cheaper in the country than the town; he thought that he could save between 150 and 200 florins a year, especially on rent. In one of his letters, Vincent confided to Theo that he proposed to do a lot of work in the Drenthe, and added : *I will need to renew myself there.* In an earlier letter, he had already underlined that : *To live for a time under a peasant's roof, far, very faraway, very far from here, there where nature is real,* was necessary to him if he was to progress. Vincent had certainly not forgotten, although he did not breathe a word of it, that two years previously, Mauve had spent some weeks in the Drenthe.

Vincent was to stay there three months.

THE RETURN OF THE PRODIGAL SON 1884 - 1885

From the standpoint of artistic production, the three months spent in the Drenthe allowed Vincent to conduct certain experiments concerning "local tones", as the professionals put it. The countryside lent itself to these attempts, and Vincent knew how to take advantage of it.

The artistic output of these three months was not enormous ; it consisted of 42 works, inasmuch as we can tell from existing pictures and drawings or from sketches illustrating letters. The technical result was very important.

A careful study shows that Vincent, before the Drenthe period, had not escaped the influence of the Hague School. Of course, nothing was more normal, since he had made his first excursions into the world of colour in painting watercolours under the guidance of Antoine Mauve. He was also connected with Weissenbruch, another of the School's authorities. From the beginning, Vincent's robust temperament and subtle intuition inspired him with a very personal audacity. The strength, the vigour of his touch are particularly distinctive. The Drenthe period was distinguished by an evolution which, from the first glance, strikes the viewer: the very apparent darkening of the palette. This tendency had already appeared, but very much less strongly, in the cloudy sky of *Scheveningen Square*. On the other hand, a systematic change is apparent when looking at the landscapes painted at Hoogeveen.

In fact, we are spectators of a complete renewal in his painting style, practically unconnected to his previous manner. From the first Drenthe picture, *Thatched Cottage on the Heath*, until *The Potato Eaters*, that masterpiece that crowned the Nuenen experiments, we can follow a constant progression in Vincent's ideas.

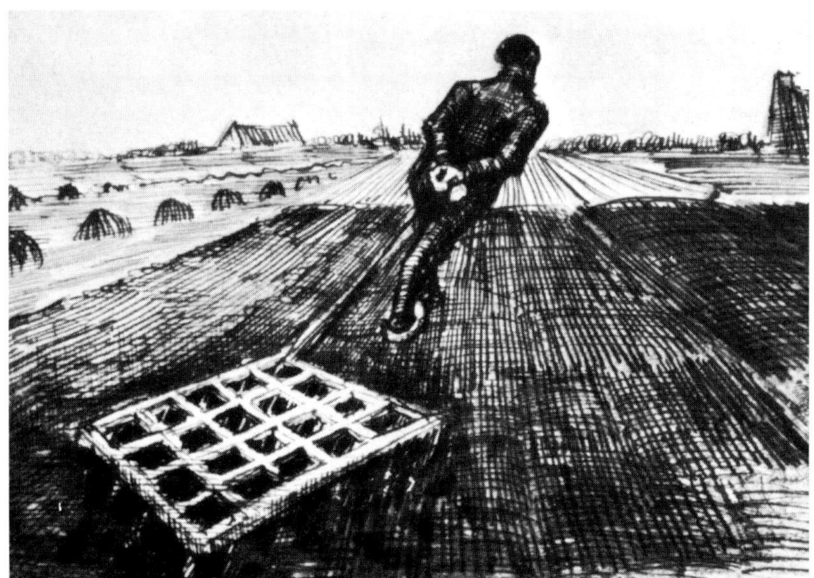
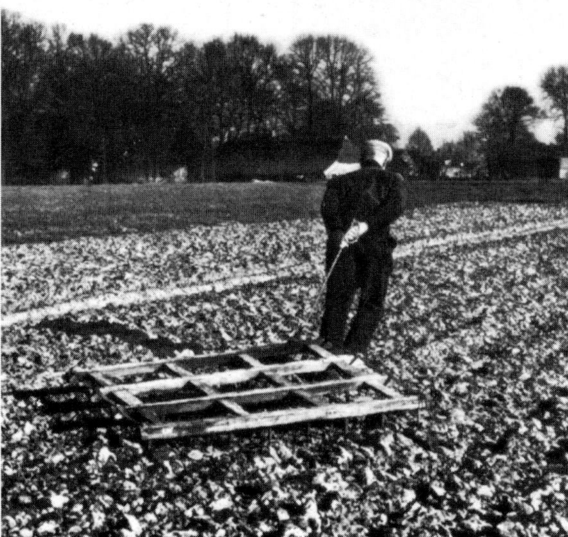

This sketch of a planter was enclosed in one of the painter's letters

However, the pleasure of walking and drawing the thatched cottages in the peat bogs did not last for long. Winter was coming, and Vincent lamented : *Painting outside has finished, it has been very cold these days.*

Not being able to put up with the loneliness, he decided to return to his parents' house at Nuenen, where he was to stay for more than two years.

Country people and weavers

Vincent told himself that it would suit him, all things taken into account, to stay at Nuenen where he could continue with his studies started in the Drenthe. Like Millet, his hero, ever since he became interested in painting and drawing, he lived as a country man among country people.

His desire to again express himself in colour was however so ardent, that all these unfortunate losses of time did not prevent him from getting down to work. He made, as he informed his friend Furnée, a surveyor, watercolours showing weavers, a wood sale, an interior with a little seamstress, and a gardener. He only painted watercolours and some hurried sketches.

Vincent was drawn, from the psychological point of view, to the theme of weavers in their workshops. These workers were the equivalent of the miners he knew in the Borinage, whom he had seen work ing in the underground galleries like bees in their honeycombs, a place where he felt himself sheltered. Later, at Arles, his dream came true when he moved into the "maison jaune"; however, his happiness only lasted eight months at the most. The weavers stayed at home and lived on the produce of their work. To highlight the homeliness of the surroundings, Vincent drew, beside the loom, a child's chair with a baby.

The weaver theme continued to absorb him for months; he took it up, in oils and watercolours, at least a dozen times. Through this, van Gogh exalted that which he most missed : the possibility, to gain his daily bread, like they did, by devoting himself to his art in a modest room that was his own.

In August 1884, Margot Begemann, a neighbour, fell in love with him; she tried to poison herself because her family opposed the marriage. Vincent was shaken. For the first time, it was someone else who had fallen for him. Margot was the only woman to fall in love with Vincent.

The time of fruitful meetings

On the financial side, an arrangement was reached : every month Vincent sent his works to Theo, who became their owner with the absolute right to dispose of them. Thus Vincent had the feeling that he was no longer solely dependent on Theo's charity.

In September 1884, a lucky chance occurred. Vincent met at Eindhoven, at his paint shop, a retired goldsmith who had just moved into a house where he was decorating for himself the walls and ceilings. Six wide panels still remained to be decorated in the dining room, for which he wanted representations of the lives of different saints and even a Last Supper, of which he had made a beginning in

The little church in the Drenthe, drawn on Novemeber 22, 1883

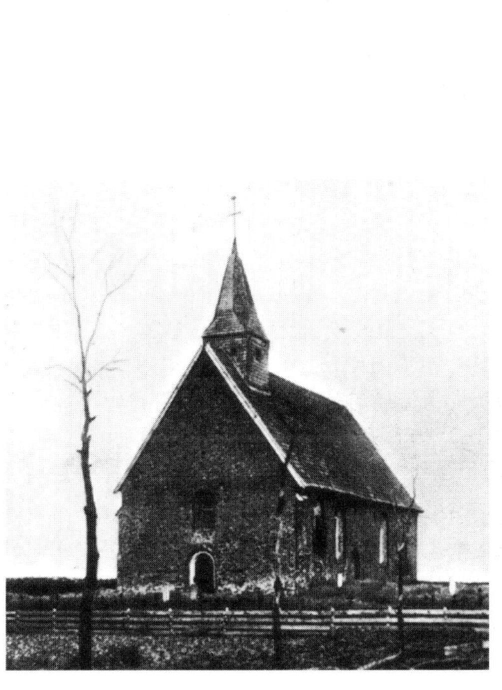

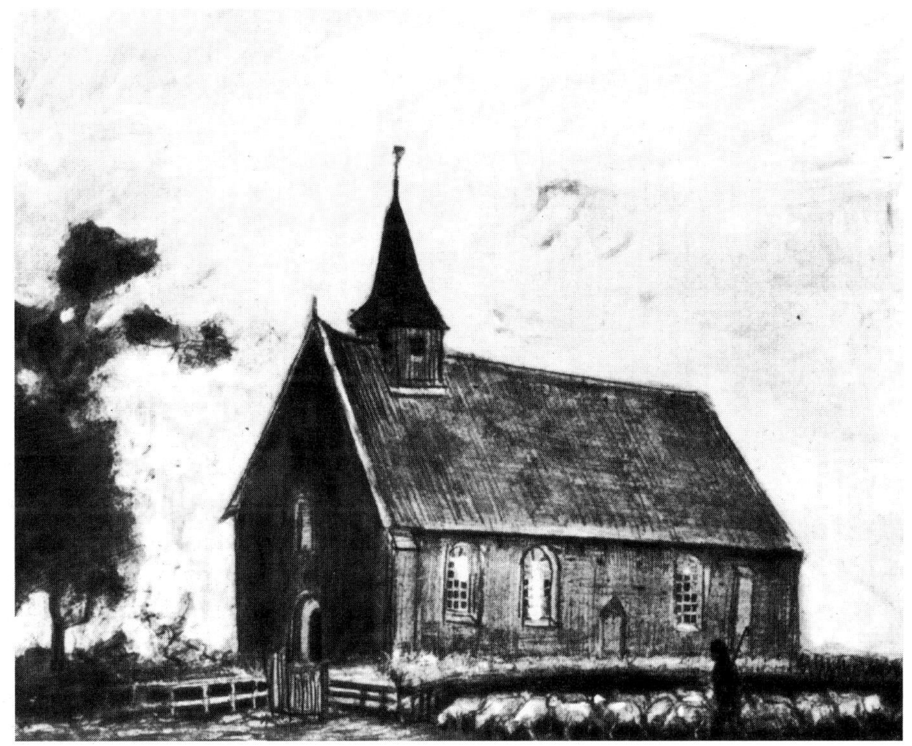

a modern gothic style. Vincent made him change his mind, suggesting to him that six pictures, inspired by Brabançon peasant life and at the same time symbolising the four seasons, would better contribute to the appetite of his guests.

The idea was accepted with enthusiasm and, after having seen Vincent's studio, the goldsmith insisted that Vincent paint the pictures. He decided on the following themes : a sower, a labourer, a shepherd, the harvest, the apple harvest and an ox cart in the snow. During the whole of one week in August, he went to the fields every day to see the harvest, and sketch.

Vincent came into contact with other inhabitants of Eindhoven. After getting to know the goldsmith Driek van Gardinghe, he met the organist of St. Catherine's Church, Vandersanden. He set himself to seriously study colour theory, in books by Delacroix and other specialists. He tried to discover relations and affinities existing between colours and sounds, and with this aim, he took solfeggio and piano lessons with Vandersanden.

The latter suggested that Vincent draw parallels between paint ing and music, in order to bring out the values and nuances of tones. During the lessons, he constantly compared the notes of the piano with Prussian blue, green, dark ochre and light cadmium.

In November, Vincent informed Theo that three people at Eindhoven wanted to paint, and that he was going to teach them to make still lifes. Vincent a drawing master: there was a new departure when it is considered that Mauve and Tersteeg thought him an amateur not worth troubling about.

Nevertheless, Vincent did not become puffed up because art students had asked him to initiate them into painting techniques. His only idea was to help them, to help his neighbour. He was starting to understand the reason for painting and the precise role of the painter.

View from Vincent's window on the first floor of the Hotel Scholte, overlooking a drawbridge

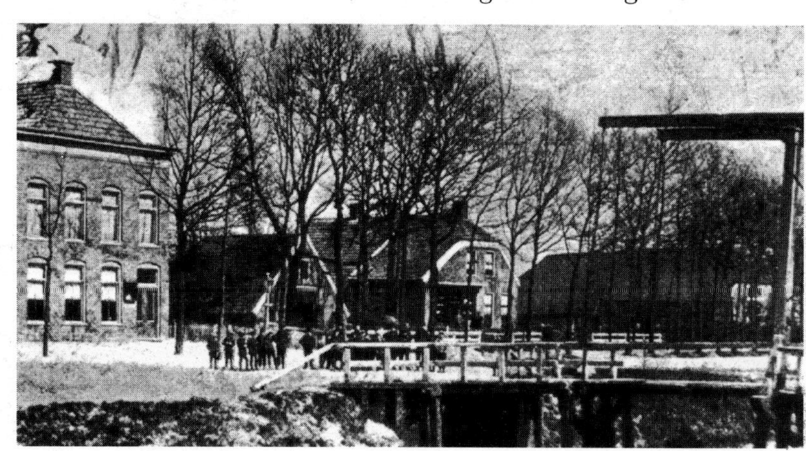

Vincent at work

Hardly four months later, he created a masterpiece, *The Potato Eaters*, which is generally considered today to be the first act of the expressionist movement. It was not necessary to wait long before seeing that Vincent, despite his undeniable modesty, was perfectly aware of the value of his work.

Convinced that a drawing or a painting was not made by thoughts alone, but also with crayons and colours - as Renoir said so well "To paint is not to dream" - Vincent shared with his pupils his own experiences. By now he had consolidated the principles of design, colour and technique. He had made great progress since that time at Cuesmes, when he first decided to devote himself to art.

Despite the piercing cold, Vincent regularly painted outdoors. At Gennep, near Eindhoven, he energetically worked on a study of an old watermill. This was a canvas more that three feet wide, thanks to which he made, still at Eindhoven, a new contact in Antoine Kerssemakers. Kerssemakers, a man of about 40, tanner by trade, was well enough off to be able to afford the luxury of concentrating on painting. Vincent's first impression was favourable : *This new chap*, he wrote to Theo next day, *I've an idea that he will quickly learn to see colour.*

Vincent and Kerssemakers often tackled the same subject; a number of landscapes made by Kerssemakers, among them some canvases of old watermills, show the direct influence of Vincent.

Weaver in his house in Nuenen

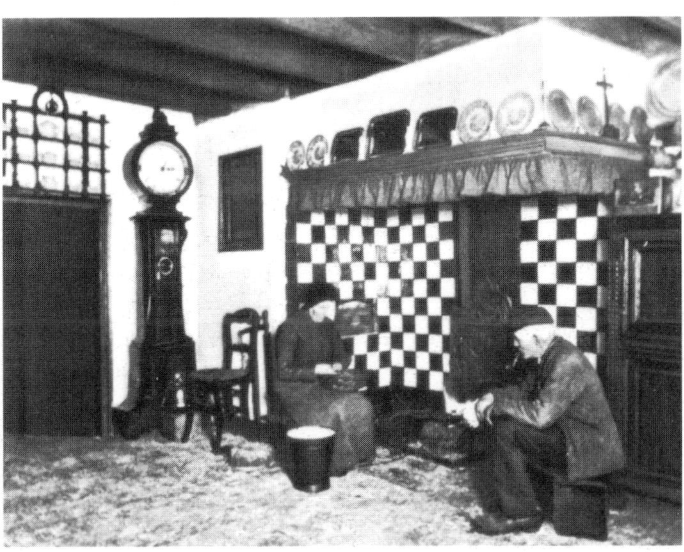

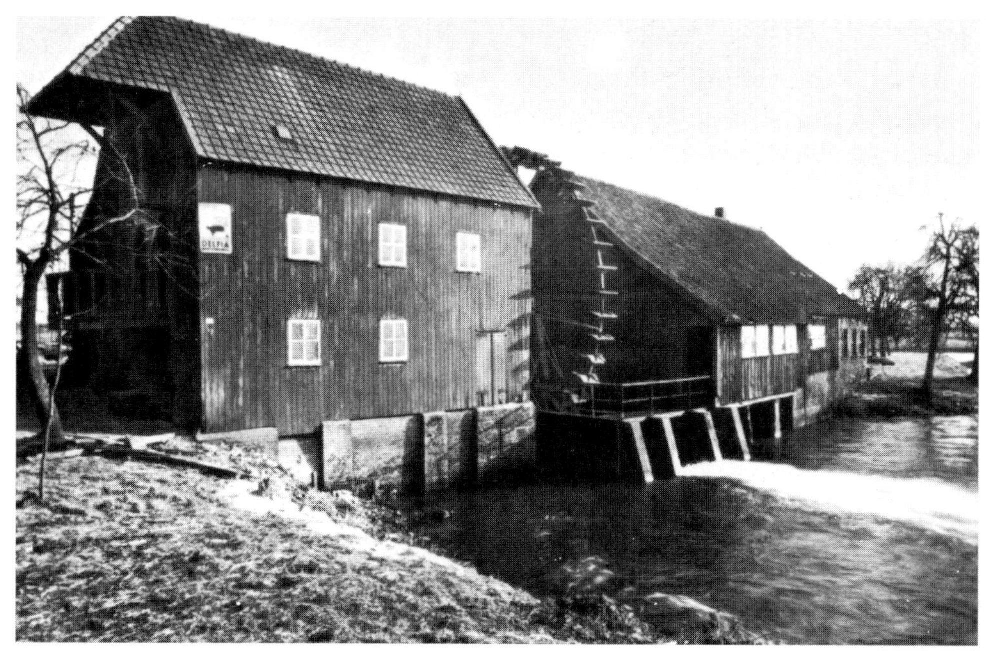

Watermill at Nuenen which Vincent drew

Kerssemakers kept a small study that Vincent had quickly painted at his house, in front of the window to serve as an example. The difficulties that Vincent found with his colours are clear. It was winter and the snow was melting ; liquid white ran over the landsacpe. This picture, made under unfavourable conditions, in a few brush strokes evokes the dull atmosphere of a grey day, with a sky threatening snow; we see in it a typical example of Vincent's skill.

Many accounts describe Vincent at work.

Once he had settled to the task, he would not stop until he had finished what he wanted to do. Besides, he worked extremely quickly, with wide powerful strokes, never correcting and never reworking what he had done. He chose as models the ugliest peasants, and did not pay them in money but in kind, with packets of coffee that he bought in Eindhoven.

His capacity fo work was huge; he left before daybreak to find his subjects, walking along the side of the road, alone, always wrapped in his thoughts, his head bent towards the ground.

When accompanying Vincent on his rambles, Gestel, one of his pupils, noticed that he started very early in the morning on a landscape of sheep and their shepherd on a heath. The picture was fin ished before midday, and after lunch, Vincent went back to the heath with the intention of painting two or three more big canvases. The last months of his stay in Nuenen, Vincent worked so feverishly that he could not even find an hour to spend with his friends.

Attraction to cemeteries

It is an established fact that Vincent, from his earliest youth, had always been drawn to cemeteries, where the sobriety, the calm and the tranquil order appeared to be in harmony with the simple lives and manners of the local people.

He even asked himself if he had not inherited from his father this predilection for wandering in graveyards : *Didn't father say : I prefer to talk in a cemetery because we are all there on an equal footing, not only because the earth there is the same for us all, but because we really find it so the moment we walk there.*

Near Hoogeven in the Drenthe, Vincent discovered an abandoned Jewish graveyard. During his first stay in Paris, he visited Père-Lachaise. In his own words, he entertained an indescribable respect for the marble tombs. Later in Paris, he drew the Common Grave, and made a watercolour of it ; at Arles, he made several pictures of the tombs in the Alyscamps. It is possible, without exaggeration, to conclude that Vincent felt a curious attraction towards graveyards. Again, all the works which Vincent made of the old church at Nuenen show the graveyard.

The death of his father

Vincent had intended to finish 50 peasants heads during the winter months ; while he was undertaking this task, he learned, on March 26, 1885, that his father, returning from a long walk on the heath, had collapsed at the parsonage door, struck down by a heart attack.

At the beginning of April 1885, only a few days after the pastor's death, Vincent's first reaction can be noted. His work had not gone forward as usual, but he intended to return to the graveyard theme as soon as weather permitted.

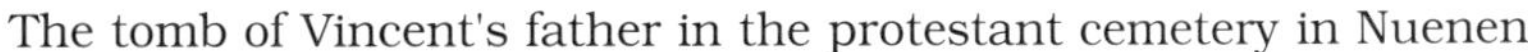

The tomb of Vincent's father in the protestant cemetery in Nuenen

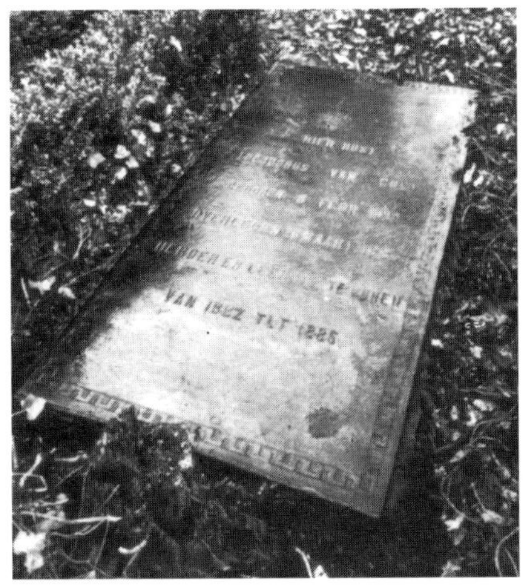

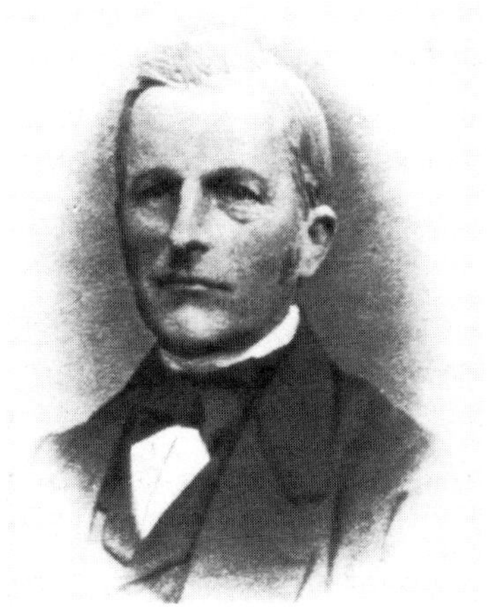

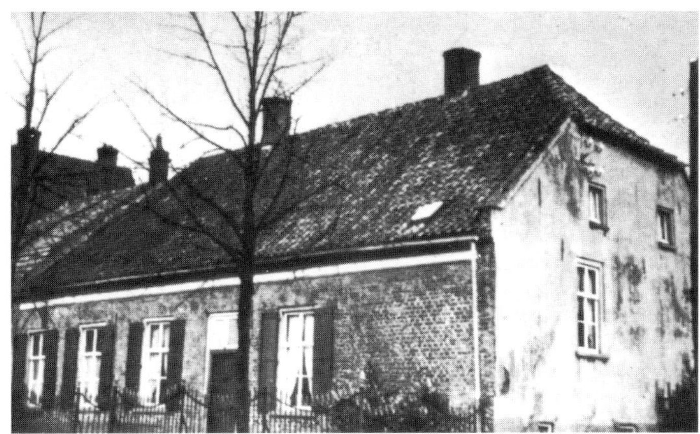
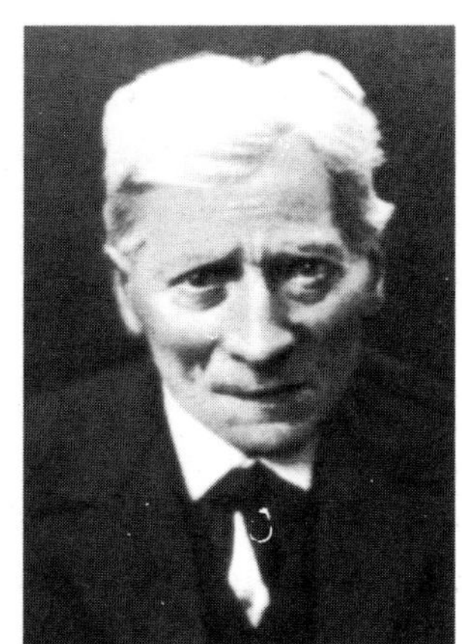

Home of the sacristan Schafrath, in which
Vincent painted the Potato Eaters

I am still greatly affected by what has just happened, wrote Vincent, who enclosed in his letter the outline of a still life which he was painting : it shows large flower stems, and in the foreground, his father's tobacco pouch and pipe.

In October the same year, Vincent made a still life containing an open Bible of which he sent a description to Theo as follows : *An open Bible (thus off white) bound in leather, on a black background, with a yellow brown foreground, and a lemon yellow note as well. I painted it at a sitting, the same day.*

Several of the biographies of Vincent have remarked on the contrast, in the picture, between the theme of the Old Testament (Isaiah) and the title of one of Zola's books, "The Joy of Life": the allusion is however fairly clear, since the reading of the novelist's works had caused grave difficulties between father and son.

After the death of his father, Vincent plunged more than ever into his work. The time was not far off when, to crown his struggle with colour, he would try to approach Rembrandt, even though his humility would never allow him to think, say or write such a thing. Nevertheless, it was really that that he sought, even if the thought was not expressed.

The potato eaters

One evening, he went into the small house of the Groot family to rest a little. Everyone was round the table under the lamp, starting to eat. Struck by a mysterious light such as he had once found at the bottom of a mine in the Borinage, he set out at once to depict the gripping atmosphere.

He wanted it to be possible to distinguish clearly the scene and the characters, despite the dark tones of the whole. He tried, in fact, to render the obscurity visible, thus continuing what Rembrandt and other great artists before him had done, but in his own individual way. While trying to scale the same summits as Rembrandt in light and shade, he was also ambitious to equal the vivacity and fullness of that virtuoso, Frans Hals.

In painting his *Potato Eaters*, Vincent threw down the gauntlet to his illustrious fellow-countrymen and predecessors, whom he was at least to equal as much in depth as in power.

After having finished his *Potato Eaters*, he attempted to push his experiments further into the realm of light and shade. It was thus that he tried to give a particular importance to some potatoes, and to bring out the intimate warmth and the symbolic force arising from a bird's nest, which, in his eyes, stood for the home he lacked so much. No other artist was able to express with such strength the power of absence, and to give free rein to the feelings of desolation that ravaged his being.

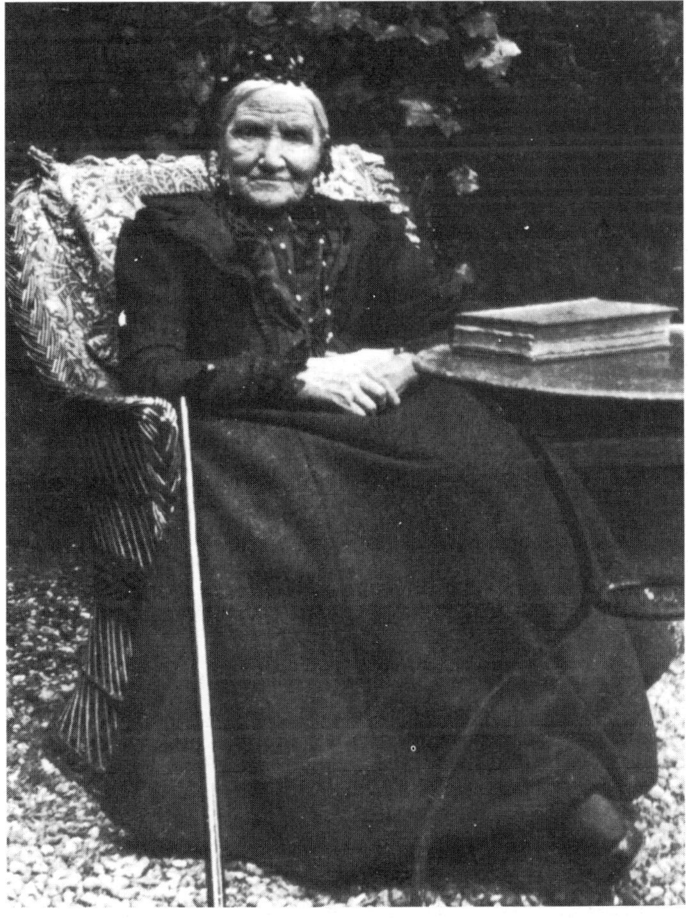

Vincent's mother

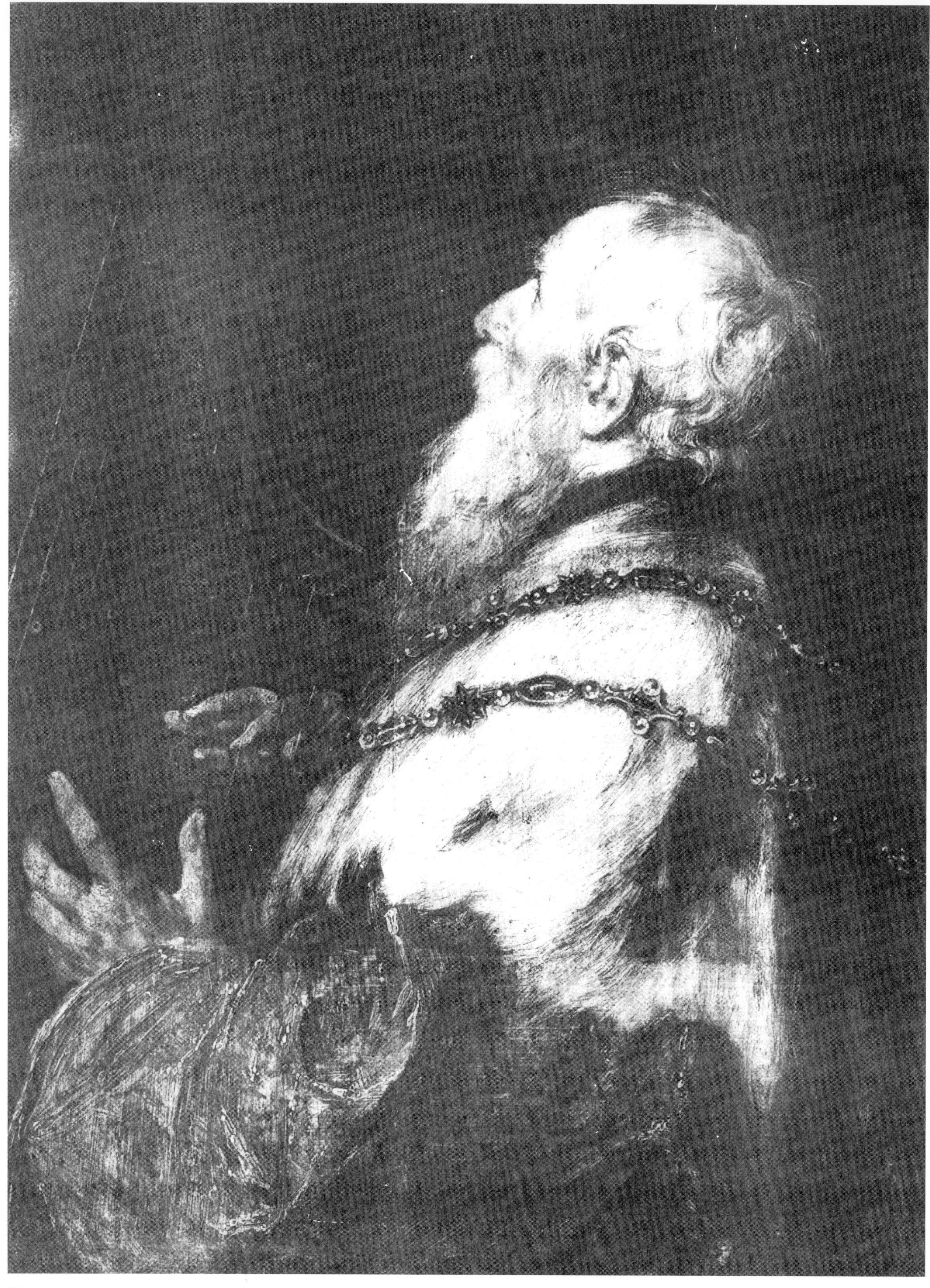

ANVERS : THE DISCOVERY OF RUBENS 1885 - 1886

On November 27, 1885, Vincent left Nuenen for Anvers where he had decided to sell his pictures himself.

He rented, for 25 francs a month, a little room at number 194, rue des Images, over a colour shop. *My studio is good enough, above all since I have pinned to the walls a whole collection of Japanese prints which please me very much.*

He avidly took in the town, going for long walks, particularly in the watermen's quarter, on the quays, where an eclectic world could be found.

At Nuenen, he discovered the potato eaters ; at Anvers, he learned to know the beer drinkers.

He visited the Musée d'art ancien and the Musée d'art moderne. In the first, he looked at the works of Rubens, Hals, Jordaens, van Goyen, Ruysdaêl, Quentin Metsys, van Eyck and other masters of former times. In the second, he was attracted by the pictures of Mols, Henri De Braekeleer, De Codk, Lamorinière, Coosemans, Asselbergs, Rosseels, Baron, Munthe, Achenbach, Leys, Ingres, David, Verbroeckhoven, and many others.

Above all, Rubens excited Vincent. There are no letters in the correspondence of the first six weeks of Vincent's stay in Anvers in which this painter does not take more or less first place.

In a letter in which he placed him in the first rank, in the company of Rembrandt and Hals, he wrote: *In fact, of the pictures, it is the "Fisherman's Son" by Frans Hals, "Saskia" by Rembrandt, and a large number of faces by Rubens, smiling or crying, that are the most vivid in my mind. Ah! a picture should be painted, and why not simply? When I look at life, I have a similar impression. I see people in the street, good. But often, I find the servant- girls more interesting than ladies, the work-*

King David, painted by Rubens

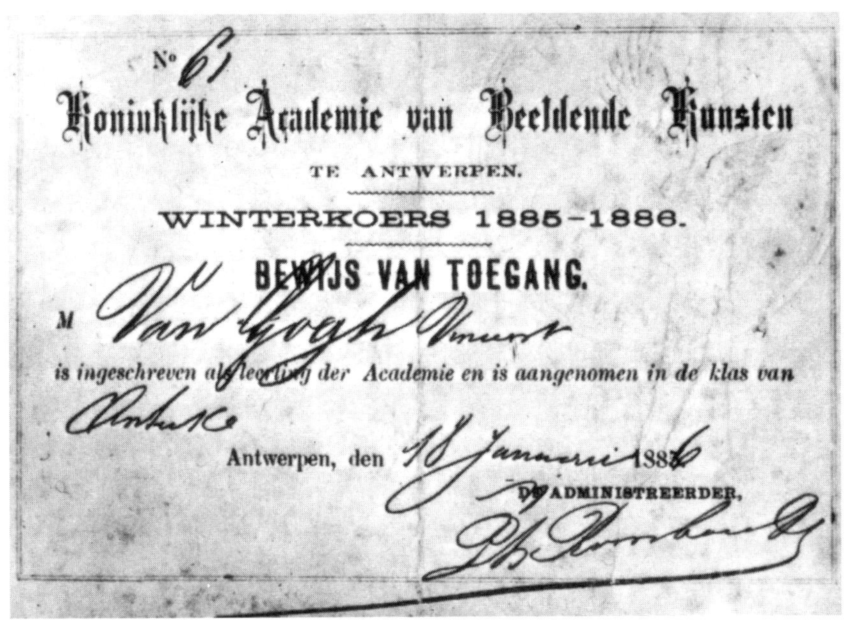

No 61

Koninklijke Academie van Beeldende Kunsten

TE ANTWERPEN.

WINTERKOERS 1885-1886.

BEWIJS VAN TOEGANG.

M Van Gogh Vincent

is ingeschreven als leerling der Academie en is aangenomen in de klas van

Antieke

Antwerpen, den 18 Januari 1886

De ADMINISTREERDER,

Entrance card to the Royal Academy of Art

men more interesting than the gentlemen. In common boys and girls, I find a strength, a life which, if they are to be expressed with their particular character, needs to be painted with firm brush strokes, and with a very simple technique.

Hardly had he arrived in Anvers than Vincent set himself to his work, in order not to lose his usual rhythm. He thought that he could make some money by painting portraits : *My best chance, he wrote, is the figure, for it interests relatively few painters. I should take advantage of that chance. I need to find my direction in this style and to contact good figure painters.*

The some 50 heads of country people that he had painted as preliminary studies for the *Potato Eaters* indicated that he had felt attracted to the portrait for months. Thus, his predilection for Ruben's heads and his decision to pursue his researches in that direction are understandable.

In studying them, Vincent arrived at the heart of a problem which haunted him ; he quickly understood that Rubens had mixed white with carmine, a colour that Vincent, limiting himself to the nine colours of his austere palette, had purposefully neglected up to then.

His first effort so pleased him that from then on, he used this procedure in all the portraits he attempted, for example when painting

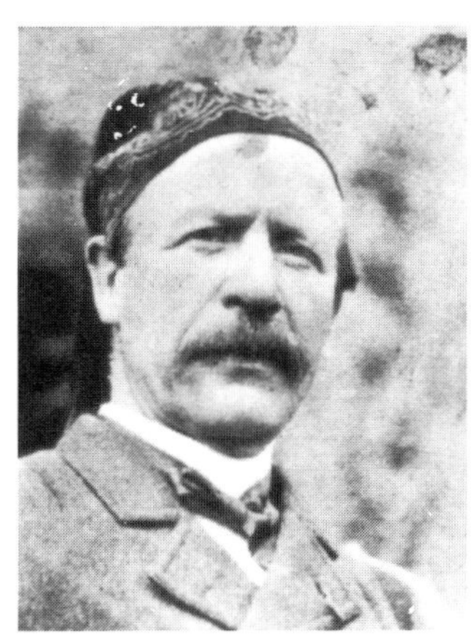

Piet van Havermaet, with whom Vincent studied drawing from nature and from classical models; Victor Hageman, like Vincent a native of Holland, imparted very helpful recollections of his time at the Academy with Vincent.

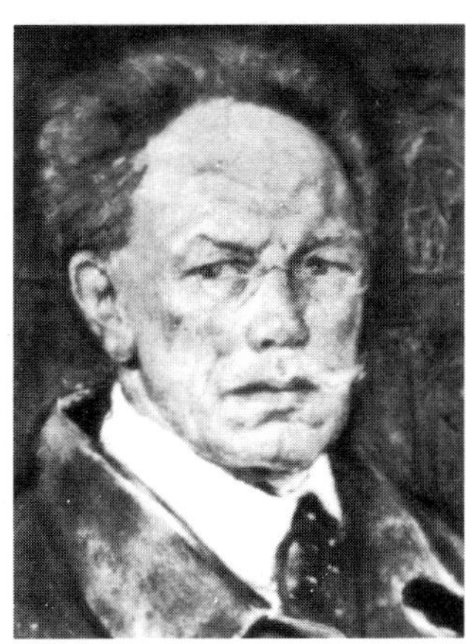

men's faces, such as *Man with a Head like Victor Hugo* (which was what Vincent himself called it.

Looking for a model

He saw very quickly that it was not easy to find a model in a town that he did not know. Nevertheless, he managed to make a bargain with two cabaret girls : they would pose for him, he would make two or even three portraits of them, and as payment, he would give them a copy.

So he painted *Woman in a Café Singing* and *Woman in Blue.*

A letter sent to Theo in the first half of December 1885 starts : *I wanted to write to you to tell you that I have continued to work with a model... The model is a cabaret girl, which has not prevented me from trying to give her an expression, this is what I wanted to to make her say, because I make myself stay within the truth, although I try to express an idea. When the model came in, it was obvious that she had*

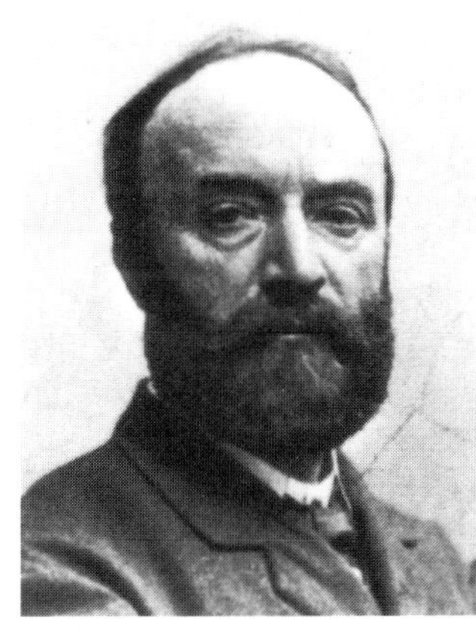

Charles Verlat, director of the Academy and a well-known painter; Eugene Sieberdt, one of the professors with whom Vincent had violent disagreements.

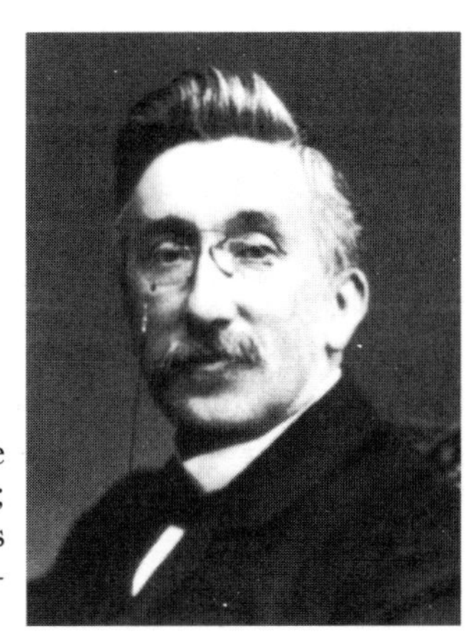

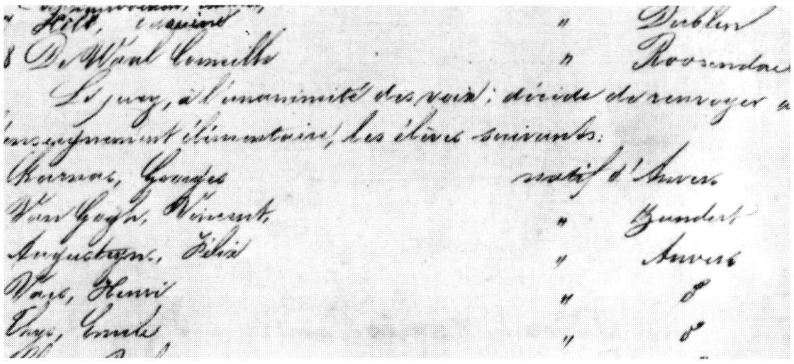

Results of the exams from the Academy on April 3, 1886,
showing that Vincent was left back by the unanimous vote of the examiners.

been busy for several nights, and she was eloquent enough : champagne does not cheer me up, it makes me very sad. I then saw what to grasp, and I made myself express an abstraction that was voluptuous and troublesome at the same time. And Vincent further added : What pleased me was that the girl who posed for me wanted to own her portrait painted by me, and in the same style as the one that I had just painted ... If I manage to sell something, so that I earn a little more, I shall continue my work even more vigorously.

When the colour on the cheeks of the two portraits of women is examined, the lightening of the palette is quickly seen.

His fascination for Rubens led Vincent to transform his dark palette of the Nuenen period to a lighter range of colours that thereafter would stay unchanged.

Fear of Death

Vincent pursued his ends assiduously ; he wanted to attain perfection by the shortest route, and worked ceaselessly. Instead of buying food, he often preferred to go without in order to use the money saved to buy canvas, brushes and colours. He relied too much on his own strength, and worn out, he fell ill, losing at 32 some dozen teeth.

His fear of dying before becoming known as a talented painter resurfaced. He was also frightened of going mad. This state of mind shows us the source of inspiration for a masterpiece which is not always appreciated at its just value. We refer to the *Skull with Cigarette.* We should at the same time draw attention to a marvellous little drawing, made during the same period, the *Hanging Skeleton.*

The sudden appearance of such a theme, which had never before been treated by Vincent, is linked with the confrontation with the idea of death.

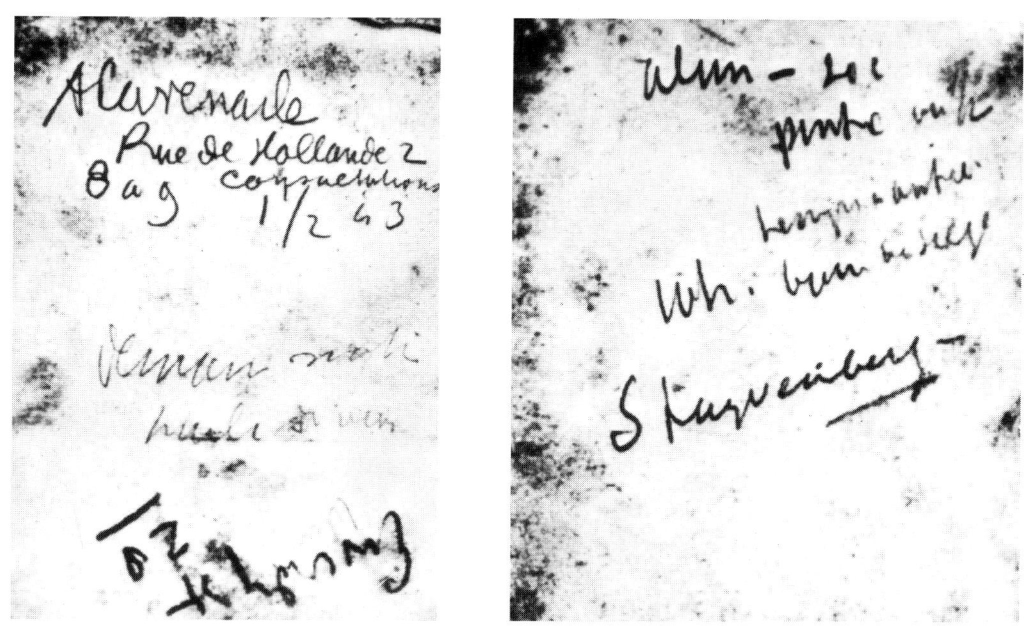

Leaf from a notebook that Vincent carried with him in Anvers

After having become, with the *Potato Eaters,* the spiritual found er of the expressionist movement, Vincent, by painting the *Skull with Cigarette*, became a precursor of surrealism.

These preoccupations are linked with another phenomenon, the appearance in his works of self portraits. Doubtless, it was when he looked at himself with anxiety in the mirror that he had the idea of making his own portrait.

During his three months stay in Anvers, Vincent made at least four, two in oils on canvas, and two pencil drawings in the pages of his sketchbook. A quick glance is enough to show that these portraits reveal faithfully the evolution he underwent. More than the paintings, the sketches show us the ravages of illness.

Back to school again

On 18 January 1886, Vincent put his name down for the Anvers Academy of Art as a student. The first time he attended, he was wearing a blue smock, as worn at that time by Flemish cattle drivers; on his head he wore a fur cap. He spread out his drawings, which everyone looked at with some bewilderment; for a palette, he used a plank taken from a sugar crate. Then he started to paint the two nude models posing in front of the class.

This account corresponds to Vincent's own description of his first work at the Academy : *This week, I have painted a large canvas showing two wrestlers, one of Verlat's poses. The work pleases me very much.*

Hageman the painter recalled that one day Vincent used such a thickness of paint that the colours literally ran off the canvas onto the parquet. While at the Anvers Academy, Vincent did not abandon his habit of sometimes substituting his fingers for brushes. When, at the Hague, Mauve reproached him for stroking the canvas with his fingers, Vincent became angry and turned on him : *What's it matter! I would even use my nails if it would be useful to do so and to give an effect.*

Victor Hageman noted that Vincent painted and drew with ardour, being determined, even though suffering, to grasp the form; he worked quickly, without retouching, very often tearing up his drawing and throwing it behind him when he had finished. He made sketches of everything that he found in the classroom: students, clothing, furniture, without forgetting the plaster model he had to copy. The speed with which Vincent worked was astonishing; he would remake the same drawing a dozen times.

One day, struck by one of the salient characteristics of a model, he strongly emphasised the width of the thighs. Under his pencil, the beautiful Greek became a robust Flemish matron. When the professor saw this, he furiously corrected the drawing. Beside himself, Vincent flew into a rage and said to the professor : *You don't know what a woman is ! A woman should have thighs, a bottom, a lap to hold a child!* That was the last lesson that Vincent took at the Academy.

Before leaving Anvers for Paris, he had made 64 works, of which 15 were paintings.

PARIS : MEETING THE IMPRESSIONISTS 1886 - 1888

In March 1886, Vincent found himself in Paris, staying with his brother Theo. While at the Anvers Academy, Vincent had often heard tell of the Paris studio of Fernand Cormon, which was then the most renowned in the capital. It was there that Gauguin and Toulouse-Lautrec had made a part of their apprenticeships. It was there also that Vincent was to meet Emile Bernard, the only colleague that Vincent was to be friends with for life, without even the smallest shadow darkening their relations.

Vincent only stayed three months at the studio, but that short time was enough for him to make great advances.

Certain drawings dating from this epoch not only show an academic perfection, but also demonstrate that Vincent was really able to apply to his studies of nude models "the overwhelming knowledge and feeling for truth of the ancients."

In June, three months after Vincent's arrival, the brothers moved to rooms on the third floor of a building dominating Paris, number 54, rue Lepic, Montmartre, not far from the Boulevard Clichy, which Vincent was to draw and paint.

When Emile Bernard visited him, in the living room he saw a quite good collection of paintings from the Romantic School, and many Japanese prints, Chinese drawings, and engravings after Millet. The drawers of a large piece of Dutch furniture were full of balls of wool mixed together, forming unexpected juxtapositions of colours.

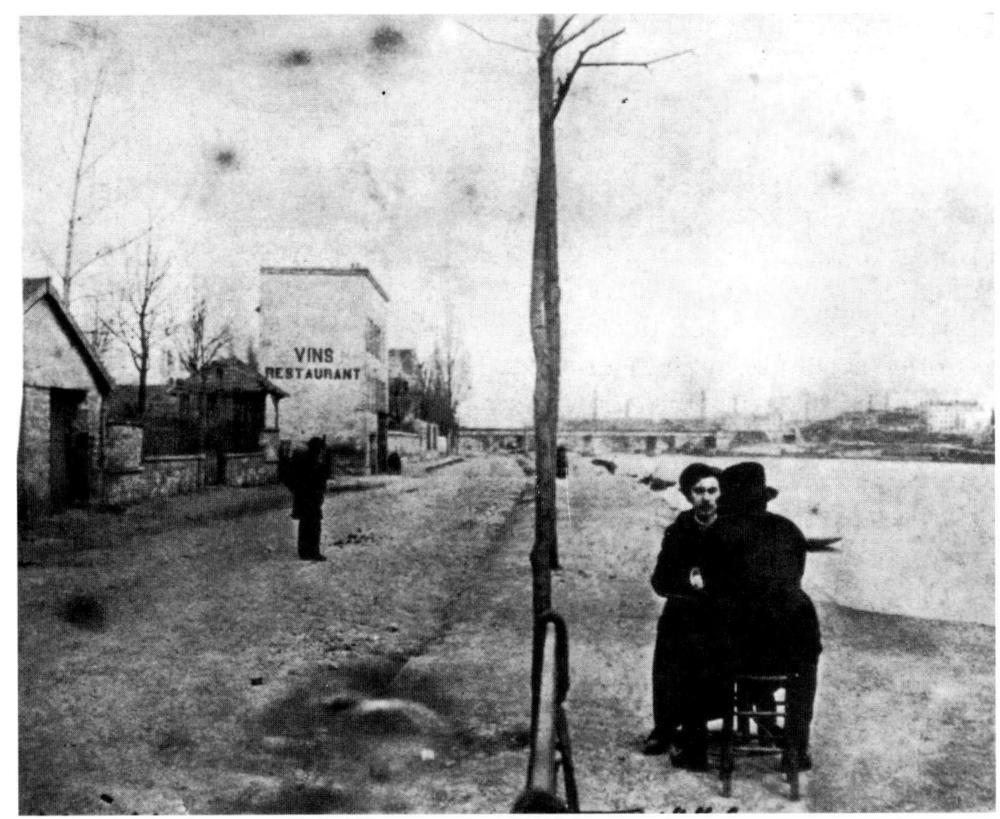

Vincent and Emile Bernard

At first, Vincent found his sources of inspiration very close by in Montmartre. Climbing the rue Lepic, that long winding street of pavé that led from the rue des Abbesses to the Moulin de la Galette, in a few minutes he reached the old Montmartre village ; there he painted the tiny gardens, the music halls, but above all, the old Moulin de la Galette from various angles.

Later, he did not confine his wanderings to his own quarter; his search for subjects led him into the suburbs. Covering many miles, he even took long walks as far as Asnières, Joinville, Suresnes and Chatou; he was also a visitor to the Isle of the Grande Jatte, following in Seurat's footsteps.

Emile Bernard: a friend for life

Most of the time, it was the Asnières bridges that aroused Vincent's interest, close by where Emile Bernard lived.

Vincent often went to see his friend in his wooden studio built in his parents' garden. It was there that they both painted a portrait of Père Tanguy, and Vincent started one of Emile Bernard.

In Emile Bernard's studio, Vincent painted still lifes, using slightly made dots, then complementary bands; among others, he fin ished the famous *Yellow Books*, which he exhibited at the Salon des Indépendants in 1888.

Emile Bernard not only left a fine sketch of Vincent sitting on a low stool in front a large canvas ; we also owe to him some precious memories. He related that Vincent left each morning with a large canvas. Arriving at his place of work, Vincent would divide it up into a number of boxes, according to the subjects. By the evening, the canvas was entirely covered, and looked like a small gallery, where all the feelings of the day were set down. There were depicted the banks of the Seine with some boats, islands with blue swings, restaurants with multicoloured awnings, decorated with rambler roses, corners of abandoned gardens, or houses for sale.

Emile Bernard, who knew the places very well, because just like Vincent he often wandered alone, stated that "these fragments caught on the end of the brush as though stolen from the flying hours, gave out a poetry of springtime, the charm of which he sensed, because he felt their spirit."

At the heart of impressionism

In Paris, Vincent found himself at the centre of the impression ist movement. His experiments put him in the tradition of Manet and within the "climate" of the new school. Think of the *Guinguette* and other similar canvases, where the break with light and shade left him half-way between the open air and the pointillist schools.

Cormon's studio in Paris. The group includes
Emile Bernard and Toulouse Lautrec.

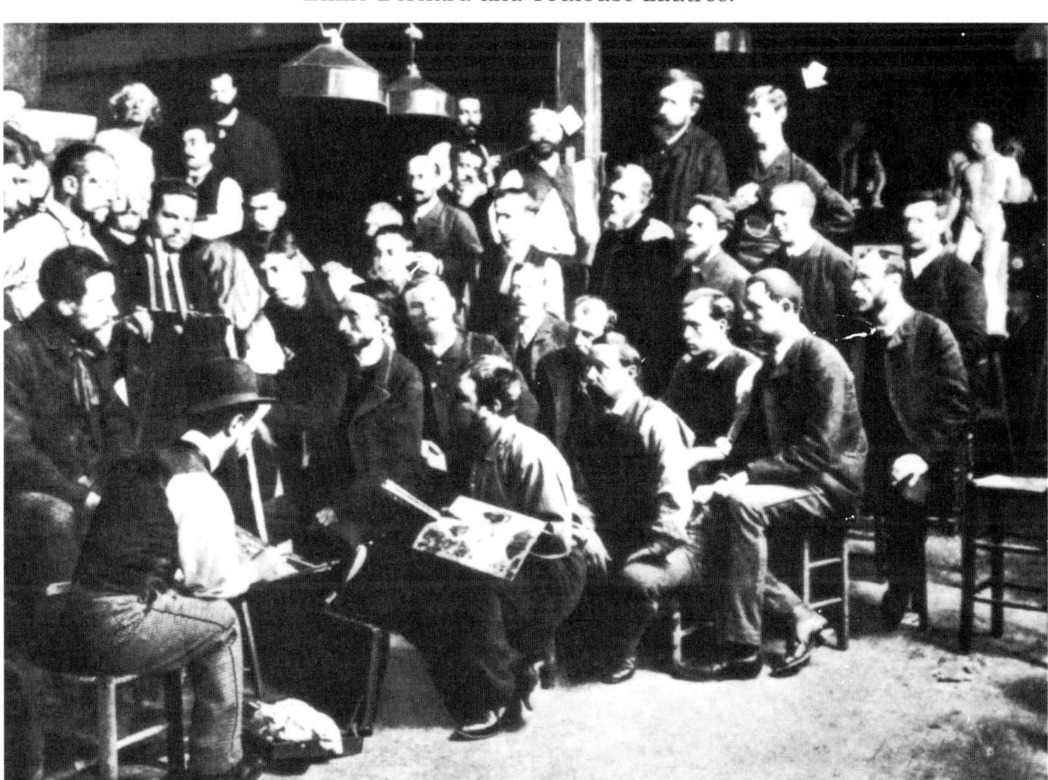

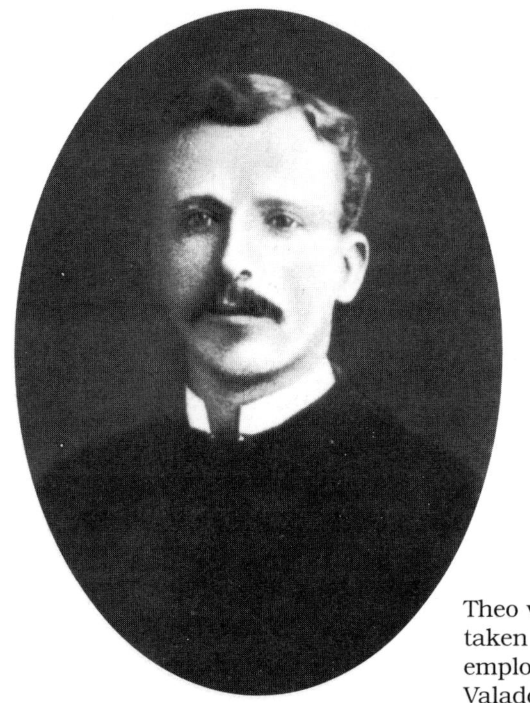

Theo van Gogh, photograph taken 1888-90, when he was employed by Boussod, Valadon and Company.

At Cormon's studio, Vincent became friendly with Toulouse-Lautrec. As a mark of his warm affection, Vincent gave him one of his best pictures, painted under the pointillist influence. Like Lautrec, Vincent was to know moments of happiness and of deep distress. His painting of a pair of old hobnailed boots, which expressed what he called the little miseries of human life, caused great excitement in the restricted circle at Cormon's studio, at a time when impressionism was sliding towards over-elaborate landscapes.

In a few months, Vincent had joined the circle of the innovators, in company with Toulouse-Lautrec, Emile Bernard, Gauguin, Anquetin, Signac, and Seurat. His fiery temperament and his combativeness led him to become one of the leaders of the new movement; he considered that impressionism was a thing of the past and recognised a new direction which was provisionally known as post- impressionism.

In 1887, the innovators organised an exhibition in one of the café-restaurants they habitually met at, the "Tambourin", on the boulevard Clichy. On that occasion, the group took the name of "peintres du Petit Boulevard", by contrast to the "peintres du Grand Boulevard", Monet, Sisley, Pissarro, Raffaëlli, Degas, Seurat and others, who exhibited at Theo's, that is at Boussod, Valadon & Cie, boulevard Montmartre.

Vincent seems to have had an affair for a time with the manager of the "Tambourin", Agostina Segatori. In any case, Vincent painted her portrait, under the title of *La femme au "Tambourin".* Toulouse-Lautrec did the same, but his picture was called *Poudre-de-Riz.*

The self portraits

At this time, Vincent painted several self portraits, probably for lack of models. Among them, there is one that seems to fully convey the character of the painter: Self-Portrait with Dark Felt Hat. His gaze reflects, on the one hand, the gentleness and the immense kindness of this man towards the humble and their human failings, while on the other, it shows an exceptional almost boundless power of penetration. In this work, Vincent looks pitilessly at himself, and his analysis lets nothing escape. It needed his sincerity, his greatness of soul, and his depth of spirit to thus strip himself naked.

This self portrait shows how he had changed, as Theo told their mother. He no longer presented himself as a peasant or a Bohemian, but as a comfortable gentleman, suitably clothed. The man shown there would certainly not have been conspicuous for extravagant outfits or artistic eccentricity.

The attraction of the East

At this time Vincent became fascinated by Japanese colour prints, which he could see at Bing's, the importer of art from the Far East. He painted three pictures in the Japanese style : *The Bridge* and *The Tree,* both after Hiroshige, and *Oiran* after Resei Yeisen.

Vincent completed during his stay in Paris, from March 1886 to February 1888, some 200 paintings and 50 drawings. But he longed

At left Boulevard Clichy and the Moulin Rouge; at the right 54 rue Lepic, where Theo put Vincent up during his stay in Paris

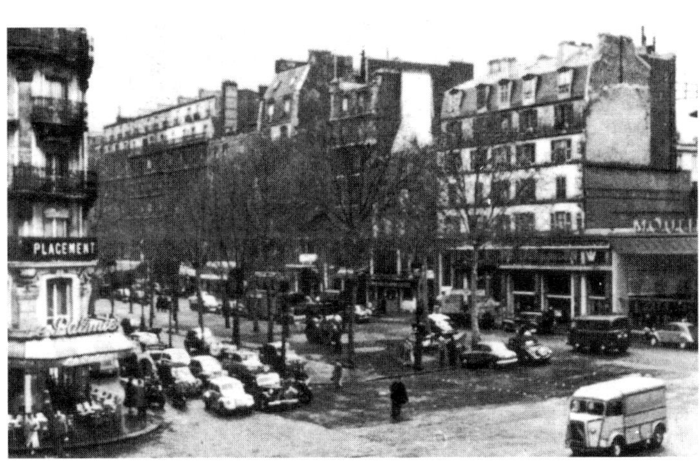

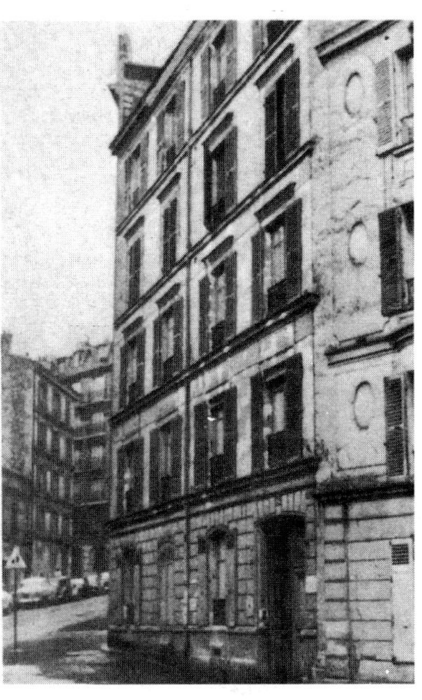

for more light and clarity. He wanted to be nearer the sun, and the desire for the South overcame him. When he announced that he was leaving for Arles, he hoped that Bernard would join him there. They walked together down to the avenue Clichy, shook hands, and it was goodbye for ever.

Thus ended Vincent's stay in Paris. Two important facts result from these two years : his palette had lightened through contact with the impressionists, but of all the painters that he had met, one alone - Gauguin - would still play a part in his life.

ARLES : THE CALL OF THE SOUTH 1888

On February 20, 1888, Vincent left Paris. He arrived at Arles the same day.

When he arrived, he saw a rare sight in Provence : it was snowing. This was a gift for a painter who, at first, could hardly believe his eyes. He seized his materials to make a very rare landscape : *Effect of Snow at Arles.* This painting, which Vincent described as *a whitened countryside with the town in the background,* is little known and probably has never been exhibited.

He rented a small room in the Hotel-restaurant Carrel, from which he could see the arena towers and those of various churches. Of course, he could not stop himself drawing this panorama.

For an idealistic painter like Vincent, a daring dream took shape, and his ideas concretised during the time he discovered and appreciated the tranquillity of Arles : *Why not,* he asked, *found a cooperative society which would share out equally among all the members the common income from works sold? An artist should be able to create free from all material cares.*

He expanded his ideas in a long letter that he wrote to Theo. He equally expected to do a packet of things for the 1890 Exposition universelle. But he was nonetheless under the spell of the countryside, and continued with his walks and his studies, for in Provence, the fruit trees blossom very early ; the almonds, well sheltered from the winds, start to put on their spring dress from January on. Vincent, more than ever invaded by nature, had arrived in time to successfully complete, working feverishly, a whole series of pictures and drawings, showing, in a prodigious succession of colours, the almond trees, the cherries, the apricots, the peaches, the plum trees, pears and apple trees. These stunning blossomings, with their white subtleties and delicate pinks, had a healthy influence on the inner state and health of Vincent.

I am in a flurry of work, because the trees are in flower and I

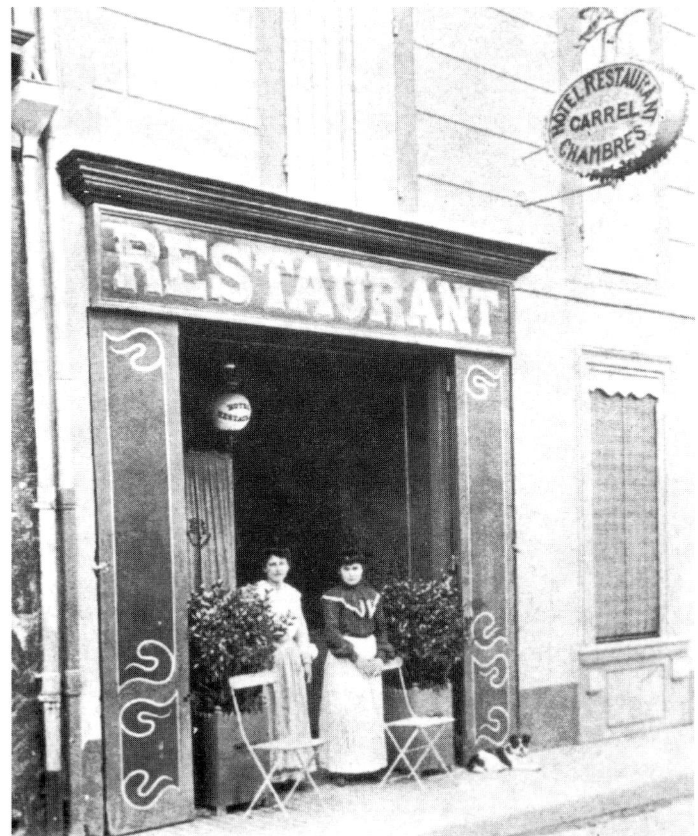

The Hotel-Restaurant Carrel, 30 rue Cavaline, where Vincent lived on arriving in Arles. The building was destroyed after the second world war.

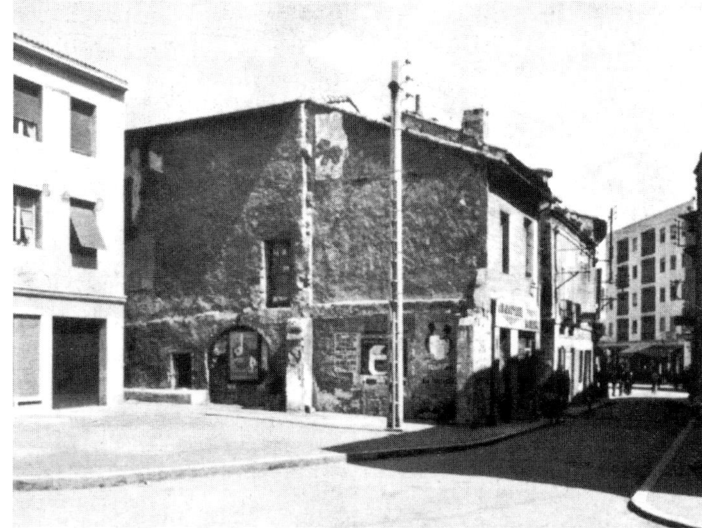

want to make a Provence orchard of enormous gaiety, he wrote in a letter at this time.

It is certain that, during his stay in Paris, Vincent was extremely interested by the avant-garde movements, and let himself be influenced by them, without, however, committing himself to any one of them. He spurned any easy imitation, for he wanted to succeed through his own originality. Again, he considered that the theories that his contemporaries used were already out of date. His own choice was exclusively directed towards individual expression, which did not stop him from finding elsewhere elements that were liable to nourish his own researches.

His rule from then on was that of "everything is allowed," provided that the final effect expresses the aim postulated. Vincent appeared to be the only one who knew how to exploit to its maximum Seurat's pointillist technique, taking it to a climax by the raging brutality of his brush strokes, their strength and their density.

The Provencal landscapes bathed in the ardent sunlight seemed to have a beneficent influence on his temperament, so prompt to react to external influences, and reality suddenly appeared to him under a flamboyant aspect, when he, so to speak, spectrographically analyzed the colours. By his small *Pont de Langlois*, more than by his orchards, Vincent taught his successors the charms of pure, violent, and striking colours.

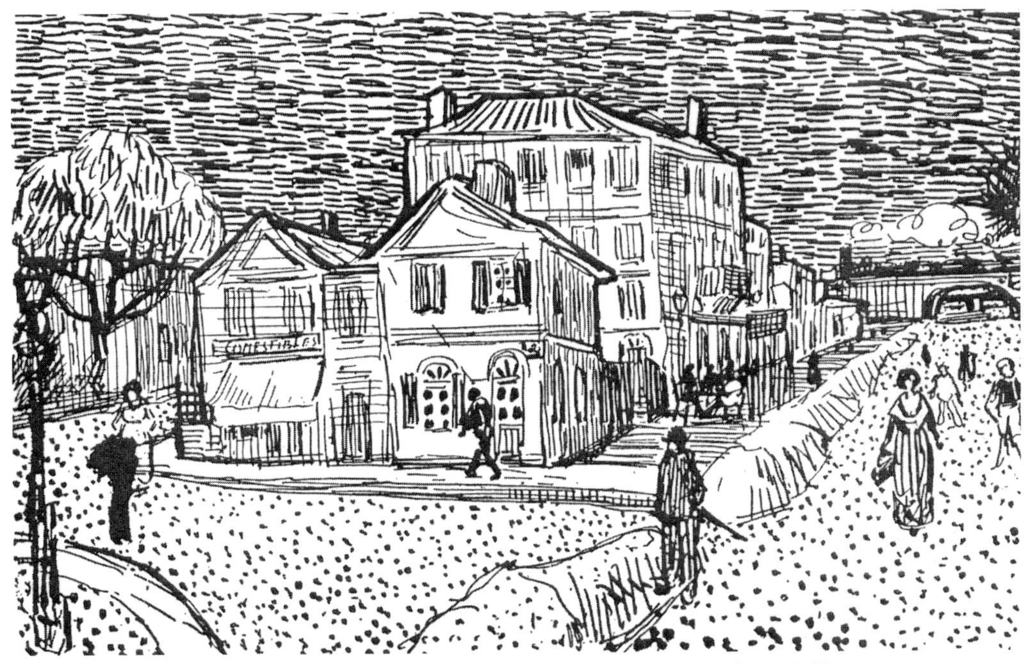

The Yellow House, drawn by Vincent in September 1888.

Thanks to his inspiration, Vincent made in a minimum of time astonishingly rapid progress. He was now in full possession of all his means, and could join beauty of expression and sobriety of style to a solid technique.

The Maison jaune

In May 1888, he rented, for 15 francs a month, the right wing of a house, number 2, place Lamartine. Because the walls were painted in yellow, Vincent straightaway called the building the "Maison jaune" (yellow house), which had a symbolic significance for him as the house of friendship.

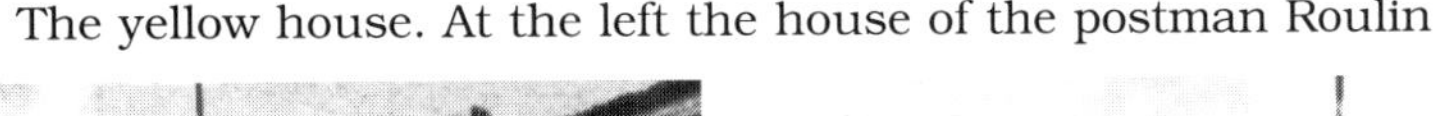

The yellow house. At the left the house of the postman Roulin

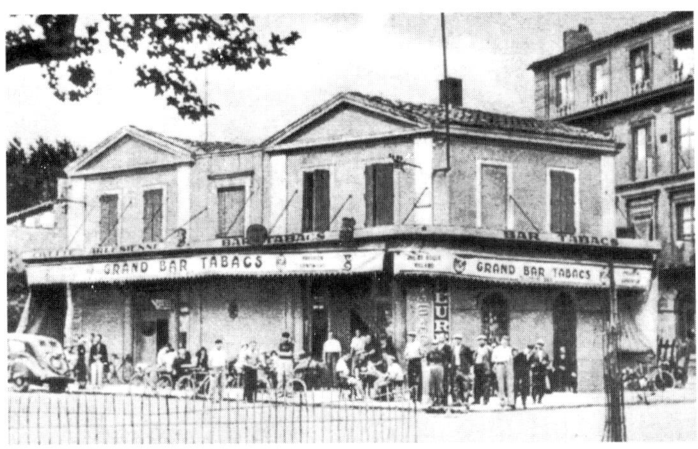

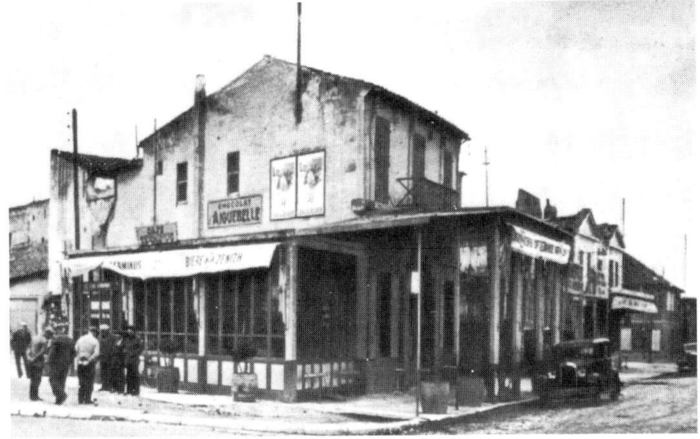

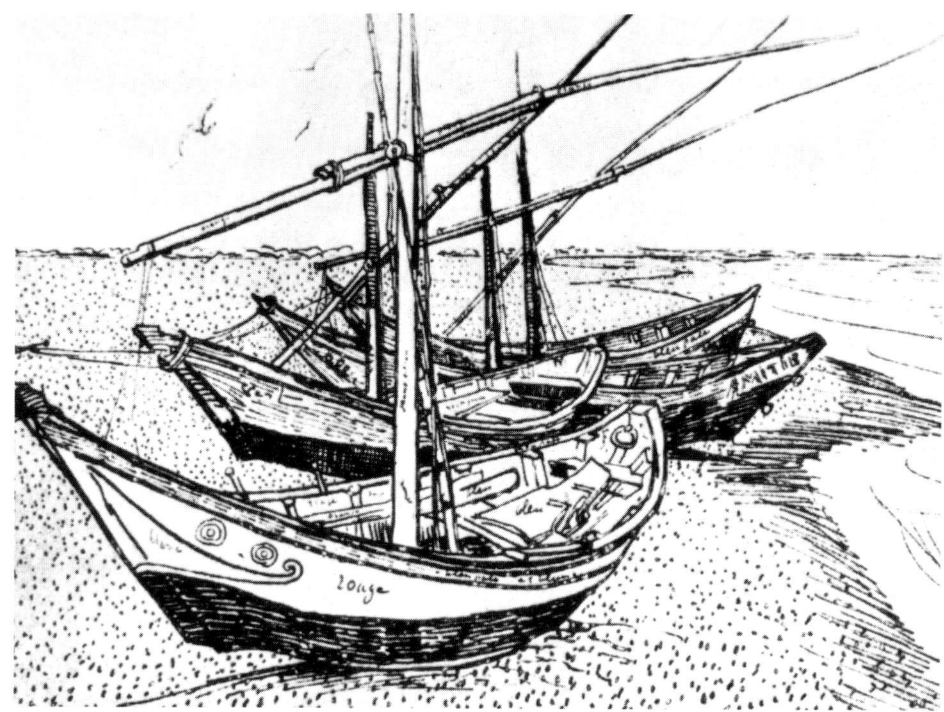

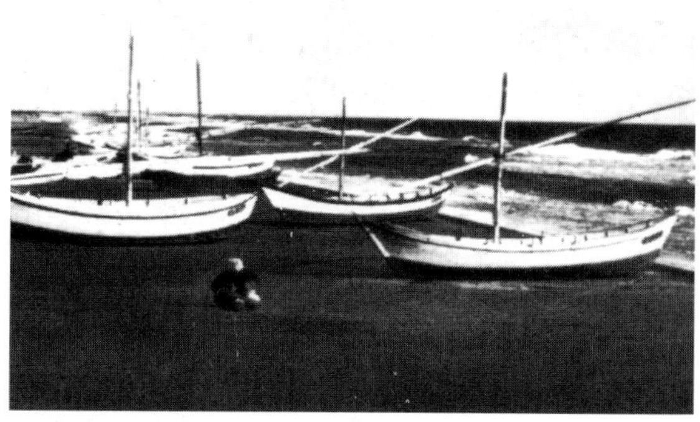

Boats on the Beach, drawn in red and black ink, in June of 1888.

While he was arranging his studio, Vincent took his meals at the Café de la Gare, kept by the Ginoux couple ; he slept at the Café de l'Alcazar, where he later painted the famous *Night Café.* He did not settle in to the "Maison jaune" before September 18.

His letters to Theo tell us how he arranged the "Maison jaune", but we can also have an idea through his works, particularly thanks to a picture, universally known, of his bedroom, with its wooden bed, washing stand, and two chairs.

The painter of the poor

At Arles, as elsewhere, Vincent recruited his models - with the exception the poet-painter Boch and Doctor Rey - from among the poor, who alas had little time, which explains why the painter had to paint so fast.

In this manner, he painted successively : *The Zouave* in June; *La Mousmé* in July ; *A Young Girl, The Postman Roulin* and *Patience Escalier* in August ; *Eugène Boch and Milliet* in September ; *Vincent's Mother,* from a photograph, in October ; *L'Arlèsienne, Armand Roulin, Camille Roulin* and *Madame Roulin* in November ; *The Actor* in December ; *Doctor Rey* in January 1889.

All these portraits, not forgetting *the Mother Rocking Her Baby*, capture the integrity of these people.

A tireless walker, Vincent covered the vicinity of Arles, looking

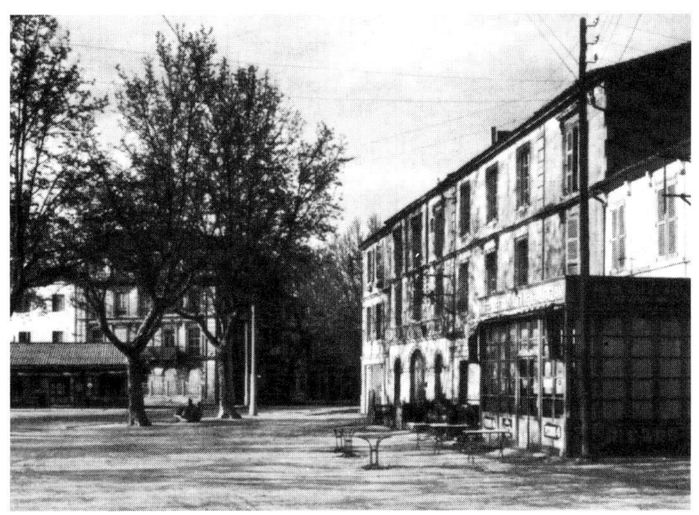

The Alcazar. It was here that Vincent painted Night Café.

for themes to paint. The country helped his vision of nature reach its full poetical expression.

In Vincent's work, the unusual arrangement of the construction of forms appears, from the technical standpoint, to be a mixture of Western traditions and Oriental techniques. Far from surprising us, this amalgam should appear logical. An inventory of the technical means Vincent used to serve his virtuosity, comes down to the simplest elements: a small dot, a straight line, and a curved line. Surfaces filled up with small dots and cross hatchings of straight or curved lines create the tones, giving the whole an impression of volume and space.

All this seems simple and naive to us, yet, before Vincent, no other European was successful with such a technique. Hokusai, who preceded him up to a point in this field, did not conceal the efforts he had to make before arriving at a similar accomplishment.

Arlésienne nights

One night in September, wandering around the centre of Arles, Vincent suddenly stopped in front of a café with a terrace lit by a gas lamp. He was so struck by the sight that he intended to make it live again on canvas.

Now that he was familiar with the effects of the Provençal light on the appearance of the town and on the countryside, even on starlit nights, he was convinced that the violent contrasts of Japanese prints would gain tremendously in depth and in beauty were they to be painted in oils on canvas. After all, the Japanese works were and continued to be mere printed coloured engravings ; they could not allow, such as they were, the mysterious vibrations of light to be felt, the subtleties of which could be rendered on canvas and made sensitive by the brush hairs. Vincent thought to obtain a striking effect by accentuating the contrast between the deep blue and the clear yellow of the prints, with the velvety blue of the night sky, the sparkling stars, hanging over the golden light of the terrace in the place du Forum. He wrote to Theo : T*he sky is blue-green, the water royal blue, the fields are mauve, the town is blue and violet, the gas is yellow and the reflections in gold and rust descend to bronze green. On the blue-green field of the sky, the Great Bear has a green and pink sparkle, of which the discreet paleness contrasts with the crude gold of the gas light.*

How could he tell in the dark his palette colours and those of the canvas ?

One night, very late, a strange figure walked the little, badly lit, narrow and winding streets; he carried all sorts of tools in his hands, and hung on his back was a wooden box suspended from a leather strap. His head was covered by a bowler hat with a wide brim, on which were fixed candles. Arriving at the place du Forum, he set up his easel in front of the café, and put a white canvas on it, also ornamented with candles, on each side and above.

When all the candles were lit, he started to paint ; the sight was truly bizarre, and the next day all Arles knew that the redhead was mad, but nobody doubted his genius.

After having painted the *Night Café*, he painted, several days later - still equipped with his candle-bearing hat- *Starry Night.*

LIVING WITH GAUGUIN OCTOBER 1888 - DECEMBER 1888

At Paris, during the discussions in the Montmartre bistros, Gauguin strongly impressed Vincent, who considered him the leader of the movement for renewal.

In keeping with the dream he had always embraced of creating a work in direct collaboration, Vincent naturally thought of asking Gauguin to come and live at the "Maison jaune".

In fact, the only thing that Gauguin had in common with Vincent was his firm determination to escape the cul-de-sac they both found themselves in due to the failings of impressionism. Gauguin was devoured by a burning ambition, which he followed with more calculation than pure artistic inspiration.

Living above all for his decorative preoccupations, Gauguin was hardly prepared to understand Vincent's work, basically directed towards realism.

Only the deep misery in which he found himself drew Gauguin to Arles, like a starving wolf leaving the forest. He went here, convinced that in doing so, he would get into Theo's good books, who would then sell his paintings for a decent price.

"From the day after (his arrival), we were at work," said Gauguin.

At first, all seemed to go well, even though Gauguin, according to his memoirs, had been shocked originally by the mess that was everywhere. This does not surprise us, for Theo had already complained of Vincent's untidiness, that had quickly changed their rooms in the rue Lepic into a junk heap.

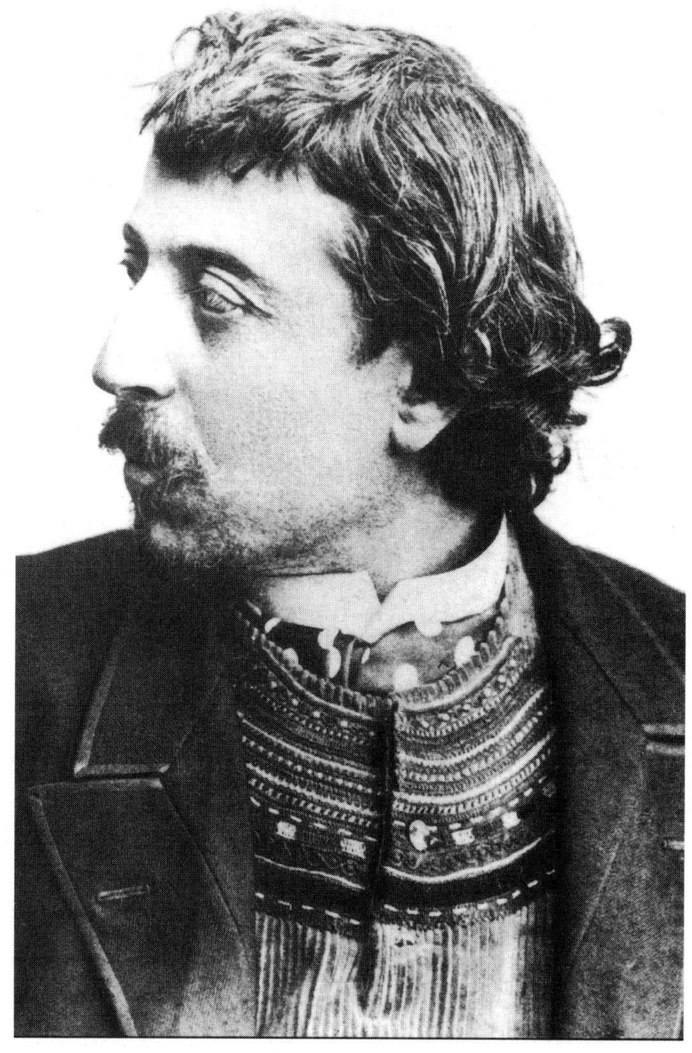

Paul Gauguin.

Vincent and Gauguin took turns cleaning and cooking ; during the day, they painted inside as well as outside; among other sites, at the Alyscamps, where one day they found themselves side by side, but looking in opposite directions. At night, they went to the brothels of the little garrison town; Gauguin called these visits : "nocturnal, hygienic walks."

Vincent, who already knew the maison Tutelle in a back street, was not at all a debauchee, but the presence of Gauguin, a great womanizer, led him to go more often to the Arles red light area.

At the beginning, there was a good understanding between the two painters. They took a trip together to Montpellier to visit the Fabre museum.

There they saw Courbet's *Bonjour, Monsieur Courbet*, which inspired Gauguin to later paint his *Bonjour, Monsieur Gauguin*. Another time, at the "Maison jaune", Gauguin made a portrait of Vincent while he was painting his famous sunflowers.

But it was clear that the two men were not made to get on together. On December 23, 1888, Vincent wrote to Theo : *I believe that Gauguin is a bit discouraged with the good town of Arles, with the little yellow house where we work, and above all, with me. In fact, there are still for him, as for me, grave difficulties to overcome here. But these difficulties lie more in ourselves than elsewhere. Altogether, I believe that either he goes away altogether or he makes up his mind to stay. Before doing anything, I told him to think about it and to redo his calculations: Gauguin is very strong, very creative, but just because of that he needs peace. Will he find it somewhere else if he can't find it here? I am waiting with absolute calm for him to make a decision.*

After two months of working together, the tension between them reached its summit. Very early on December 24, the police commissioner found Vincent in bed with his left ear lobe cut off, and he had him taken to the municipal hospital.

One can imagine an explanation for Vincent's act. As he was subject to frequent aural hallucinations, he might have heard, during his quarrels with Gauguin, a voice whispering in his ear : "Kill him!" After flinging himself on his friend with an open razor, he remembered after his moment of folly had passed, a passage from the Bible, which he knew well : "If thy limb offend thee, cut it off." And he hoped he would be absolved from his sin by punishing himself....

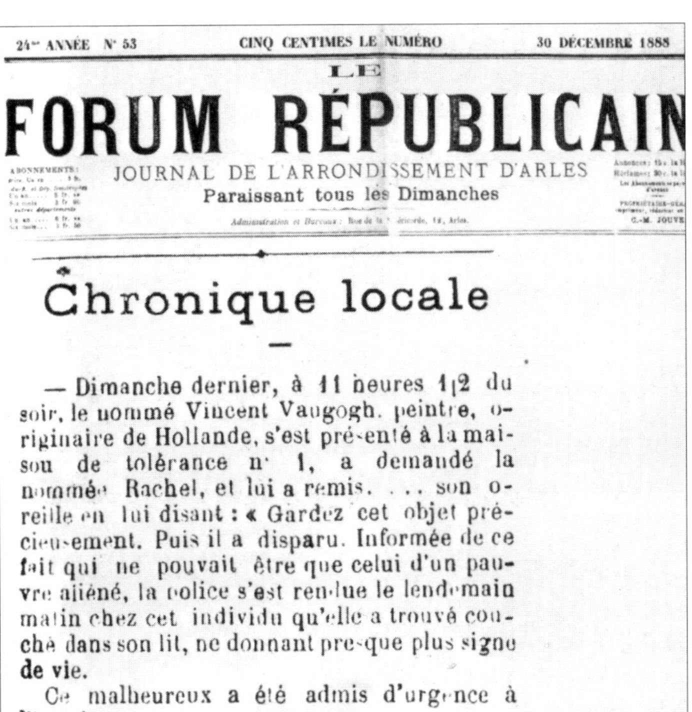

24me ANNÉE N° 53 CINQ CENTIMES LE NUMÉRO 30 DÉCEMBRE 1888

LE FORUM RÉPUBLICAIN

JOURNAL DE L'ARRONDISSEMENT D'ARLES

Paraissant tous les Dimanches

Chronique locale

— Dimanche dernier, à 11 heures 1/2 du soir, le nommé Vincent Vaugogh, peintre, originaire de Hollande, s'est présenté à la maison de tolérance n° 1, a demandé la nommée Rachel, et lui a remis. . . . son oreille en lui disant : « Gardez cet objet précieusement. Puis il a disparu. Informée de ce fait qui ne pouvait être que celui d'un pauvre aliéné, la police s'est rendue le lendemain matin chez cet individu qu'elle a trouvé couché dans son lit, ne donnant presque plus signe de vie.

Ce malheureux a été admis d'urgence à l'hospice.

Contrary to popular opinion Vincent did not cut off his entire ear, but only the lower part as the arrow indicates.

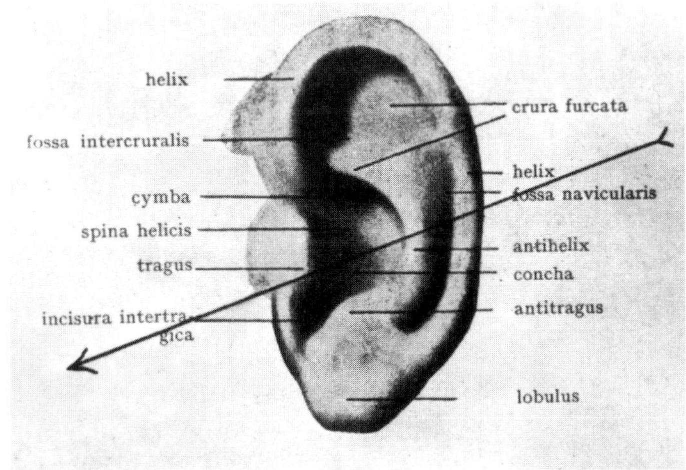

Illness progresses

One thing is sure : when Vincent found himself at the height of his powers, his mind gave way. The fury with which he attacked his work, which had already allowed him to achieve in his paintings and drawings his greatest hopes with an unbelievable ease, had to undermine little by little the strongest constitution.

Hardening himself against toil and fatigue, he never gave himself a moment's respite ; from early morning until late into the night, he worked ceaselessly at his art.

On January 7, 1889, Vincent left hospital and returned to his "Maison jaune".

Vincent's artistic heritage includes some records of his stay in hospital. We should mention his painting and his drawing of the *Garden of the Asylum.* The contrast is striking between the two scenes: the interior of the cell, dark and discouraging enough to drive one mad, and the luminous exterior like a dream from the Thousand and One Nights.

Vincent went back to work, but on February 9, he had to go back to hospital, worn out by sleeplessness and hallucinations. Other than the fear that his illness would become worse, another thing bothered Dr Rey. Ever since Vincent had left hospital the first time, he caused panic wherever he went. The inhabitants became hostile towards him, even to the point of signing a petition. On March 11, Vincent was again put into a cell in the Hôtel-Dieu.

With his health destroyed, his nerves on edge, without any support, feeling himself considered to be a mad and dangerous eccentric, Vincent broke down. Nervousness and folly overcame him following his relapse.The threats that left him no rest, no truce wherever he was, made him worse rather than better.

In these circumstances, Pastor Selles, after making enquiries, advised Vincent to go to Saint-Rémy-de- Provence, where there was an institution that would be good for him. Taking into account the isolated state that Vincent found himself in on leaving the Arles hospital, the doctors encouraged this solution.

Finally, on May 3, 1889, Vincent replied : *Alright for Saint-Rémy, then.*

SAINT-RÉMY-DE-PROVENCE : THE ASYLUM TIME 1889 - 1890

Crossing the threshold of the asylum, for a moment Vincent imagined that he had left the world of "normal" people for ever.

He found he was mistaken ; he could not escape outside influences, nor take leave of his unconquerable passion for painting and drawing, which had once elicited from him, in autumn 1887, the following confession : *When one has within one passion and a soul, one cannot snuff them out; one prefers to burn than to be snuffed. That that one has within one must come out.*

The day after his arrival, he set to work. In the garden he found two excellent subjects : violet iris flowers and a lilac bush. *The idea of the need to work,* he wrote, *came to me often and I believe that all my faculties for work will come back to me quickly.*

Vincent had the use of two cell rooms. One of them could be considered his bedroom. Vincent himself gave the following description : *I have a little room with grey- green wallpaper ;* he went on to say: *through the iron- barred window, I can see a square of wheat in a close, a perspective after van Goyen, and over which I see in the morning the sun in all his glory.*

The other room - his working cell - was on the first floor, and it must be said that Vincent had a superb view over the convent garden towards the Alpilles mountains, which stood out against the sky, showing their peculiar peaks and hollows.

Vincent at the height of his powers

It was certainly at this period of his career, in his "seeing madness", with the whirling suns and wavering of upset grounds that the deepest character of Vincent's art was revealed. He joined together an unprecedented freedom of spirit with a freedom of expression that has never been surpassed.

In his exaltation, Vincent animated elements observed in their reality with a breadth that seems to take them beyond our know ledge. He violently threw the elements and light itself into a crucible. They explode with the vast vibration of a cosmos in creation.

By this passage from the real to the reflection, which is the essential secret of art, Vincent undertook what most of his colleagues would never dare to imagine. Thanks to his remarkable clear sightedness, he became one of the greatest liberators of pictorial subjectivity, and, at the same time, one of the greatest lyric poets of nineteenth century art, perhaps of all time.

The asylum Saint Paule-de-Mausole at Saint Rémy.

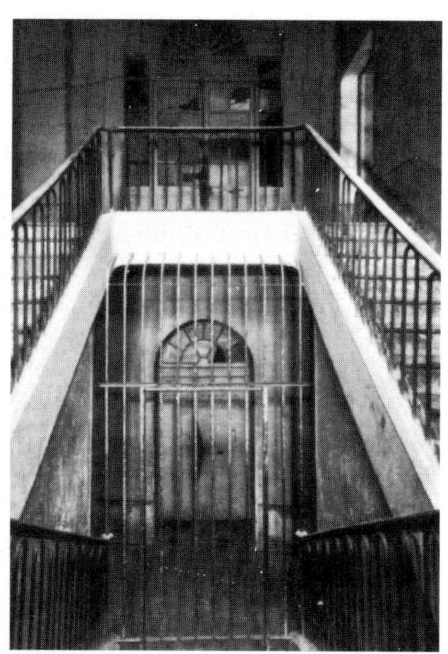

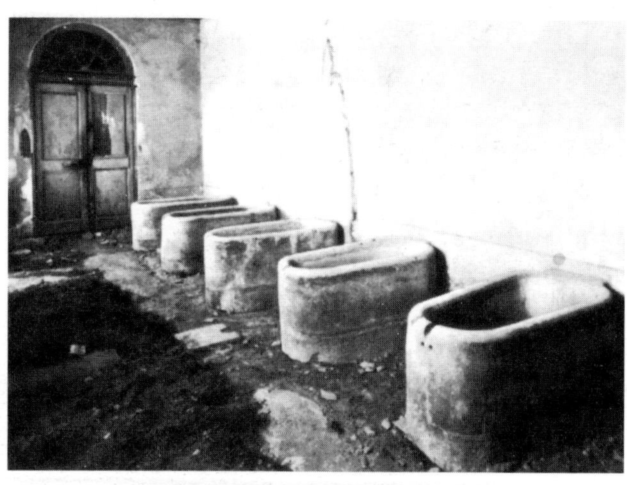

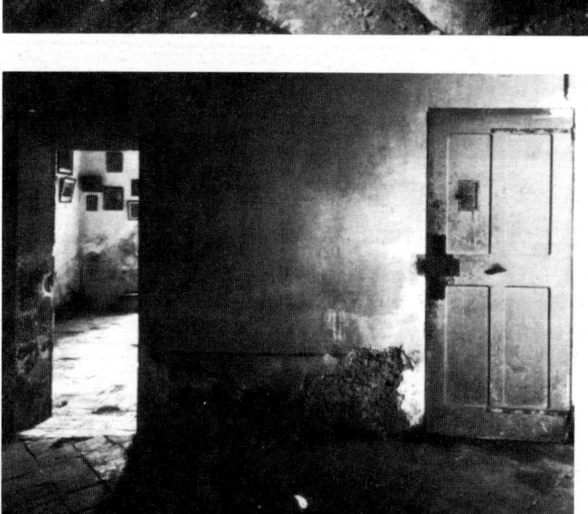

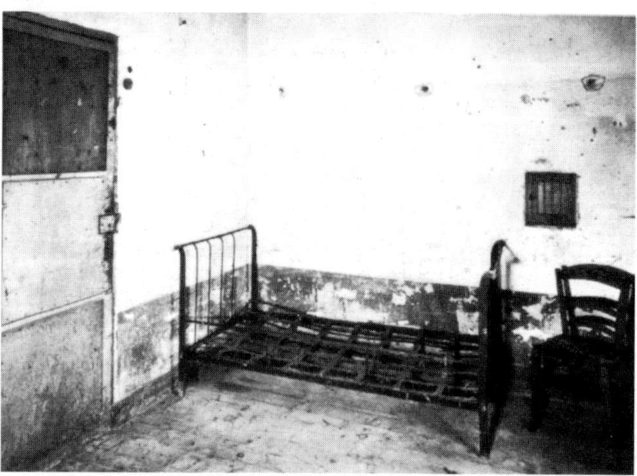

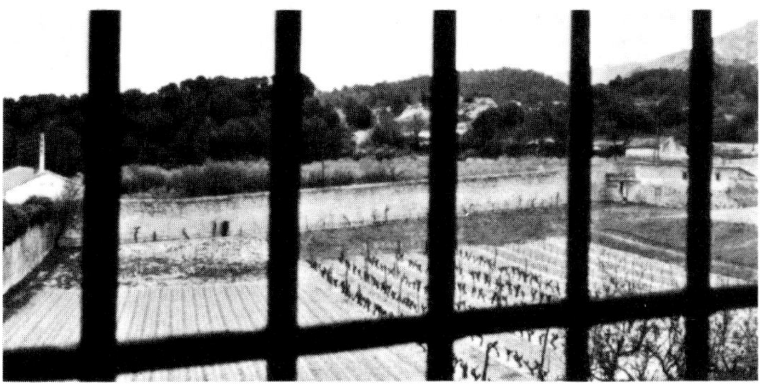
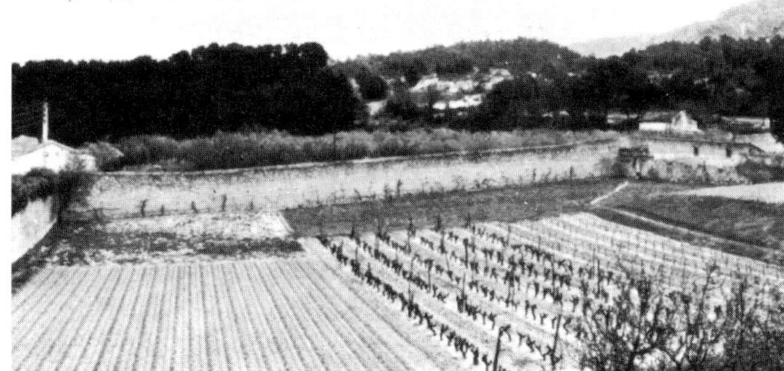

From behind these bars Vincent looked out on the countryside, which he drew and painted many times.

Within the asylum buildings, with its park oriented towards the south, and its vegetable garden, Vincent enjoyed relative freedom. He could paint there whenever he wanted. So were made several canvases, which show different views of the grounds ; some of them may be classified among his most fully realized productions.

Dr Peyron, who looked after him, had promised Theo that Vincent would be allowed to paint outside the asylum, and he kept his word.

Vincent told Theo that his work was going as he wanted, which was saying a lot for a man who was his own severest critic ; he also said that he had discovered things that he had been searching for in vain over the years. A glance at the productions dating from the first weeks at Saint-Rémy-de-Provence confirms this assessment.

Olive groves in Saint Rémy

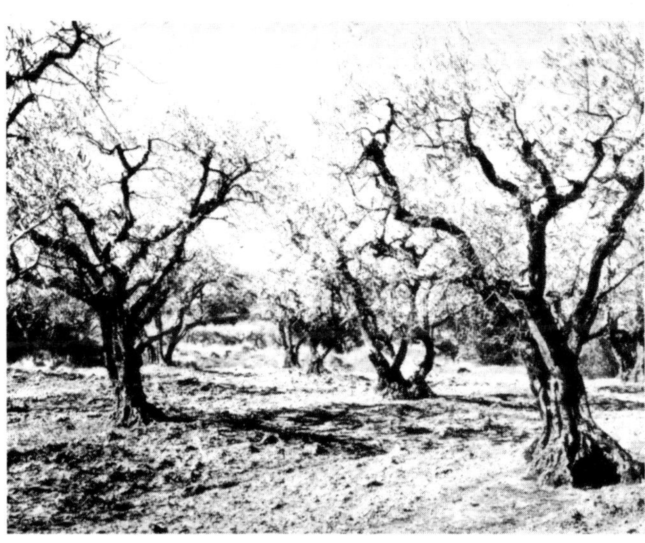
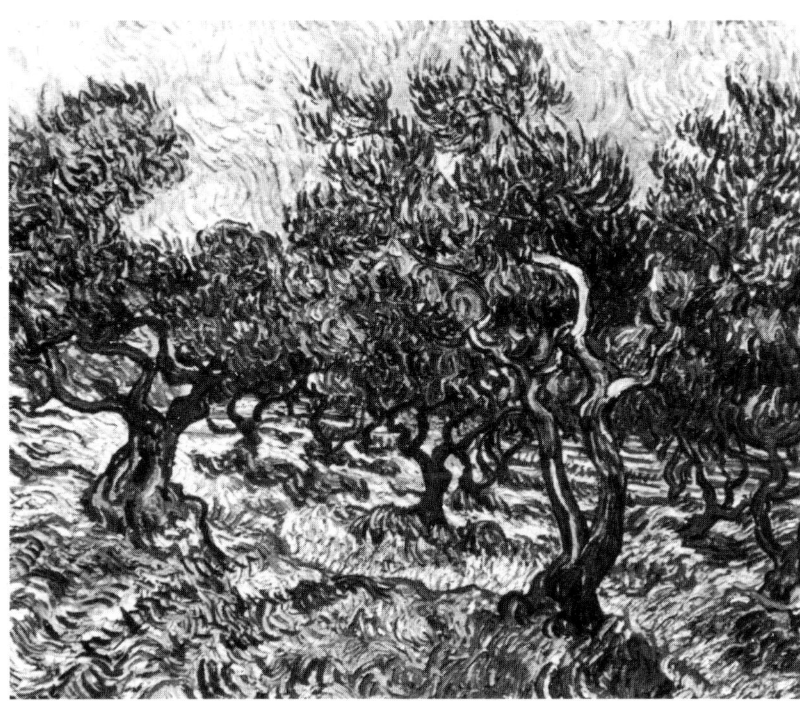

Illness omnipresent

At the beginning of July, Vincent felt his spirit break down. While he was working on a subject in the fields, he was suddenly seized by a new crisis. The acute phase of this attack lasted until the end of July, but a period of prostration and mental exhaustion stayed with him until August.

During each crisis, Vincent behaved like a lost soul for several days. Then, little by little, his strength came back to him. After these crises, Vincent regained an astonishing lucidity which enabled him to create pictures that are striking in their serenity. Some specialists have spoken of epilepsy, others of schizophrenia, while yet others have produced more complicated diagnoses.

The cypresses

Vincent's rendering of cypress trees provides a key to his mental state.

These flamboyant trees inspired Vincent to make several remarkable pictures. At the beginning, in Arles, they did not play an important part in his landscapes.

At Saint-Rémy-de-Provence, all at once they began to domin ate his compositions. On June 25, 1889, Vincent wrote to Theo that he hade made two studies of cypresses, with their delicate bottle-green nuances, while working the foreground with thick layers of white lead, to give solidity to the ground.

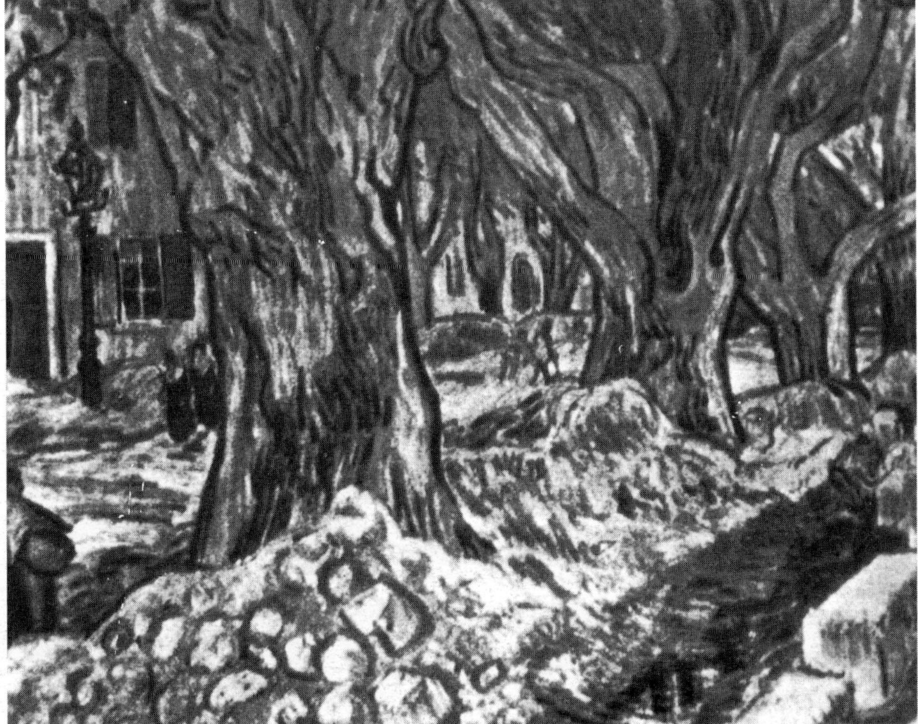

This spot that Vincent painted still exists in Saint Rémy.

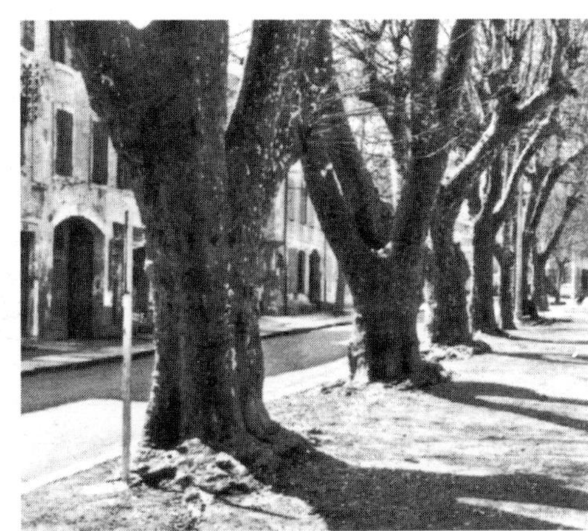

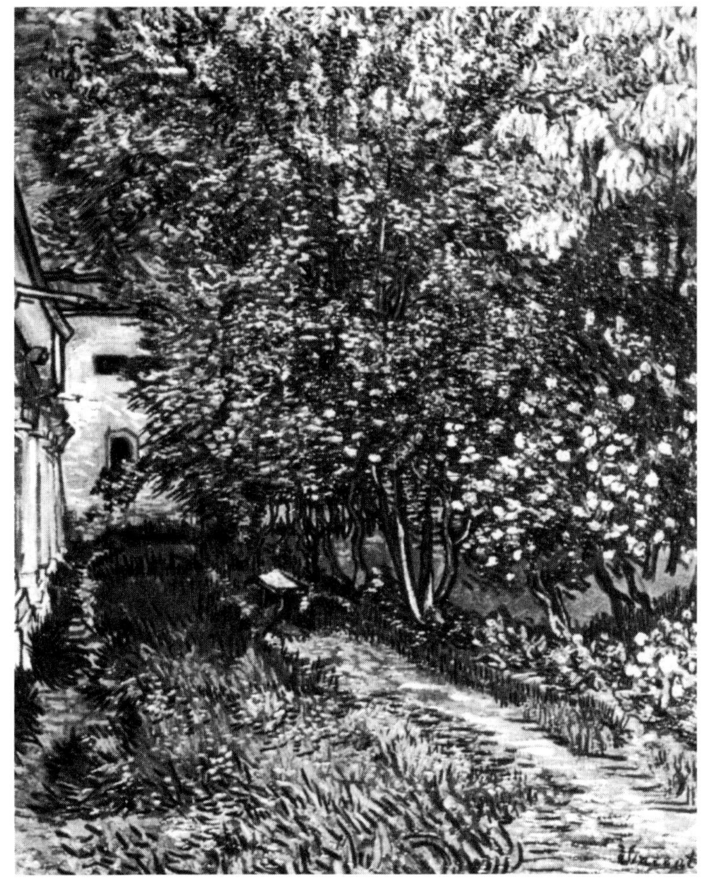

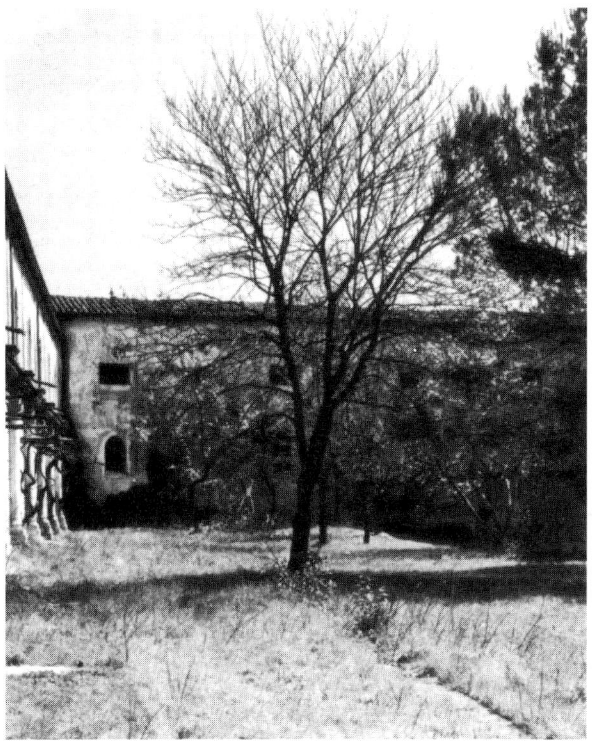

The asylum garden

The more Vincent's depression, discouragement and sadness grew, the more dramatic became his depictions of the cypresses; they ended by occupying the whole surface of his canvas, threatening to cover up completely the landscape, which was practically reduced to nothing.

On February 1, 1890, Vincent learned of the birth of his nephew. He, who liked children so much, was to become the god father of this little boy who carried his name.

A few days later, on February 15, he wrote the following in a letter addressed to his mother : *I would have much preferred that Theo had given his son Pa's name, whom I have thought about a lot these days, rather than mine. However, now that it's done, I started straightaway a picture for him, to hang in his bedroom: several big flowery almond branches against a blue sky.*

In the same letter, he added : *I should add to this that Theo told me yesterday that he had sold one of my canvases in Brussels, for 400 francs.*

The only pictures sold in his lifetime

In November, Vincent himself made the choice of several pictures that Theo could send to the Salon des XX, a Belgian artistic group who exhibited in Brussels. *Here is what I would like to exhibit,* he wrote to Theo, *1 and 2, the two Sunflower pendants, 3, the ivy, 4, the orchard in blossom (which Tanguy is exhibiting at the moment) with poplars crossing the canvas, 5, the red vineyard 6, wheatfield, sunrise, which I am working on at the moment.*

One of these six pictures found a buyer, *the Red Vineyard.* This canvas, which now delights visitors to the Hermitage in St. Petersburg, was bought by Anna Boch, the sister of the Belgian poet-painter Eugène Boch, whom Vincent knew for several weeks at Arles.

The sale comforted Vincent very much, above all when he found out that it was the sister of a friend, an artist herself, who was the buyer.

This picture along with a self portrait bought 15 months earlier by a London gallery, were the only ones sold in Van Gogh's life time.

The painter Anna Boch, who bought the Red Vineyard

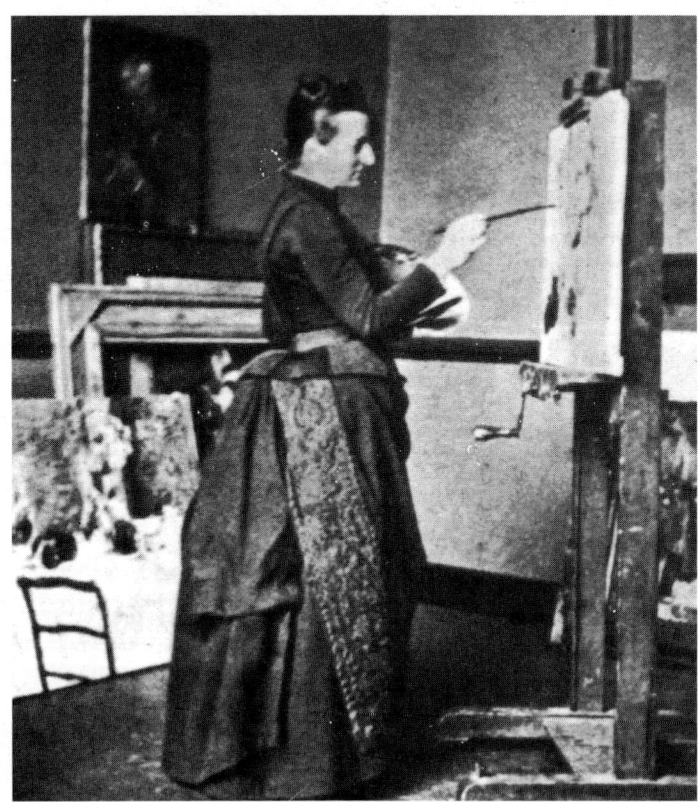

AUVERS-SUR-OISE : TO DIE IS DIFFICULT, BUT TO LIVE IS STILL MORE DIFFICULT MAY 1890 - JULY 1890

Feeling crippled by the proximity of madmen, Vincent decided to leave the asylum.

For some time now, Theo had been trying to find another lodging for Vincent, nearer to Paris, but still in the country.

Pissarro told him of a doctor who, in his spare time, painted, drew, and engraved. This original character was called Paul-Ferdinand Gachet, but in the art world, he was better known by his pseudonym: Paul van Rijssel (of Lille), after his native village. He boasted of descending, by his paternal grandmother, from Jean de Mabuse, which explained his artistic disposition.

In these two fields, medicine and art, he acted as an innovator. On the one hand, he was one of the first to practice homeopathic medicine and use the therapeutic properties of electricity. On the other, he was one of the first and the most fervent admirers of impressionist painting. His artistic leanings also explain why he had so many friends and acquaintances among painters. To the names already mentioned, those of Sisley, Renoir and Monet could be added.

After a three day stay in Paris, where he got to know his sister-in-law, previously only seen in a photograph, Vincent went to Dr. Gachet's house at Auvers-sur-Oise.

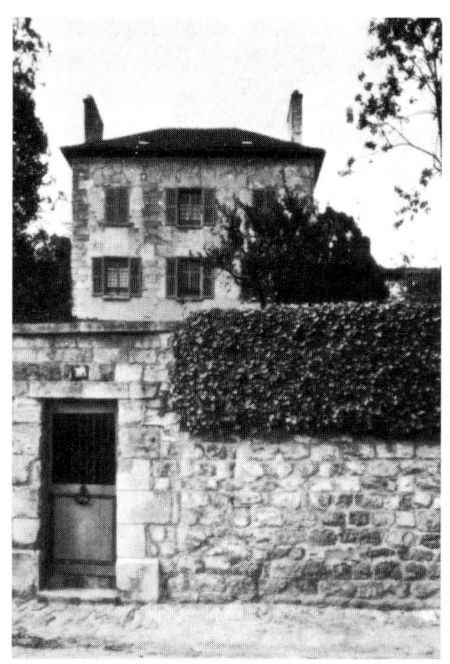

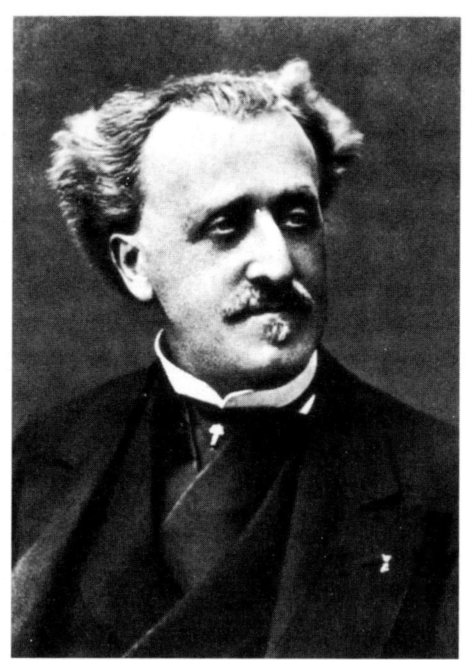

The house of Doctor Gachet

Like his predecessors, he became friends with the man he had heard so much about.

The house of this doctor-painter - a real little gallery - pleased him very much. *He has a very beautiful Pissarro, winter with a red house in the snow, and two pretty flower paintings by Cézanne,* he wrote to his brother. This was a very brief enumeration of all that was to be seen there - beautiful and interesting works by Renoir, Monet, Guillaumin, Courbet, and Sisley, even Daumier.

Vincent looked for a lodging not too far from Gachet's house; he rented an attic room in the Ravoux's café- restaurant.

The rage to paint

Always, Vincent was an prodigious worker, from the crack of dawn until night; and at Auvers, his activity attained an unprecedented rhythm. He went to bed at night fall, and rose very early, in general before sunrise. *Work,* he wrote, *is what I can do the least badly. All the rest... is very secondary.*

In a note, Dr Jan Hulsker stated that Vincent, having stayed at most 70 days at Auvers-sur-Oise, produced in that short time 70 pictures and more than 30 drawings, which is truly astonishing. From landscapes, he turned to portraits, and from portraits returned to landscapes. It often happened that he would start a new canvas when he had barely given the last touch to the preceding one.

To obtain a more or less accurate idea of this extraordinary output, it is necessary to glance at a short chronological table obtained only from information furnished by the painter himself.

In May : 21st, a study of old thatched roofs ; the 25th, a study of an old vine that Vincent proposed to make into a painting ; 30th, a study of a chestnut tree ; a study of a horse chestnut. In June : 4th, a portrait of Dr Gachet plus a second version ; a study of an aloe with marigolds and cypresses ; a study of white roses and vines ; 14th, a harvest study ; a field of daisies ; a landscape with a small cart ; a study of a vine ; 17th, a study of a bunch of wild plants ; of a white house ; a garden study ; between 16th and 23rd, a study of ears of wheat ; 24th, the portrait of Adeline Ravoux, plus a second and a third version ; a wheat field ; a thicket ; Auvers château ; 29th, a portrait of Miss Gachet at the piano ; 30th, a peasant woman ; a landscape with fields ; a thicket. In July : 9th, two wheat fields beneath troubled skies ; Daubigny garden ; 23rd, old thatched cottages.

Beyond these two dozen pictures mentioned by Vincent in his letters, we also know of three dozen canvases from his hand in which we again find the vigorous simplicity and disciplined ardour of his creation.

The room at the Auberge Ravoux where Vincent died

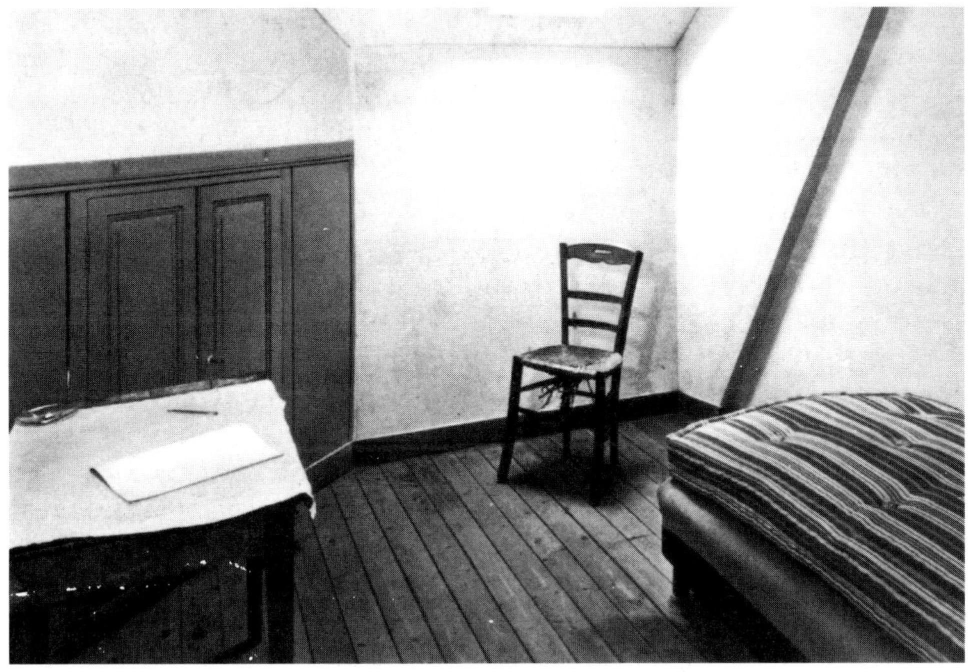

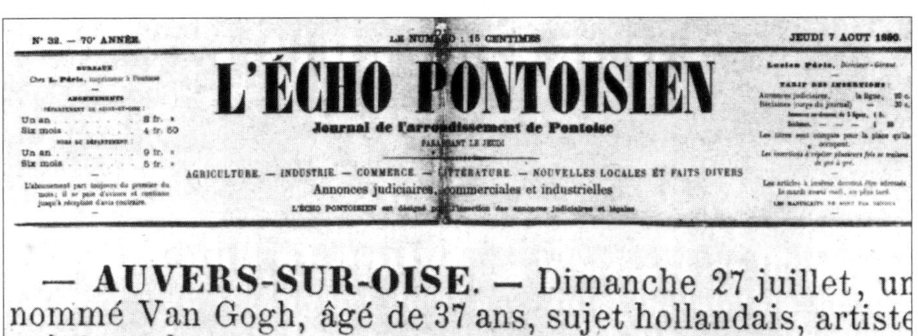

N° 32. — 70e ANNÉE — LE NUMÉRO : 15 CENTIMES — JEUDI 7 AOUT 1890

L'ÉCHO PONTOISIEN

Journal de l'arrondissement de Pontoise

PARAISSANT LE JEUDI

AGRICULTURE. — INDUSTRIE. — COMMERCE. — LITTÉRATURE. — NOUVELLES LOCALES ET FAITS DIVERS

Annonces judiciaires, commerciales et industrielles

— **AUVERS-SUR-OISE.** — Dimanche 27 juillet, un nommé Van Gogh, âgé de 37 ans, sujet hollandais, artiste peintre, de passage à Auvers, s'est tiré un coup de revolver dans les champs et, n'étant que blessé, il est rentré à sa chambre où il est mort le surlendemain.

The last days

In his letter of June 3, 1890, he wrote to Theo : *My health continues good ... I feel surer of my brush than before going to Arles. And Dr. Gachet says that he finds it very unlikely that it will happen again, and that is altogether good.*

Obviously, Dr. Gachet, as a good doctor, attempted to reassure Vincent as to an eventual return of his crises, knowing full well that otherwise his patient's nervousness would increase. But it is difficult to imagine that he did not suspect that Vincent's calm was only temporary. And the future was to show that it was an illusion.

On Sunday July 27, at the end of the afternoon, the Gachet family watched Vincent walk away, apparently calm. Some previous incidents had already disquieted Dr. Gachet. In fact, something was happening. He suspected that Vincent might have a hidden purpose.

One Sunday, while lunching with the Gachets, had not Vincent suddenly thrown down his napkin and left the table, to go back to his brushes ? Had there not also been that attempt to attack Dr Gachet because he had not taken care to frame a picture by Guillaumin ?

But that Sunday, while the Gachet family watched Vincent go off, they did not know that he was going to the place where he was to commit suicide.

Some said that he went behind the graveyard, where there stretched out immense wheat fields. The famous painting of the crows above the wheat was painted not far from there.

Others said that he went to the yard of a small farm. There he hid behind the dunghill and shot himself in the breast.

He had the strength to return to the Ravoux auberge.

"But what have you done ?" asked Dr. Gachet when he found him stretched on his bed at the auberge. *I have shot myself... Let us hope that I didn't miss...* replied Vincent.

The following morning, July 28, Theo saw, at his office, a messenger who gave him a note from Dr. Gachet, and without losing a moment, he went to Auvers-sur-Oise. In the tiny room, with breaking heart and tears in his eyes he saw his poor brother in his last agony. Observing Theo's distress, Vincent said : *Don't cry, I've done it for the good of us all.*

At one moment, he asked what the doctors thought of his condition, and when Theo assured him that they would save him, he replied : *It's useless... Sadness will last a lifetime....*

At nightfall, Vincent became weaker, and at about 1:00 in the morning of Tuesday July 29, 1890, having suddenly lost consciousness, he breathed his last in Theo's arms, who had never left him.

By 10:00 in the morning, Gachet, Ravoux, Tanguy and Emile Bernard, accompanied by Charles Laval, had joined Theo there.

Later, many others arrived, artists especially, among them Lucien Pissarro and Lauzel.

The burial took place on Wednesday July 30, at 3:00 in the afternoon. Thanks to Theo, Vincent, who had laid violent hands on himself, had a tombstone.

Six months later, Theo, worn out, went to join Vincent. In 1914, his remains were taken to Auvers-sur-Oise where now the two brothers, whom nothing could separate, lie side by side.

One day, Theo had said : "I should not be astonished if my brother was not a great genius and that he will be compared with someone like Beethoven." Theo made no mistake; the future was to prove him right.

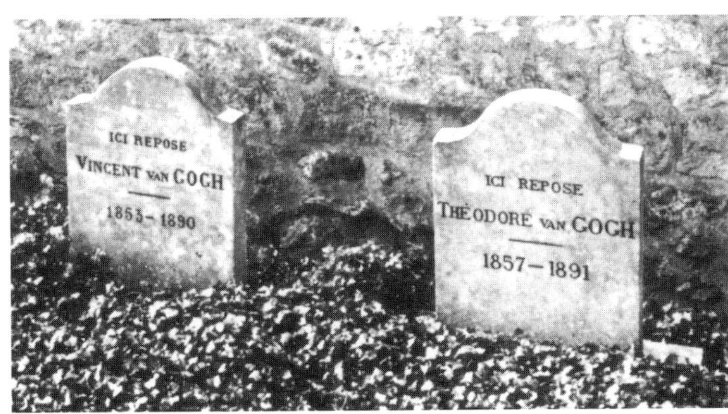

Gravestones of Vincent and Theo in the cemetery in Auvers-sur-oise

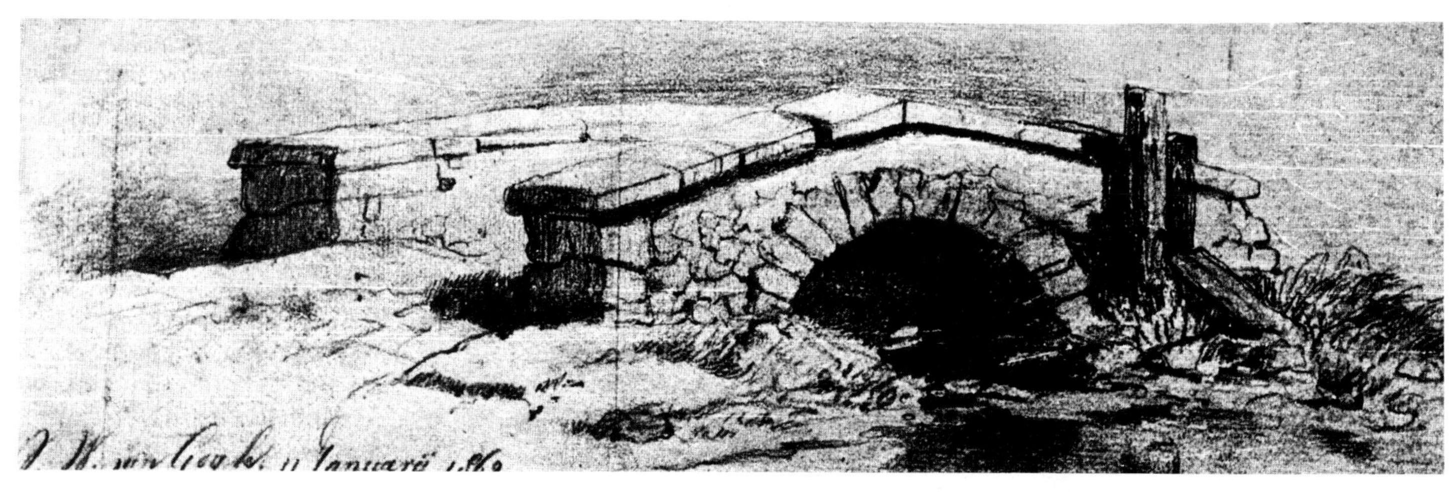

The Bridge

January 11 - pencil on Holland paper
- 12 x 36.5 cm-
Rijksmuseum Kröller- Müller, Otterlo

Milk Pitcher

September 5, 1862 - pencil on Holland paper
- 27.8 x 22 cm. -
Rijksmuseum Kröller- Müller, Otterlo

The Dog

December 28, 1862 - pencil on Holland paper
- 28 x 28.5 cm -
Rijksmuseum Kröller- Müller, Otterlo

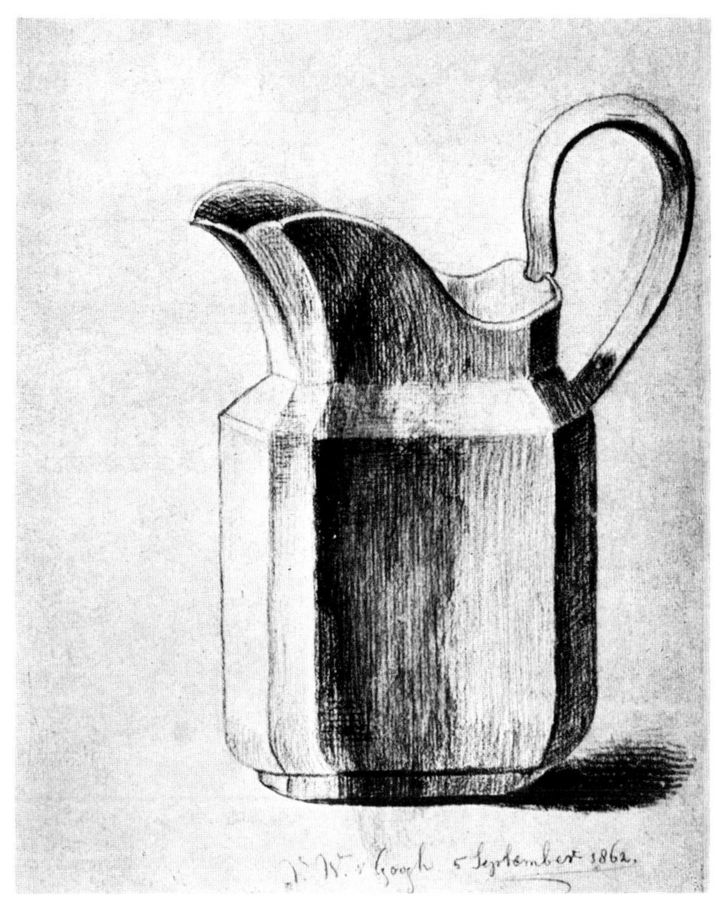

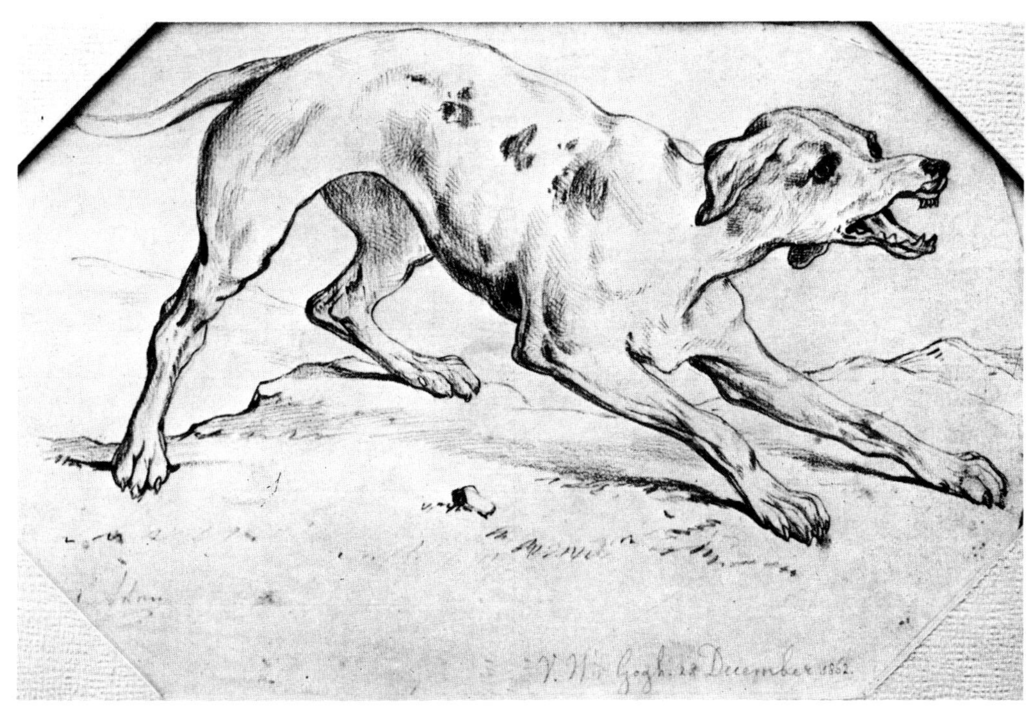

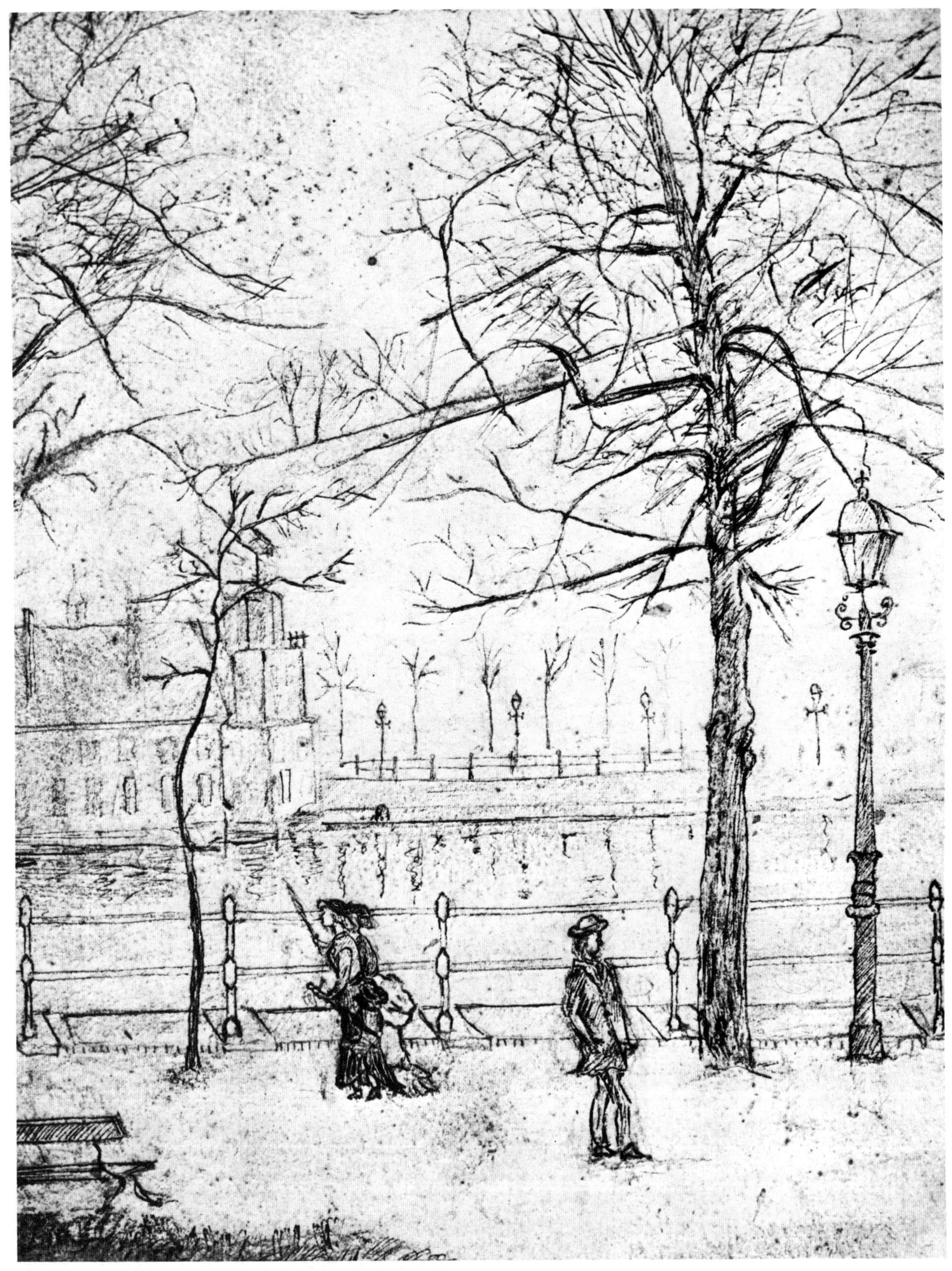

Promenade in The Hague

February 8, 1864 - ink - 22 x 17 cm -
Vincent Van Gogh Foundation, Amsterdam

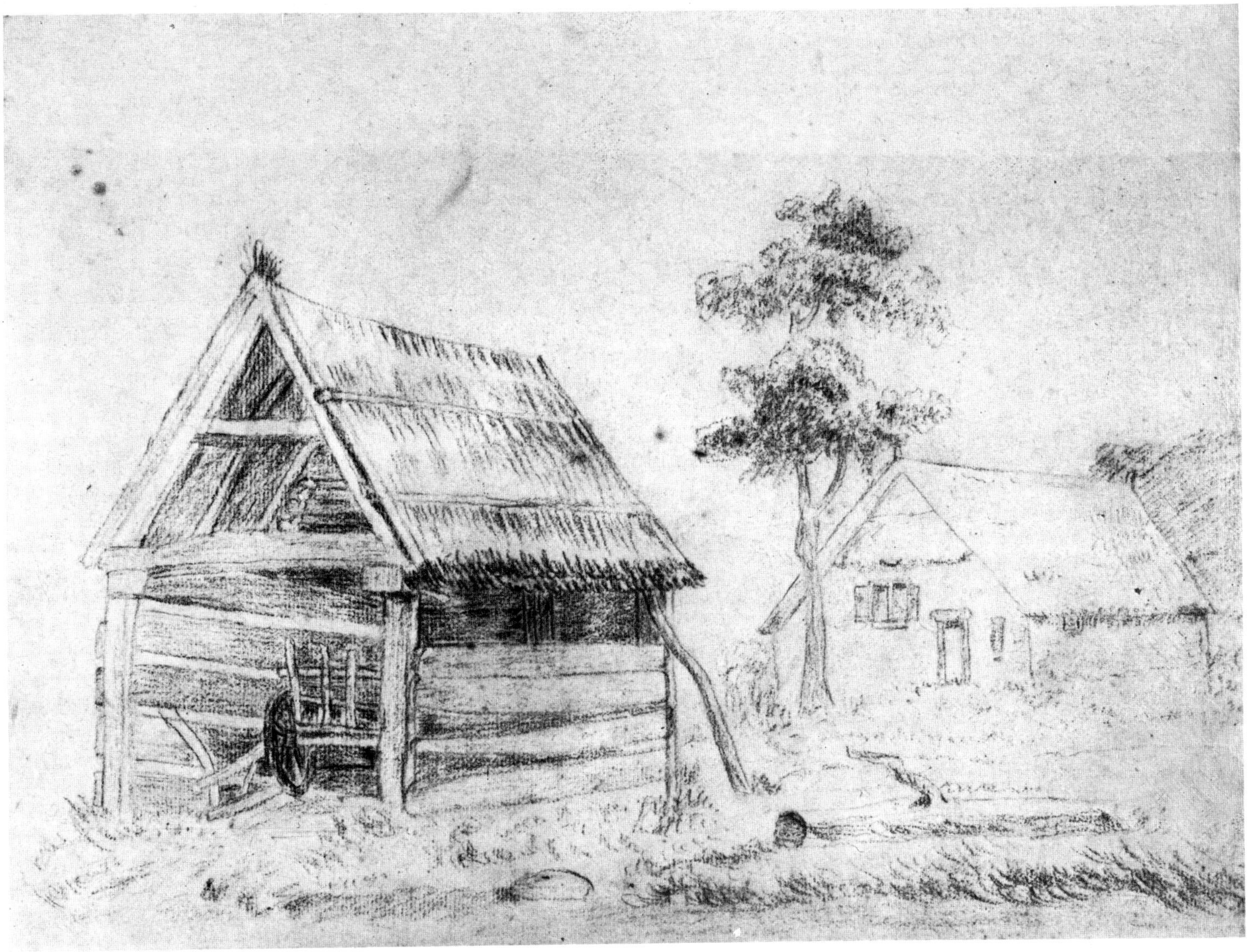

Farm and Shed

February 8, 1864 - pencil on vellum
- 22 x 27 cm -
J.P. Scholte van Hauten Collection, Lochem

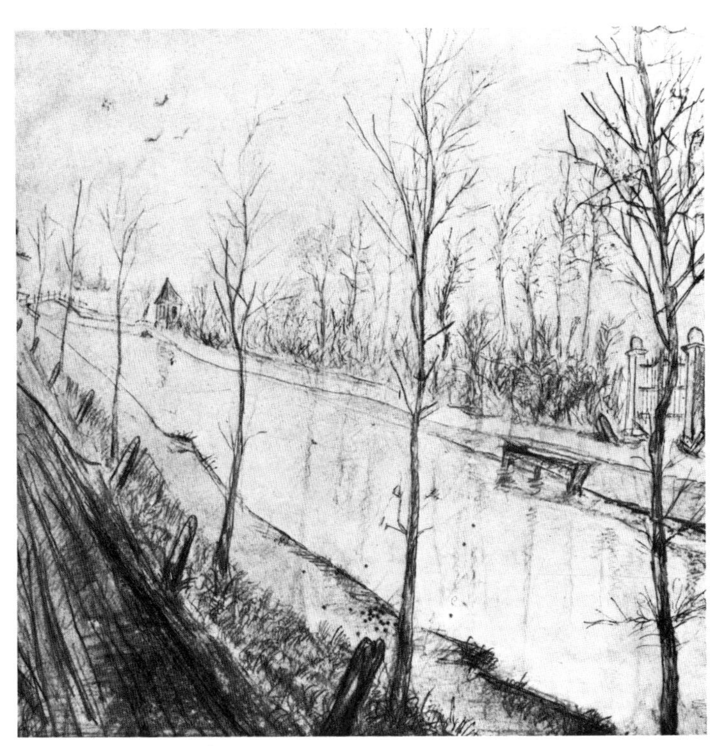

The Canal

1870-1873 - pencil sketch - 25 x 27 cm -
Vincent Van Gogh Foundation, Amsterdam

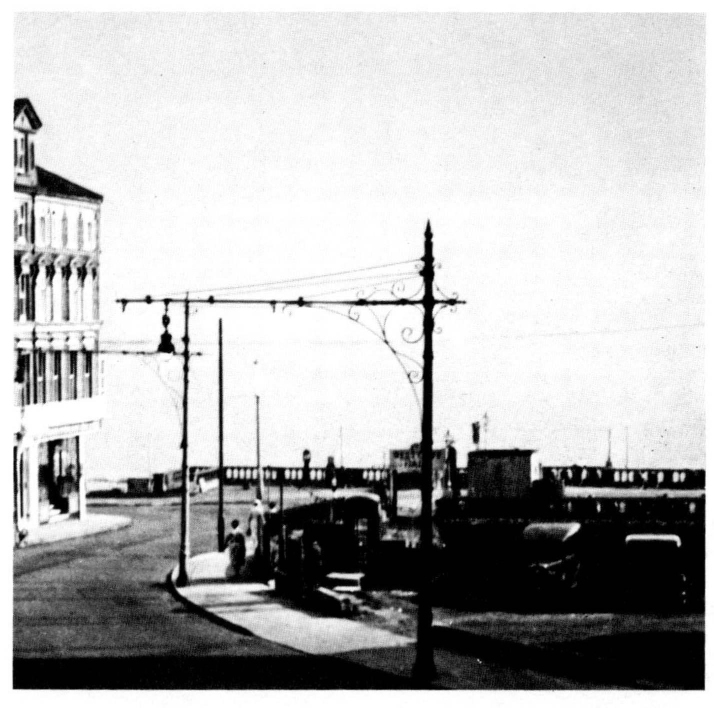

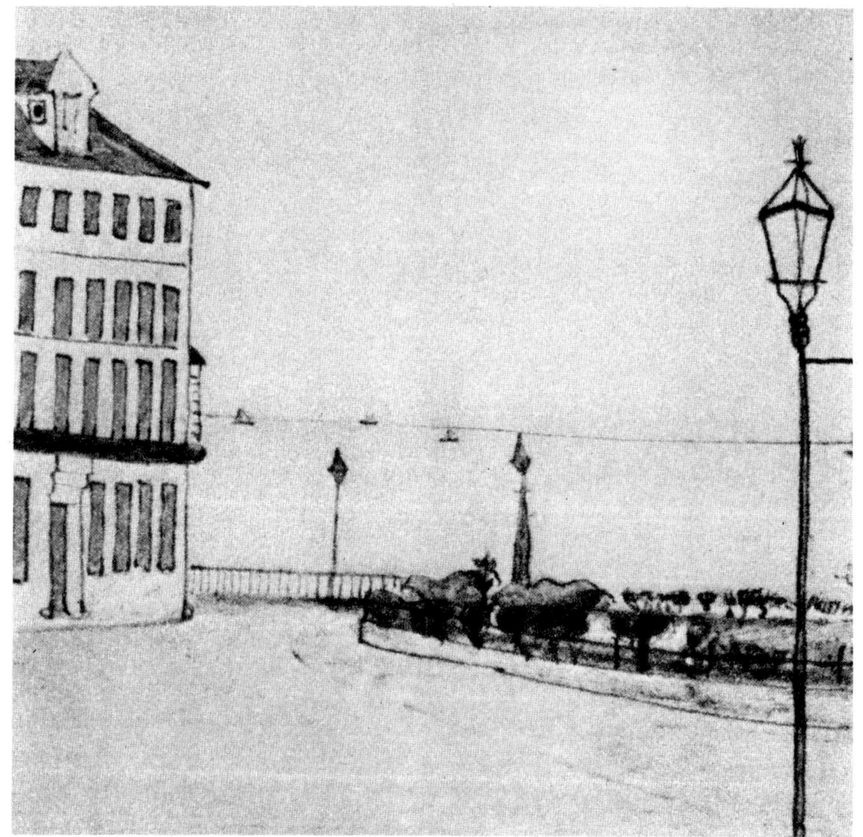

The Beach

May 31, 1876 - pen and ink - 5.5 x 5.5 cm -
Vincent Van Gogh Foundation, Amsterdam

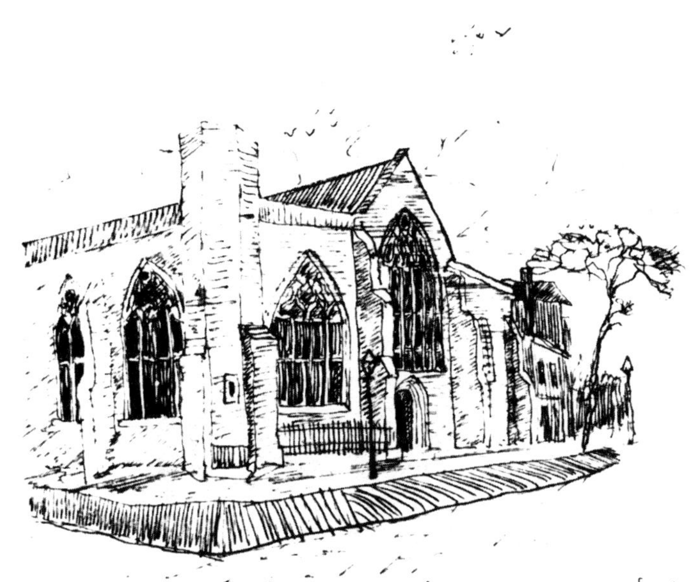

The Church of Austin- Friars

April-December 1876 - pen and ink - 10 x 17 cm -
Private collection

Churches of Petersham and Turnham Green

November 25, 1876 - pen and ink - 4 x 10 cm -
Vincent Van Gogh Foundation, Amsterdam

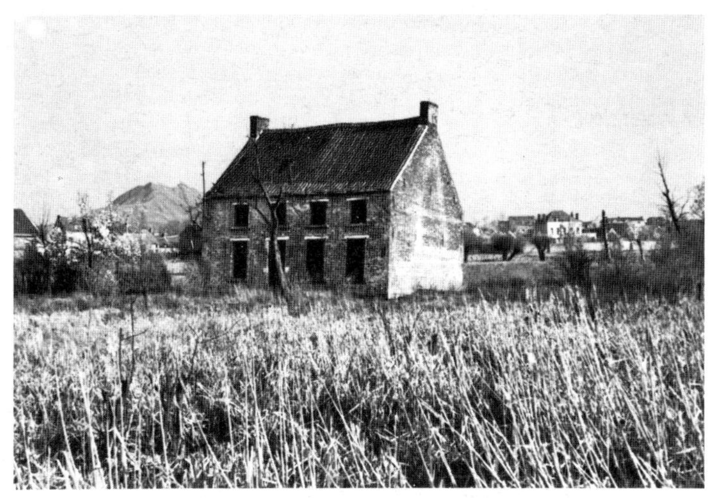

Photograph of Decrucq's house at Cuesmes

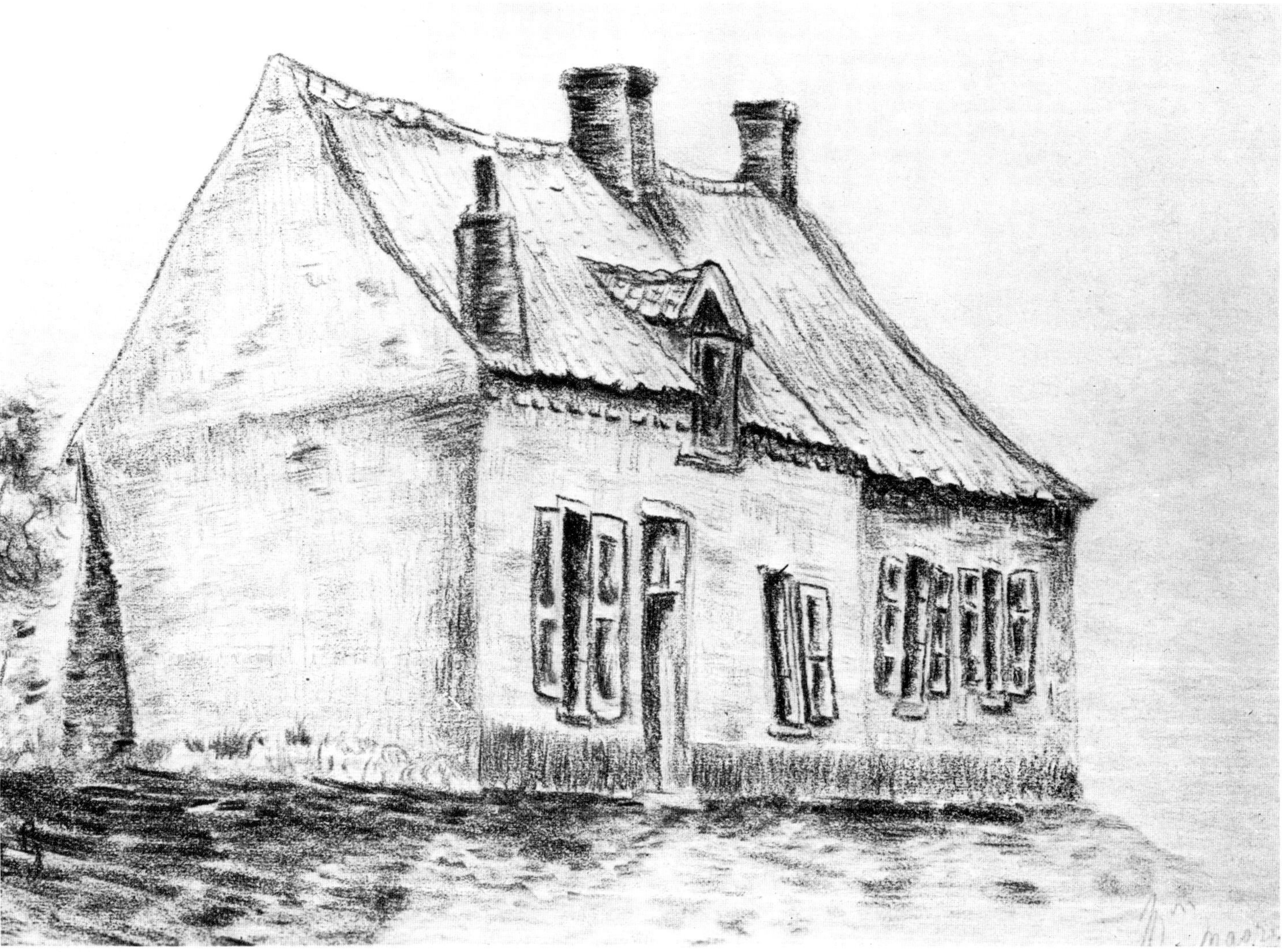

Zandmennik's House

No date - pencil sketch - 23 x 29.5 cm -
S. and C. Deslaut Collection, Cuesmes, Belgium

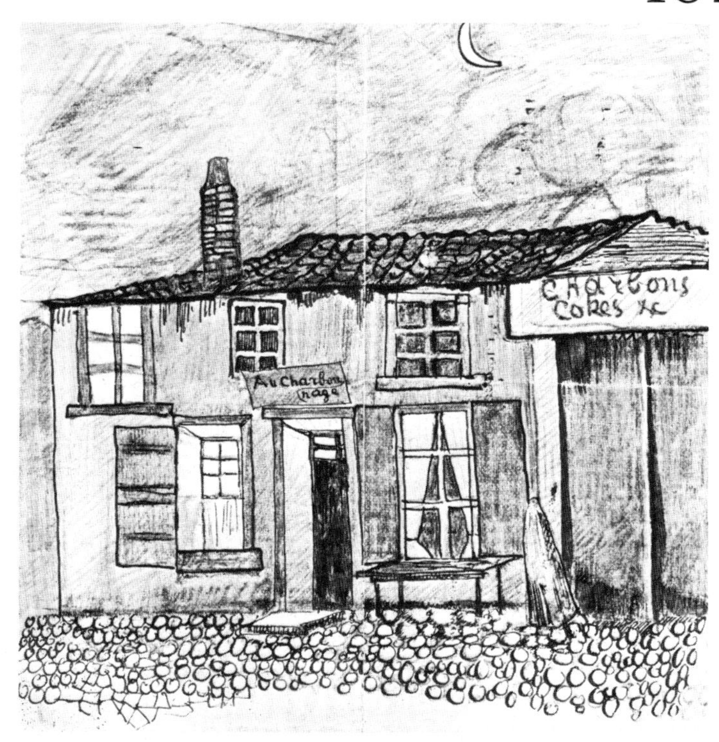

The Colliery

November 1878 - black pencil and pen - 14 x 14 cm - Vincent Van Gogh Foundation, Amsterdam

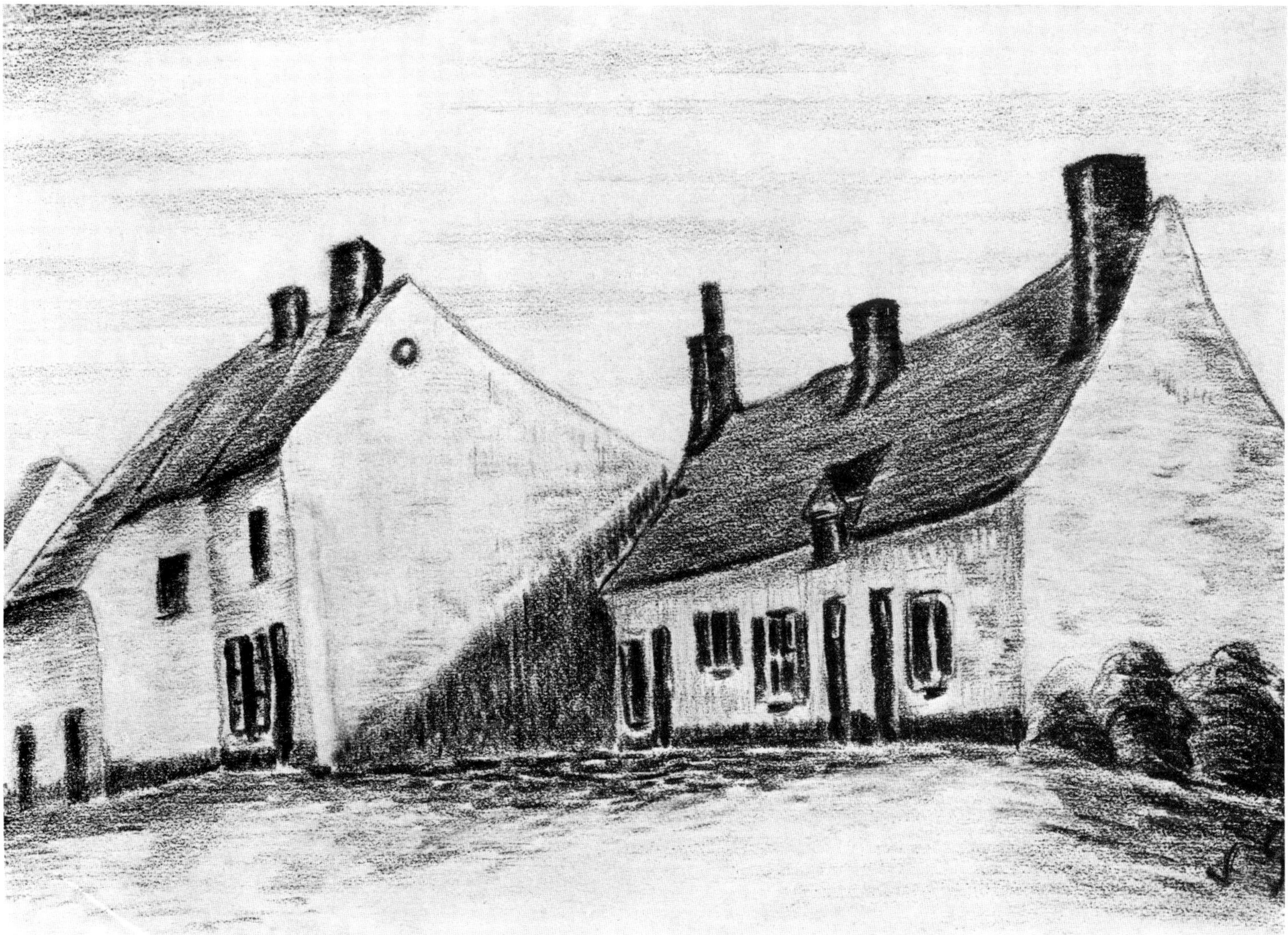

Magrot's House

No date - pencil sketch - 23 x 29.5 cm - S. and C. Deslaut Collection, Cuesmes, Belgium

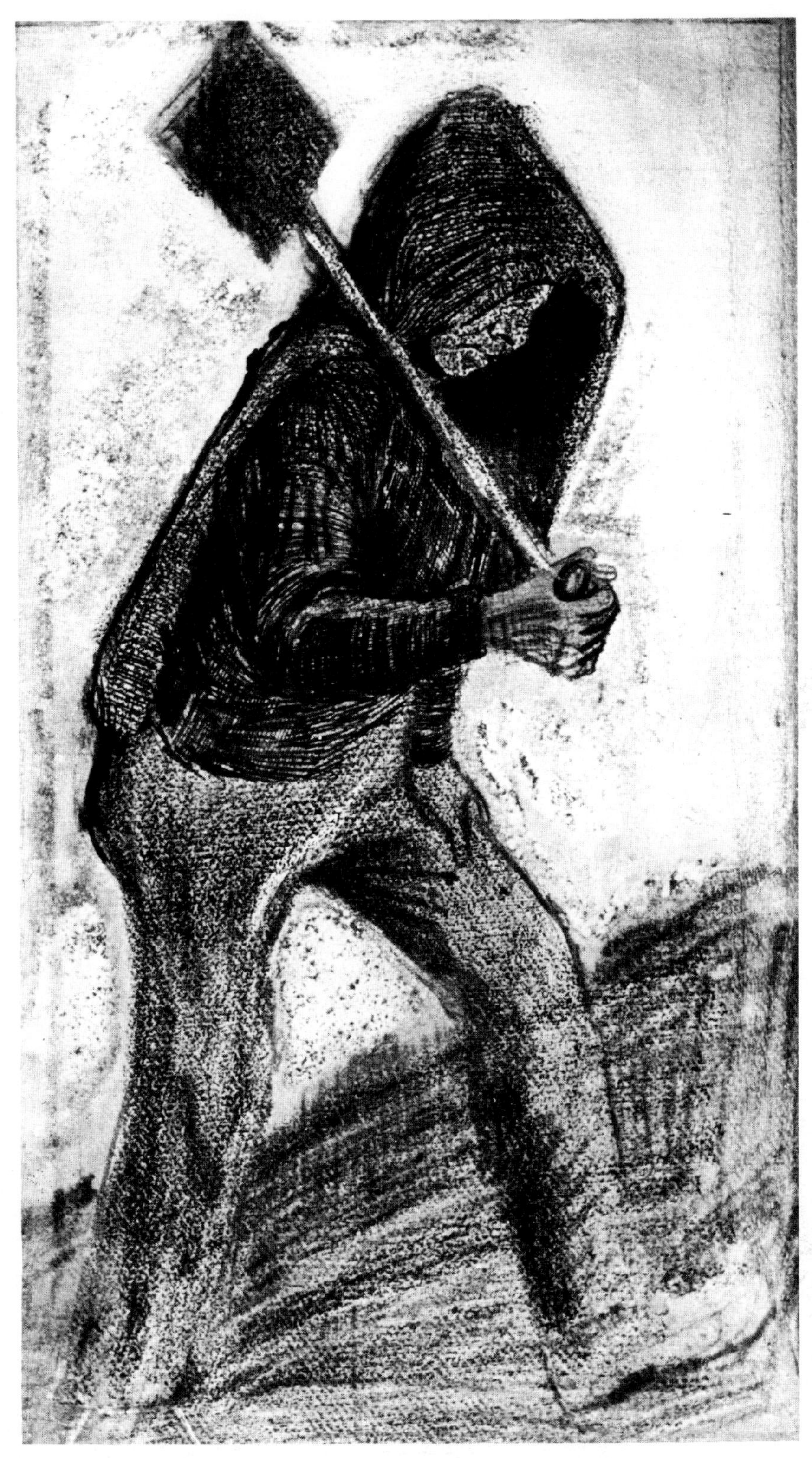

Miner Carrying a Shovel

July-August 1879 - black chalk, pencil and ink - 49.5 x 27.5 cm - Rijksmuseum Kröller- Müller, Otterlo

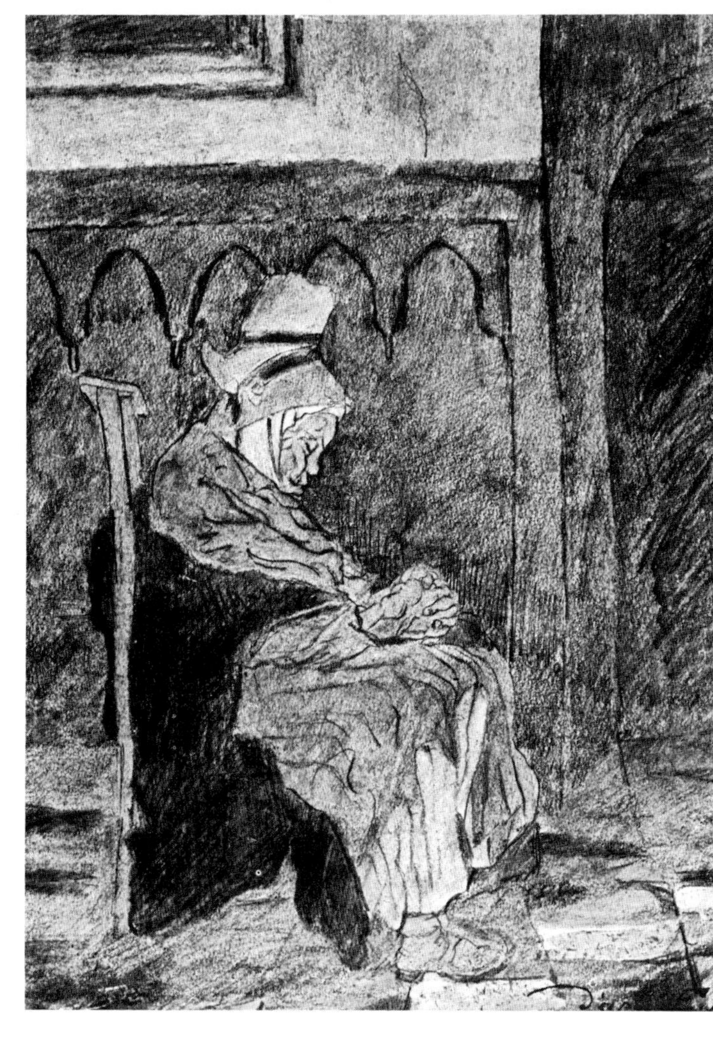

Old Breton Woman Asleep in Church

1880 - pencil with white highlights - 26.5 x 19.5 cm - Vincent Van Gogh Foundation, Amsterdam

Ditchdiggers (after Millet)

November 1880 - pencil - 26.5 x 19.5 cm - Rijksmuseum Kröller- Müller, Otterlo

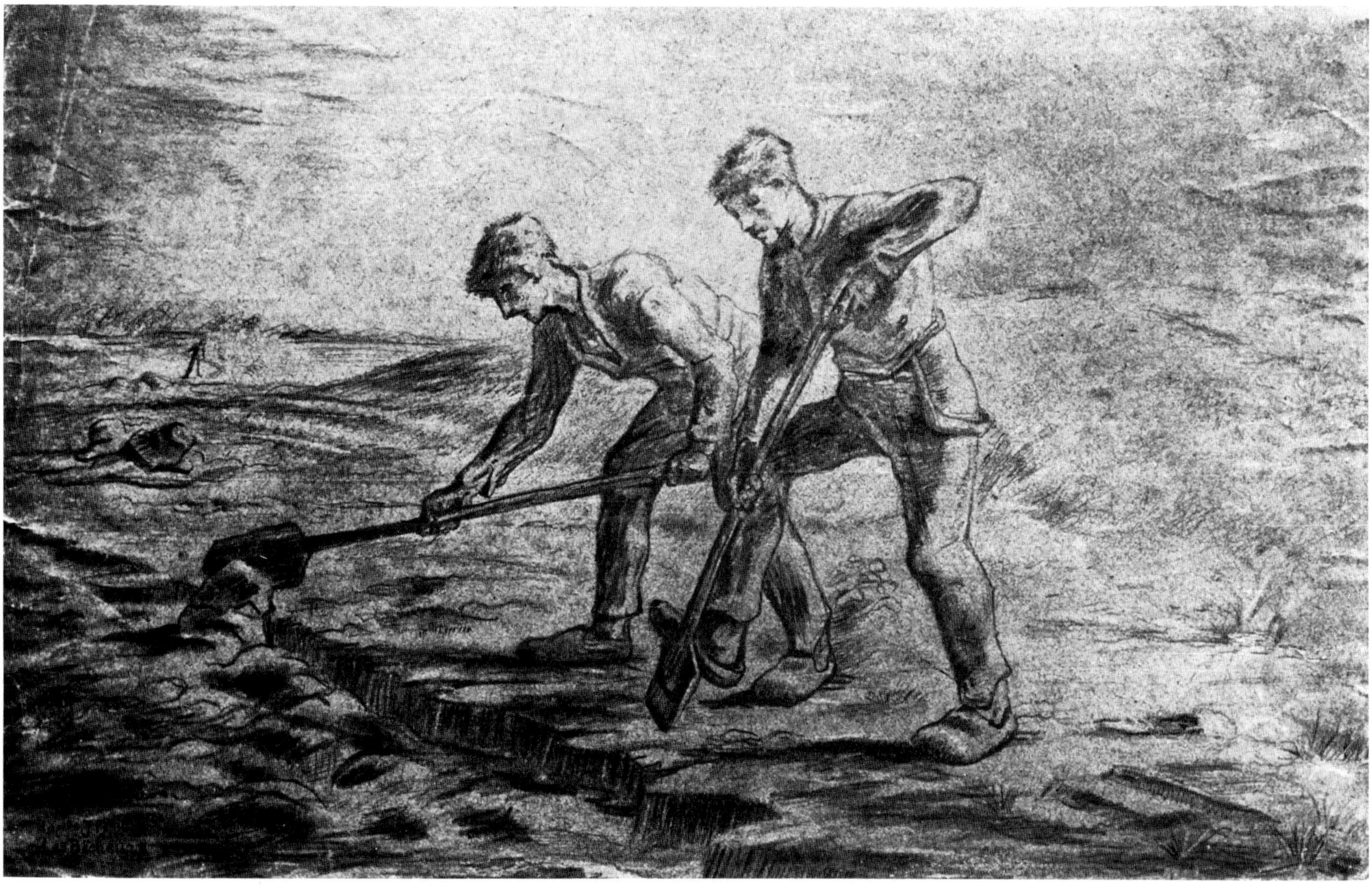

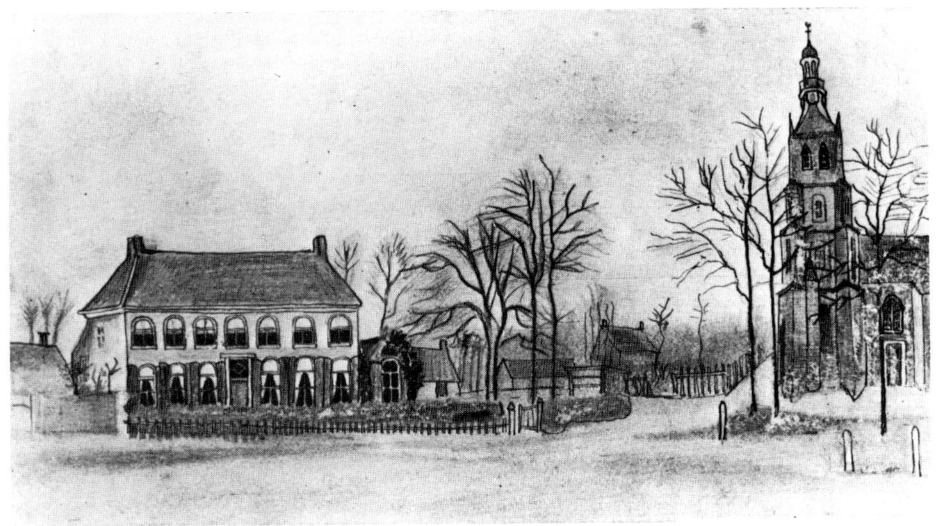

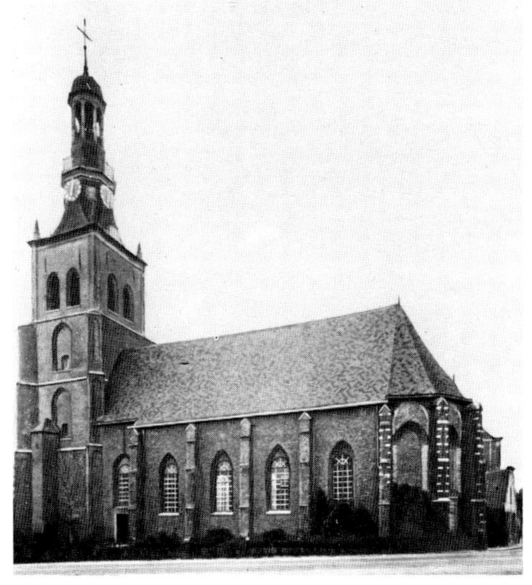

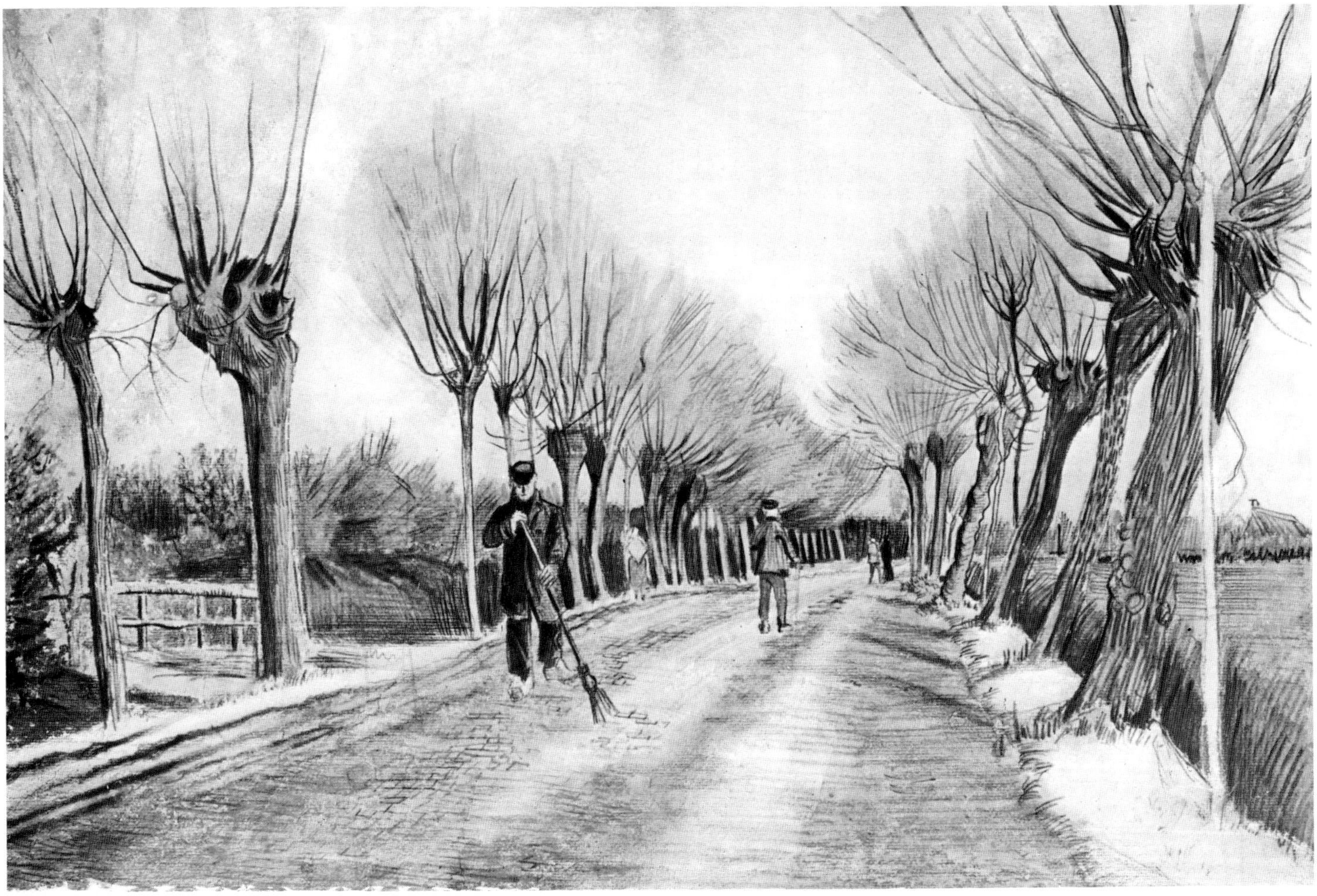

The Church and Parsonage at Etten

1881 - pencil - 9 x 17.5 cm -
Vincent Van Gogh Foundation, Amsterdam

Snow Scene at Etten

1881 - black chalk with coloured highlights - 39 x 60 cm -
Private collection

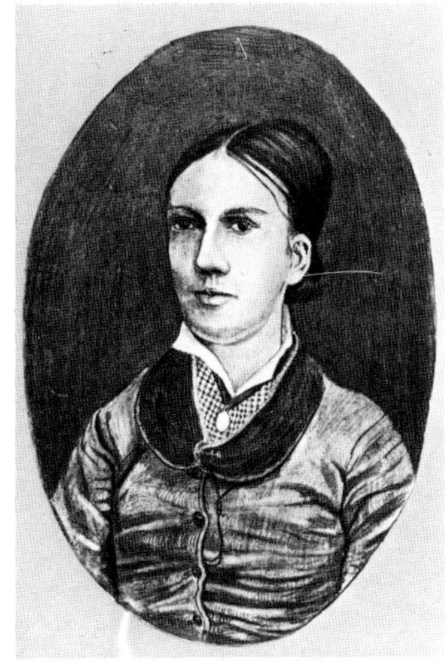

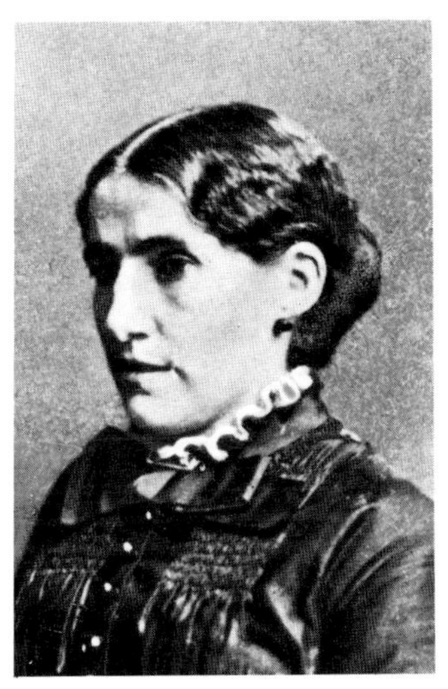

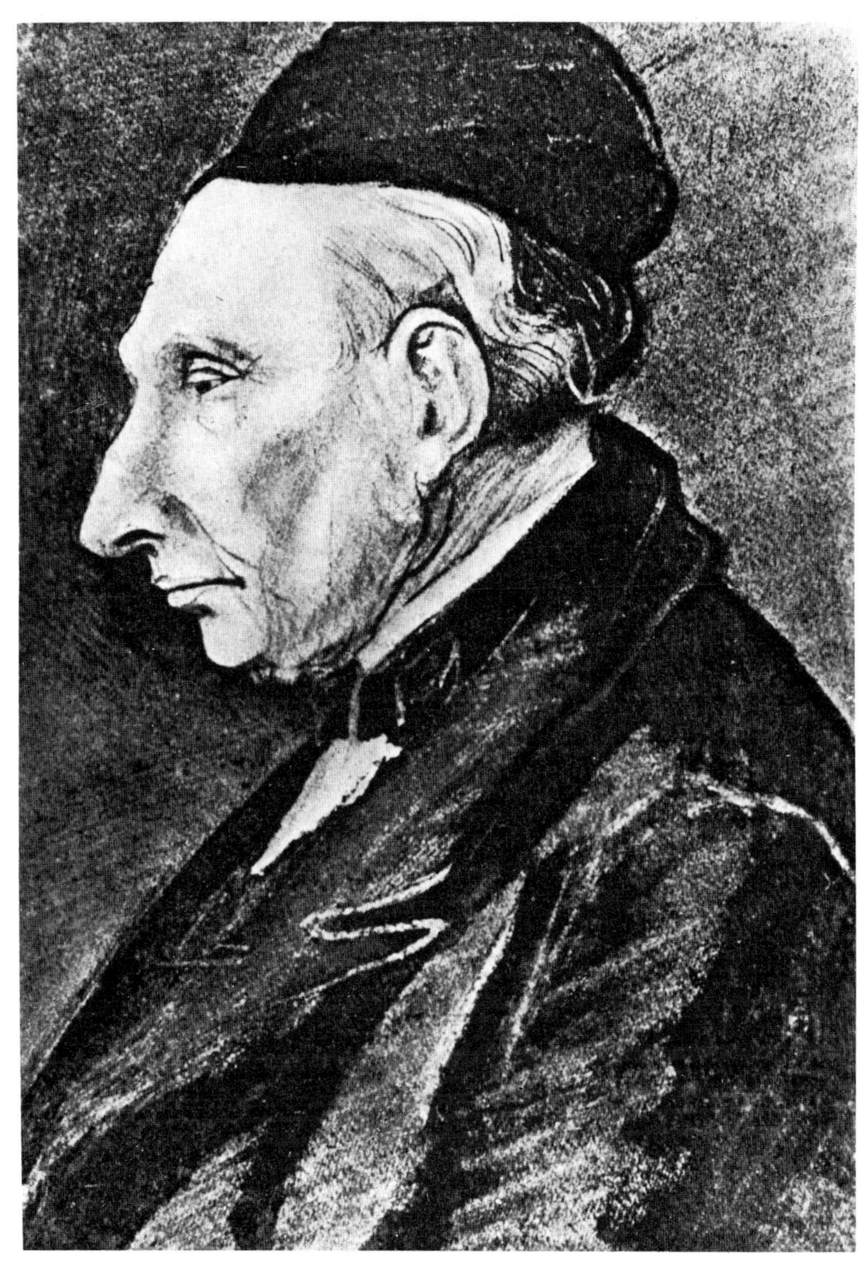

Portrait of Kee Vos- Stricker

*June-July 1881 - pencil - 35 x 24.5 cm -
Rijksmuseum Kröller- Müller, Otterlo*

*Photograph of Kee Vos- Stricker
J.P. Scholte van Hauen Collection, Lochem*

Theodorus Van Gogh

*June-July 1881 - black chalk with white highlights - 33 x 23 cm -
Van Nieuwenhuizen Segaar Collection, The Hague*

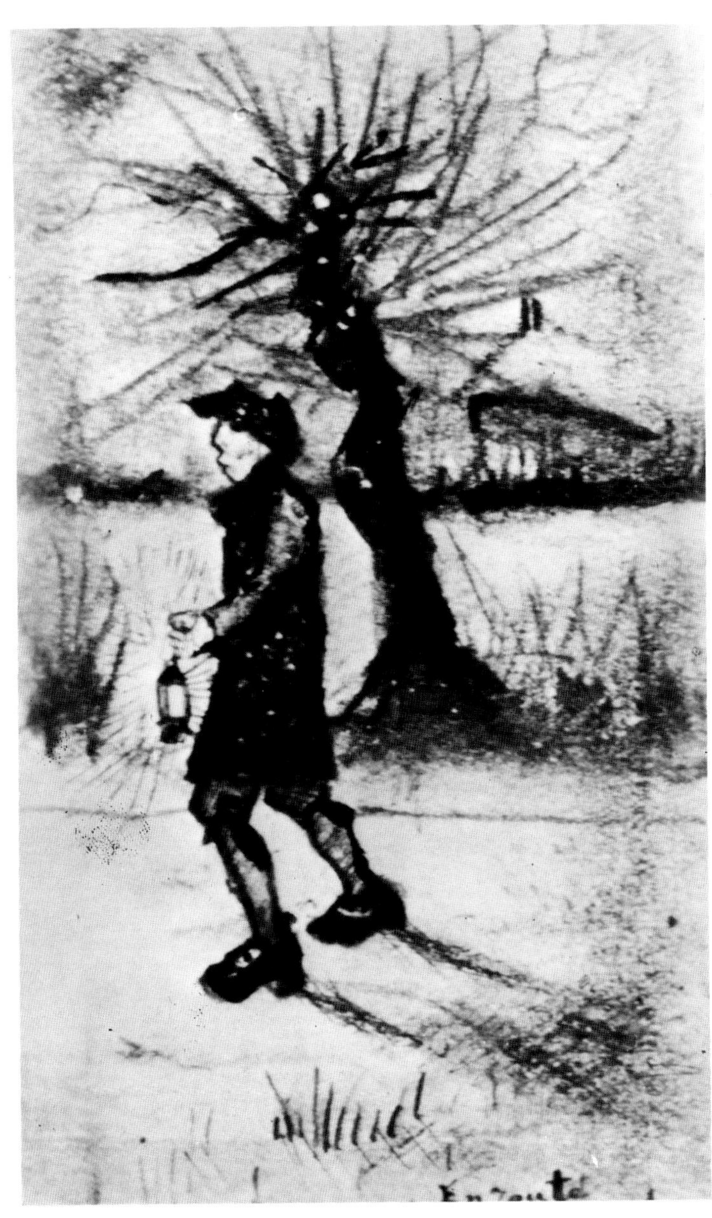

En Route

January 1881 - black chalk - 9.5 x 15.5 cm -
Vincent Van Gogh Foundation, Amsterdam

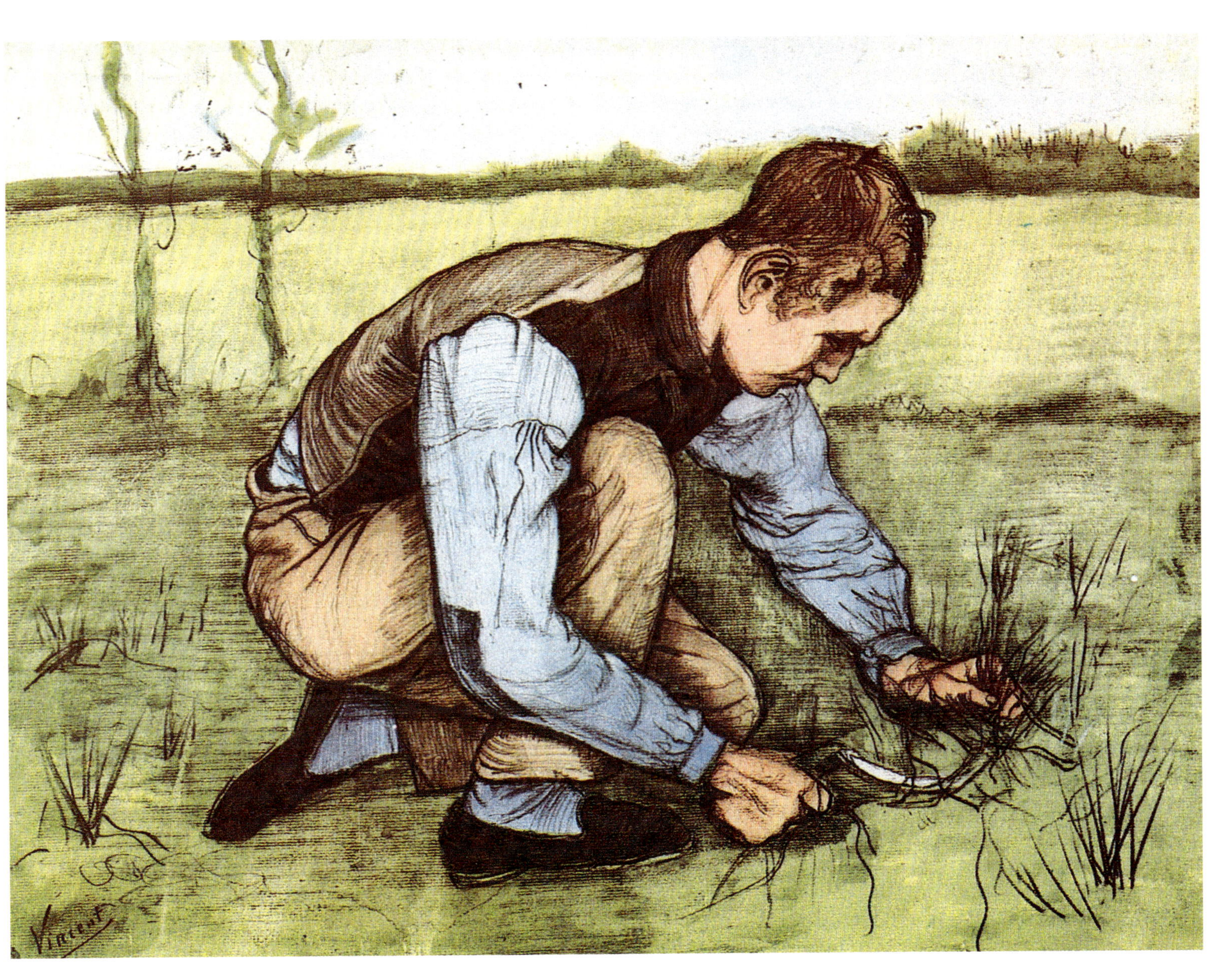

Young Boy Cutting Grass

October 1881 - black chalk and watercolour - 47 x 61 cm - Rijksmuseum Kröller-Müller, Otterlo

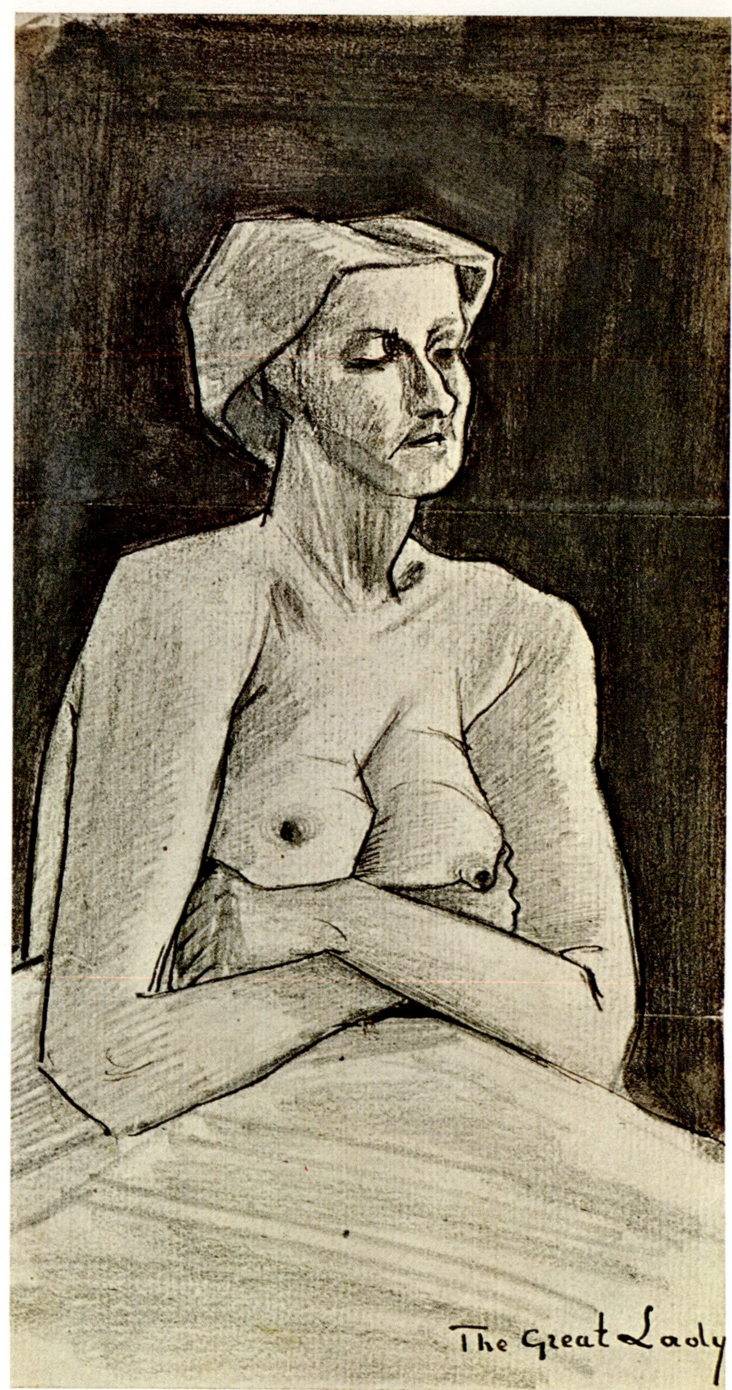

The Great Lady

April 1882 - pencil and pen - 19 x 10.5 cm -
Vincent Van Gogh Foundation, Amsterdam

The Factory of M. Enhoven

March 1882 - watercolour - 35.5 x 59.5 cm -
H.P. Bremmer Collection, The Hague

Sorrow

April 1882 - pencil - 46 x 30.5 cm -
H.P. Bremmer Collection, The Hague

Woman Peeling Potatoes

1883 - conte crayon - 59.5 x 37.5 cm -
Paul Citroen Collection, Wassenaar, Holland

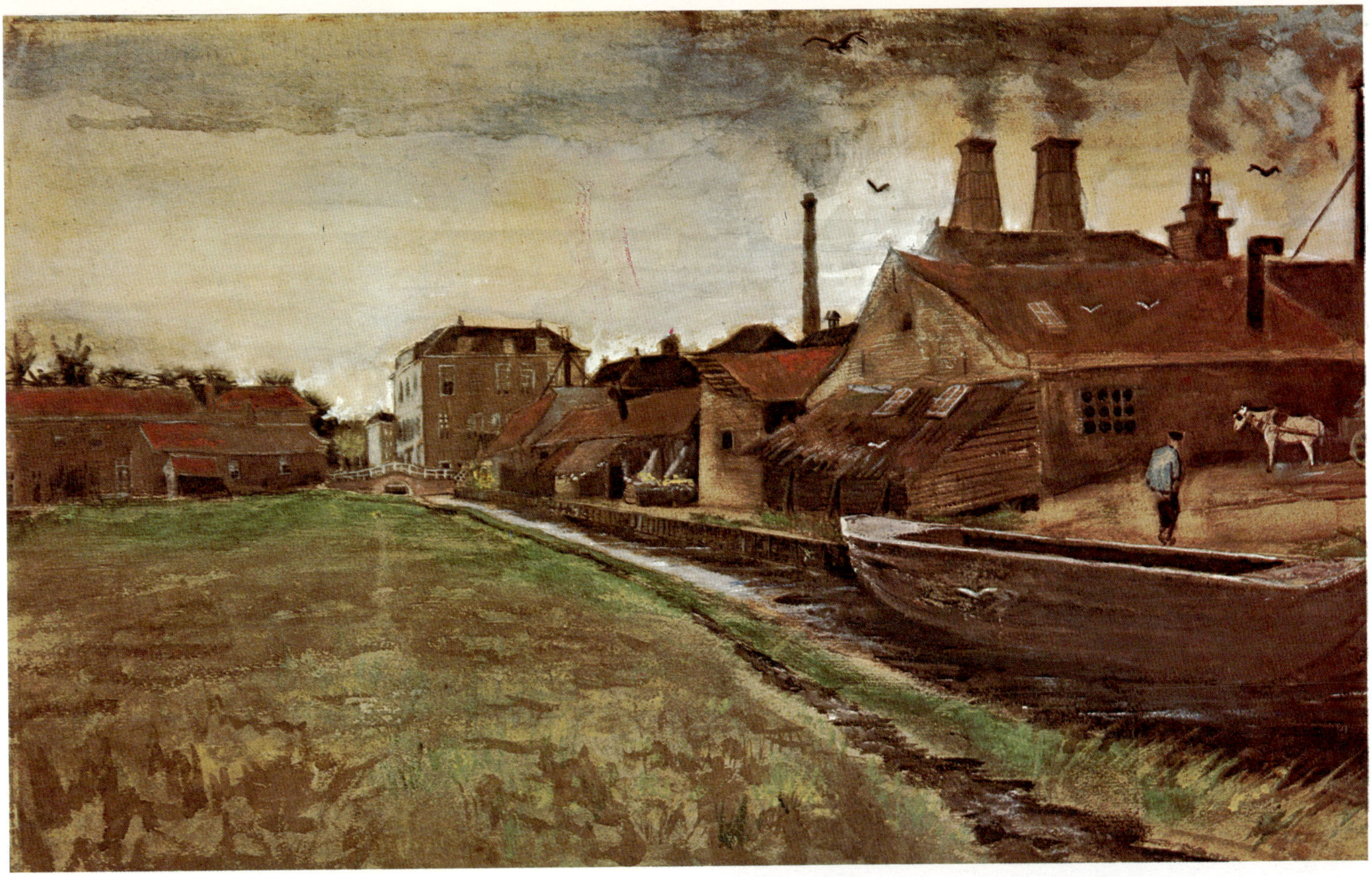

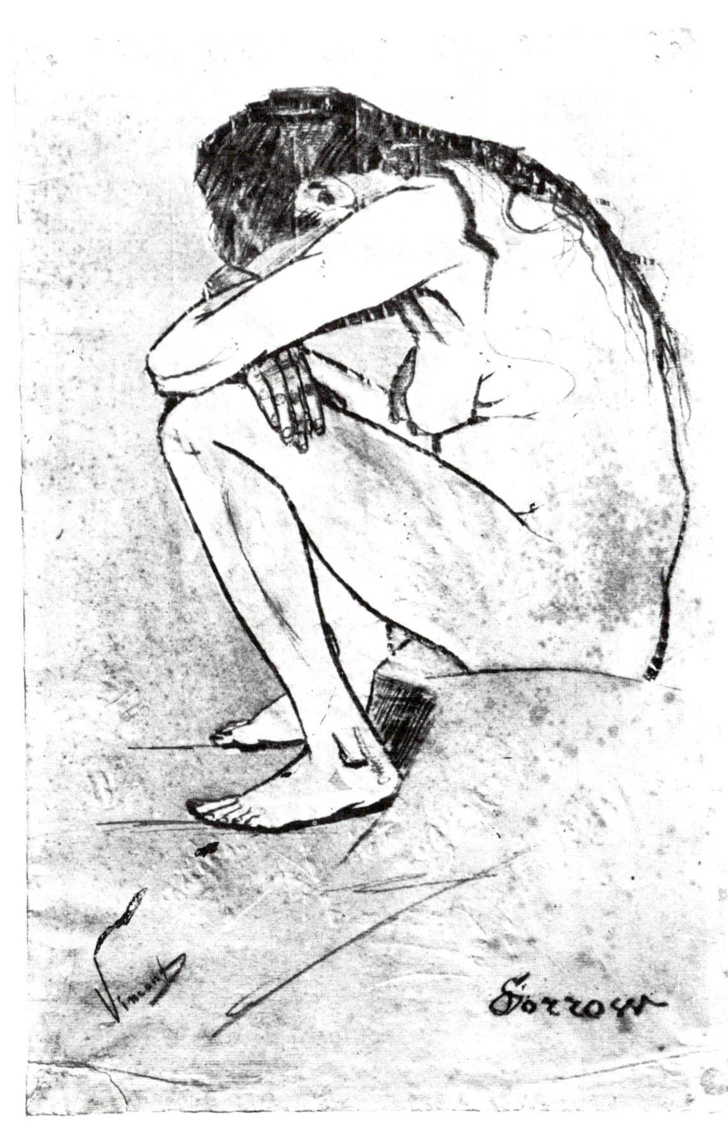
Sorrow

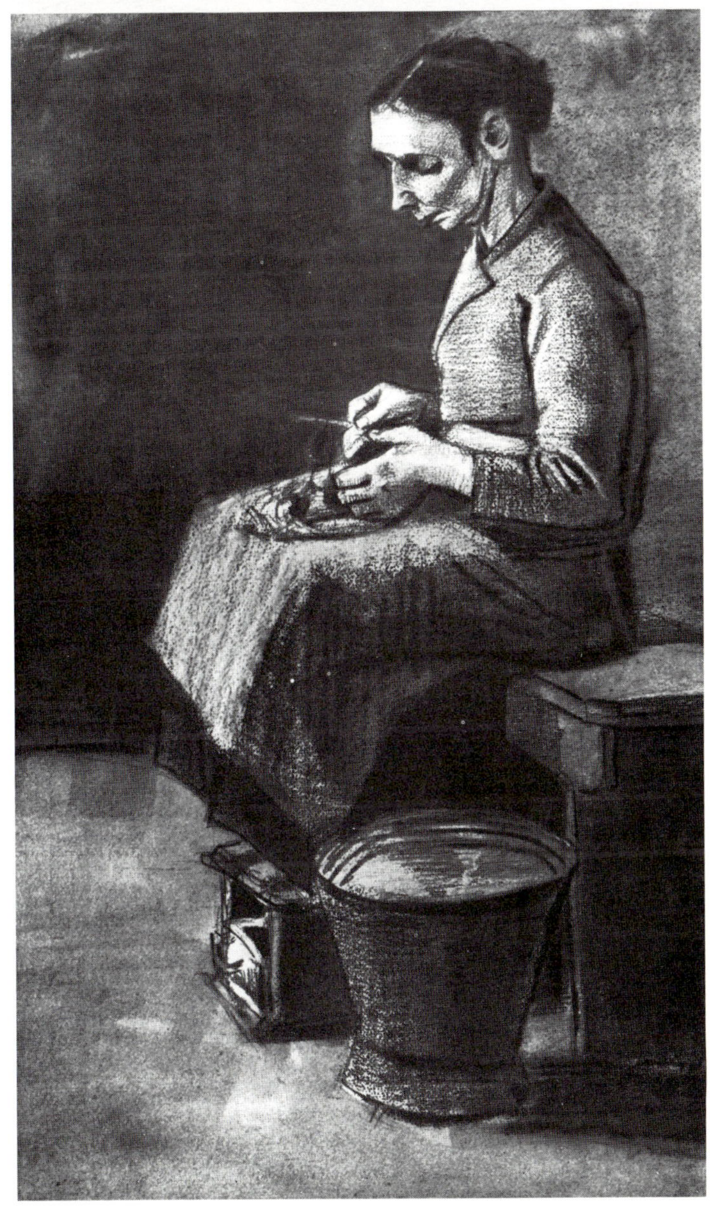

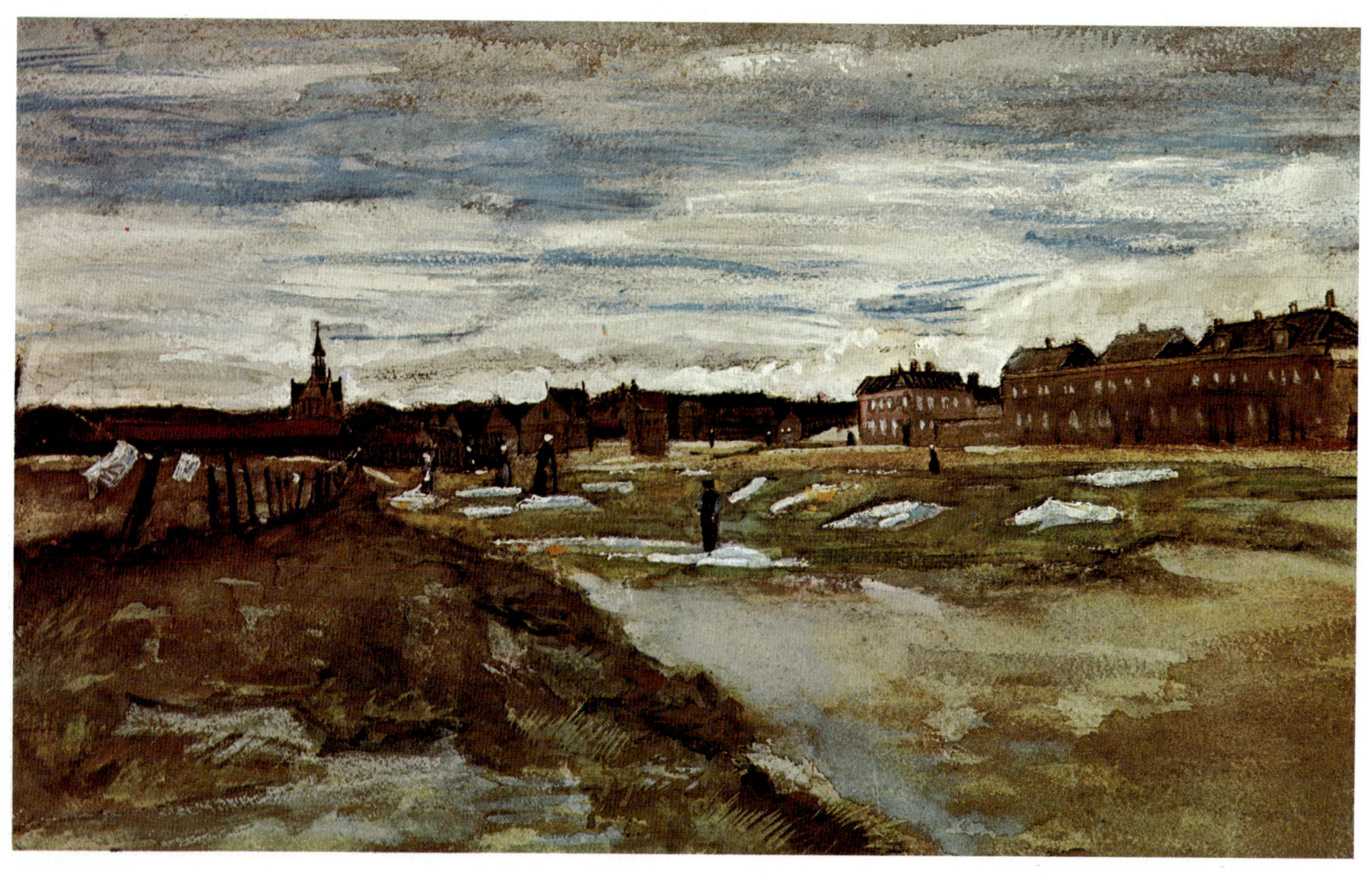

Bleaching Ground at Scheveningen

July 1882 - watercolour on waste paper - 32 x 54 cm - Private collection, Holland

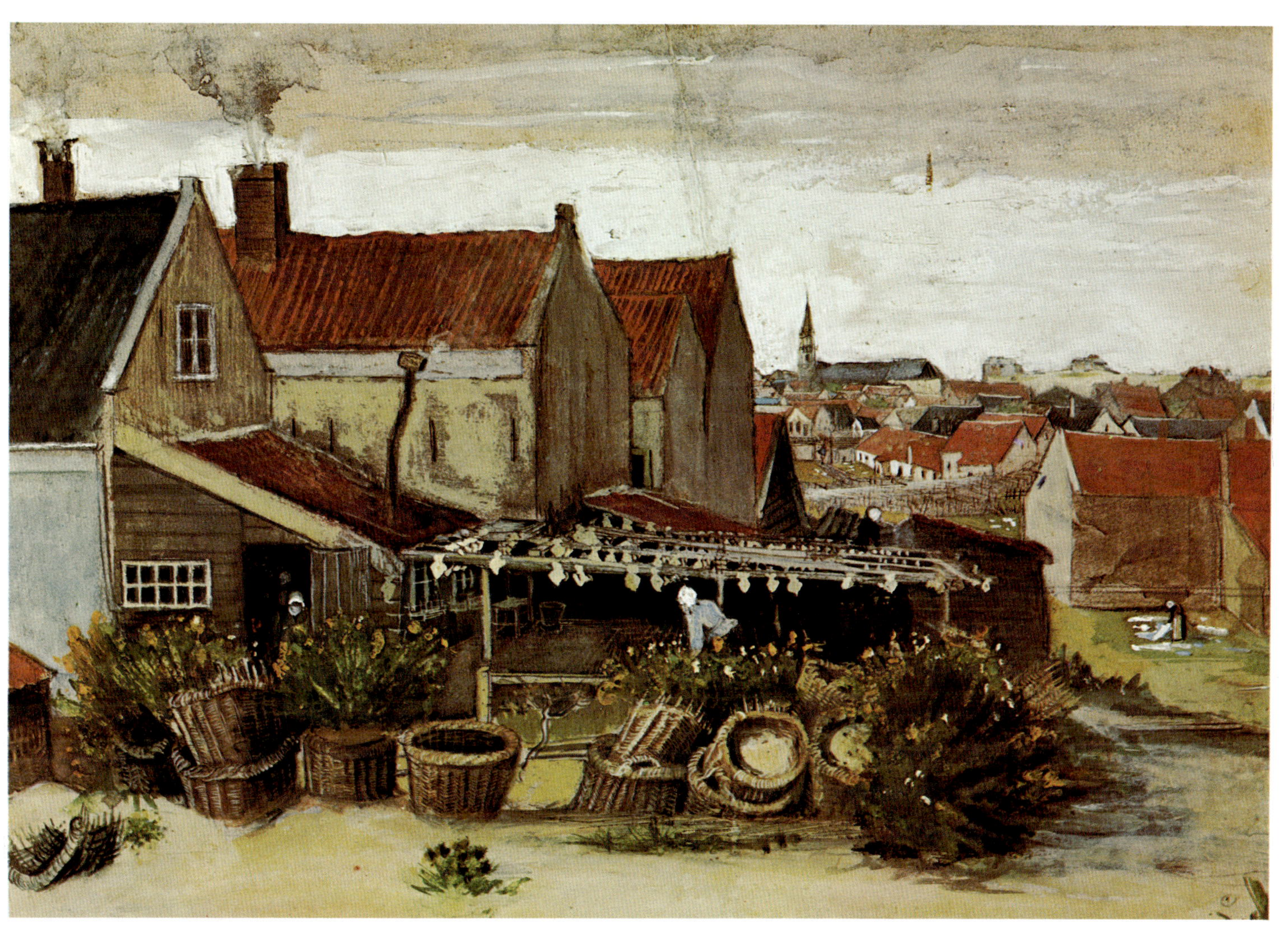

Drying House at Scheveningen

July 1882 - watercolour - 35.5 x 52 cm - H.P. Bremmer Collectin, The Hague

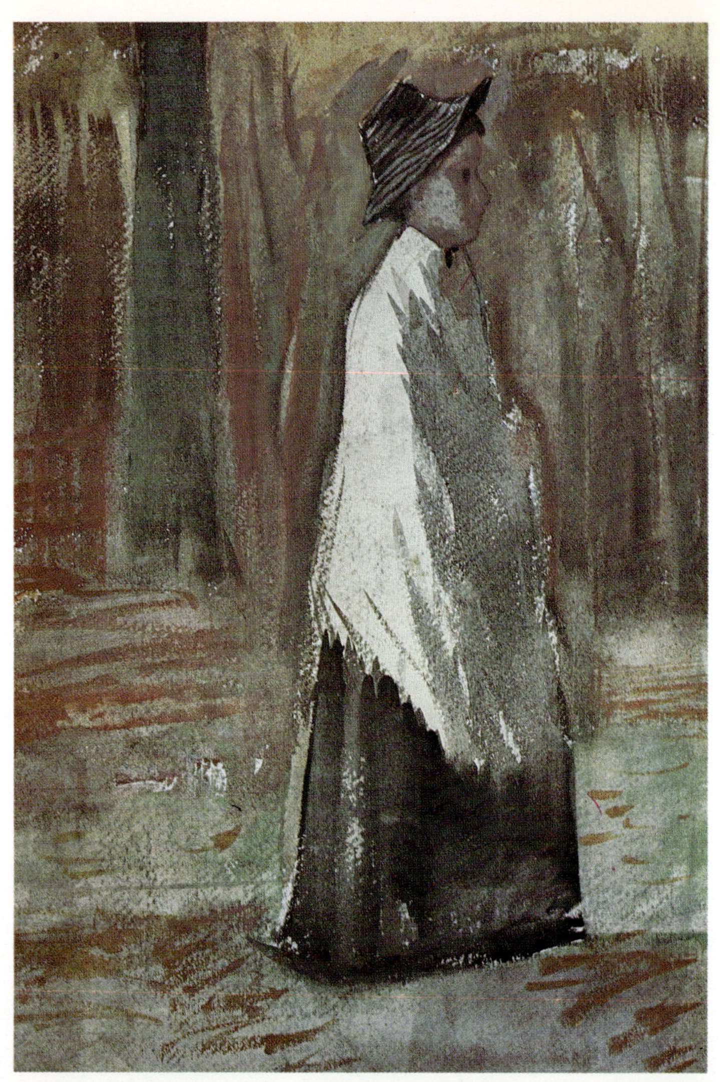

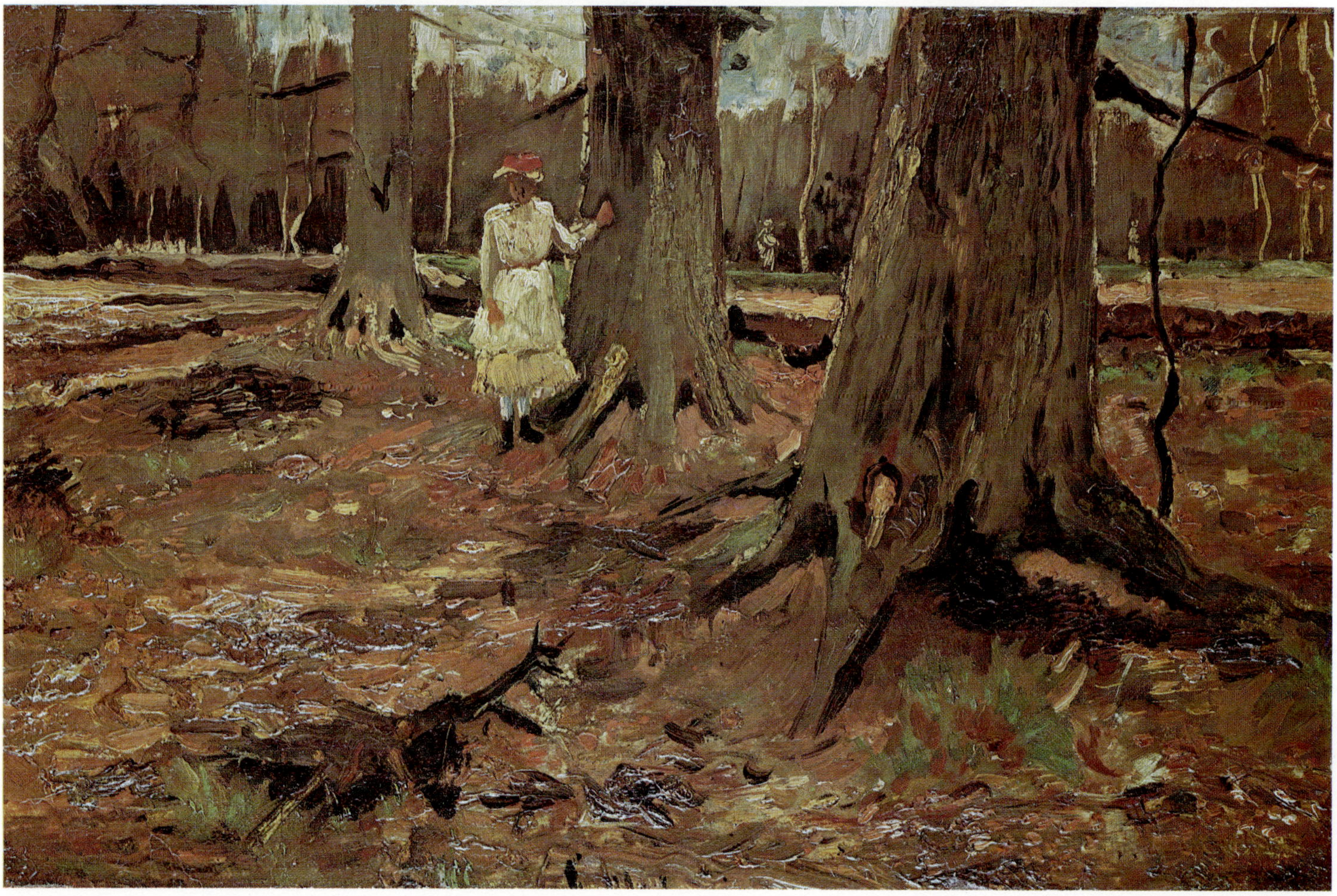

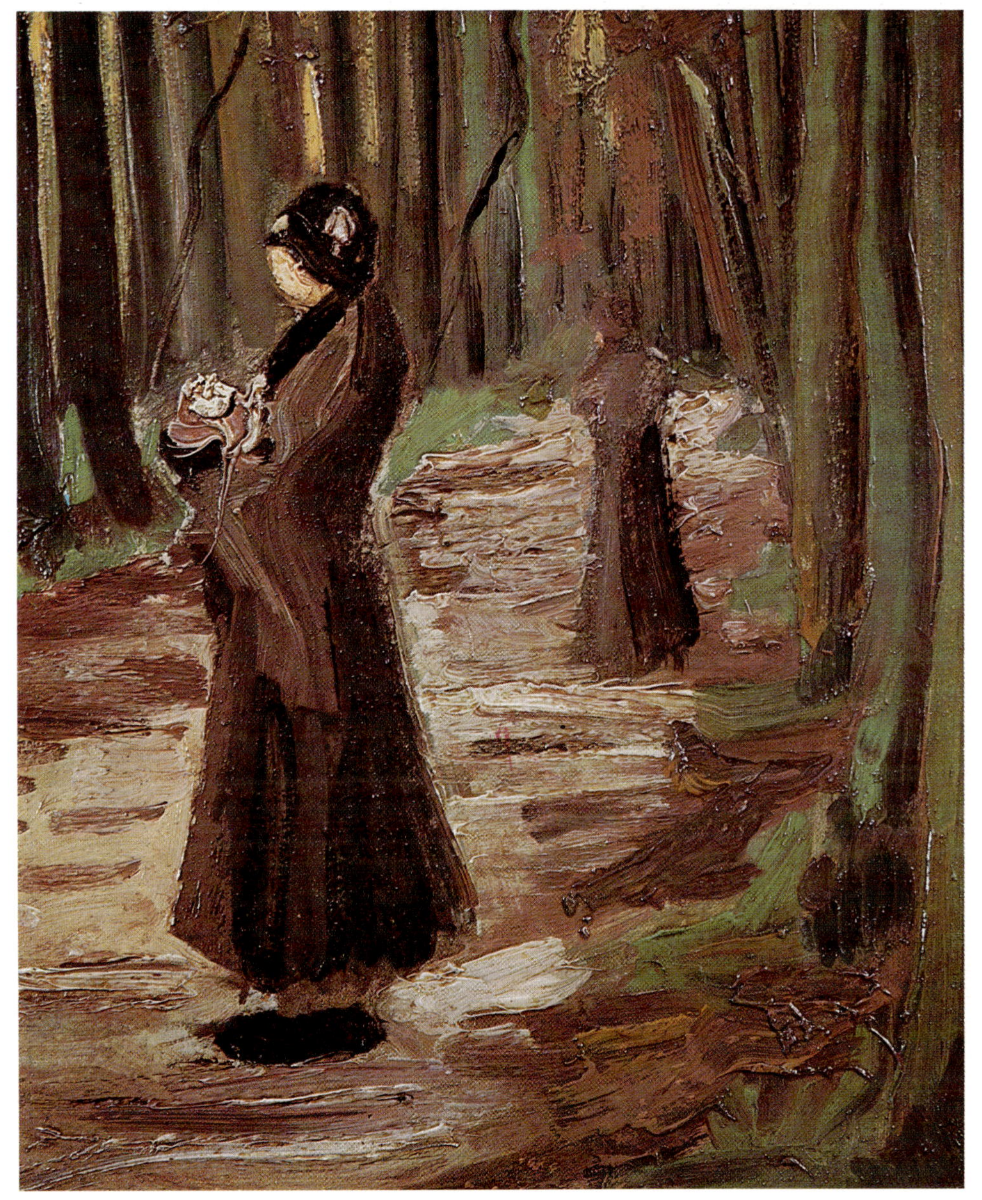

Woman in the Woods

August 1882 - watercolour - 34.5 x 24 cm -
G. Cramer collection, The Hague

Girl in White in the Woods

September 1882 - oil on canvas - 39 x 59 cm -
Rijksmuseum Kröller- Müller, Otterlo

Two Women in the Woods

Autumn 1882 - oil on wood - 31 x 24.5 cm -
Private collection, Paris

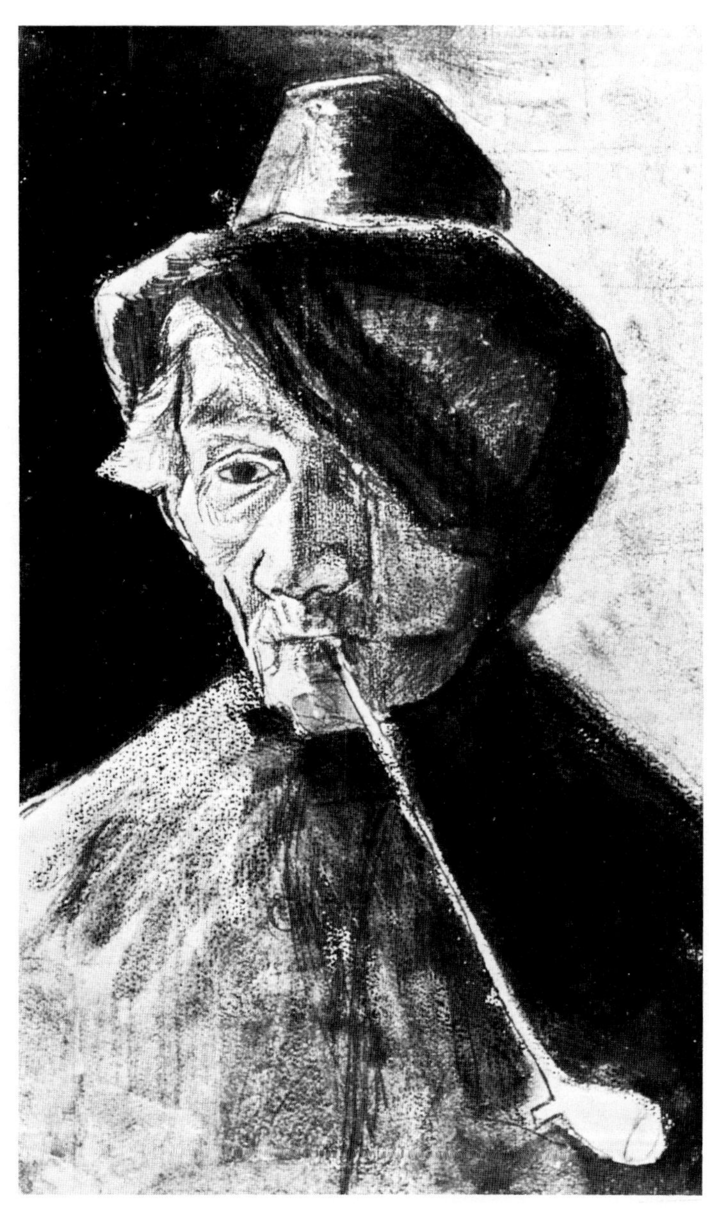

Man with Clay Pipe and Bandaged Eye

December 1882 - black chalk, wash, white highlights - 45 x 27.5 cm -
Rijksmuseum Kröller- Müller, Otterlo

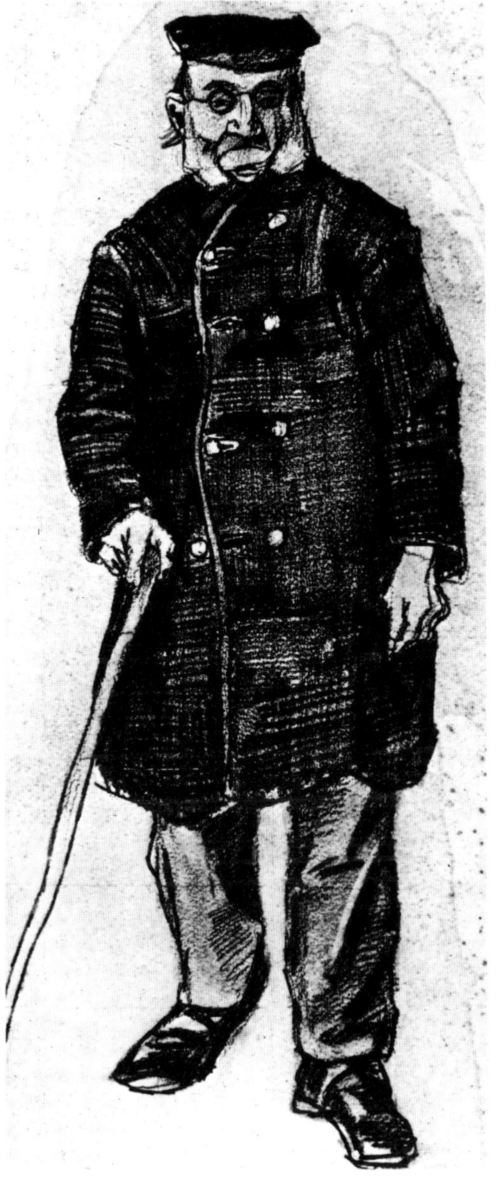

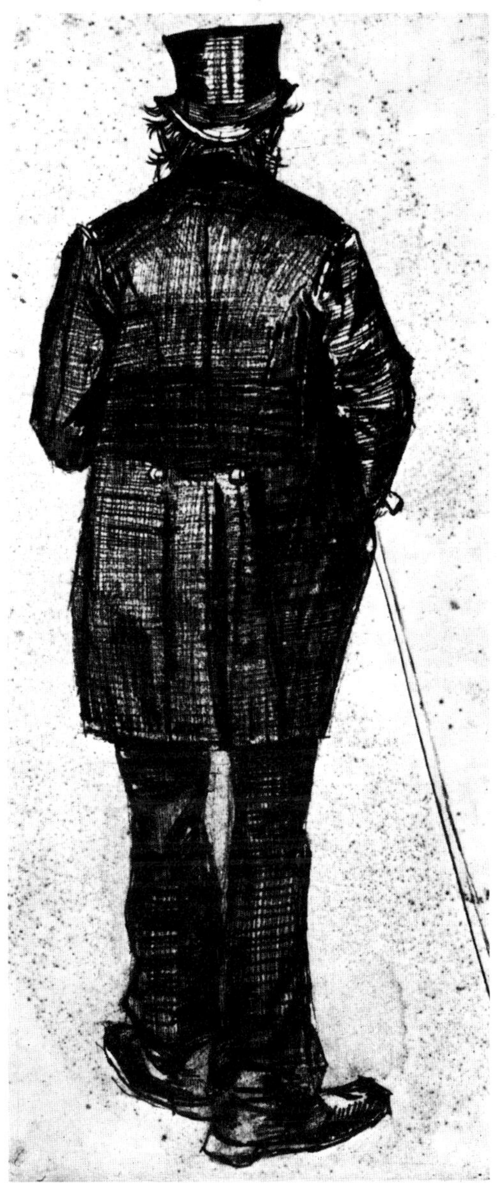

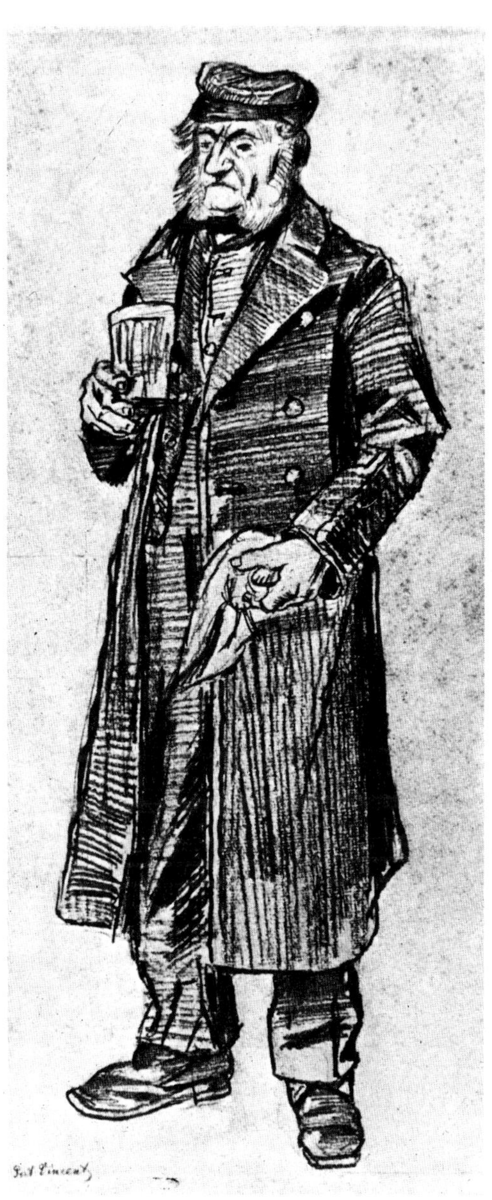

Man with Cane

October 1882 - pencil drawing - 48.5 x 26 cm - H.P. Bremmer collection, The Hague

Old Man in the Almshouse

October 1882 - pencil drawing - 47.5 x 26 cm - Vincent van Gogh Foundation, Amsterdam

Old Man in Almshouse Holding a Glass and a Handkerchief

October 1882 - crayon - 49 x 25 cm - Rijksmuseum Kröller-Müller, Otterlo

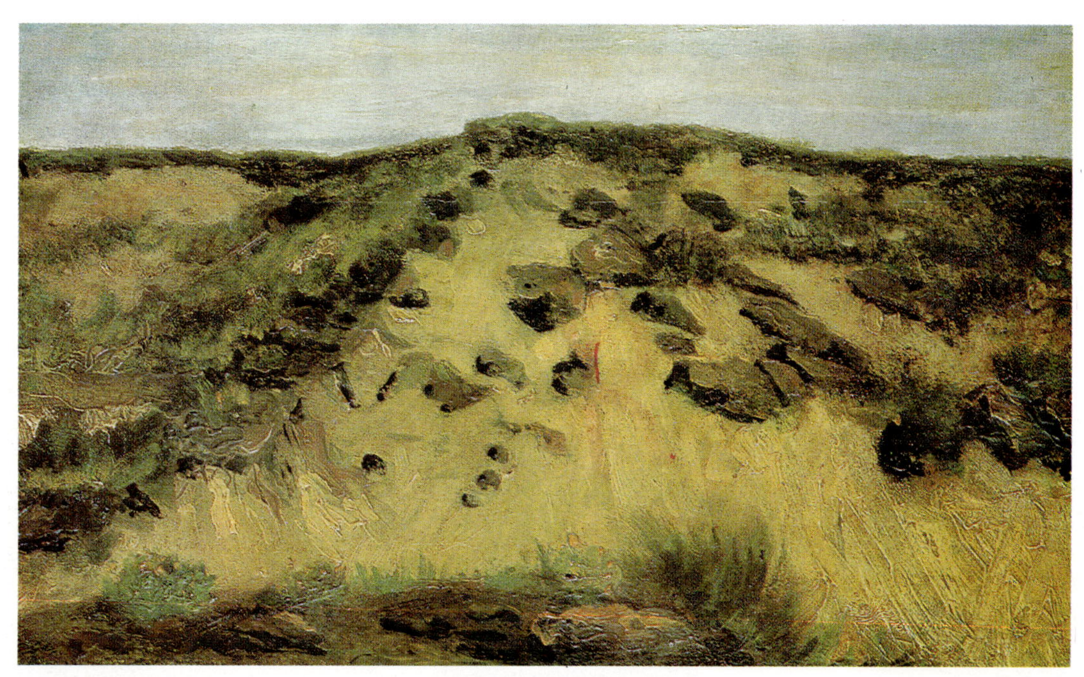

Dunes

August 1882 - canvas on wood - 24 x 32 cm - Private collection, Amsterdam

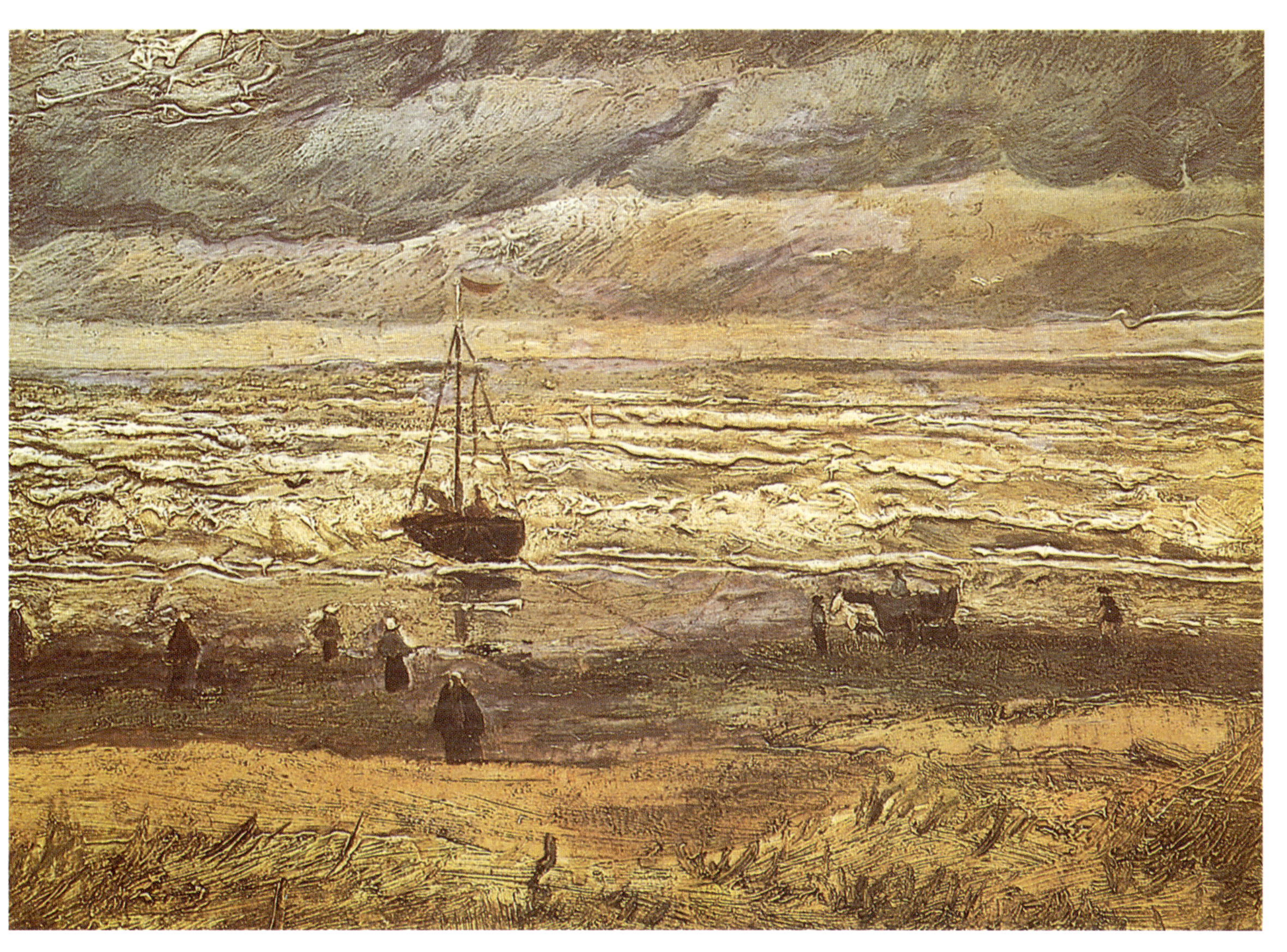

Beach at Scheveningen

August 1882 - oil on canvas on card -34 x 51 cm - Stedelijk Museum, Amsterdam

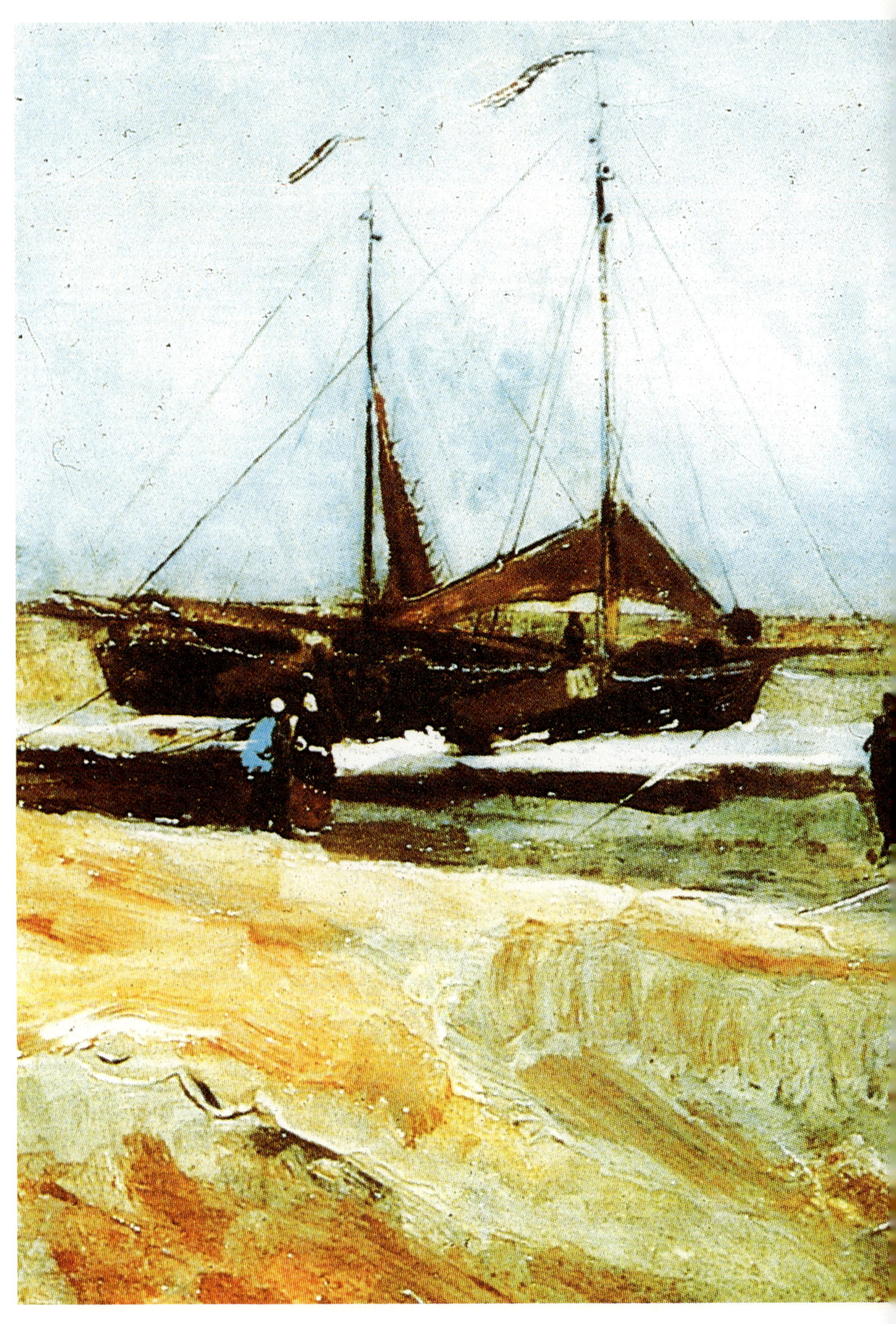

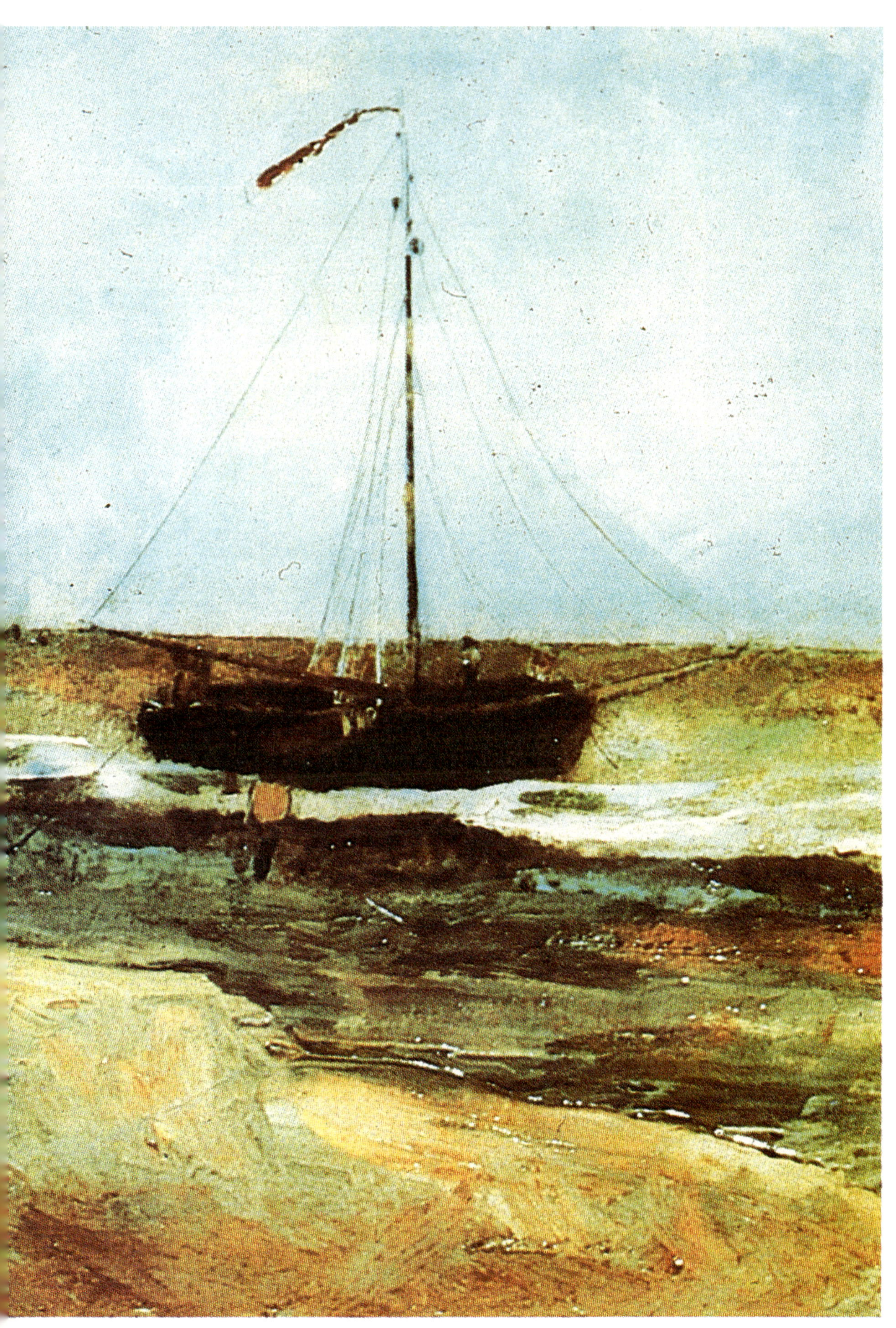

Beach at Scheveningen

August 1882 - oil on paper on wood - 35.5 x 49.5 cm - Private collection

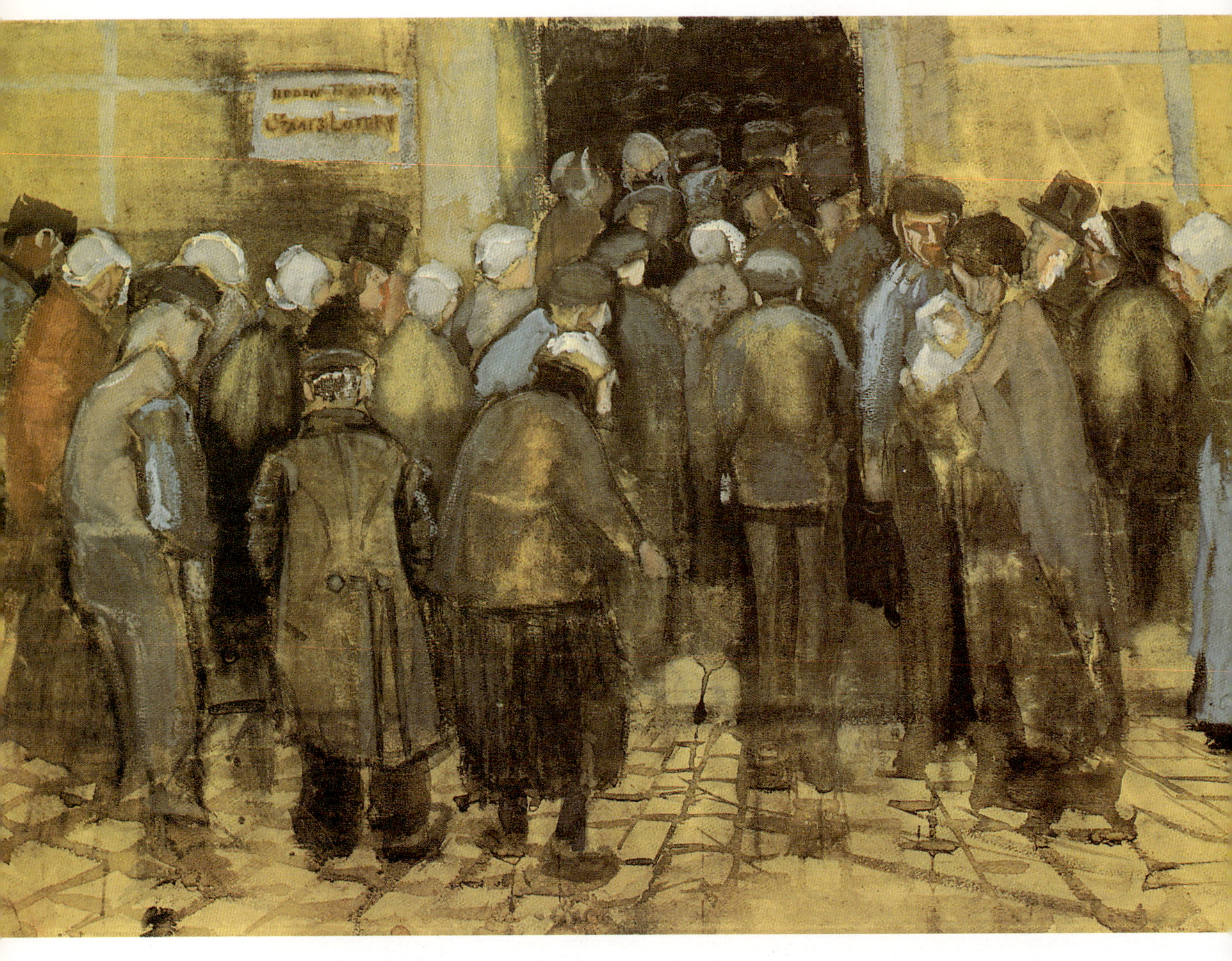

The National Lottery

September 1882 - watercolour - 38 x 57 cm - Vincent van Gogh Foundation, Amsterdam

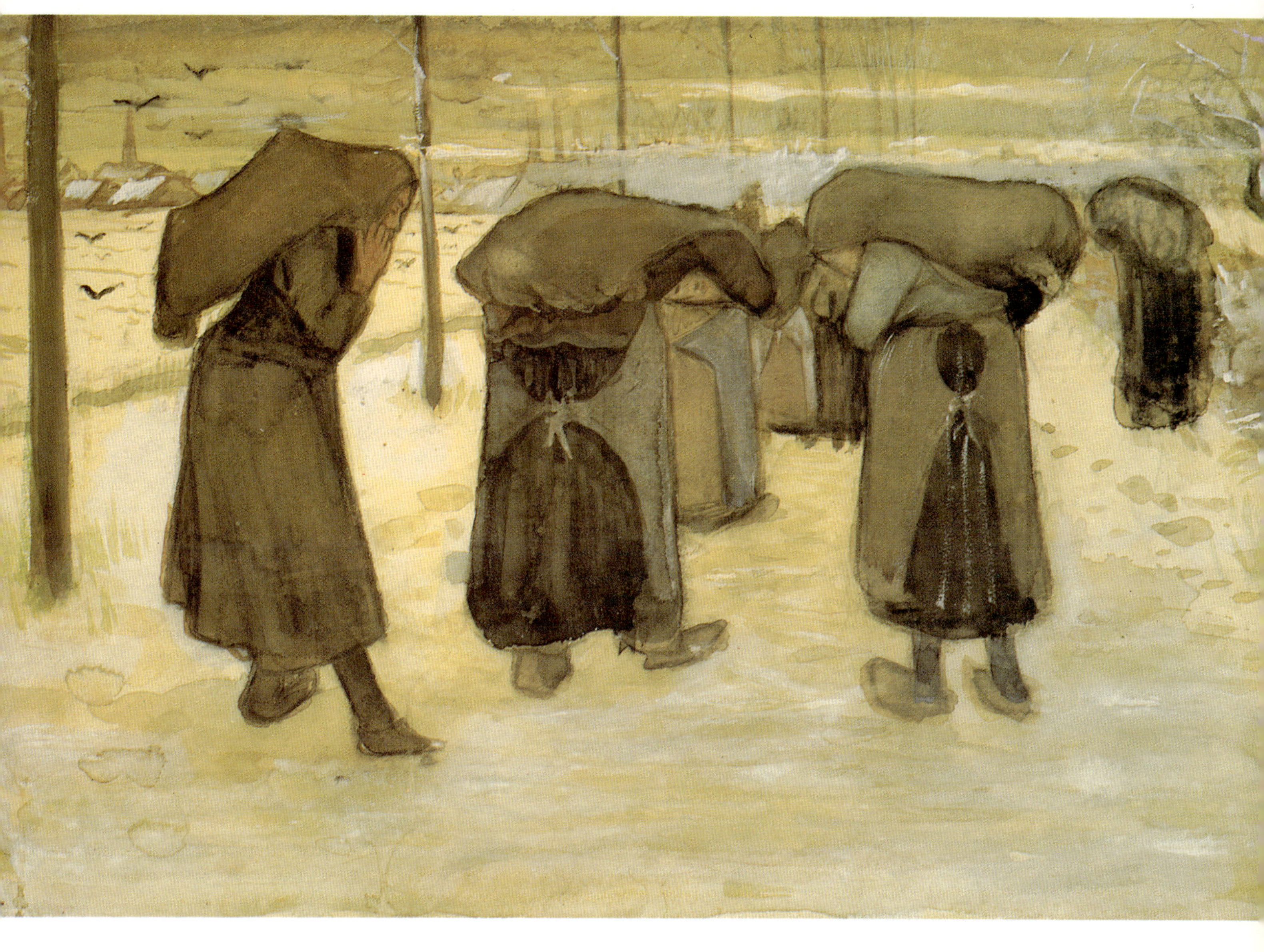

Miners' Wives

November 1882 - watercolour highlighted with white - 32 x 50 cm - Rijksmuseum Kröller- Müller, Otterlo

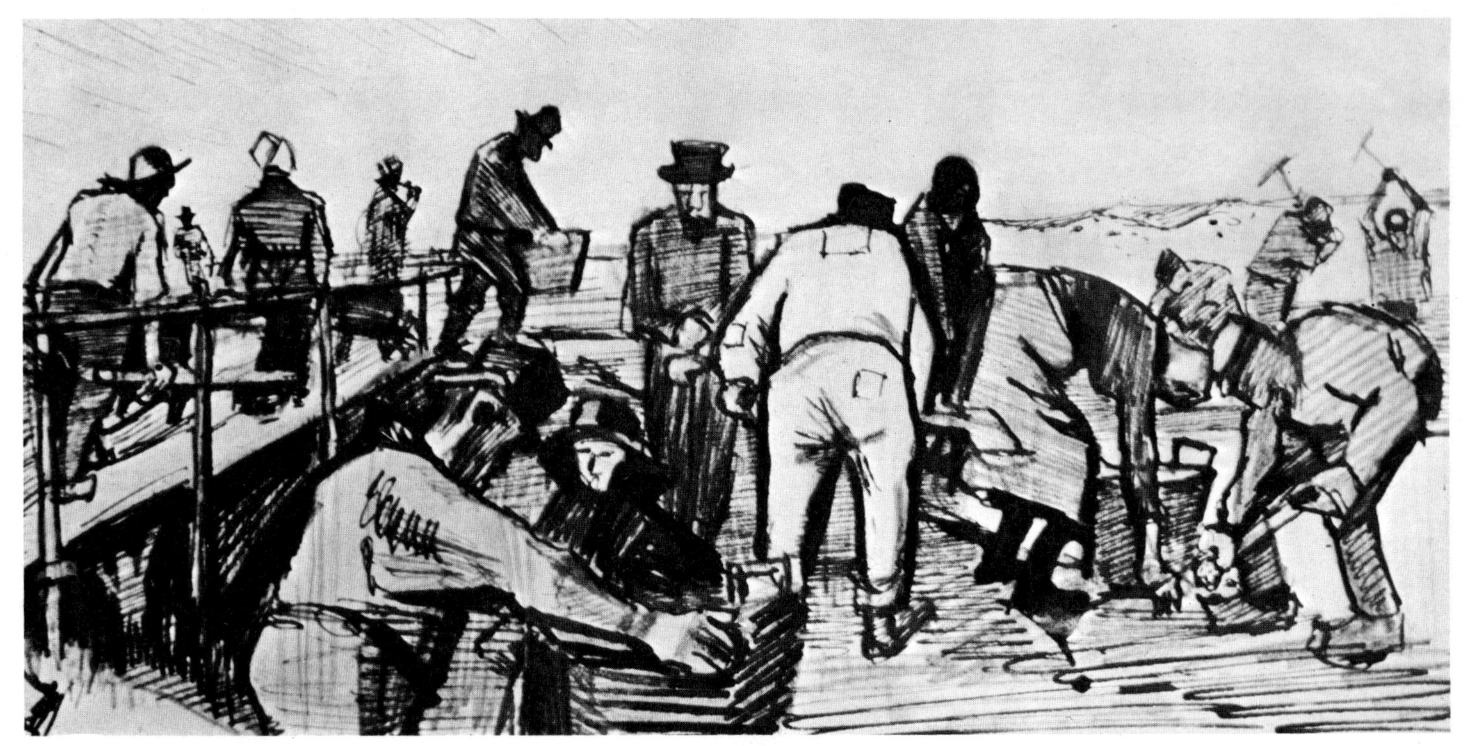

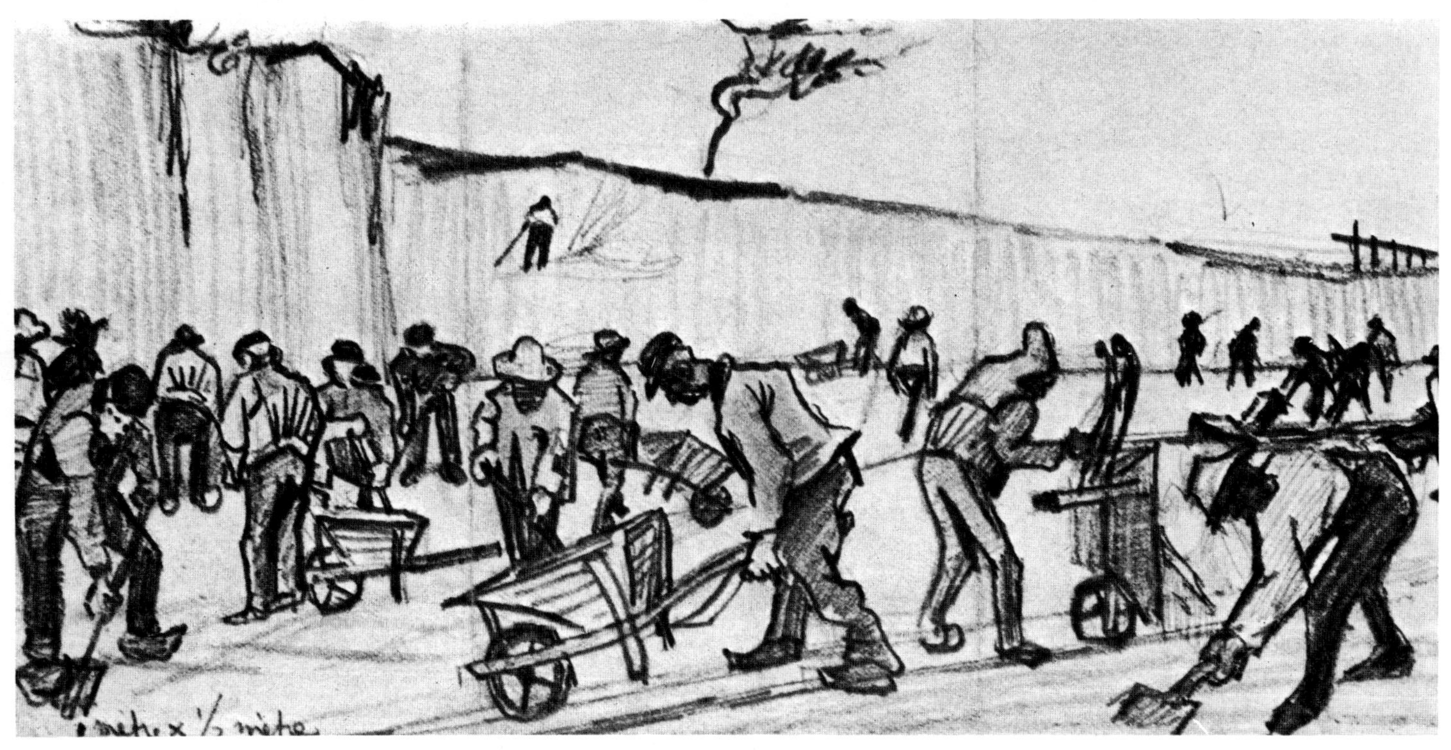

Men and Women Working

April-May 1883 - pen and pencil drawing - 11.5 x 21 cm - Vincent van Gogh Foundation, Amsterdam

The Sandpit

April-May 1883 - pencil drawing - 10.5 x 21 cm - Vincent van Gogh Foundation, Amsterdam

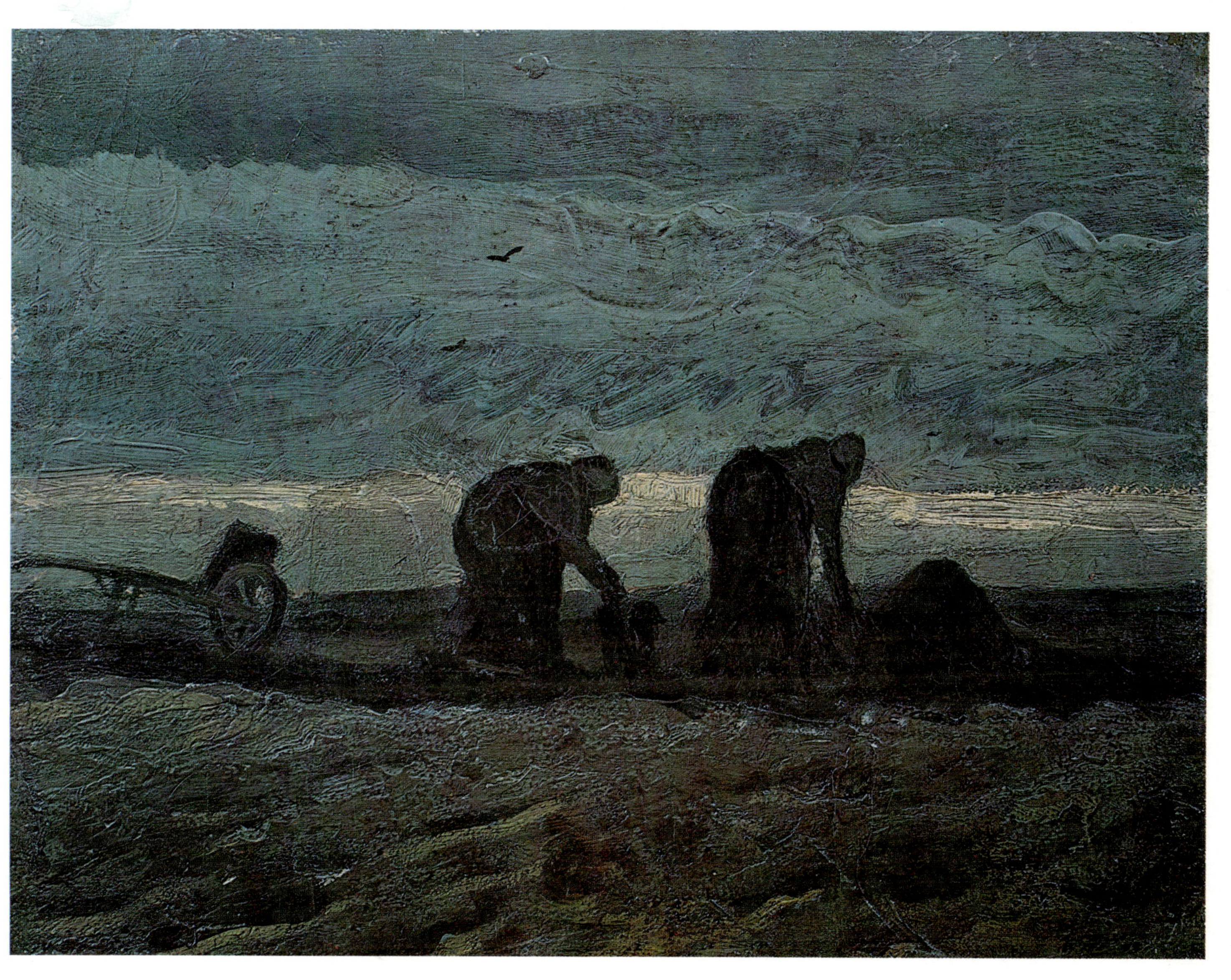

Two Peasant Women in Peat Field

September 1883 - oil on canvas - 27 x 35.5 cm -
Vincent van Gogh Foundation, Amsterdam

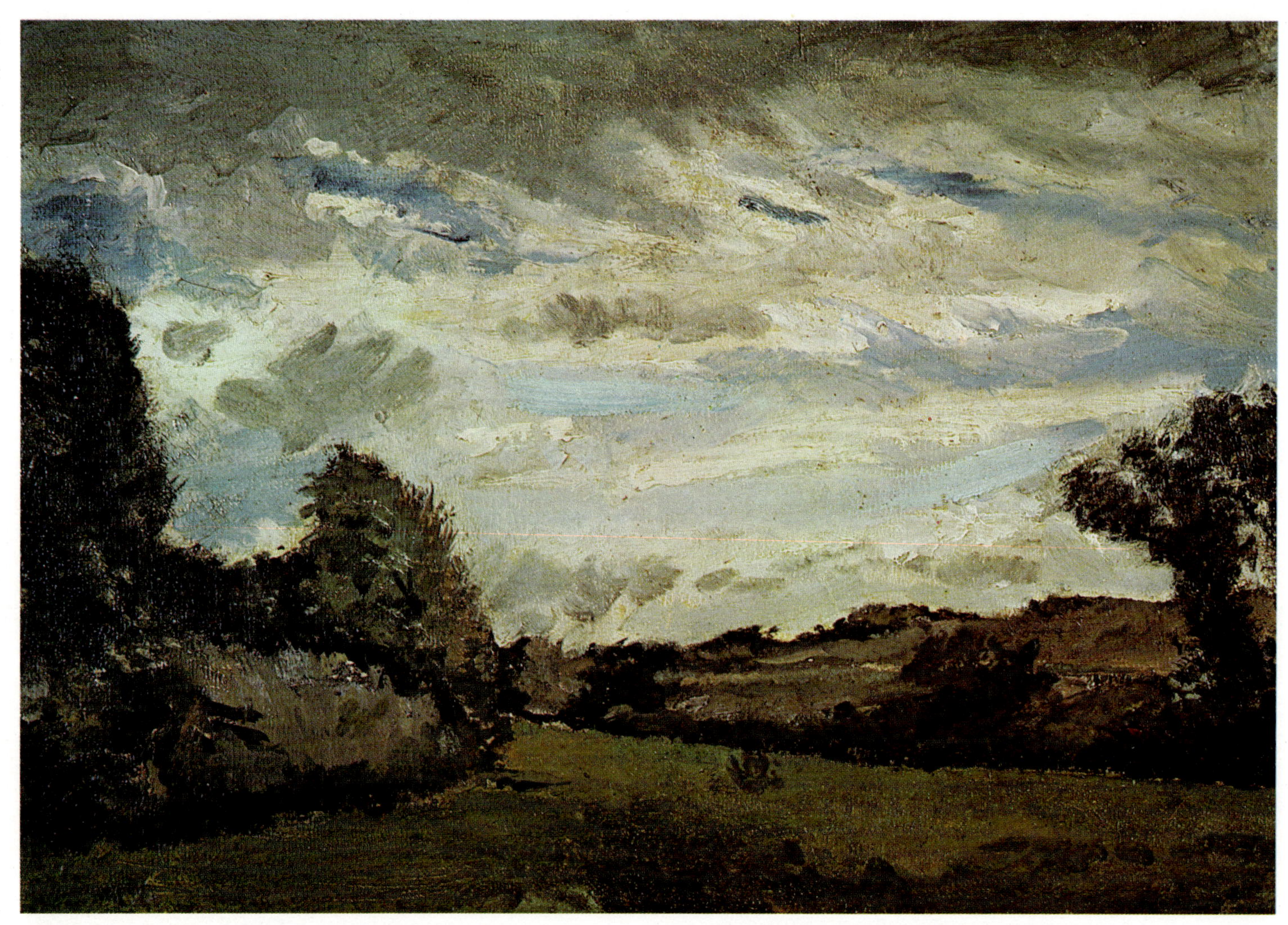

Landscape with Dunes

September 1883 - oil on canvas - 33.5 x 48.5 cm -
Mrs A.M. Sythoff-Burgerhout collection, Wassenaar, Holland

The Village of Loosduinen Seen from a Dune

1883 - pencil - 26.5 x 48.5 cm -
Groningen musueum, Holland

Farm Houses

September 1883 - oil on canvas on card -36 x 55.5 cm -
Vincent van Gogh Foundation, Amsterdam

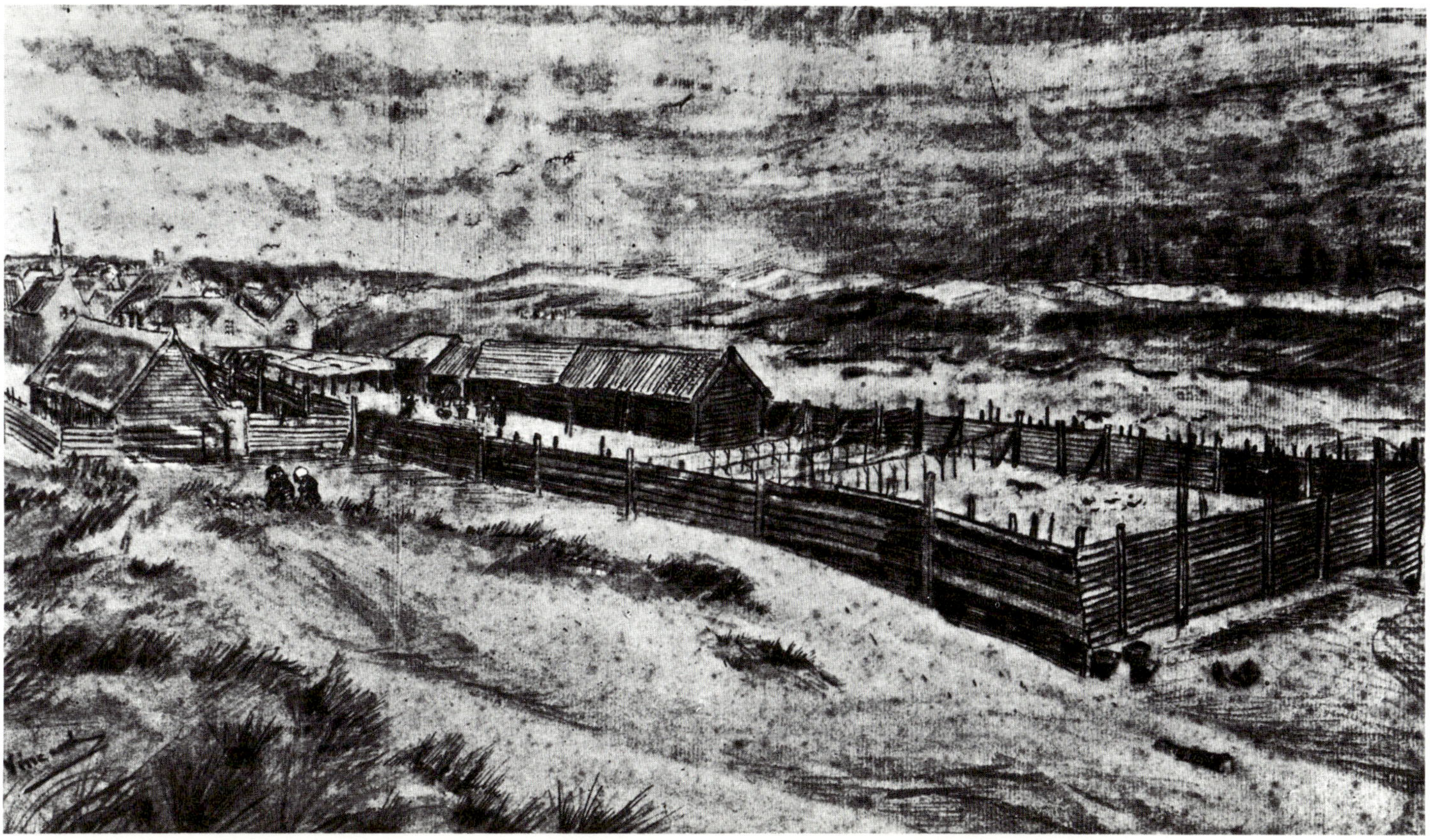

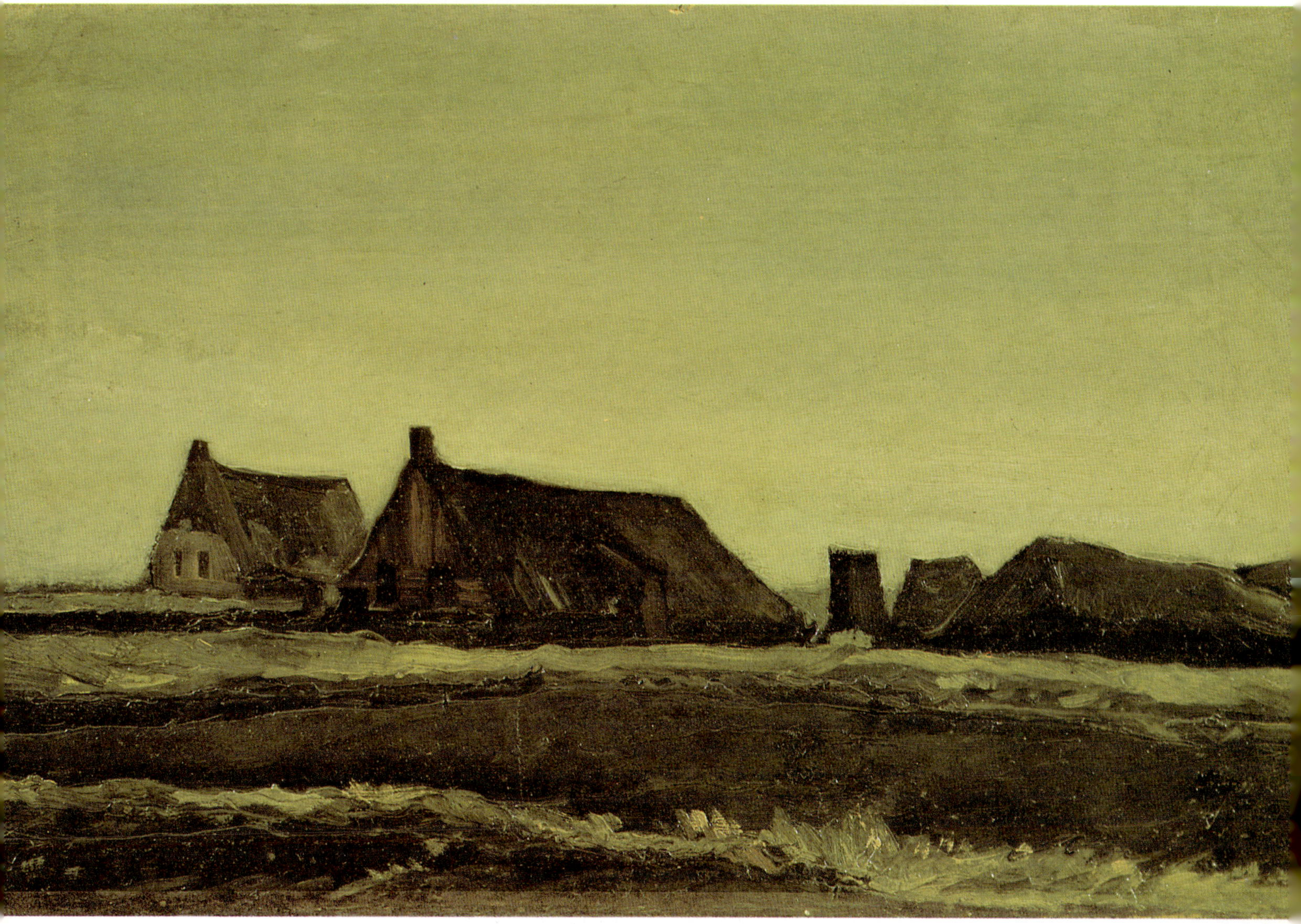

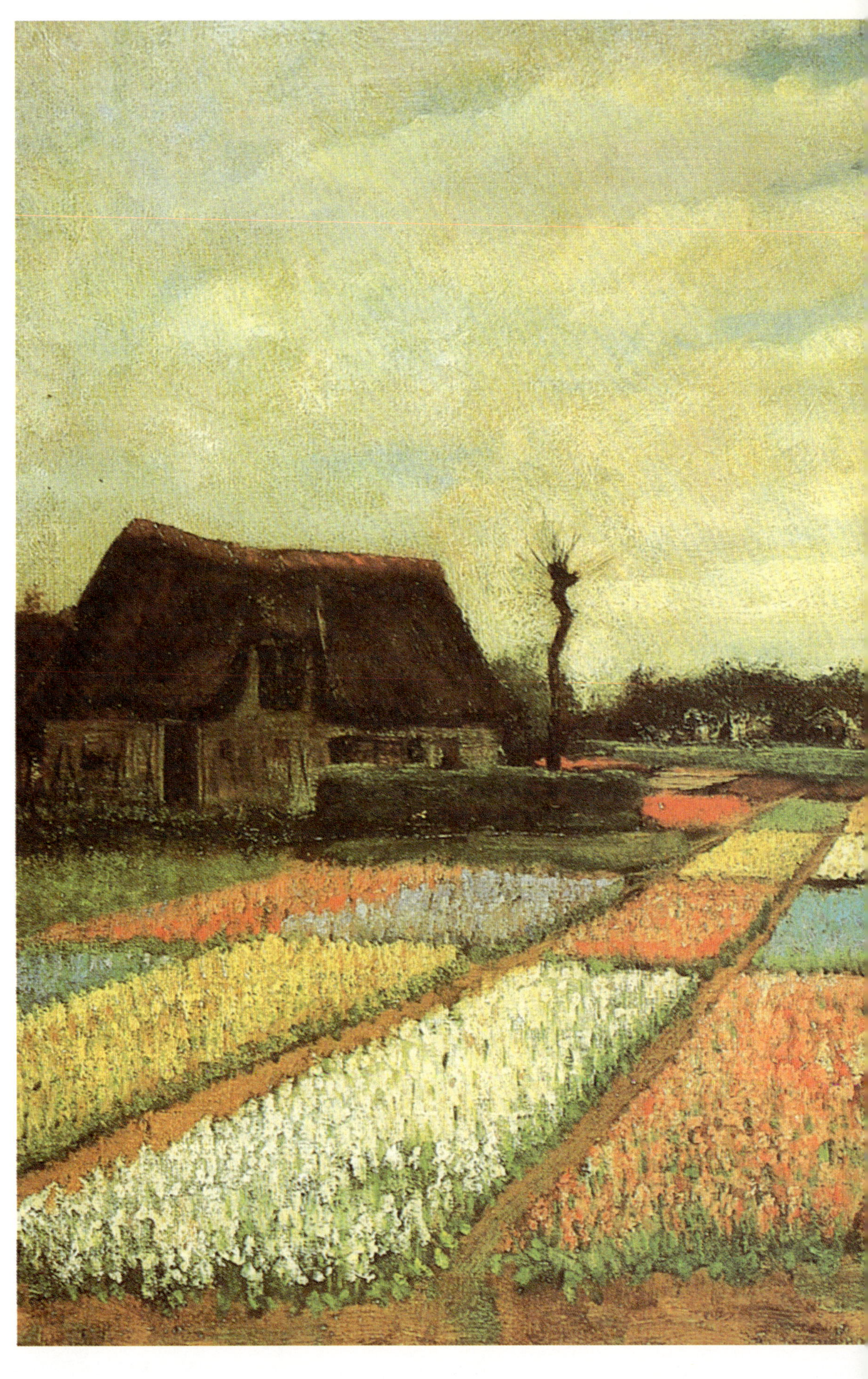

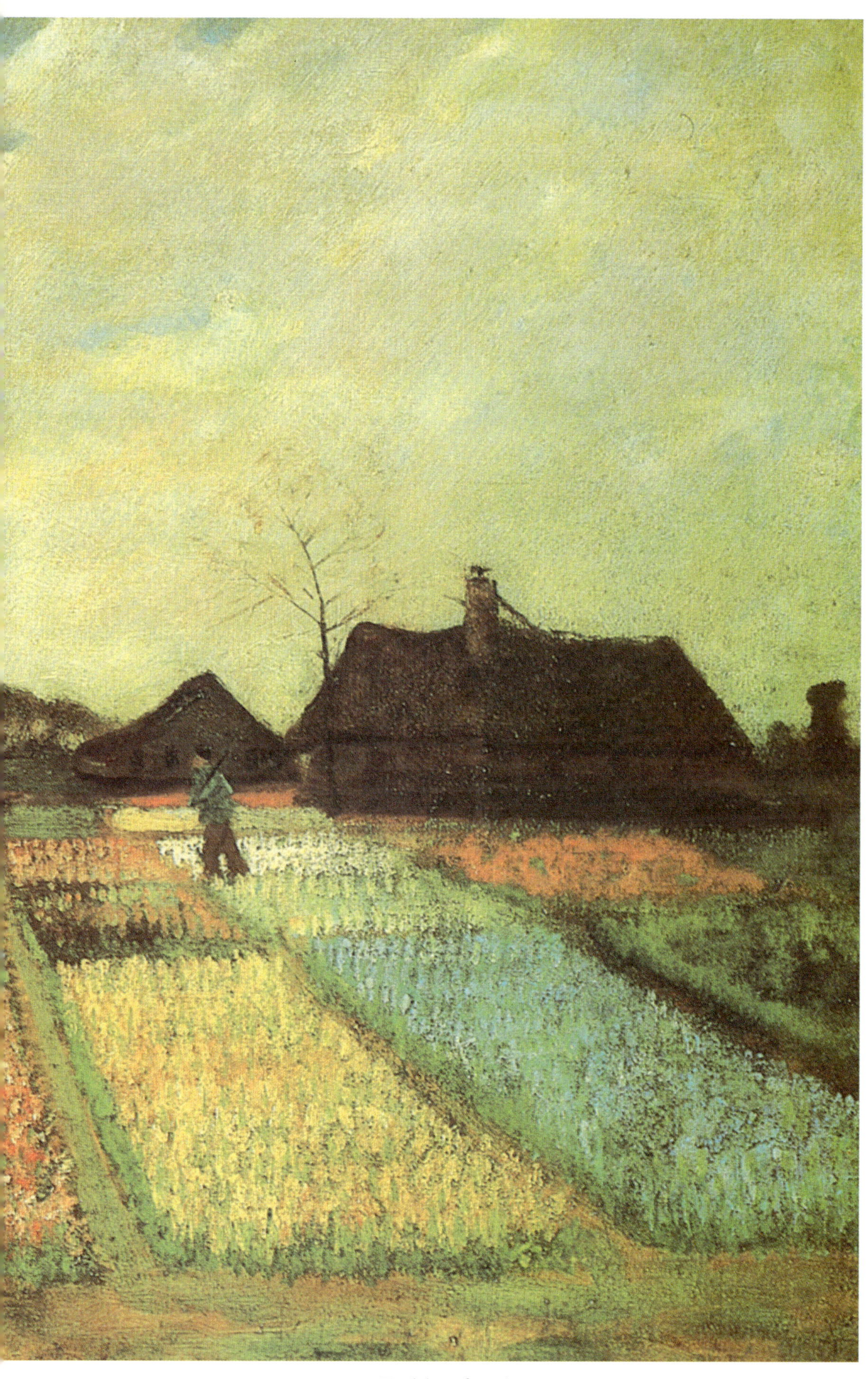

Fields of Tulips

April 1883 - oil on canvas on wood - 48 x 65 cm -
Mr. & Mrs. Paul Mellon Collection, National Gallery of Art,
Washington D.C.

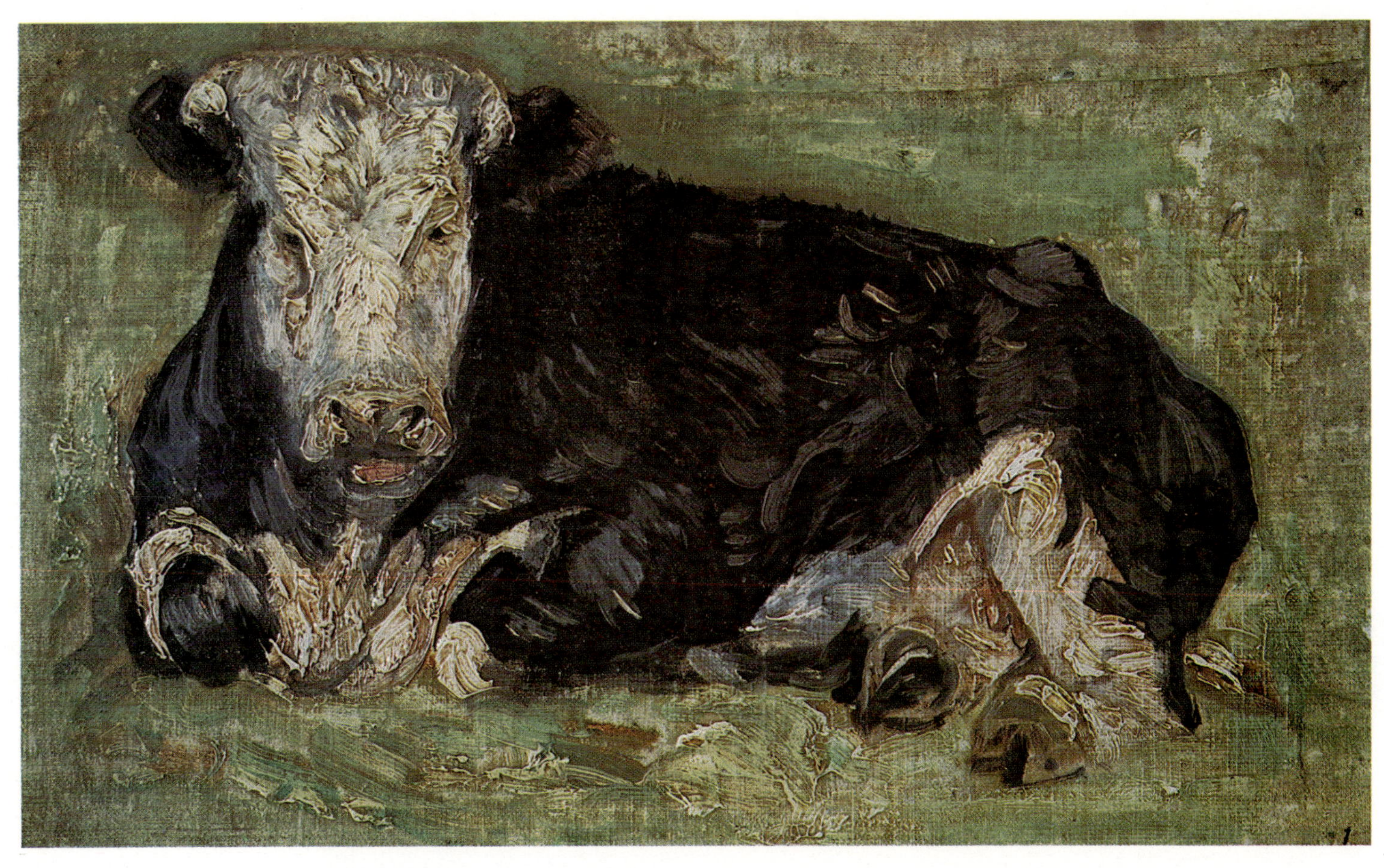

Cow Lying Down

1883 - oil on canvas on a panel - 30 x 50 cm -
Private collection, Paris

Young Girl Kneeling before
a Sleeping Baby

April 1883 - charcoal with white highlights - 48 x 32 cm -
Vincent van Gogh Foundation, Amsterdam

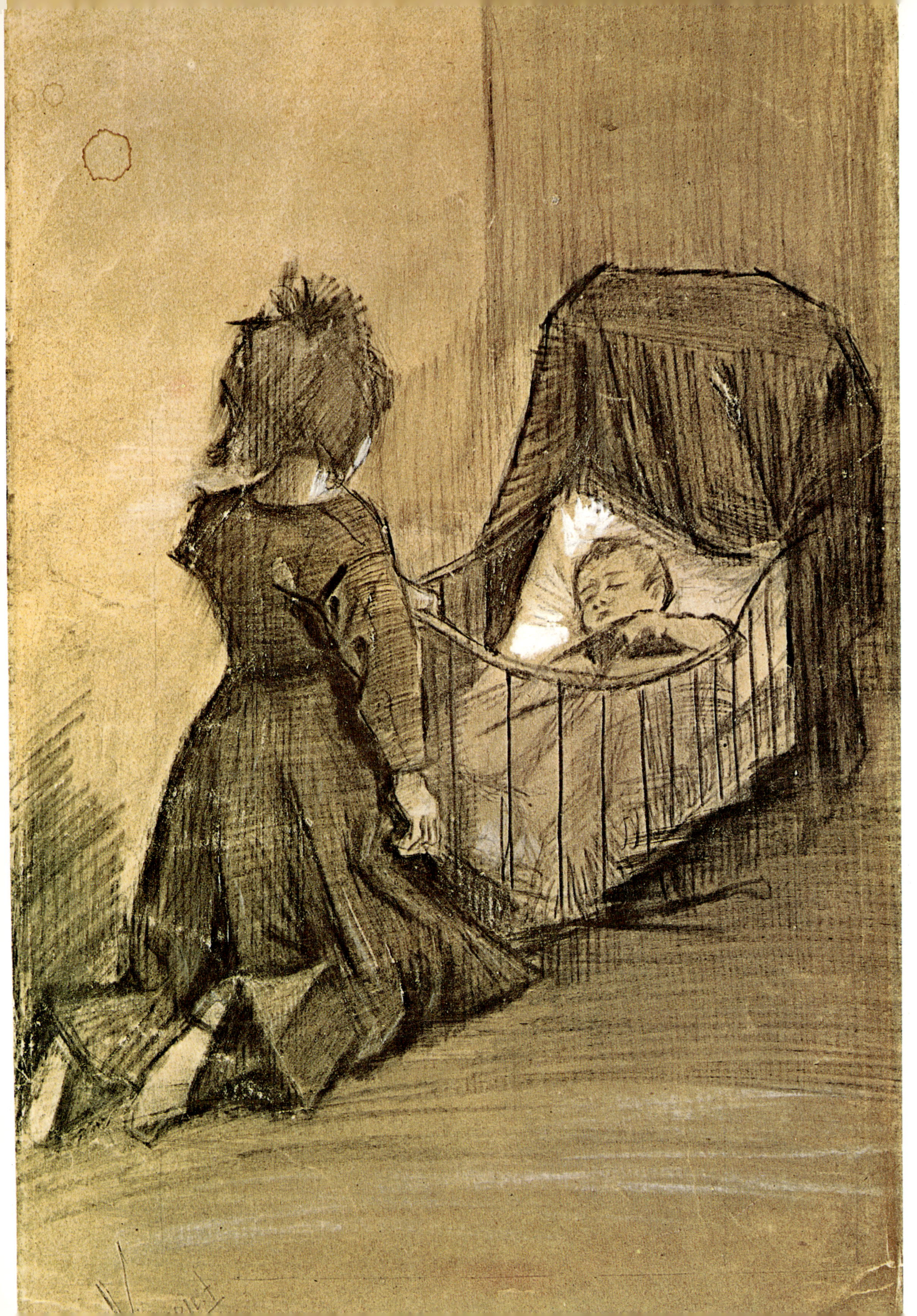

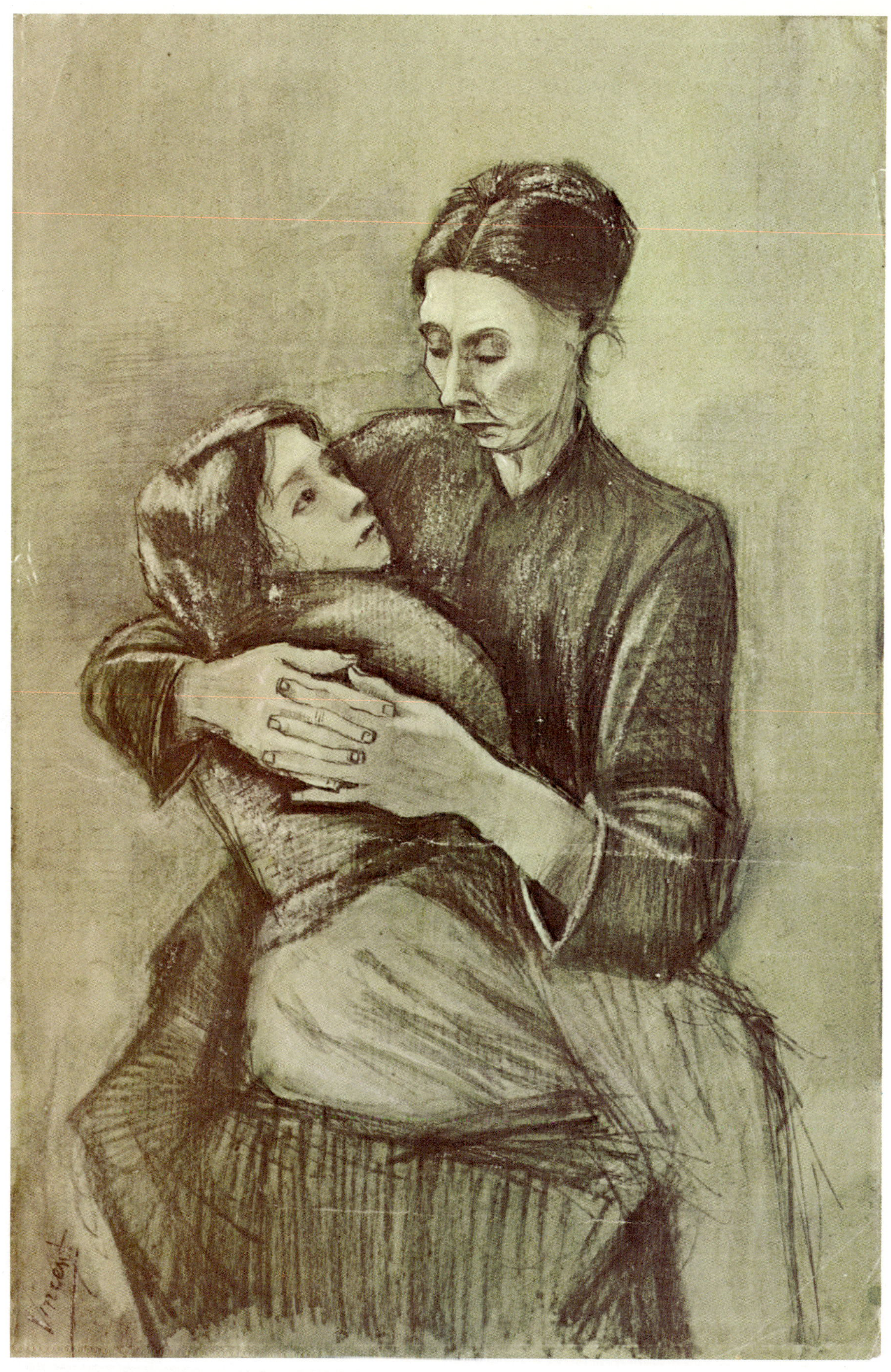

Mother and Child

Spring 1883 - charcoal and pencil drawing, with white highlights and wash - 53.5 x 35 cm - Vincent van Gogh Foundation, Amsterdam

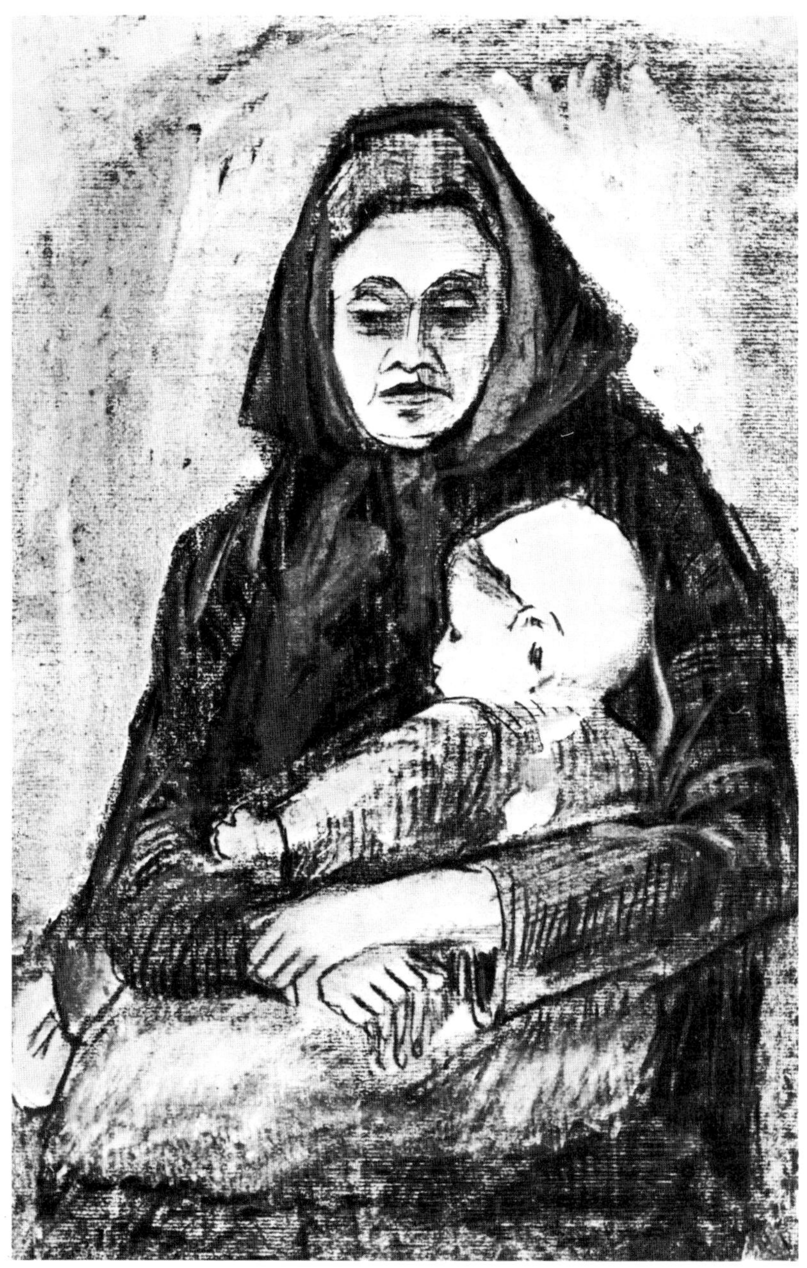

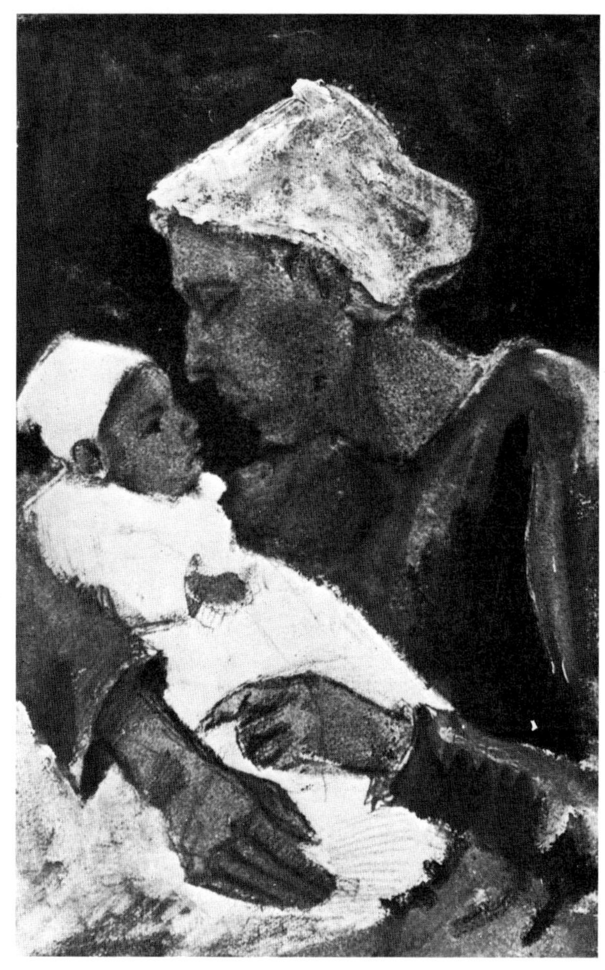

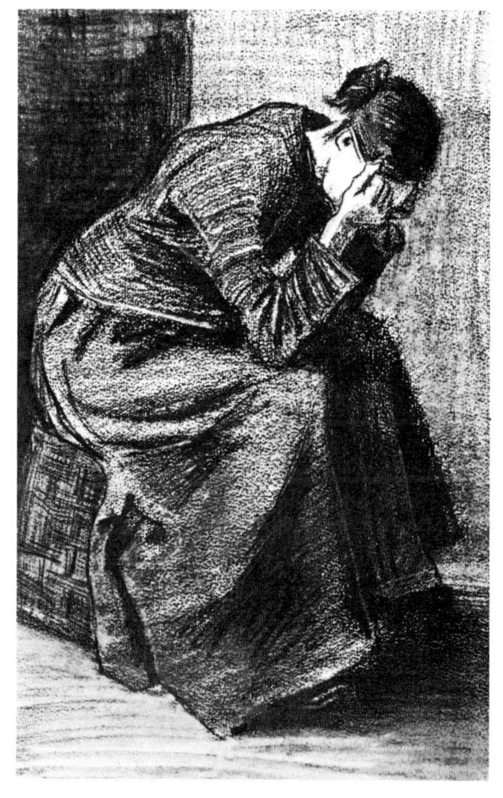

Mother Holding Her Child in Her Right Arm

April 1883 - watercolour, crayon, highlighted with white oil - 40.5 x 20 cm - Rijksmuseum Kröller- Müller, Otterlo

Mother in Tears, Seated on an Upturned Basket

March-April 1883 - black chalk, wash, white highlights - 47.5 x 29.5 cm - Rijksmuseum Kröller- Müller, Otterlo

Mother Holding Her Child on Her Knees

Spring 1883 - black chalk, wash, white highlights - 41 x 27 cm - Rijksmuseum Kröller- Müller, Otterlo

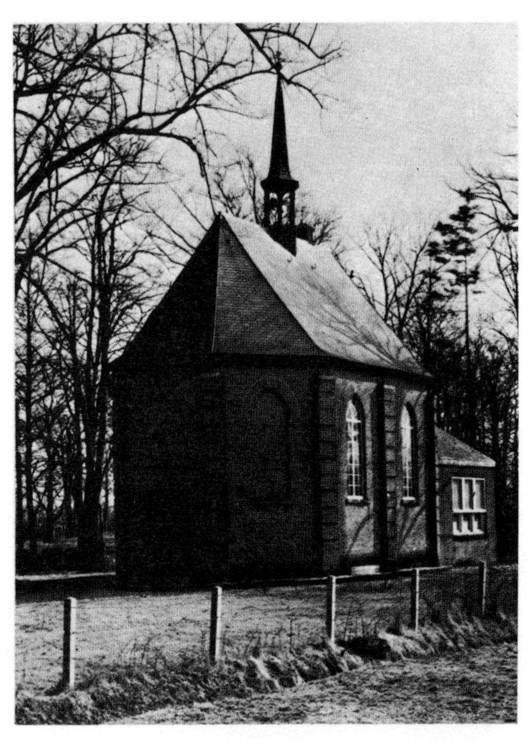

Photograph of the little church at Nuenen

The Little Church at Nuenen

January 1884 - oil on canvas -41 x 32 cm - Vincent van Gogh Foundation, Amsterdam

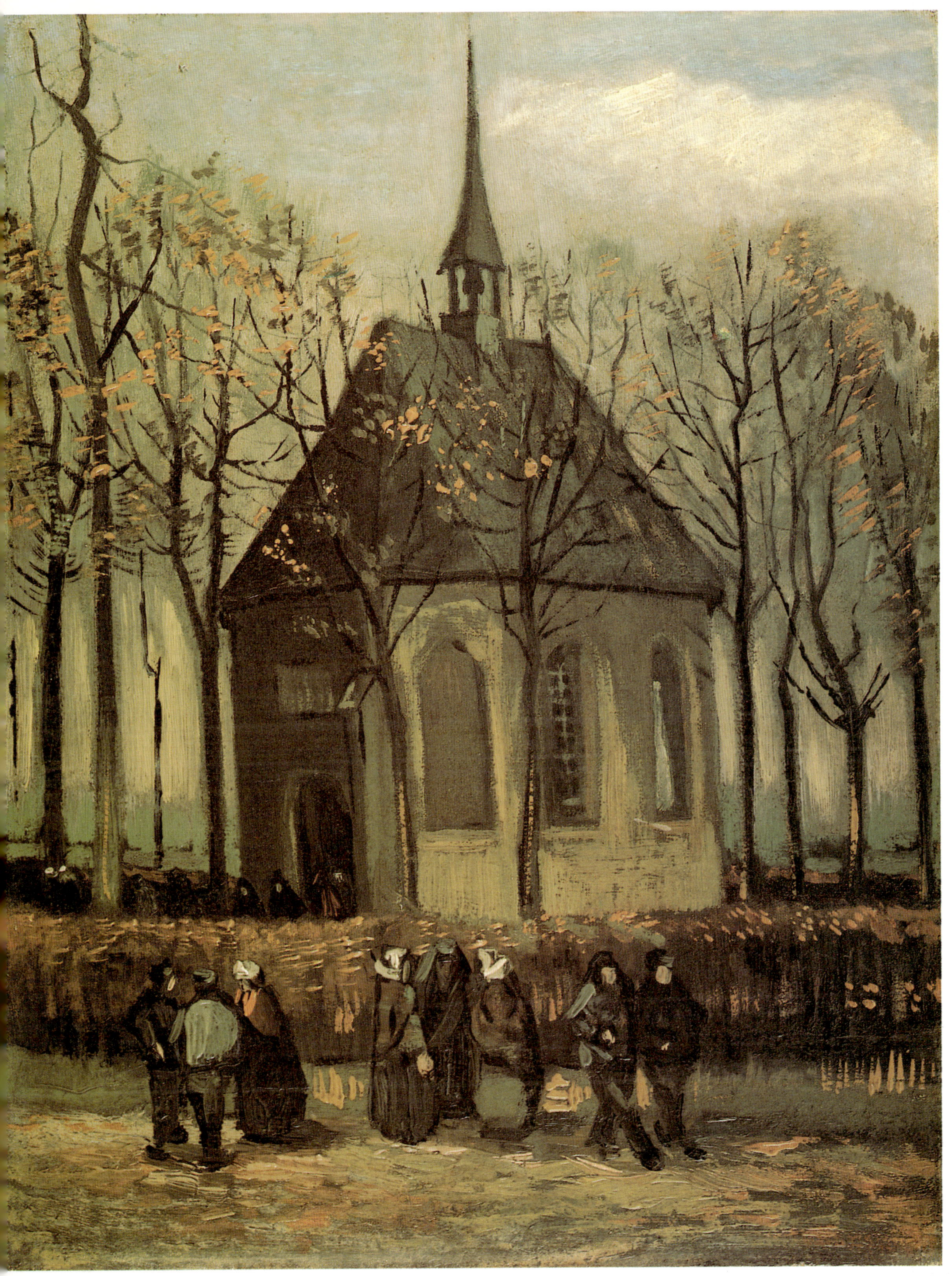

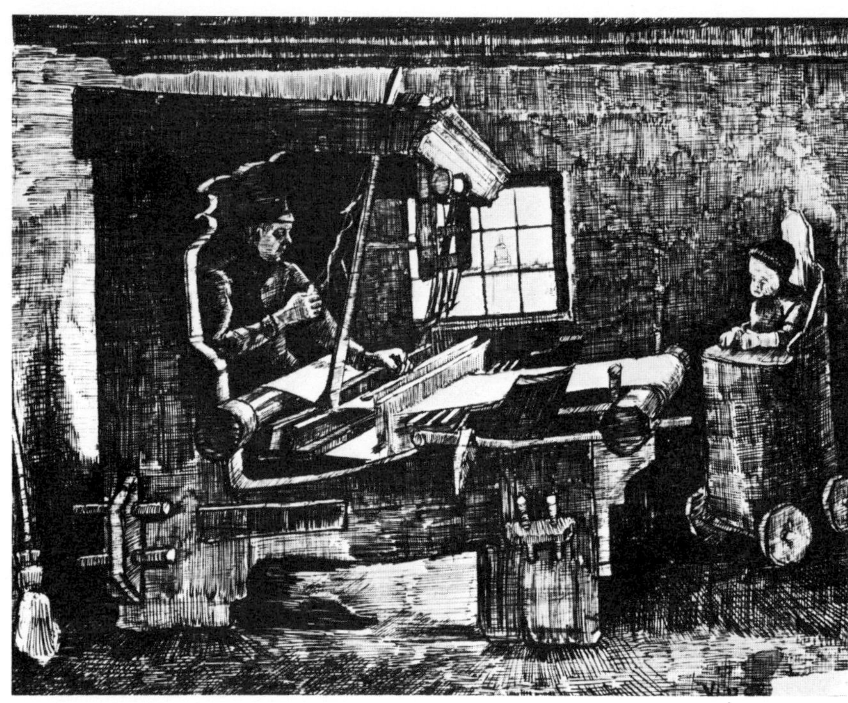

Inside the Weaver's

February 1884 - pen - 32 x 40 cm -
Vincent van Gogh Foundation, Amsterdam

Weaver Repairing Thread

March 1884 - oil on canvas - 61 x 85 cm -
Museum of Fine Arts, Boston

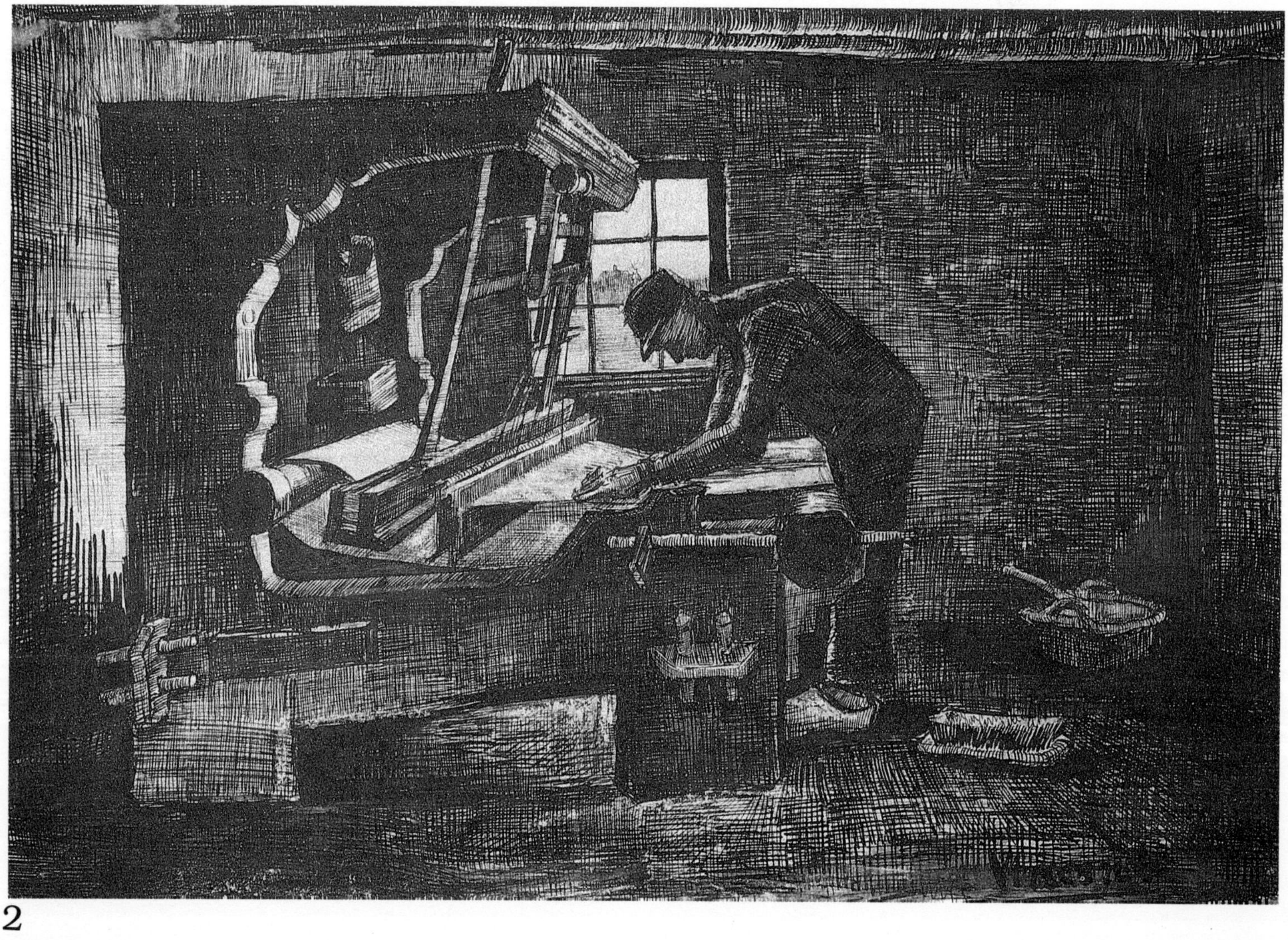

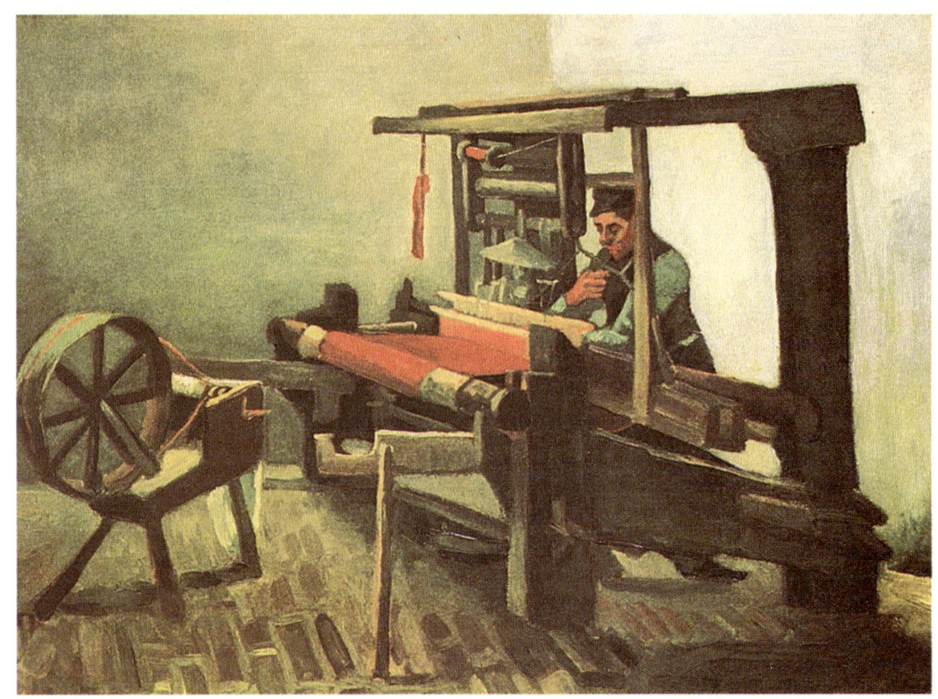

Weaver Standing in front of a Loom

May 1884
- crayon, pen and indian ink -27 x 40 cm -
Rijksmuseum Kröller- Müller, Otterlo

Weaver with Loom

May 1884 - oil on canvas - 70 x 85 cm -
Rijksmuseum Kröller- Müller, Otterlo

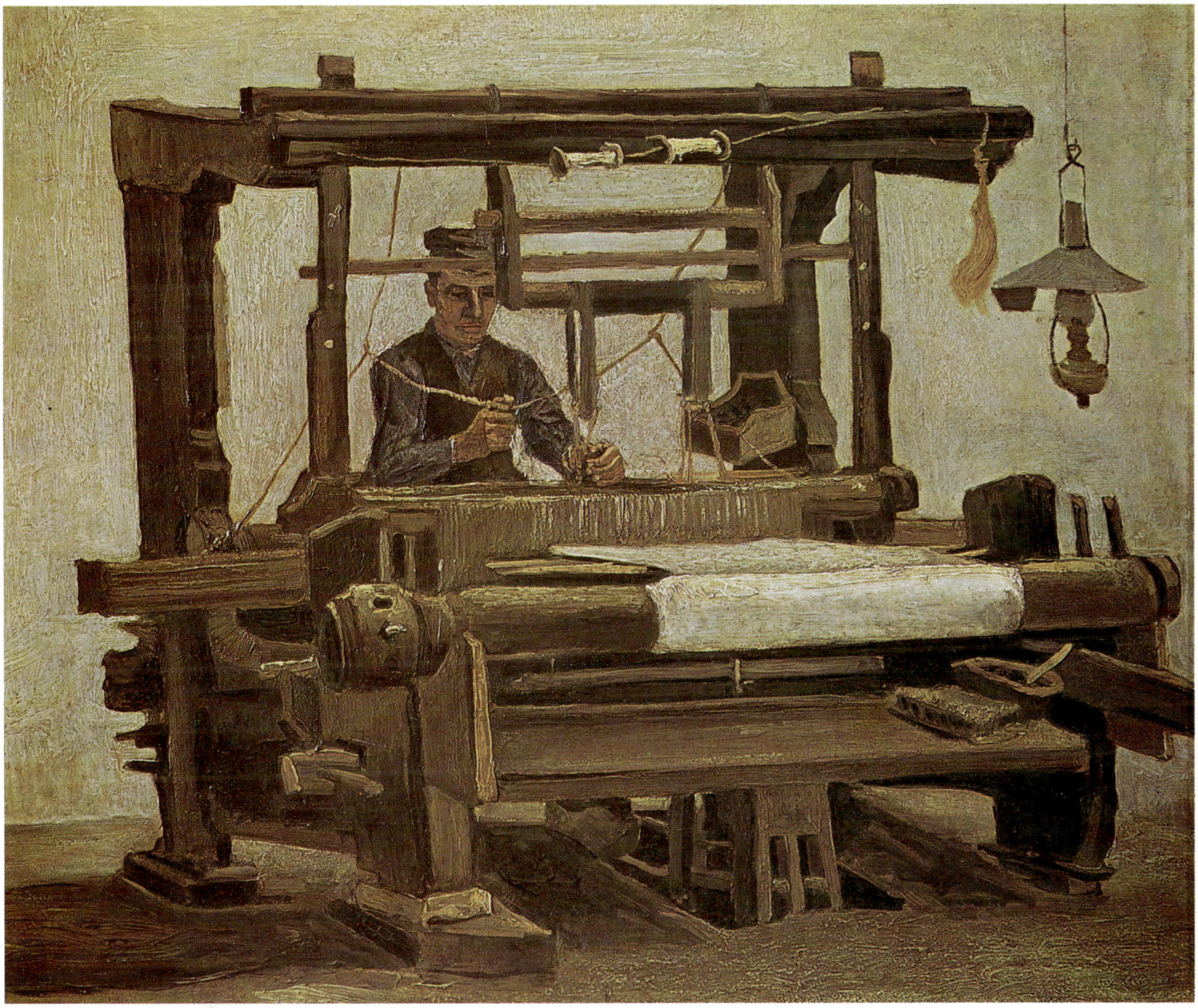

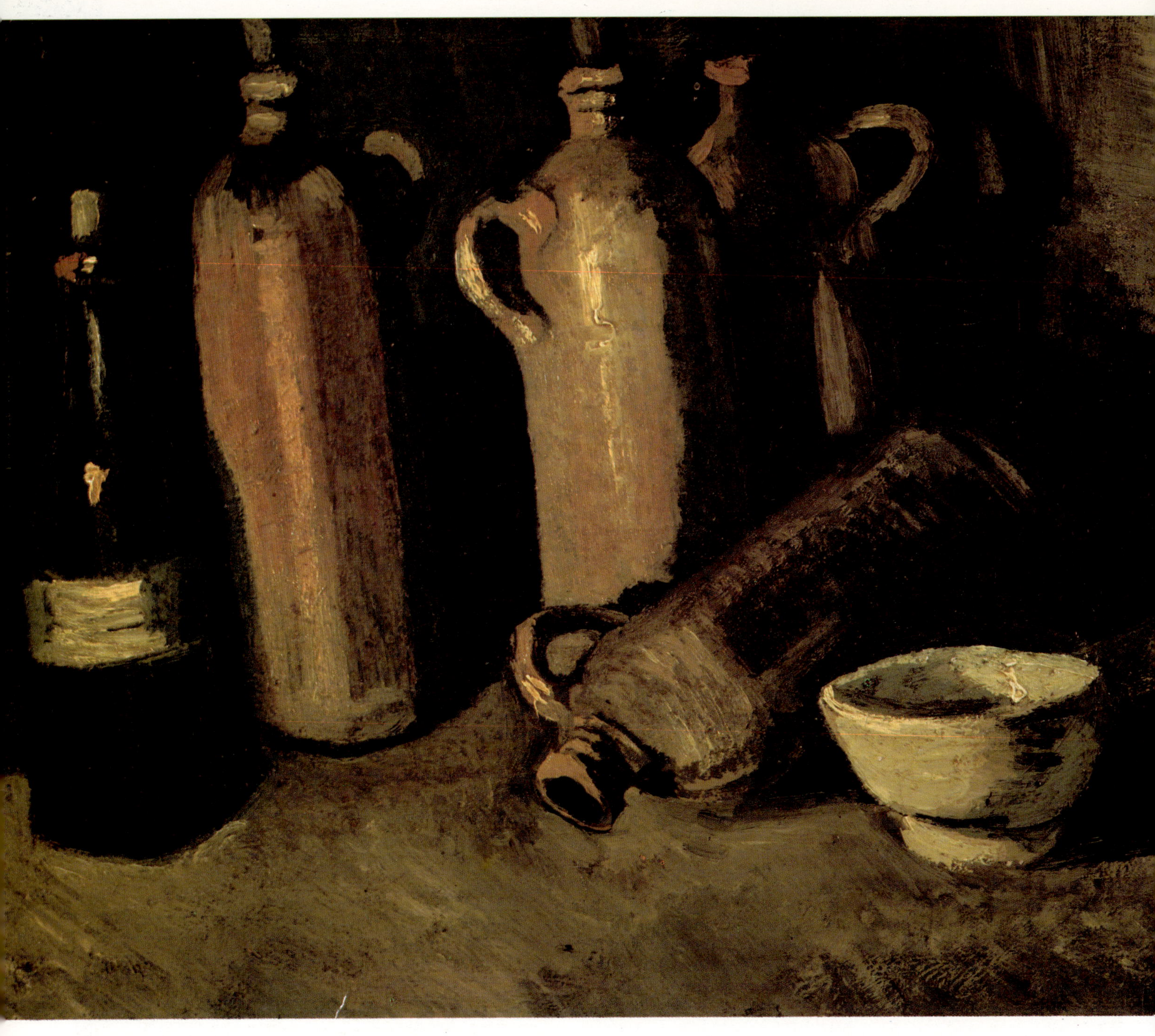

Still Life: Bottles

November 1884 - oil on canvas - 33 x 41 cm -
Rijksmuseum Kröller- Müller, Otterlo

Ox-drawn Cart

July 1884 - oil on wood - 57 x 82.5 cm -
Rijksmuseum Kröller- Müller, Otterlo

The Old Station at Eindhoven

1884 - oil on canvas - 15 x 26 cm -
H. Korting collection, Gilze, Holland

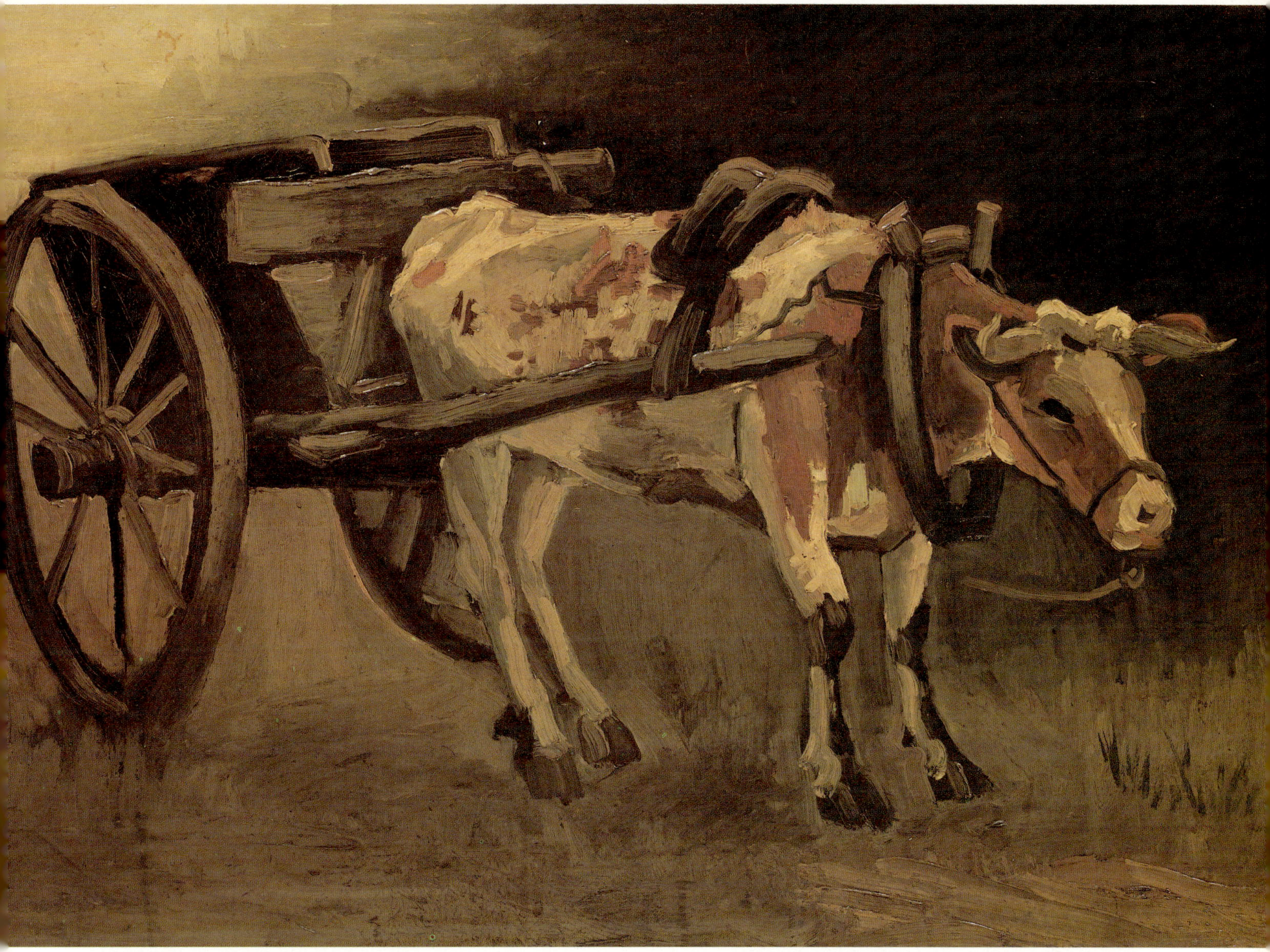

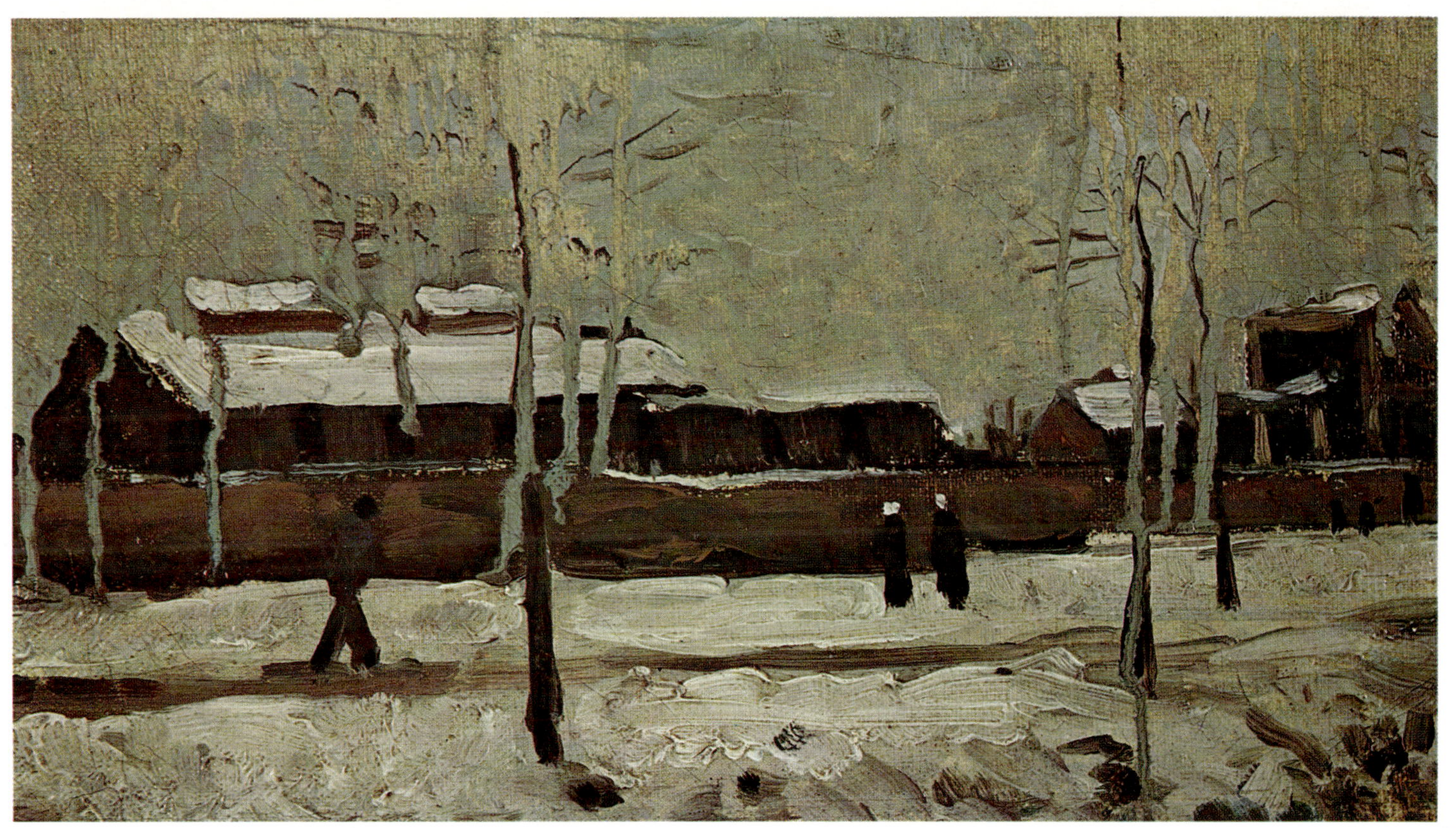

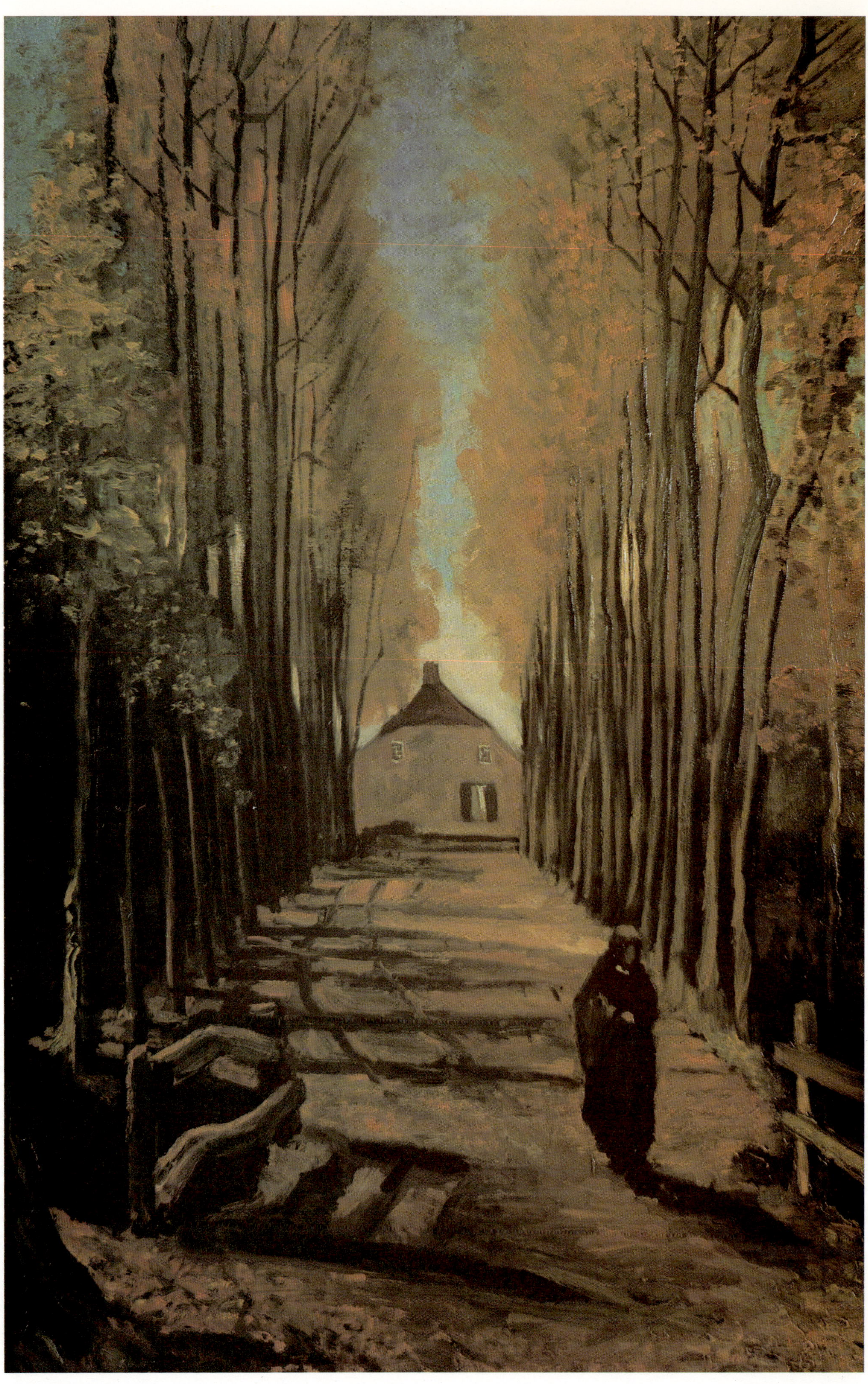

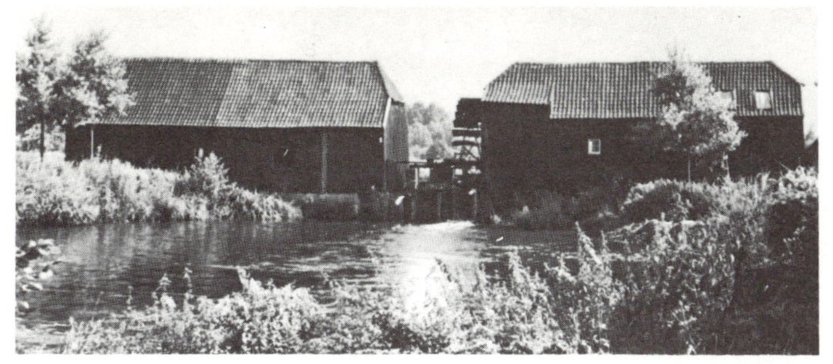

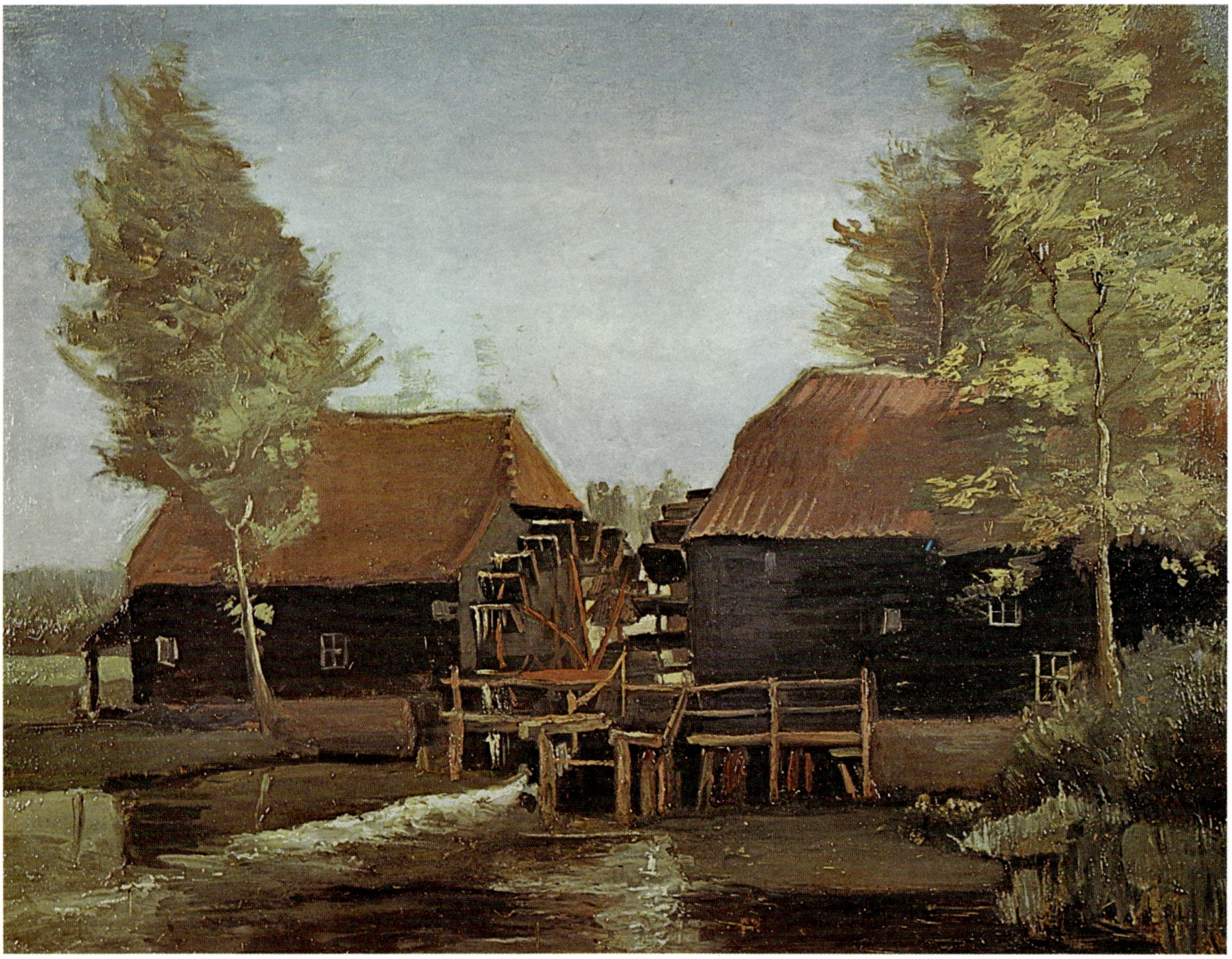

Photograph of a watermill at Nuenen

Water Mill at Krollen

November 1884 - oil on card - 58 x 78 cm -
Private collection

Avenue of Poplars in Autumn

October 1884 - oil on canvas on wood -99 x 66 cm -
Rijksmuseum Kröller- Müller, Otterlo

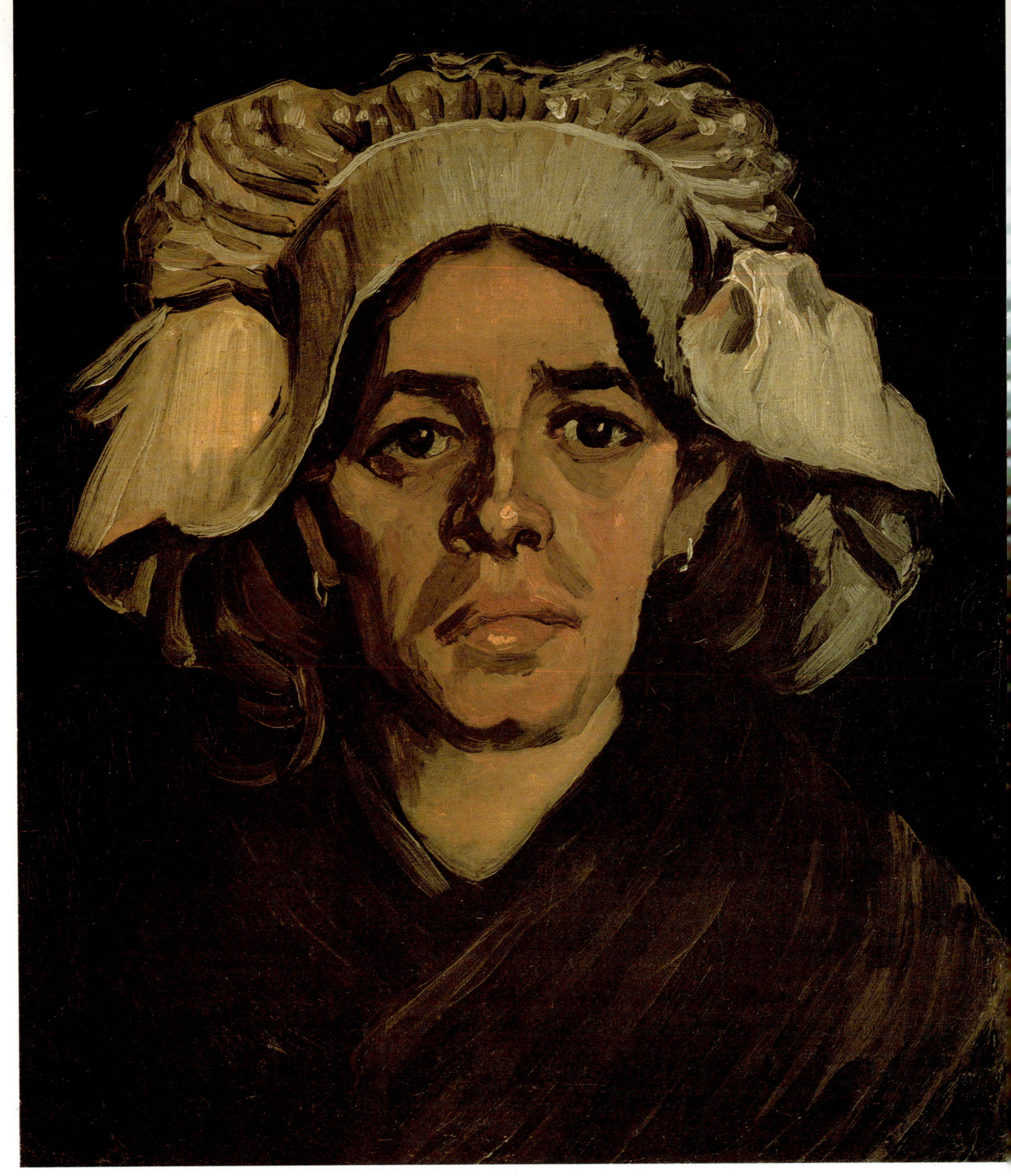

Head of Peasant Woman with White Cap

March 1885 - oil on canvas - 43 x 33.5 cm -
Vincent Van Gogh Foundation, Amsterdam

Head of a Peasant Woman

March 1885 - oil on canvas on wood - 45 x 36 cm -
Musée d'Orsay, Paris

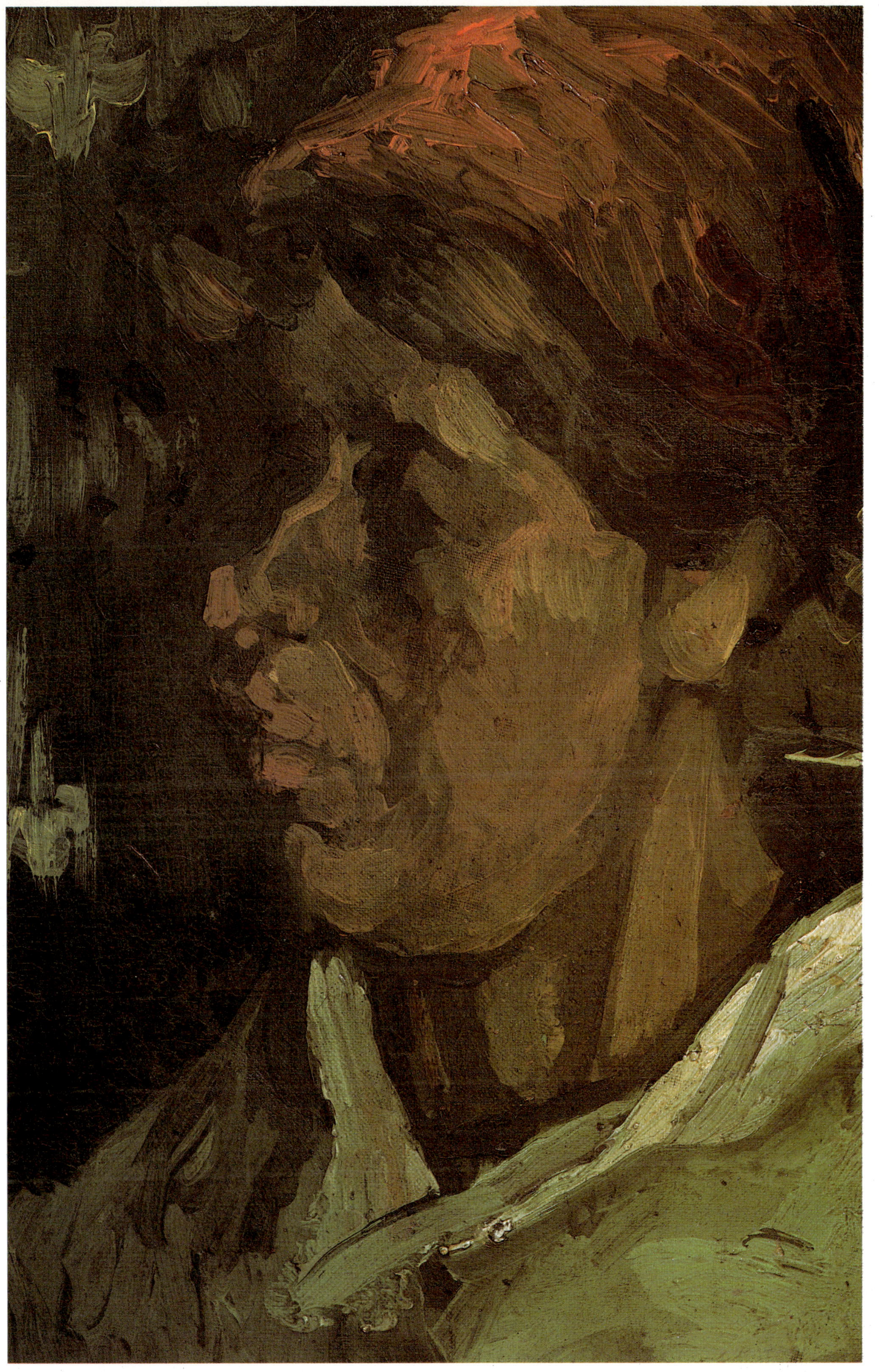

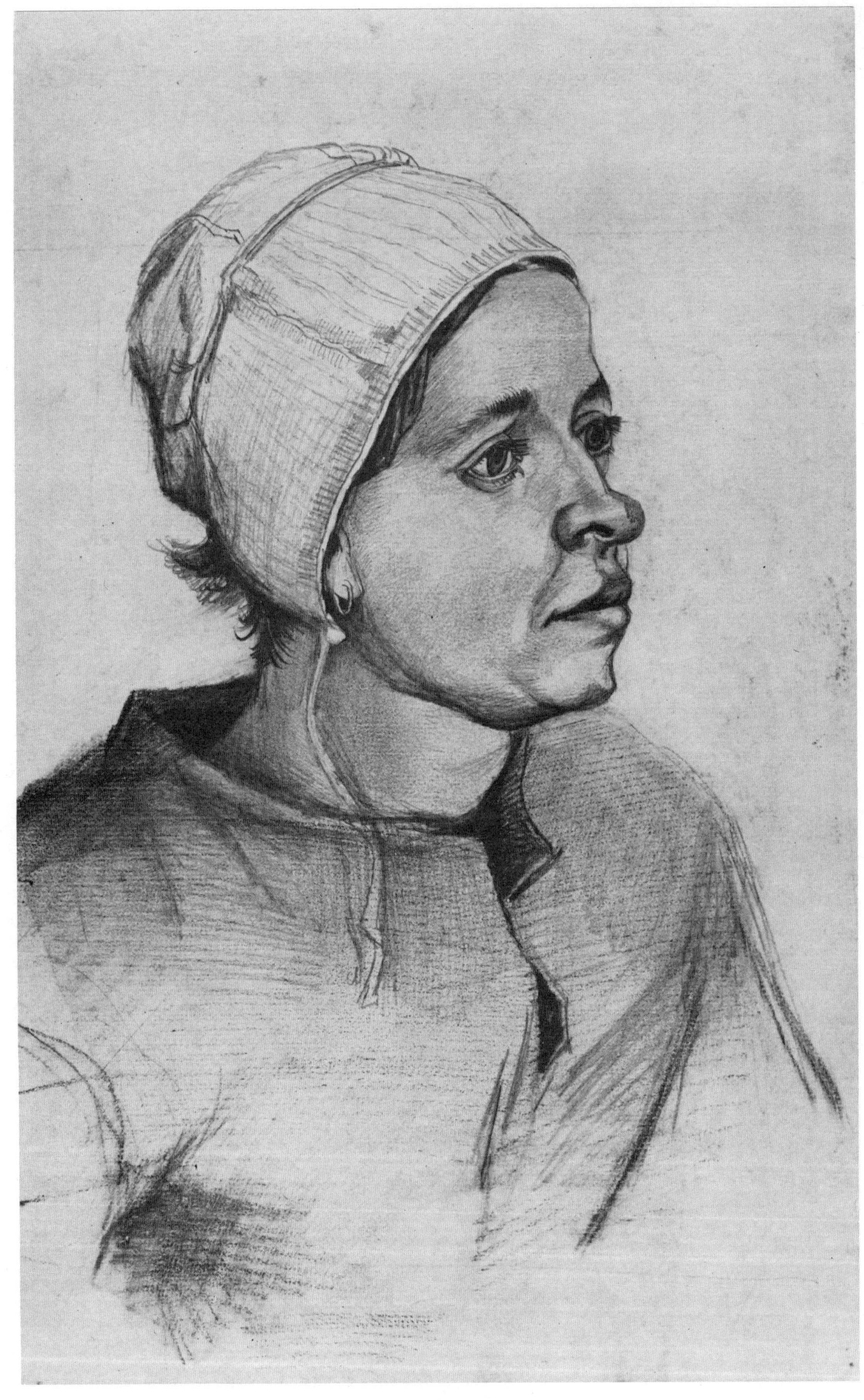

Peasant Woman with a White Cap

January 1885 - pencil and charcoal - 33.5 x 84 cm - Vincent van Gogh Foundation, Amsterdam

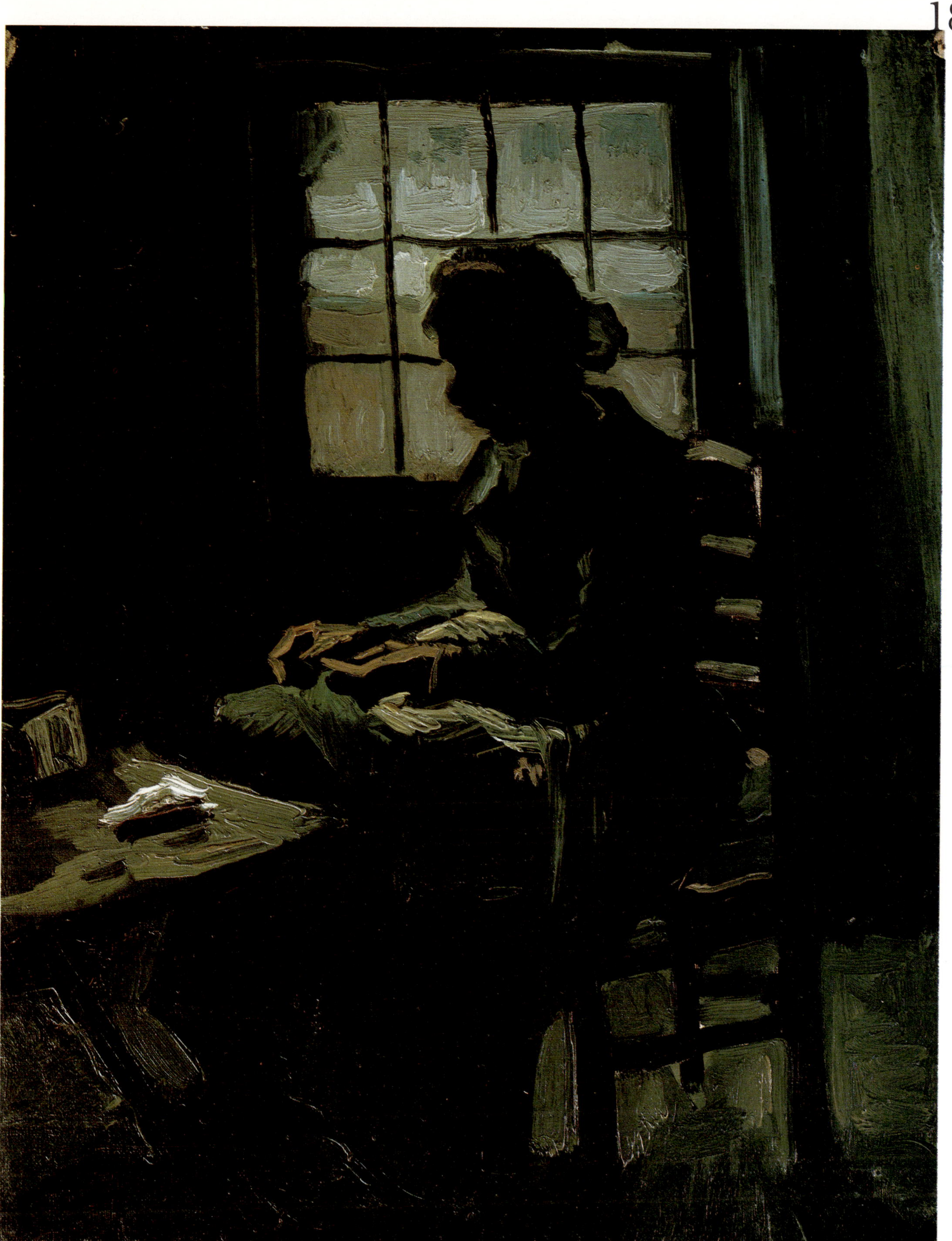

Seamstress

March 1885 - oil on canvas - 43.5 x 34.5 cm -
Vincent van Gogh Foundation, Amsterdam

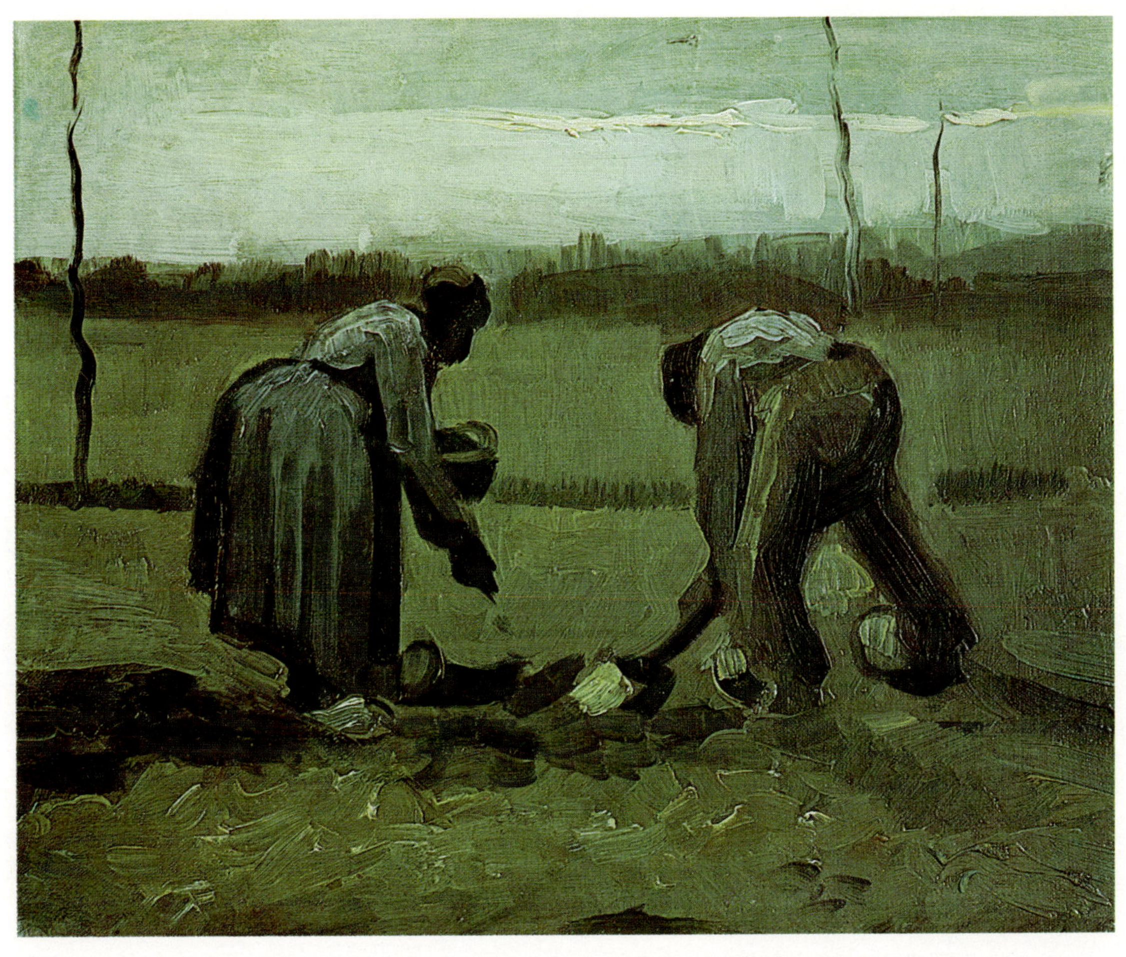

Field Work

April 1885 - oil on canvas - 31 x 39.5 cm -
Kunsthaus, Zurich

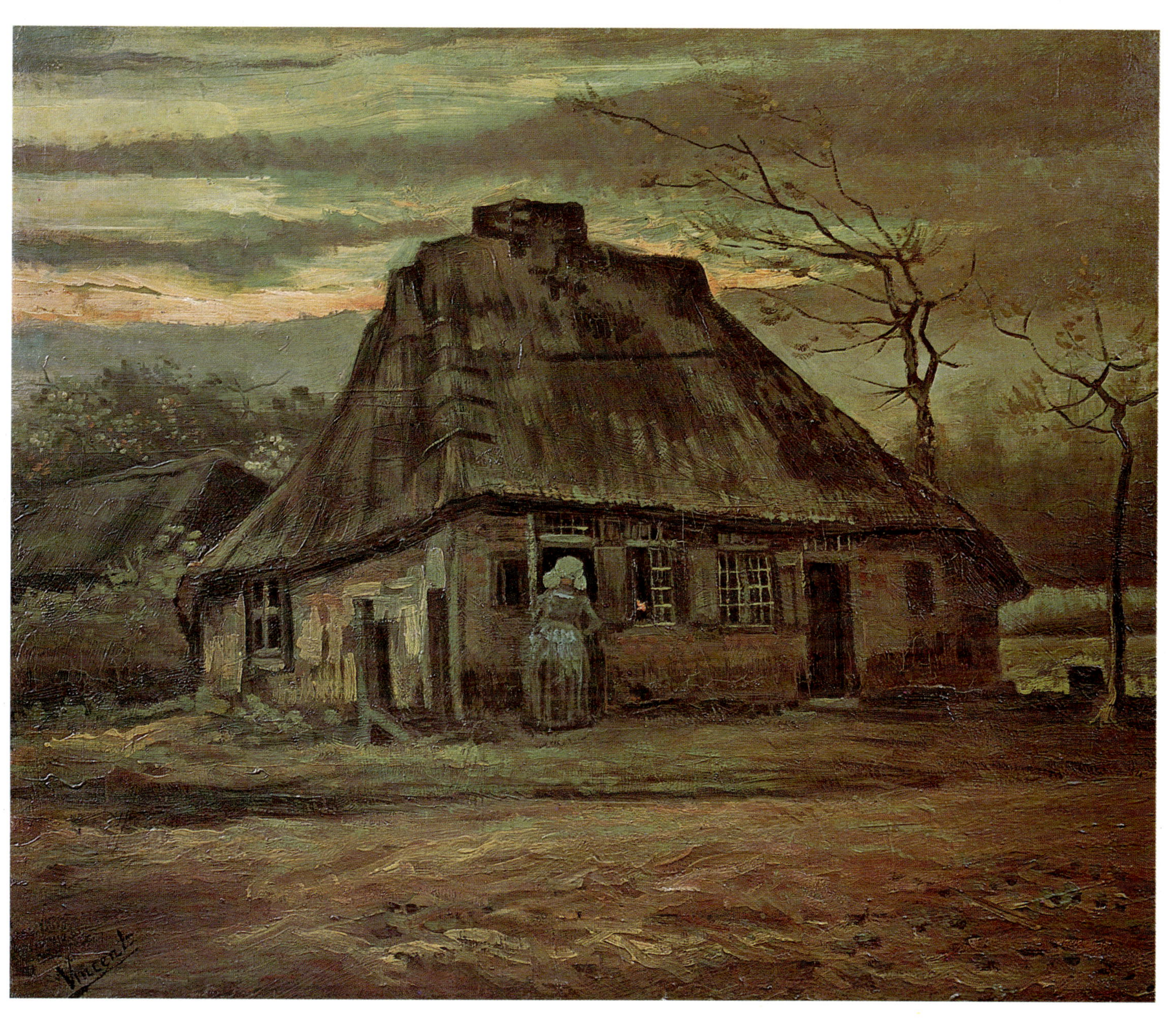

Cottage at Nightfall

May 1885 - oil on canvas - 64 x 78 cm - Vincent van Gogh Foundation, Amsterdam

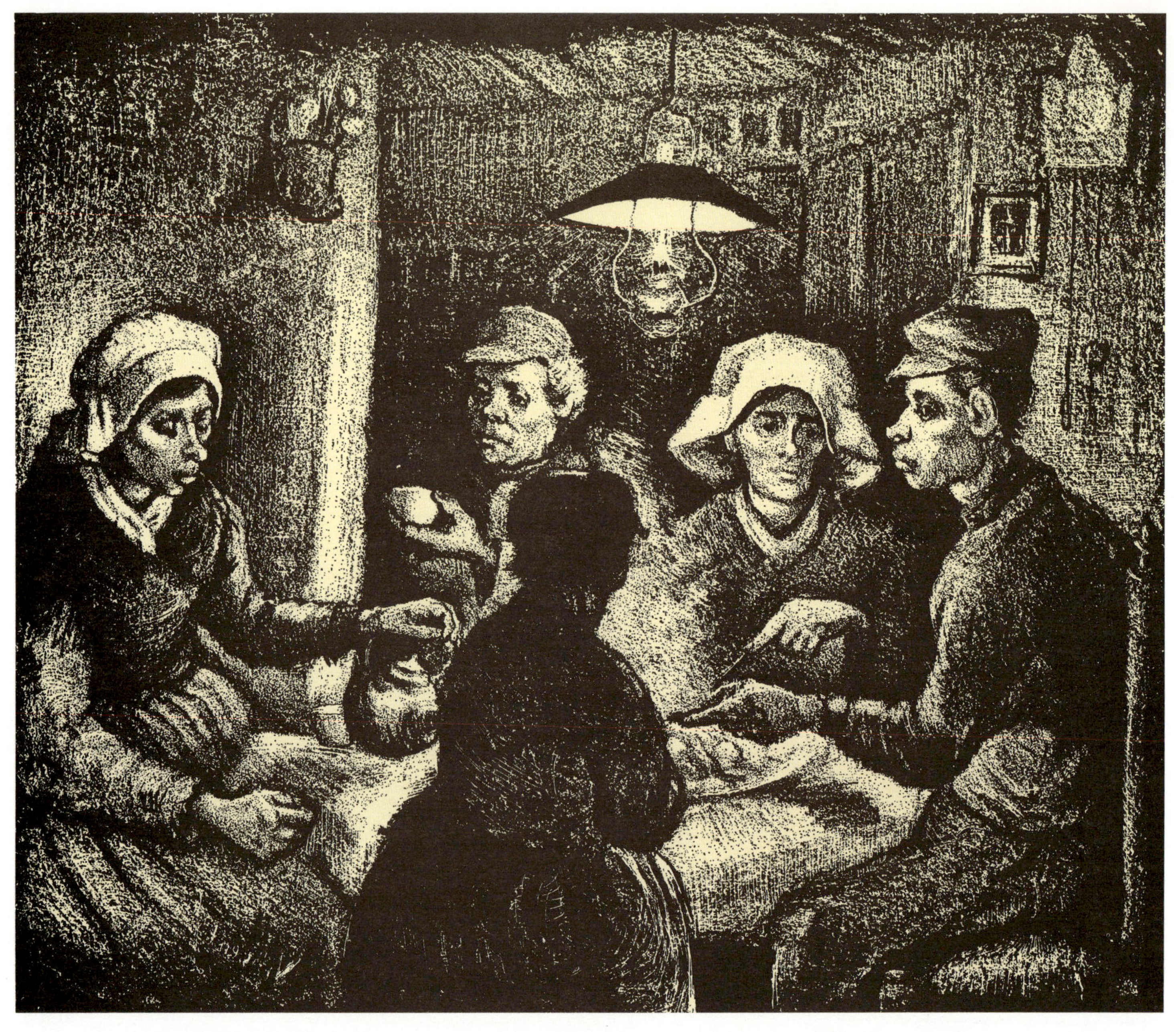

The Potato Eaters (Lithograph)

April 1885 - 25.5 x 30.5 cm

The Potato Eaters

April 1885 - pen - 5 x 8.5 cm -
Vinvent van Gogh Foundation, Amsterdam

The Potato Eaters

April 1885 - oil on canvas - 81.5 x 114.5 cm -
Vincent Van Gogh Foundation, Amsterdam

Ik kom er daarnet van thuis - en heb bij het
lamplicht nog gewerkt er aan - ofschoon
ik het bij dag dit maal heb aangezet.

Zie hier hoe de compositie nu geworden is
Ik heb het op een vrij groot doek geschilderd
en zooals de schets nu is zit geloof ik er wel

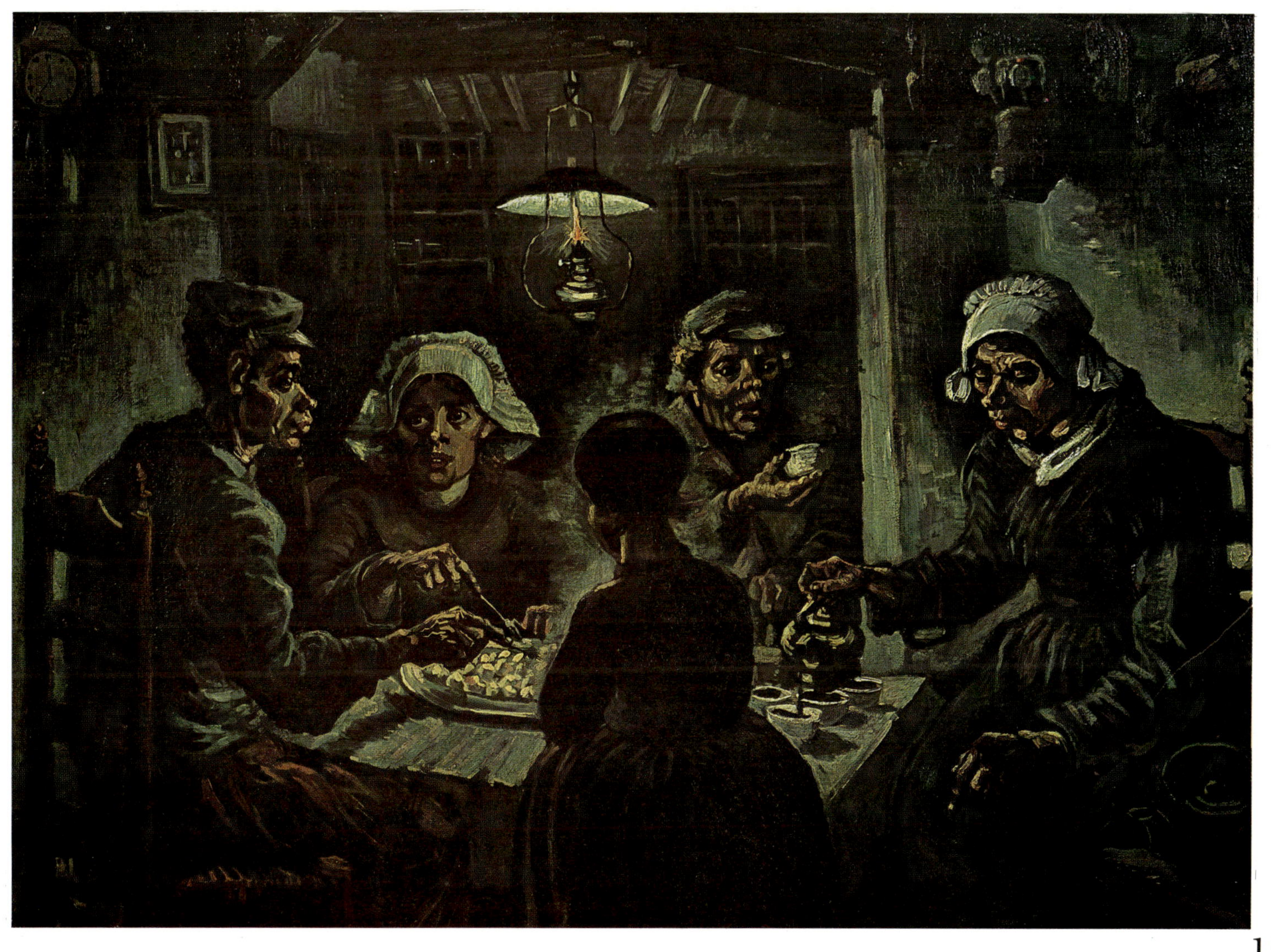

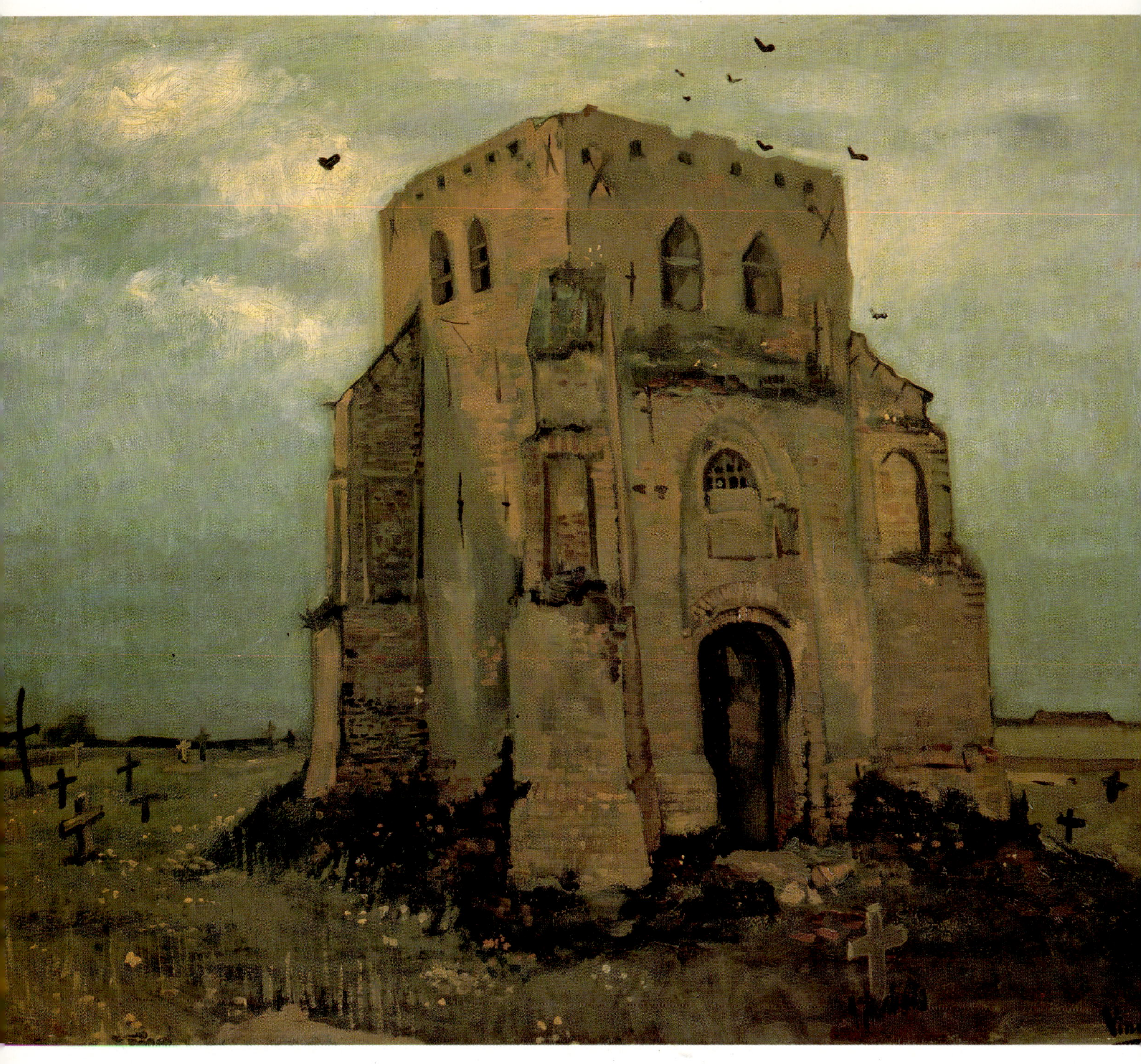

The Old Cemetery Tower at Nuenen

May 1885 - oil on canavs - 63 x 79 cm -
Vincent van Gogh Foundation, Amsterdam

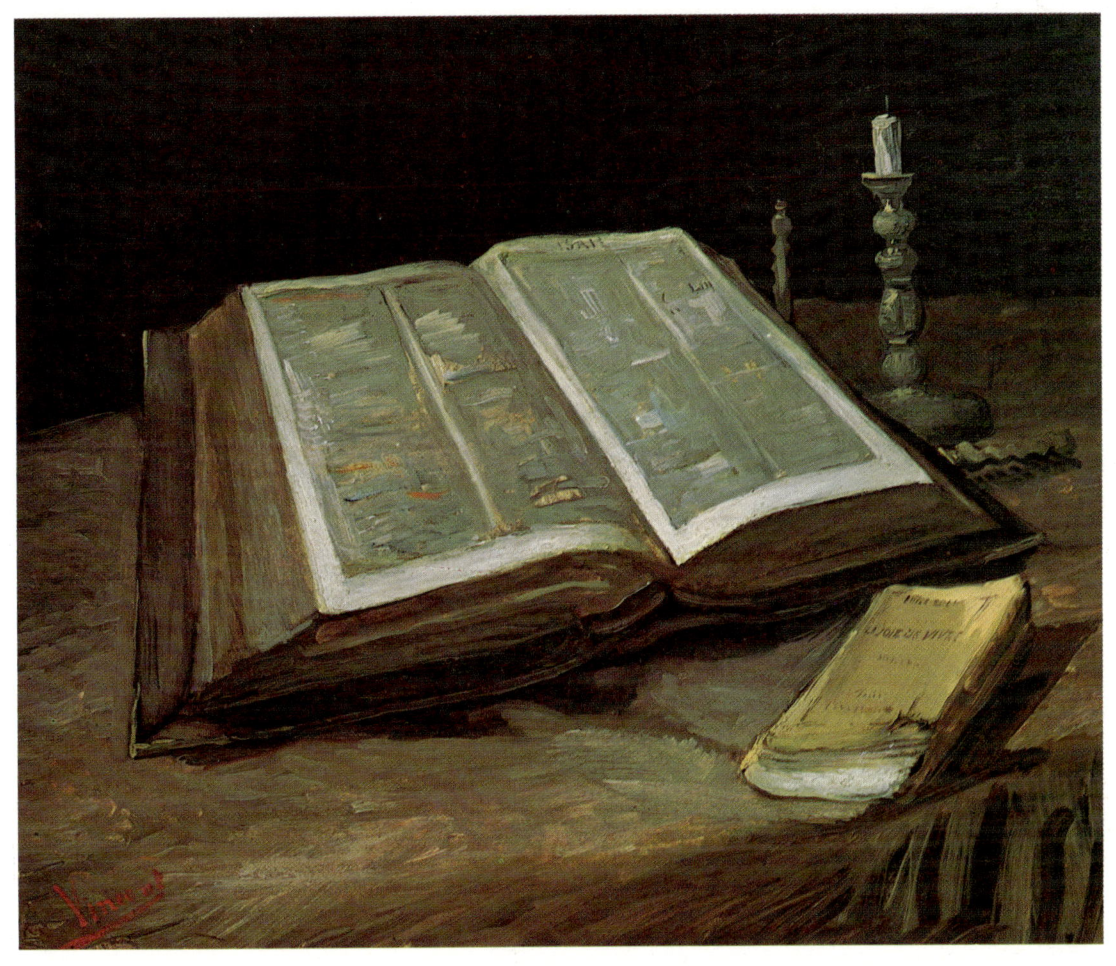

Still Life with Bible

October 1885 - oil on canvas - 65 x 85 cm -
Vincent van Gogh Foundation, Amsterdam

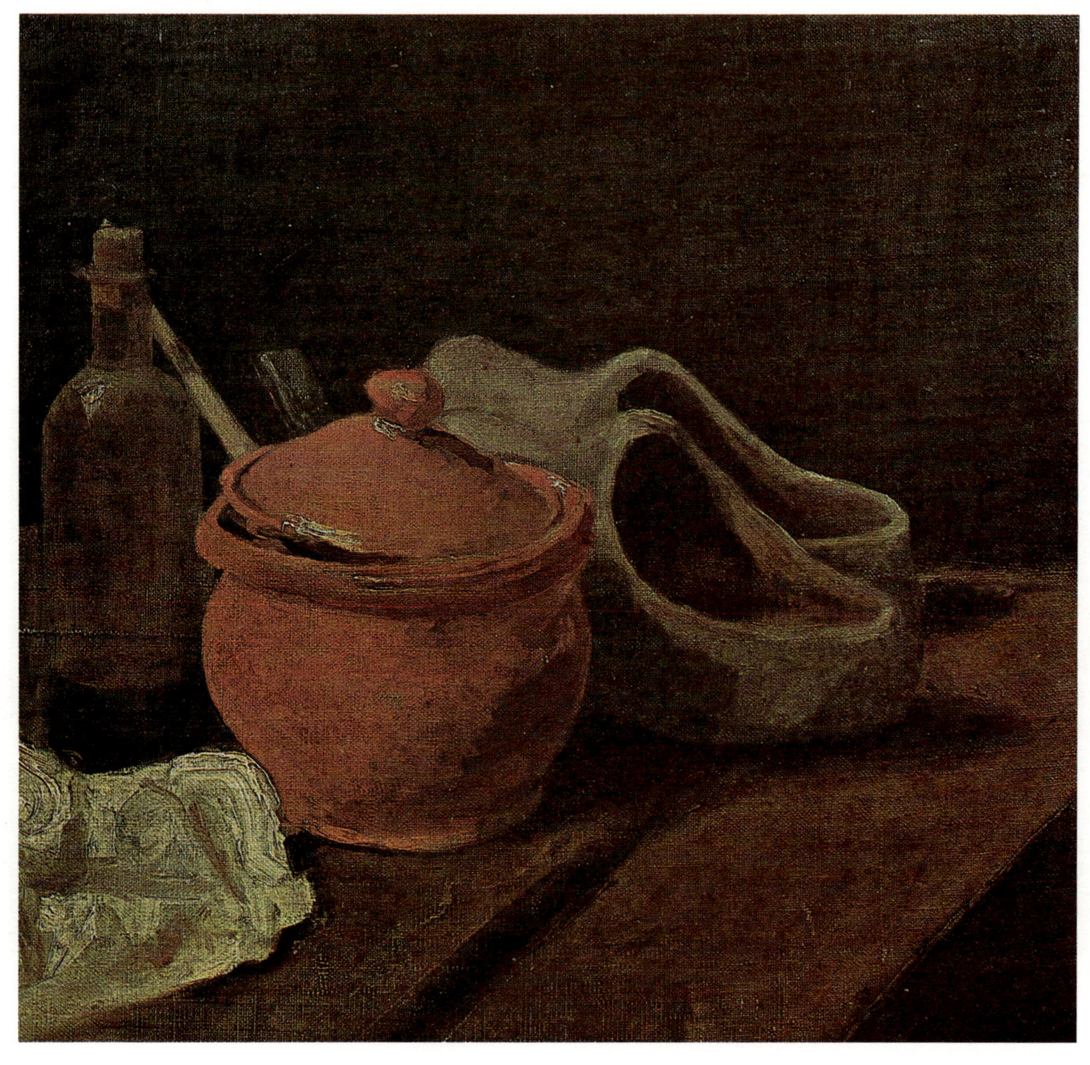

Still Life with Earthenware, Bottle and Clogs

1885 - oil on canvas on panel - 39 x 41.5 cm -
Rijksmuseum Kröller- Müller, Otterlo

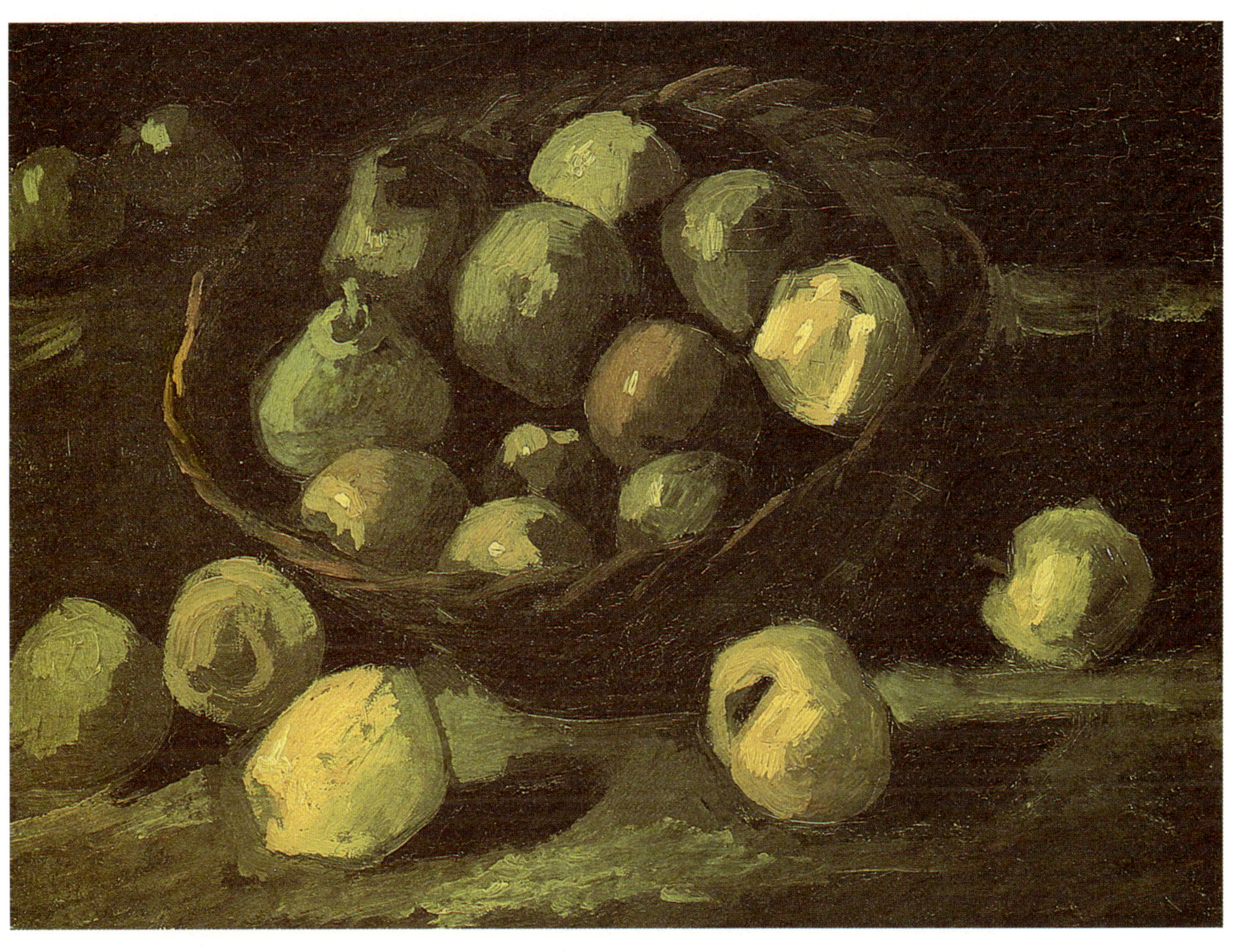

Still Life with Apples in a Basket

September 1885 - oil on canvas - 33 x 43.5 cm -
Vincent van Gogh Foundation, Amsterdam

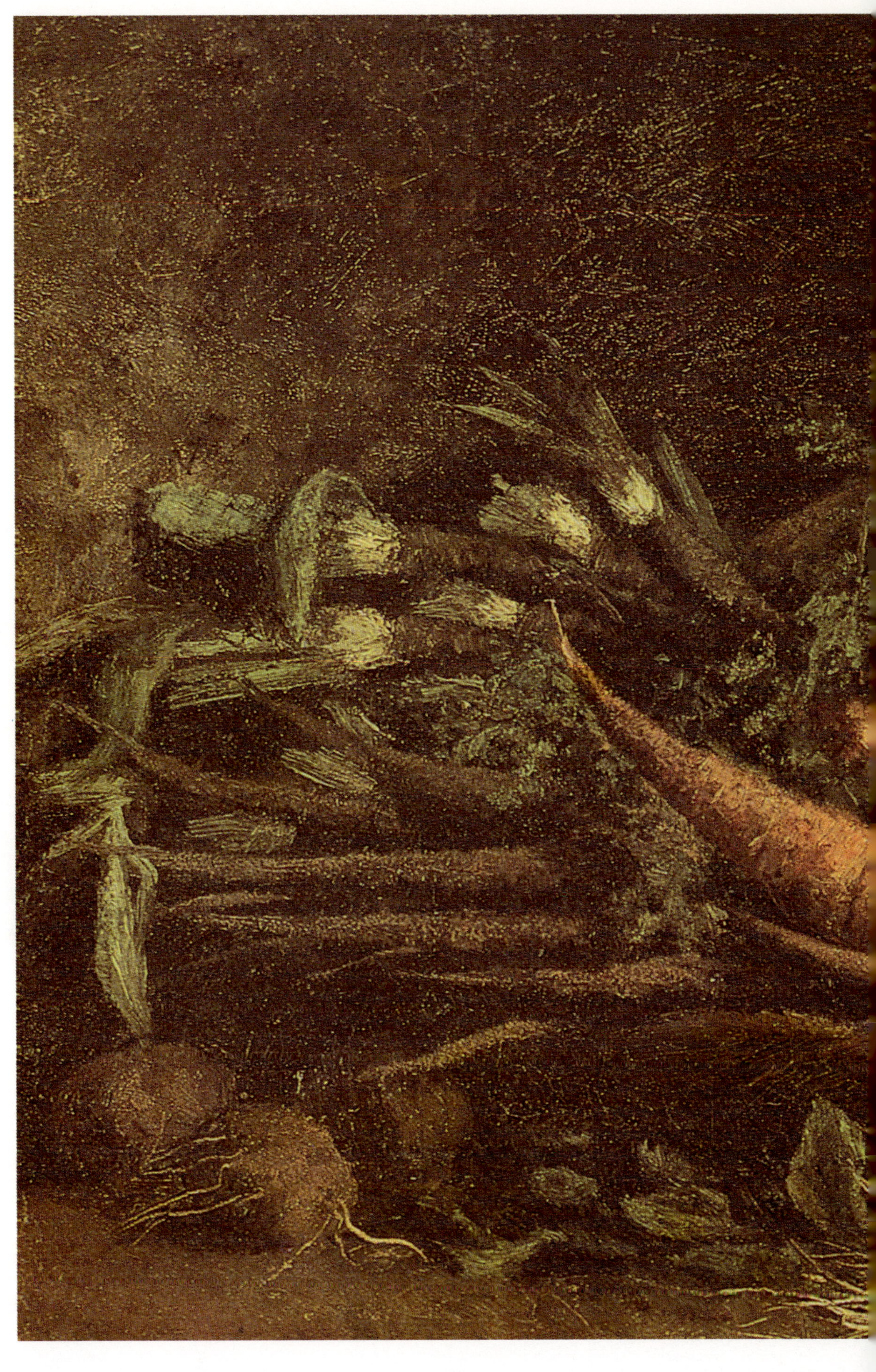

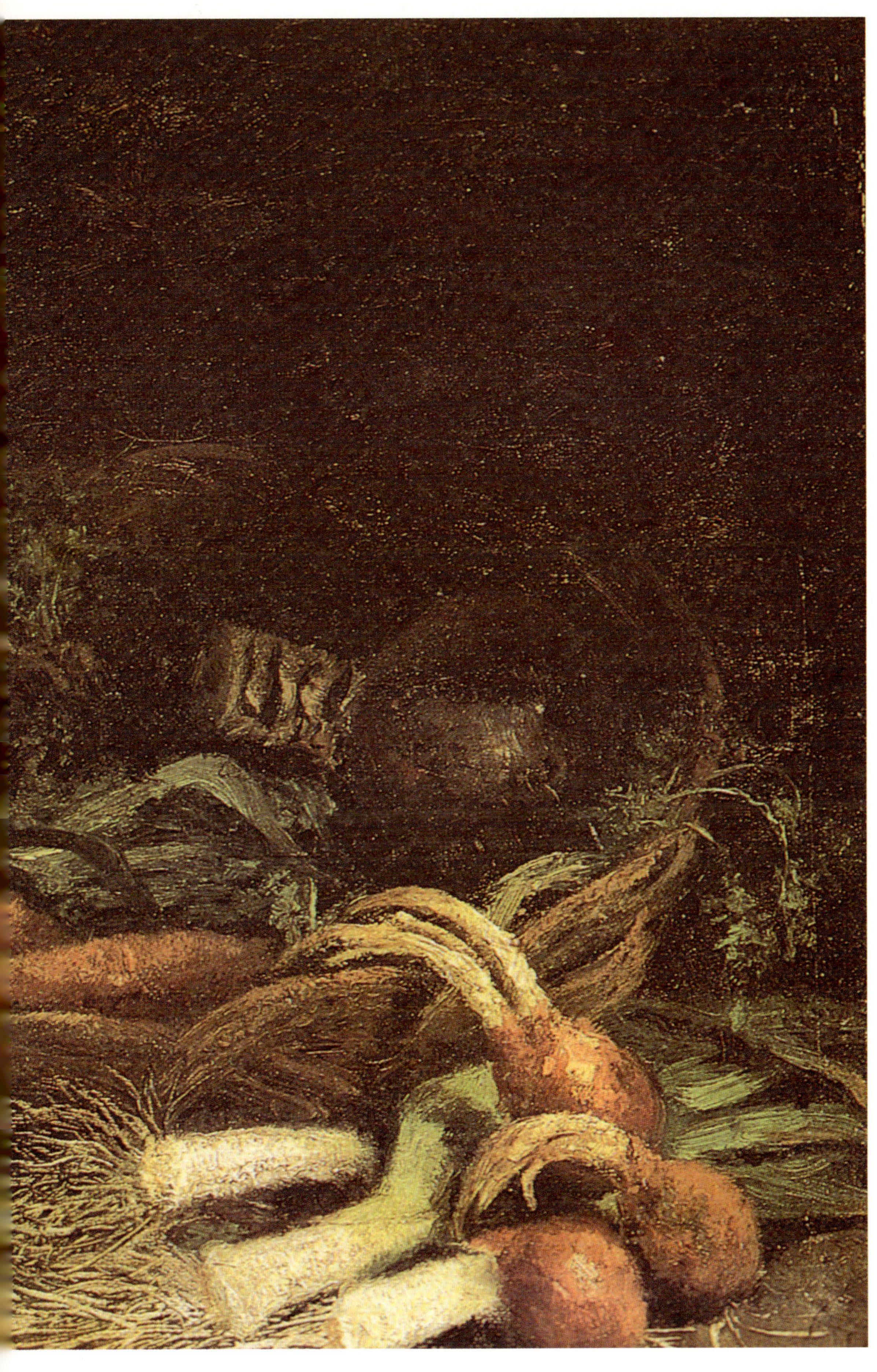

Still Life with a Basket of Vegetables

September 1885 - oil on canvas - 33.5 x 45 cm - Annelise Brand Collection, Landsberg/Lech, Germany

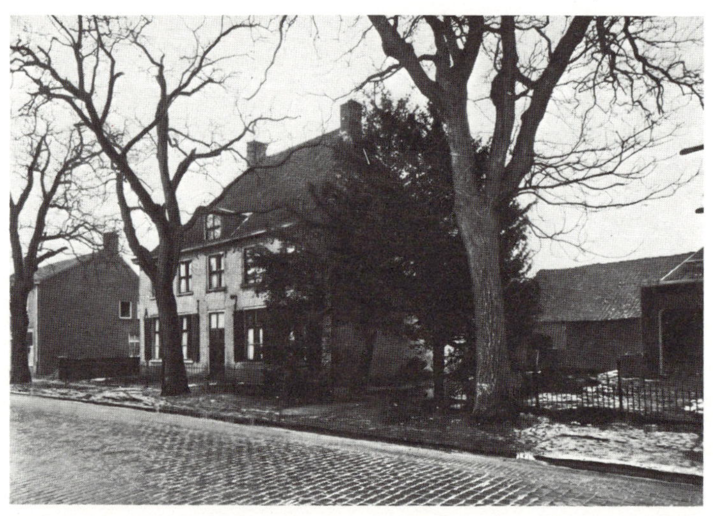

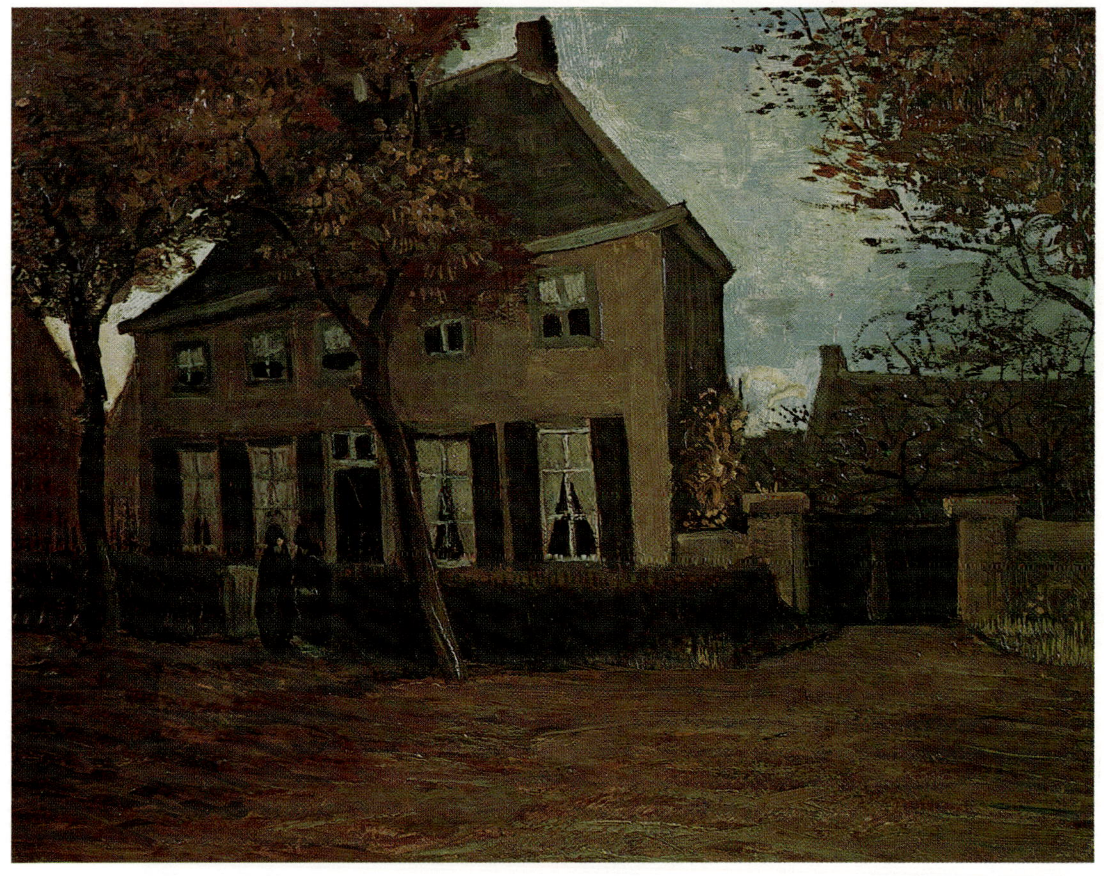

Photograph of Vincent's father's house in the Brabant

The Parsonage at Nuenen

Autumn 1885 - oil on canvas - 33 x 43 cm -
Vincent van Gogh Foundation, Amsterdam

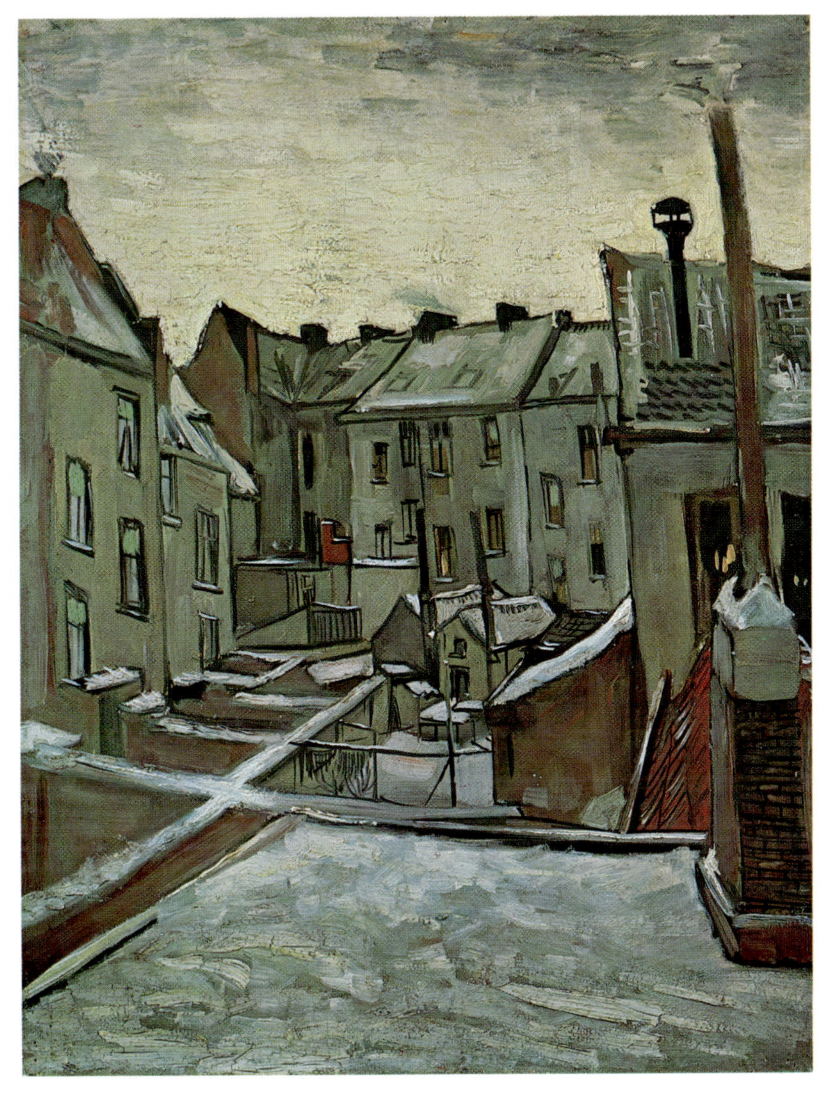

Backyards of Old Houses

December 1885 - oil - 44 x 33.5 cm -
Vincent van Gogh Foundation, Amsterdam

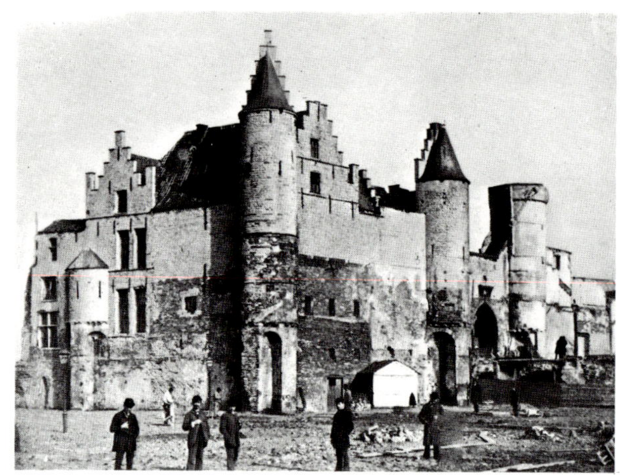

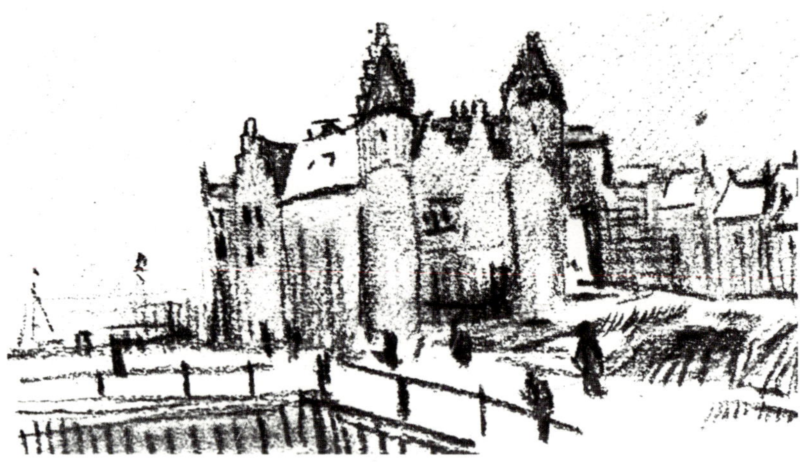

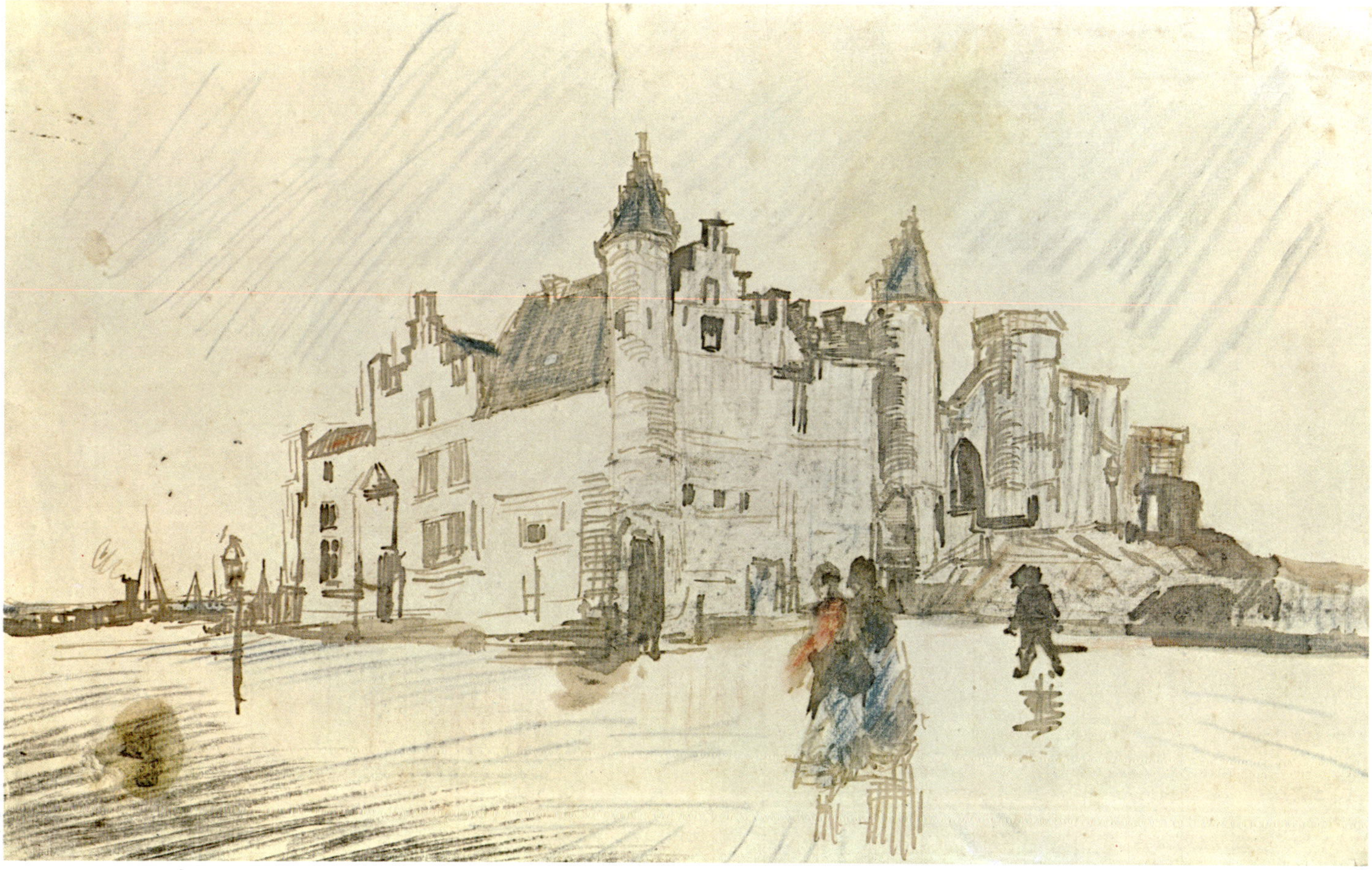

Photograph of Anvers, Anvers City Archives

The Castle

December 1885 - black chalk with coloured highlights
- 9.5 x 16.5 cm -
Vincent van Gogh Foundation, Amsterdam

The Castle

December 1885 - pen with coloured highlights
- 13 x 21 cm -
Vincent van Gogh Foundation, Amsterdam

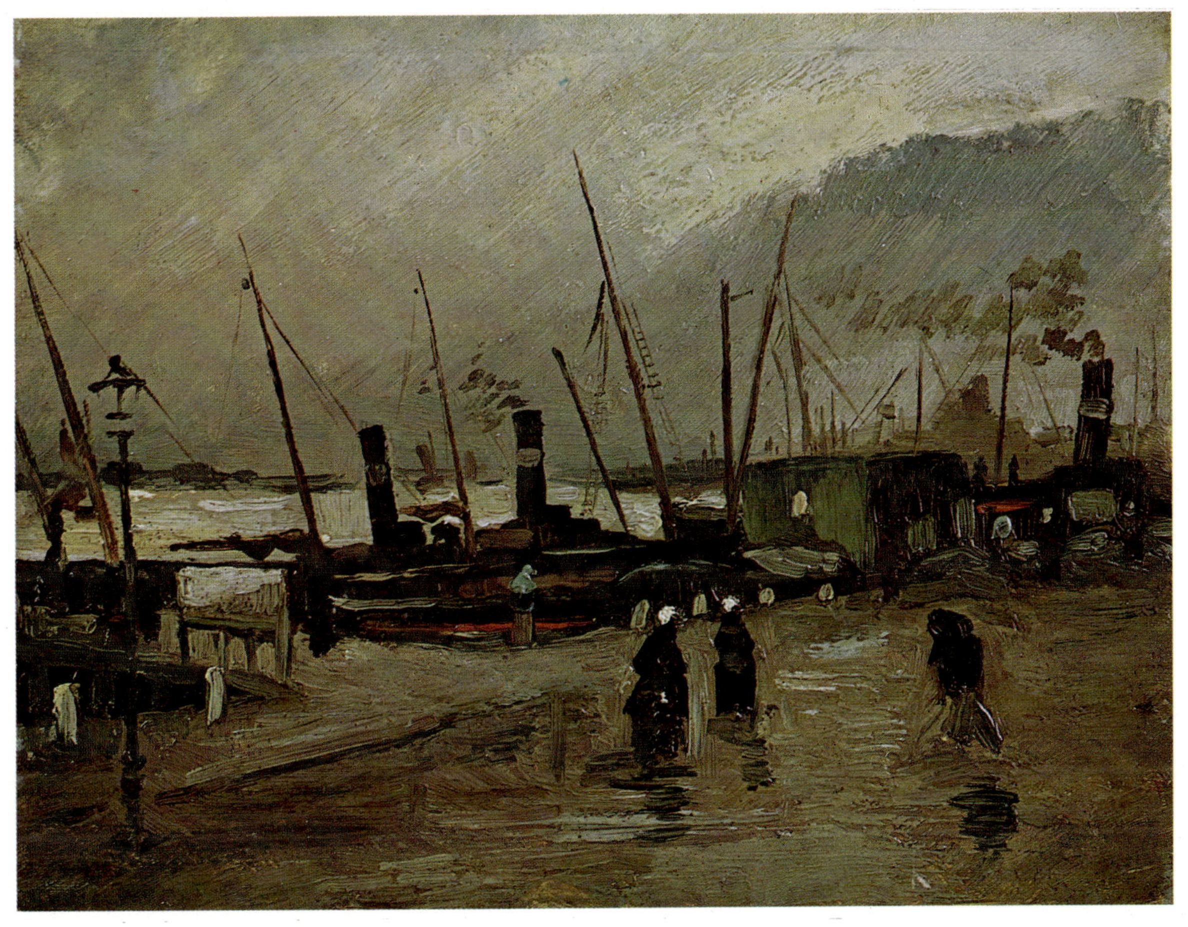

Quayside with Ships at Antwerp

Early December 1885 - oil on panel -20.5 x 27 cm -
Vincent van Gogh Foundation, Amsterdam

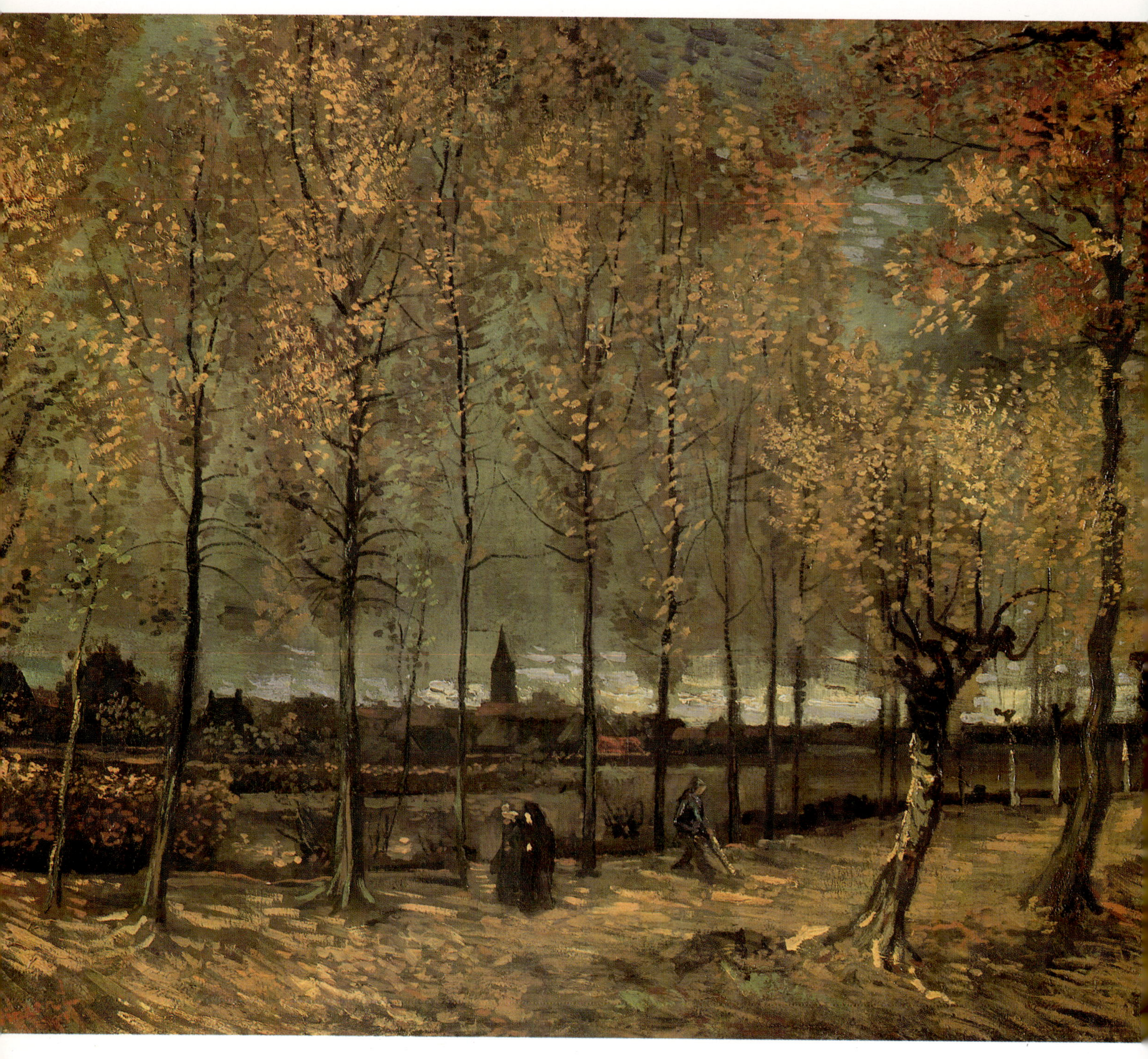

Avenue of Poplars

November 1885 - oil on canvas - 78 x 97.8 cm -
Boymans-van Beuningen Museum

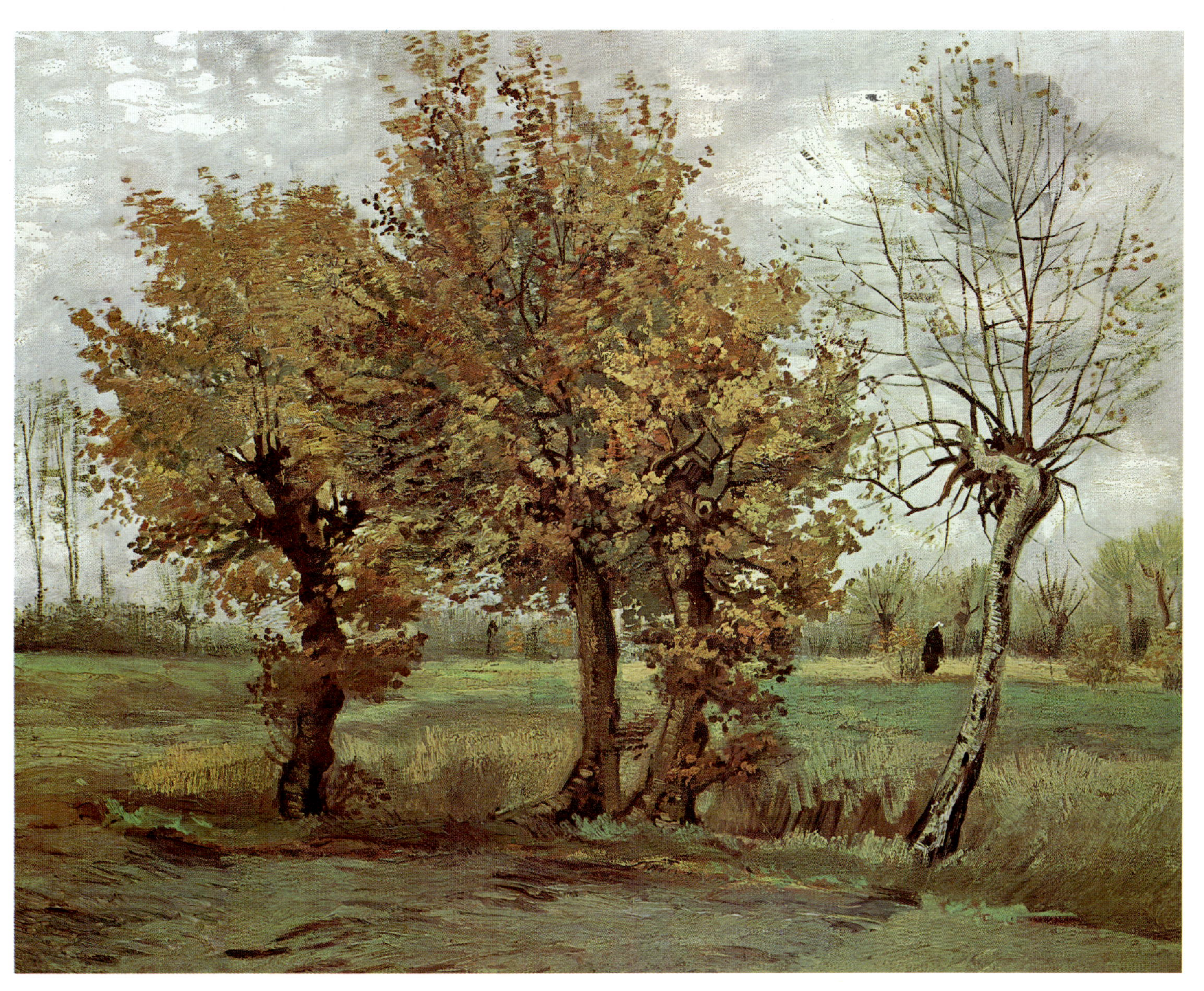

Autumn Landscape

November 1885 - oil on canvas - 64 x 89 cm - Rijksmuseum Kröller- Müller, Otterlo

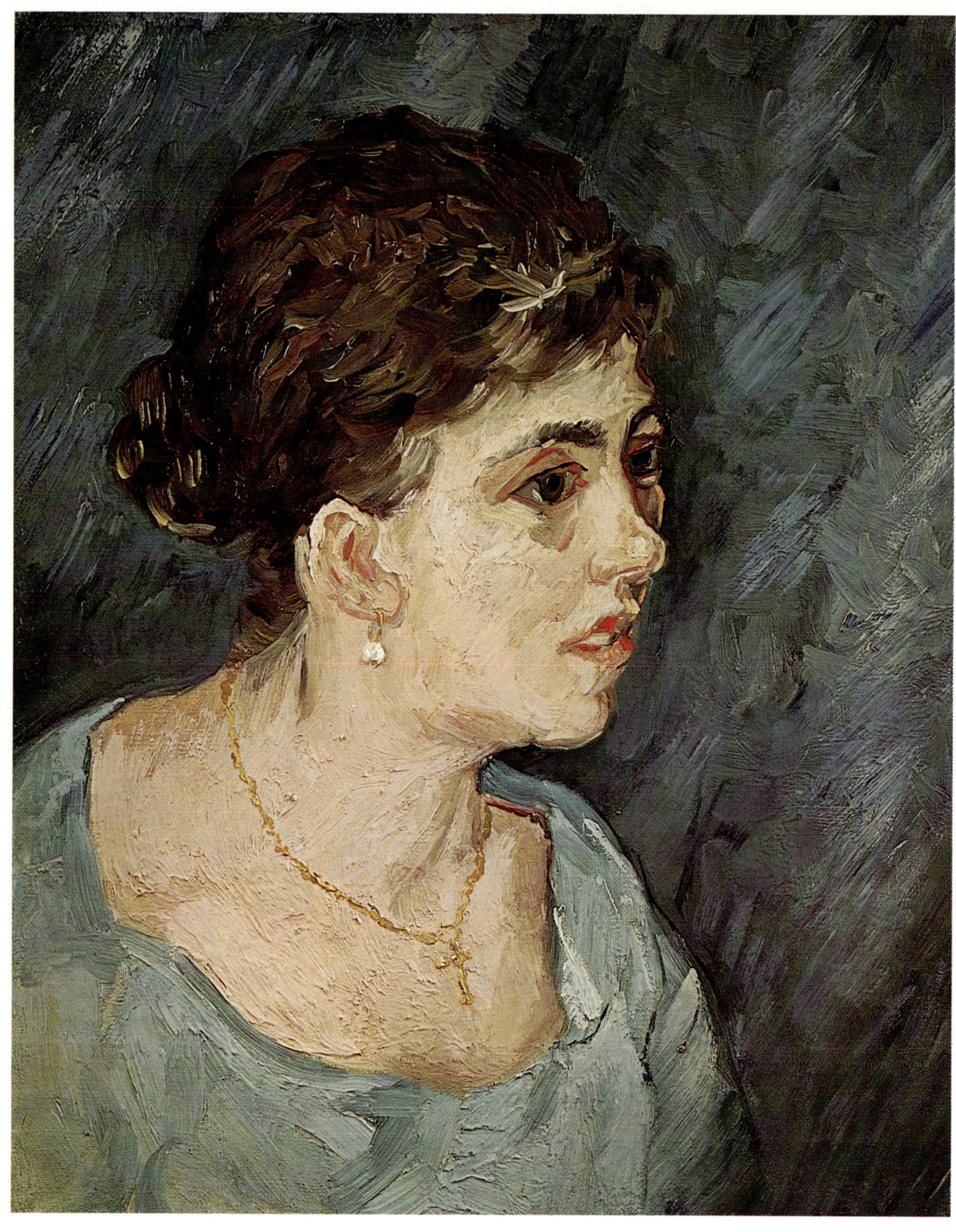

Woman in Blue

December 1885 - oil on canvas - 46 x 38 cm -
Vincent van Gogh Foundation, Amsterdam

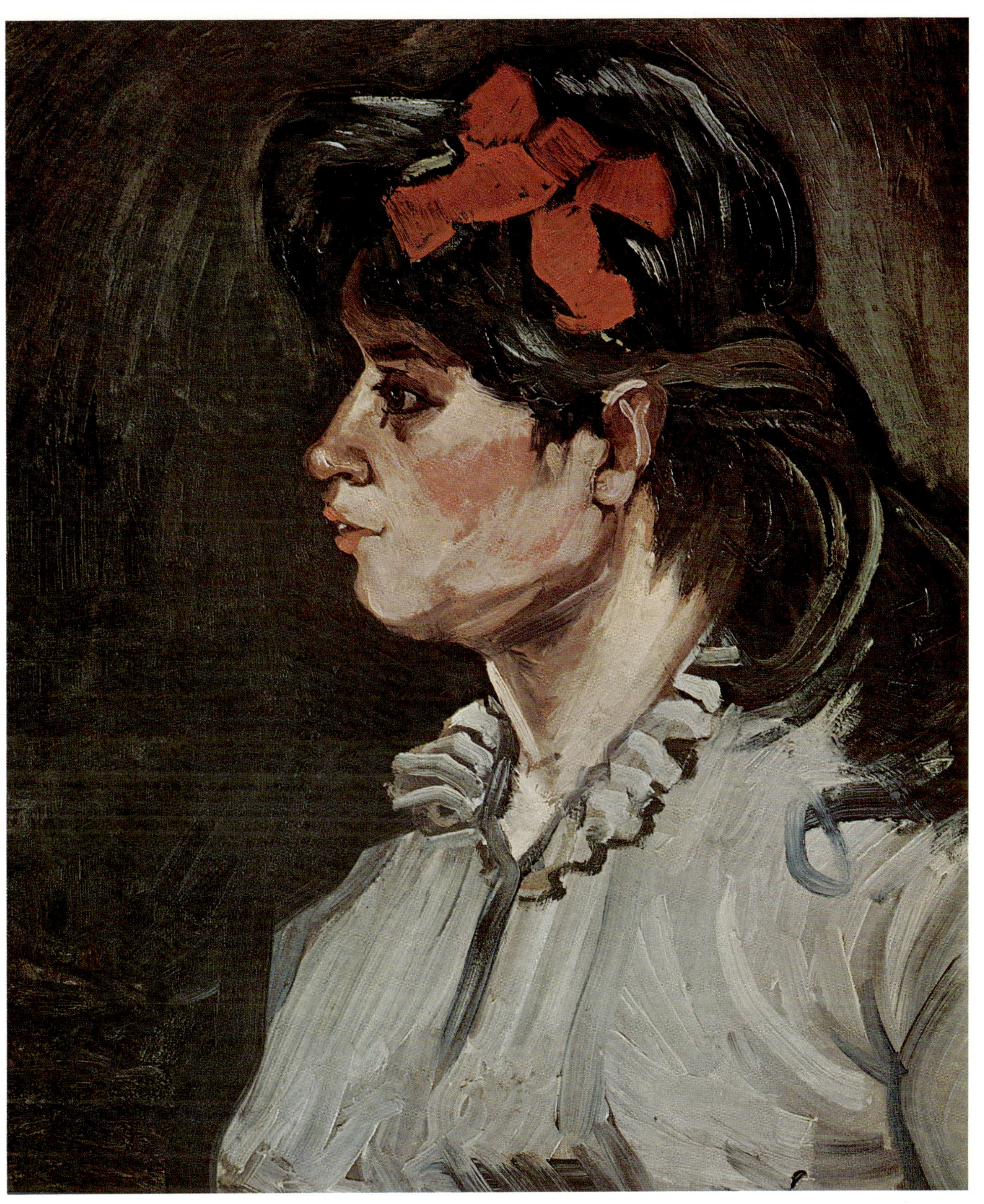

Portrait of a Woman with Red Ribbon

End December 1885 - oil on canvas - 60 x 50 cm -
A. Wyler collection, New York

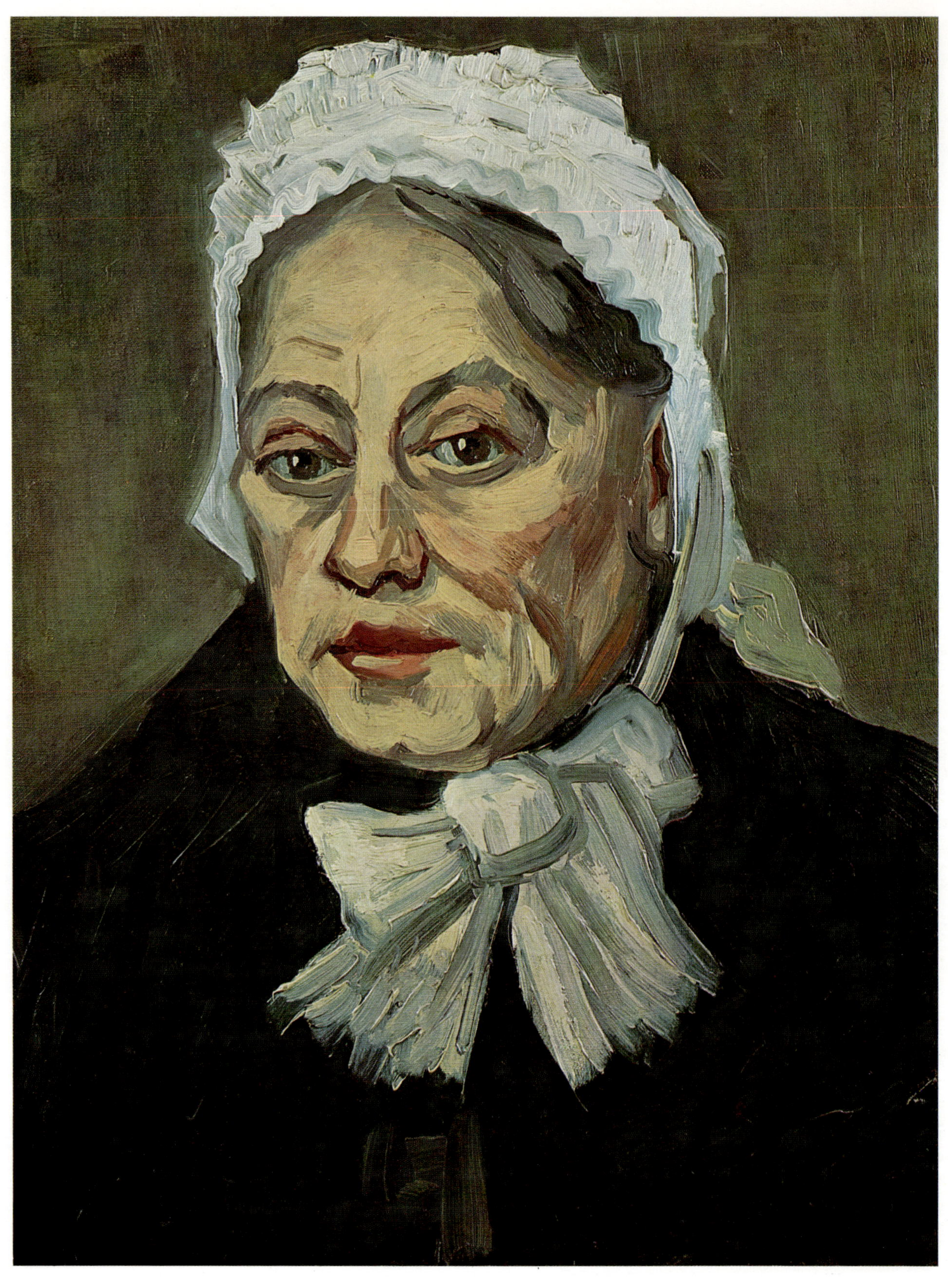

The Midwife

December 1885 - oil on canvas - 50 x 40 cm -
Vincent van Gogh Foundation, Amsterdam

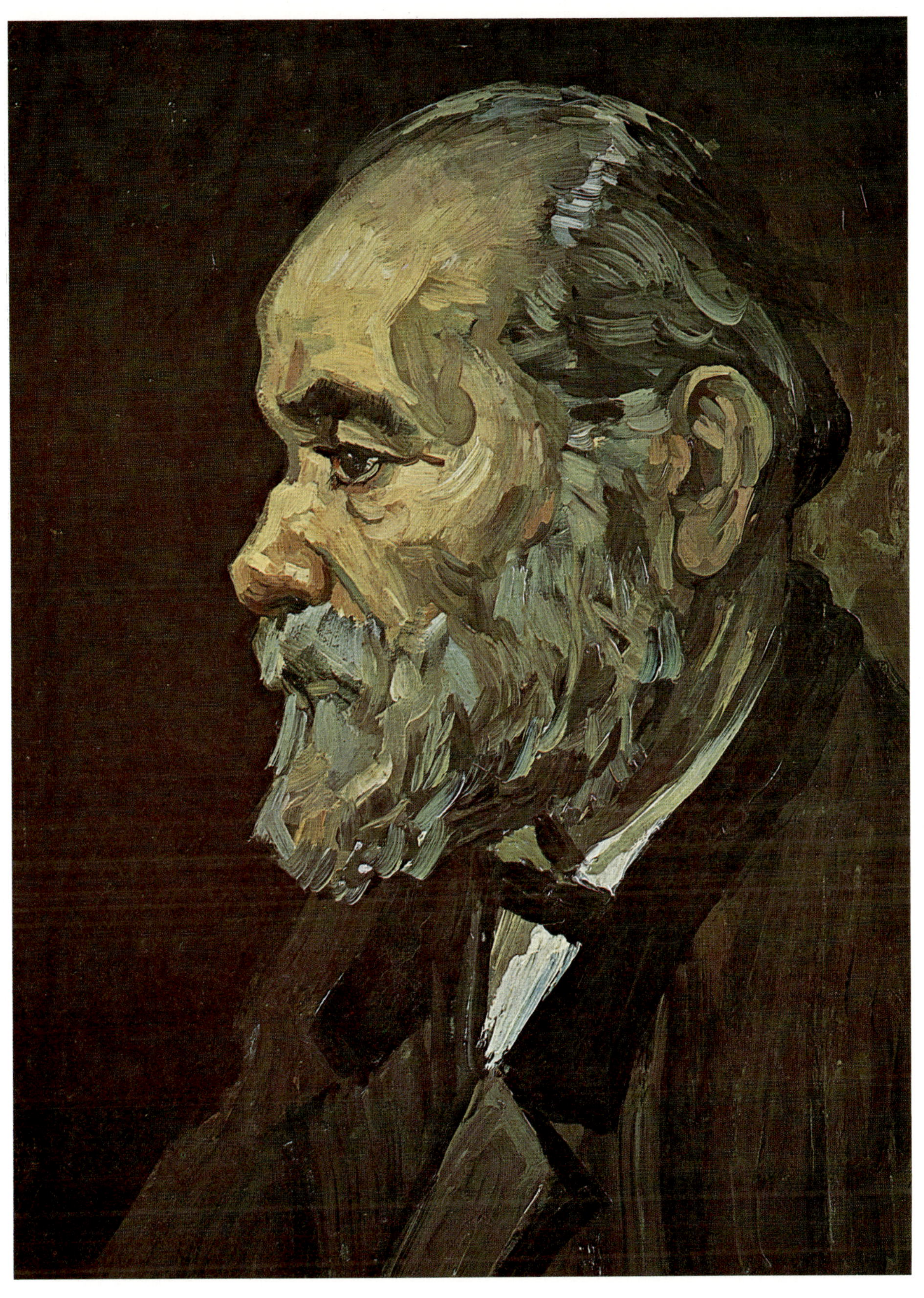

Portrait of an Old Man with a Head Like Victor Hugo

December 1885 - oil on canvas - 44 x 33.5 cm -
Vincent van Gogh Foundation, Amsterdam

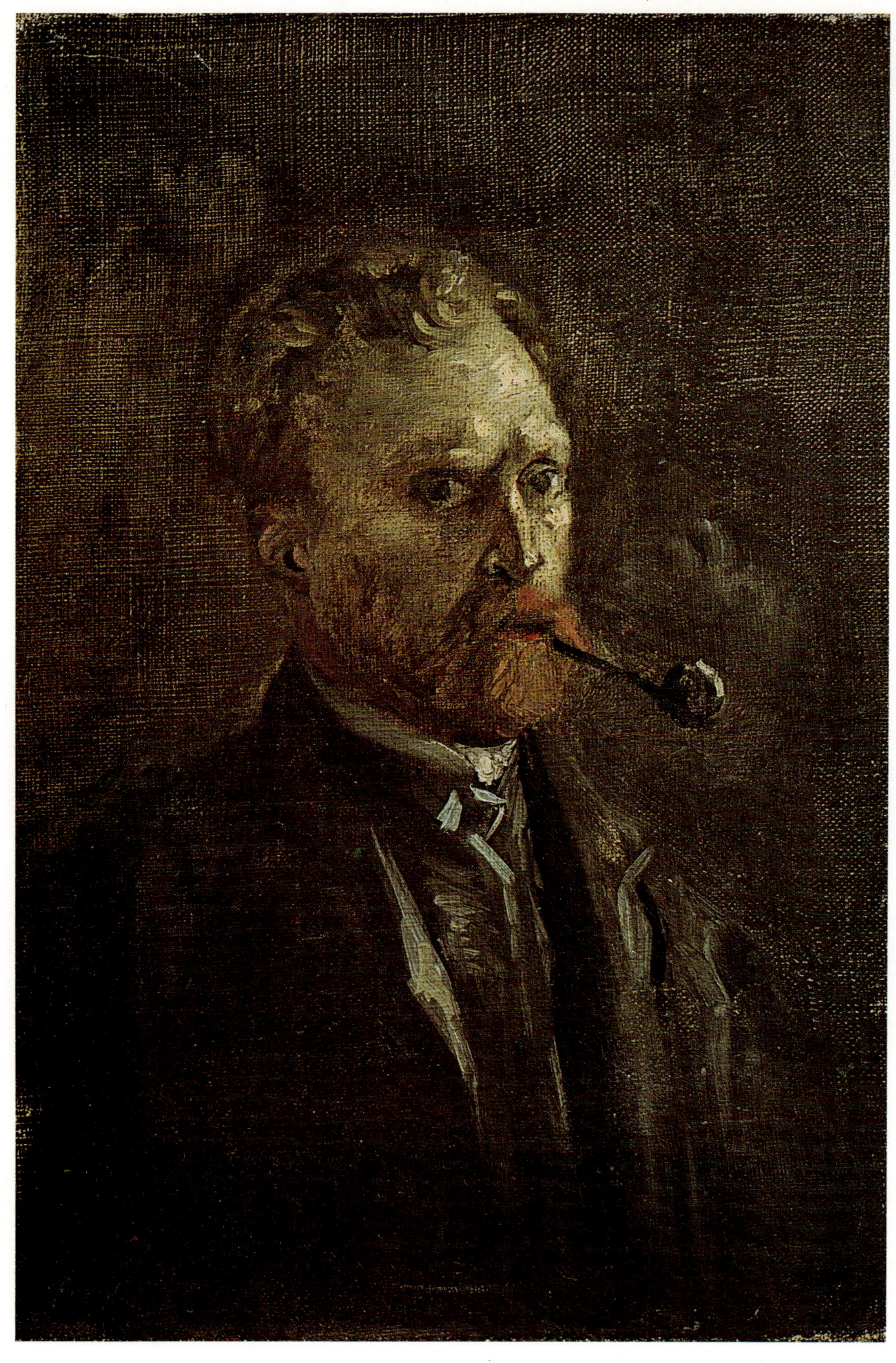

Self-Portrait

1885 - oil on canvas - 27 x 19 cm -
Vincent van Gogh Foundation, Amsterdam

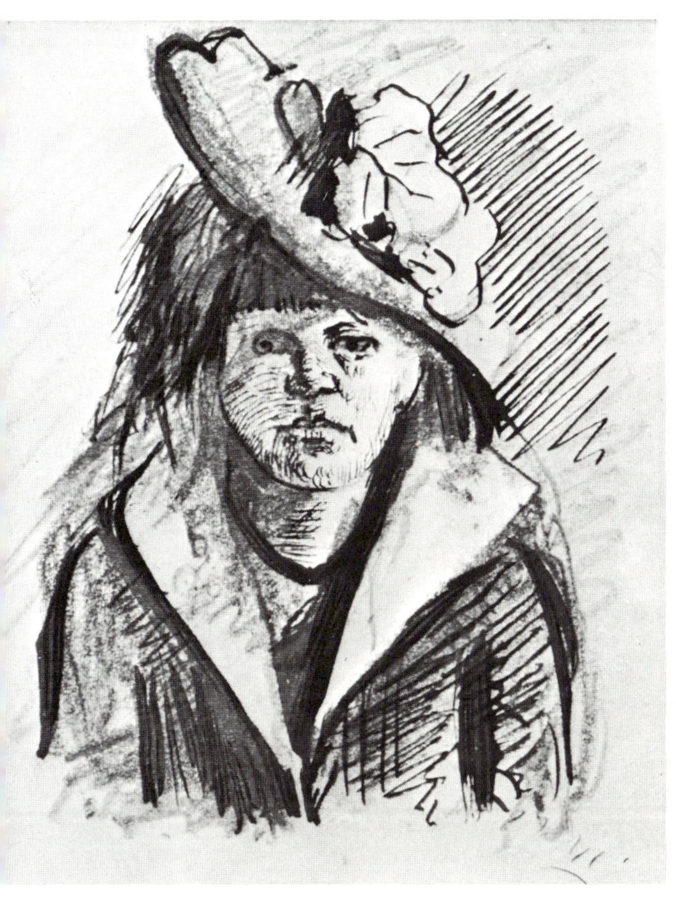

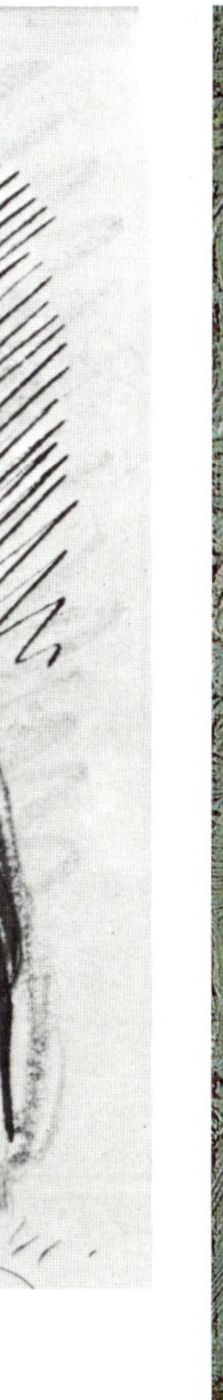

Streetwalker

December 1885 - pencil, pen - 13 x 9.5 cm - Dr H. Wiegersma Collection, Deurne, Holland

Head of a Woman with Her Hair Loose

December 1885 - oil on canvas - 35 x 24 cm - Vincent van Gogh Foundation, Amsterdam

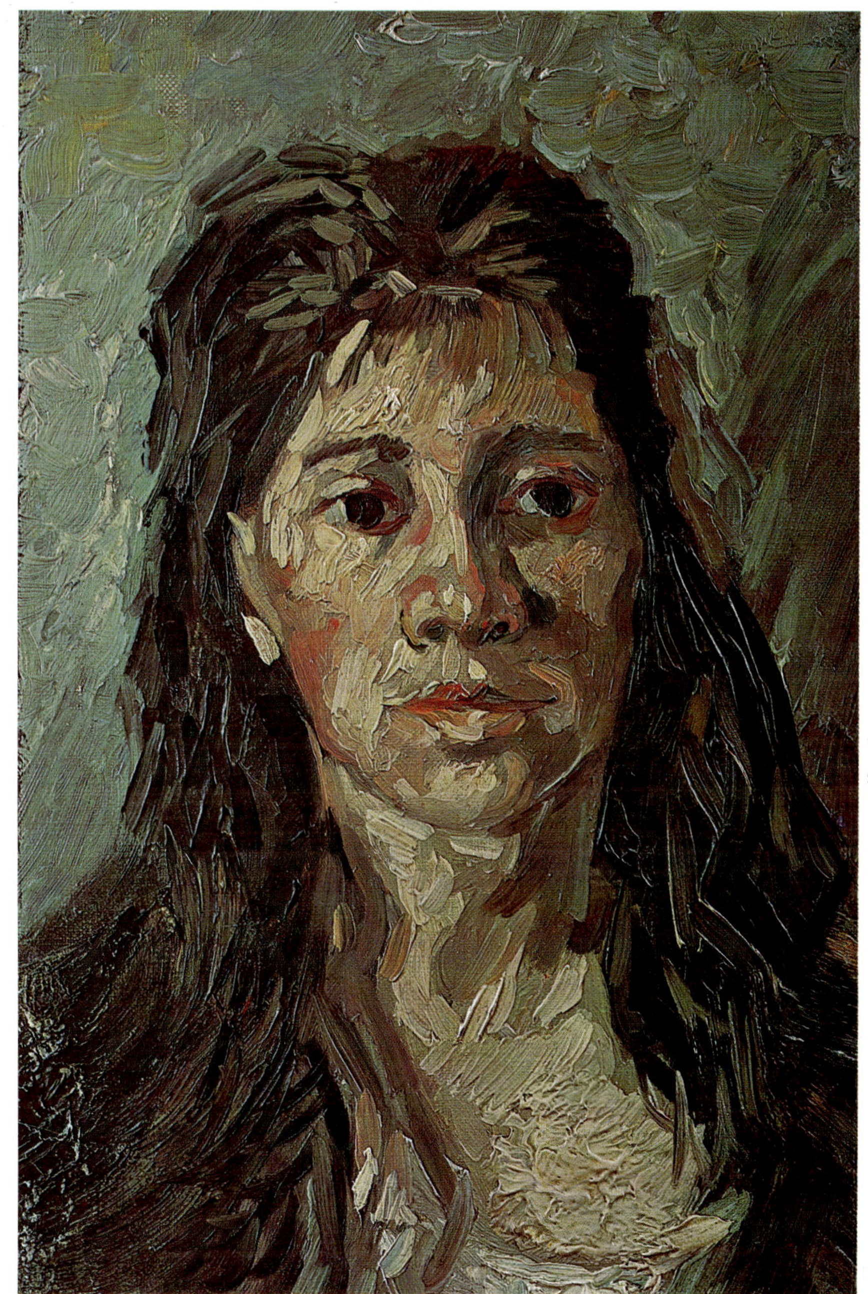

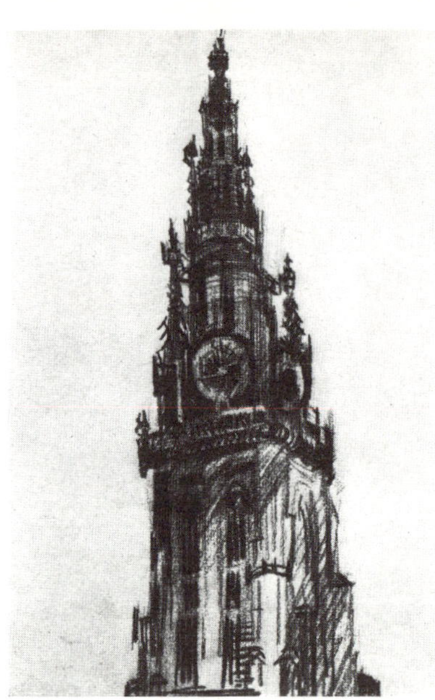

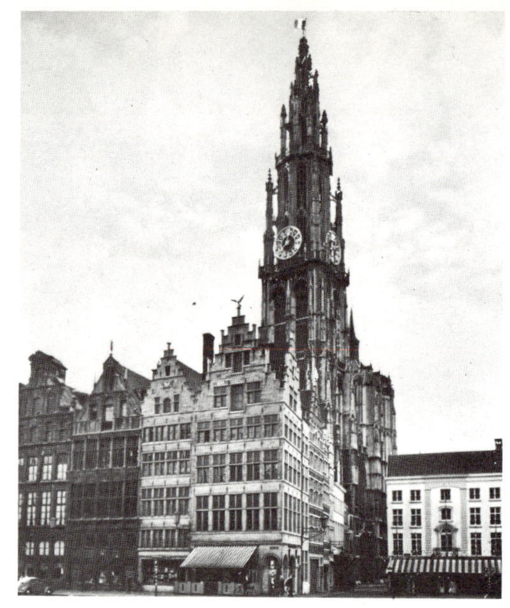

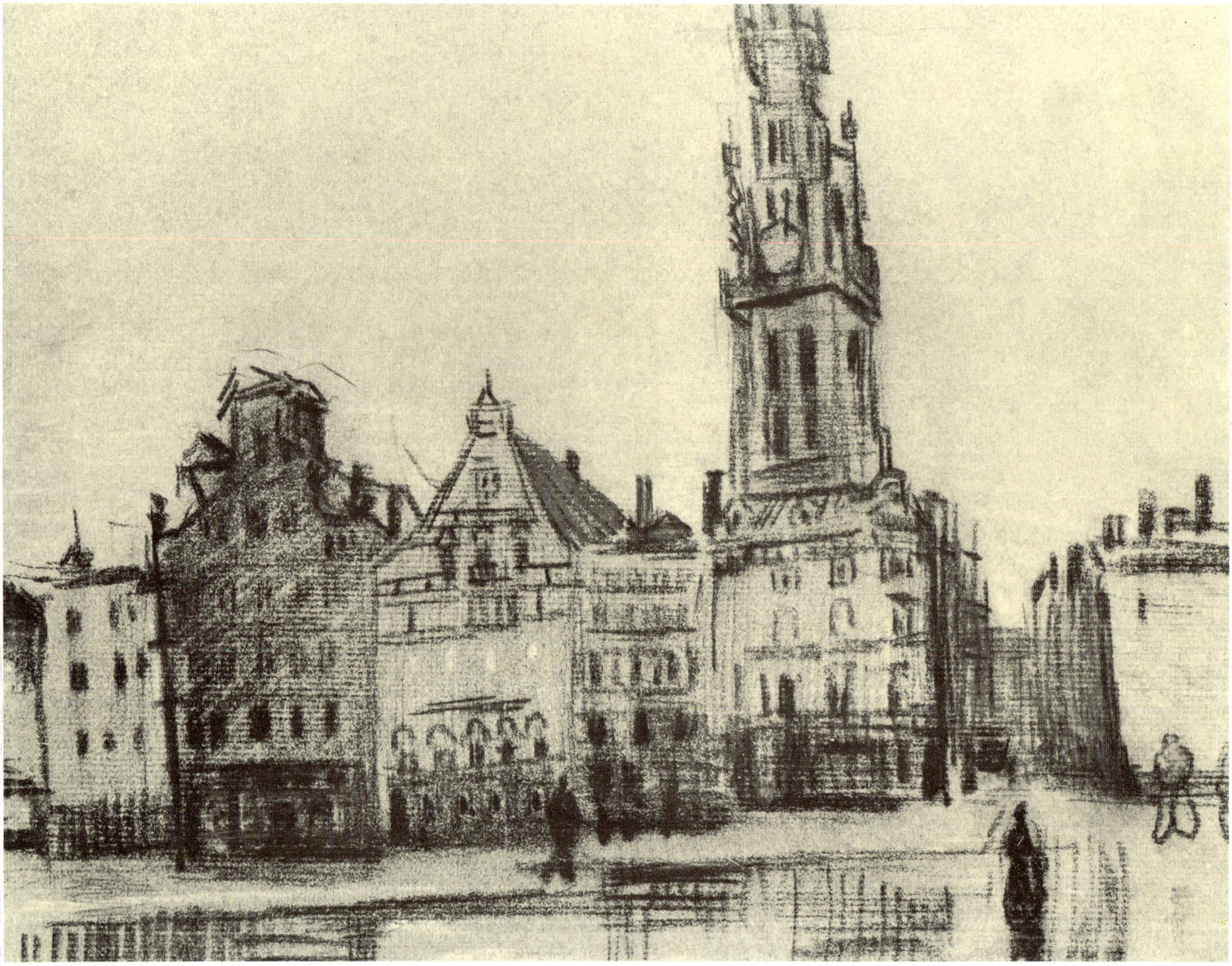

Cathedral Tower

December 1885 - black chalk on Ingres paper - 30 x 22.5 cm - Vincent van Gogh Foundation, Amsterdam

Photograph of the cathedral tower taken in 1958

La Grand-Place

December 1885 - Conté crayon on Ingres paper - 30 x 22.5 cm - Vincent van Gogh Foundation, Amsterdam

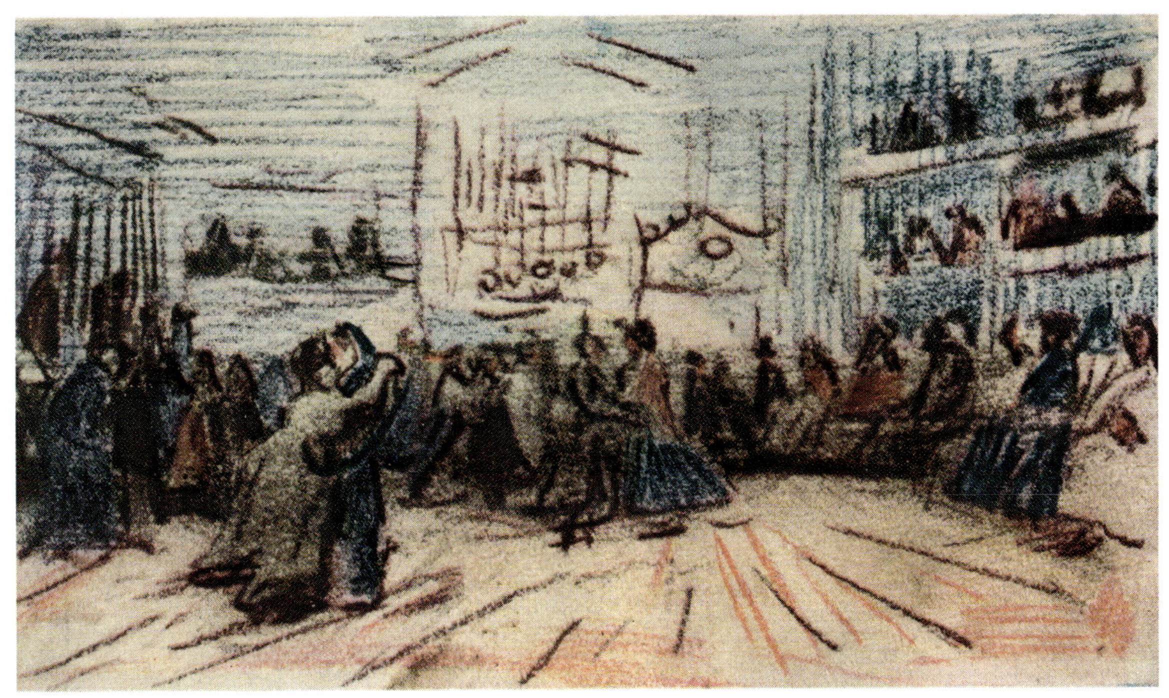

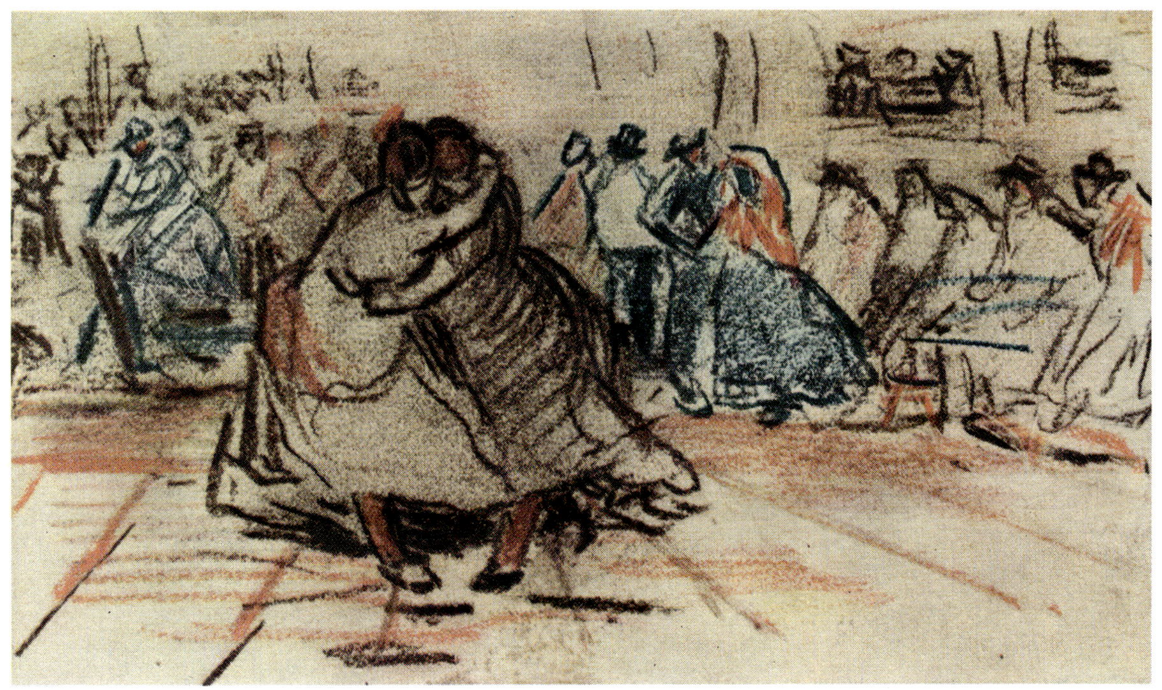

Dance in the Shipmen's Quarter

Early December 1885 - coloured crayons - 9 x 15 cm - Vincent van Gogh Foundation, Amsterdam

Women Waltzing

Early December 1885 - coloured crayons - 9 x 16 cm - Vincent van Gogh Foundation, Amsterdam

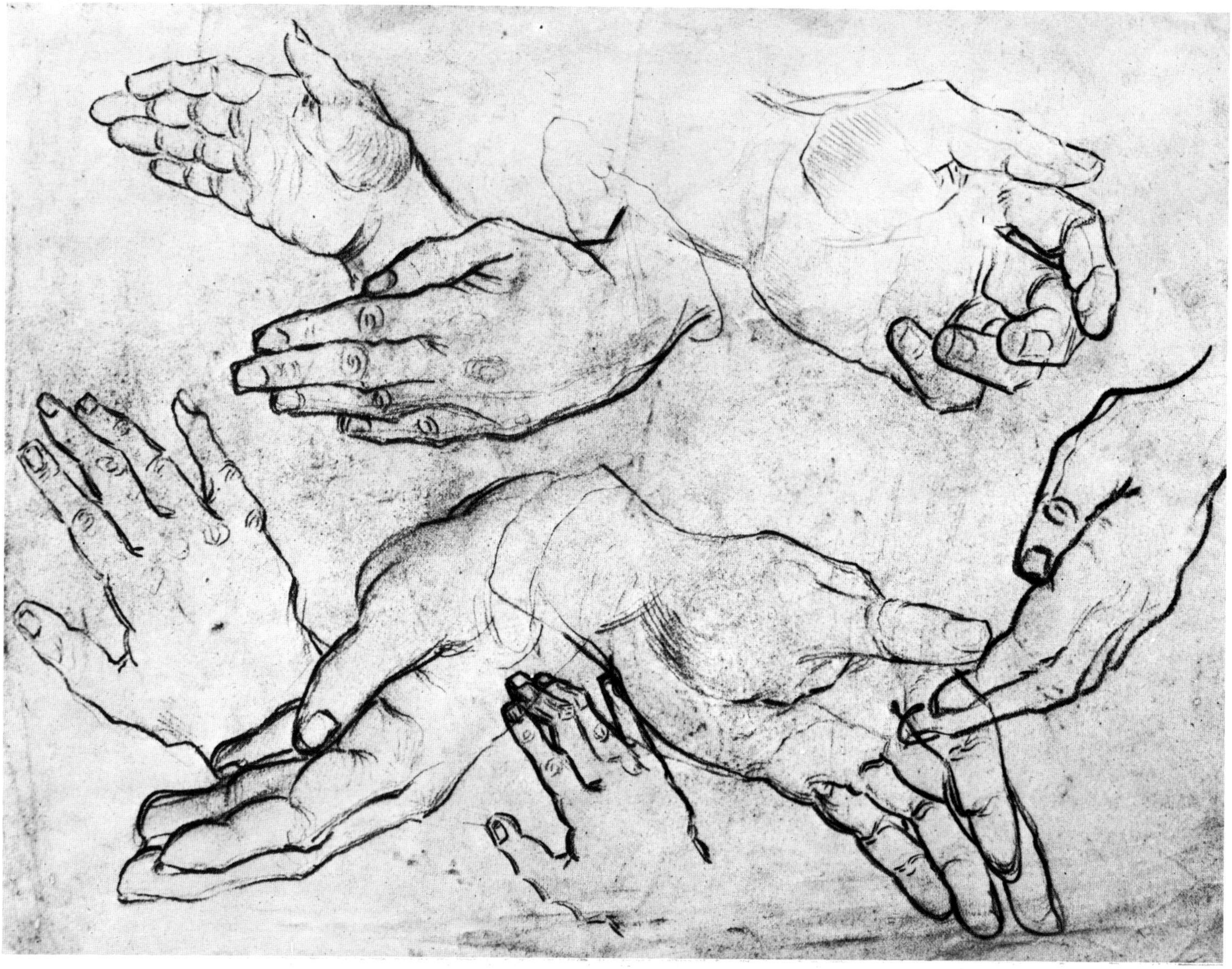

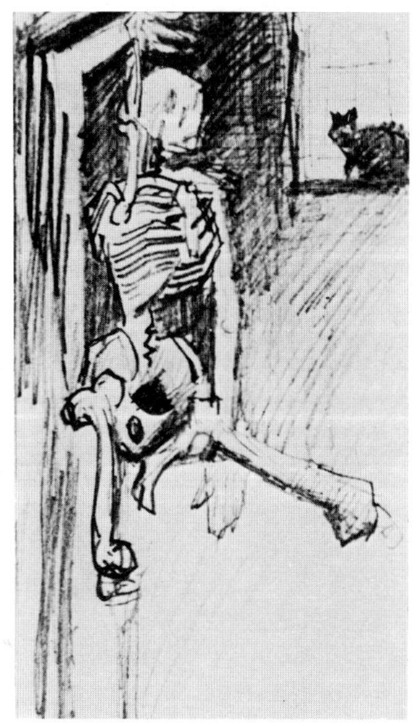

Study of Hands

January 1886 - black crayon - 32 x 24 cm - Vincent van Gogh Foundation, Amsterdam

Hanging Skeleton

February 1886 - pencil - 10.5 x 6 cm - Vincent van Gogh Foundation, Amsterdam

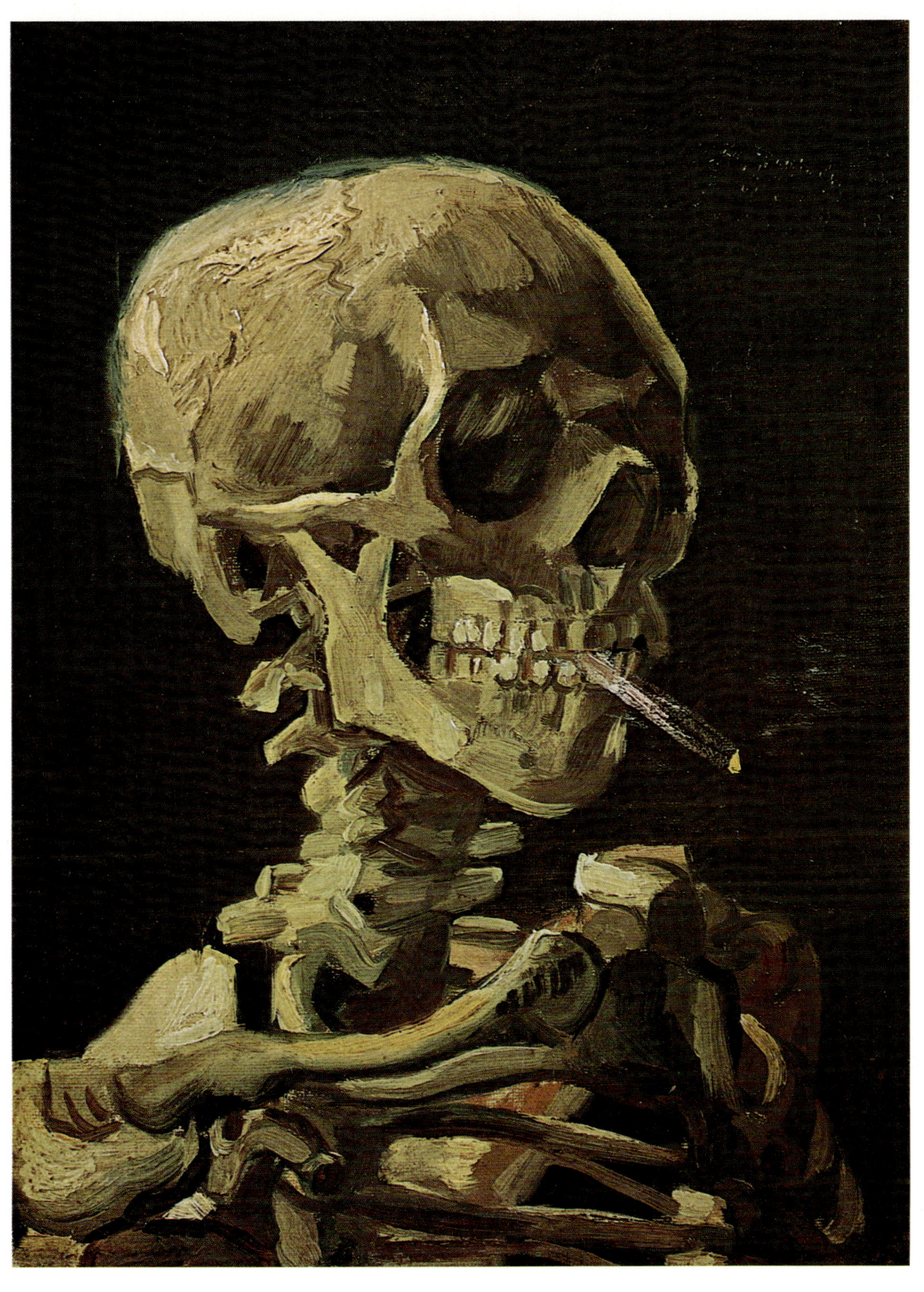

Skull with Cigarette

January 1886 - oil on canvas -32.5 x 24 cm -
Vincent van Gogh Foundation, Amsterdam

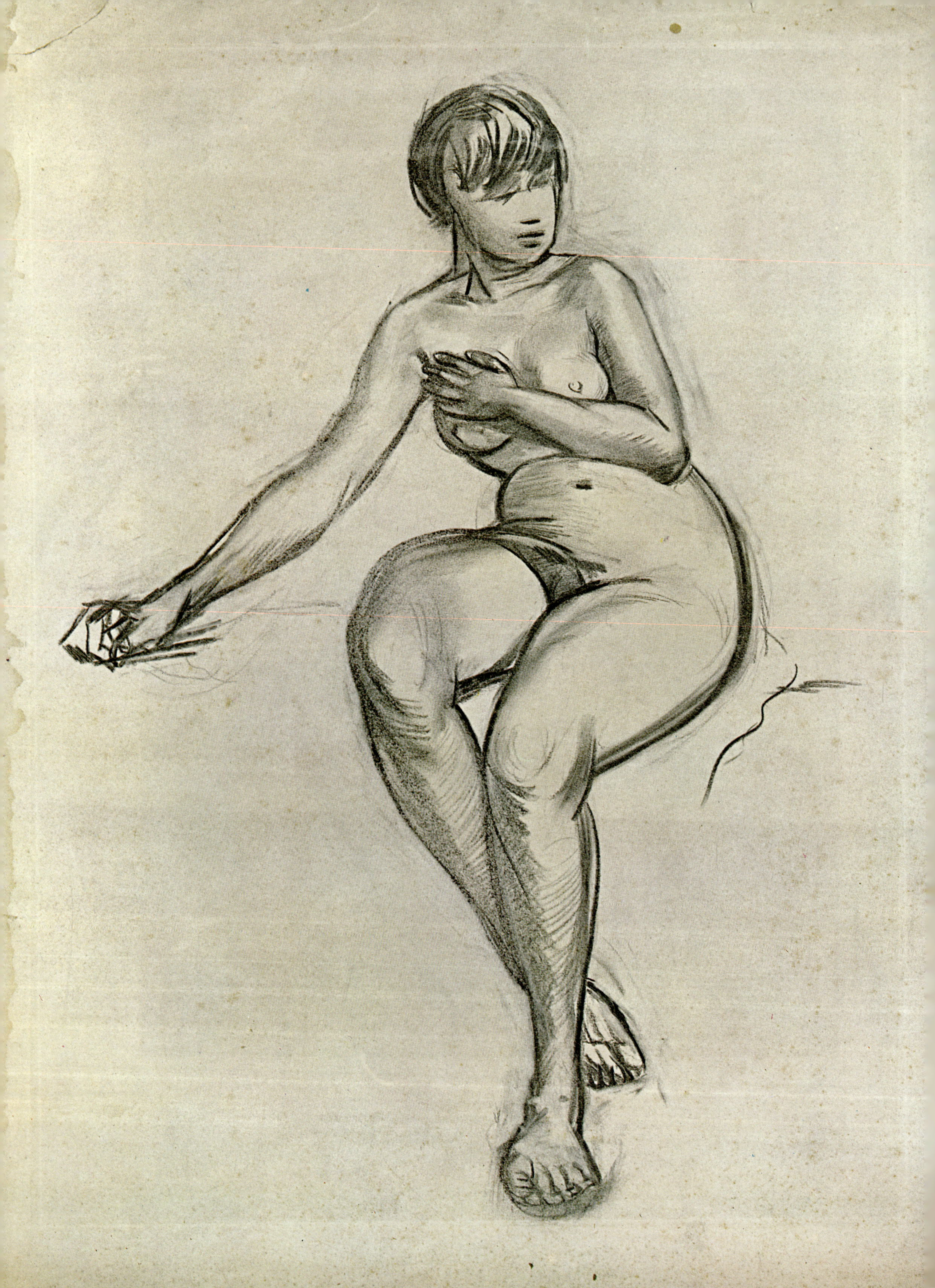

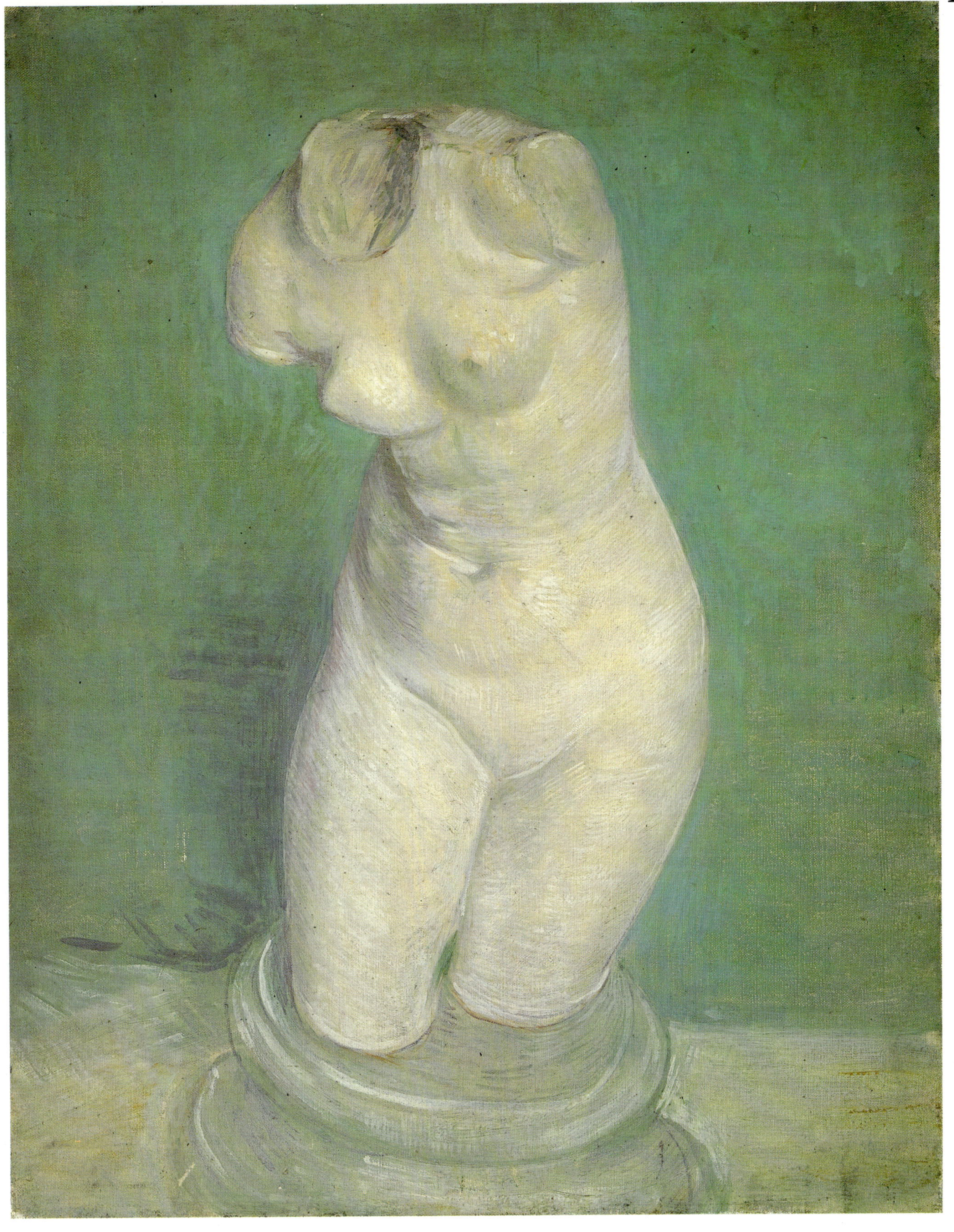

Plaster Study of a Female Torso

April-June 1886 - oil on canvas - 41 x 32.5 cm - Vincent van Gogh Foundation, Amsterdam

Nude

1886 - black chalk and charcoal - 73.5 x 59 cm - Vincent van Gogh Foundation, Amsterdam

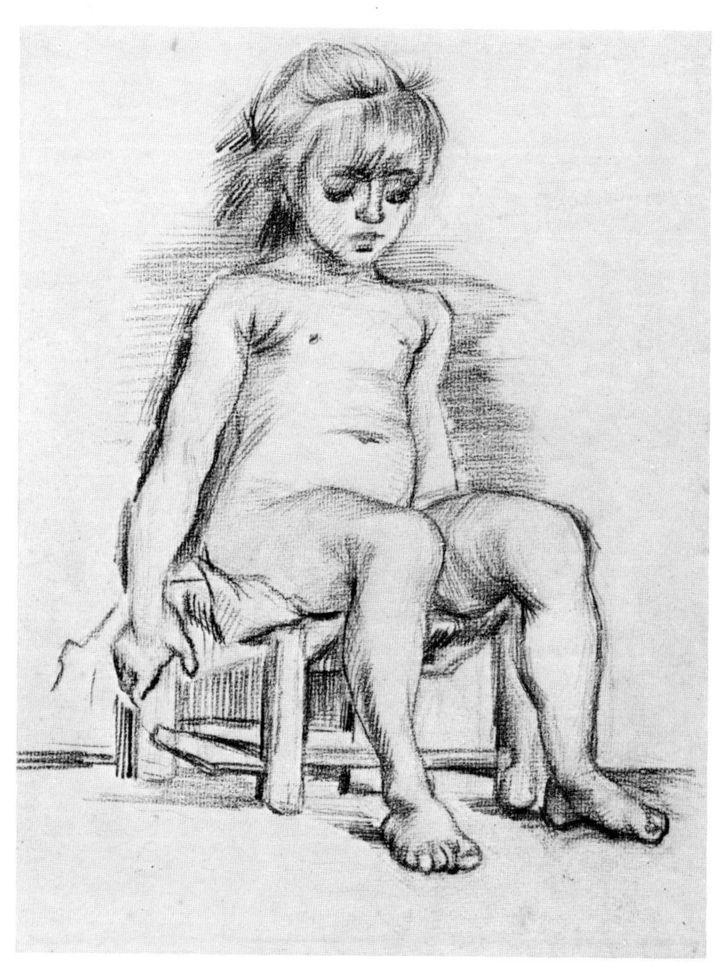

Nude Study of a Little Girl Seated

1886 - black chalk - 30 x 23.5 cm -
Vincent van Gogh Foundation, Amsterdam

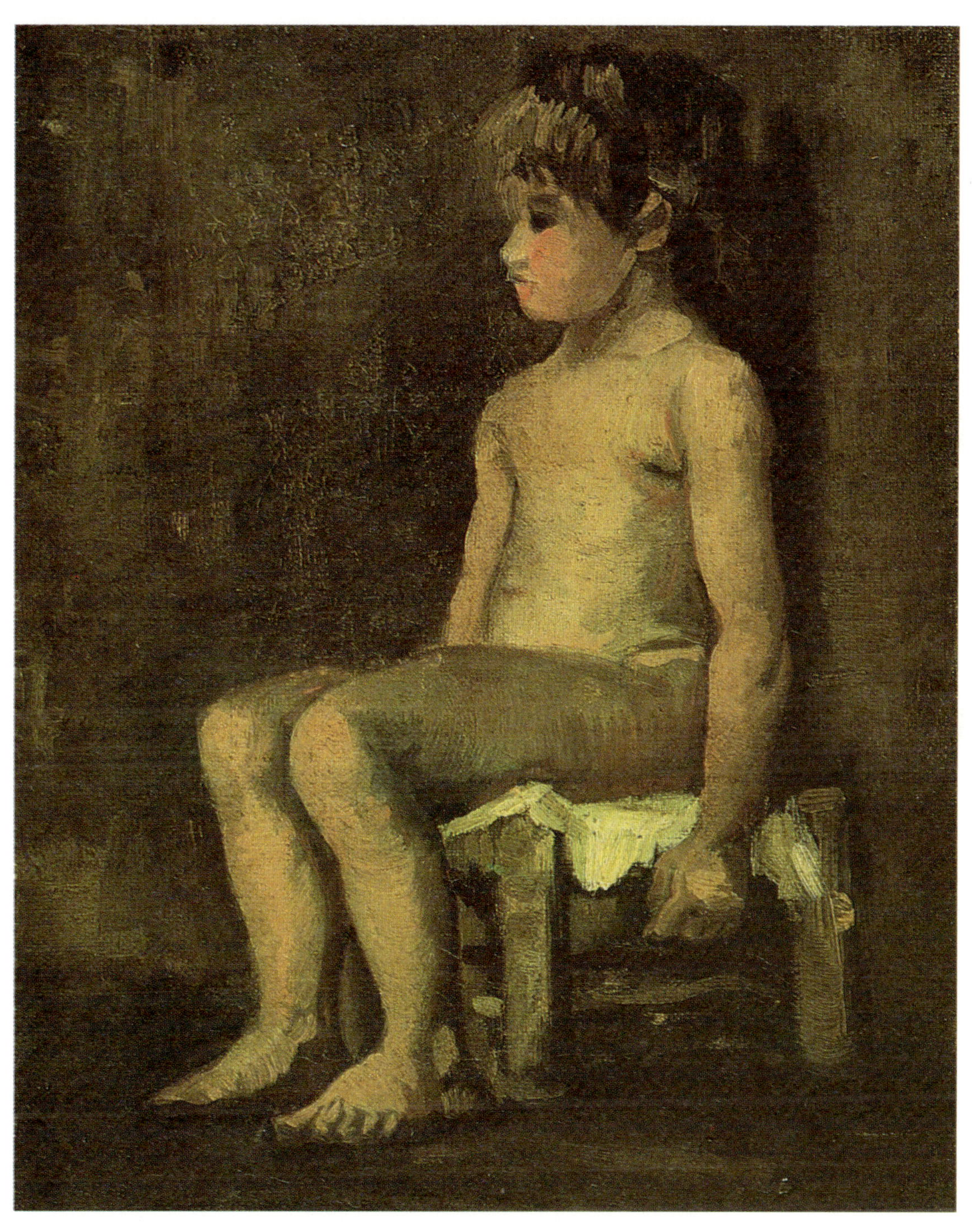

Nude Study of a Little Girl Seated

Spring 1886 - oil on canvas - 27 x 22.5 cm -
Vincent van Gogh Foundation, Amsterdam

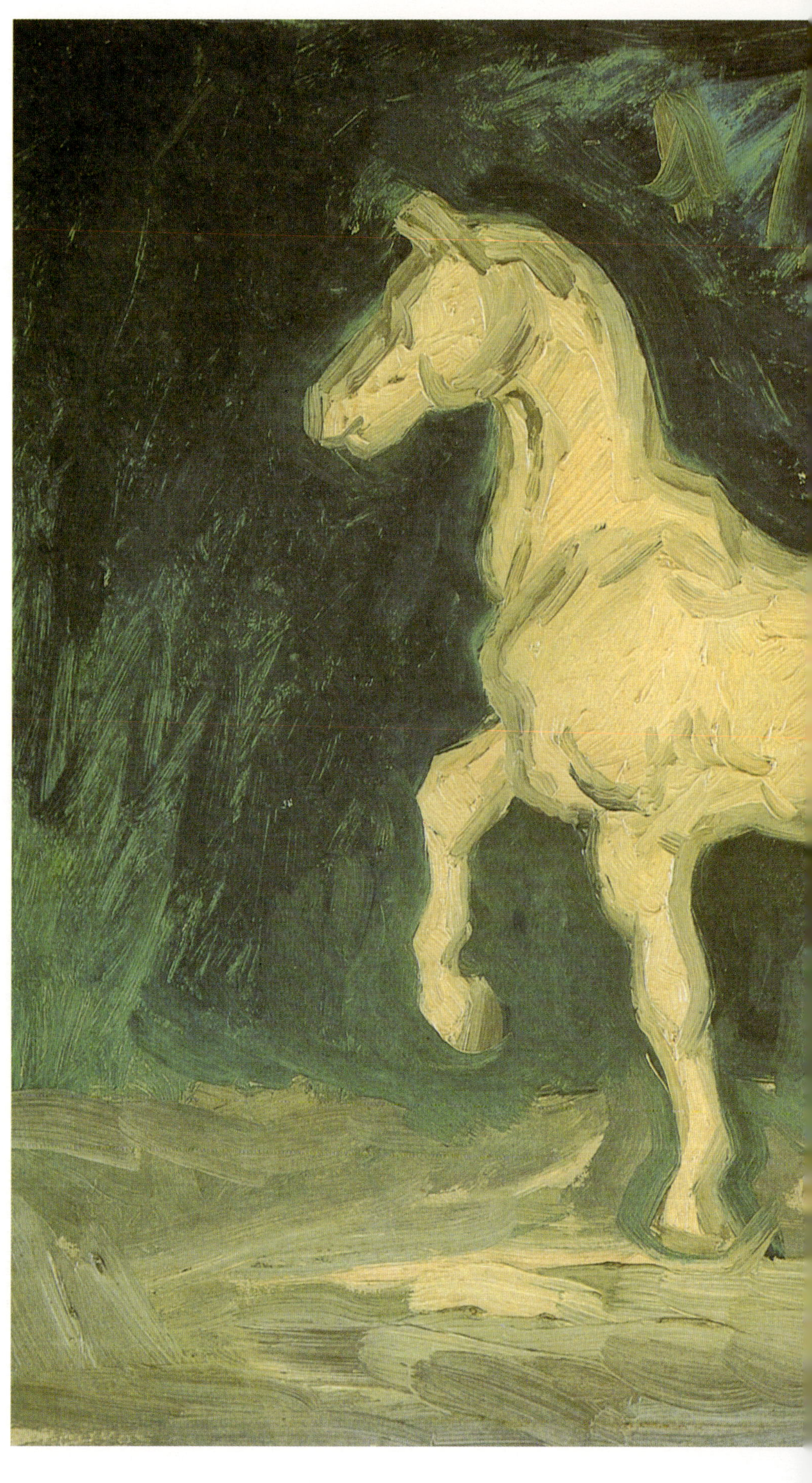

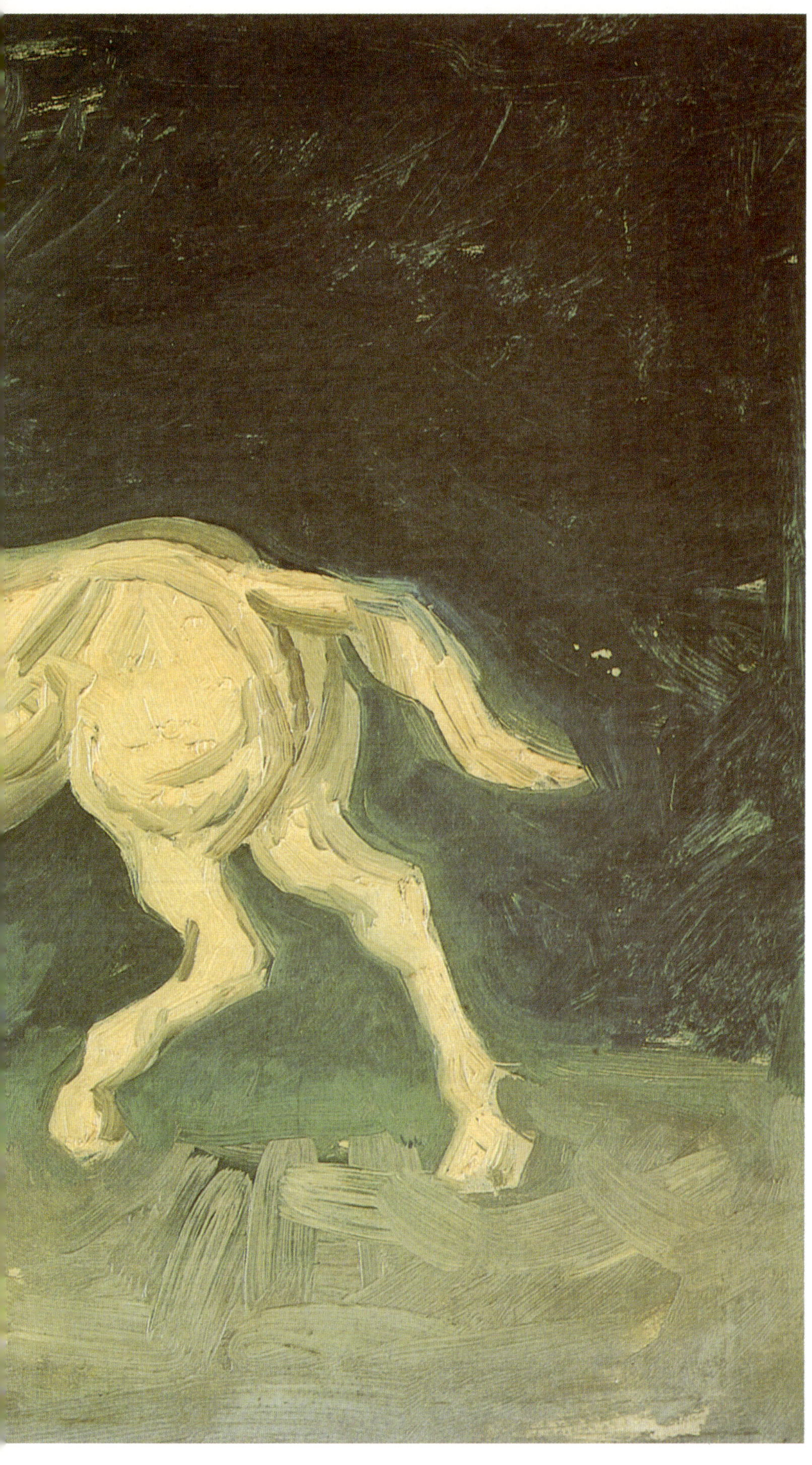

Plaster Statue of a Horse

Spring 1886 - oil on card on multiplex board - 33 x 41 cm - Vincent van Gogh Foundation, Amsterdam

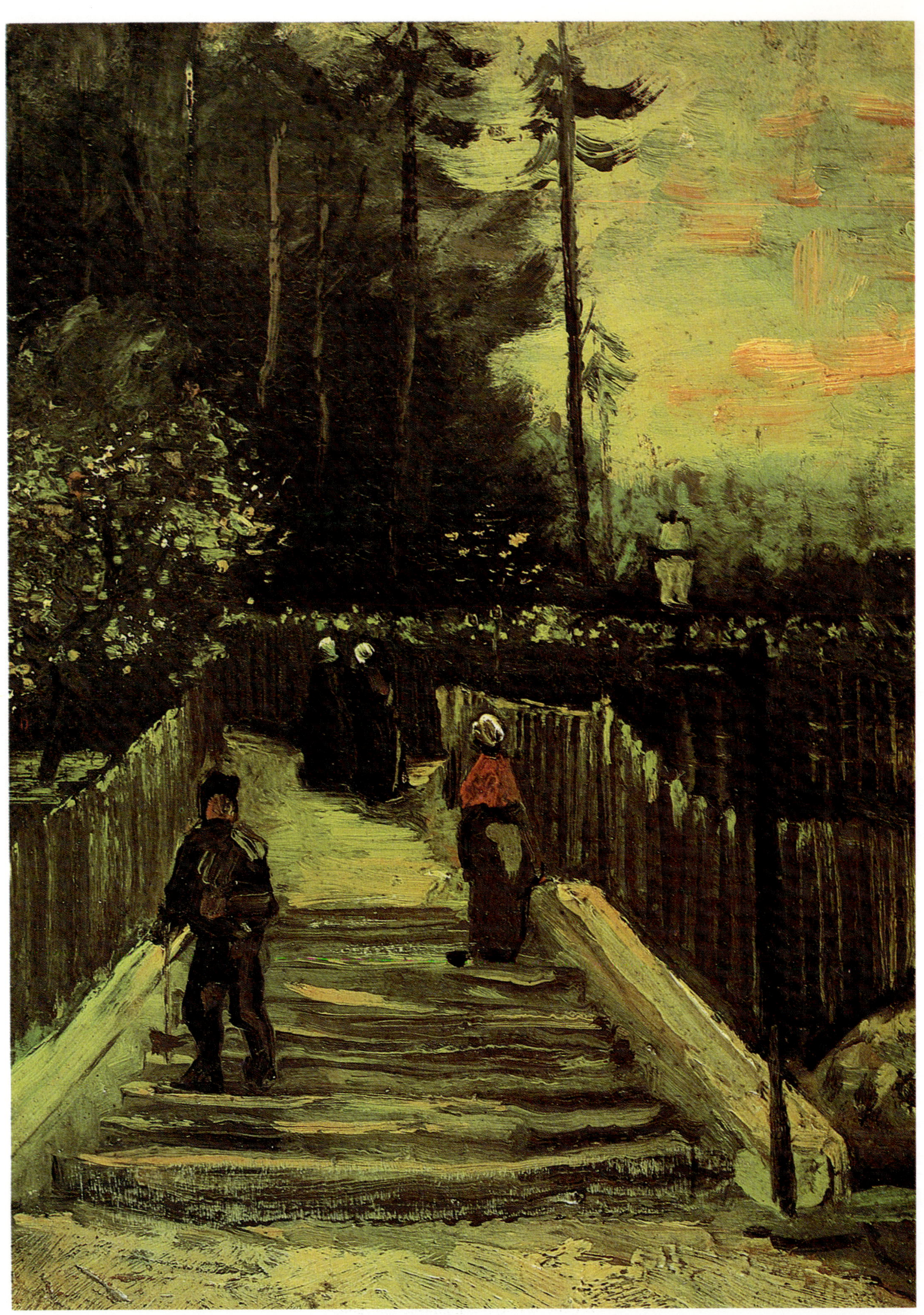

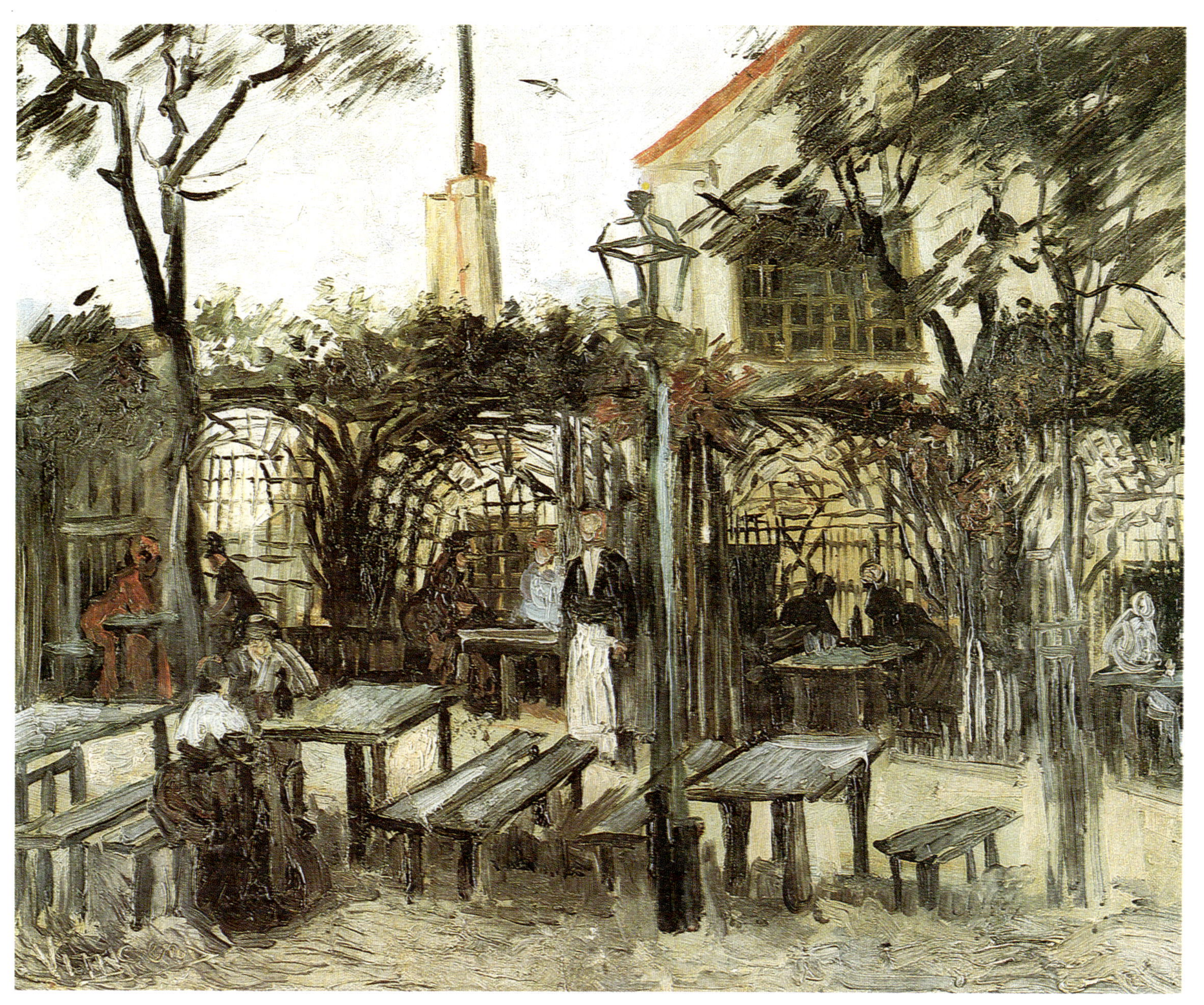

The Tavern

1886 - oil on canvas - 49.5 x 64.5 cm -
Musée d'Orsay, Paris

Path in Montmartre

Spring 1886 - oil on card on multiplex board - 22 x 16 cm -
Vincent van Gogh Foundation, Amsterdam

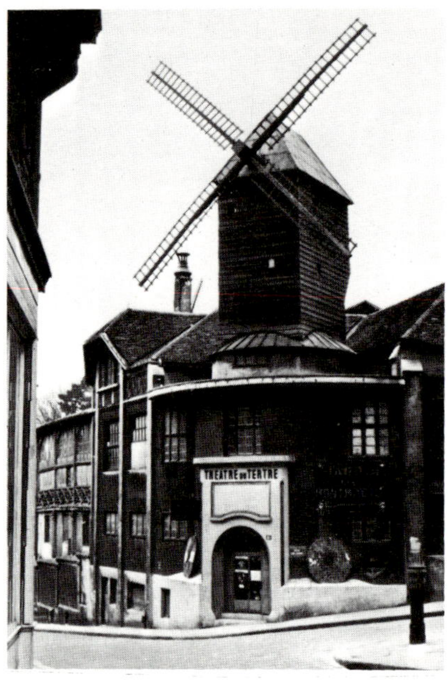

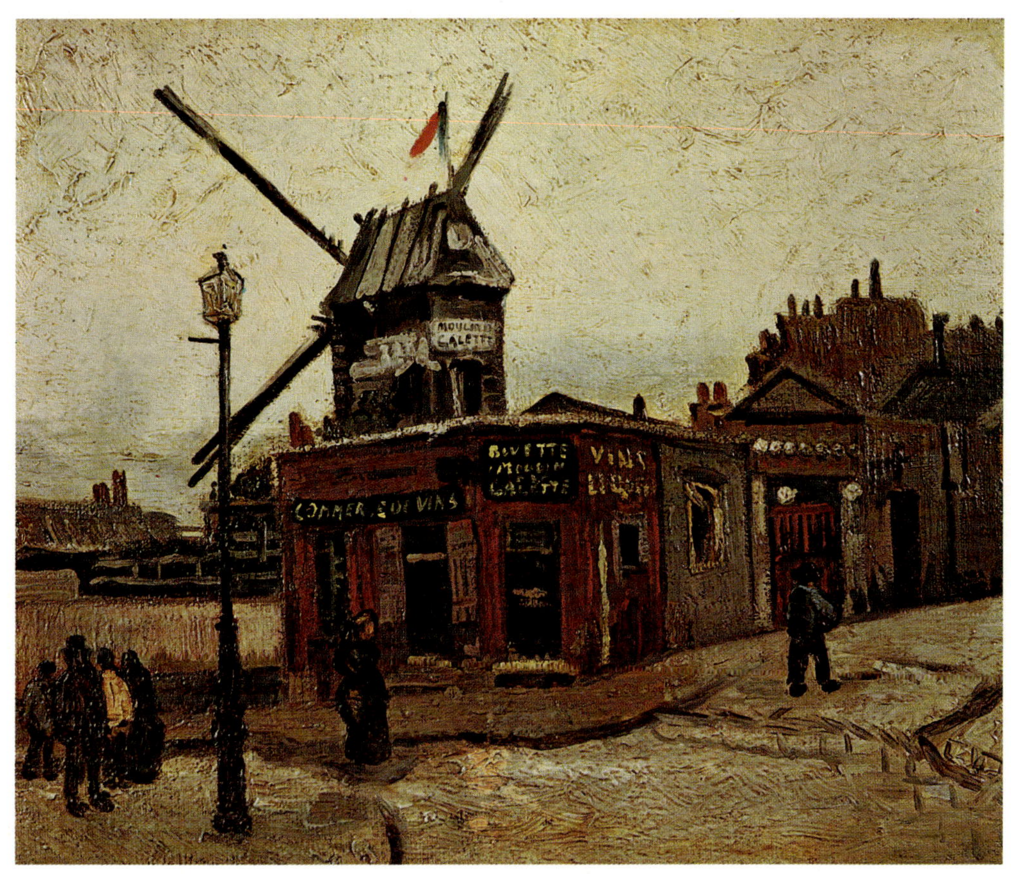

Photograph of the Moulin de la Galette

The Moulin de la Galette seen from rue Girardon

1886 - oil on canvas - 38 x 46.5 cm -
Picture Gallery, Berlin-Dahlem

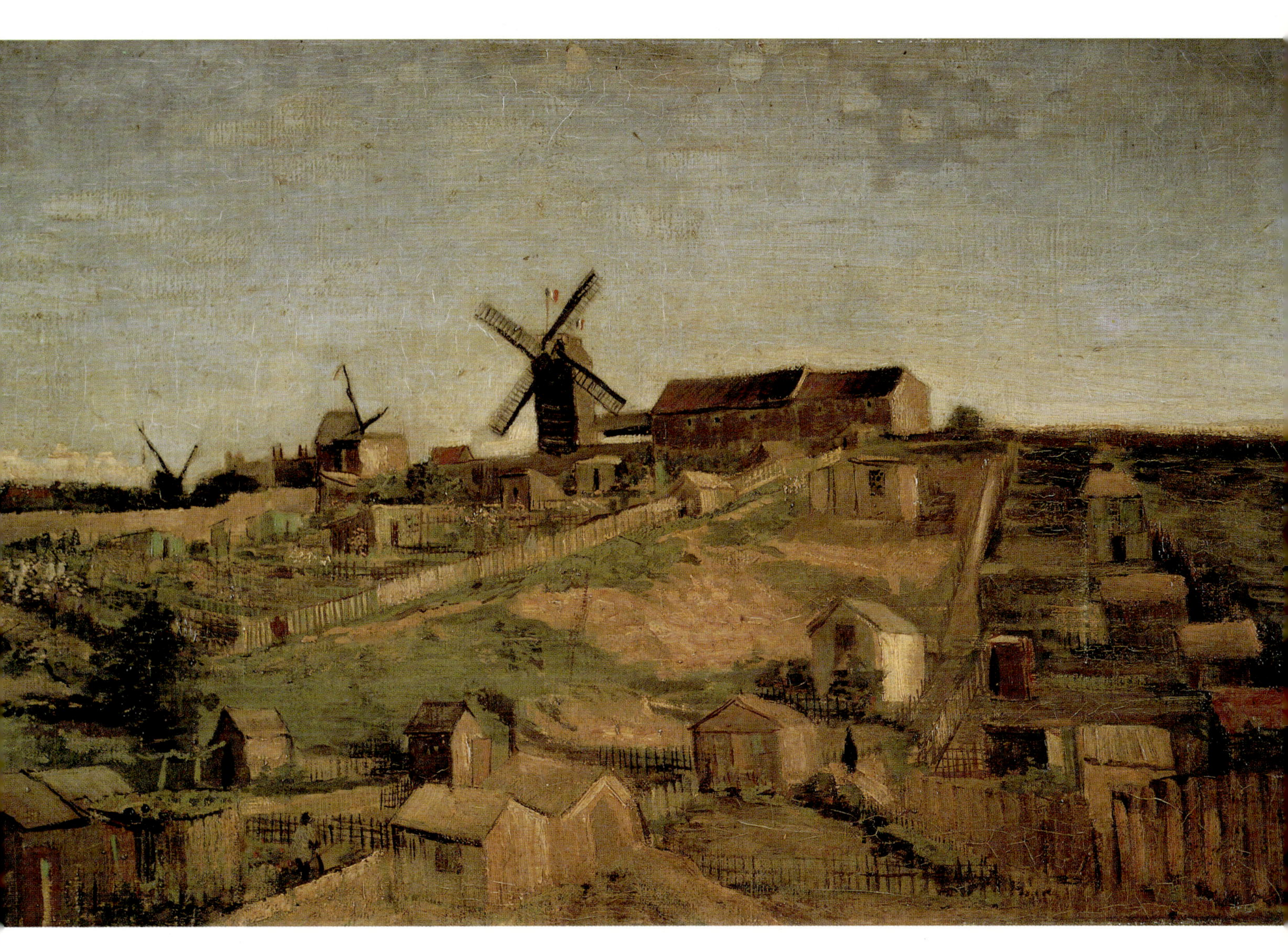

View of Montmartre with Windmills

October-December 1886 - oil on canvas - 36 x 61 cm -
Musée d'Etat Kröller- Müller, Otterlo

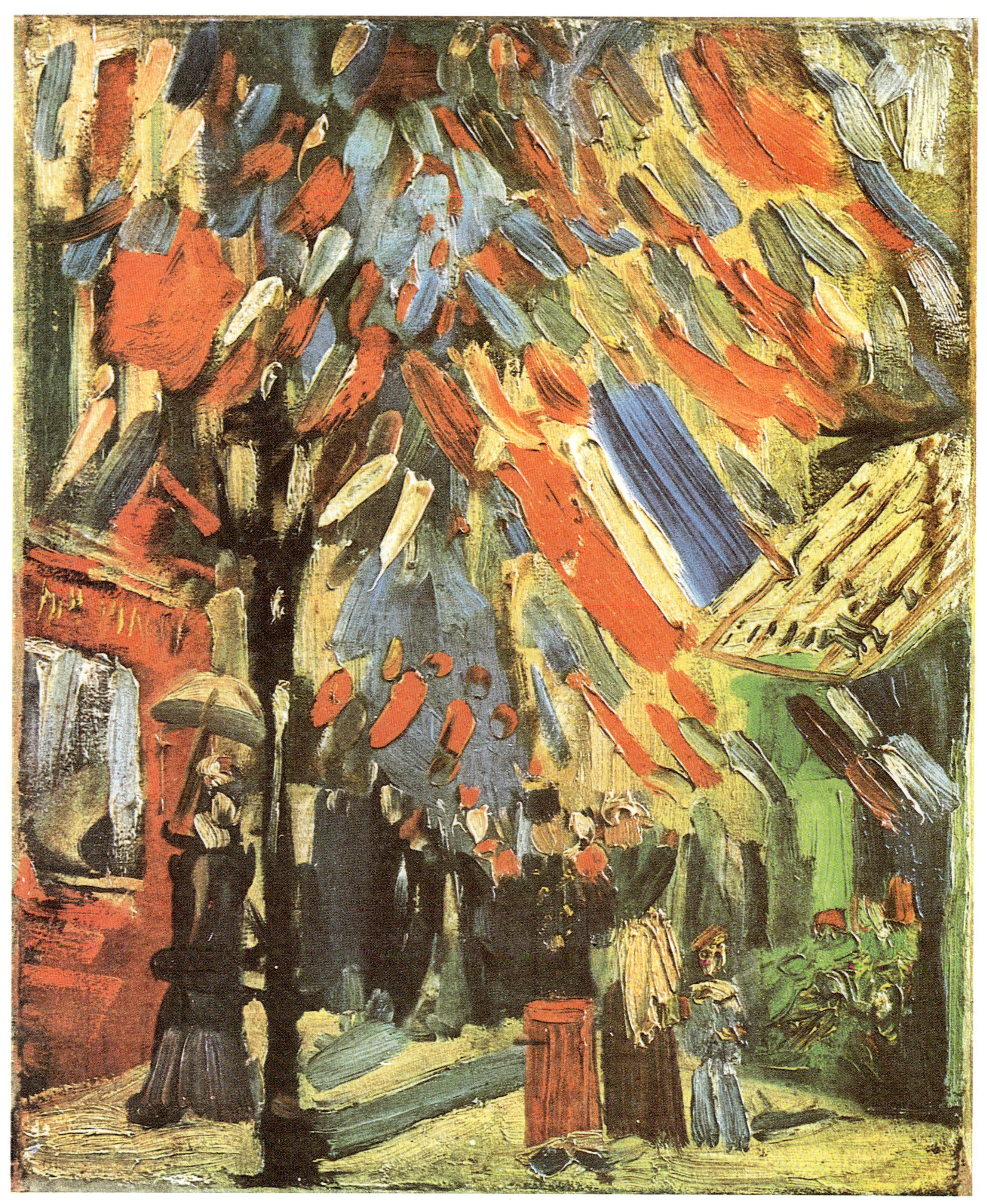

Bastille Day Celebration

Summer 1886 - oil on canvas - 44 x 39 cm -
L. Jäggli-Hahnloser collection, Winterthur, Switzerland

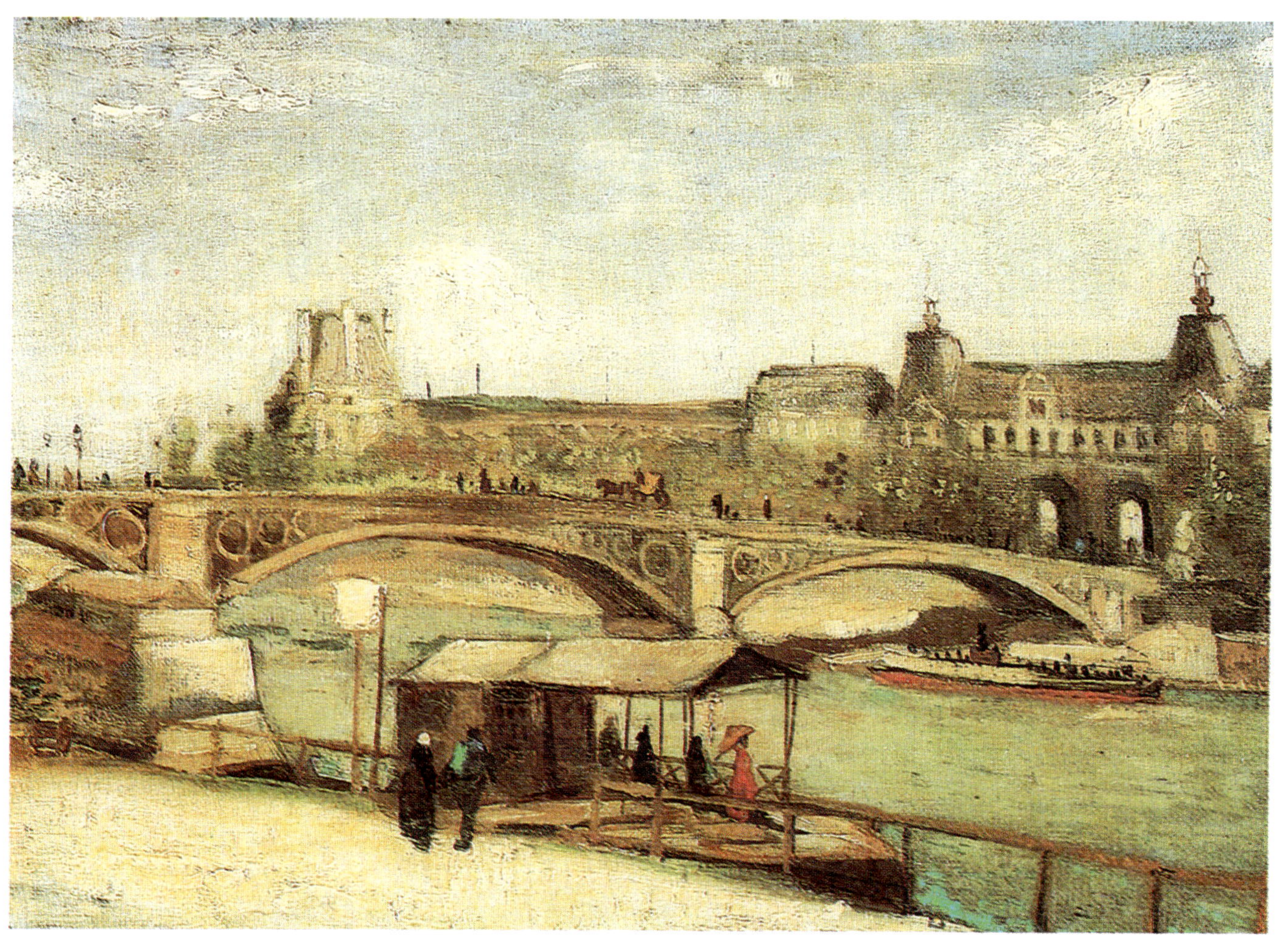

The Pont du Carrousel and the Louvre

June 1886 - oil on canvas - 31 x 44 cm -
Private collection

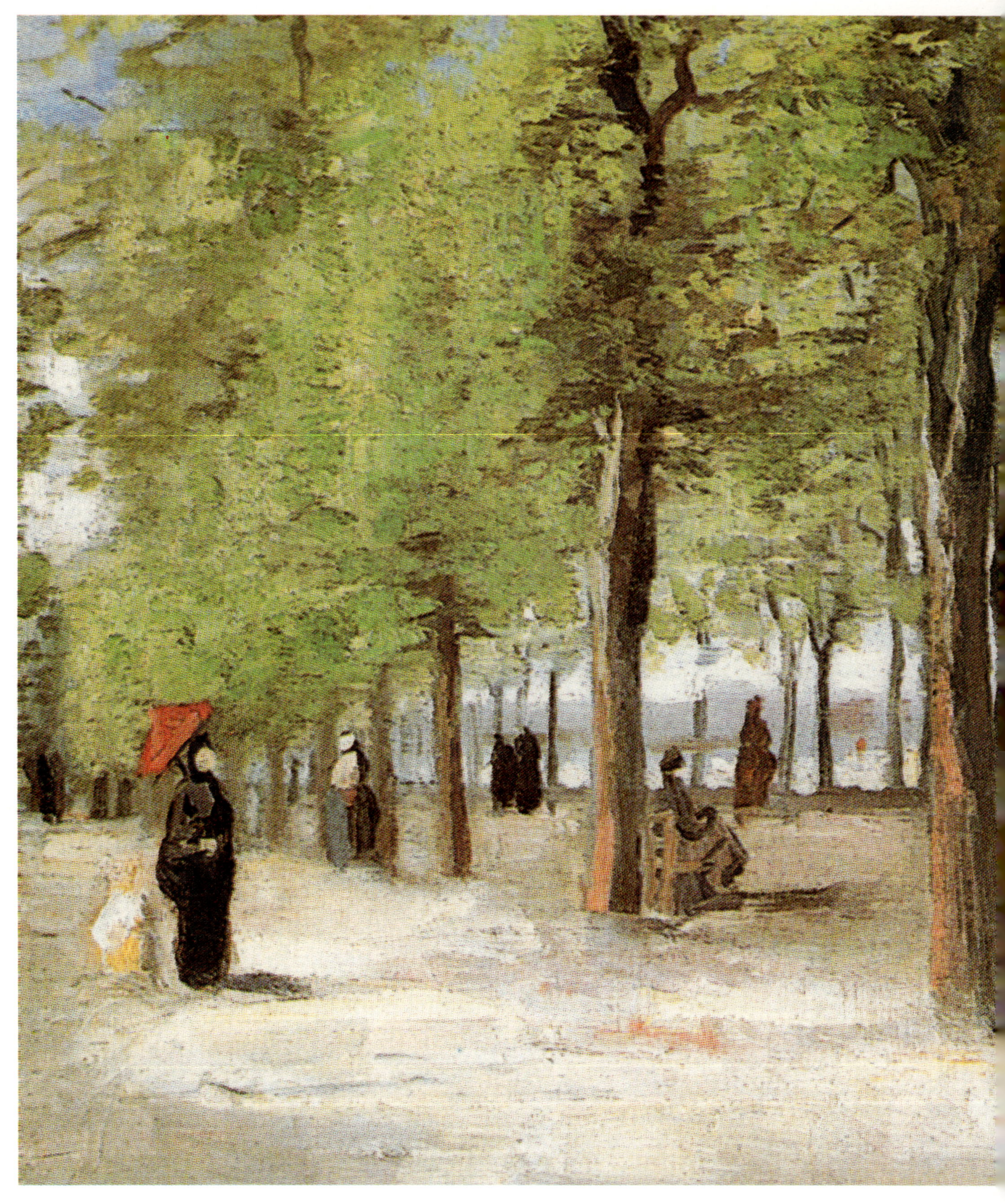

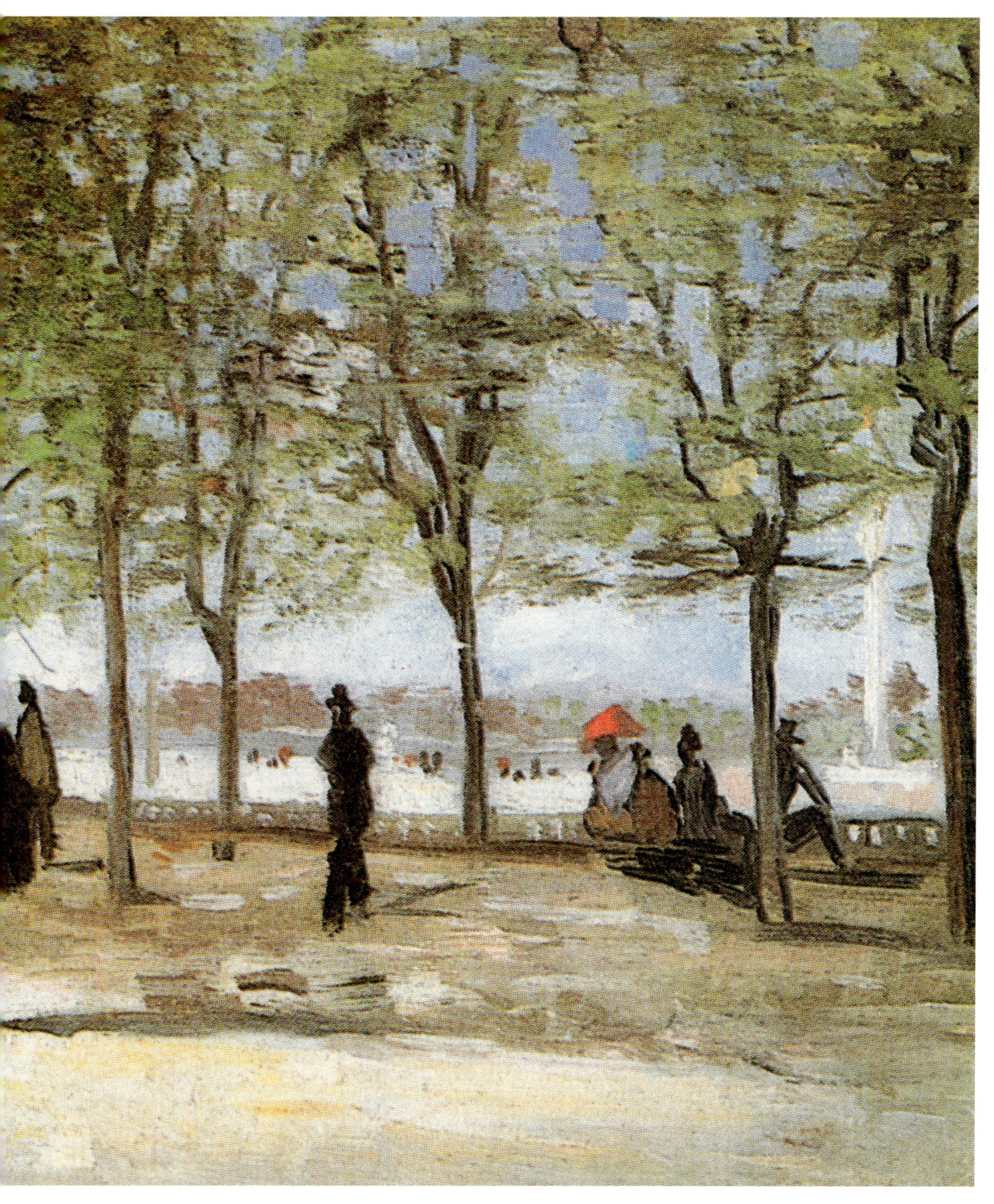

Terrace at the Jardin de Luxembourg

June-July 1886 - oil on canvas - 27.5 x 46 cm -
Sterling and Francine Clark Art Institute, Williamstown, Mass.

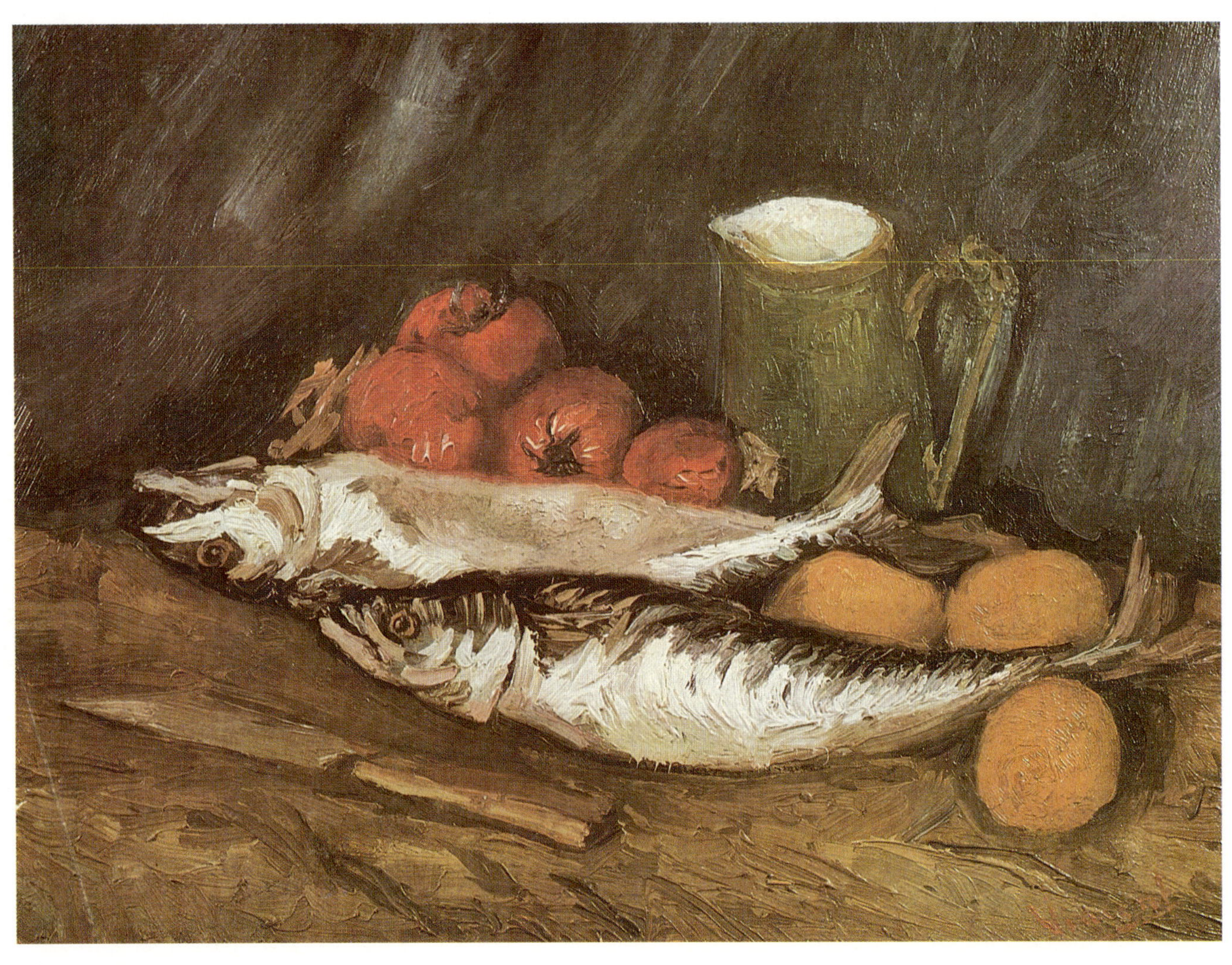

Still Life with Mackerel

Summer 1886 - oil on canvas - 39 x 56.5 cm -
Oskar Reinhart collection, Winterthur, Switzerland

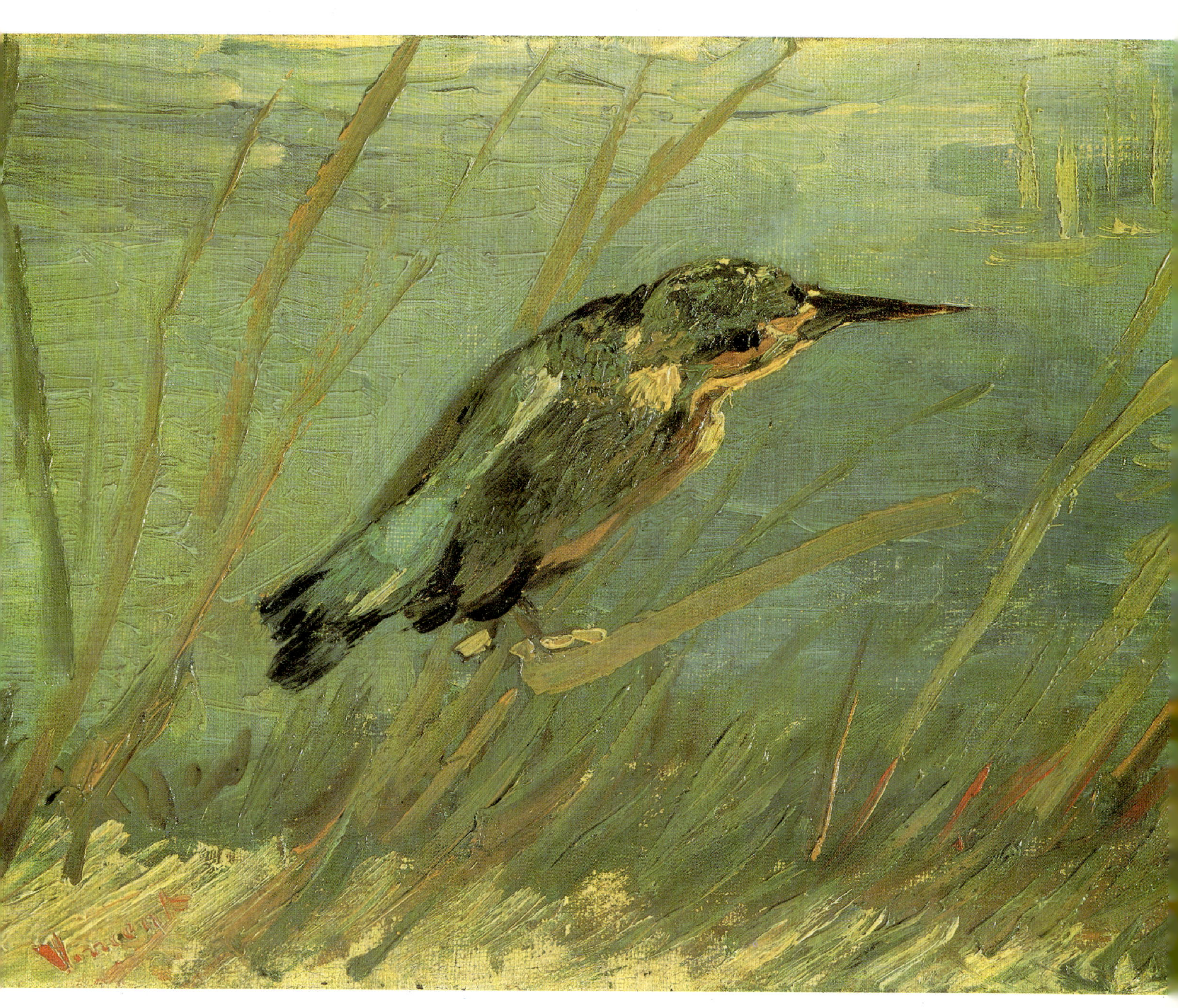

The Kingfisher

*December 1886 - oil on canvas - 19 x 26.5 cm -
Vincent van Gogh Foundation, Amsterdam*

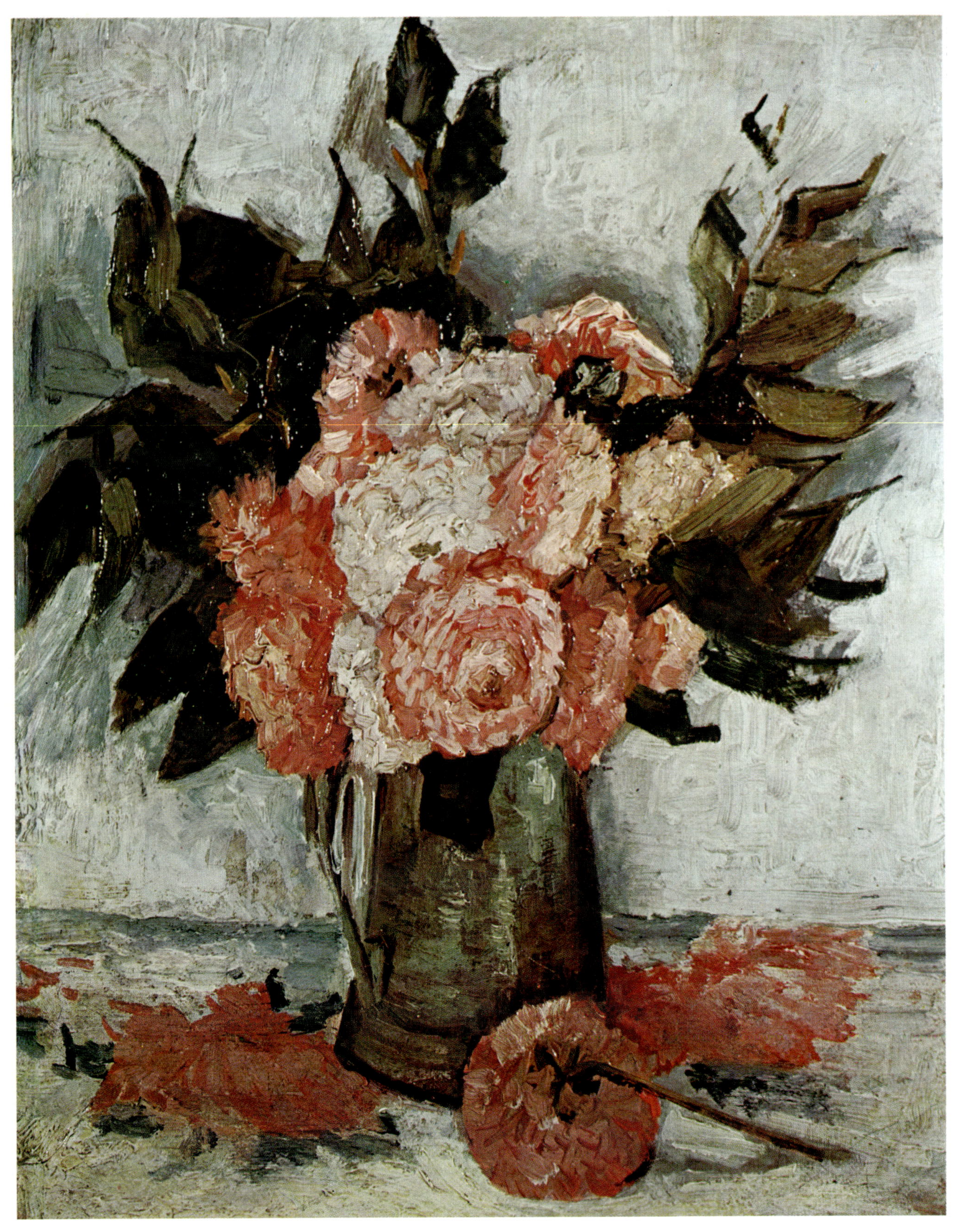

Flowers

1886 - oil on canvas - 46.5 x 38.5 cm -
Bridgestone Gallery, Tokyo

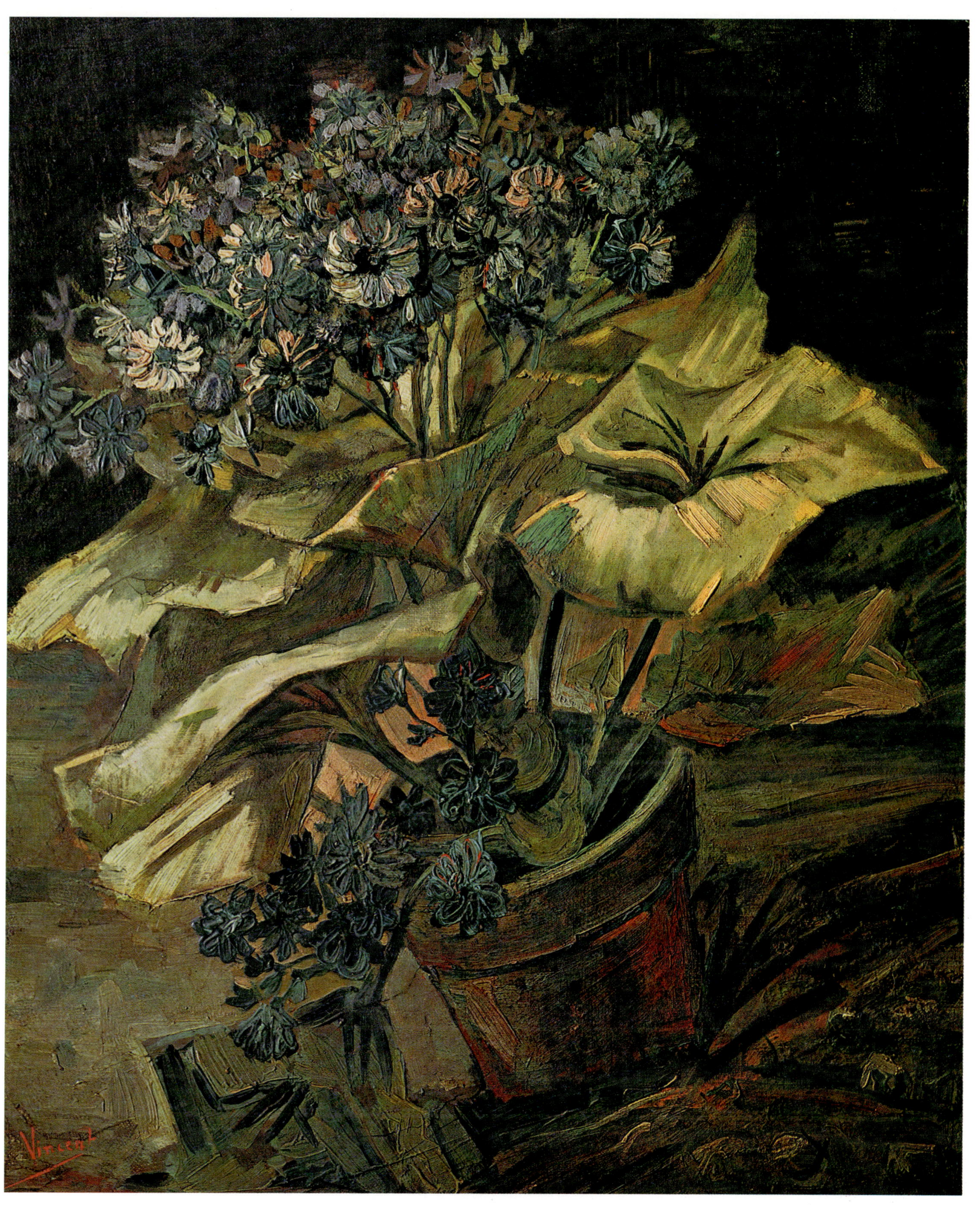

Cineraria

1886 - oil on canvas - 54 x 45 cm -
Boymans-van Beuningen Museum, Rotterdam

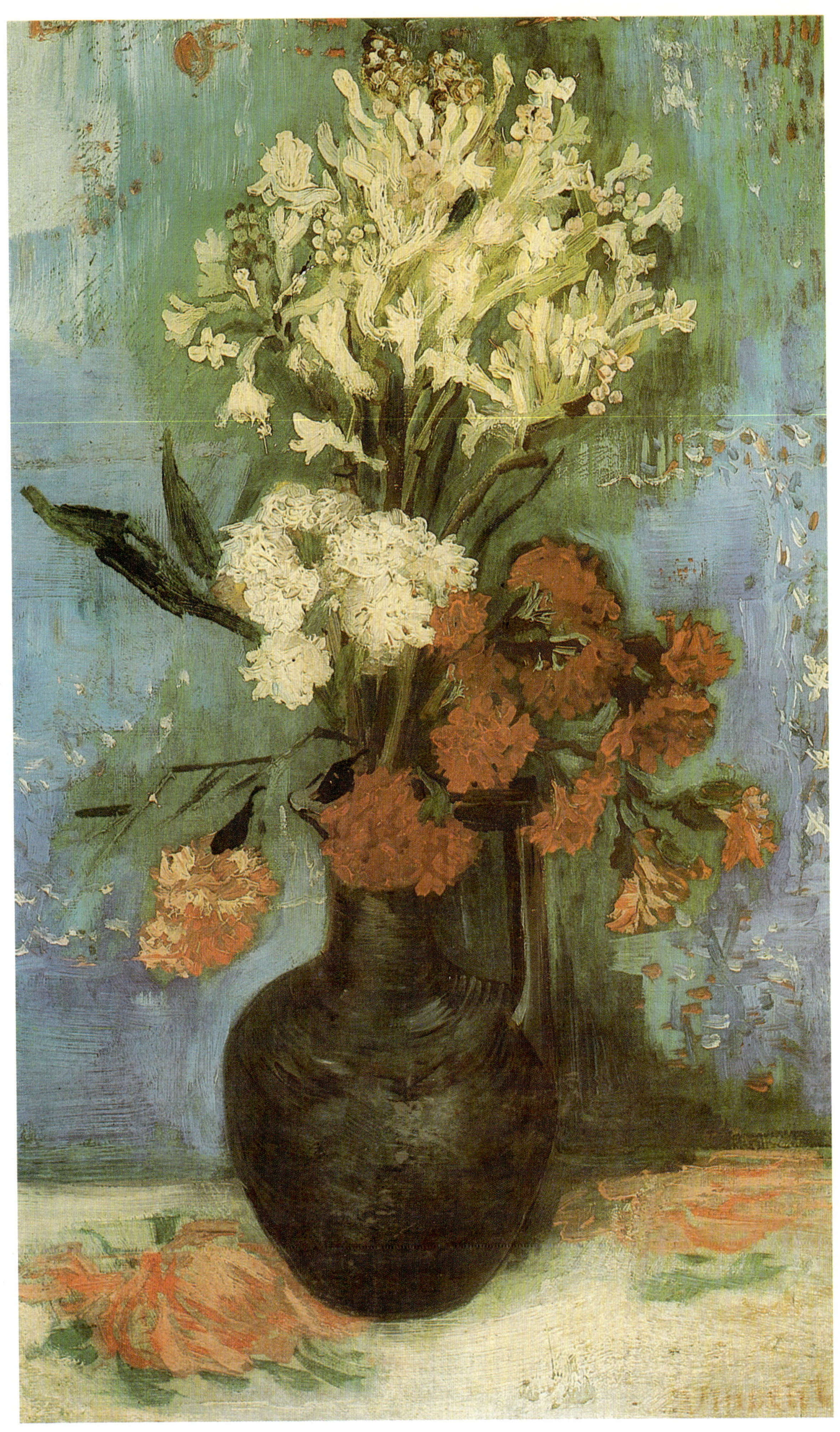

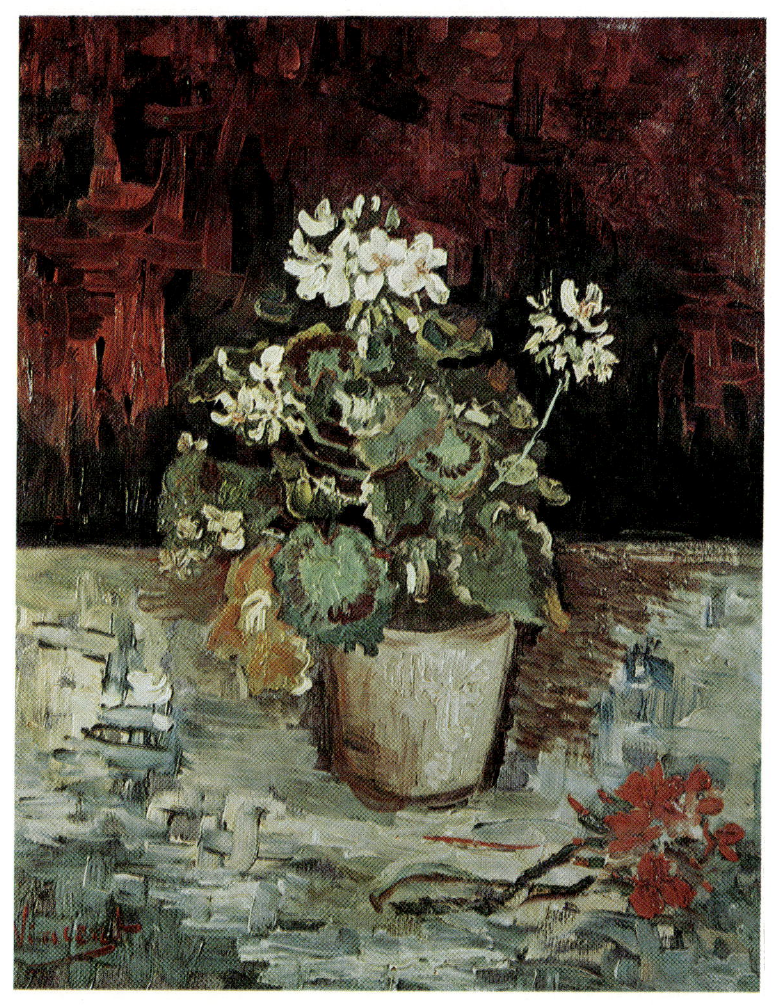

Pot with Geranium Plant

1886 - oil on canvas - 46 x 38 cm -
J.P. Scholte-van H. Gouten colection, Lochem, Holland

Vase with Carnations and Other Flowers

Summer 1886 - oil on canvas - 61 x 38 cm -
David Lloyd Kreeger Collection, Washington D.C.

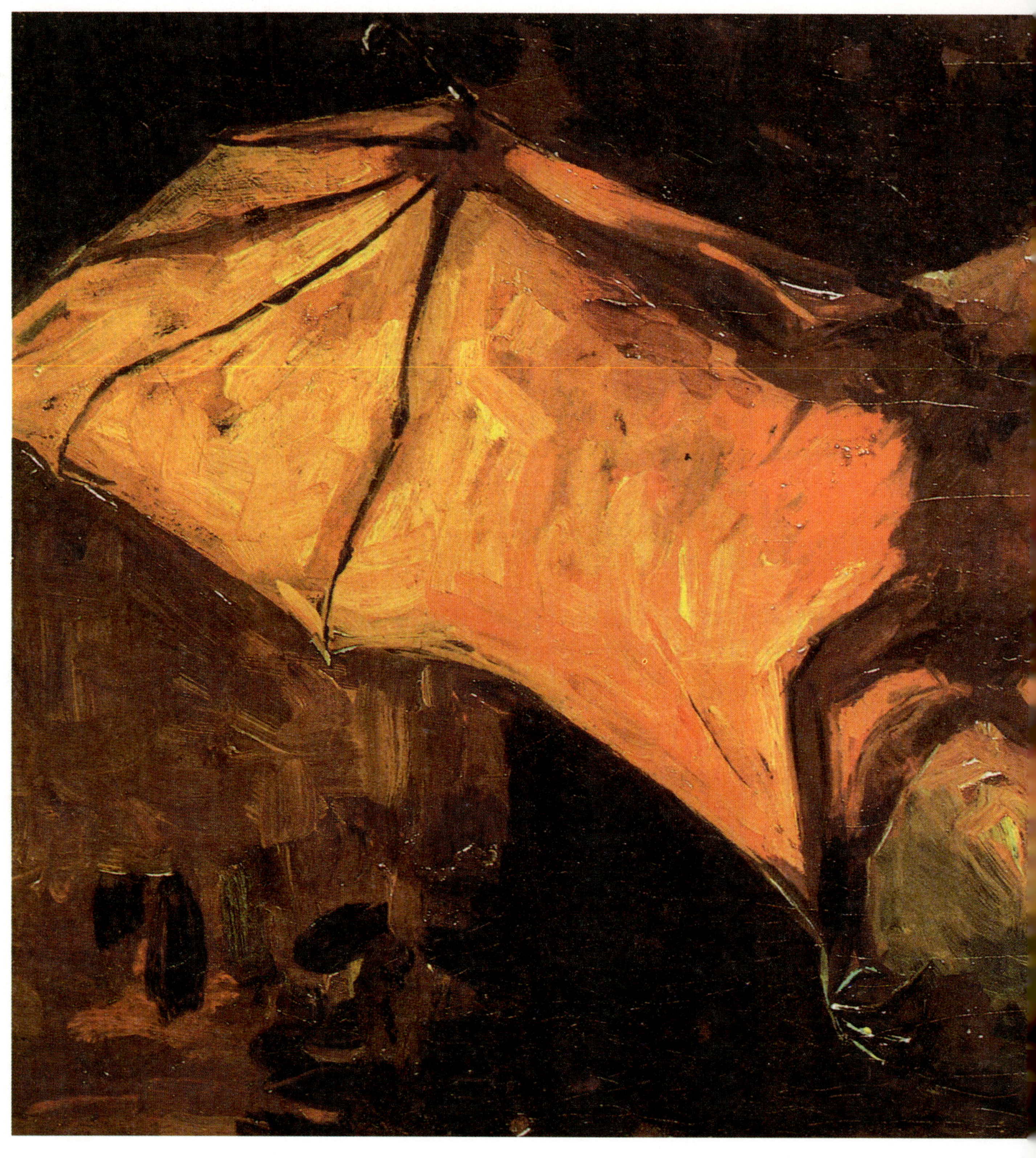

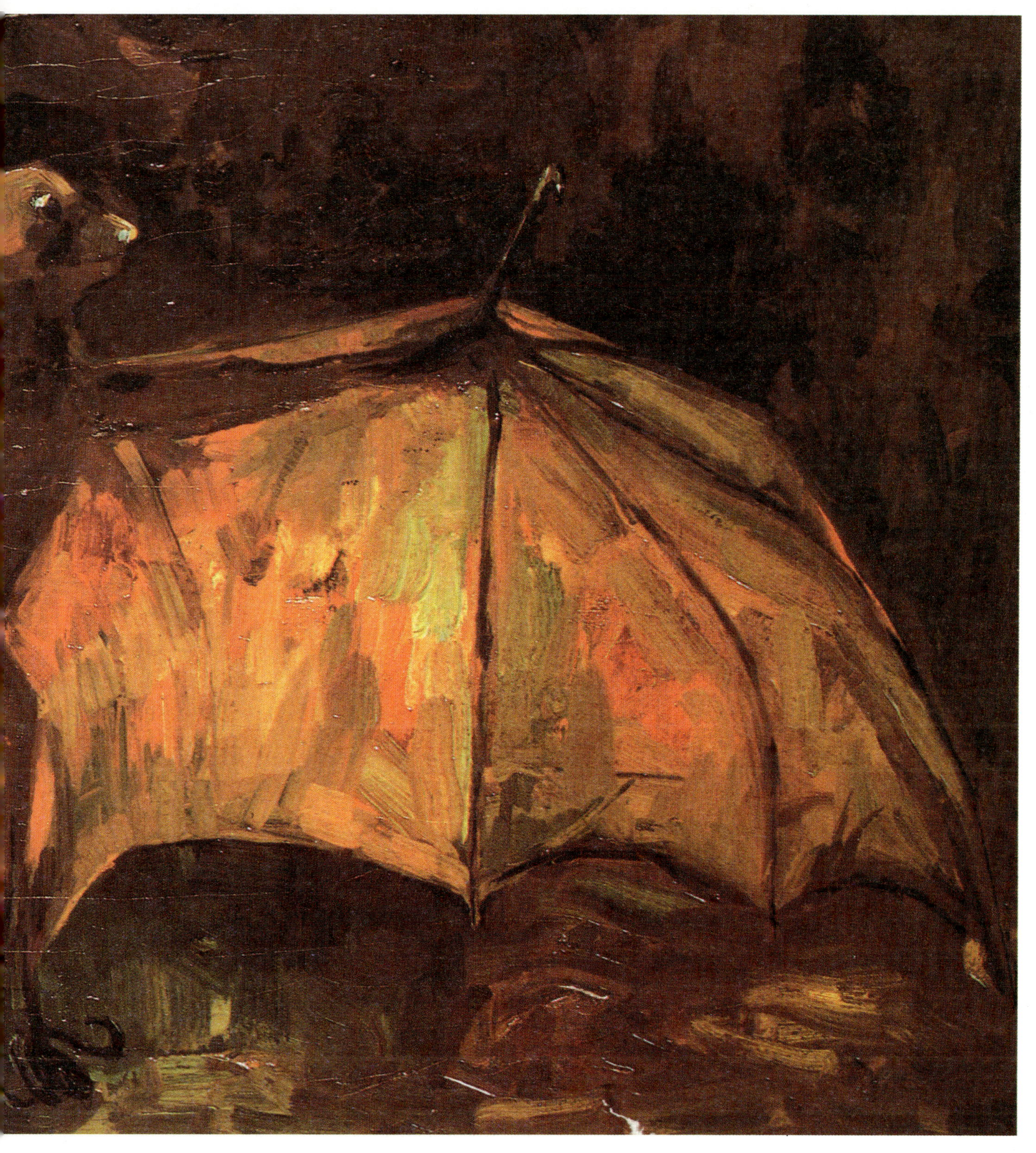

The Bat

1886 - oil on canvas - 41 x 79 cm -
Vincent van Gogh Foundation, Amsterdam

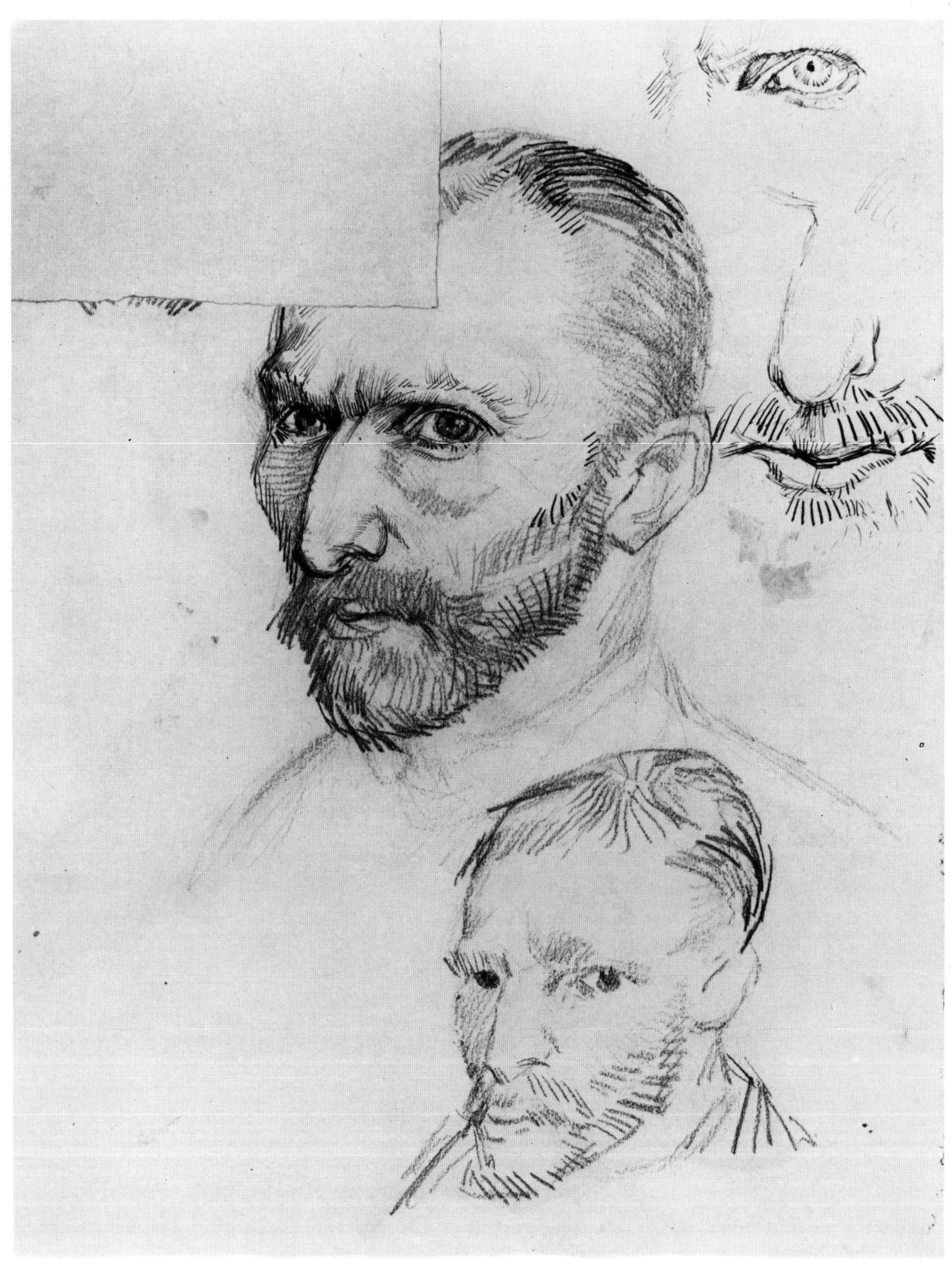

Two Self-Portraits

October-December 1886 - crayon and pen - 32 x 24 cm -
Vincent van Gogh Foundation, Amsterdam

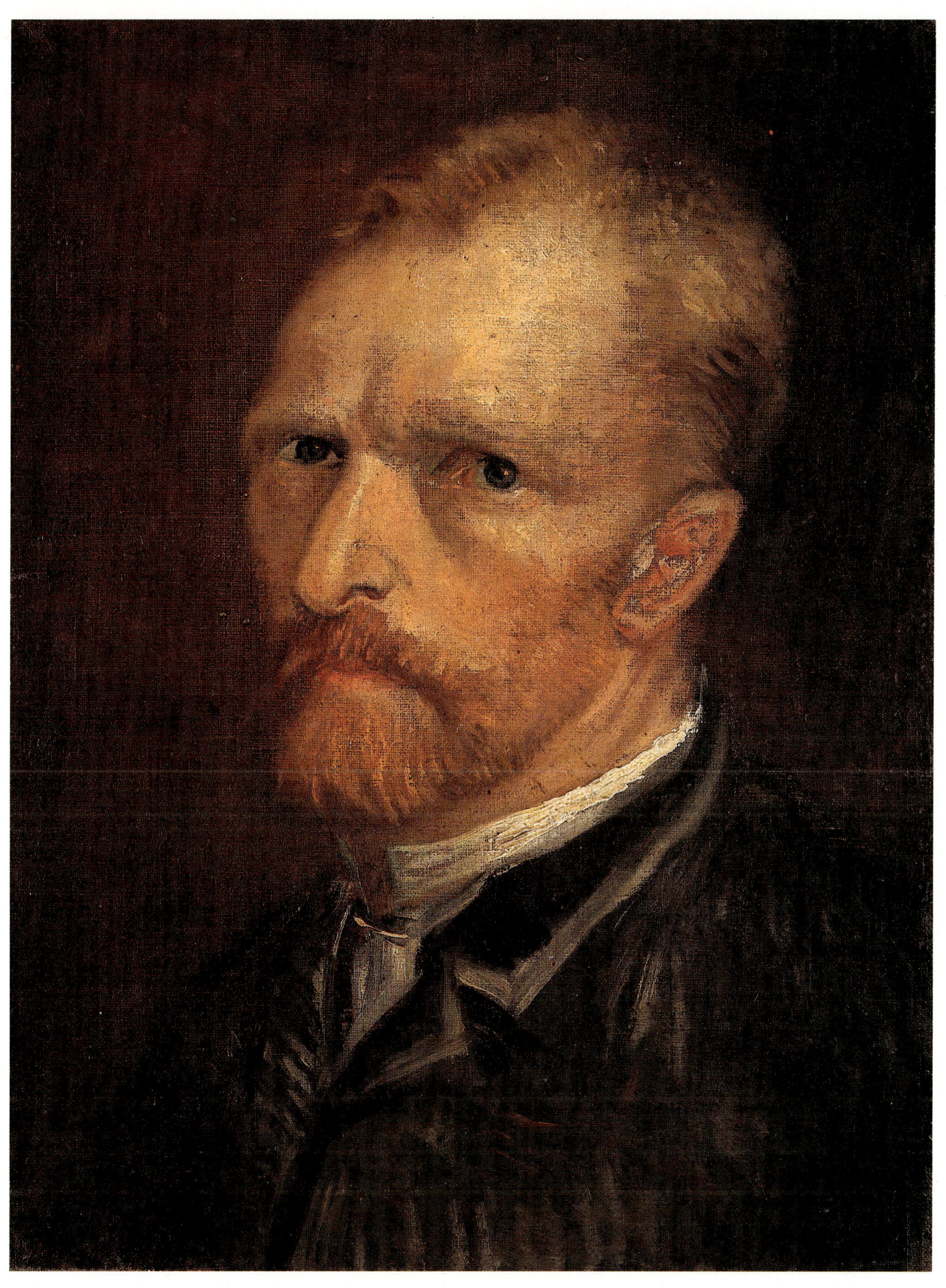

Self-Portrait

October-December 1886 - oil on canvas - 39.5 x 29.5 cm - Gemeentemuseum, The Hague

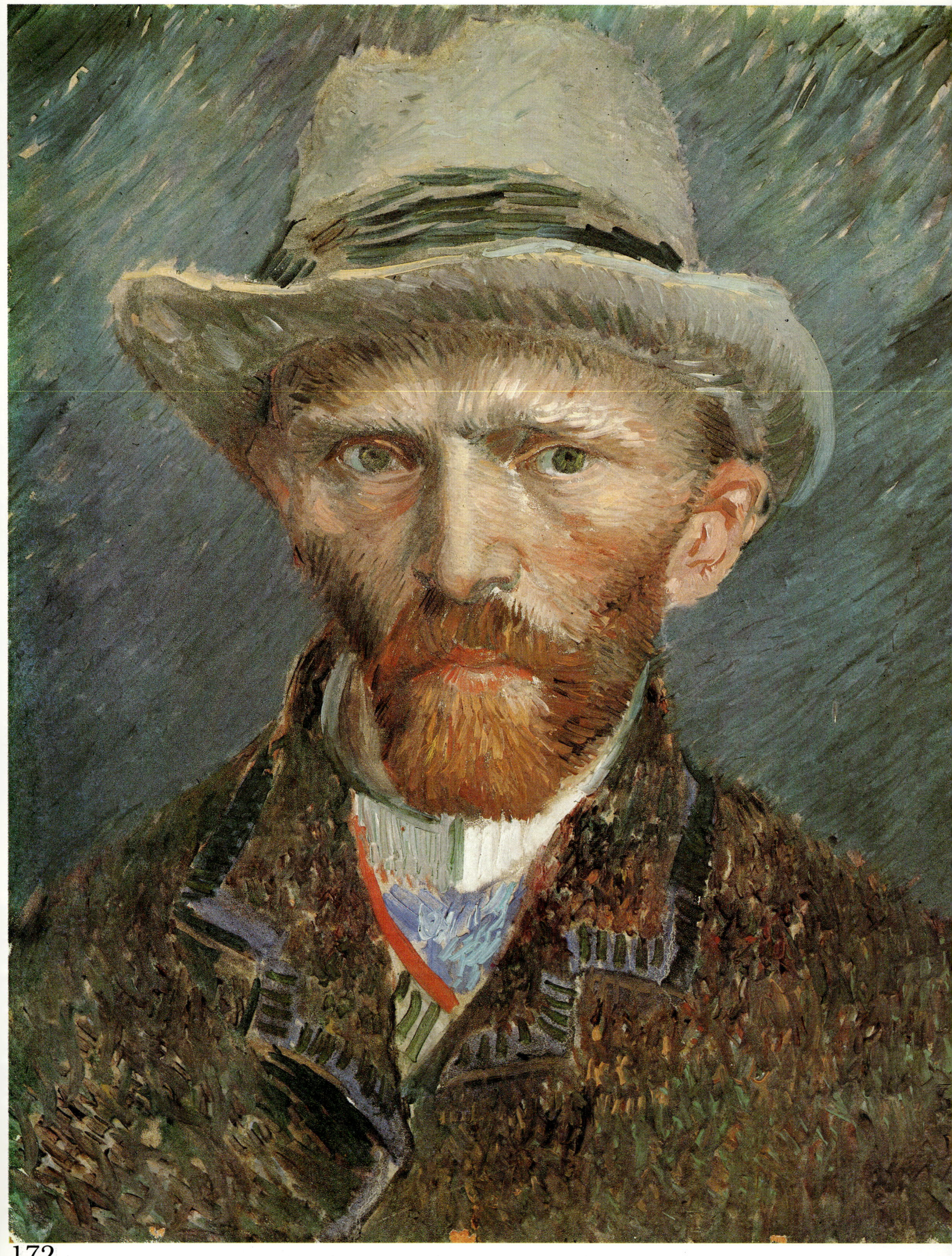

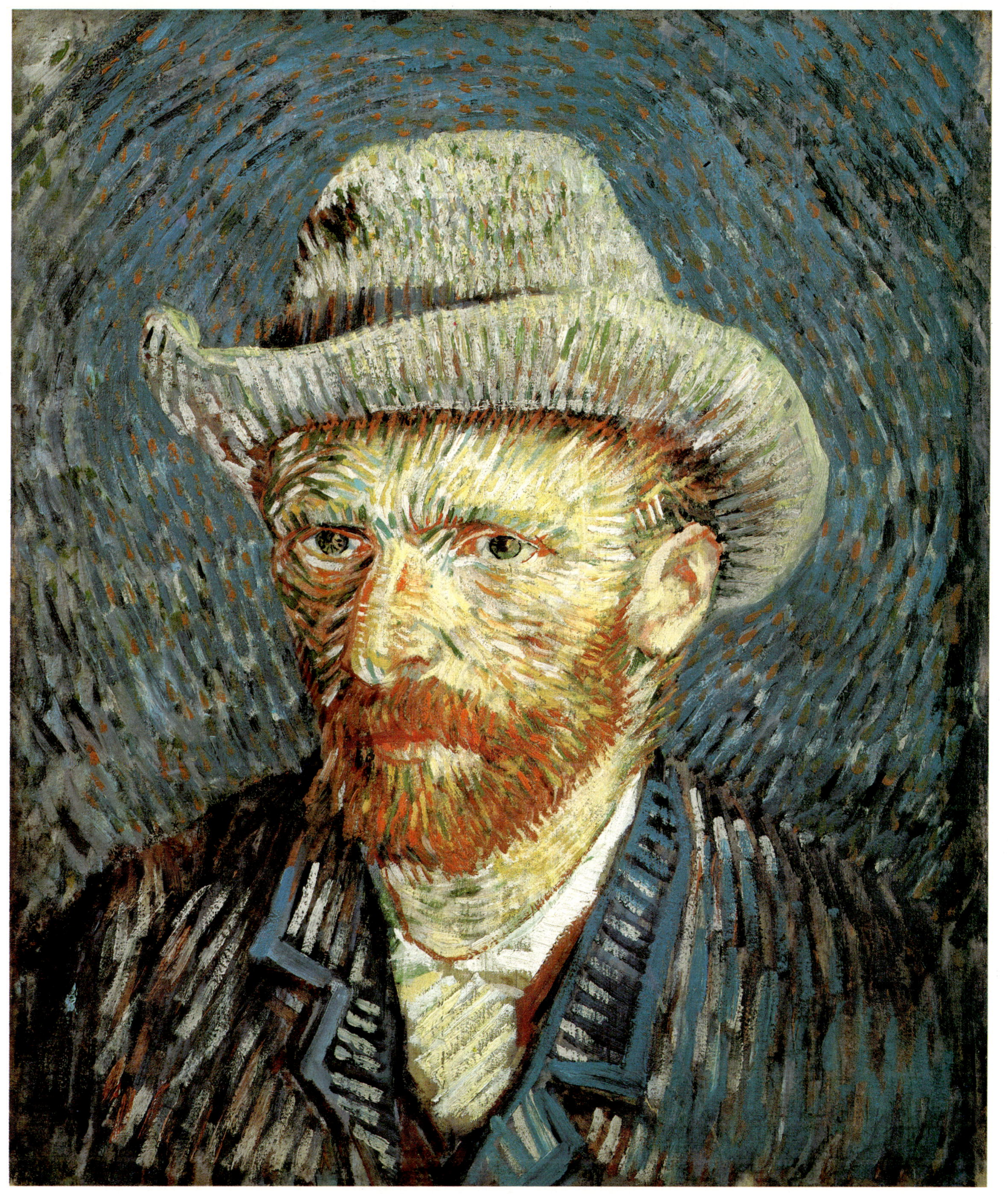

Self-Portrait with Gray Felt Hat

Winter 1887 - oil on canvas - 44 x 37.5 cm - Vincent van Gogh Foundation, Amsterdam

Self-Portrait with Gray Felt Hat

January-March 1887 - oil on card - 41 x 32 cm - Stedelijk Museum, Amsterdam

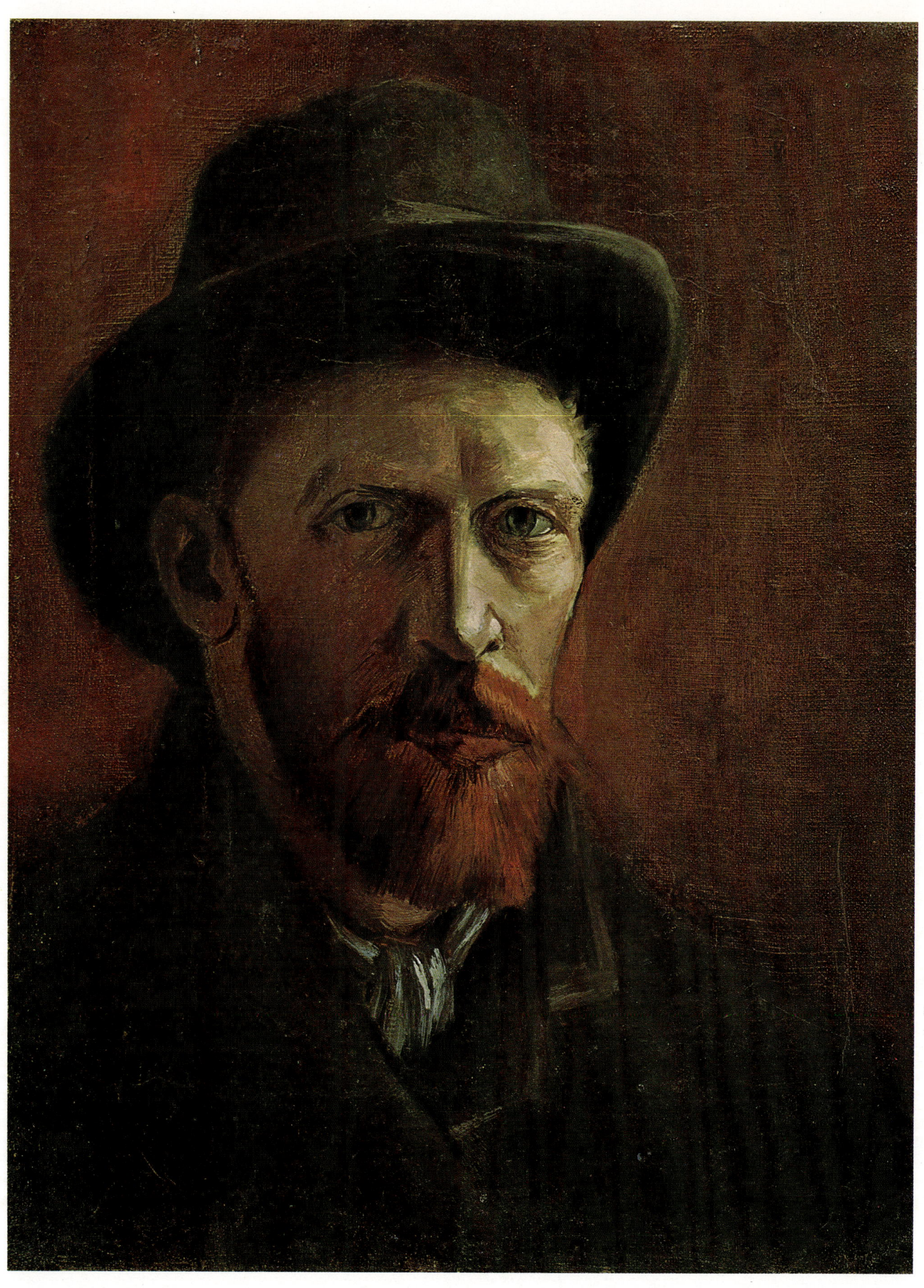

Self-Portrait

1887 - oil on canvas - 41 x 32.5 cm - Vincent van Gogh Foundation, Amsterdam

Self-Portrait with a Straw Hat

July-September 1887 - oil on cardboard - 41 x 33 cm - Vincent van Gogh Foundation, Amsterdam

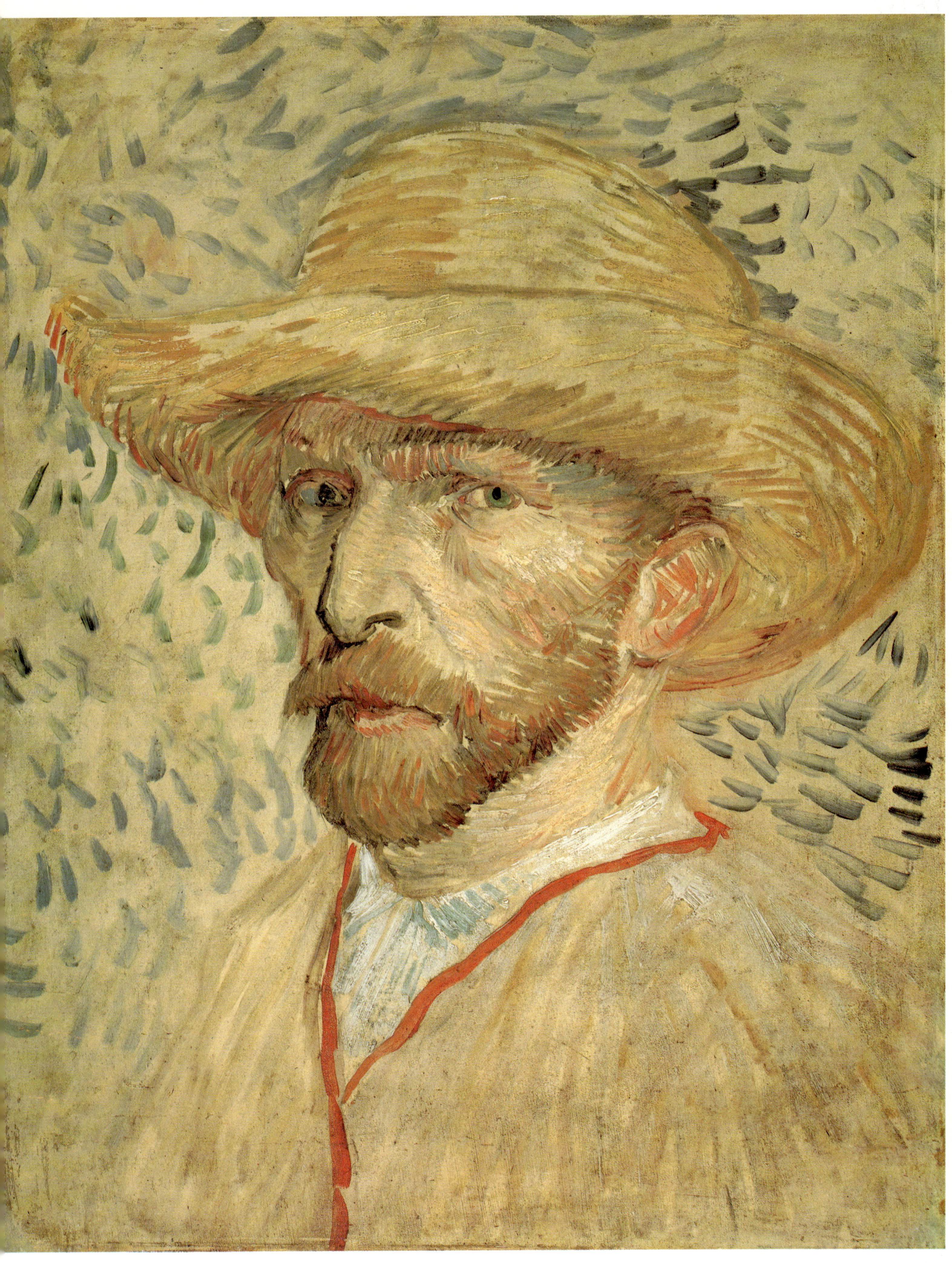

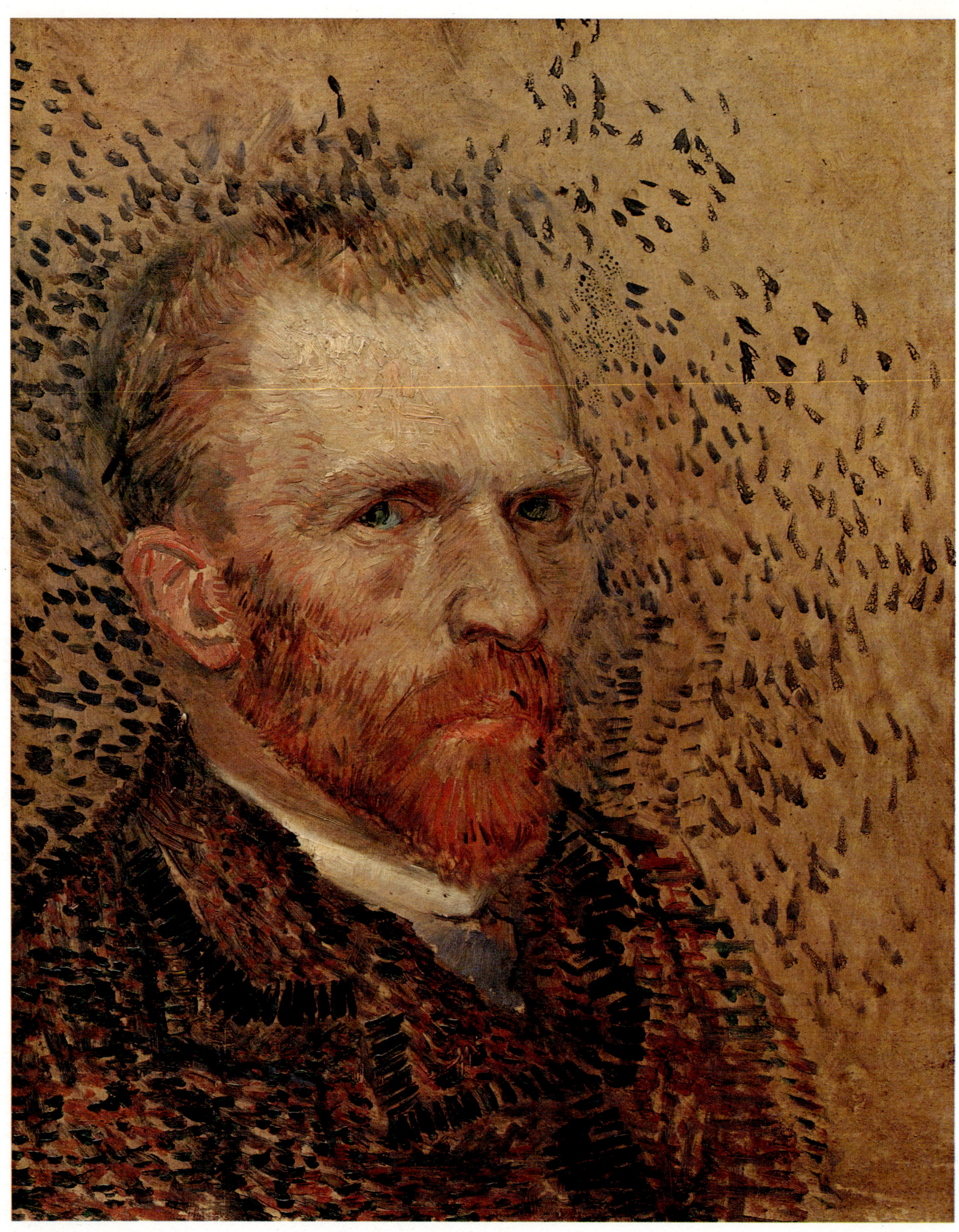

Self-Portrait

April-June 1887 - oil on canvas - 41 x 33 cm - Vincent van Gogh Foundation, Amsterdam

Self-Portrait: The Painter at Work

Winter 1887 - oil on canvas - 65 x 50.5 cm - Vincent van Gogh Foundation, Amsterdam

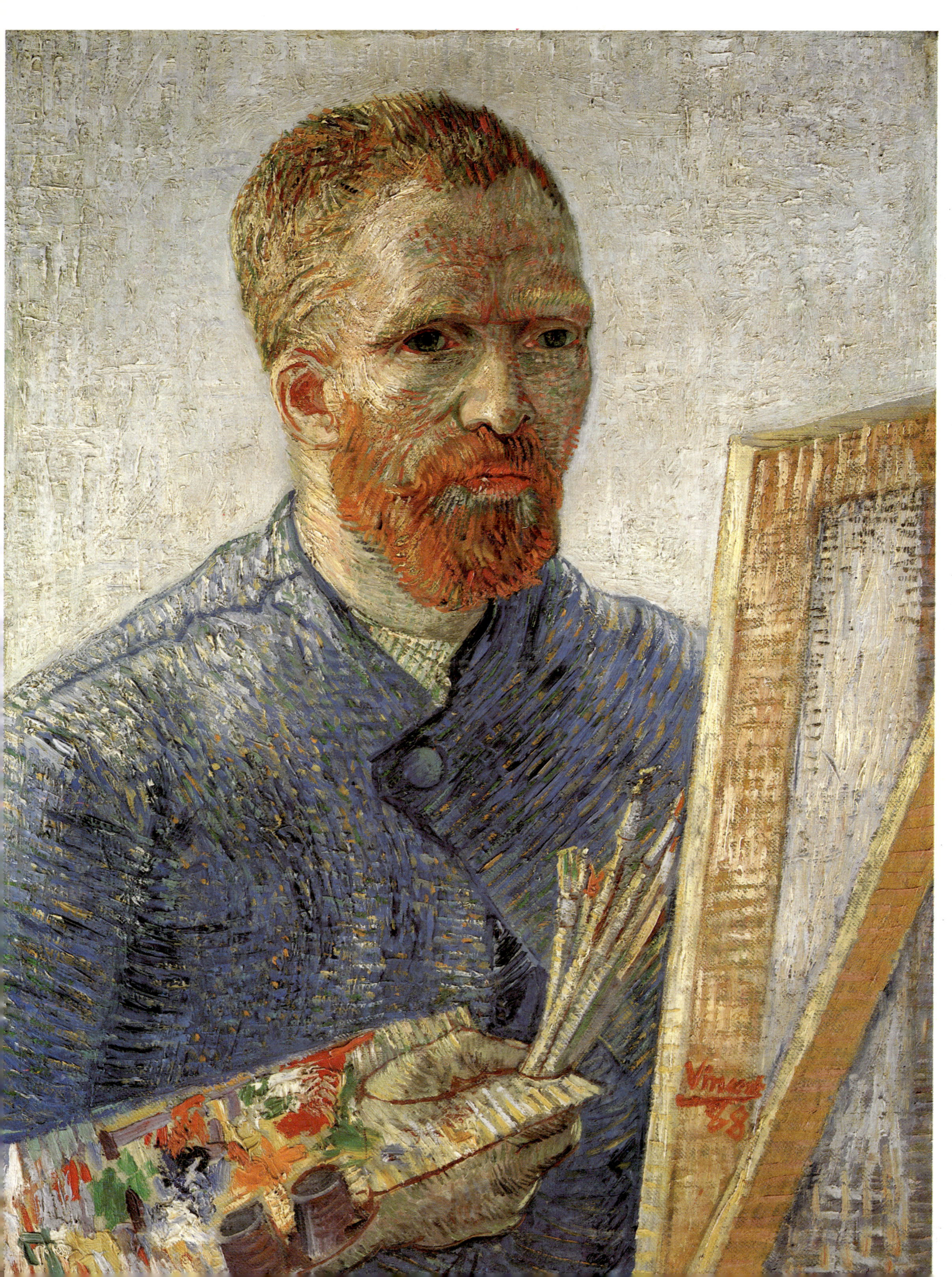
Vincent
88

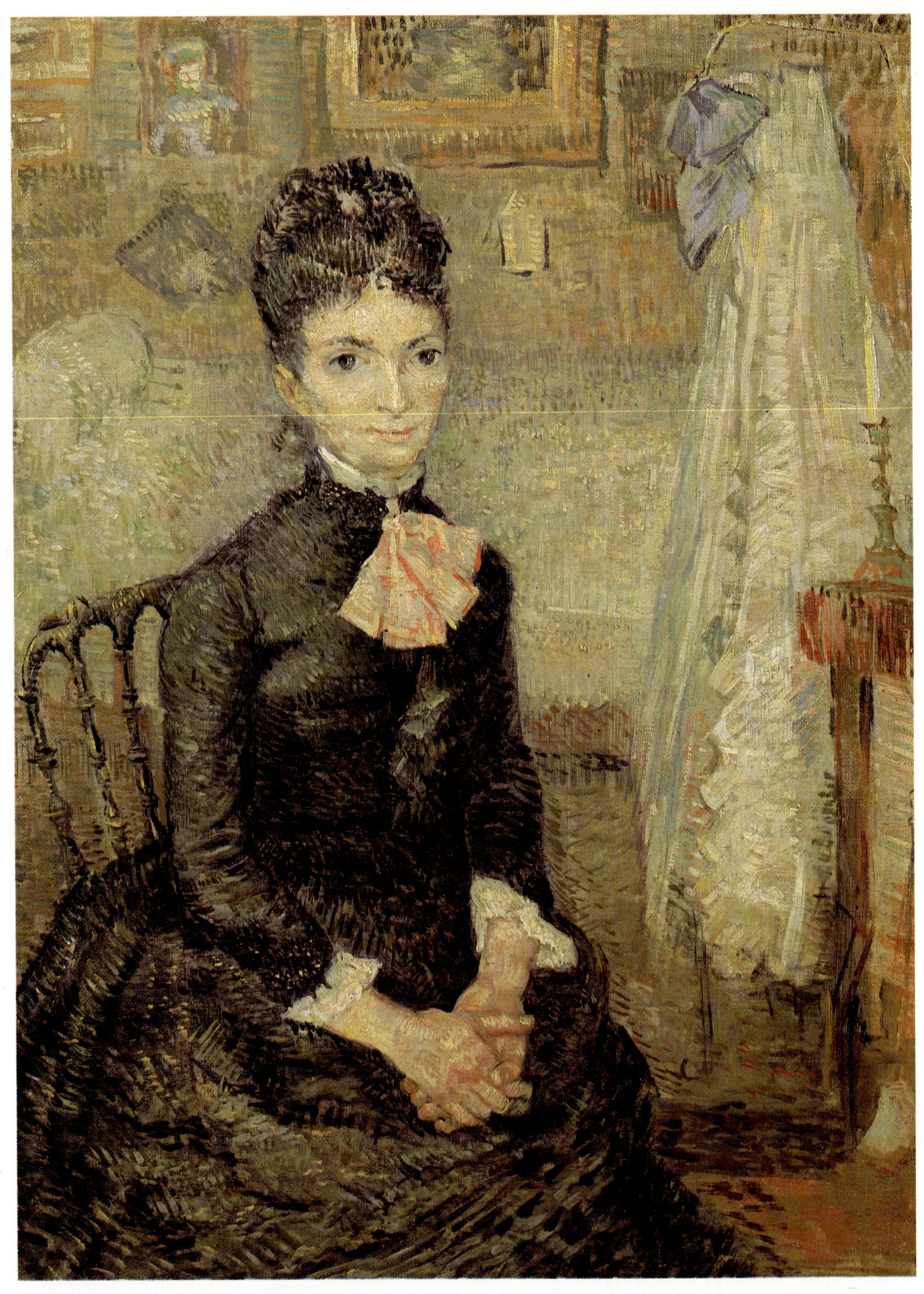

Woman Seated by a Cradle

January-March 1887 - oil on canvas - 61 x 46 cm - Vincent van Gogh Foundation, Amsterdam

Portrait of père Tanguy

Winter 1887-1888 - oil on canvas - 492 x 75 cm - Musée Rodin, Paris

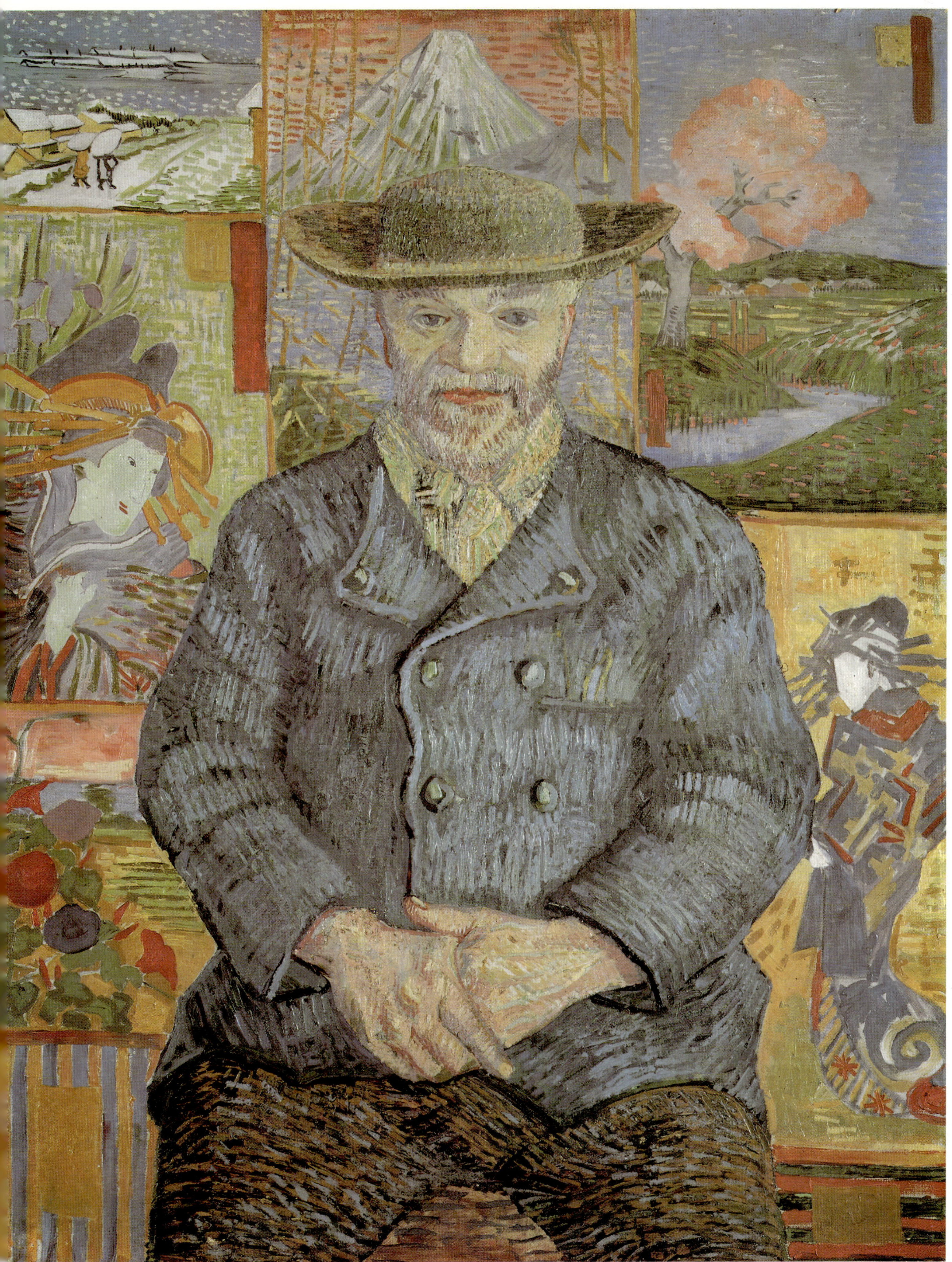

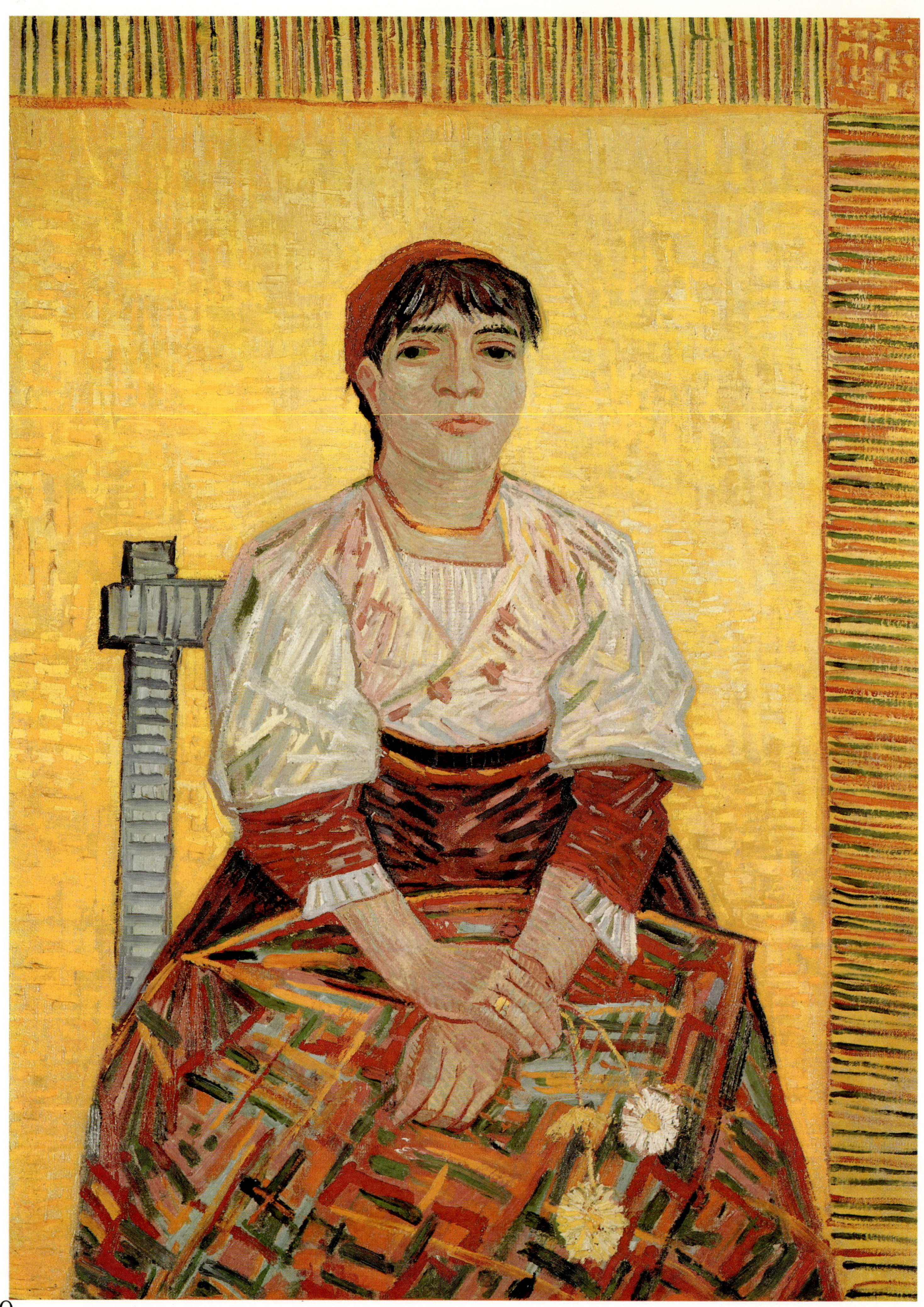

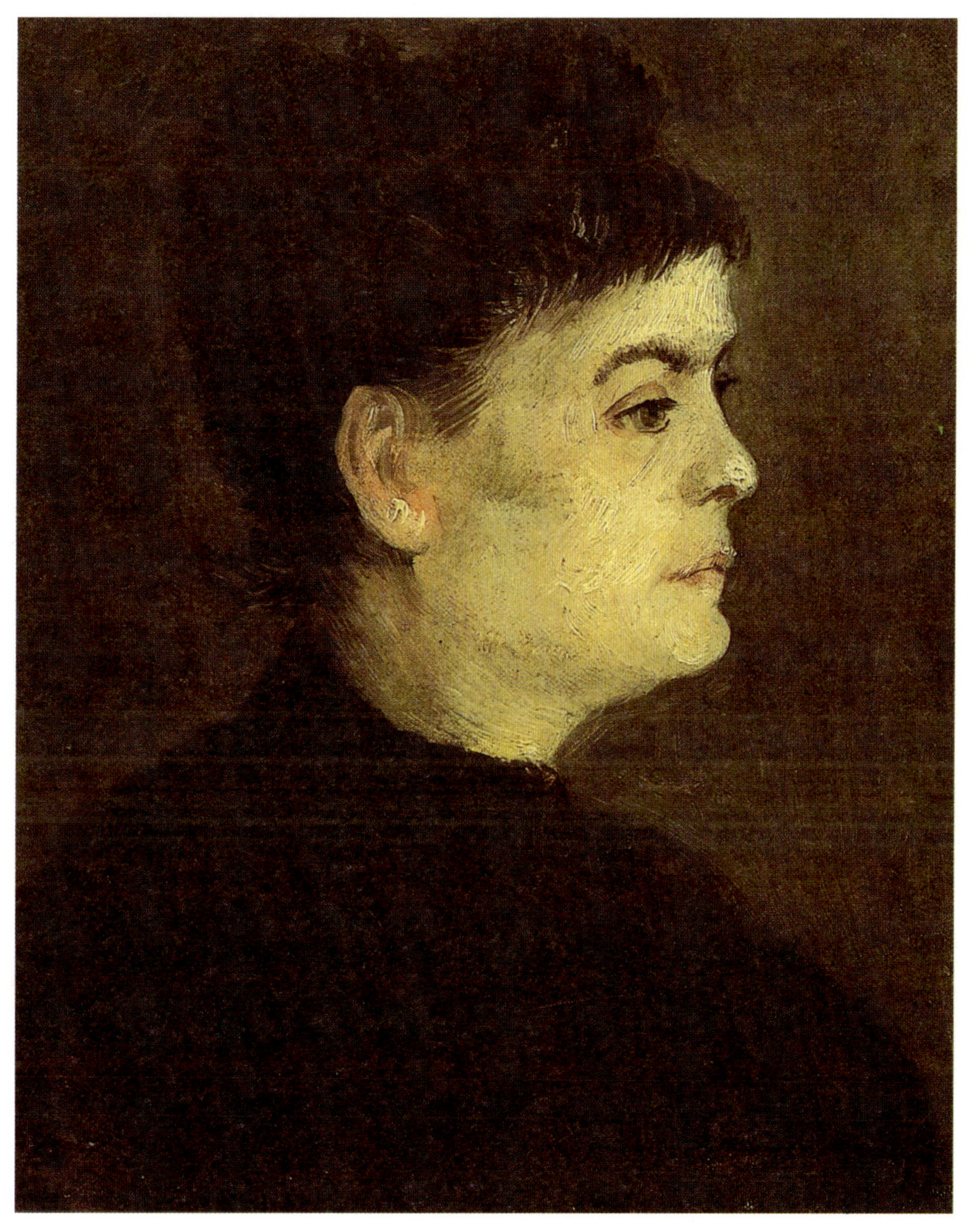

Portrait of a Woman

Winter 1886-1887 - oil on canvas - 27 x 22 cm - Vincent van Gogh Foundation, Amsterdam (attribution doubtful)

Italian Woman: la Segatori

Winter 1887-1888 - oil on canvas - 81 x 60 cm - Musée d'orsay, Paris

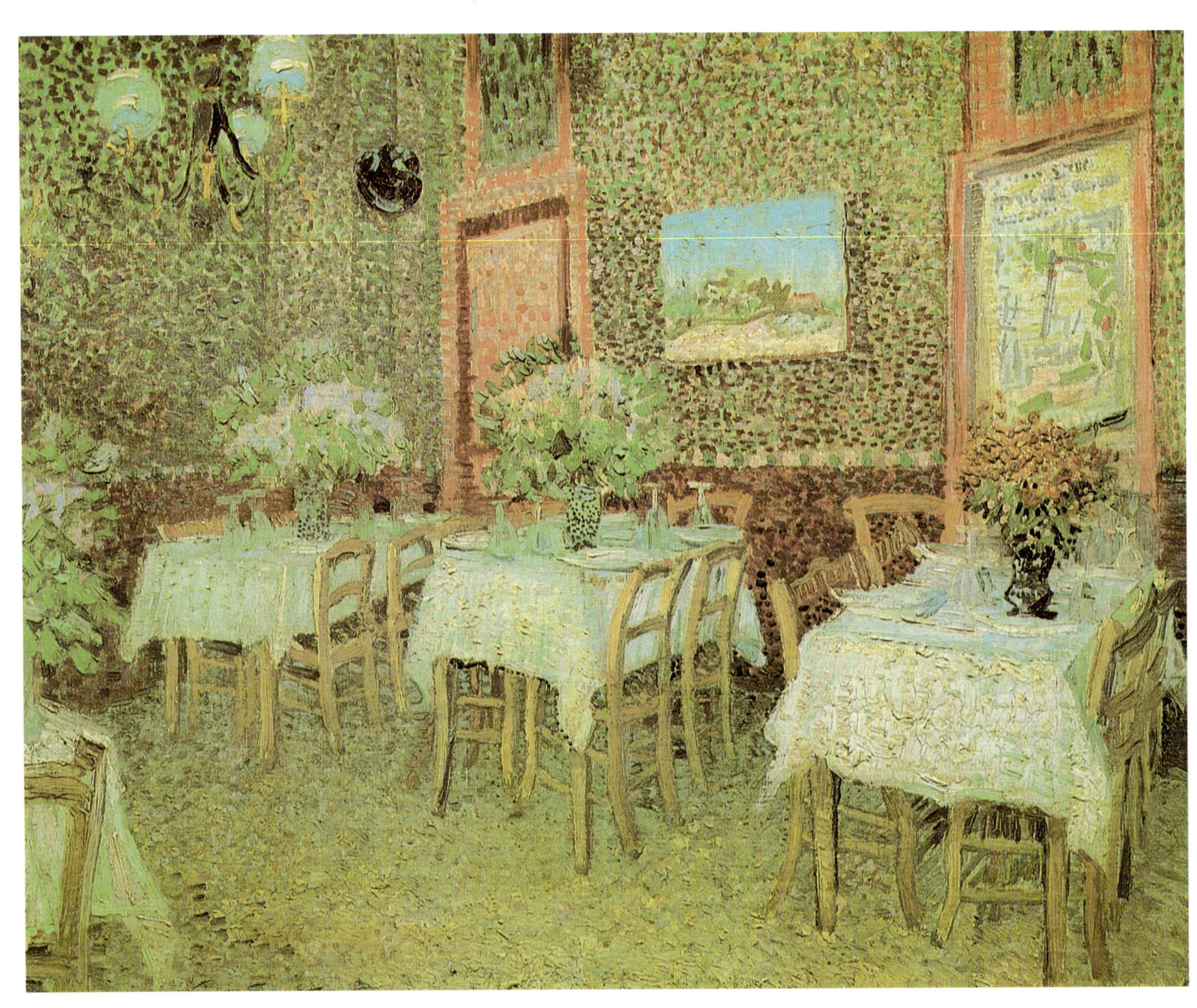

Interior of a Restaurant

April-June 1887 - oil on canvas - 45.5 x 56.5 cm - Rijksmuseum Kröller- Müller, Otterlo

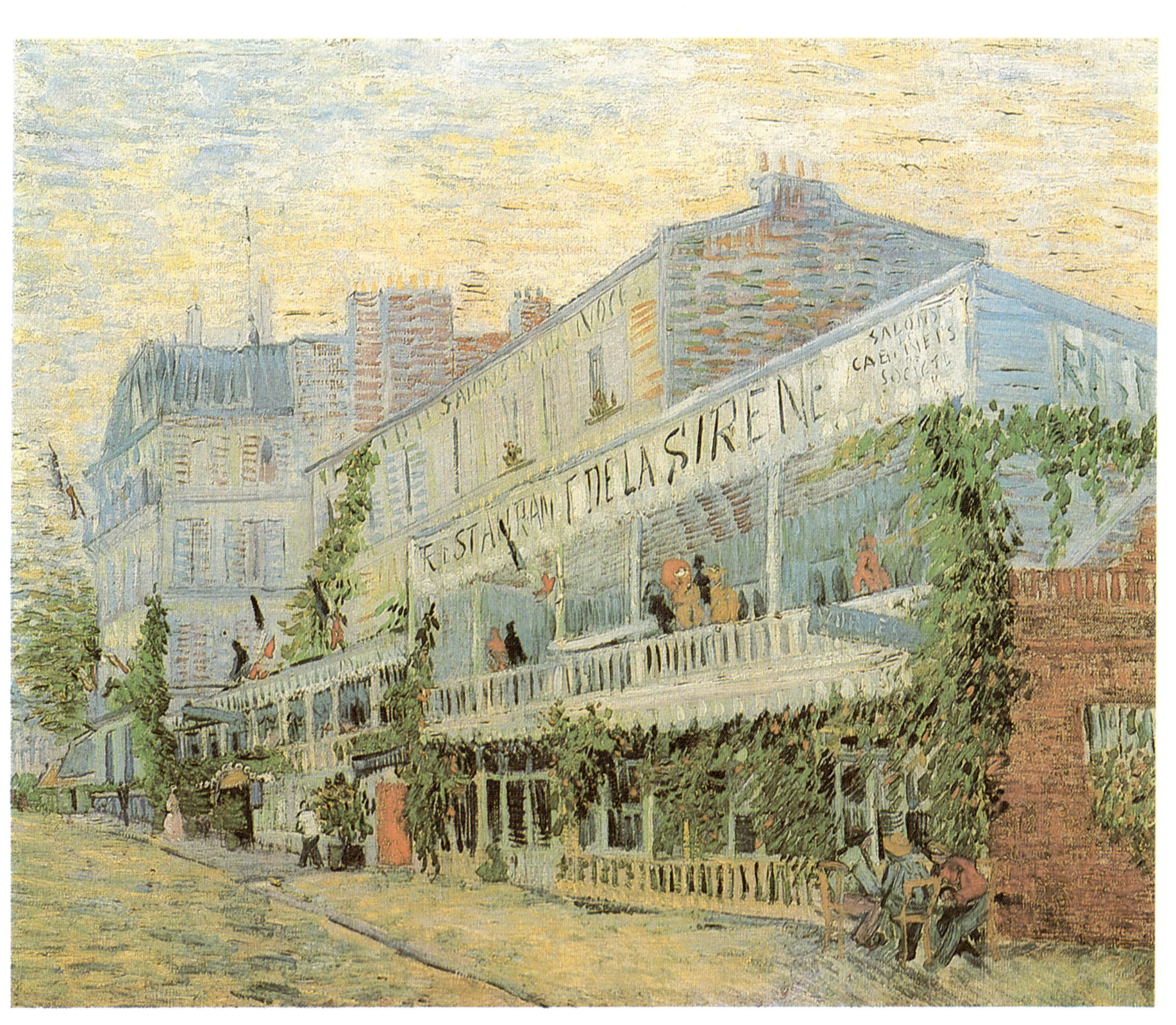

Restaurant de la Sirène at Asnières

April-June 1887 - oil on canvas - 54 x 65 cm -
Musée d'Orsay, Paris

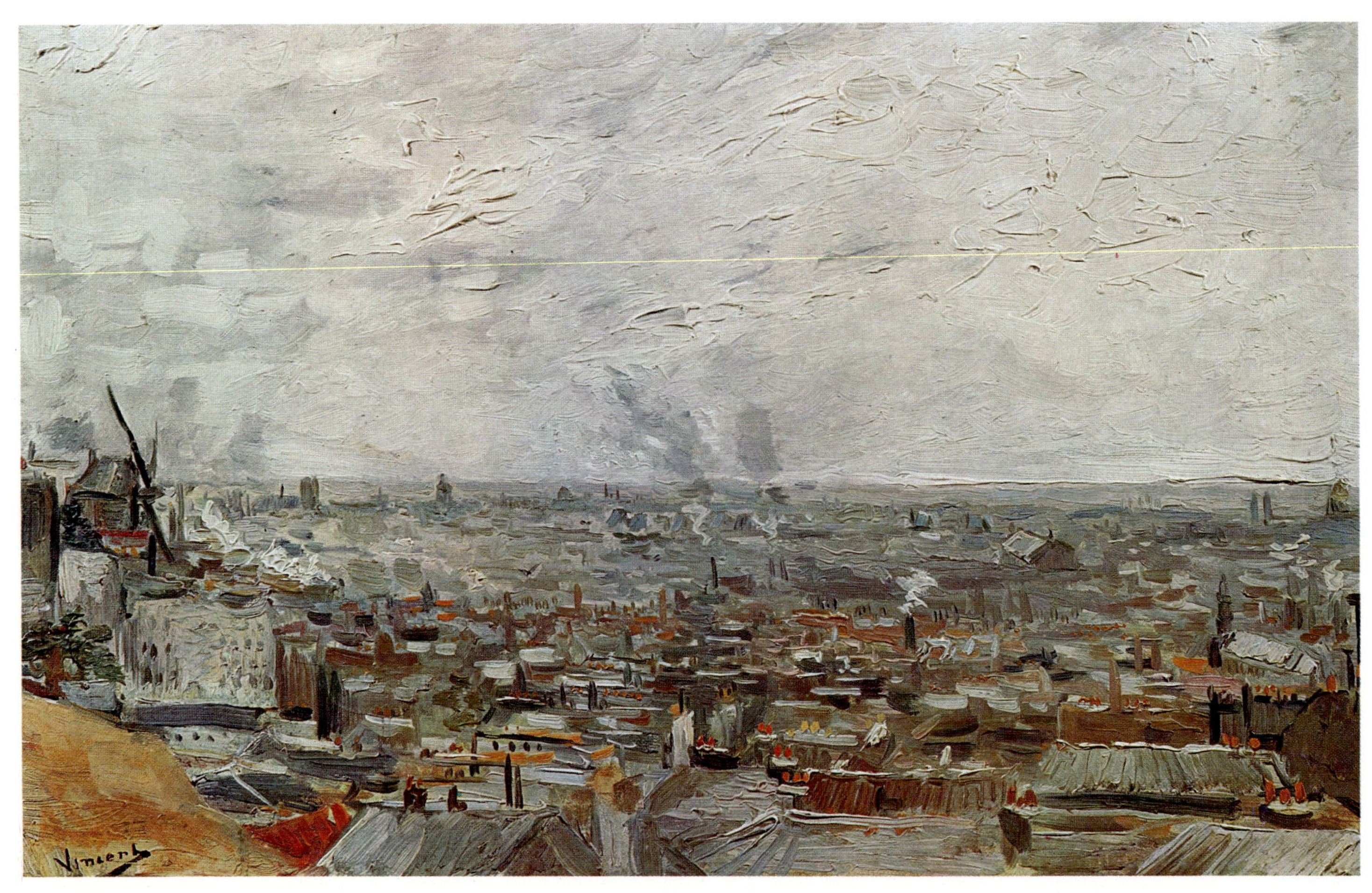

View of Paris

1887 - oil on canvas - 37.5 x 61.5 cm - Kunstmuseum, Basle

Photograph of Boulevard Clichy

Boulevard de Clichy

1887 - oil on canvas - 46.5 x 55 cm - Vincent van Gogh Foundation, Amsterdam

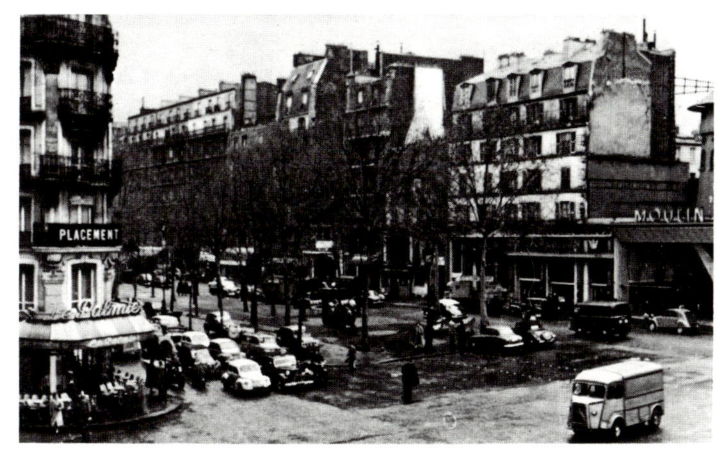
PLACEMENT
MOULIN

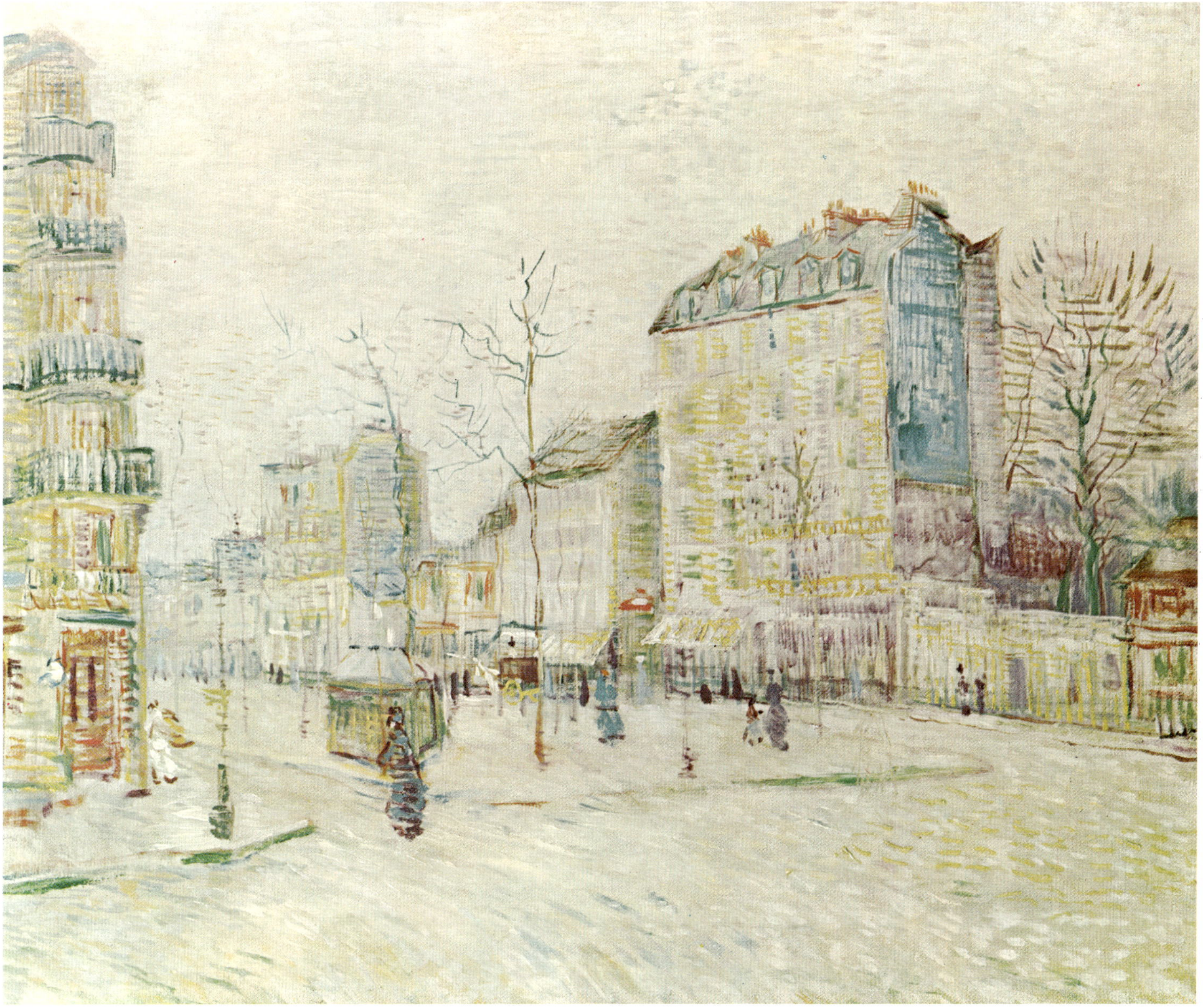

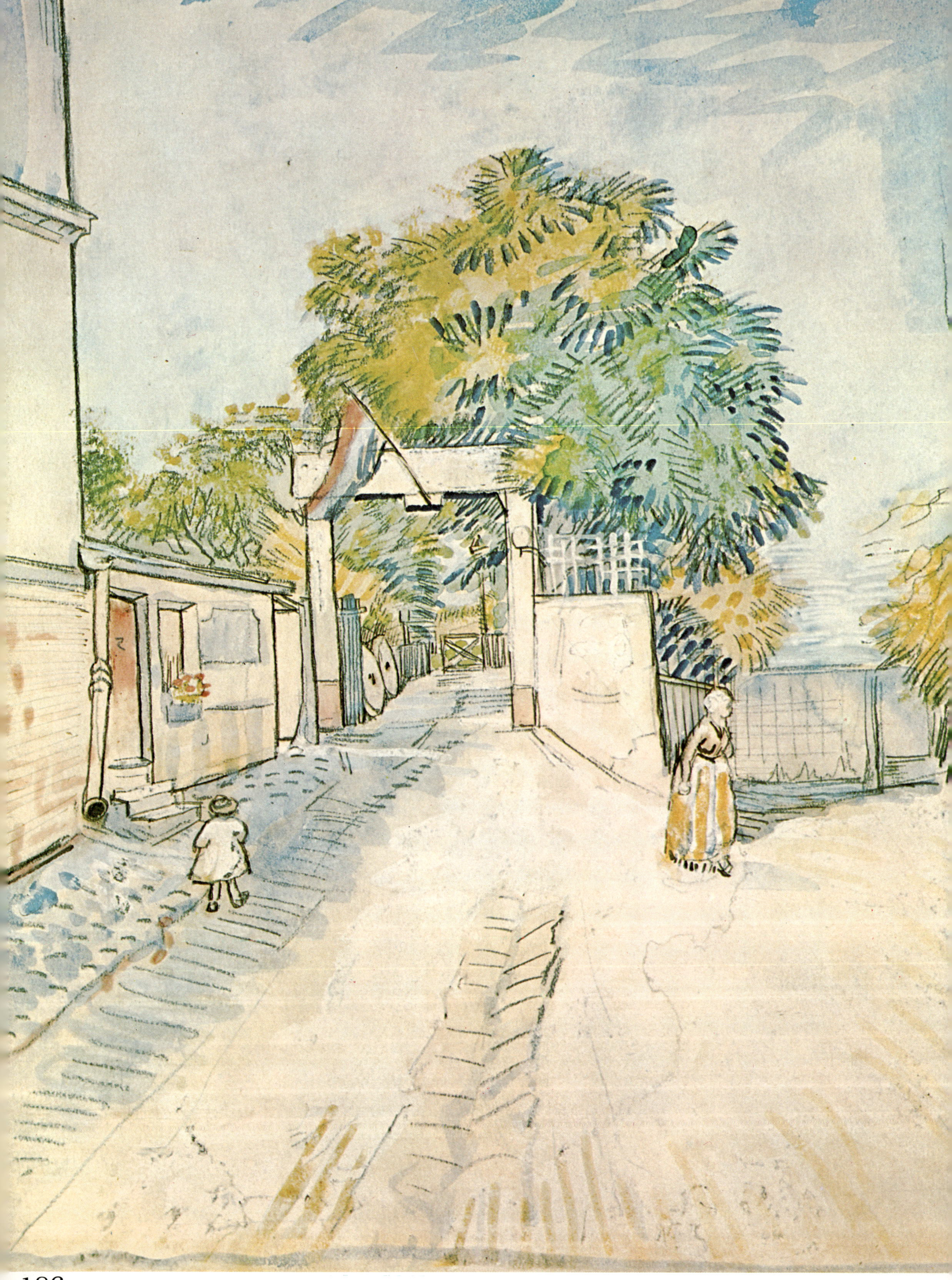

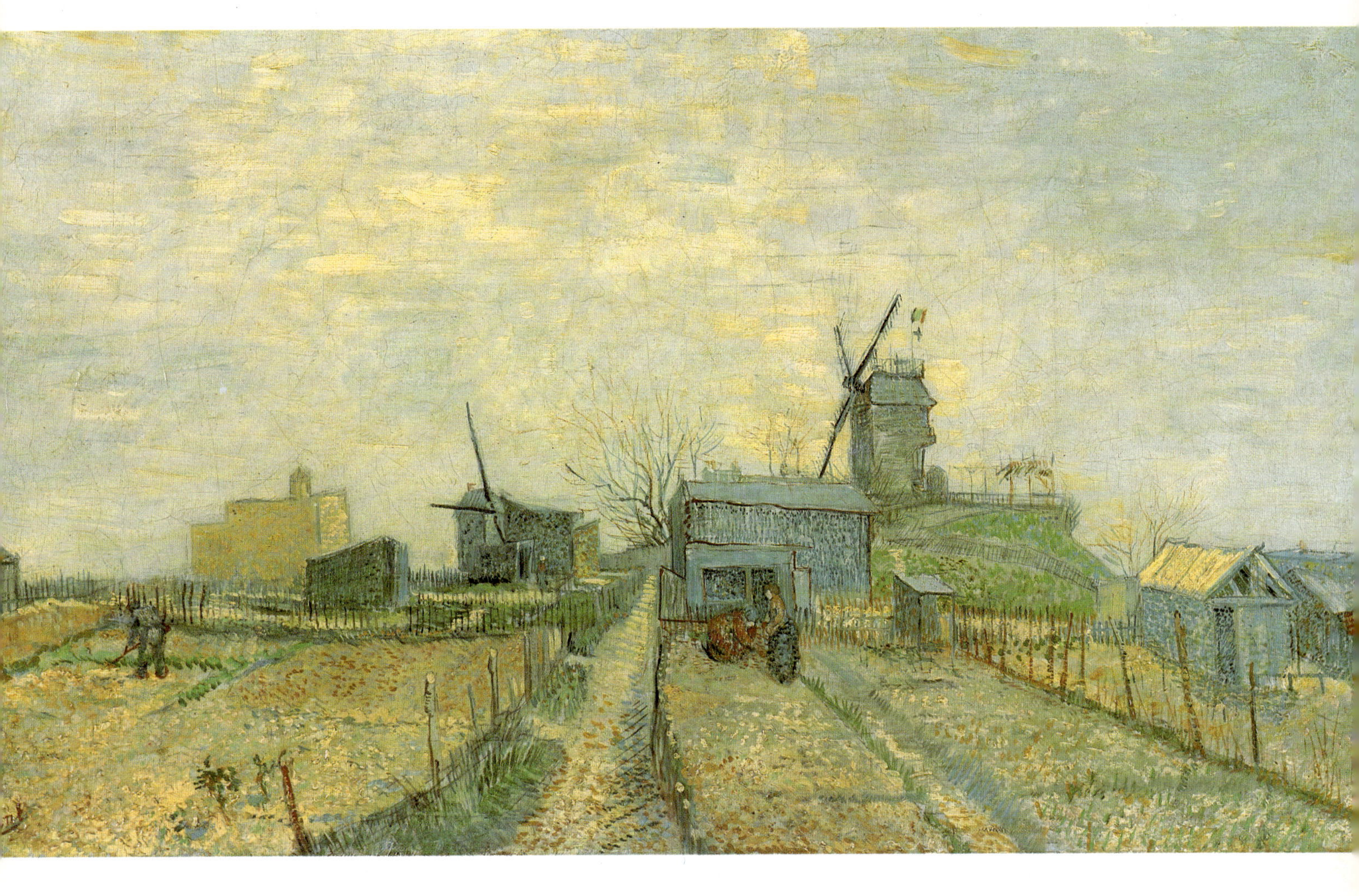

Vegetable Gardens in Montmartre

April-June 1887 - oil on canvas - 43 x 80 cm -
Vincent van Gogh Foundation, Amsterdam

Sunny Day (14th of July)

1887 - crayon, pen, watercolour and gouache - 31 x 24 cm -
Vincent van Gogh Foundation, Amsterdam

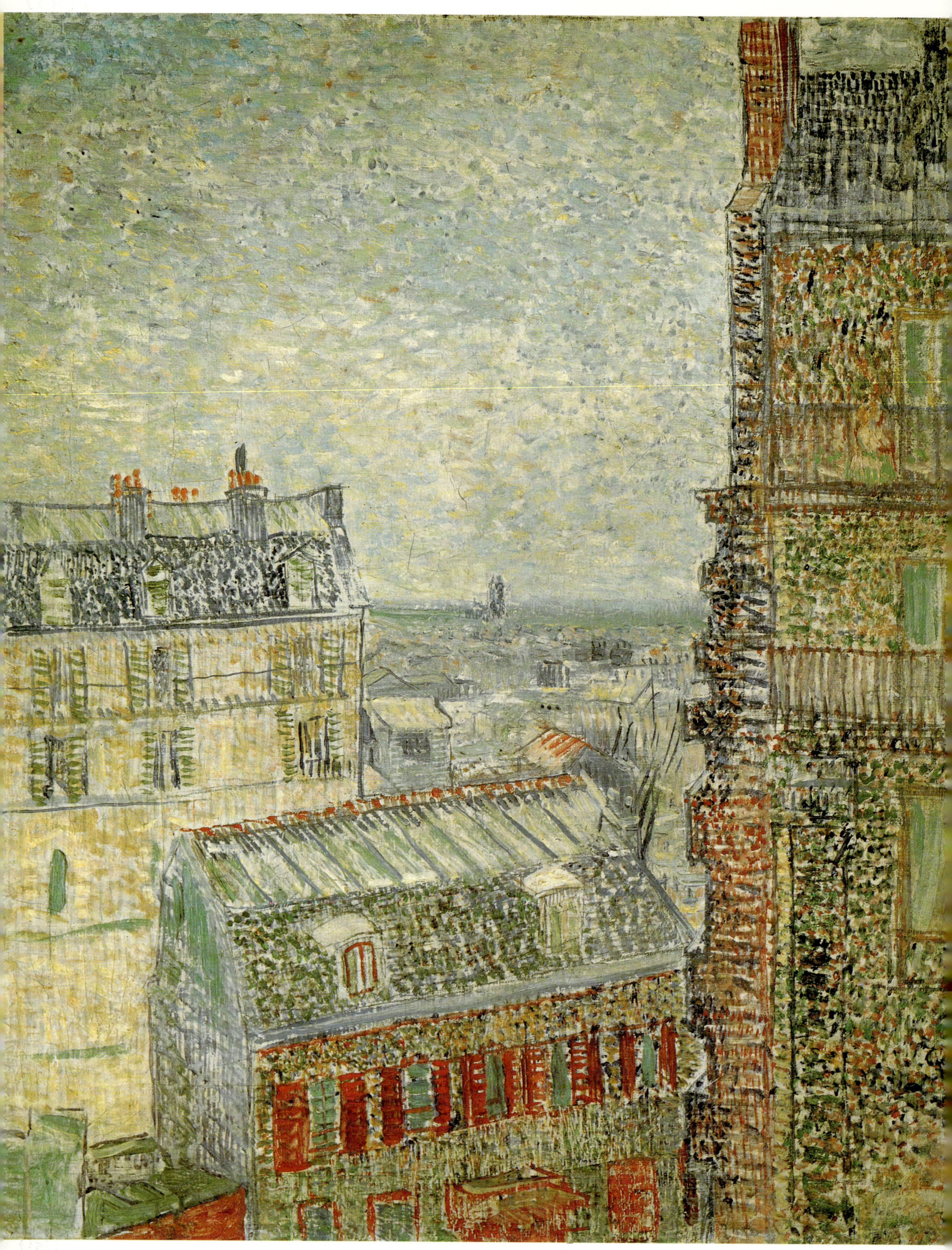

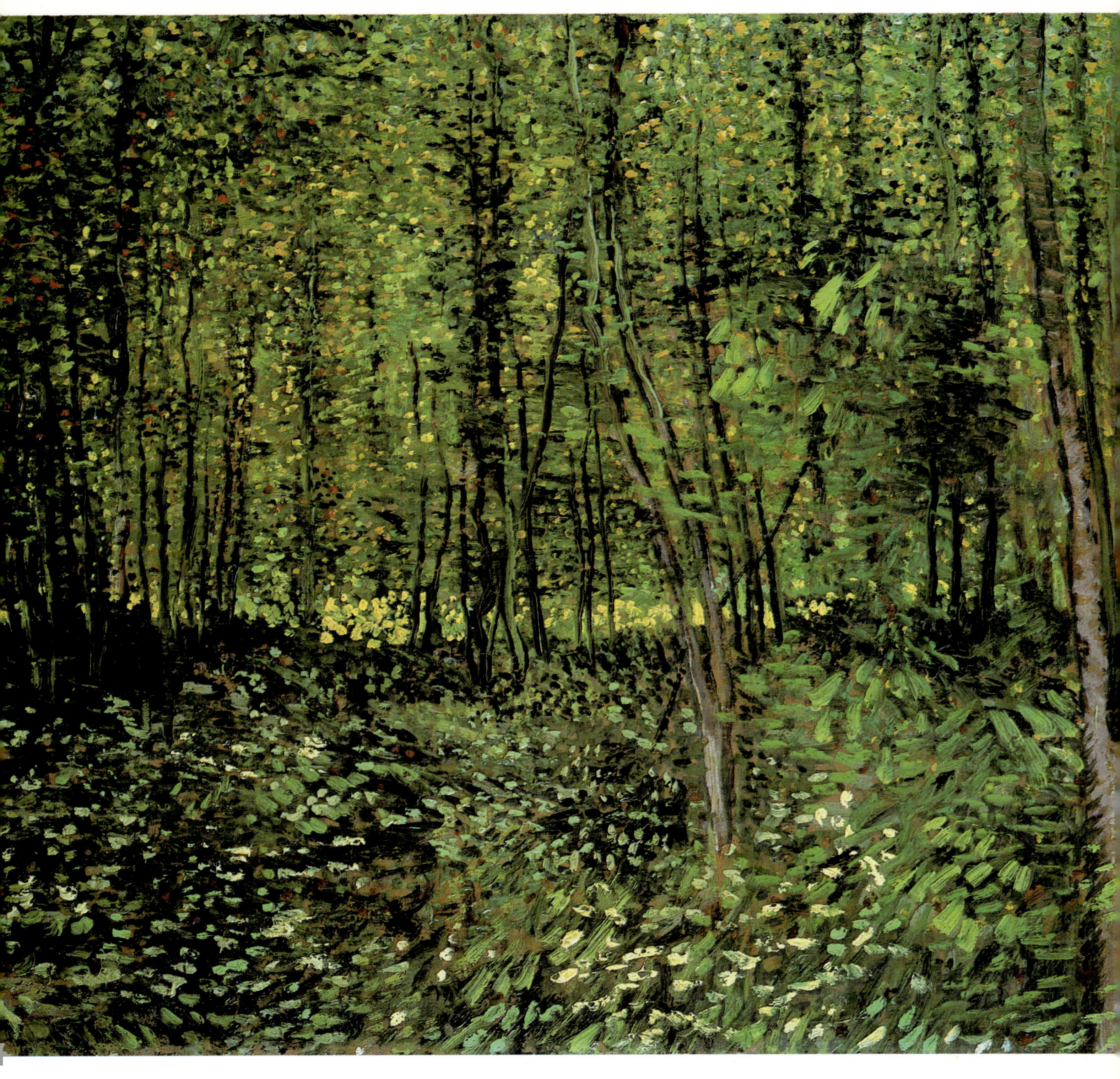

Trees and Undergrowth

April-June 1887 - oil on canvas - 46 x 55.5 cm -
Vincent van Gogh Foundation, Amsterdam

View of Paris from Van Gogh's Room in the rue Lepic

April-June 1887 - oil on canvas - 46 x 38 cm -
Vincent van Gogh Foundation, Amsterdam

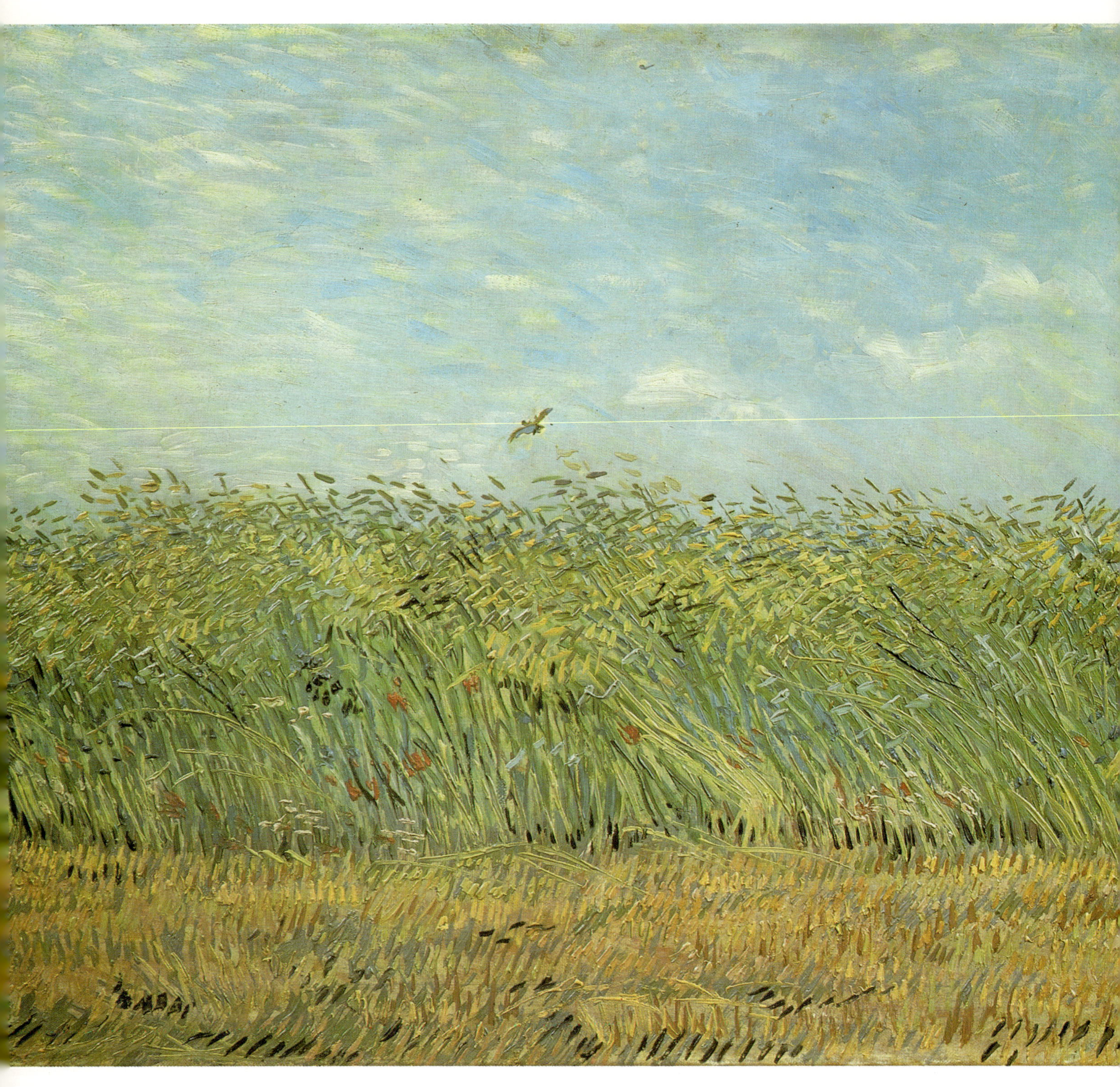

Field of Wheat

April-June 1887 - oil on canvas - 54 x 64.5 cm -
Vincent van Gogh Foundation, Amsterdam

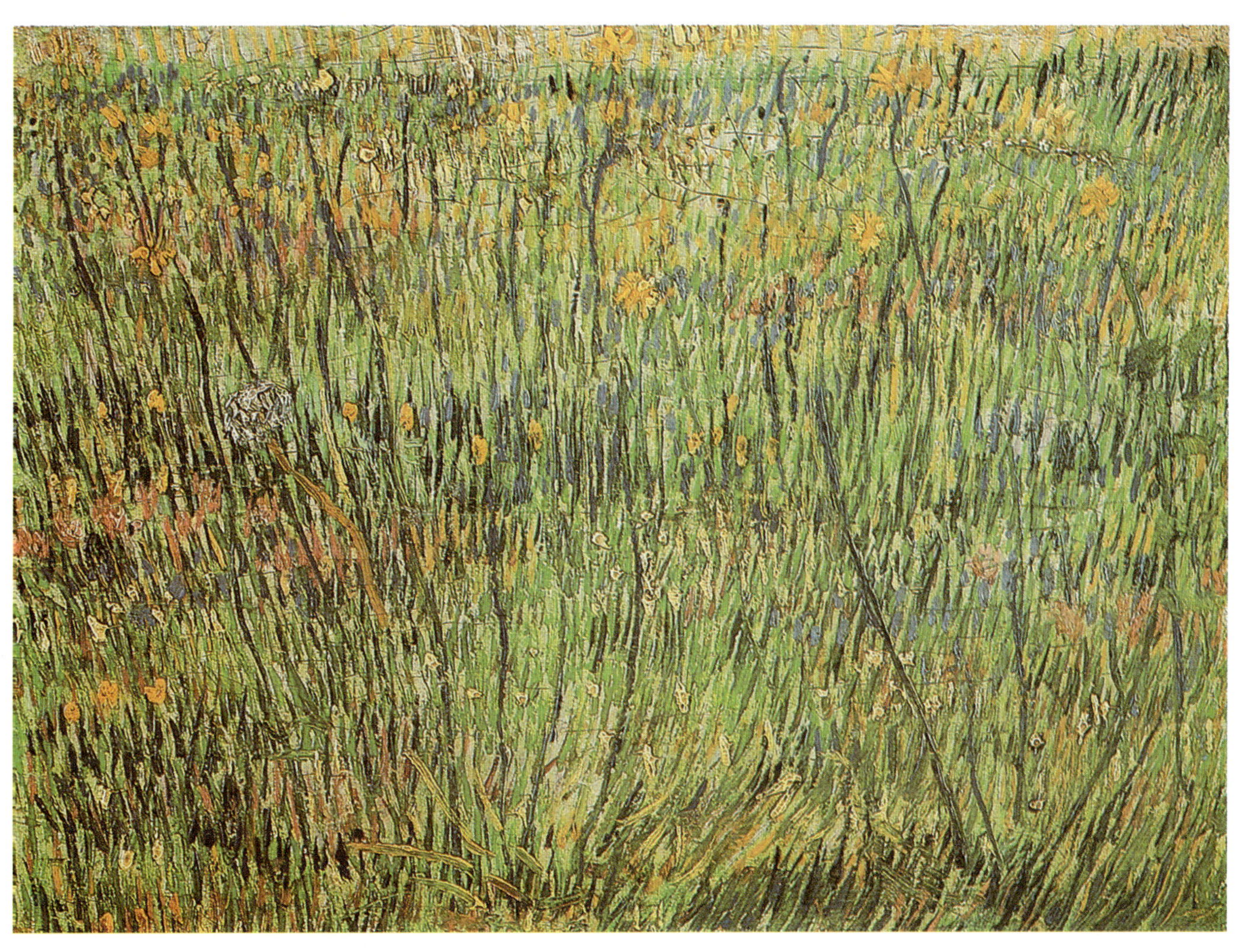

Pasture in Bloom

Spring 1887 - oil on canvas - 31.5 x 40.5 cm - Rijksmusueum Kröller- Müller, Otterlo

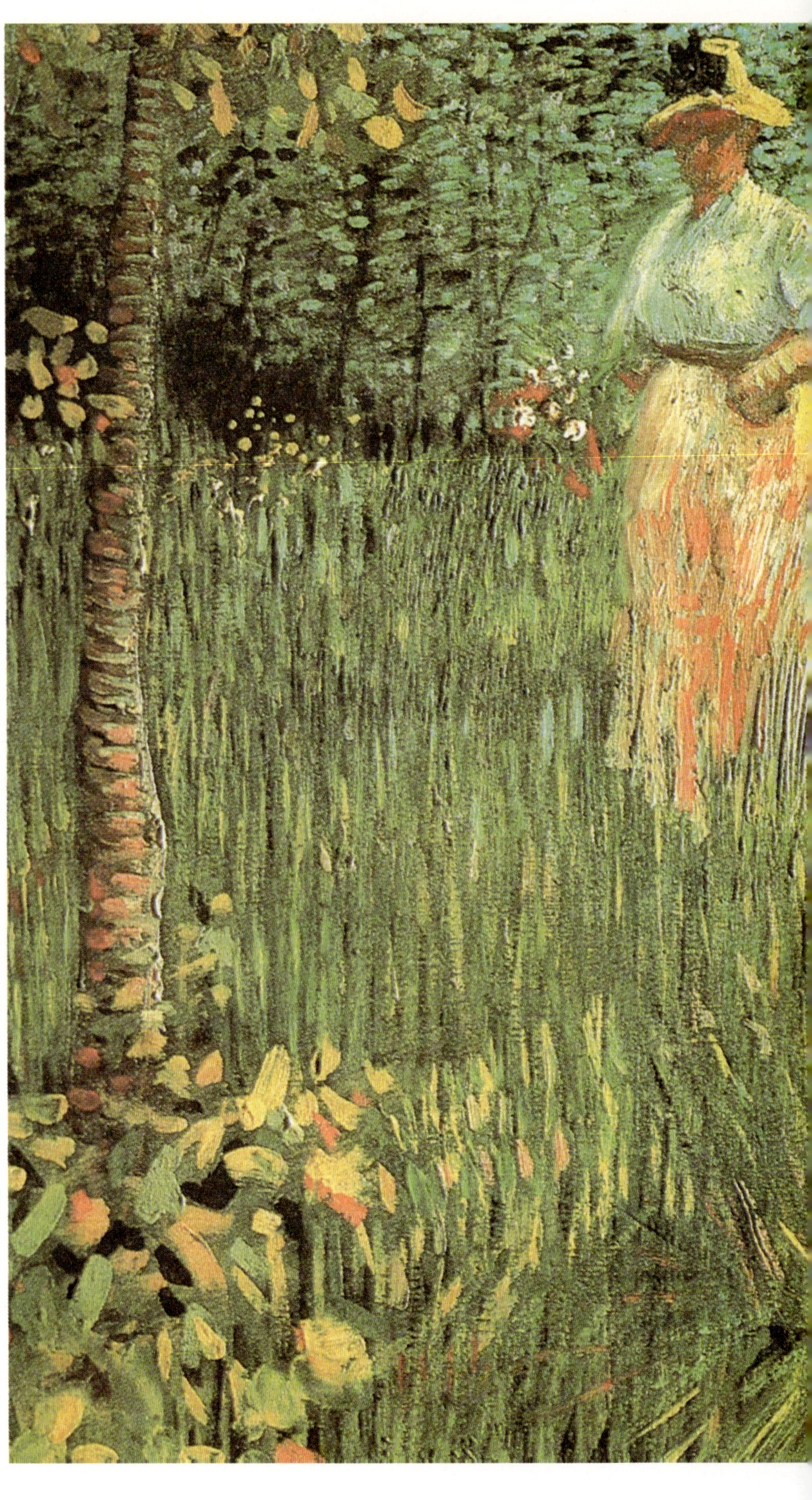

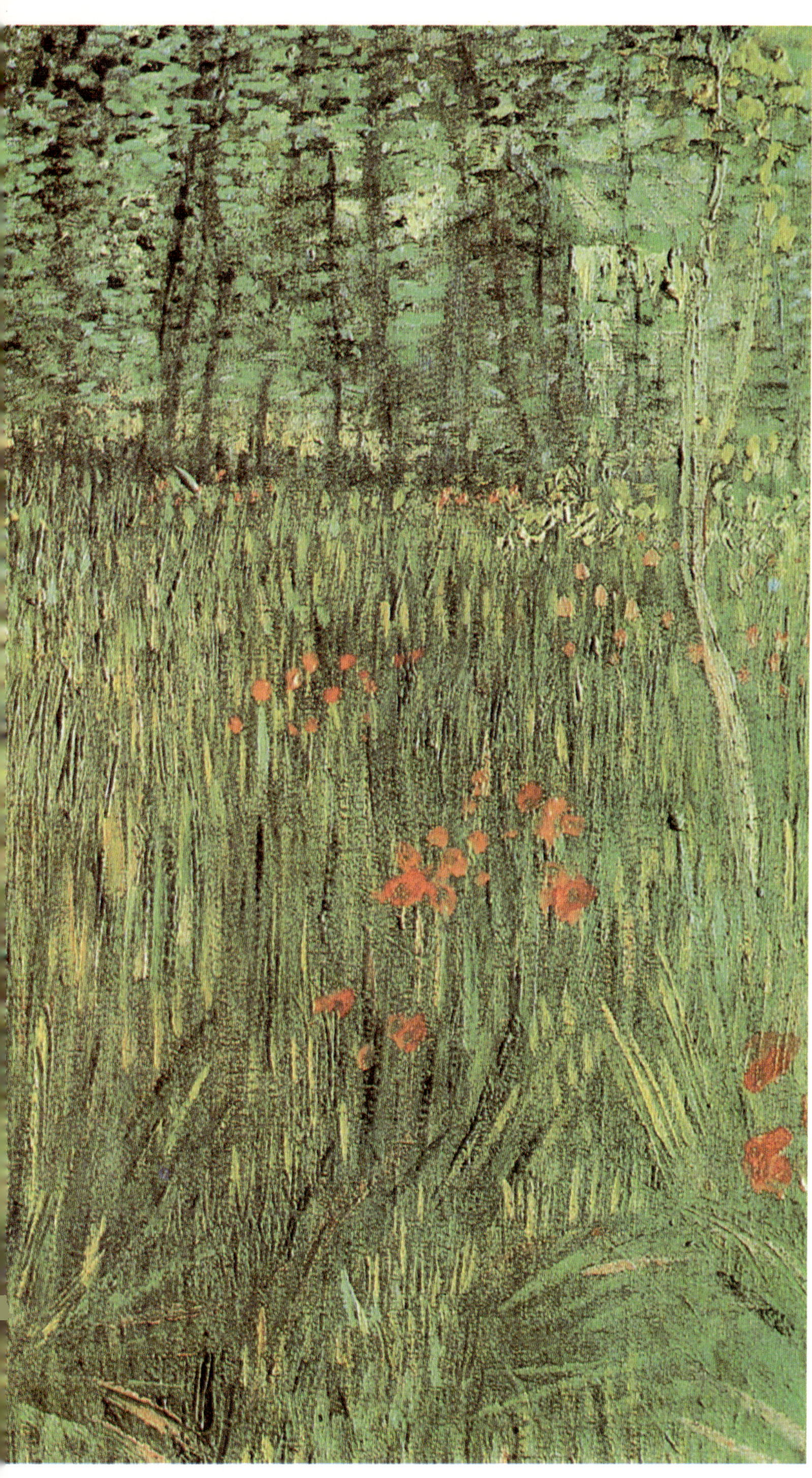

Woman Walking in a Garden

June-July 1887 - oil on canvas - 58 x 60 cm - E.J. Bowes collection, USA.

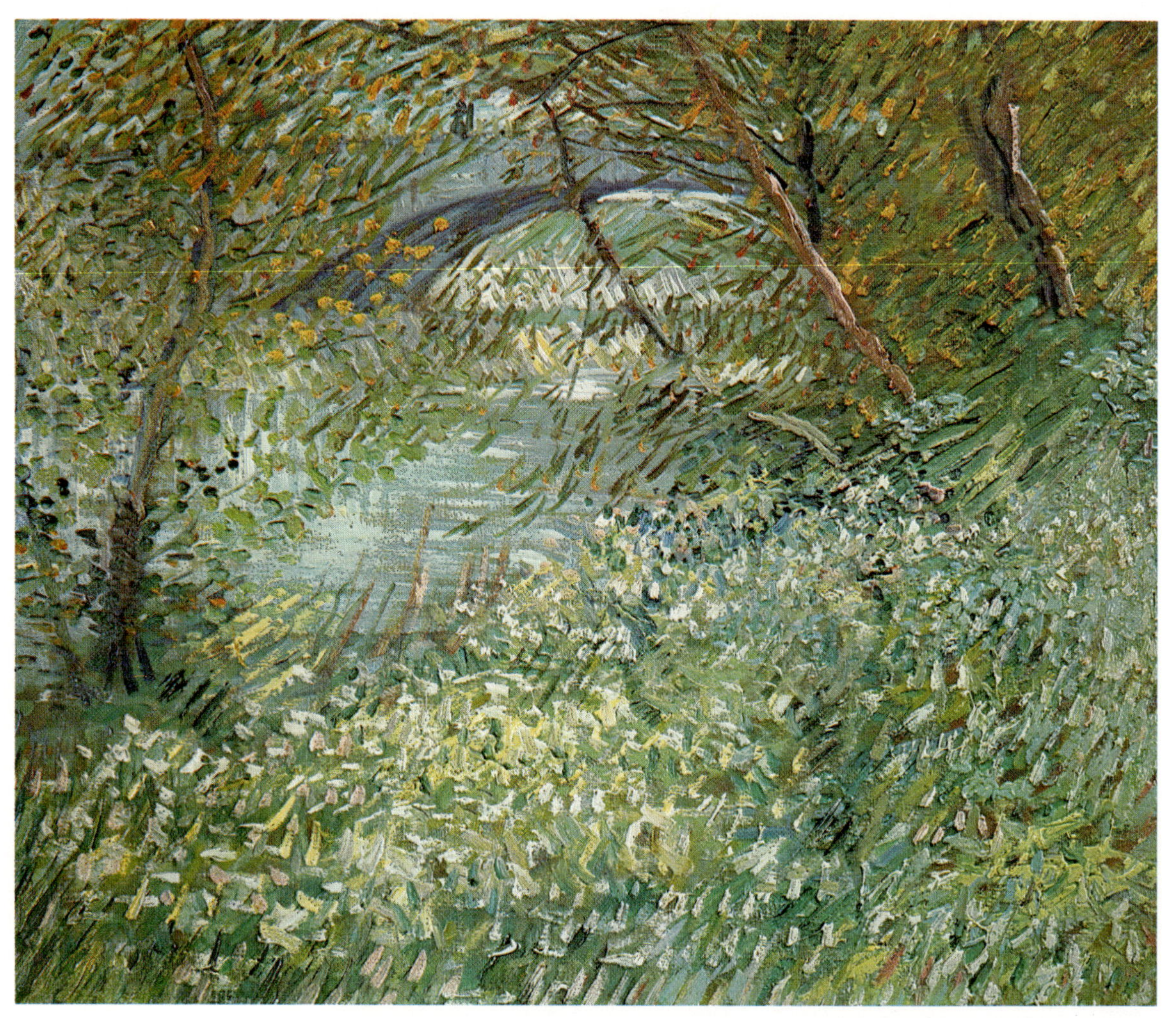

River Bank in Springtime

1887 - oil on canvas - 50 x 60 cm -
Private collection, Paris

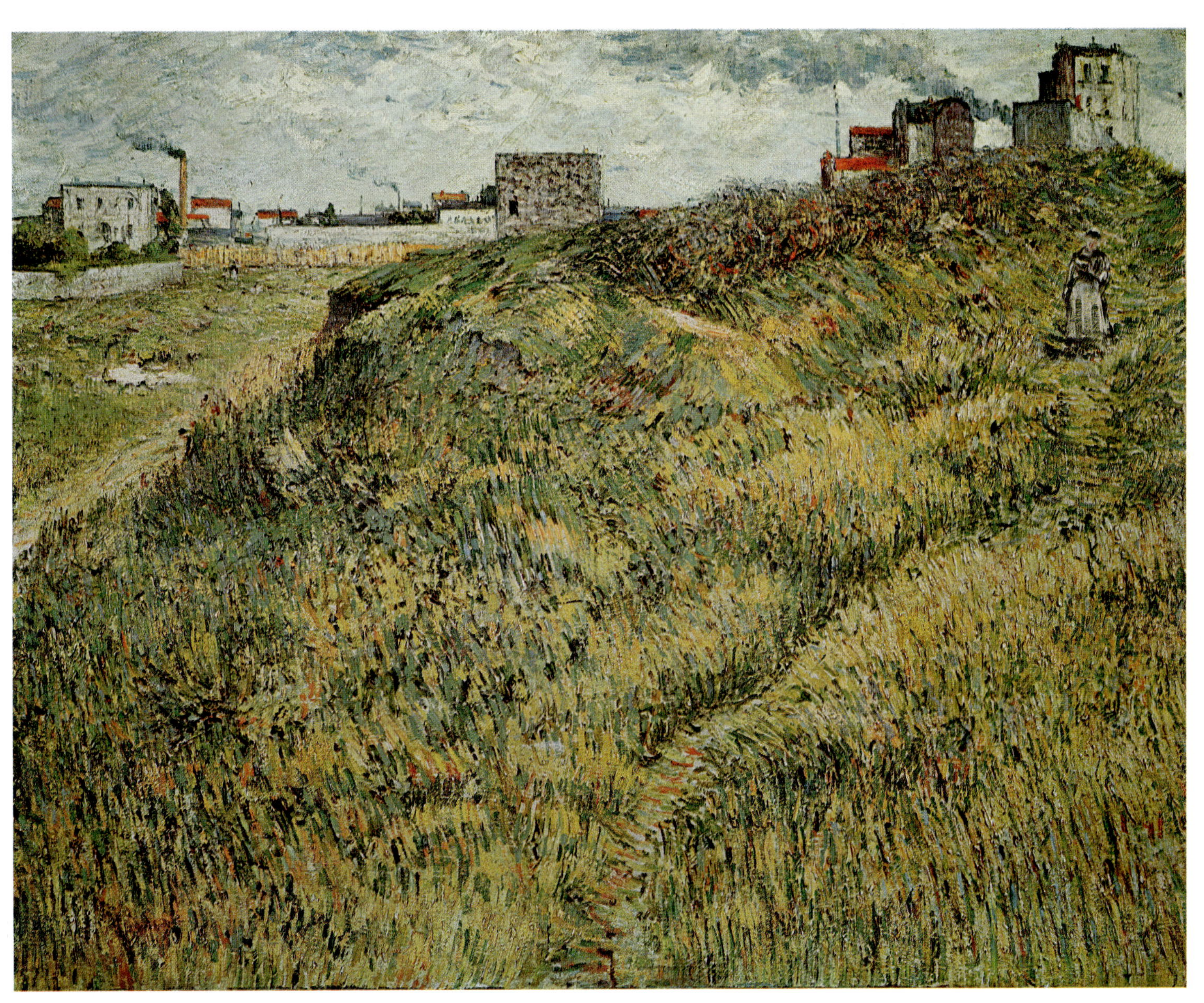

Countryside near Paris

Early September 1887 - oil on canvas - 73 x 92 cm - Private collection, Basle, Switzerland

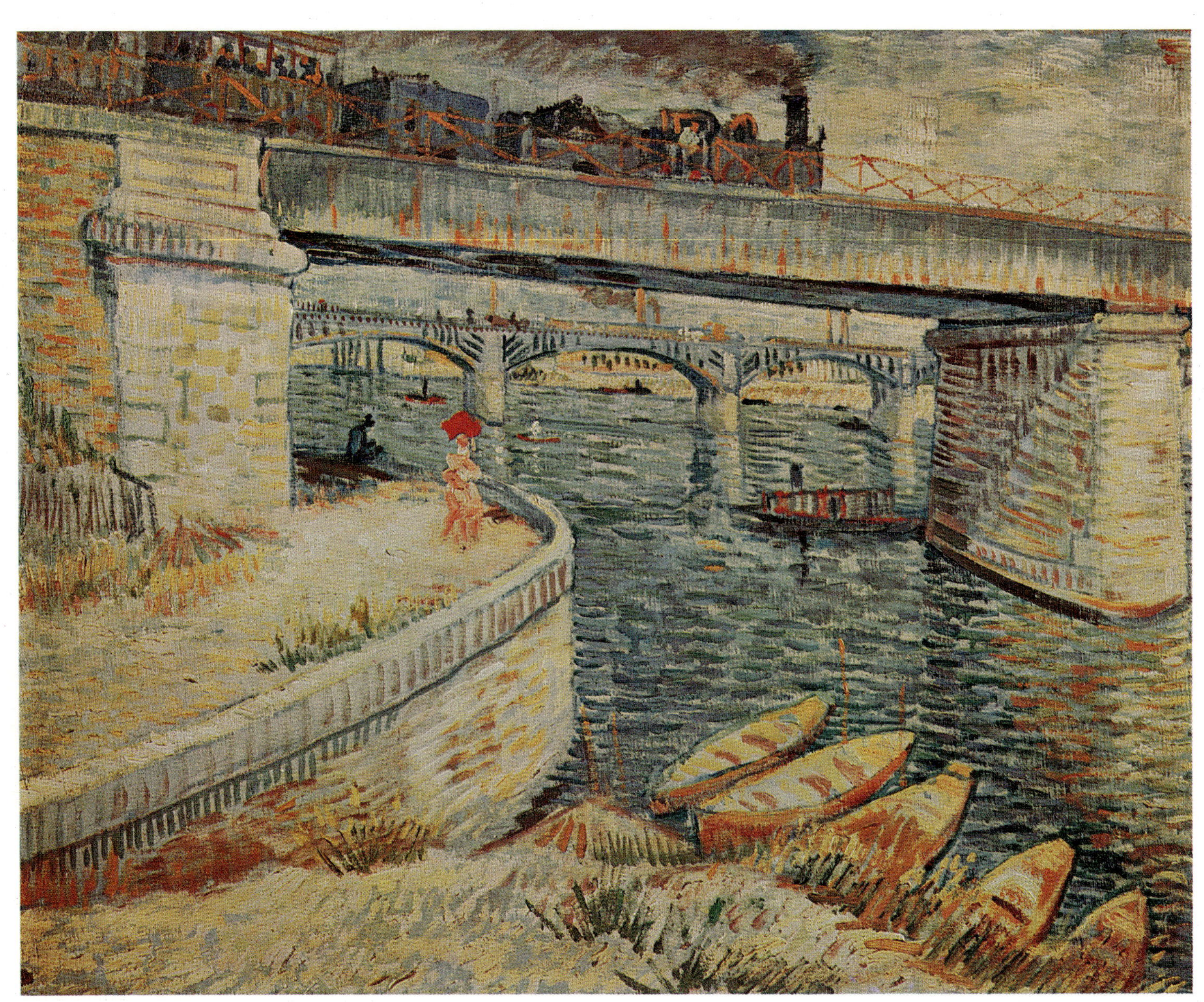

The Pont d'Asnières

1887 - oil on canvas - 52 x 65 cm -
C. Bührle collection, Zurich, Switzerland

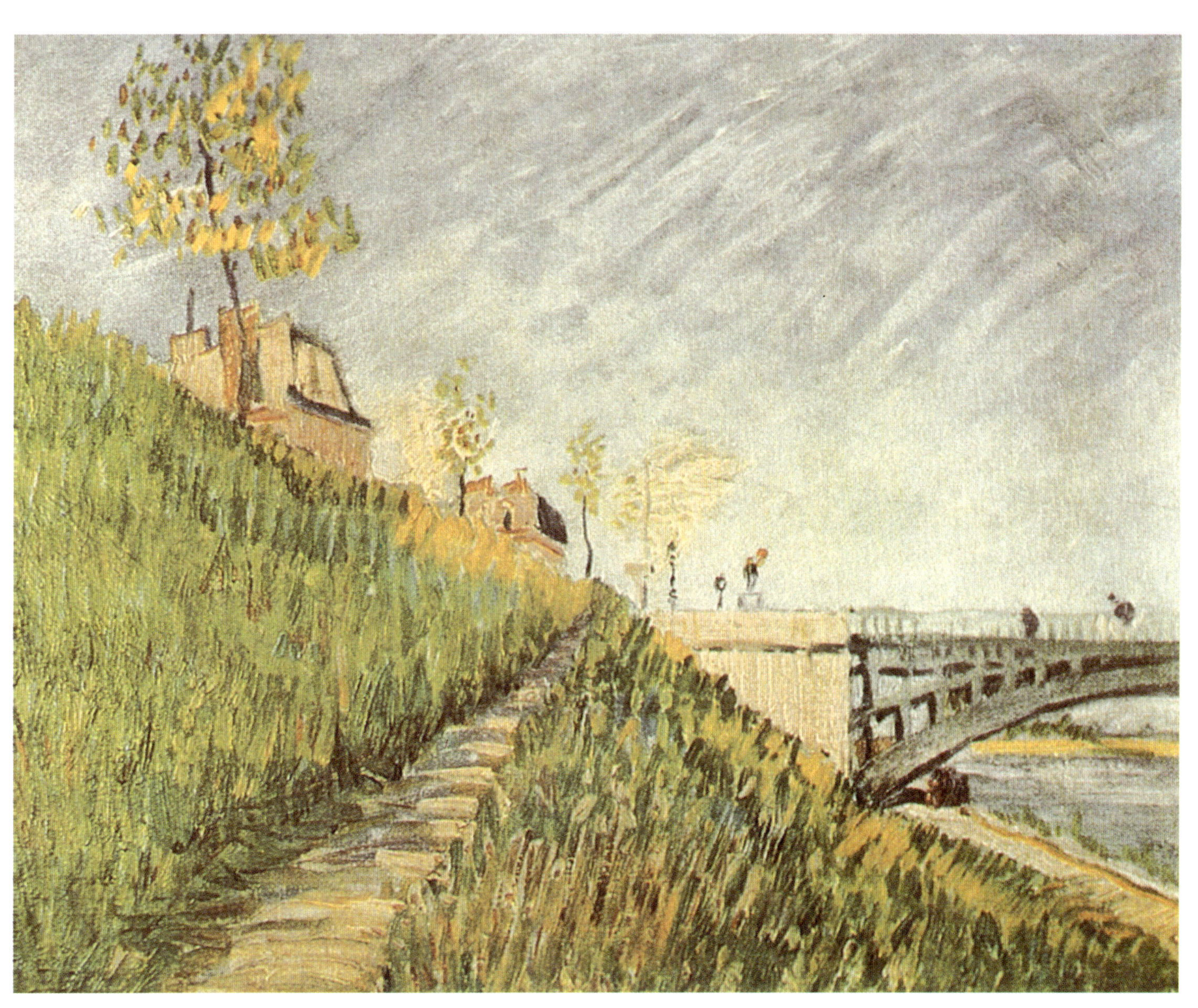

The Pont Clichy

Summer 1887 - oil on cardboard - 30.5 x 39 -
Stavros S. Niarchos Collection

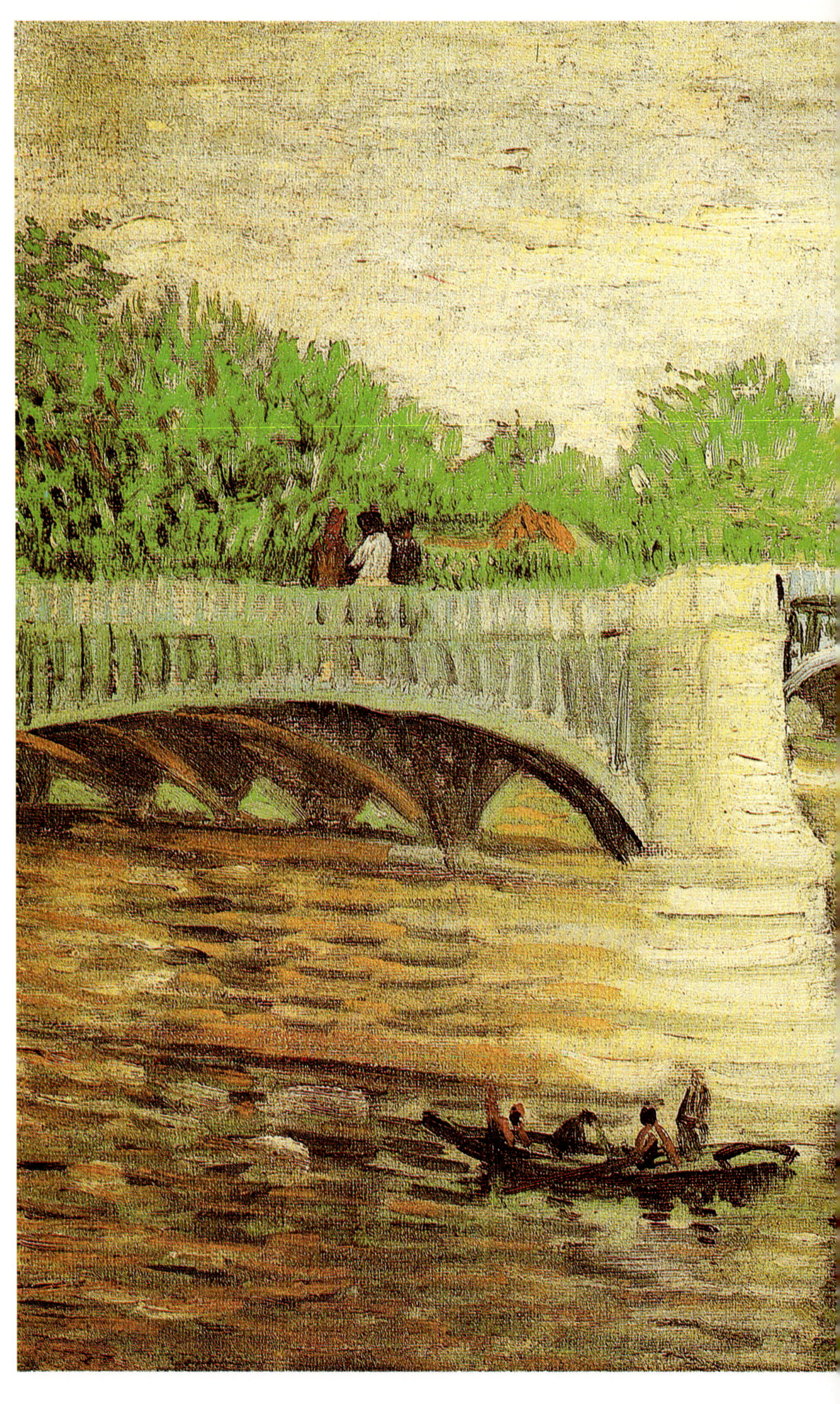

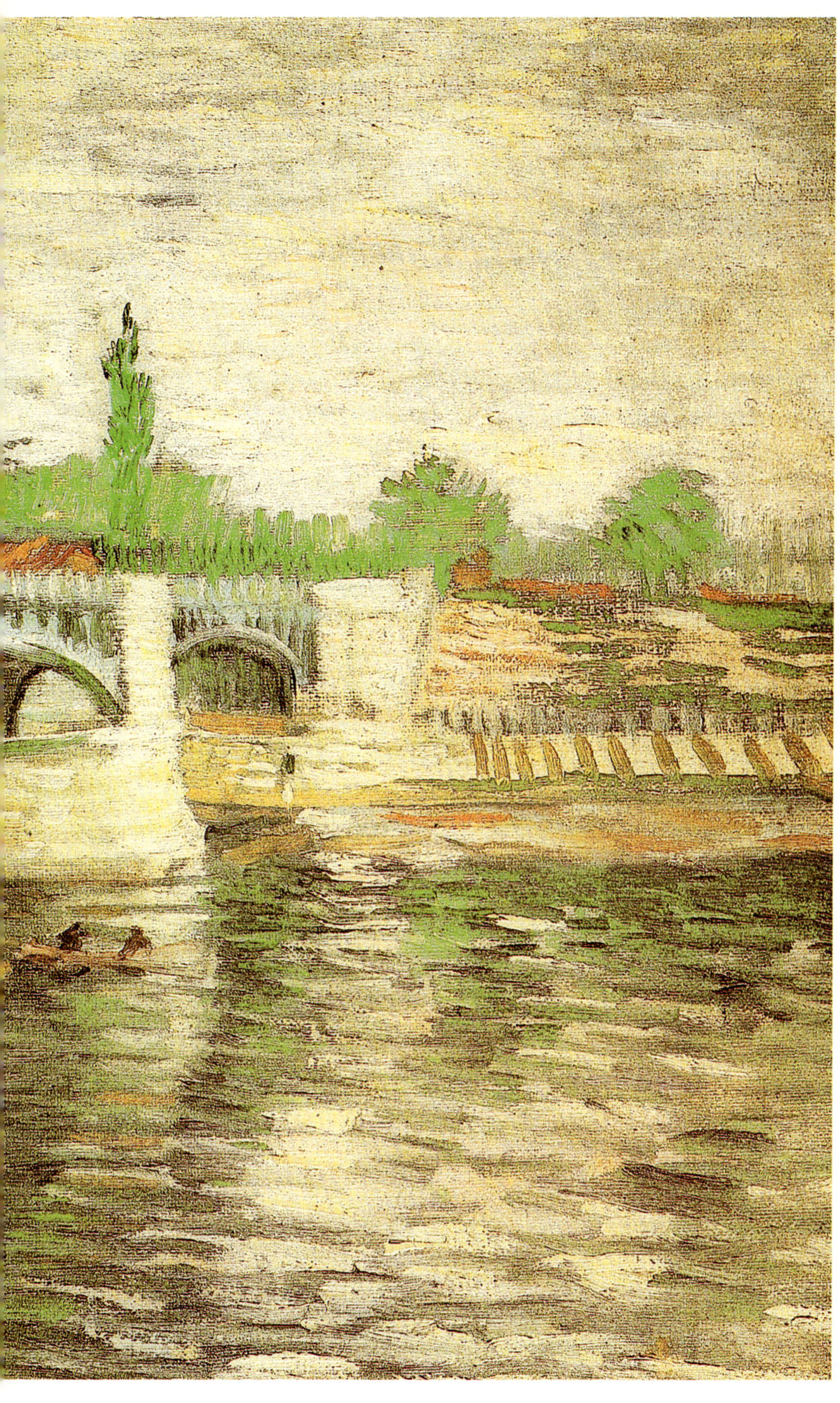

The Pont de la Grande Jatte

Summer 1887 - oil on canvas - 32 x 40.5 cm - Vincent van Gogh Foundation, Amsterdam

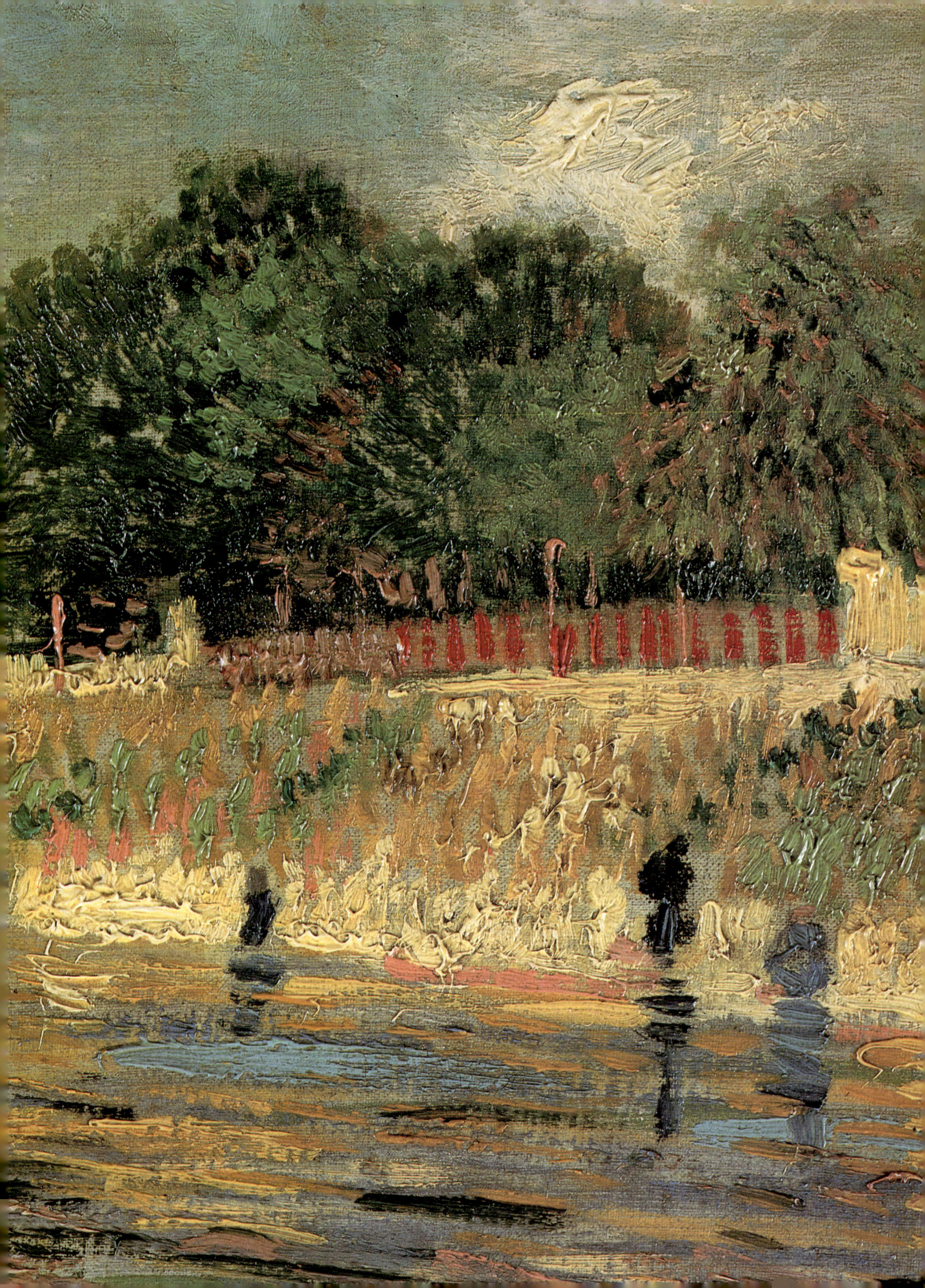

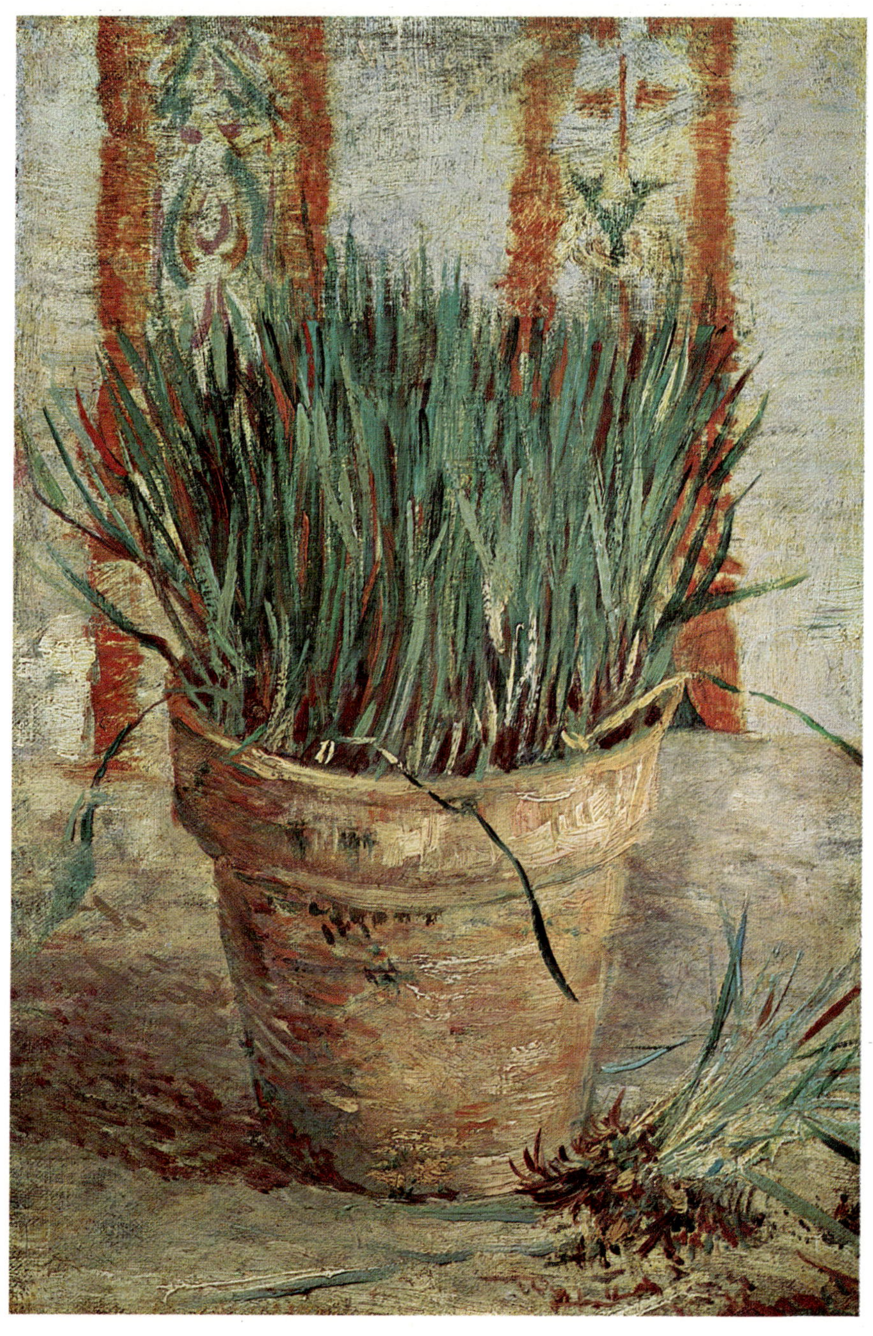

Flower Pot with Herbs

1887 - oil on canvas - 32 x 22 cm - Vincent van Gogh Foundation, Amsterdam

Banks of the Seine (detail)

April-June 1887 - oil on canvas - 32 x 45.5 cm - Vincent van Gogh Foundation, Amsterdam

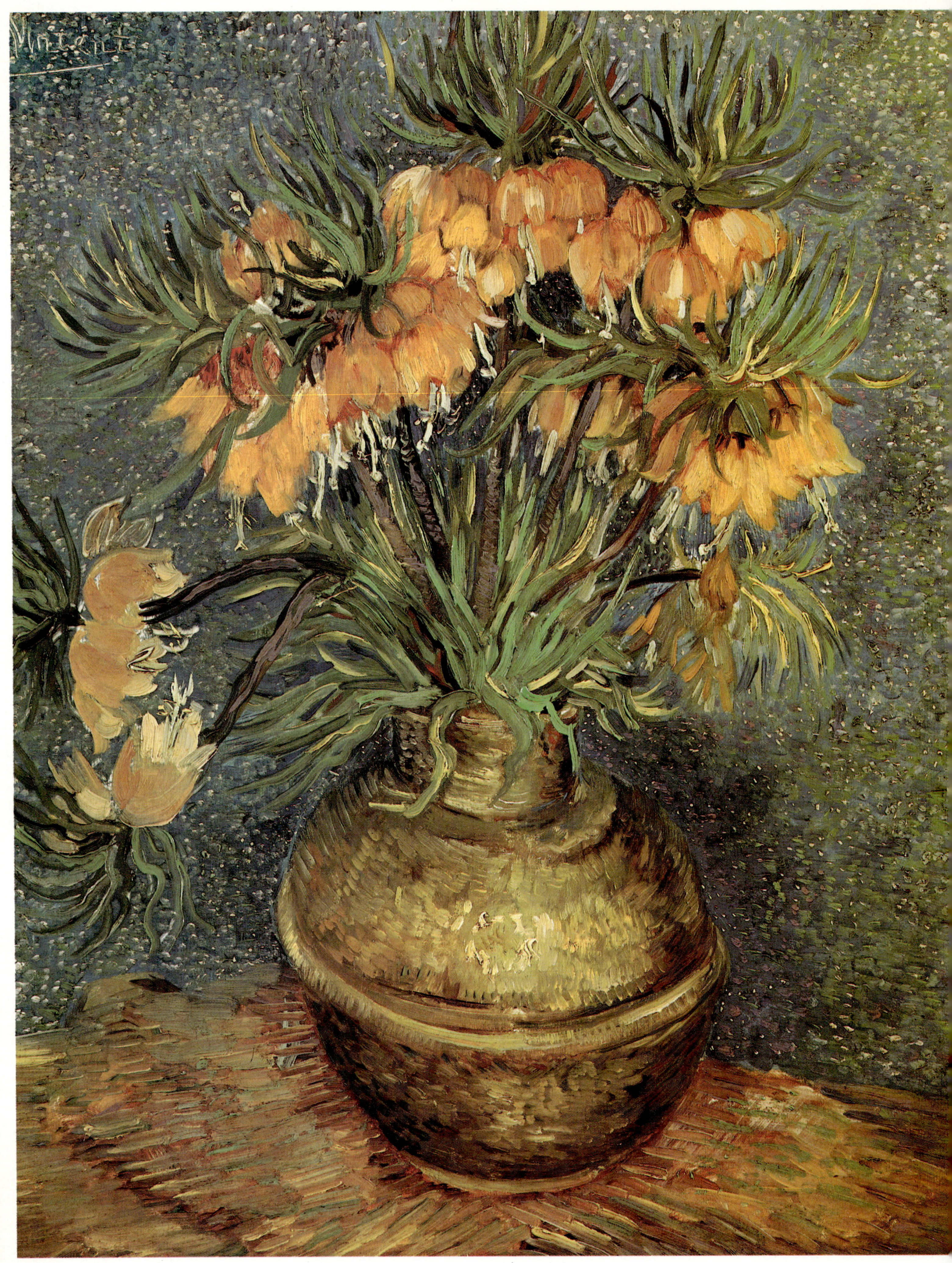
Vincent

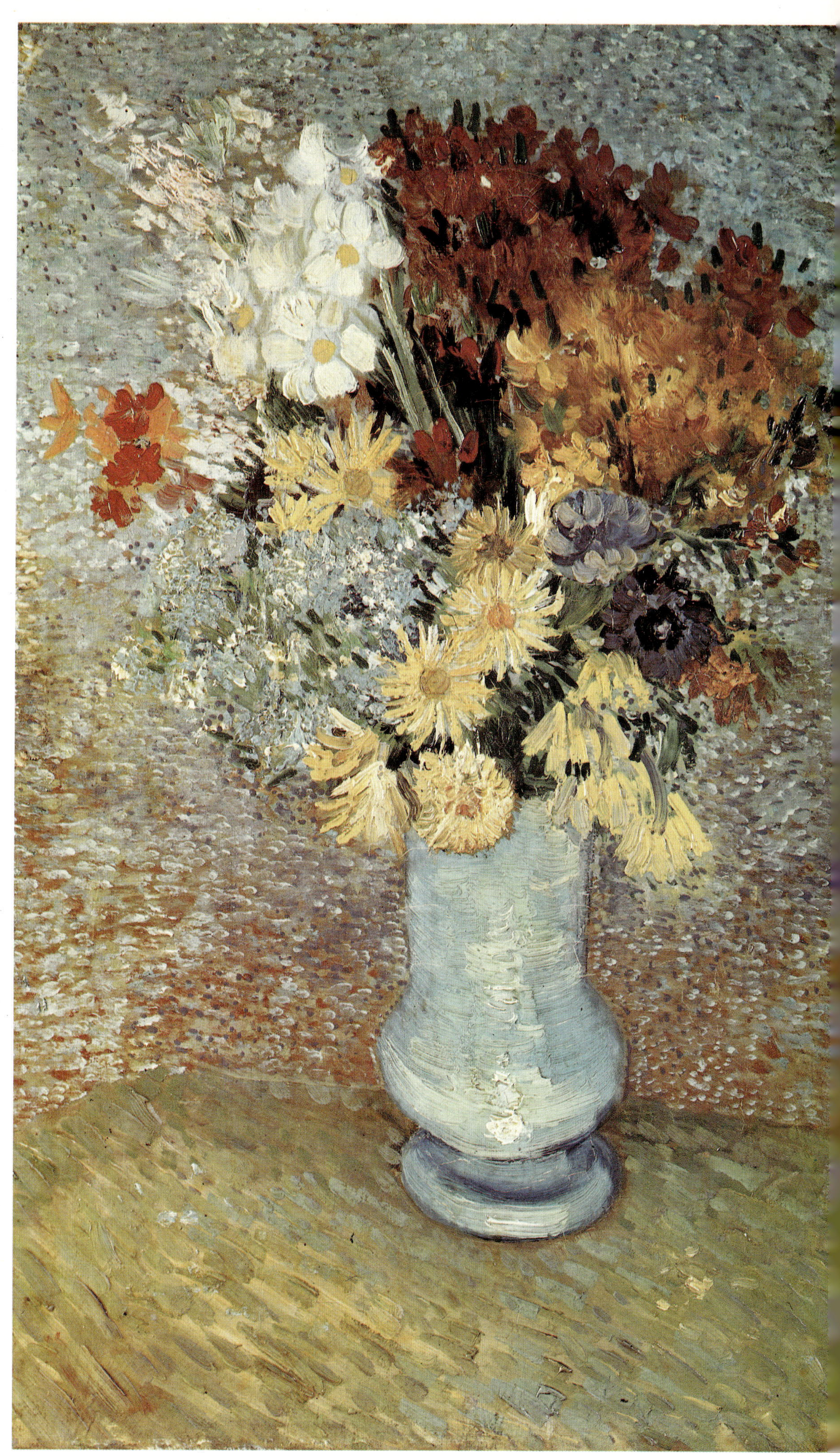

Fritillaires in a
Copper Pot

April-June 1887 - oil on canvas
- 73.5 x 60.5 cm -
Musée d'Orsay, Paris

Bouquet of daisies
and anemones

July-September 1887 -
oil on canvas
- 61 x 38 cm -
ksmuseum Kröller- Müller, Otterlo

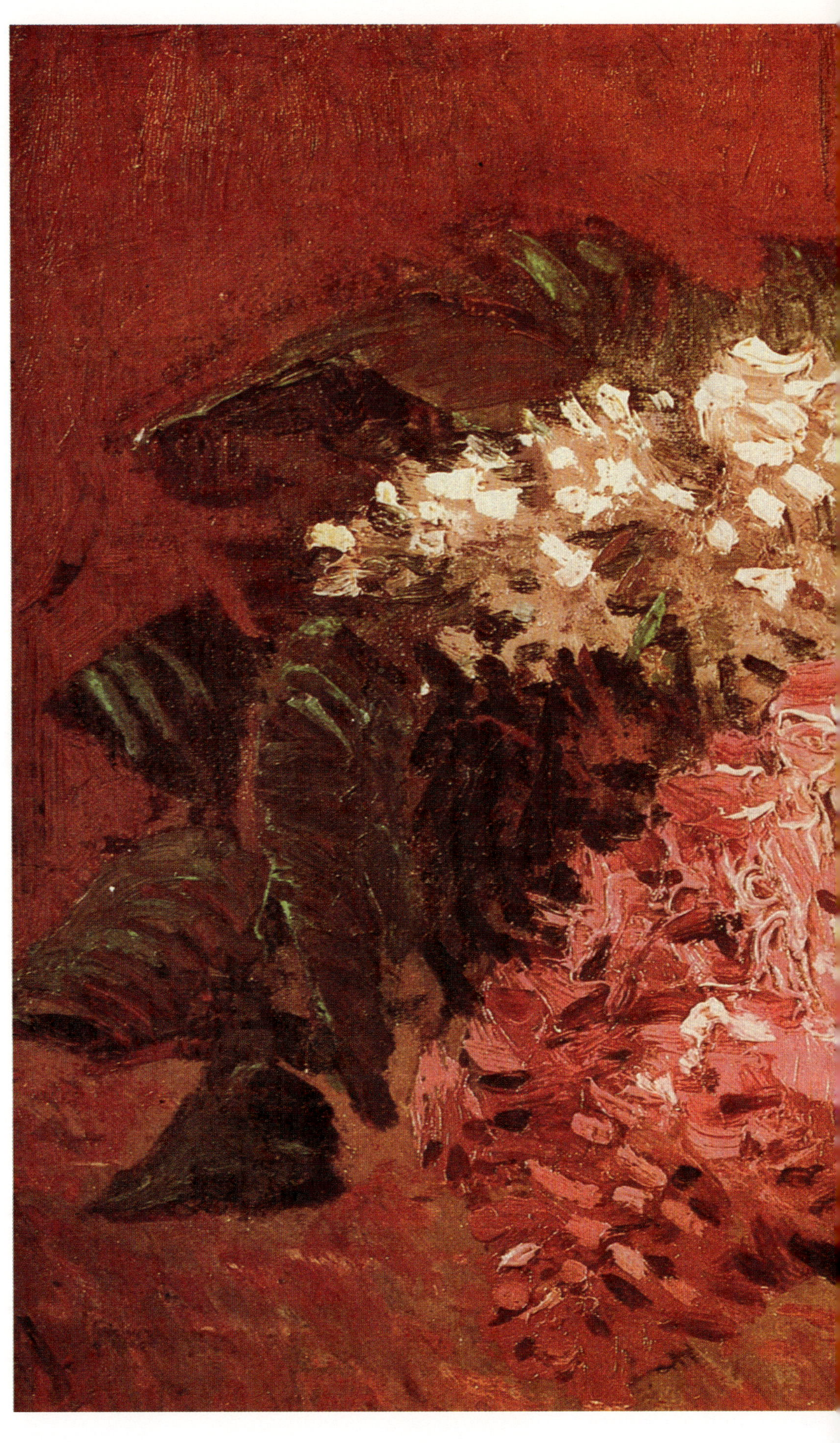

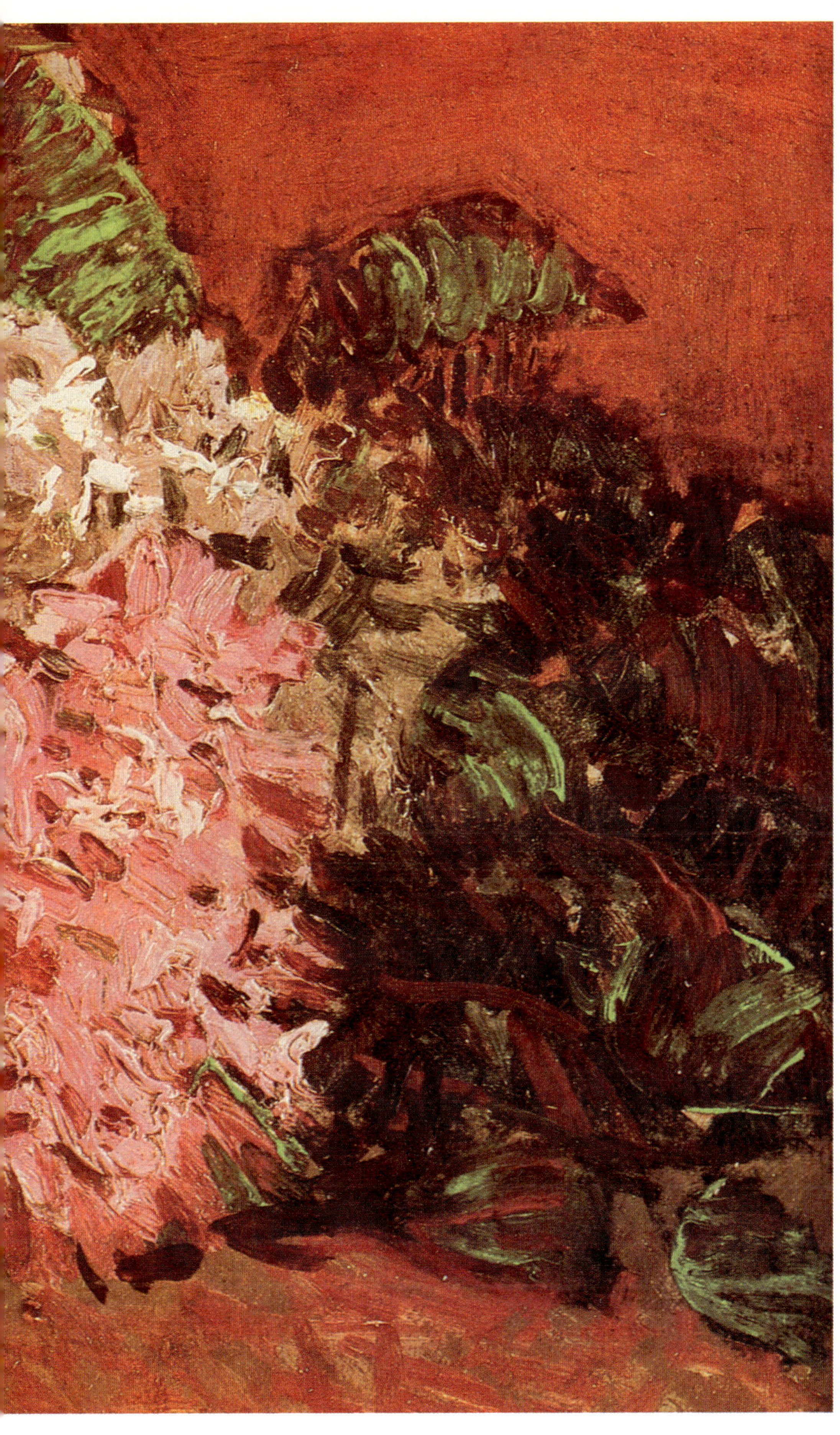

Lilacs

Summer 1887 - oil on canvas - 27.3 x 35.3 cm -
Armand Hammer Museum of Art, Los Angeles,

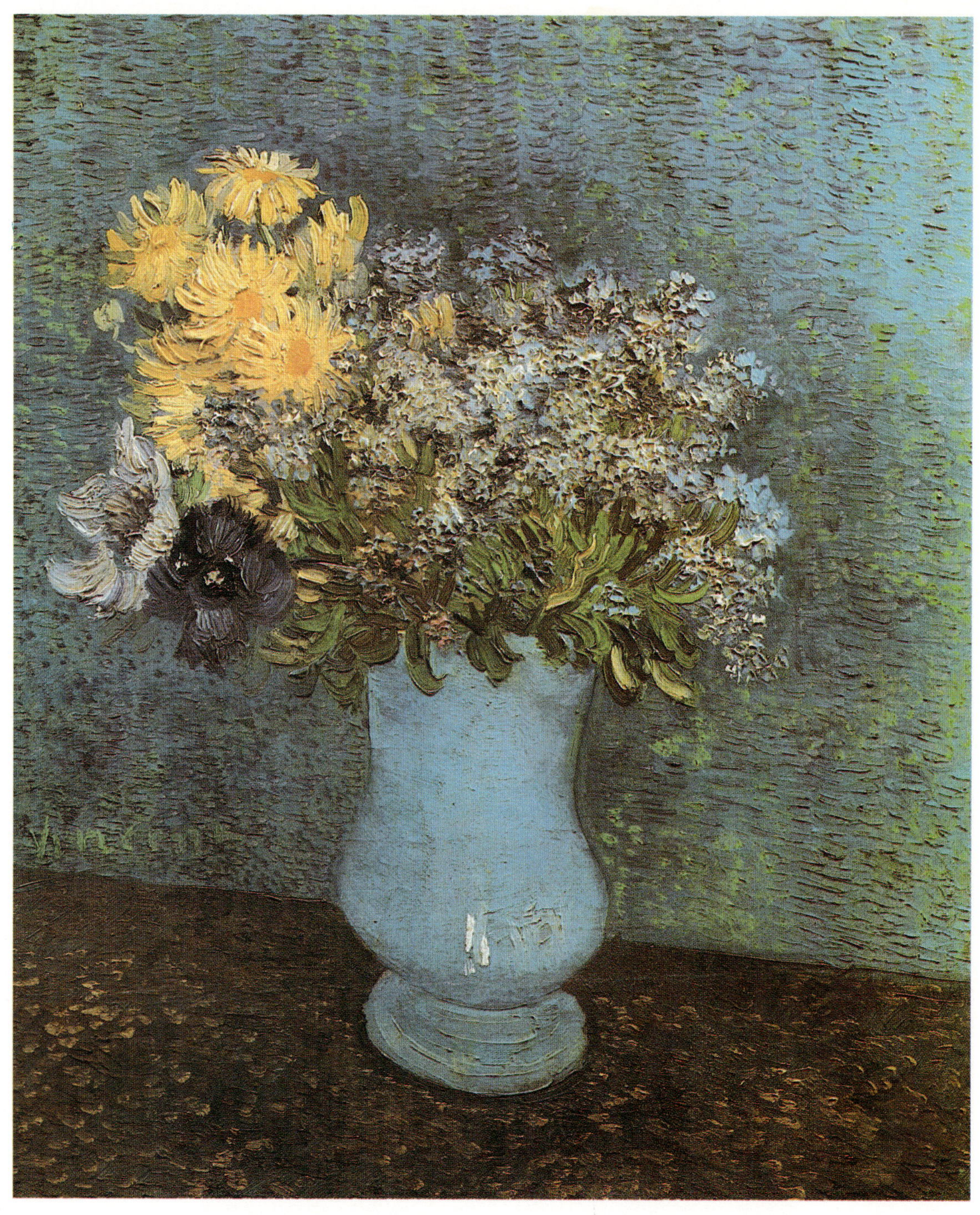

Vase with Lilacs, Daisies and Anemones

Summer 1887 - oil on canvas - 46.5 x 37.5 cm - Private collection, Geneva

Still Life : Absinthe

April-June 1887 - oil on canvas - 46.5 x 33 cm - Vincent Van Gogh Foundation, Amsterdam

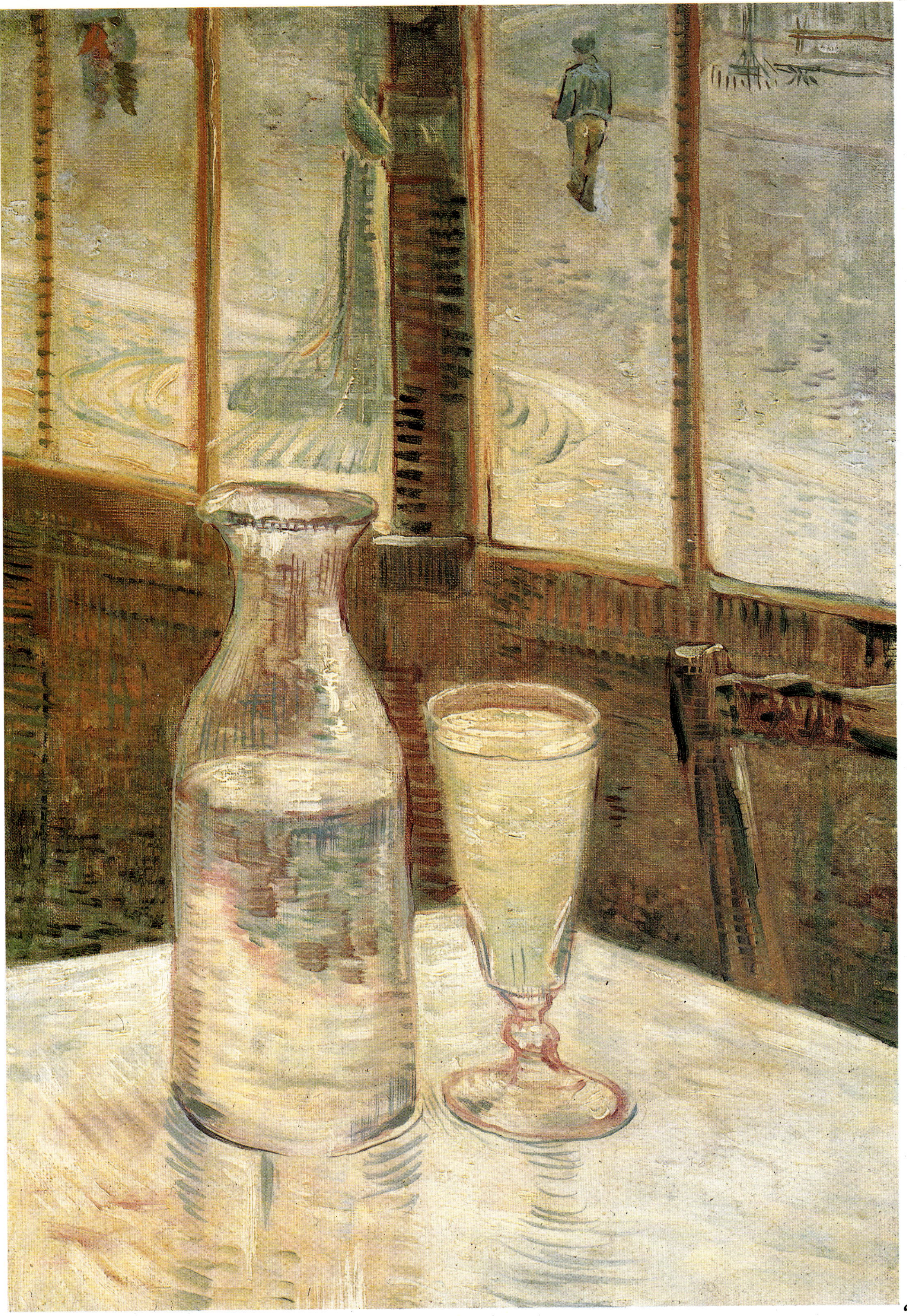

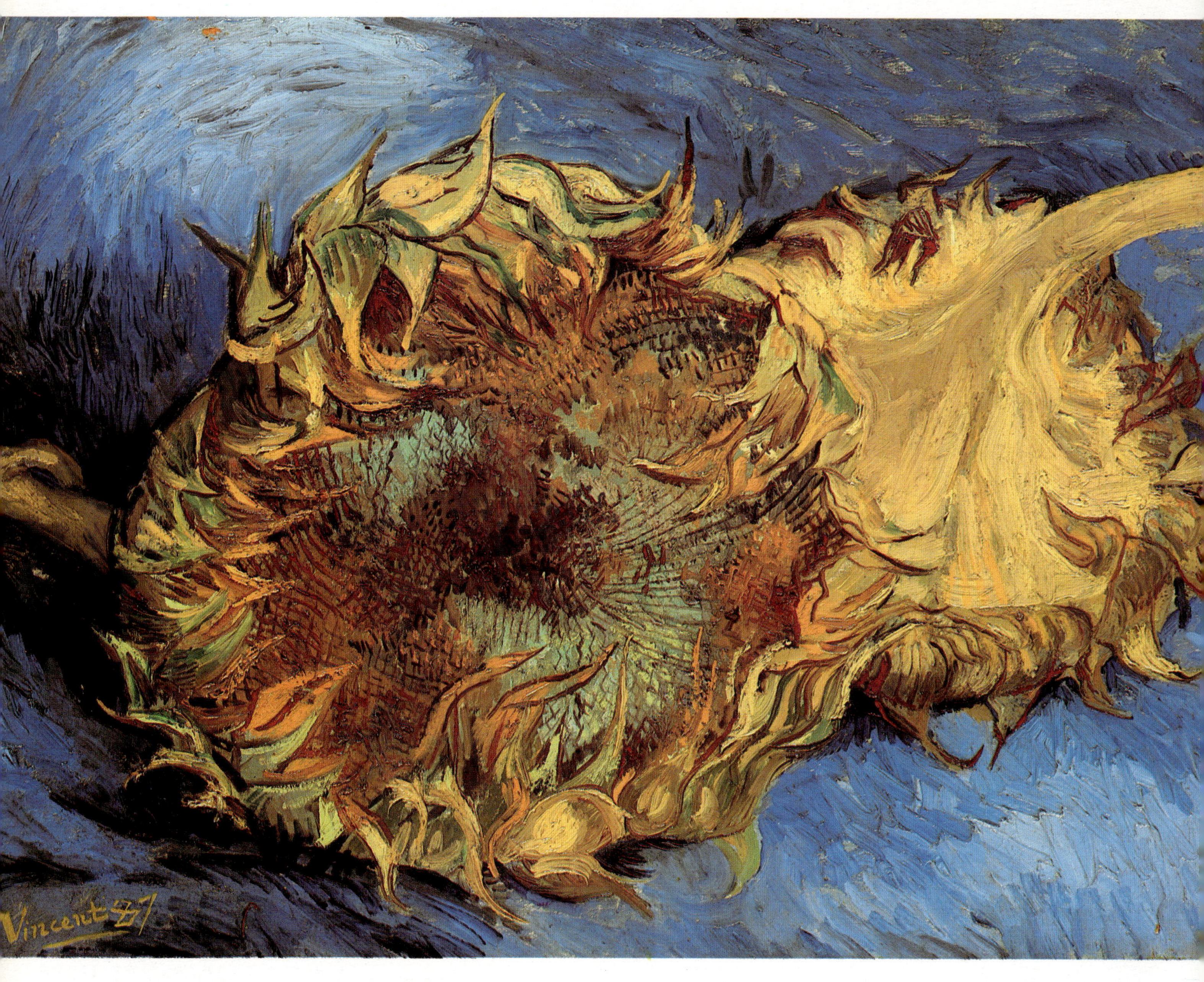

Two Cut Sunflowers

August 1887 - oil on canvas - 43 x 61-
Metropolitan Museum of Art, New York

Still Life with Lemons and Carafe

April-June 1887 - oil on canvas - 46 x 38 -
Vincent Van Gogh Foundation, Amsterdam

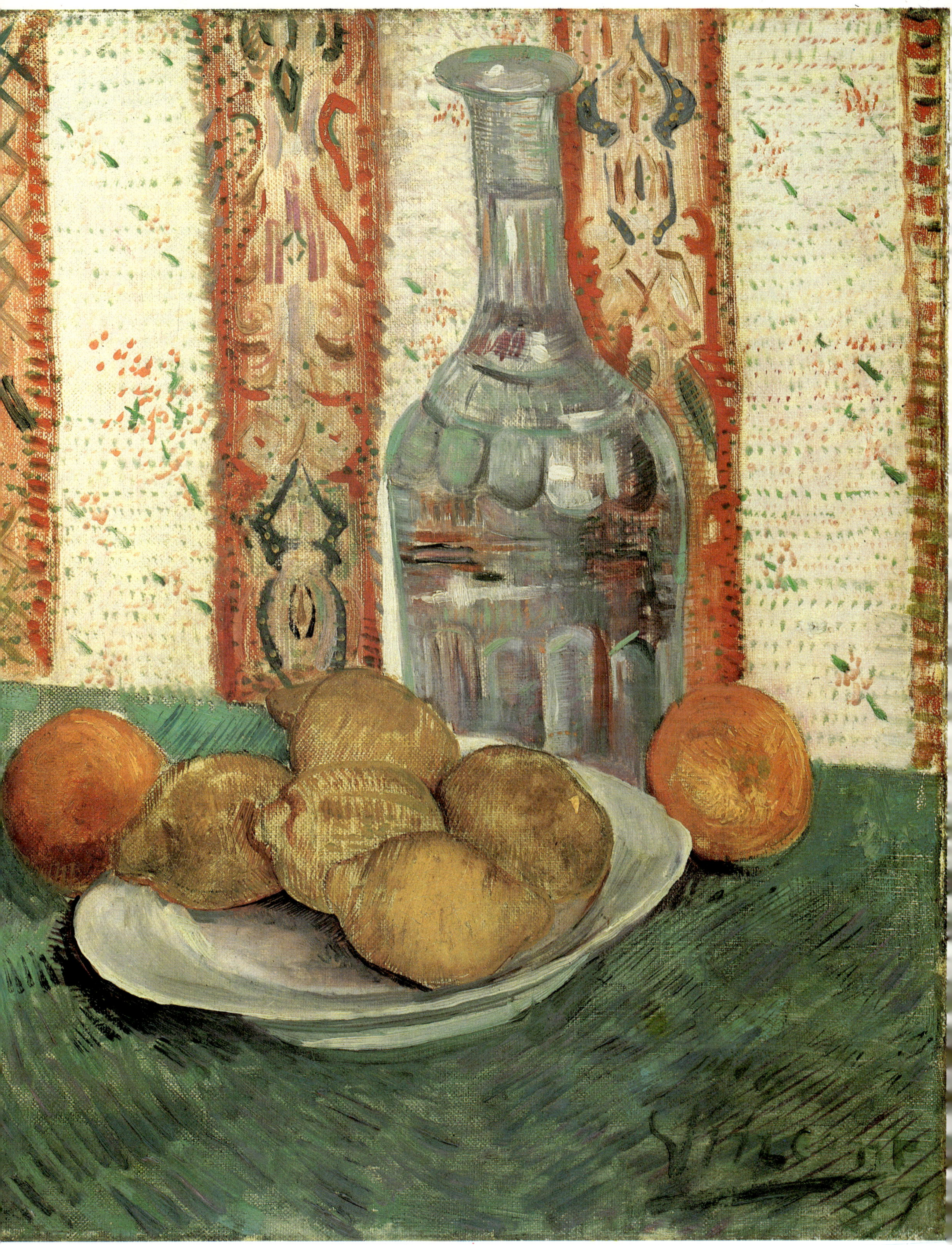

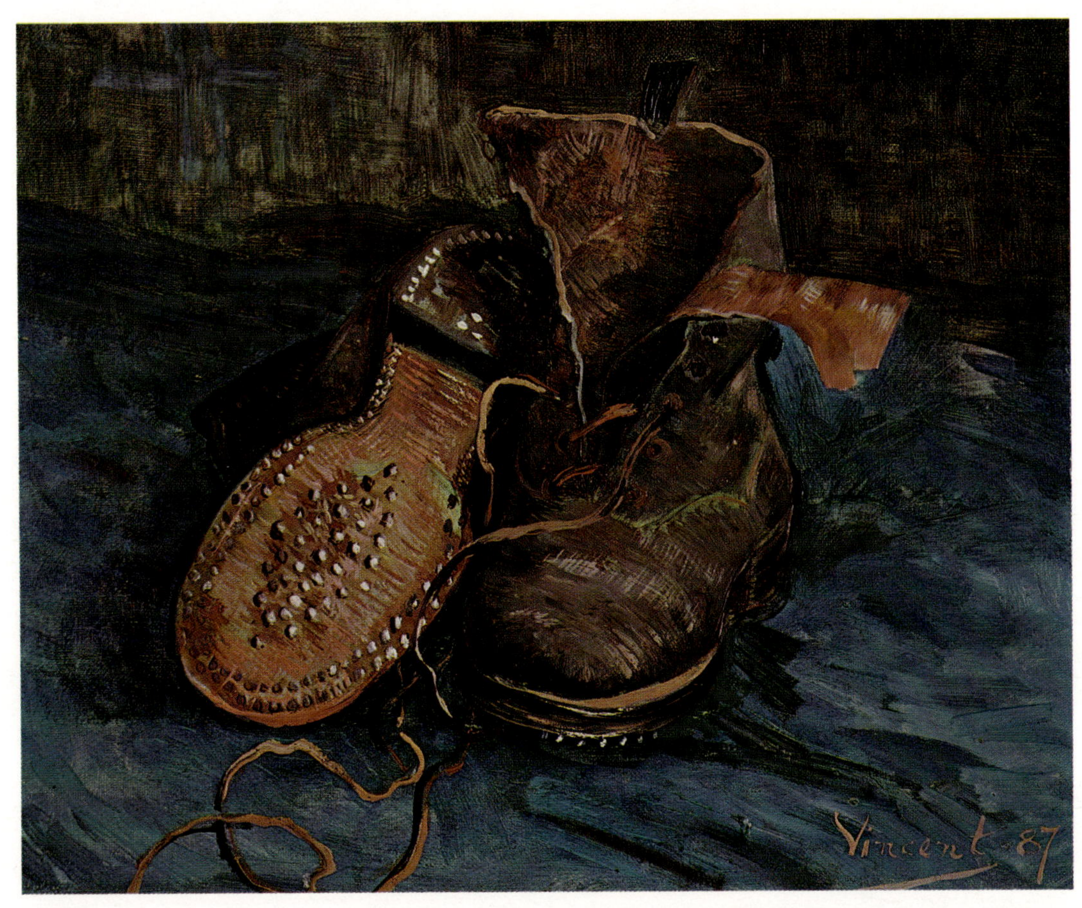

A Pair of Shoes

Early 1887 - oil on canvas - 33 x 41 cm -
Baltimore Museum, Baltimore

Still Life with Plaster Statuette,
a Rose and Two Novels

(Bel-Ami by Guy de Maupassant and Germinie lacerteux
by Jules and Edmond de Goncourt)
December 1887 - oil on canvas - 55 x 46.5 cm -
Rijksmuseum Kröller- Müller, Otterlo

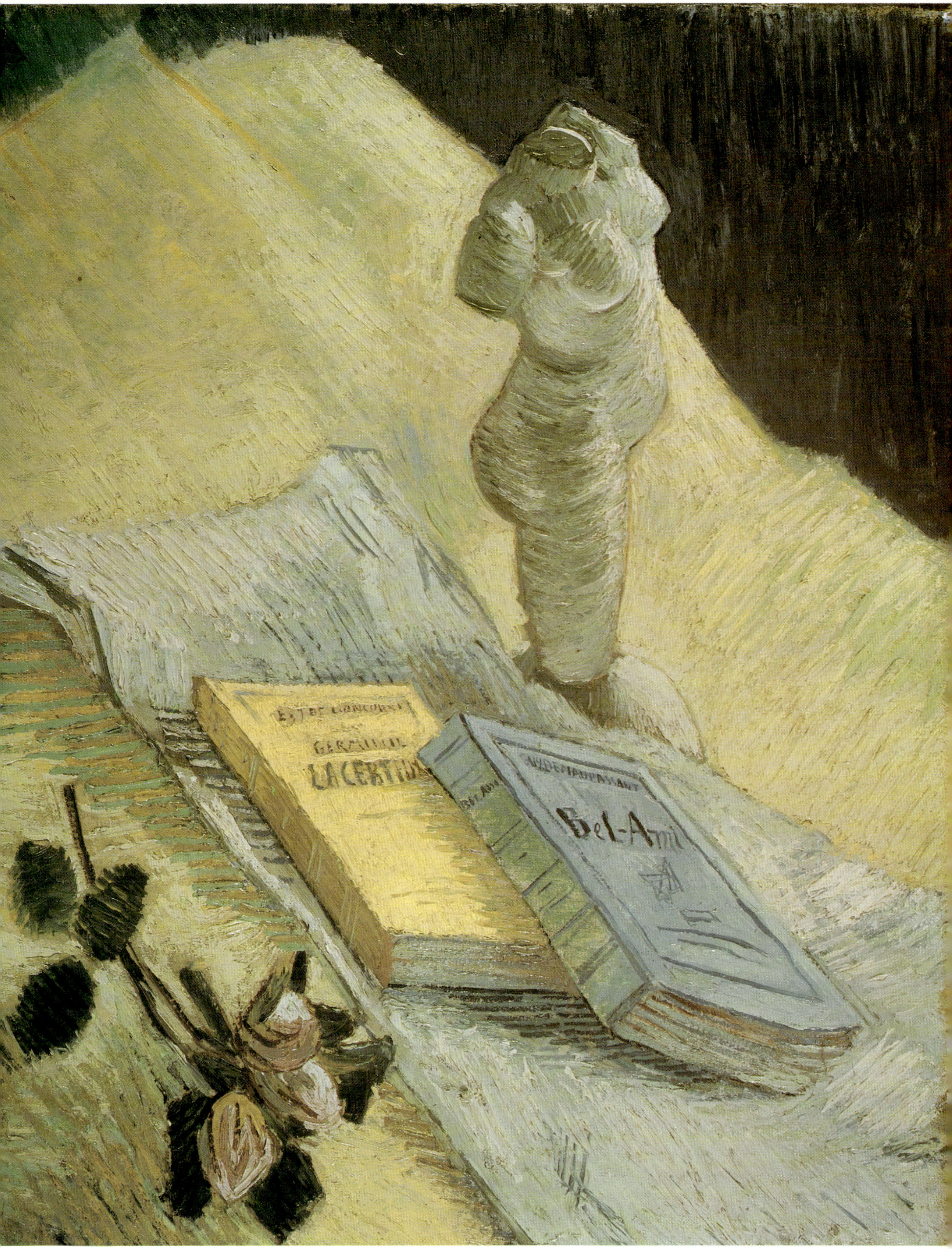
Bel-Ami

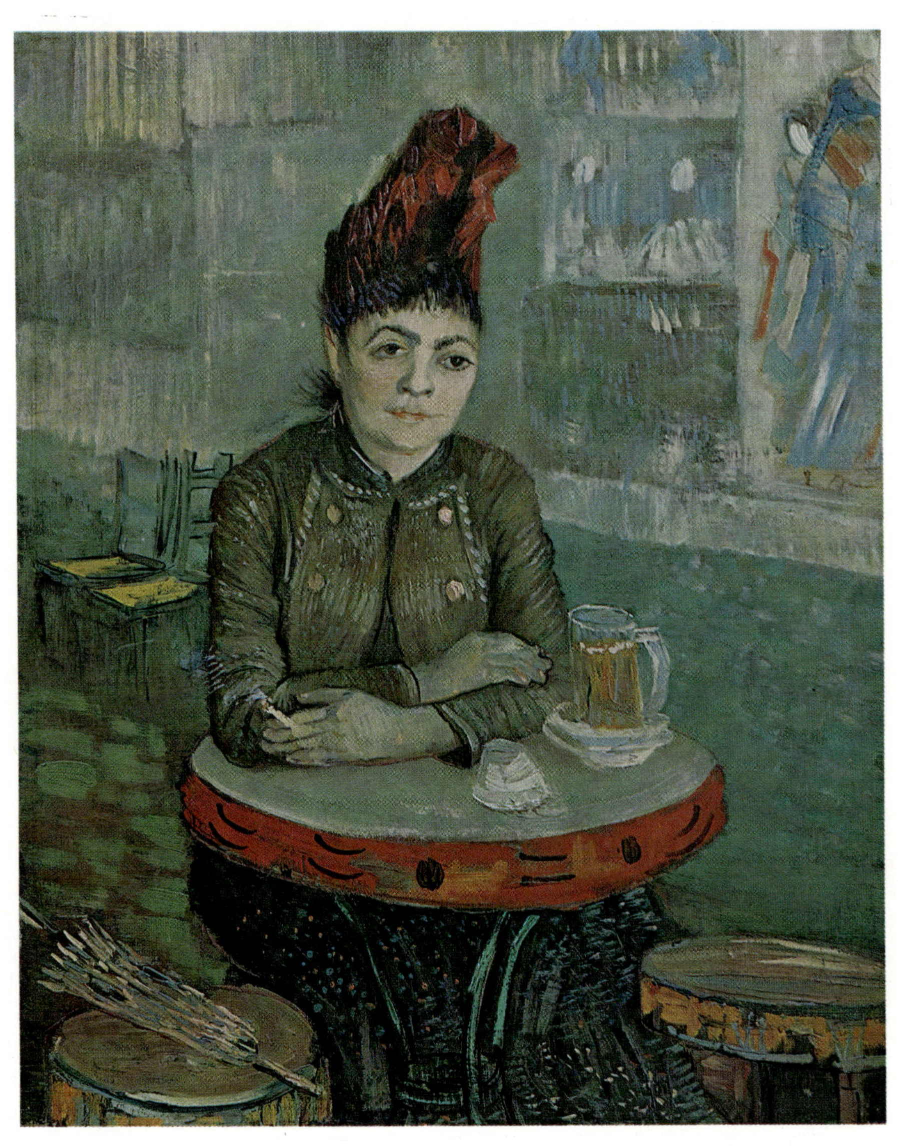

Woman in a Bar (le Tambourin)

Beginning 1888 - oil on canvas - 55.5 x 46.5 cm -
Vincent van Gogh Foundation, Amsterdam

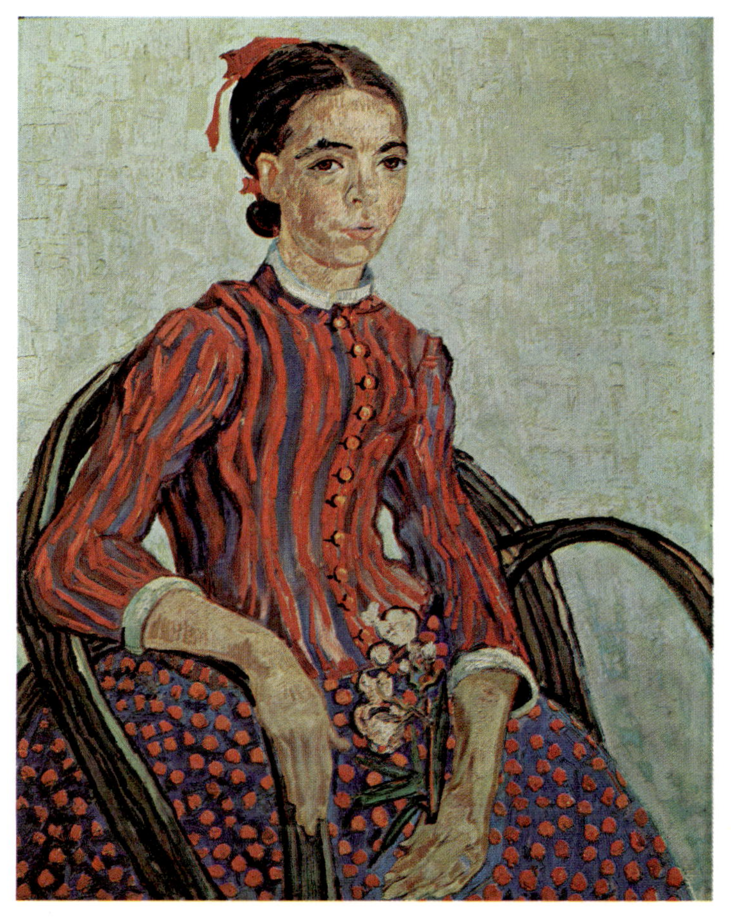

La Mousmé

July 1888 - oil on canvas - 74 x 60 cm -
Chester Dale collection, National Gallery, Washington D.C.

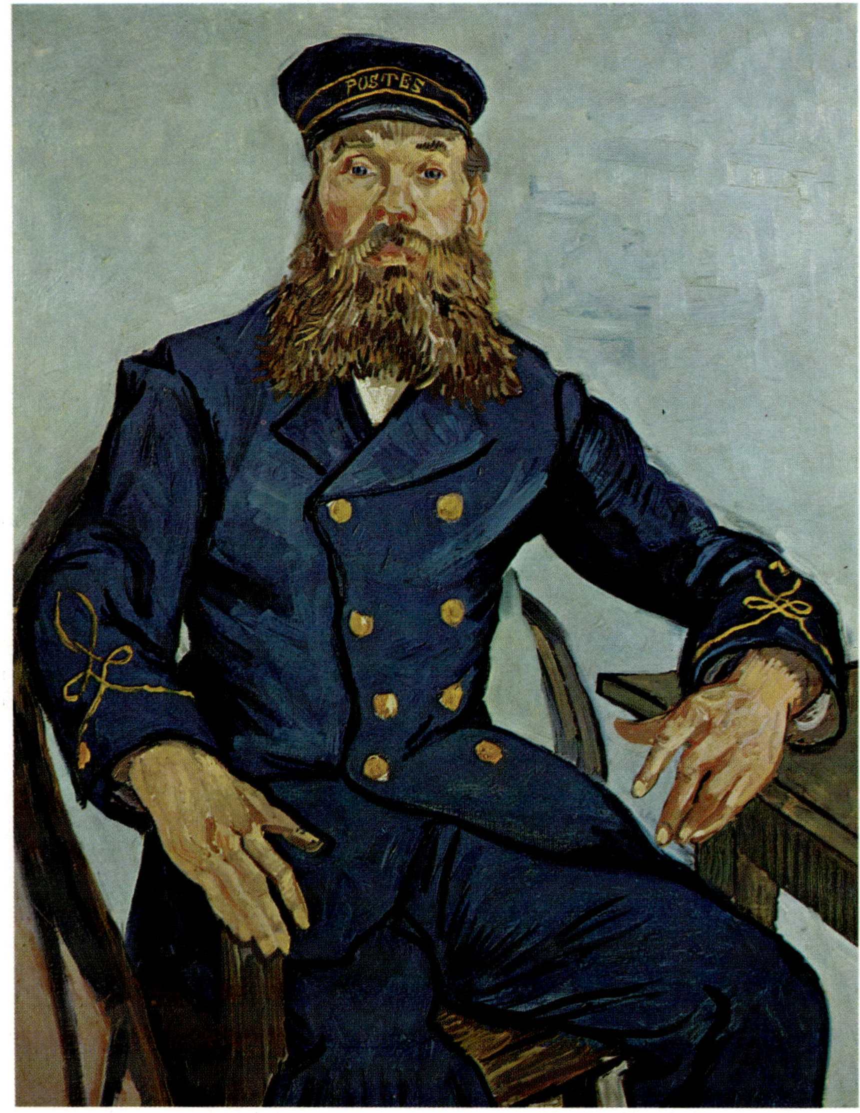

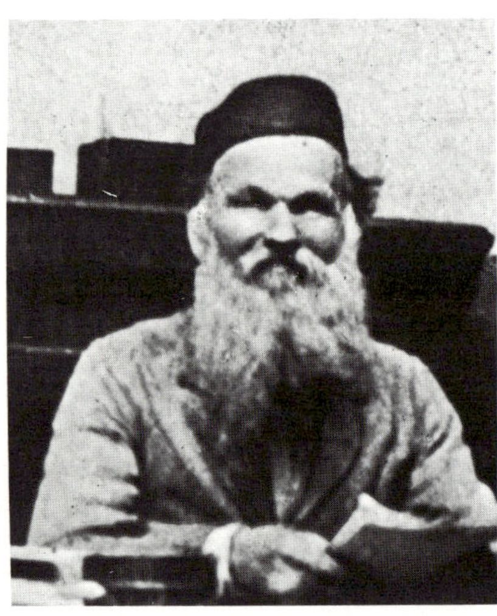

Roulin the Postman

August 1888 - oil on canvas - 79.5 x 63.5 cm -
Robert Treat Paine Collection, Boston, USA

Photograph of Joseph Roulin, taken in 1902 at Marseilles, shortly before his death

The Zouave

June 1888 - oil on canvas - 65 x 54 cm -
Vincent van Gogh Foundation, Amsterdam

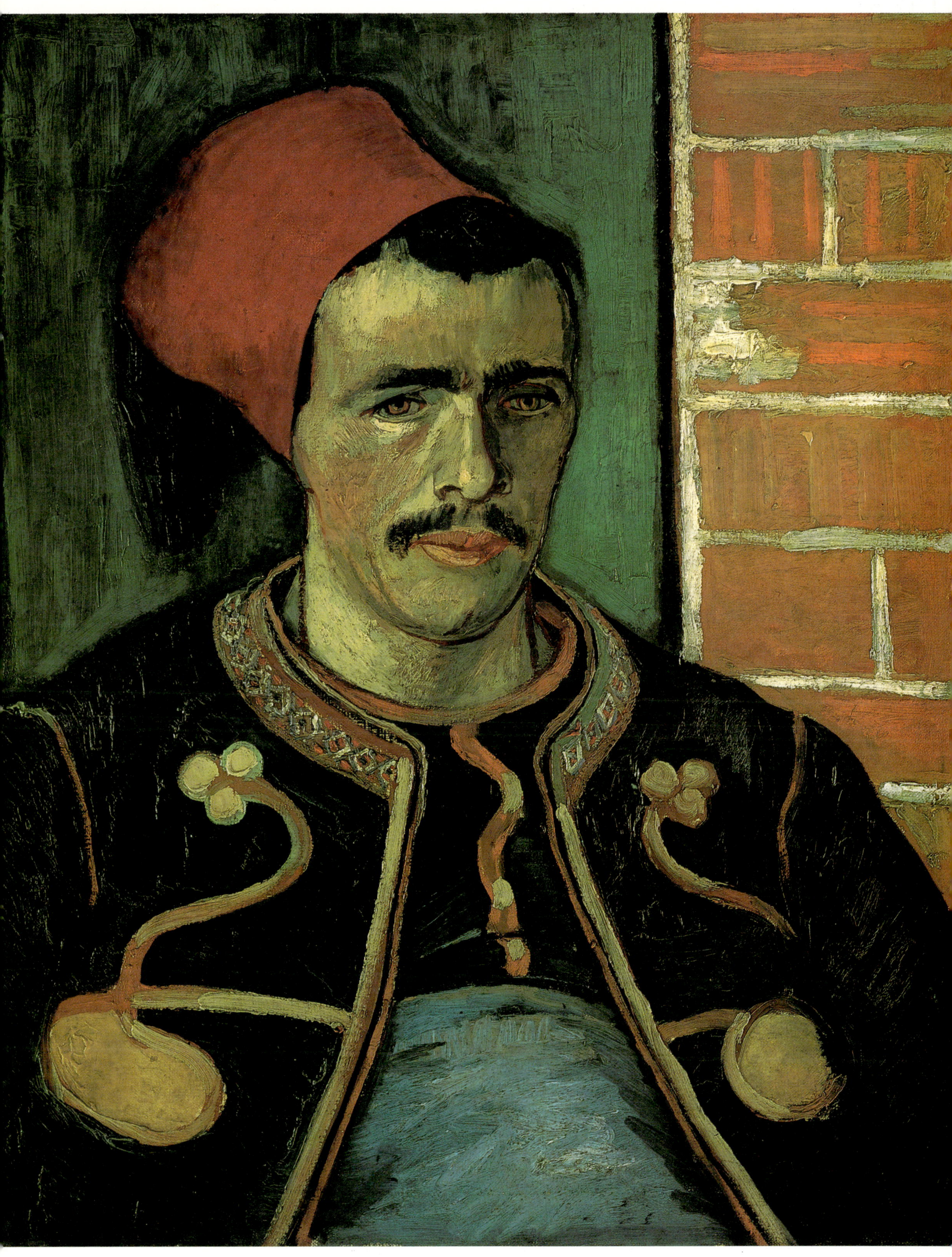

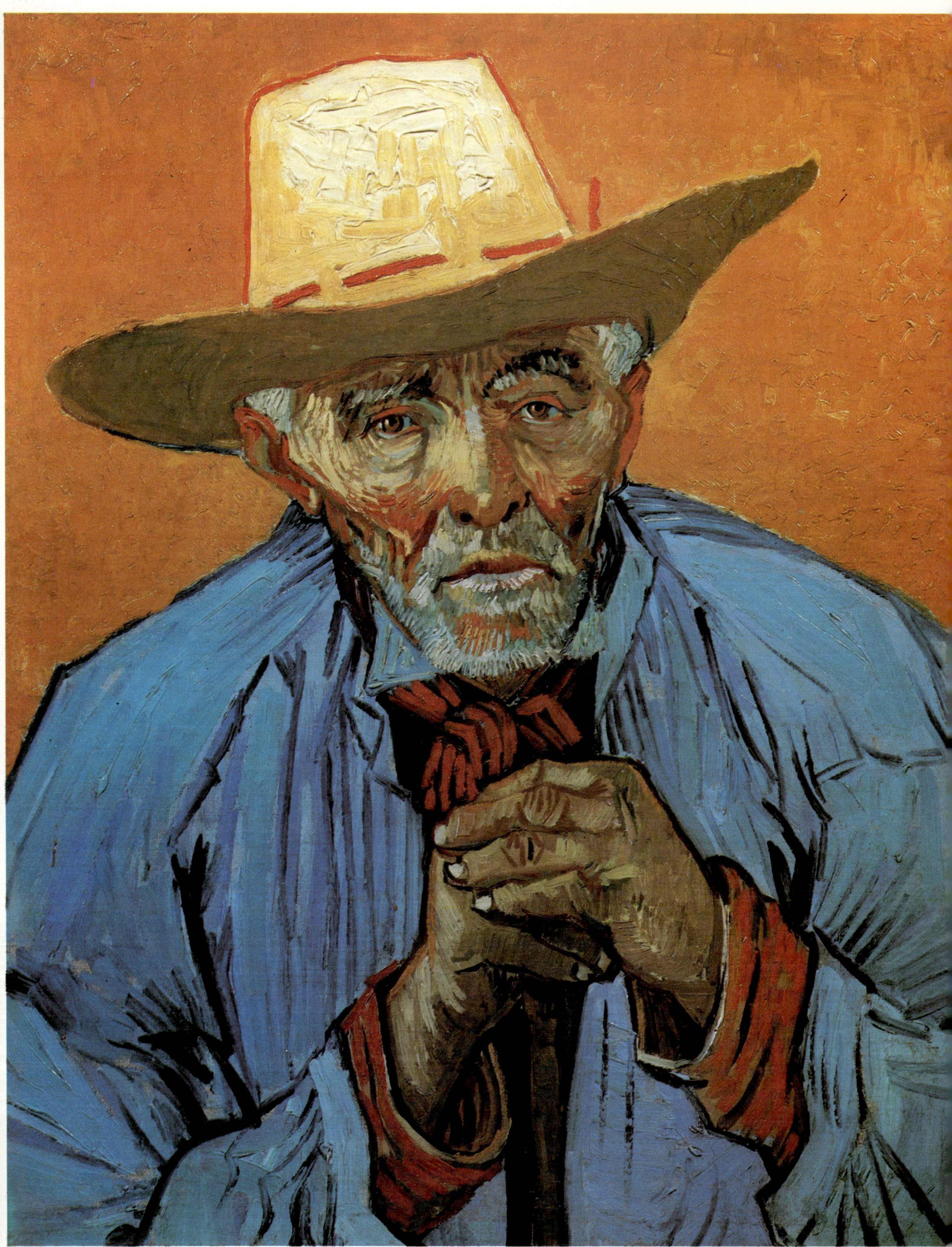

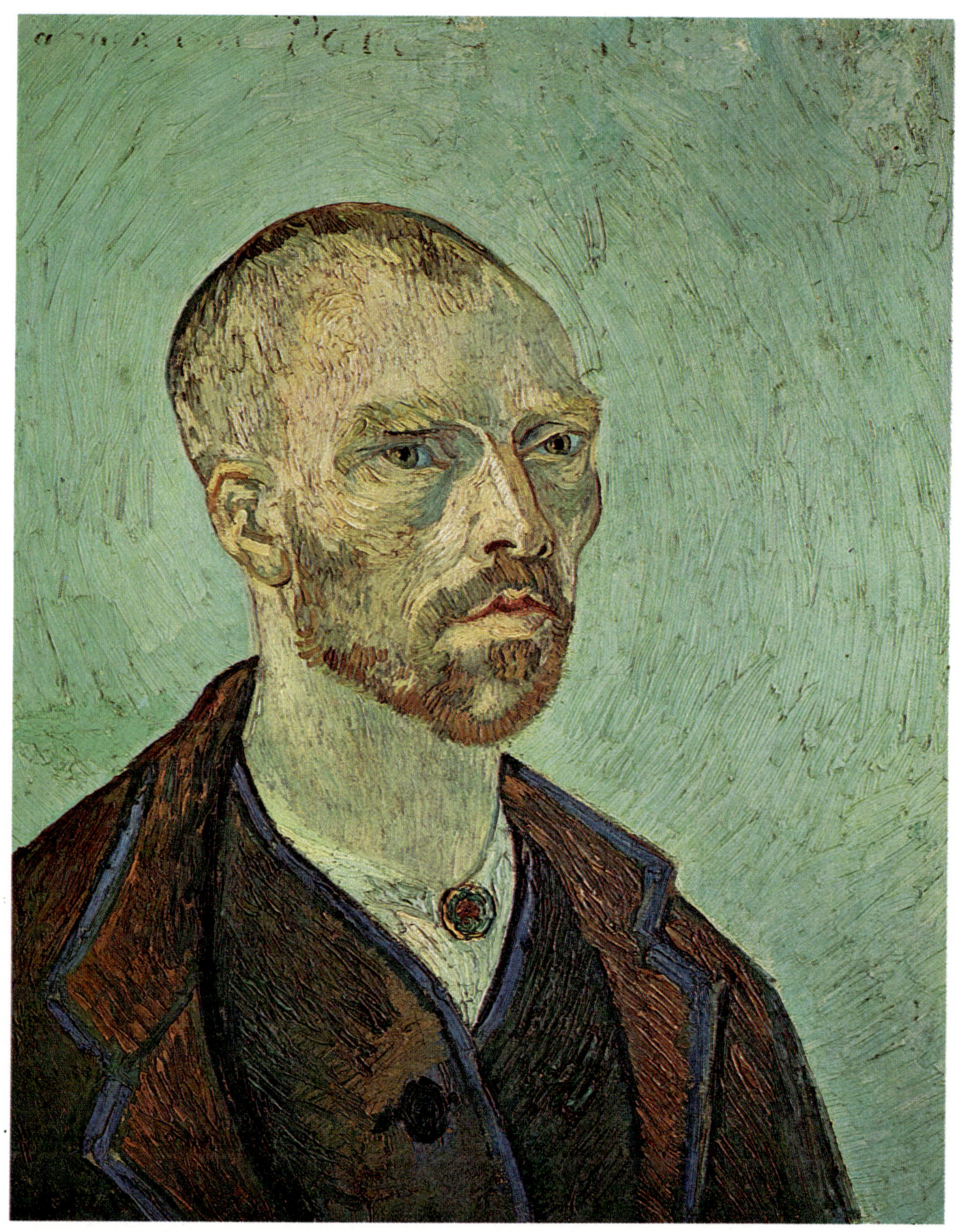

Self-Portrait

September 1888 - oil on canvas - 62 x 52 cm -
signed top left: l'ami Paul Gauguin -
Fogg Art Museum, Cambridge, Mass.

Portrait of Patience Escalier

August 1888 - oil on canvas - 69 x 54 cm -
Private Collection

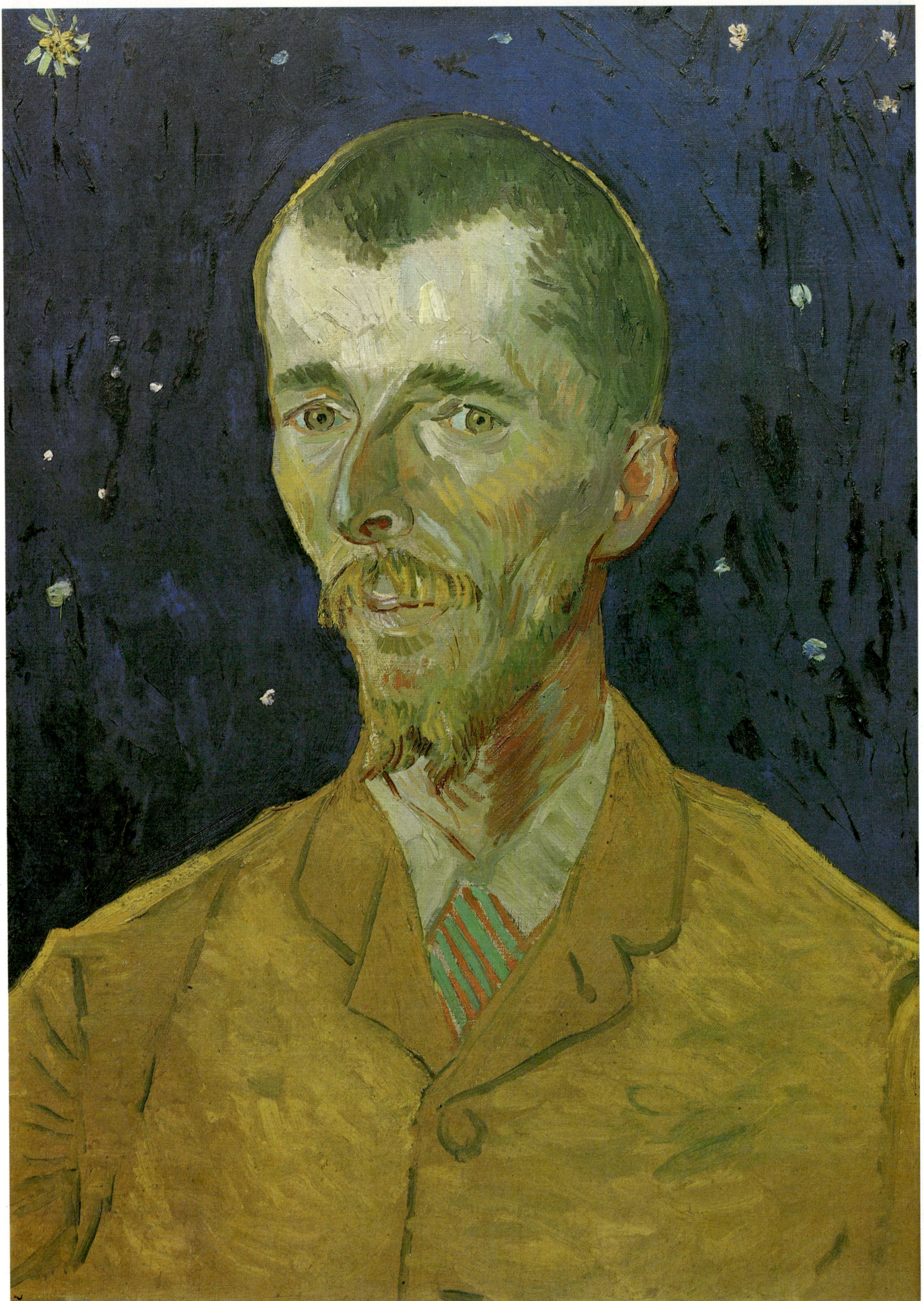

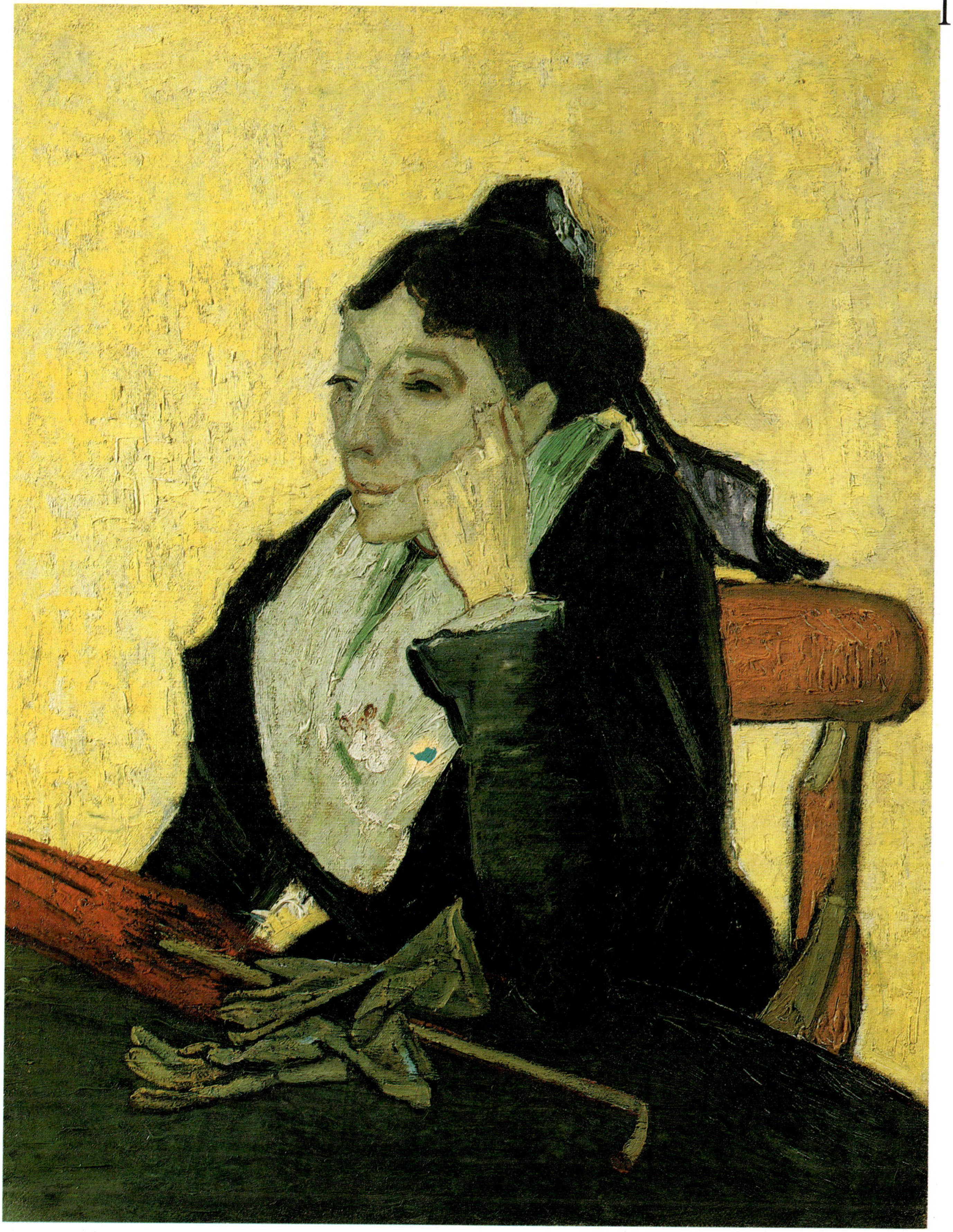

L'Arlésienne, Madame Ginoux

November 1888 - oil on canvas - 93 x 74 cm - Musée d'Orsay, Paris

Portrait of Eugène Boch

September 1888 - oil on canvas - 60 x 45 cm - Musée d'Orsay, Paris

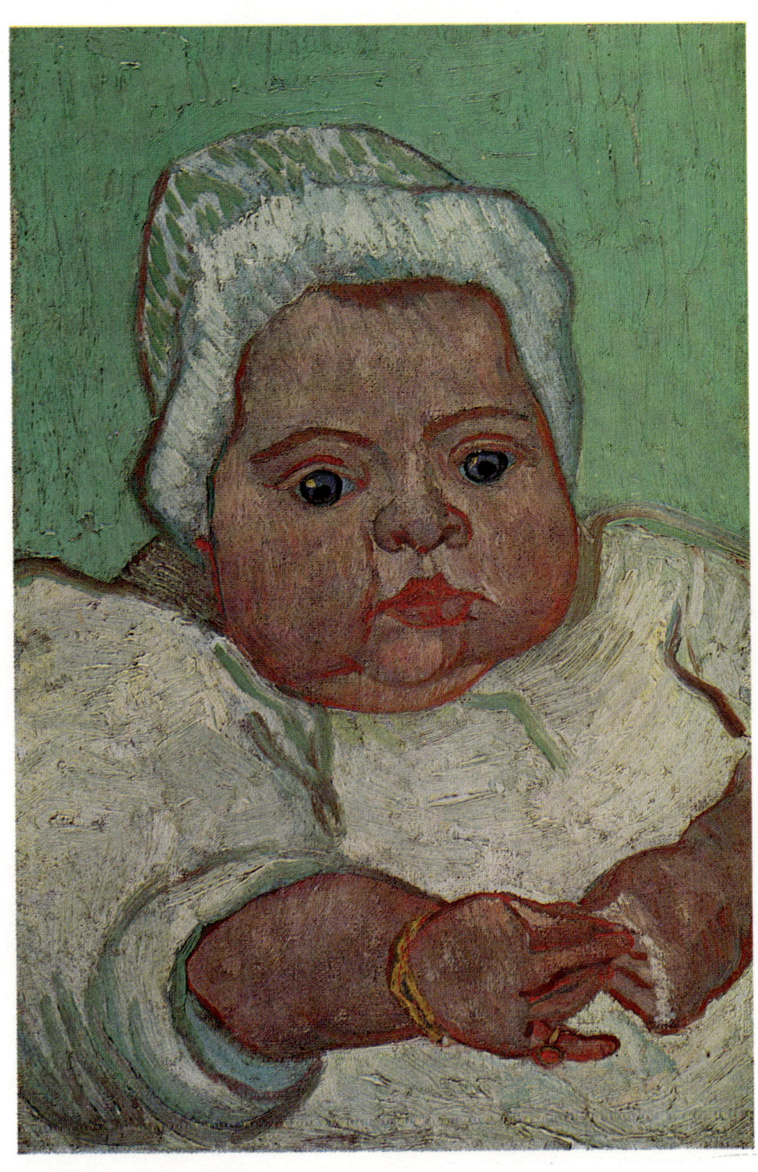

The Baby (Marcelle Roulin)

*November 1888 - oil on canvas - 35.5 x 24.5 cm -
Vincent van Gogh Foundation, Amsterdam*

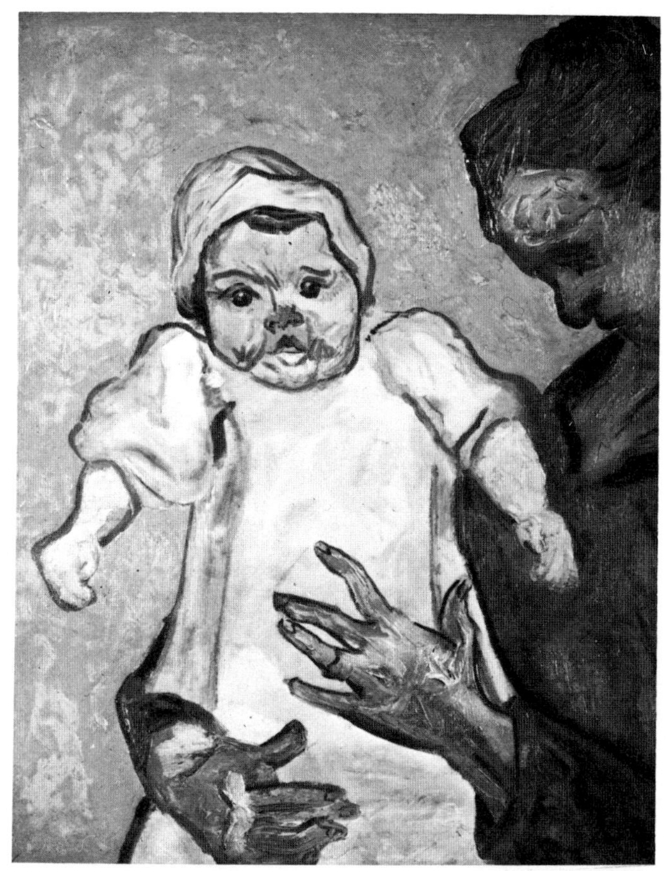

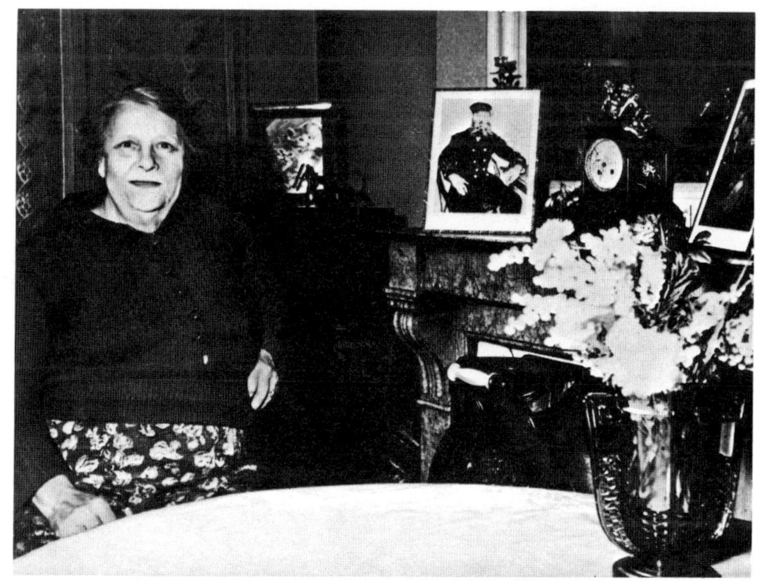

Madame Roulin and Her Baby

1888 - oil on canvas - 63,5 x 51 cm
Lehman collection, New York

Photograph of Marcelle, Mme Roulin's daughter, taken in 1955 in front of the portrait of her father, the postman

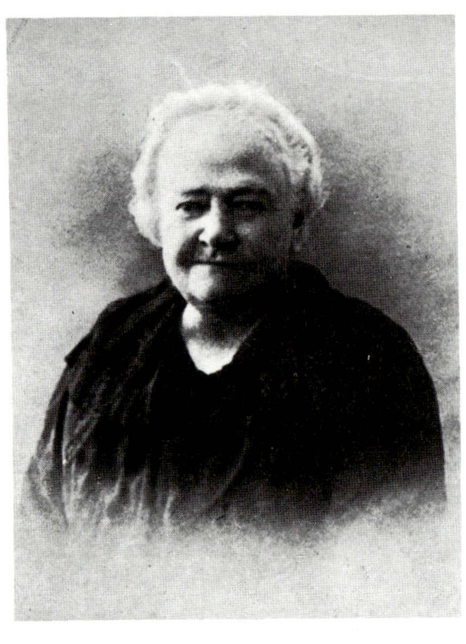

Photograph of Mme Roulin, the postman's wife, taken when she was 70

Augustine Roulin: la Berceuse

December 1888 - oil on canvas - 92 x 73 cm - Rijksmuseum Kröller- Müller, Otterlo

Madame Roulin

November 1888 - oil on canvas - 55 x 65 cm - Oskar Reinhart Collection, Winterthur, Switzerland

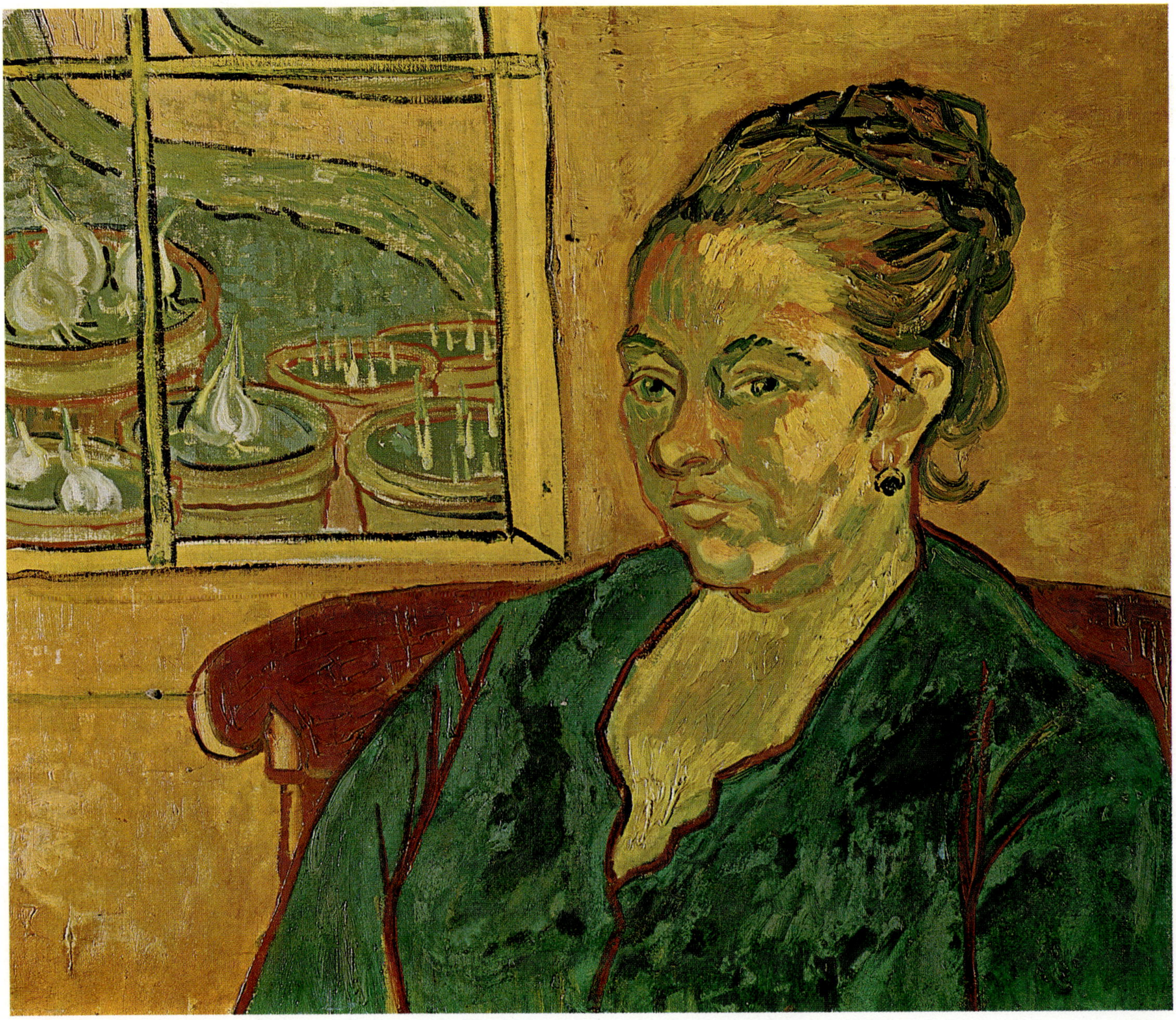

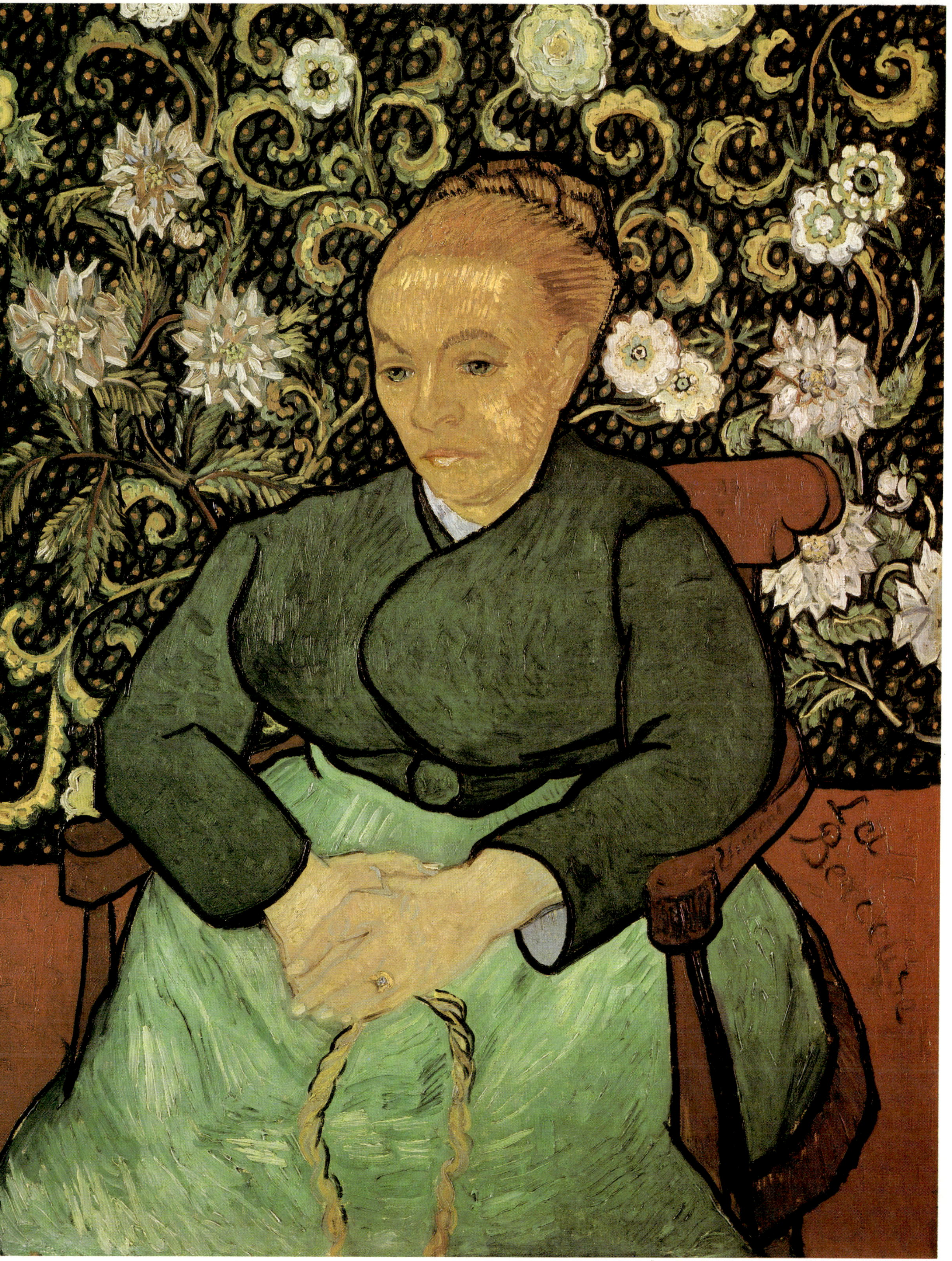
La
Berceuse

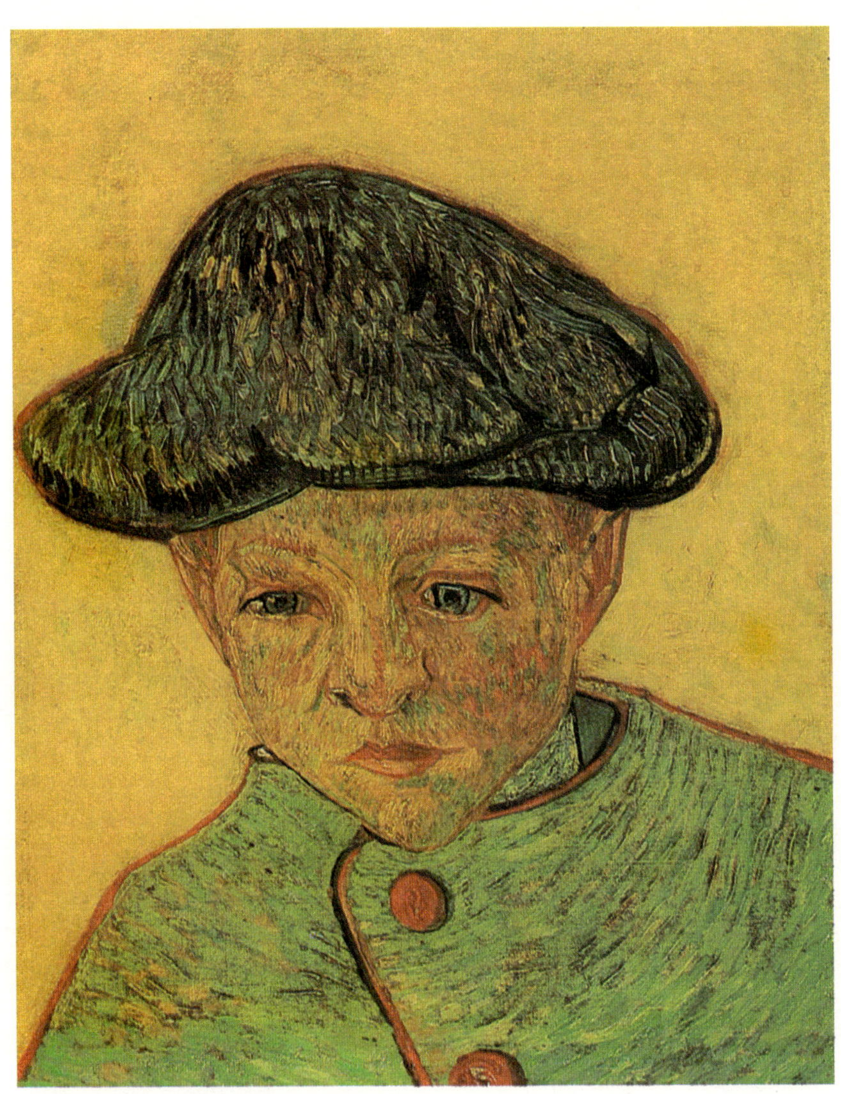

Portrait of Camille Roulin

November-December 1888 - oil on canvas - 43 x 35 cm -
Mrs. Rodolphe Meyer de Schauensee,
Mr. & Mrs. Walter H. Annenberg Collection, Philadelphia Museum of Art,

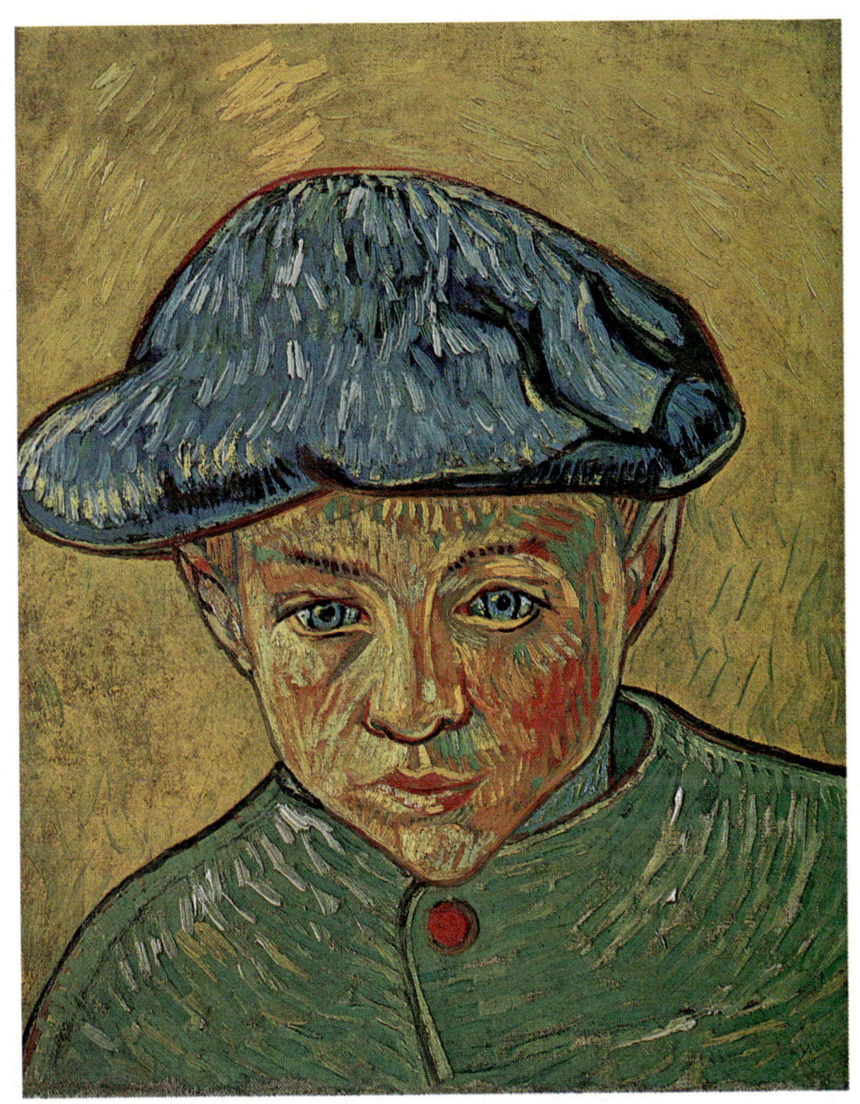

Camille Roulin

November 1888 - oil on canvas - 37.5 x 32.5 cm - Vincent van Gogh Foundation, Amsterdam

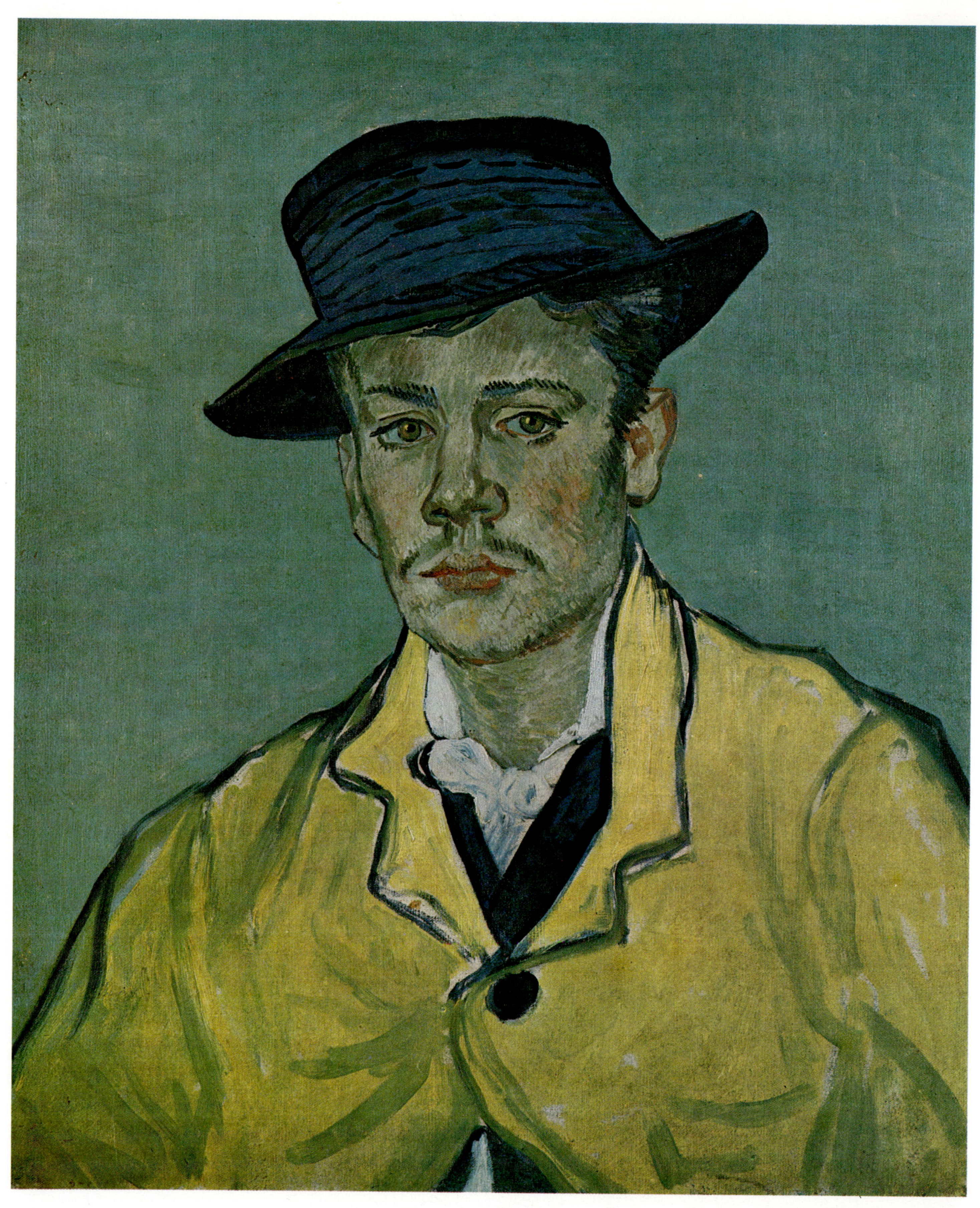

Armand Roulin

November 1888 - oil on canvas - 66 x 55 cm - Folkwang Musuem, Essen

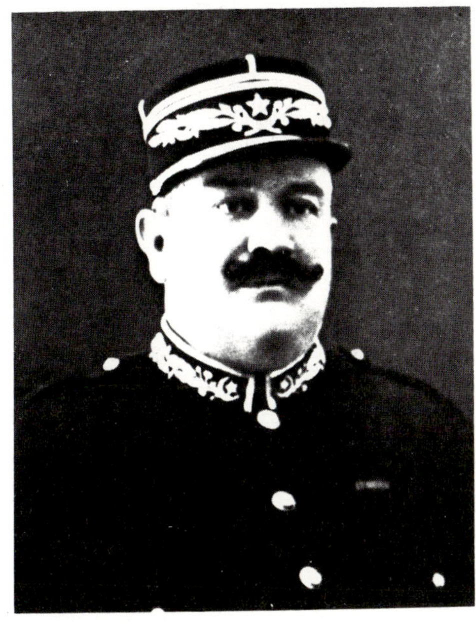

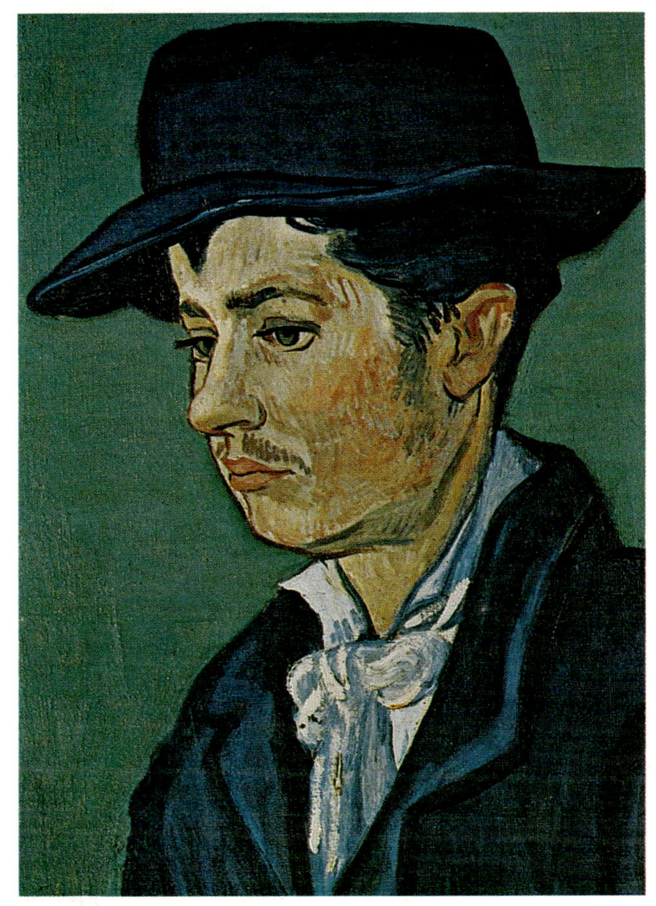

Photograph of Armand Roulin taken 33 years after Vincent had painted his portrait

Armand Roulin

November 1888 - oil on canvas - 65 x 54 cm - Boymans-van Beuningen Museum, Rotterdam

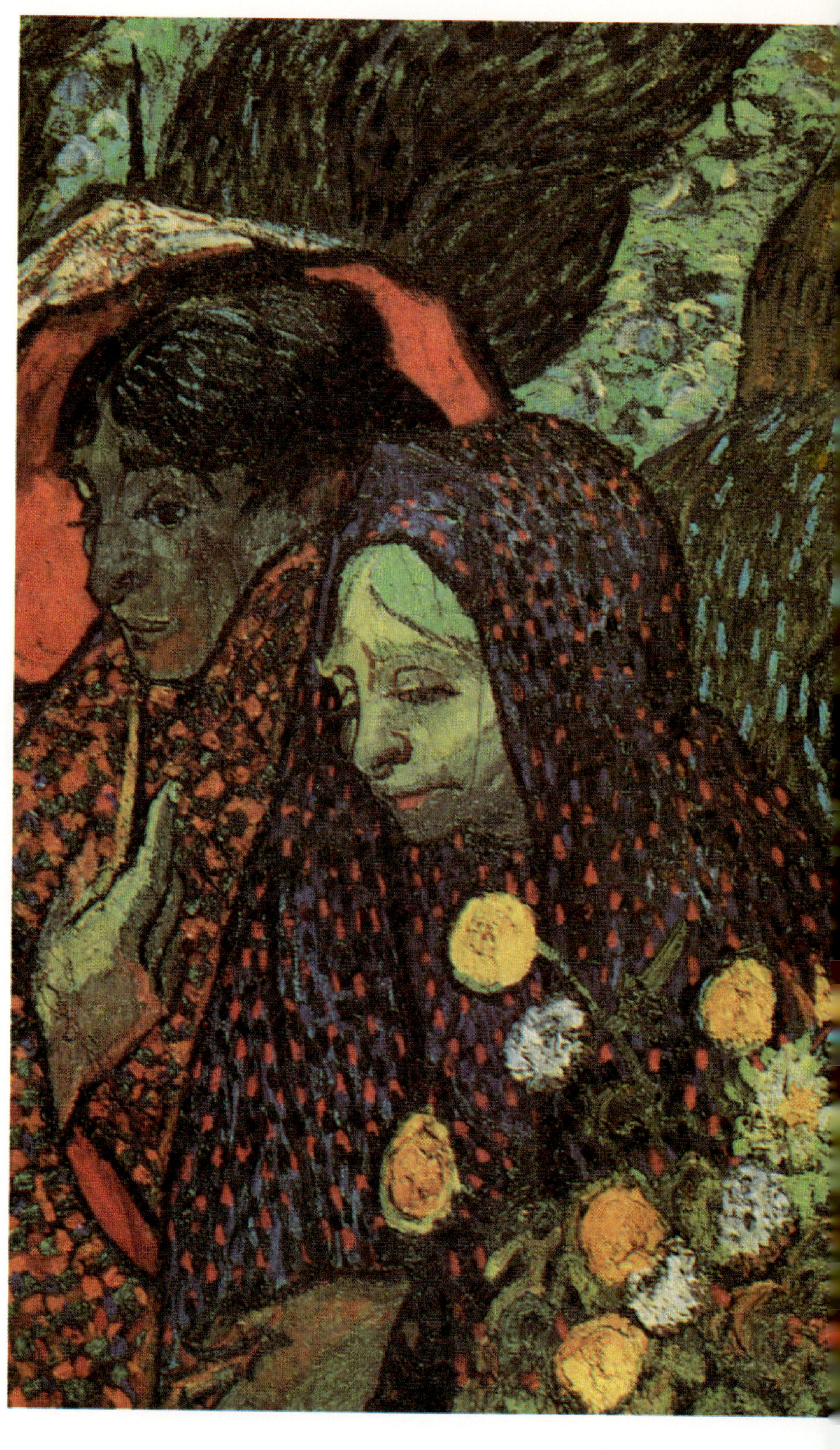

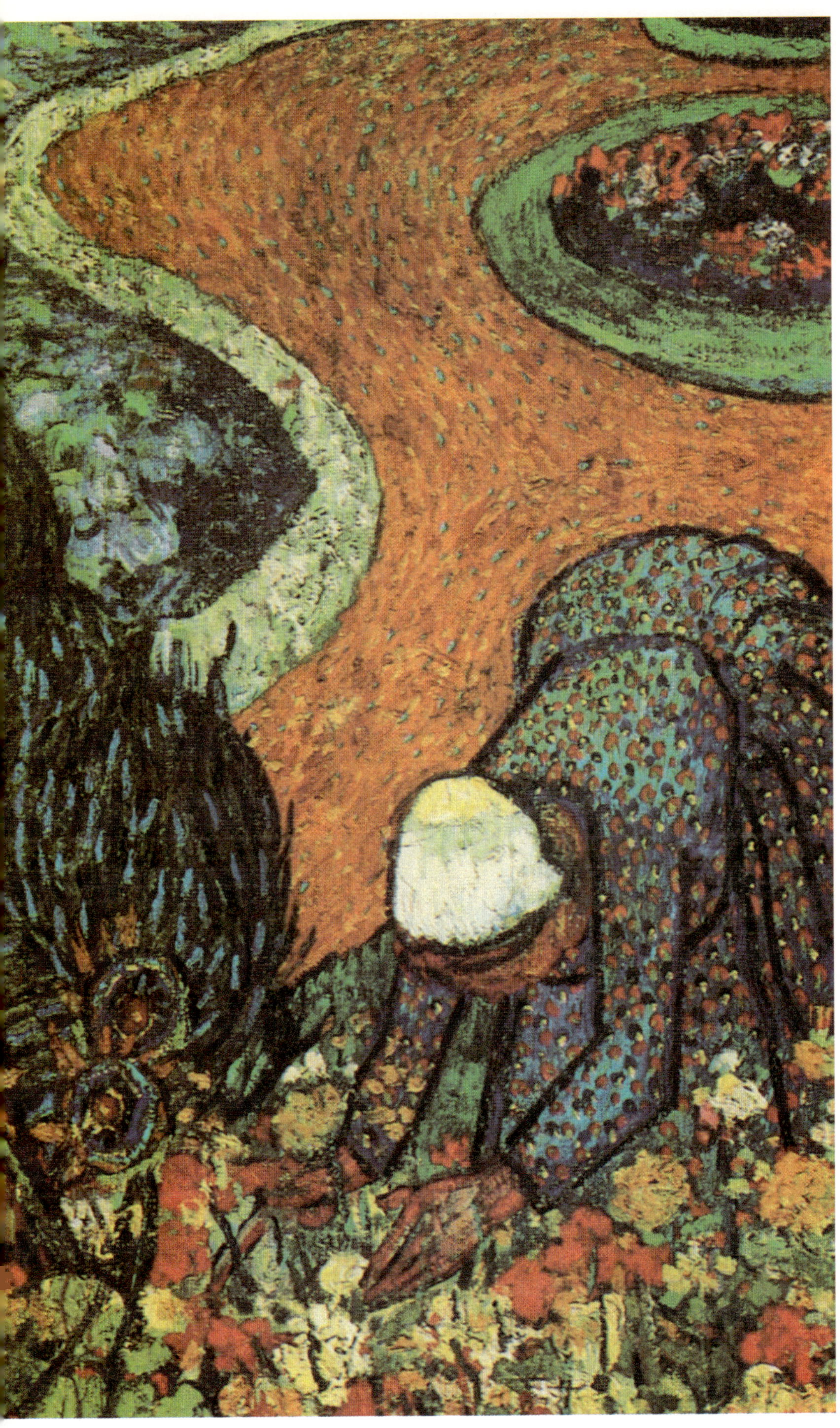

Memory of an Etten Garden (also called Promenade at Arles)

November 1888 - oil on canvas - 73.5 x 92.5 cm -
Hermitage, St Petersburg,

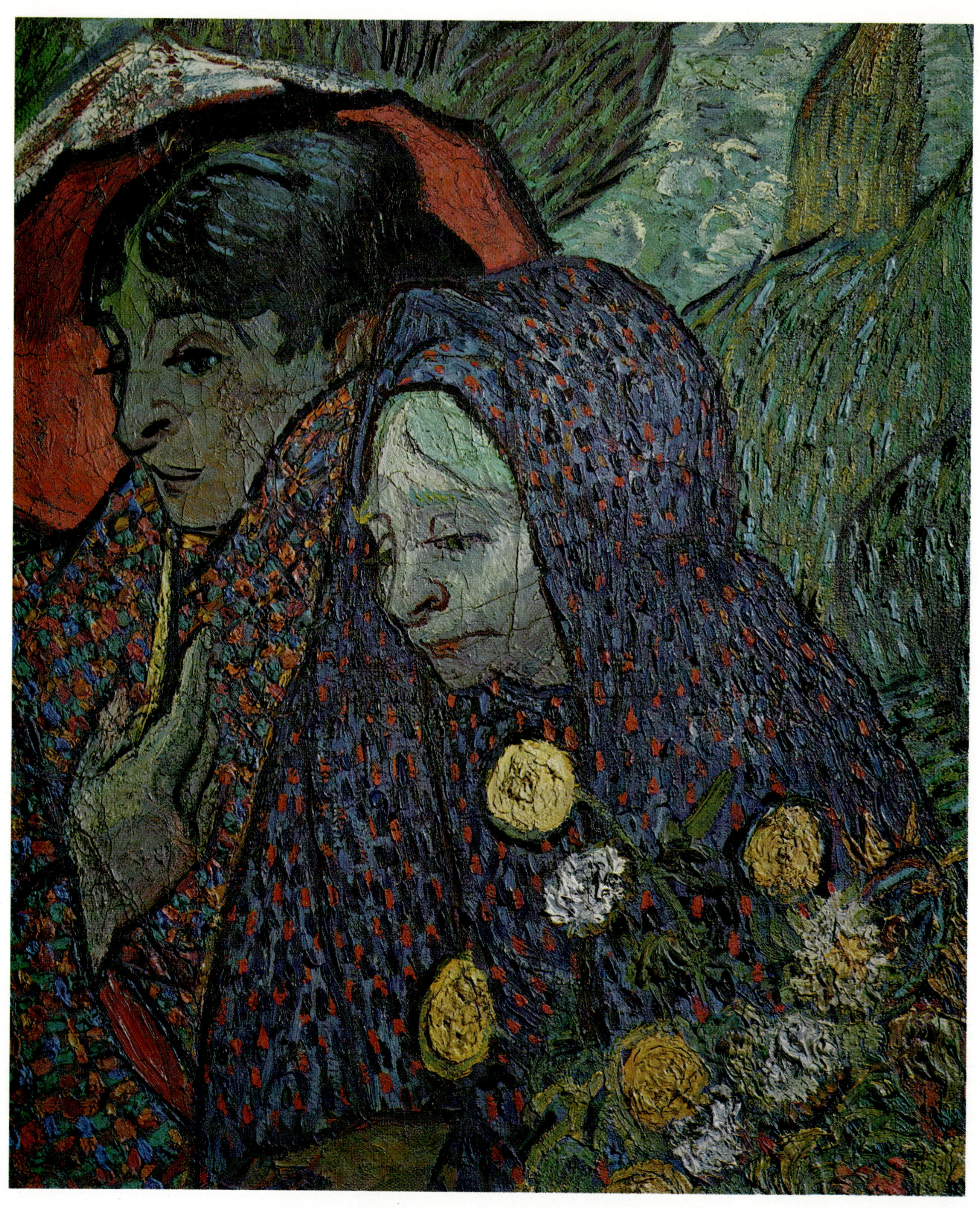

Memory of an Etten Garden (detail)

November 1888 - oil on canvas - 73 x 92 cm -
Hermitage, St Petersburg

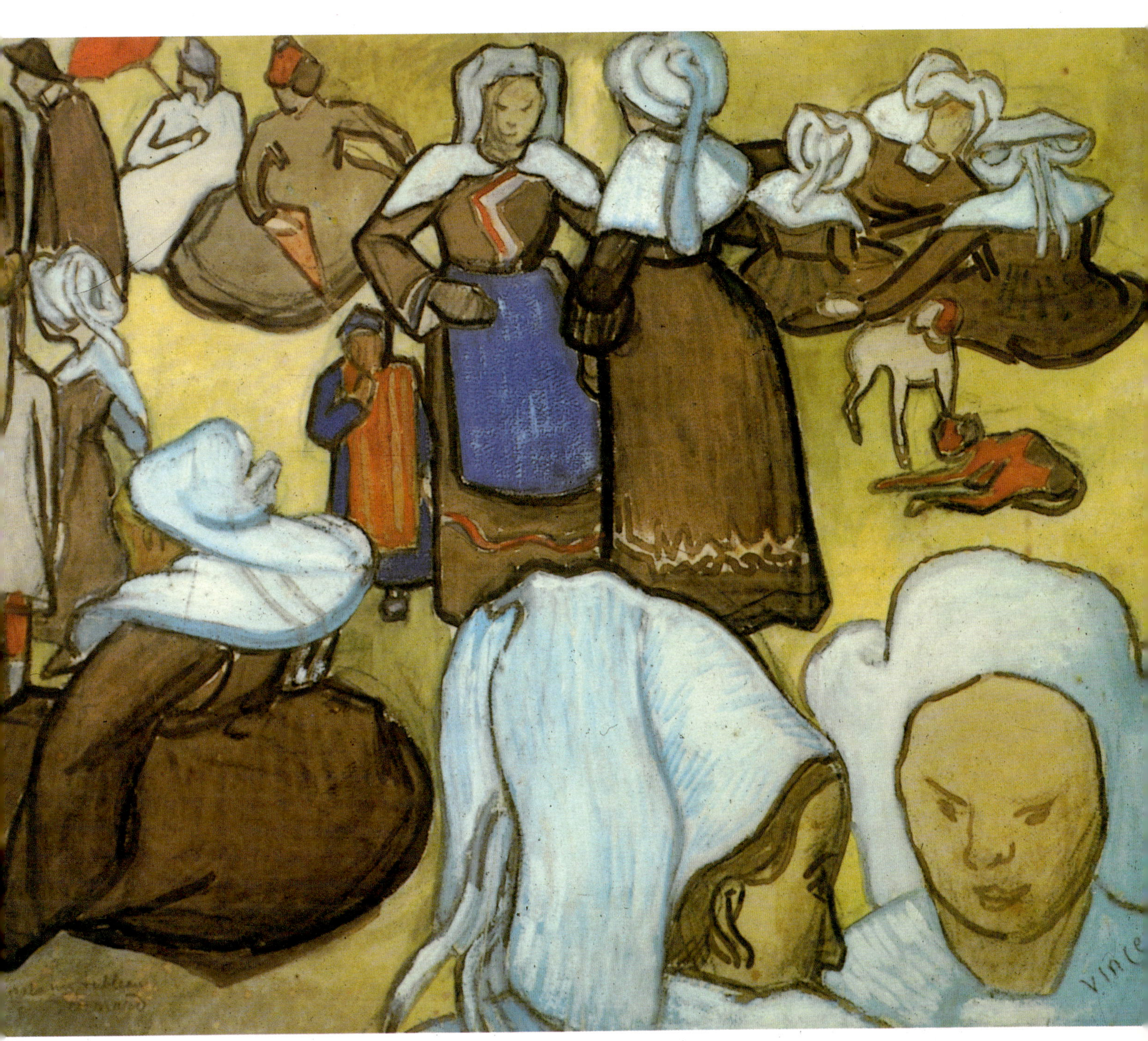

Breton Women (after Emile Bernard)

December 1888 - watercolour - 47.5 x 62 cm -
Civica Galleria d'Arte Moderna, Milan

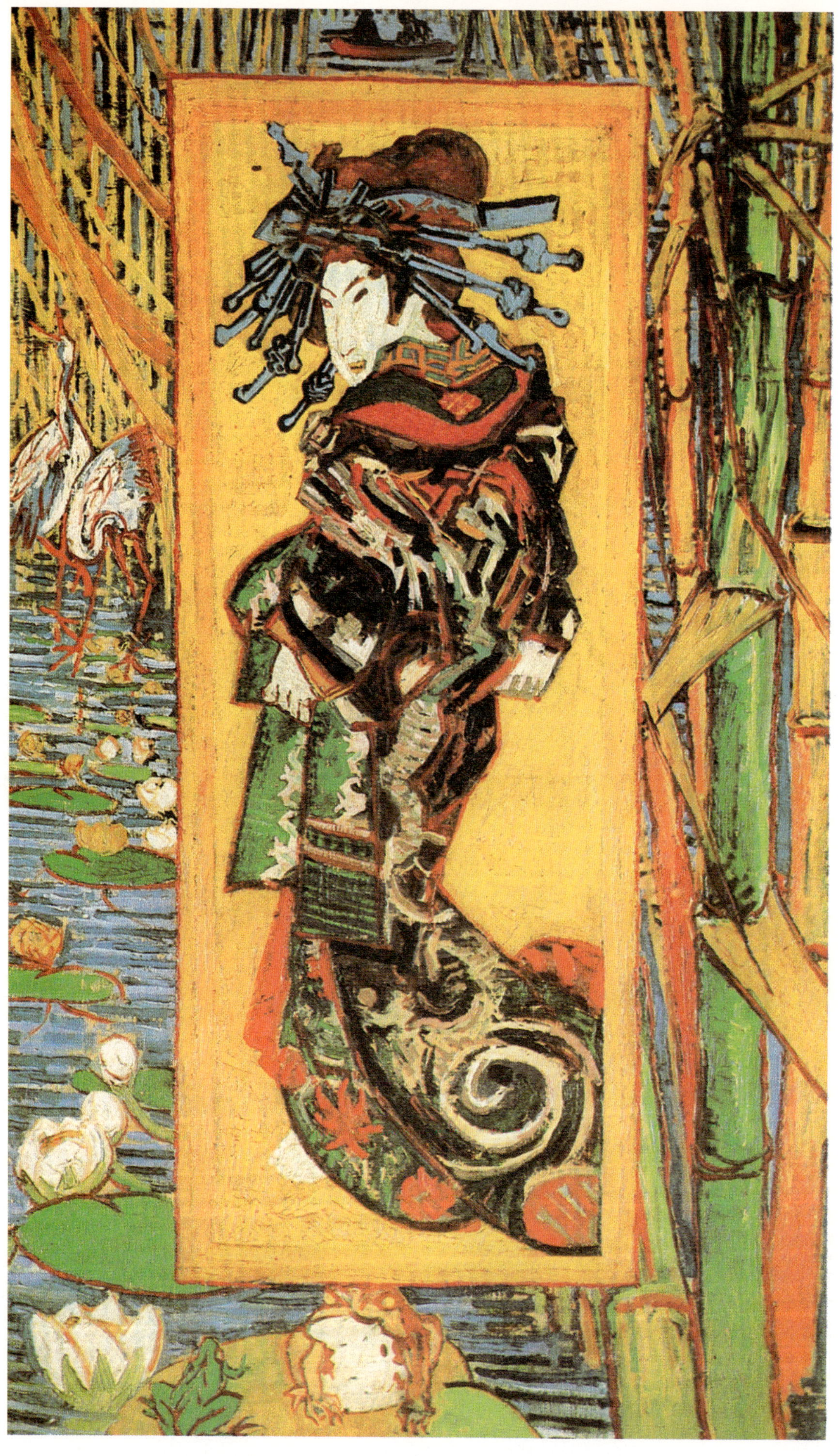

Japonaiserie: Oiran (after Kesaï Eisen)

September-October 1887 - oil on canvas - 105.5 x 60.5 cm -
Vincent van Gogh Foundation, Amsterdam

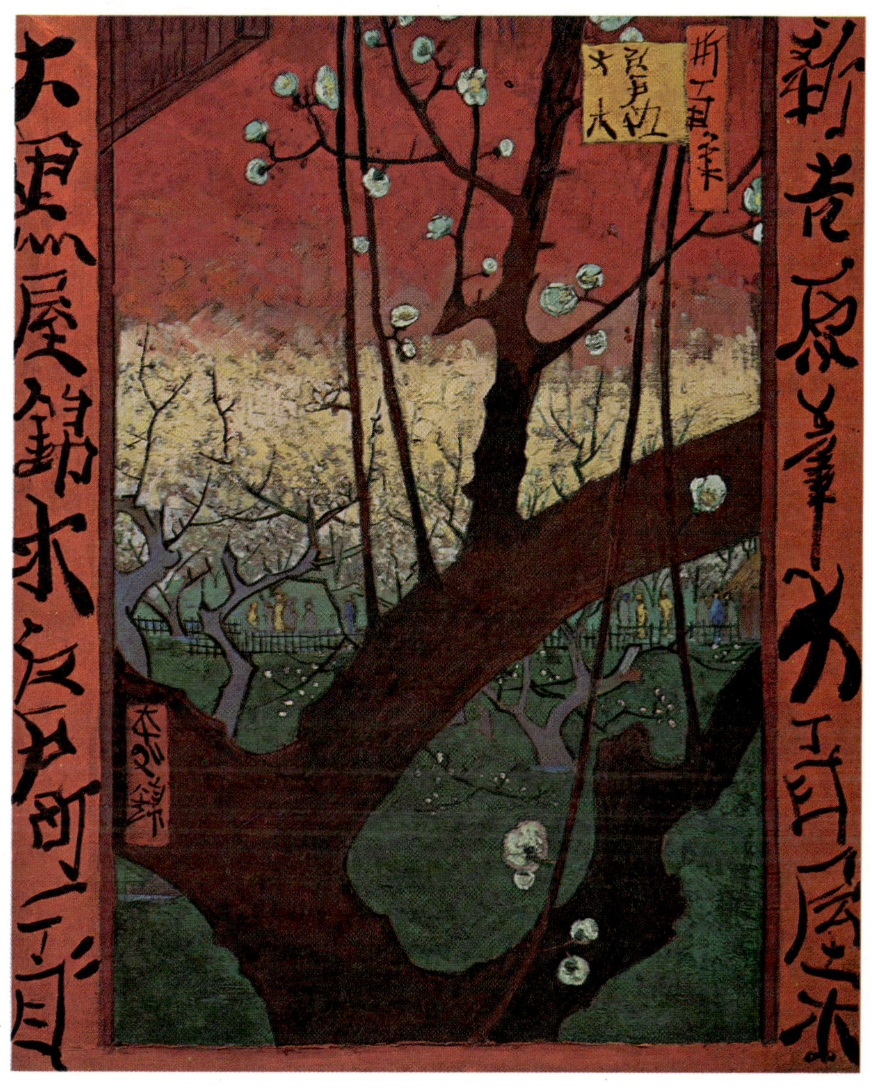

Flowering Plum Trees (after Hiroshige)

1888 - oil on canvas - 55 x 46 cm -
Vincent van Gogh Foundation, Amsterdam

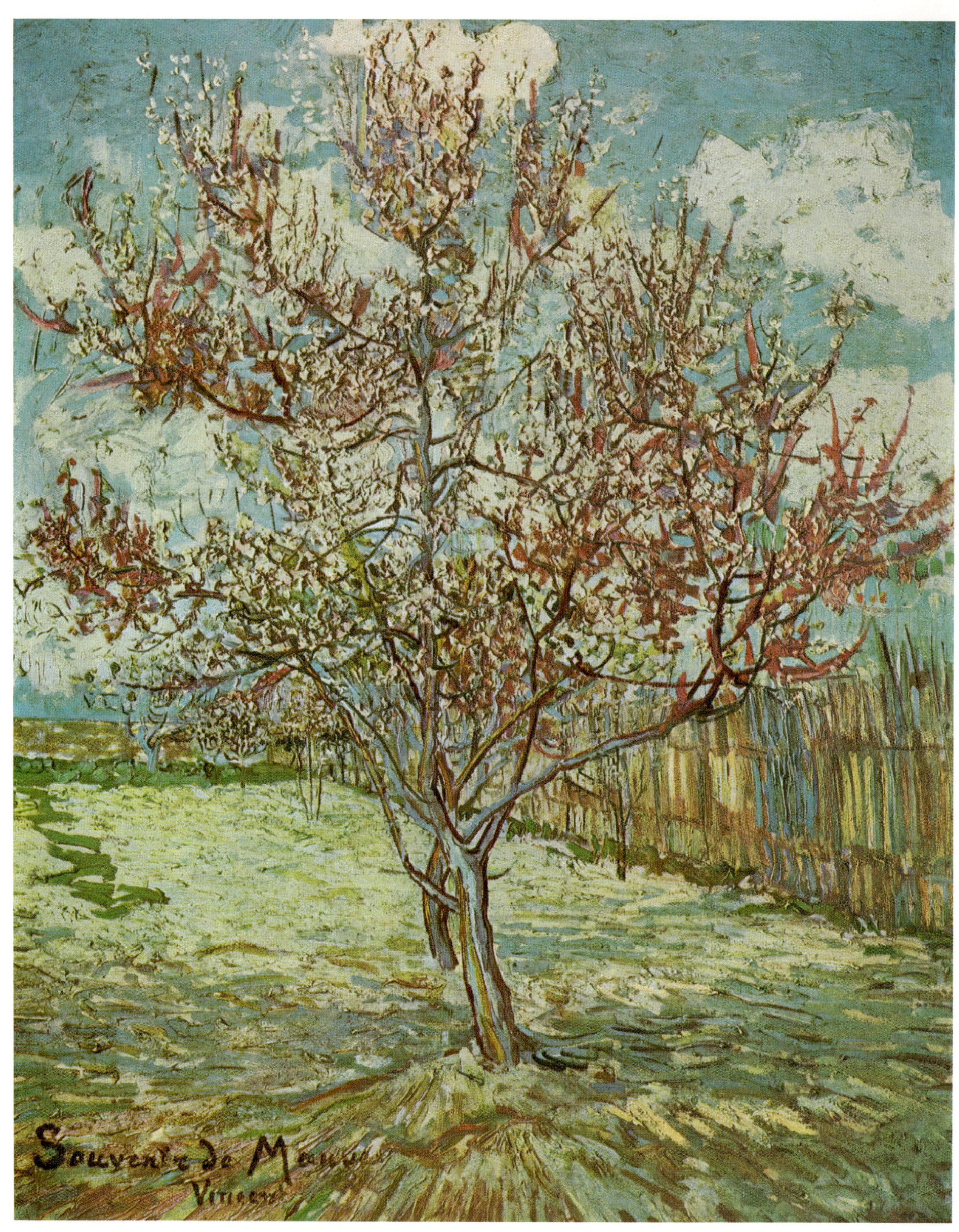

Blossoming Peach Tress (Remembrance of Mauve)

April 1888 - oil on canvas - 73 x 59.5 cm -
Rijksmuseum Kröller- Müller, Otterlo

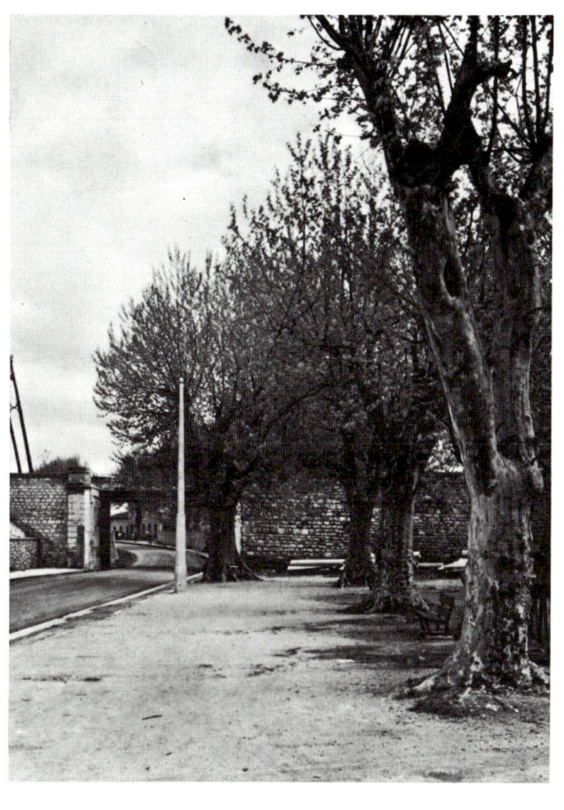

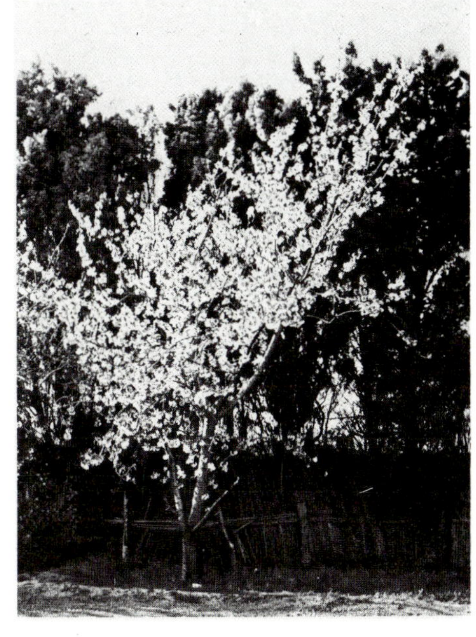

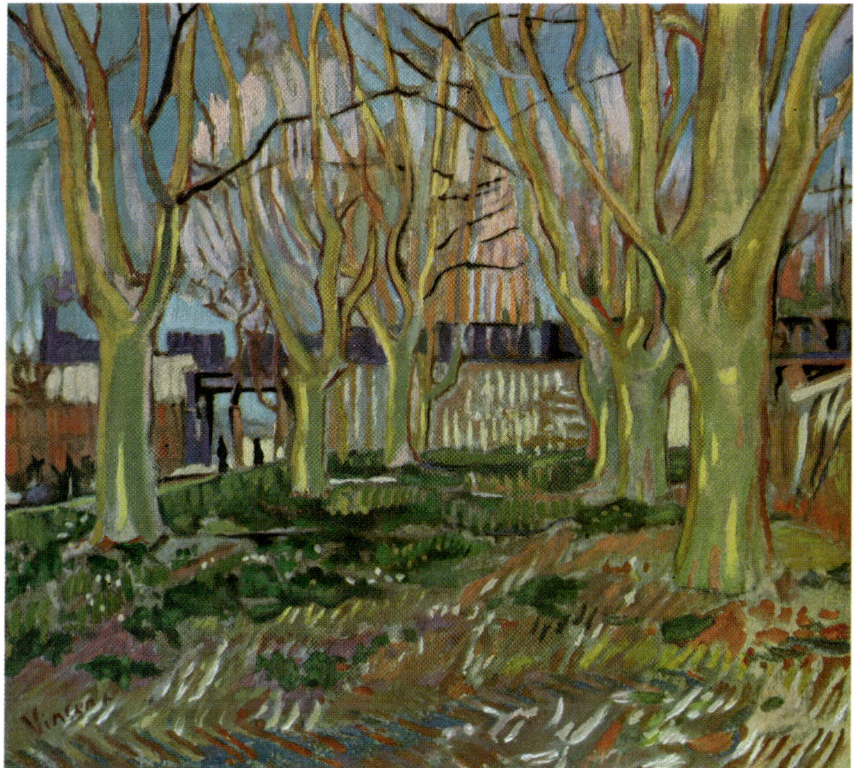

Photograph of the tree on the preceding page

Nowadays, only a part of the viaduct is left and some trees, as the photograph shows

The Viaduct near the Station

March 1888 - oil on canvas - 45 x 49 cm - Musée Rodin, Paris

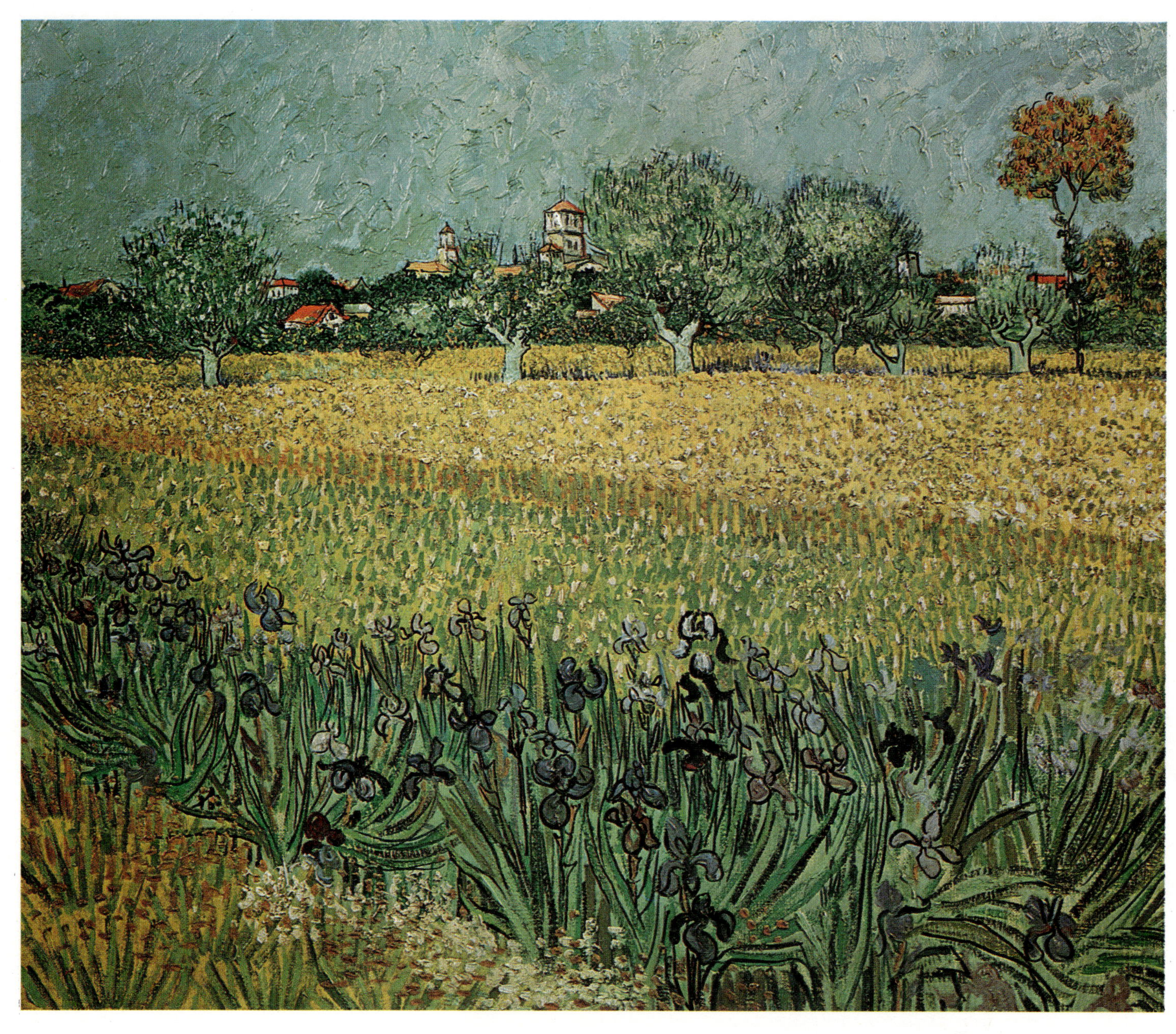

View of Arles with Irises in the Foreground

May 1888 - oil on canvas - 54 x 65 cm -
Vincent van Gogh Foundation, Amsterdam

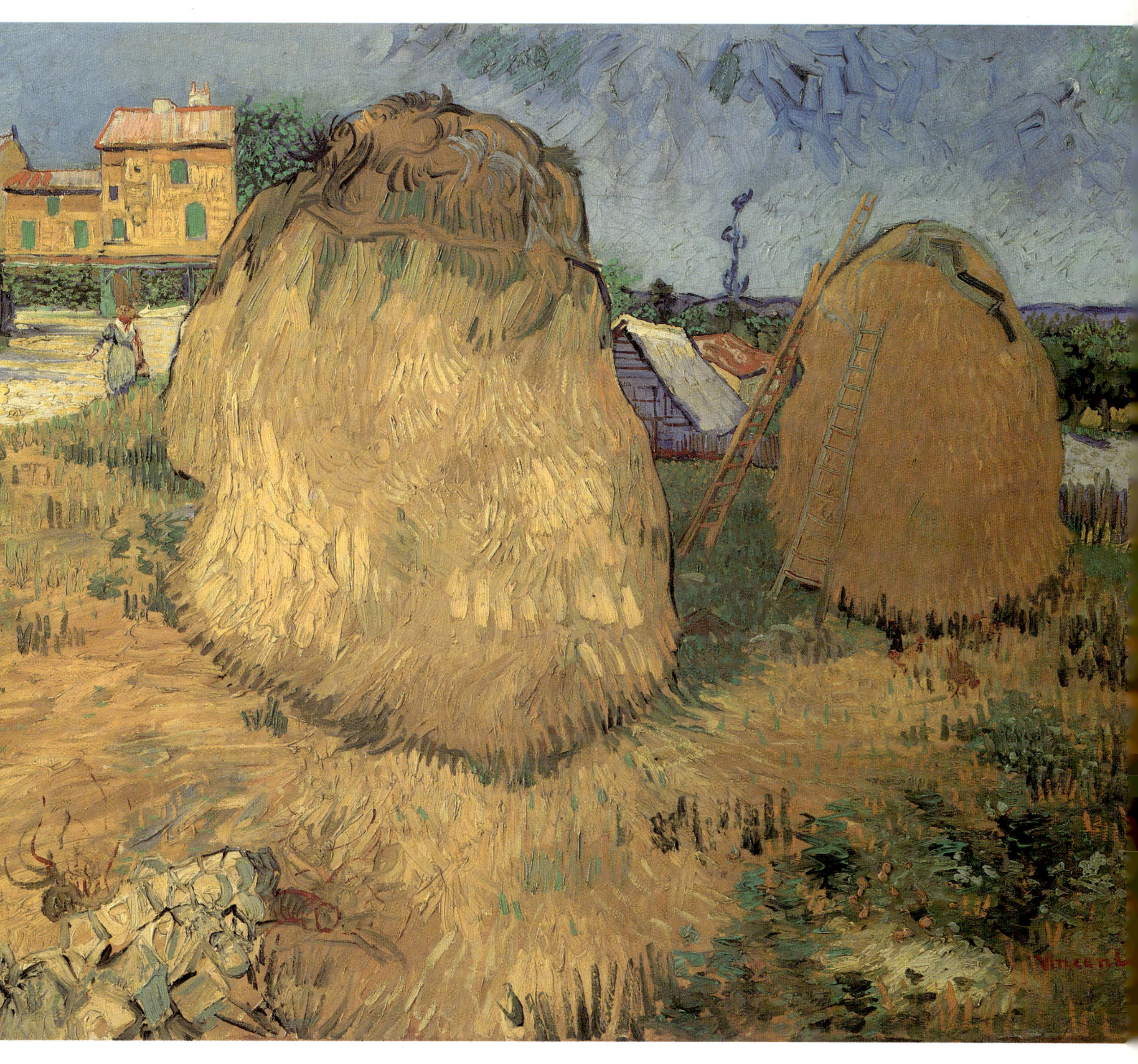

Haystacks

June 1888 - oil on canvas - 67.3 x 92.5 cm -
Rijksmuseum Kröller- Müller, Otterlo

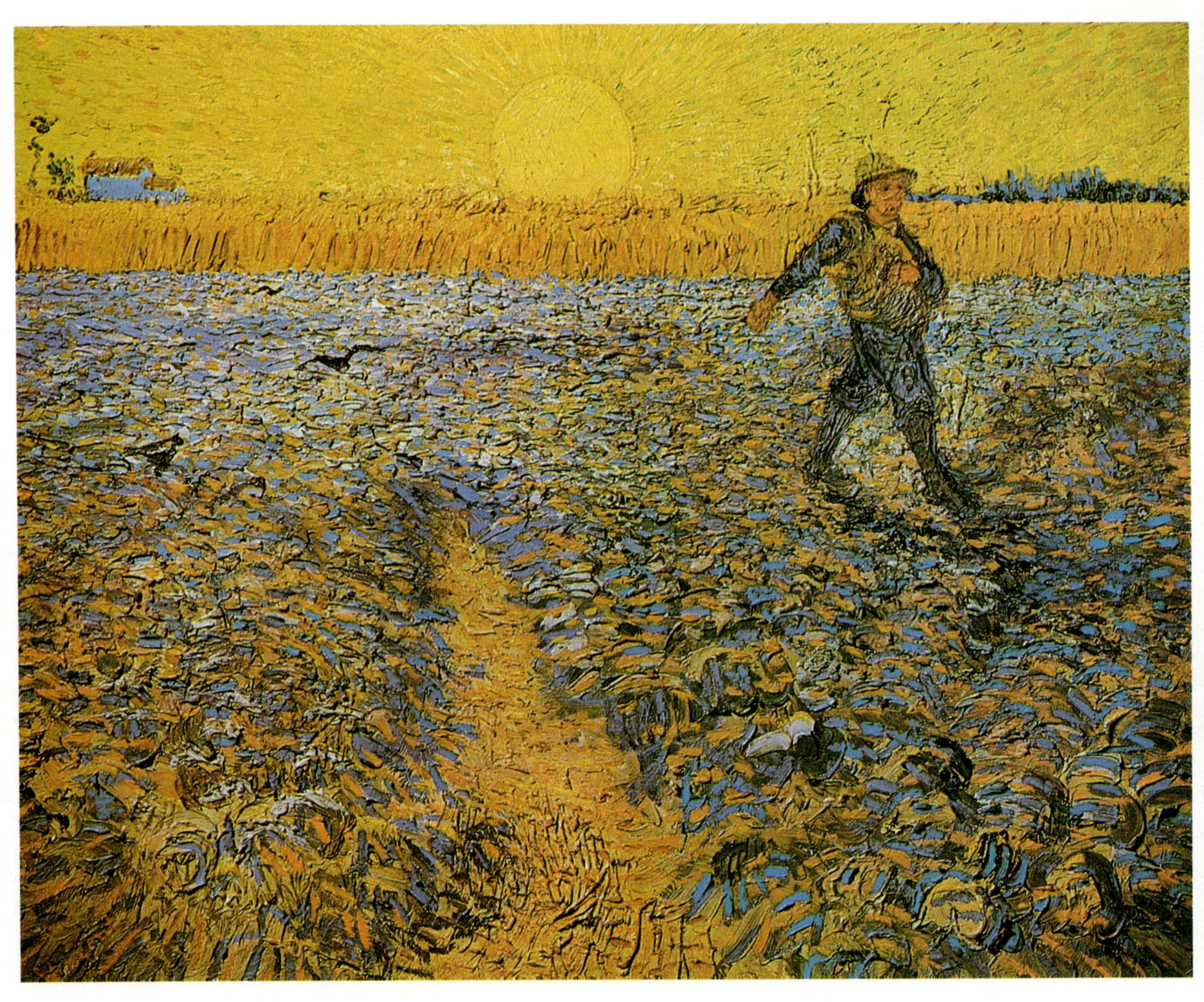

The Sower

June 1888 - oil on canvas - 64 x 80.5 cm -
Rijksmuseum Kröller- Müller, Otterlo

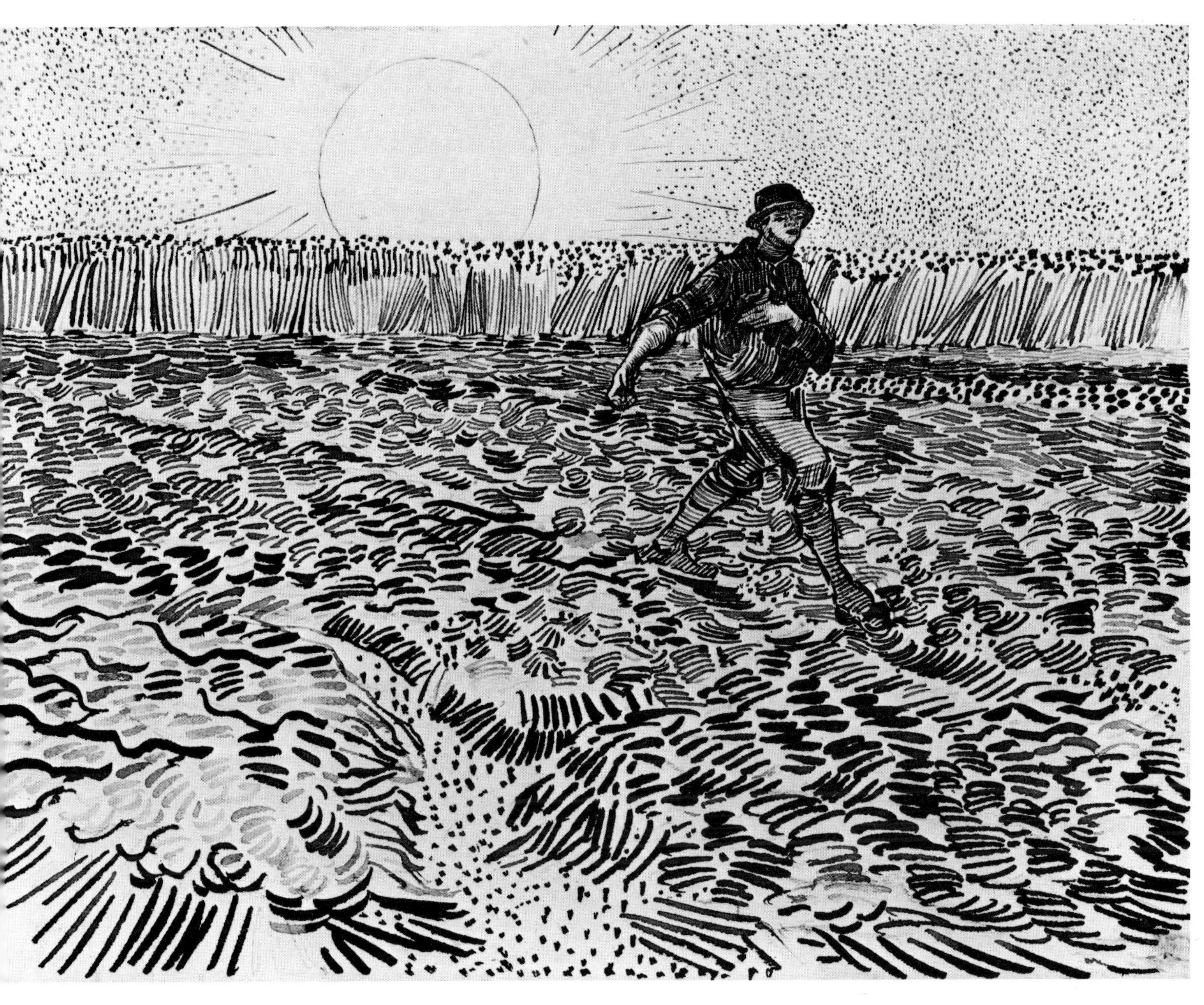

The Sower

August 1888 - pen - 24.5 x 32 cm -
Vincent van Gogh Foundation, Amsterdam

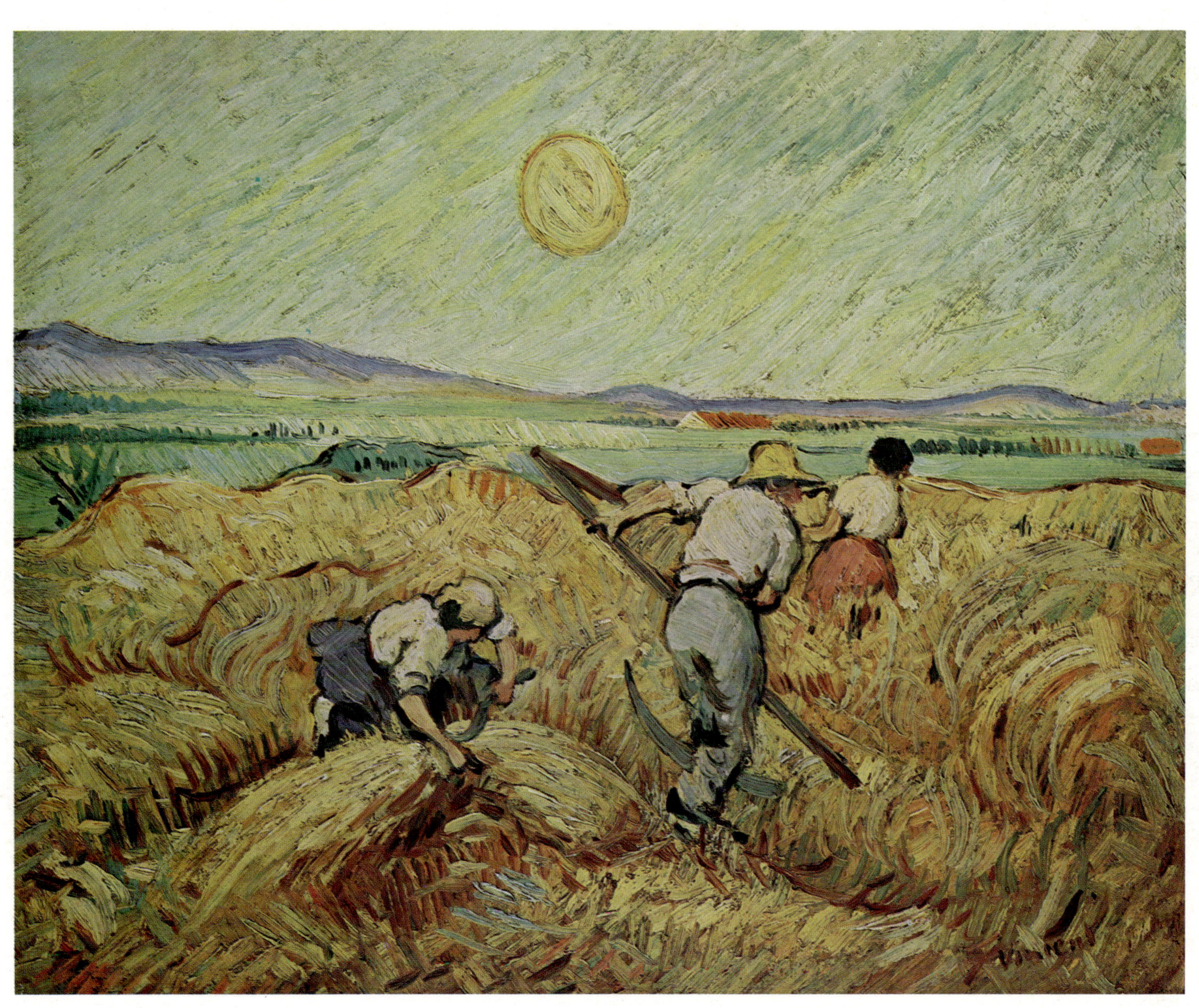

Wheat Harvest in the Fields below the Alpilles

June 1888 - oil on canvas - 30 x 40 cm - Private collection, Los Angeles

Flowering Garden (detail)

July 1888 - oil on canvas - 72 x 91 cm - Gemeentenmuseum, The Hague

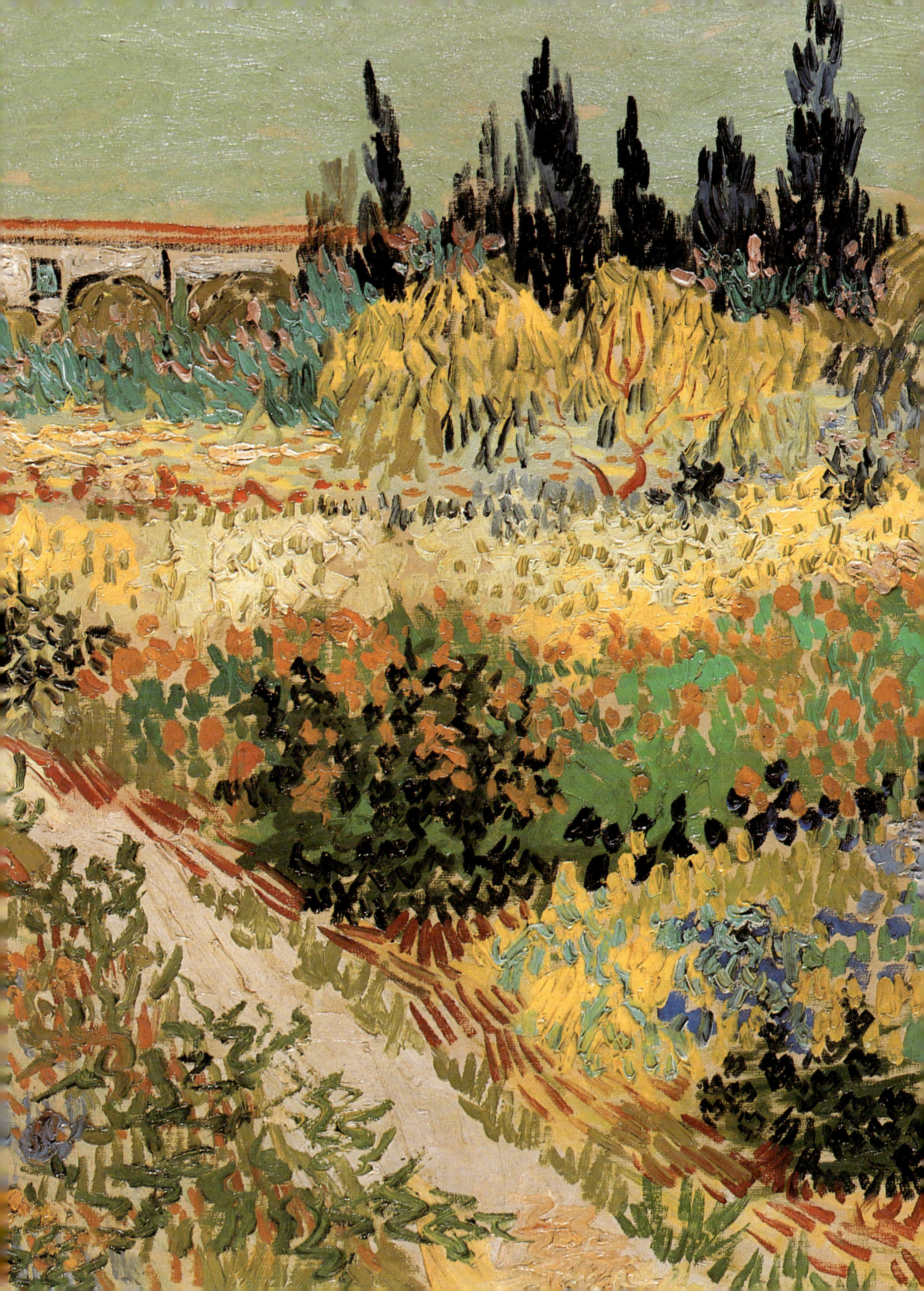

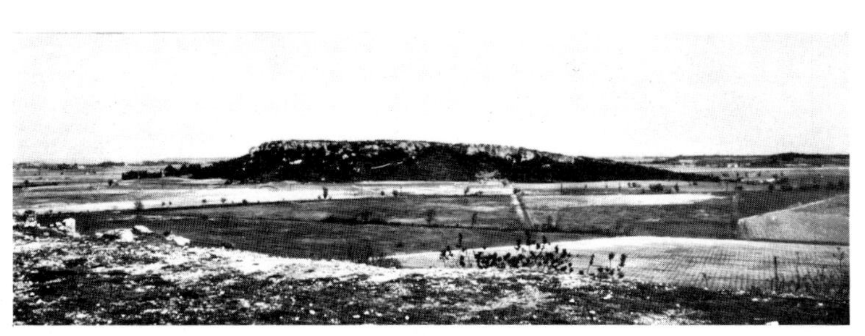

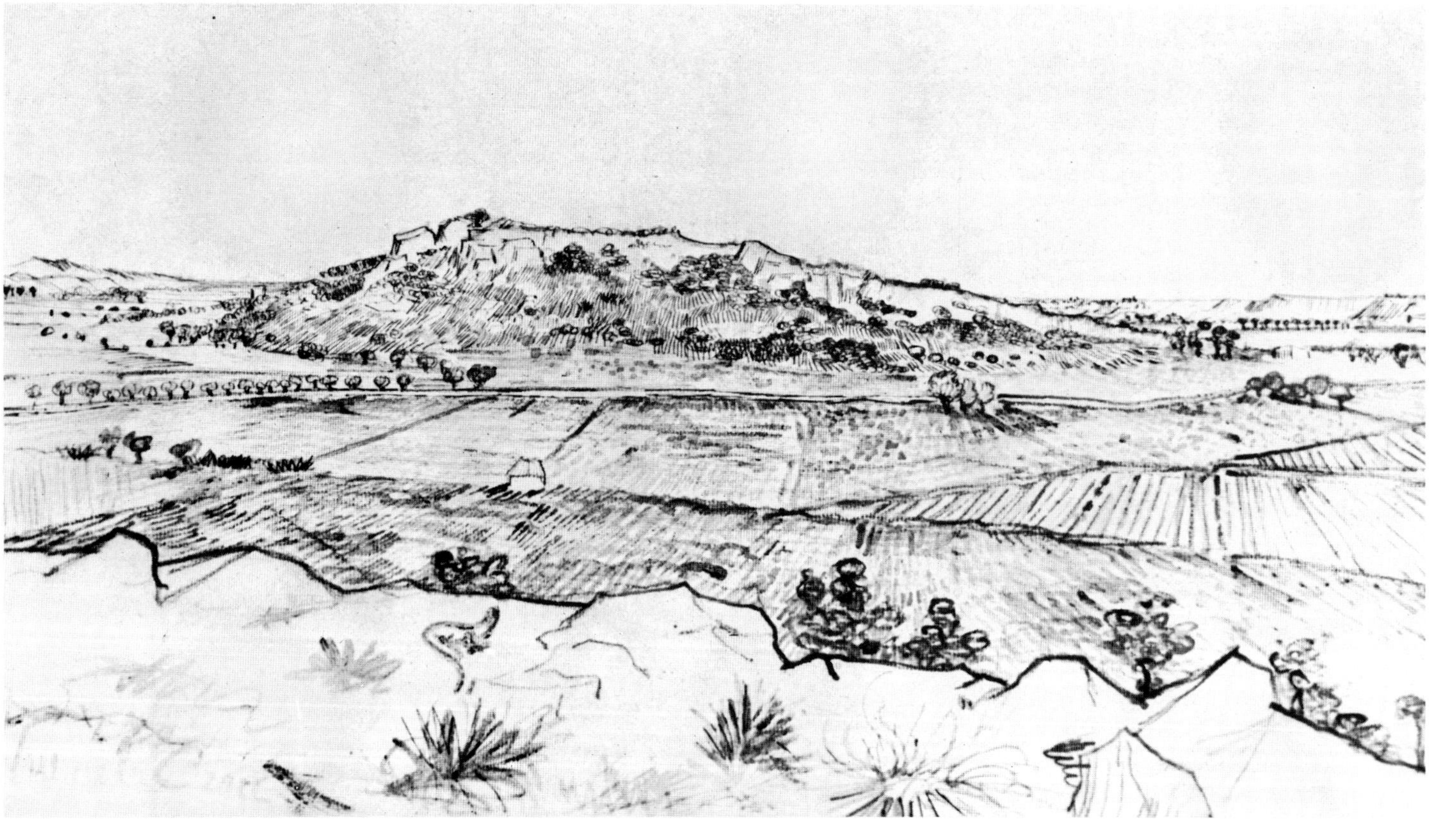

Photograph of the "Montagne de Corde" taken from the ruins of the Abbaye de Montmajour

View of the Plain, Taken from Montmajour

May-June 1888 - pen and black crayon - 28 x 47 cm - Folkwang Museum, Essen

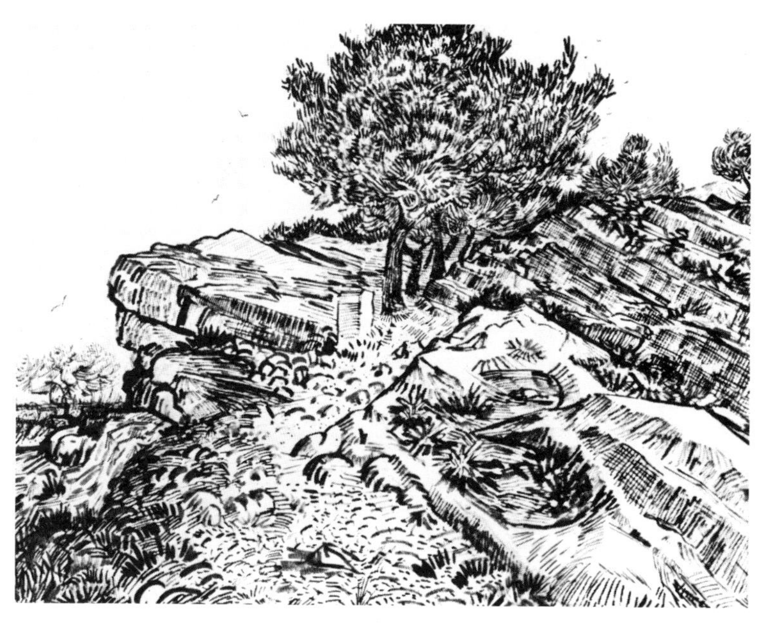

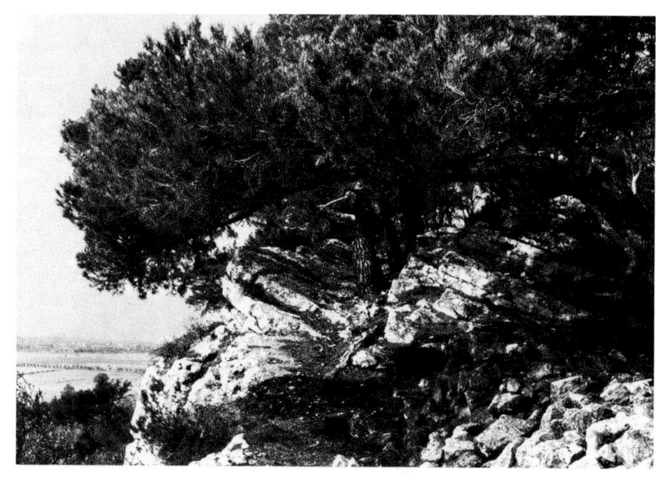

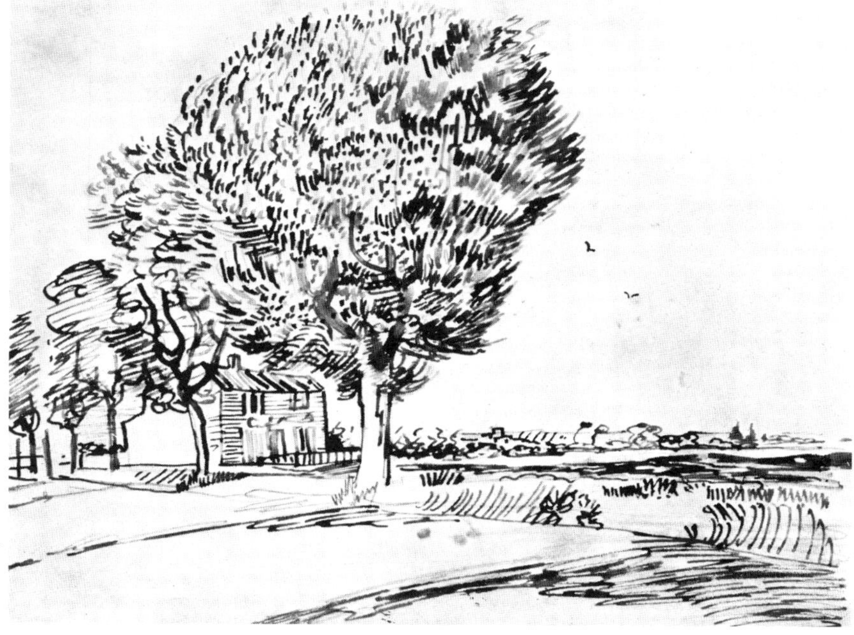

Photograph of the rock Montmajour

The rock

July 1888 - indian ink, pencil traces - 29 x 61 cm - Vincent van Gogh Foundation, Amsterdam

Road near Arles

July 1888 - crayon and sepia - 24.6 x 23.9 cm - Albertina, Vienna

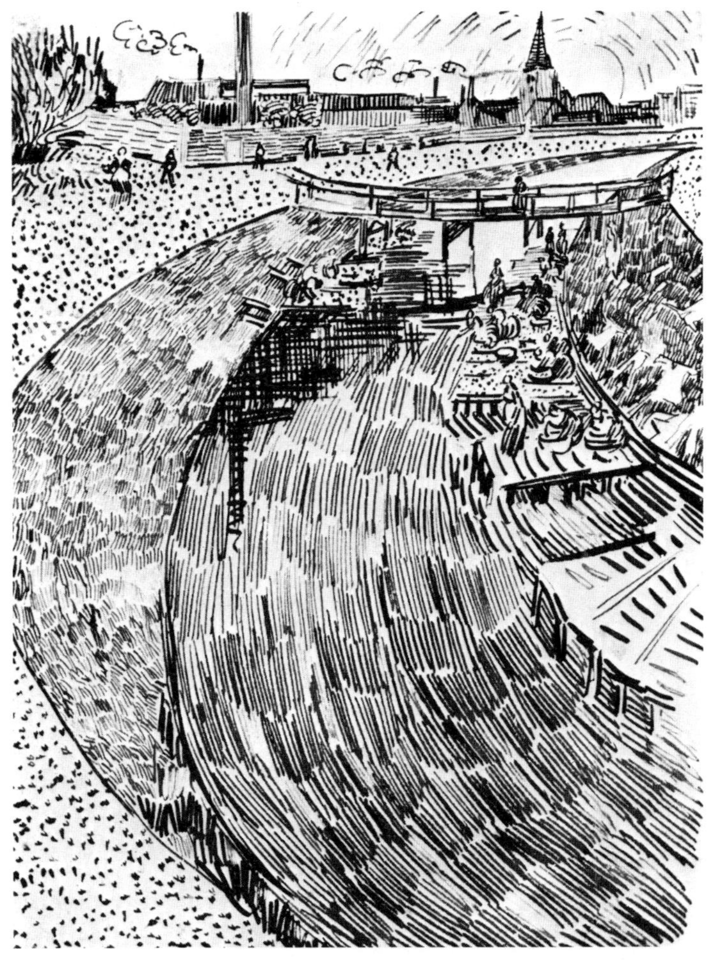

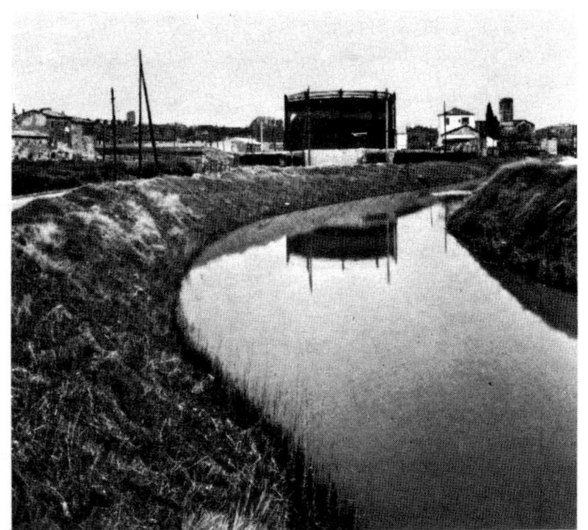

Washerwomen at the canal

Summer 1888 - indian ink - 31.5 x 24 cm -
Rijksmuseum Kröller- Müller, Otterlo

Photograph of the canal at the place called "Roubine du Roy".

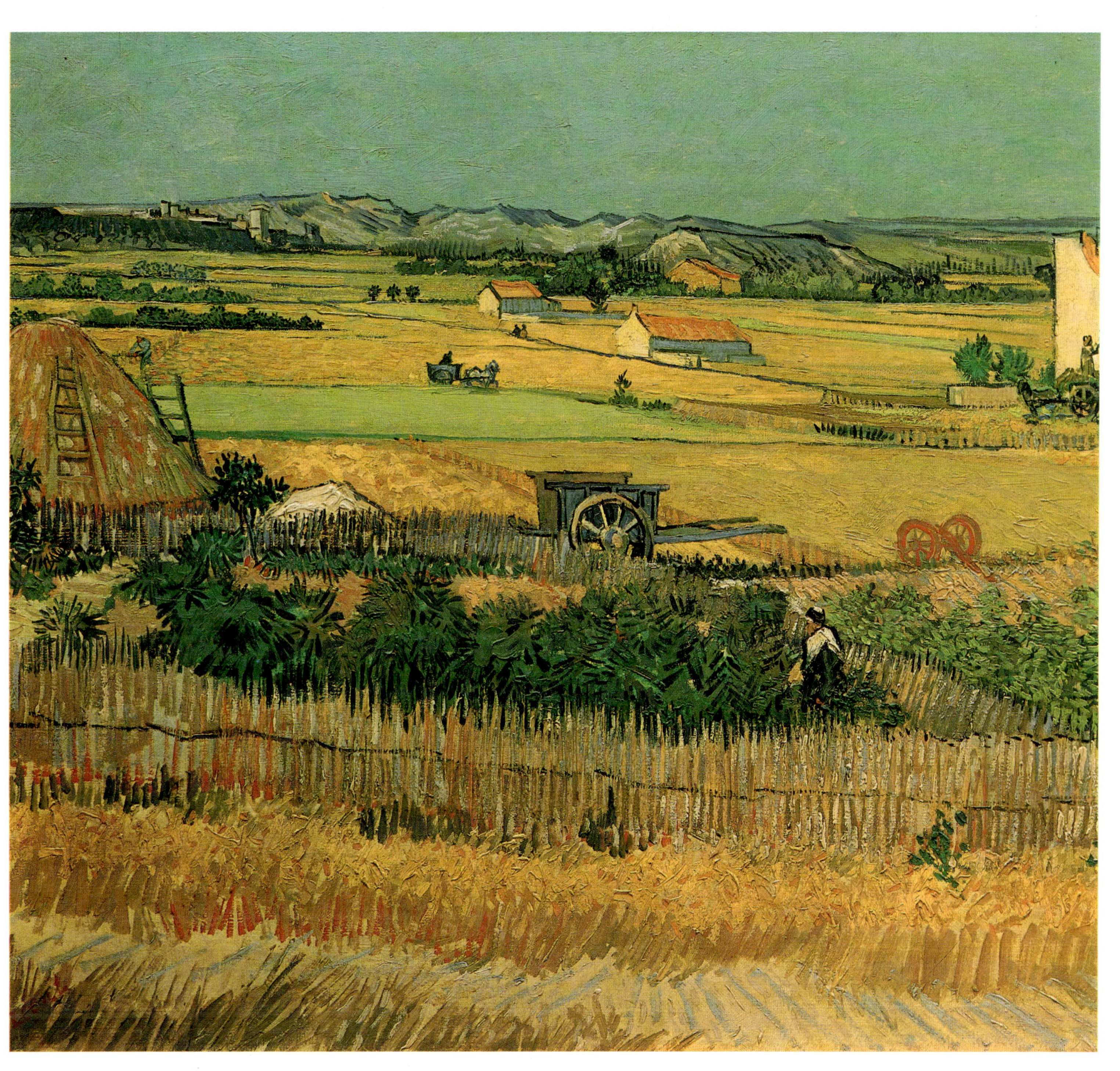

Harvest at La Crau, with Montmajour in the Background

June 1888 - oil on canvas - 72.5 x 92 cm -
Vincent van Gogh Foundation, Amsterdam

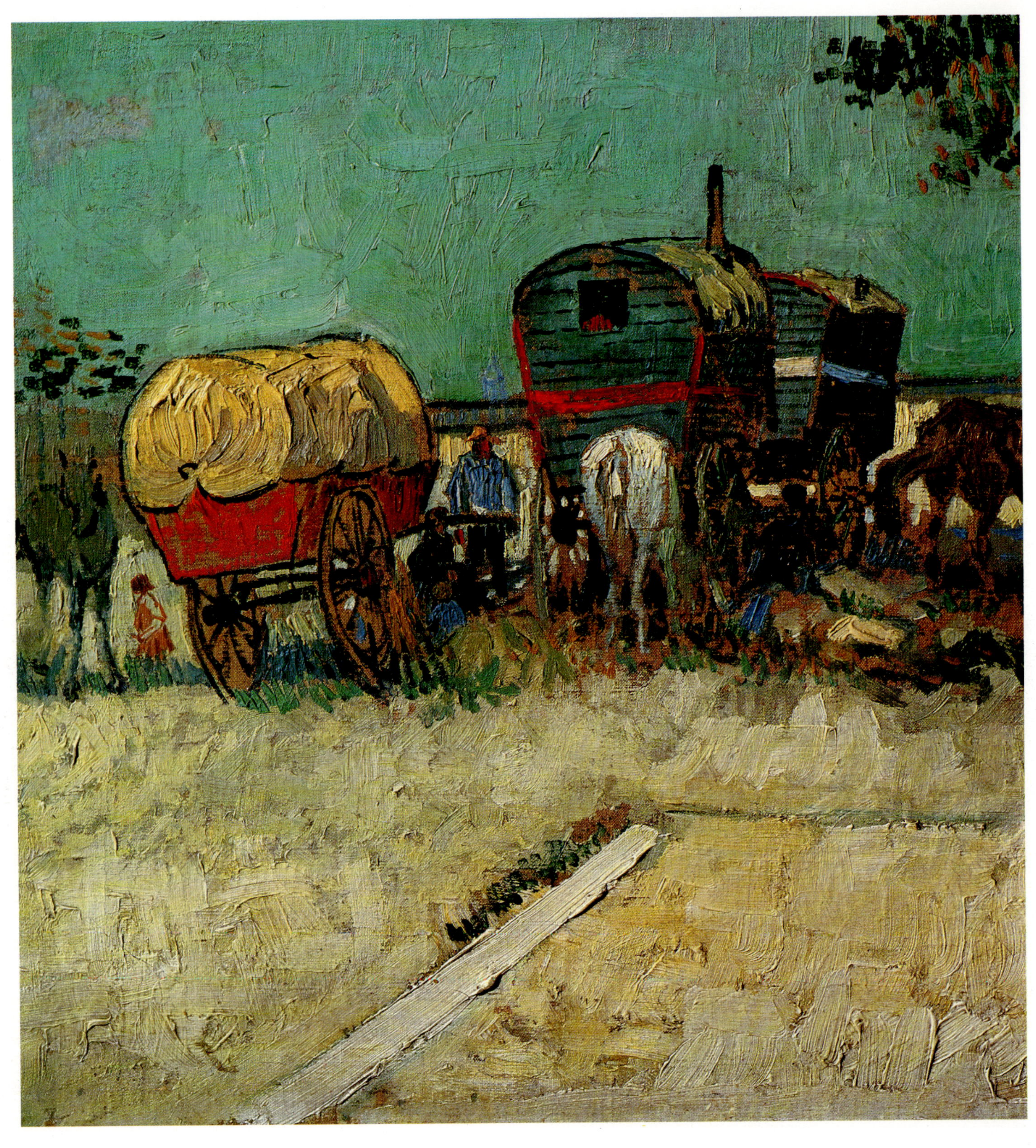

Gypsy Camp

August 1888 - oil on canvas - 45 x 51 cm -
Musée d'Orsay, Paris

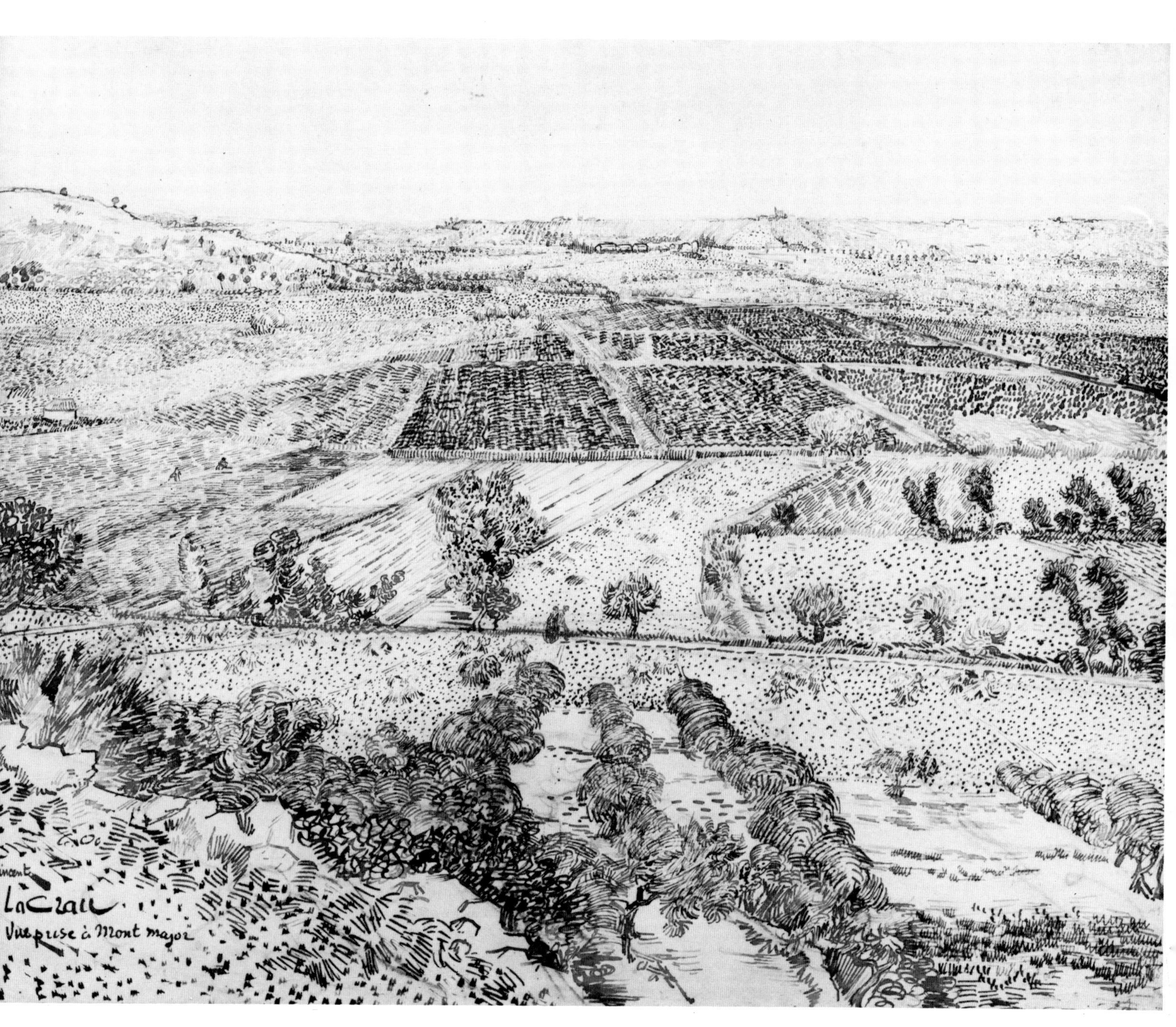

La Crau, Seen from Montmajour

July 1888 - pen, black crayon - 49 x 61 cm - Vincent van Gogh Foundation, Amsterdam

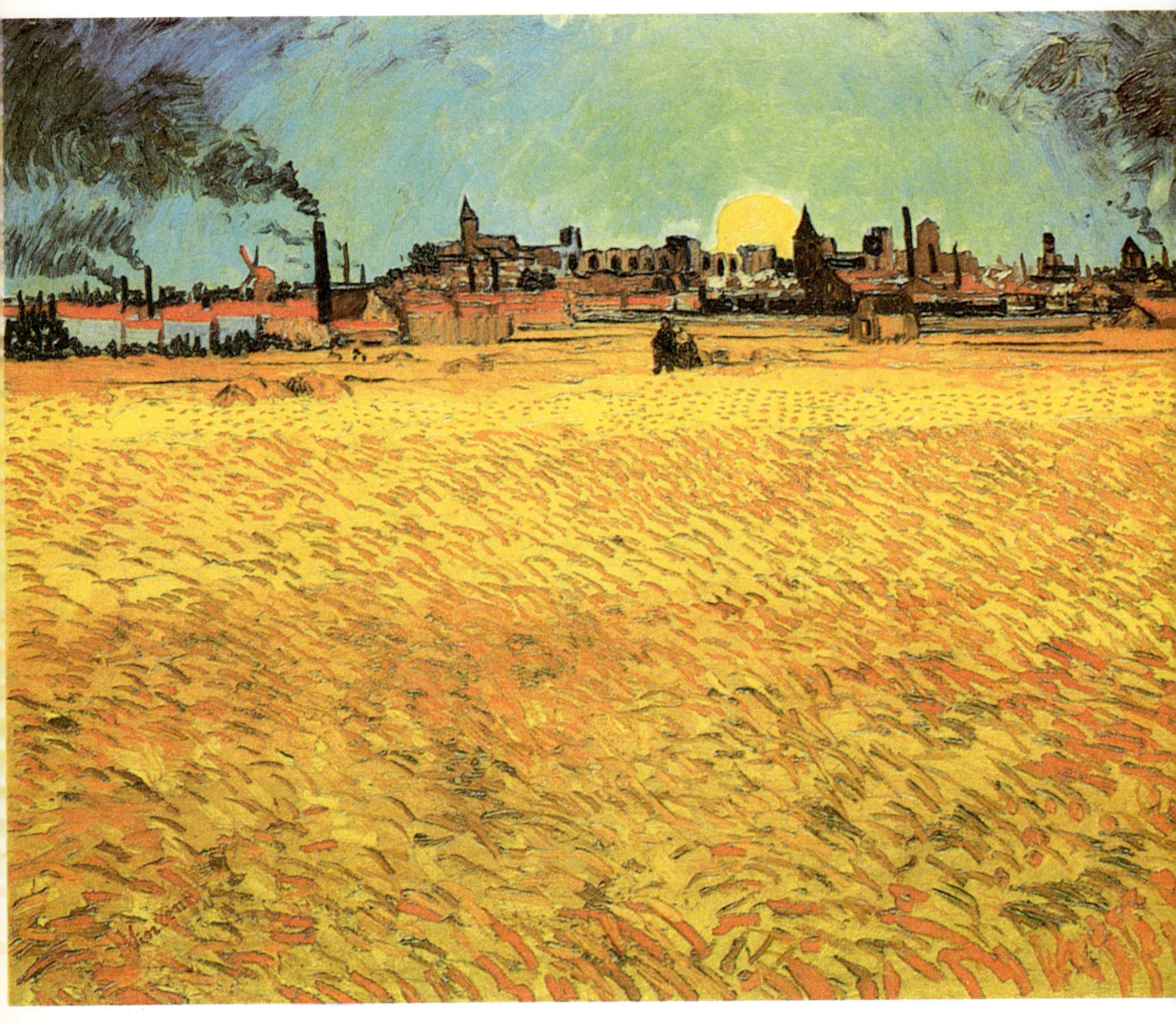

Sunset with View of Arles

1888 - oil on card - 31.5 x 34.5 cm -
Kunstmuseum, Winterthur, Switzerland

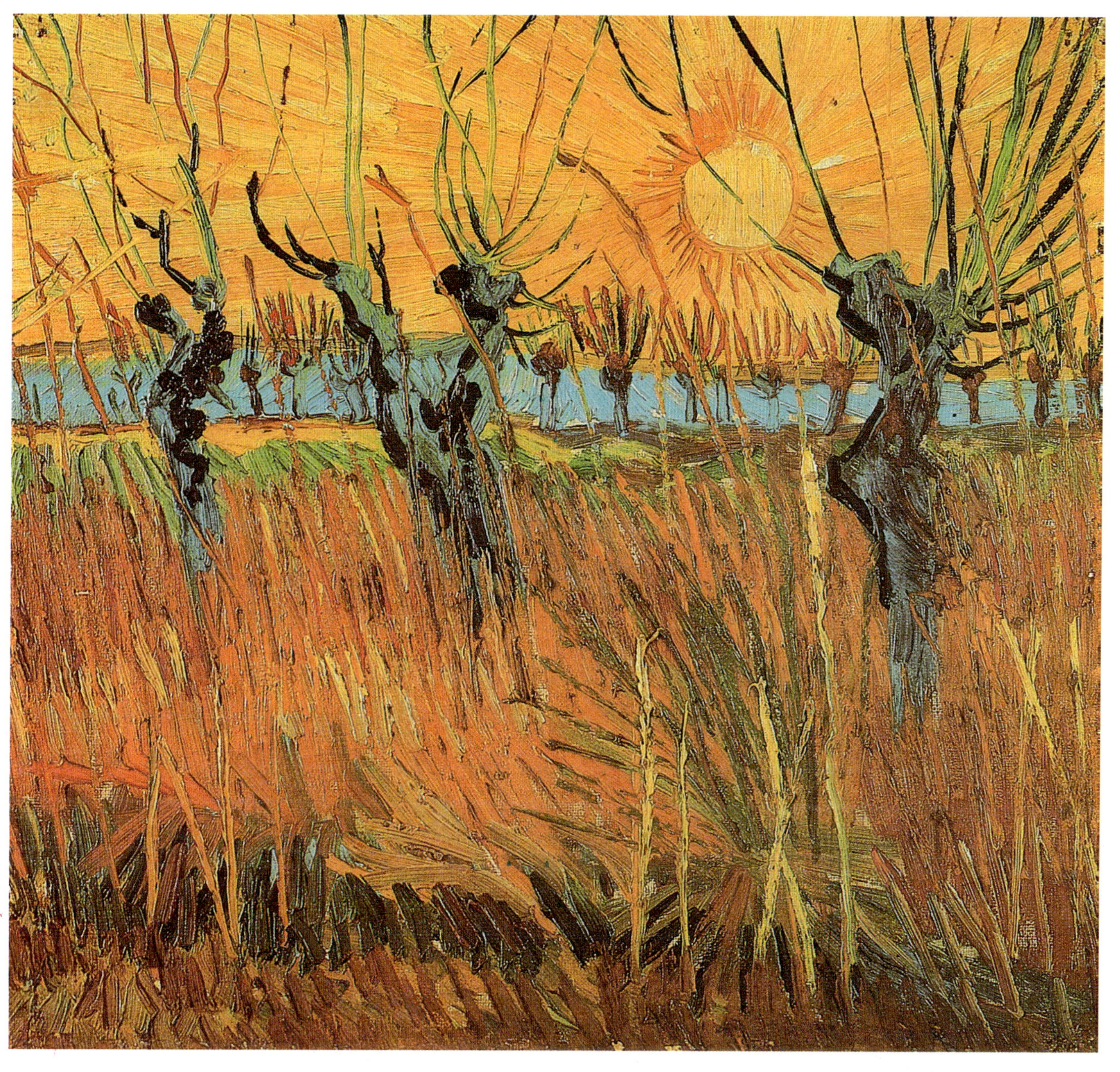

Willows at Sunset

Autumn 1888 - oil on cardboard - 31.5 x 34.5 cm - Rijksmuseum Kröller- Müller, Otterlo

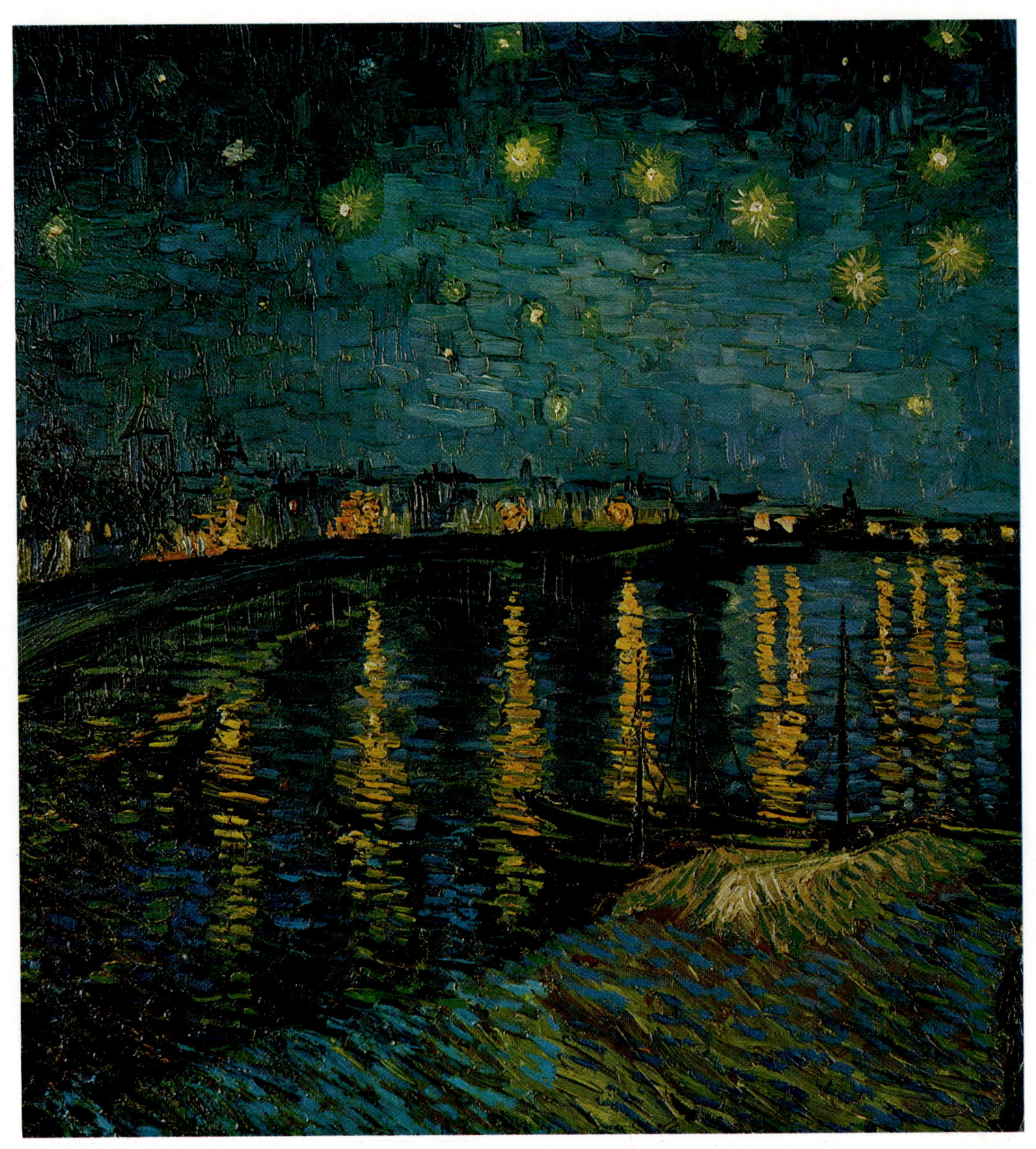

Starry Night

September 1888 - oil on canvas -72.5 x 92 cm -
Moch collection, Paris

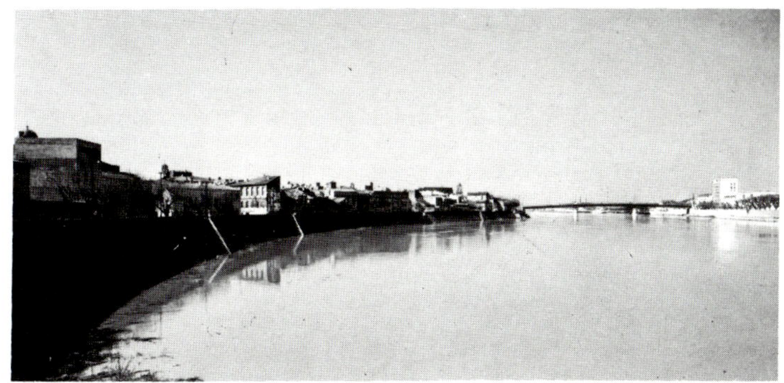

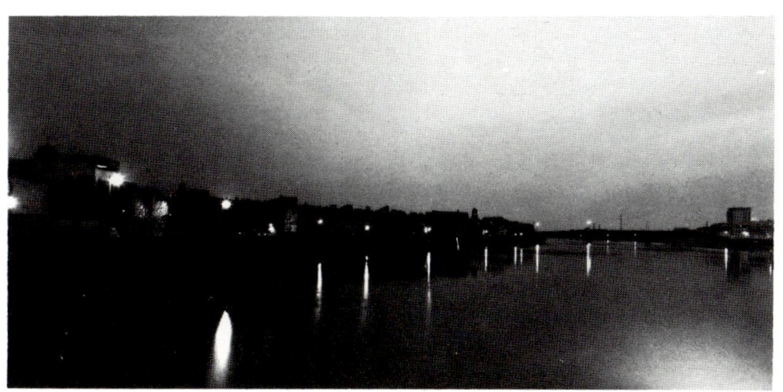

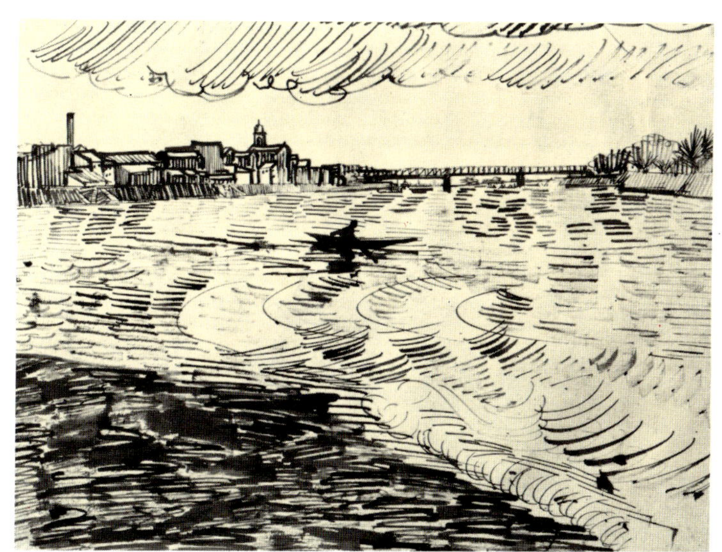

Photograph of the Rhône by day

Photograph of the Rhône by night

The Rhône by Day

Summer 1888 - indian ink - 25.5 x 34.5 cm -
Neue Pinakothek, Munich

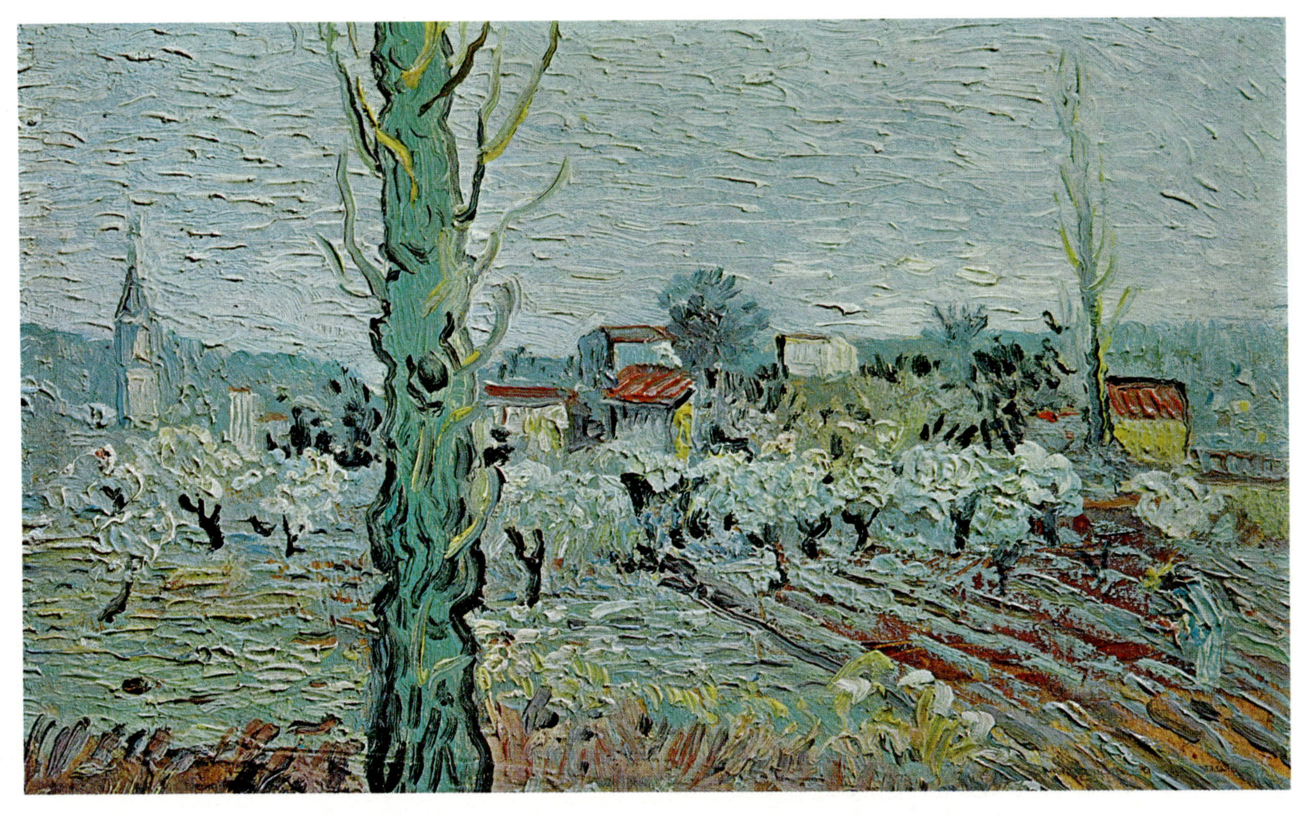

Countryside near Arles

1888 - sketch in oils - 10.5 x 17.5 cm -
George Renand collection, Paris

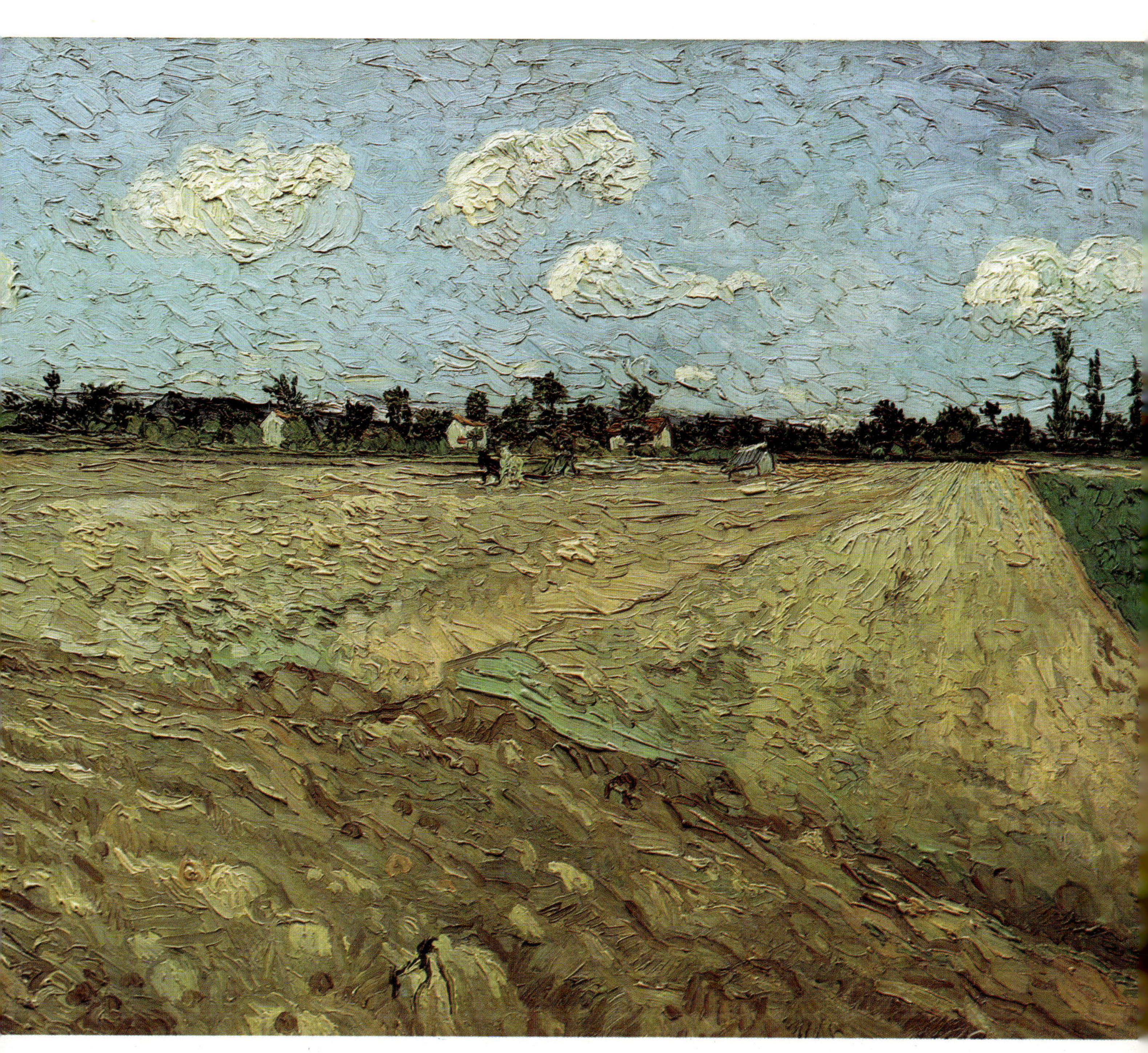

Plowed Field

September 1888 - oil on canvas - 72.5 x 92 cm - Vincent van Gogh Foundation, Amsterdam

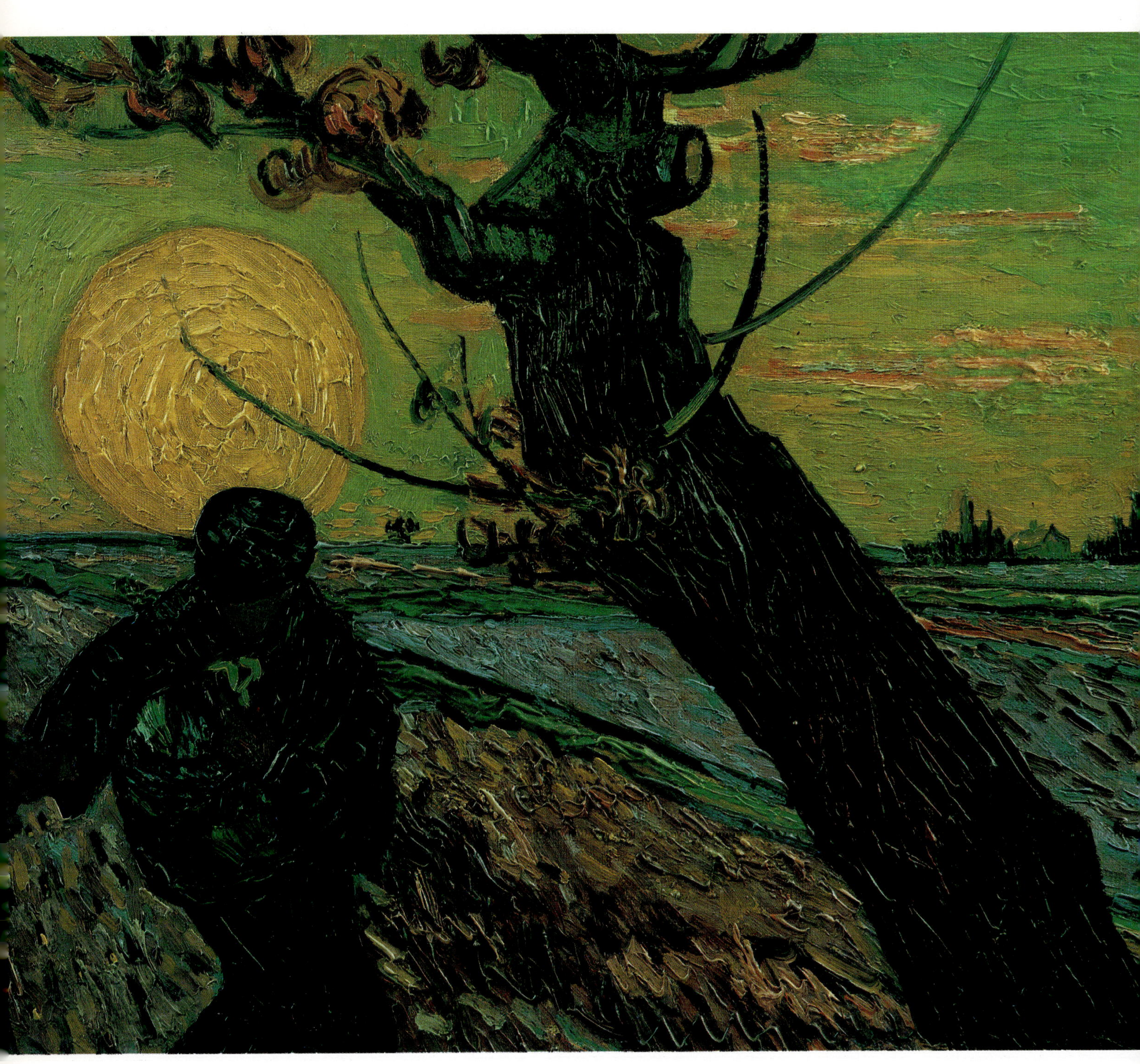

The Sower

November 1888 - oil on canvas - 32 x 40 cm -
Vincent van Gogh Foundation, Amsterdam

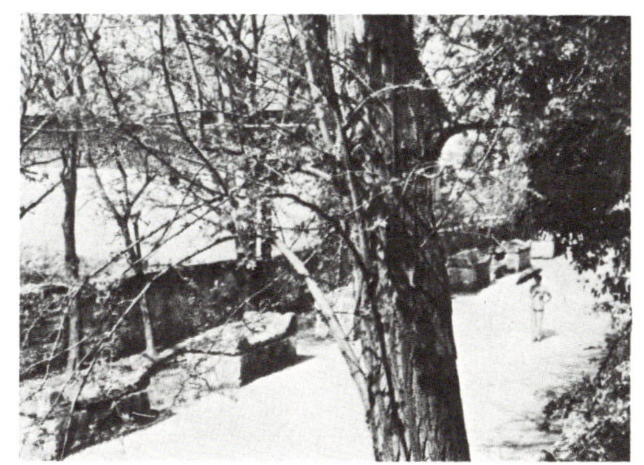

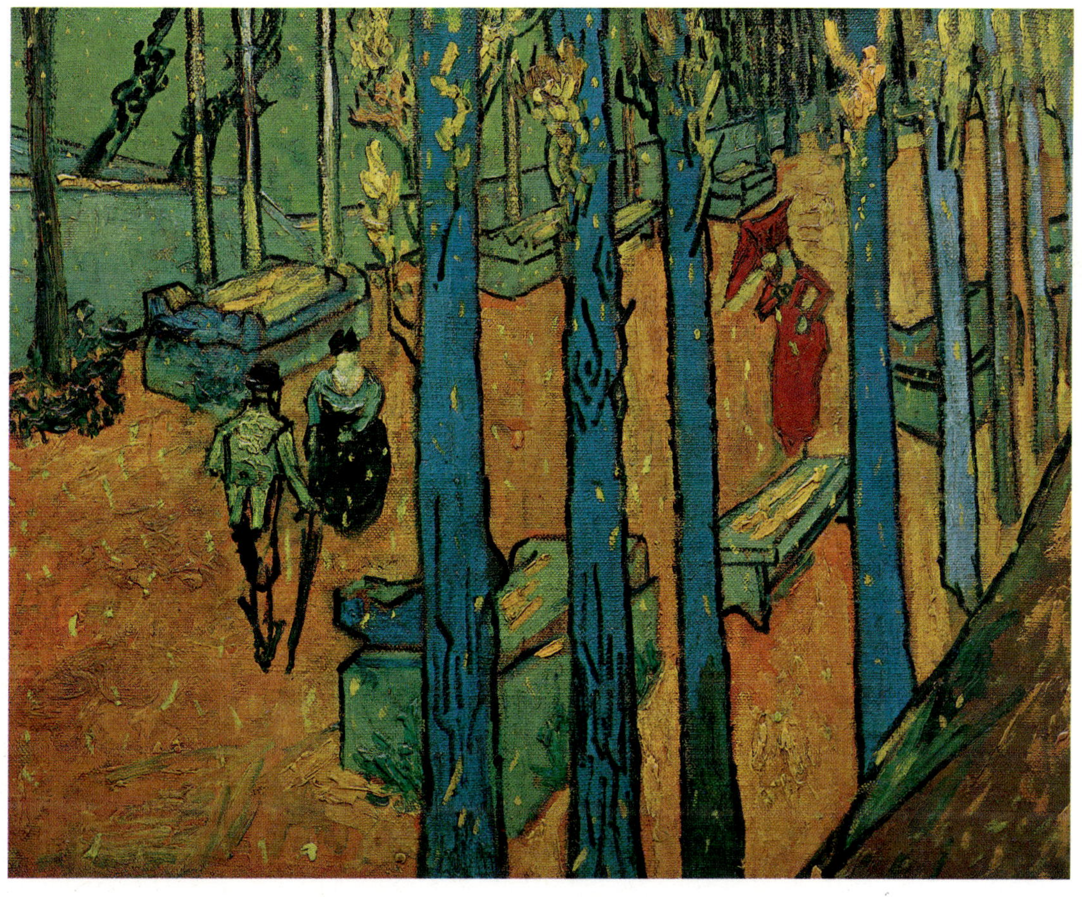

Photograph corresponding to the painting - the old wall on the left is still there

Les Alyscamps, Falling Leaves

November 1888 - oil on canvas - 73 x 92 cm - Rijksmuseum Kröller- Müller, Otterlo

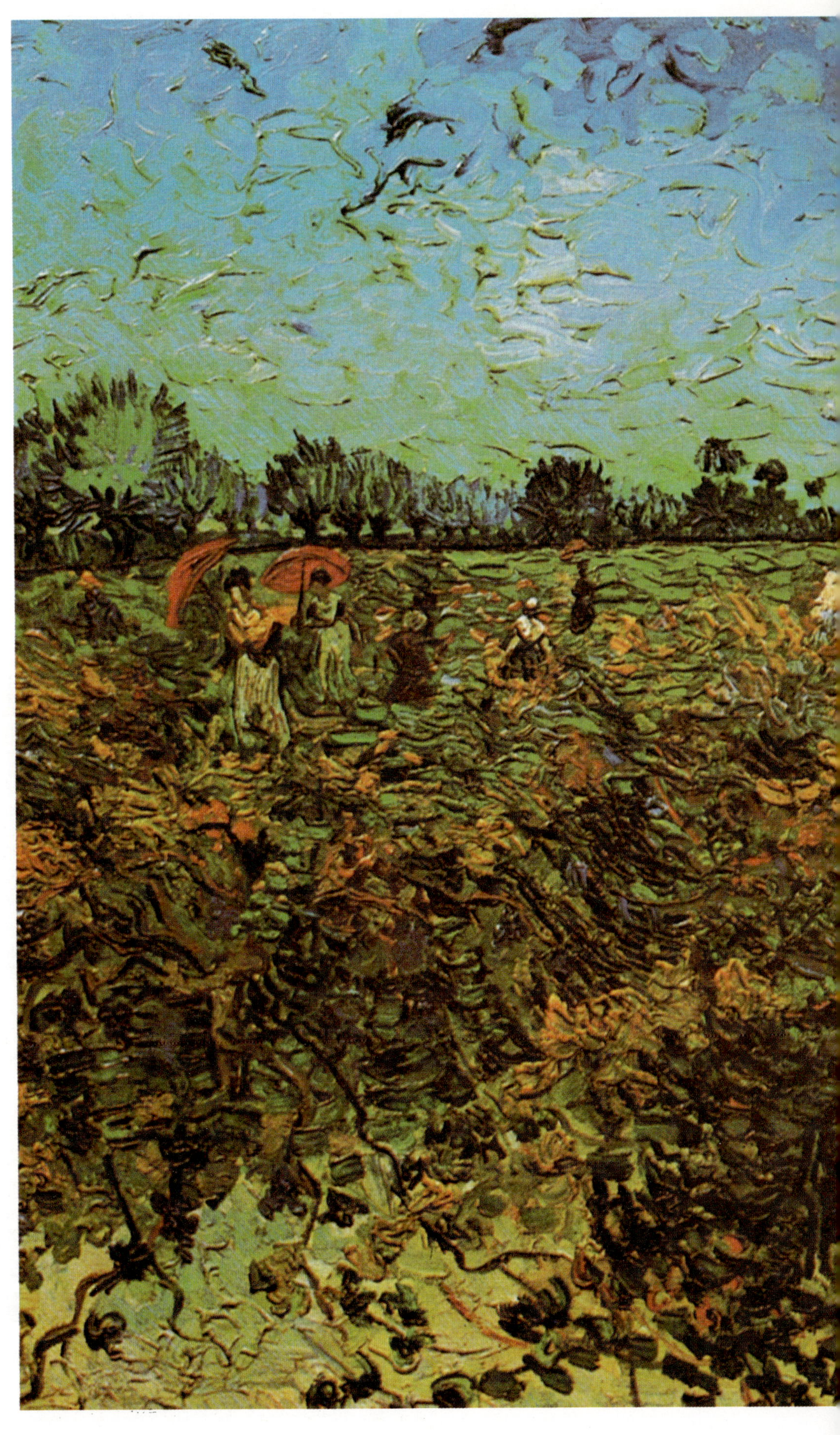

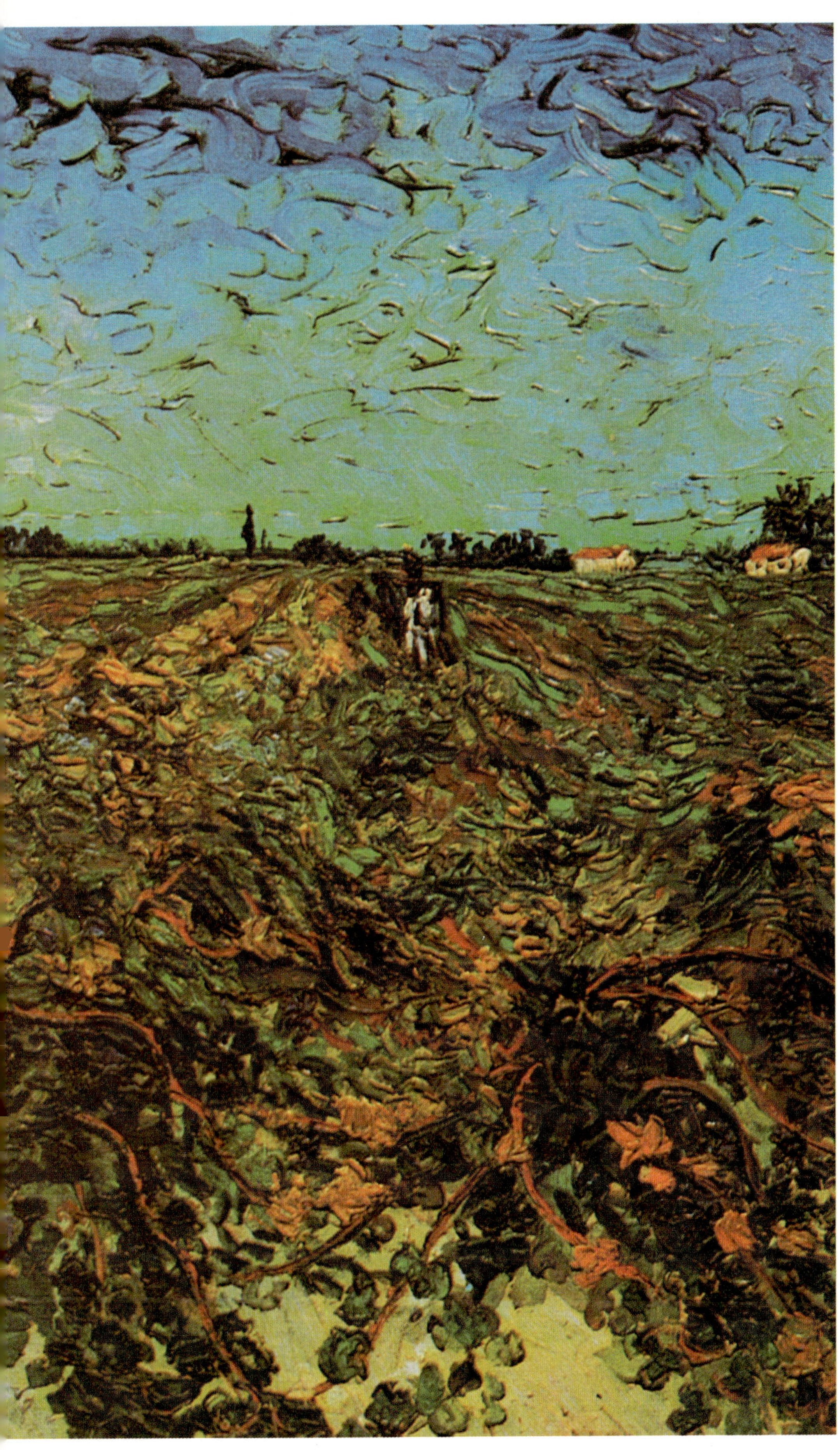

The Green Vineyard

September 1888 - oil on canvas - 372 x 92 cm - Rijksmuseum Kröller- Müller, Otterlo

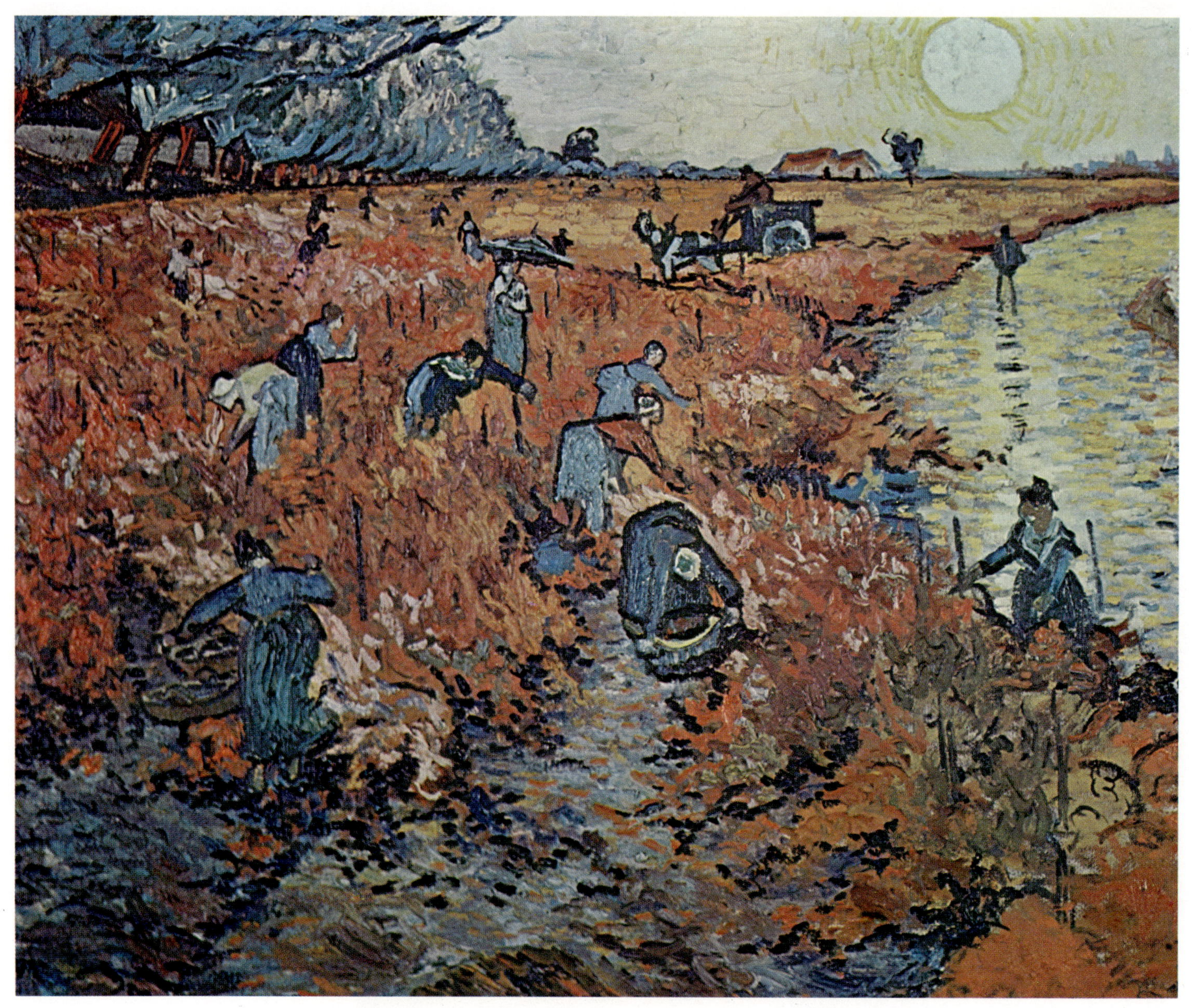

The Red Vineyard

November 1888 - oil on canvas - 373 x 92 cm -
Hermitage, St Petersburg

Photograph of the charcuterie

The Butcher Shop

February 1888 - oil on canvas on cardboard - 39.5 x 32.5 cm -
Vincent van Gogh Foundation, Amsterdam

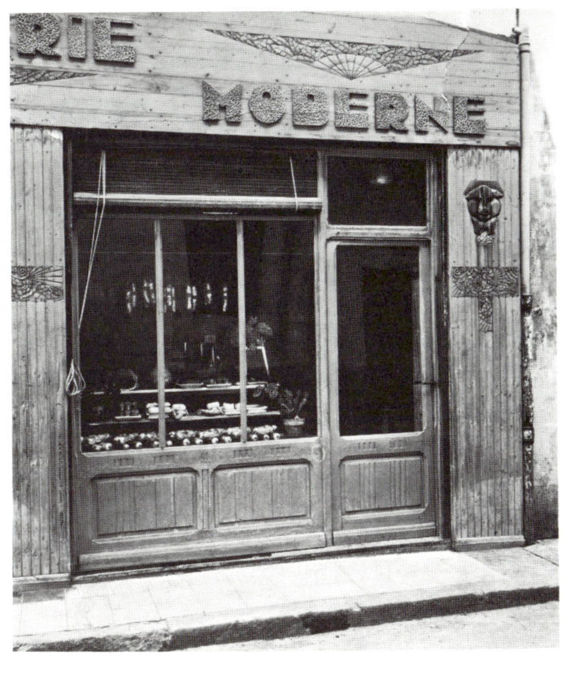
RIE
MODERNE

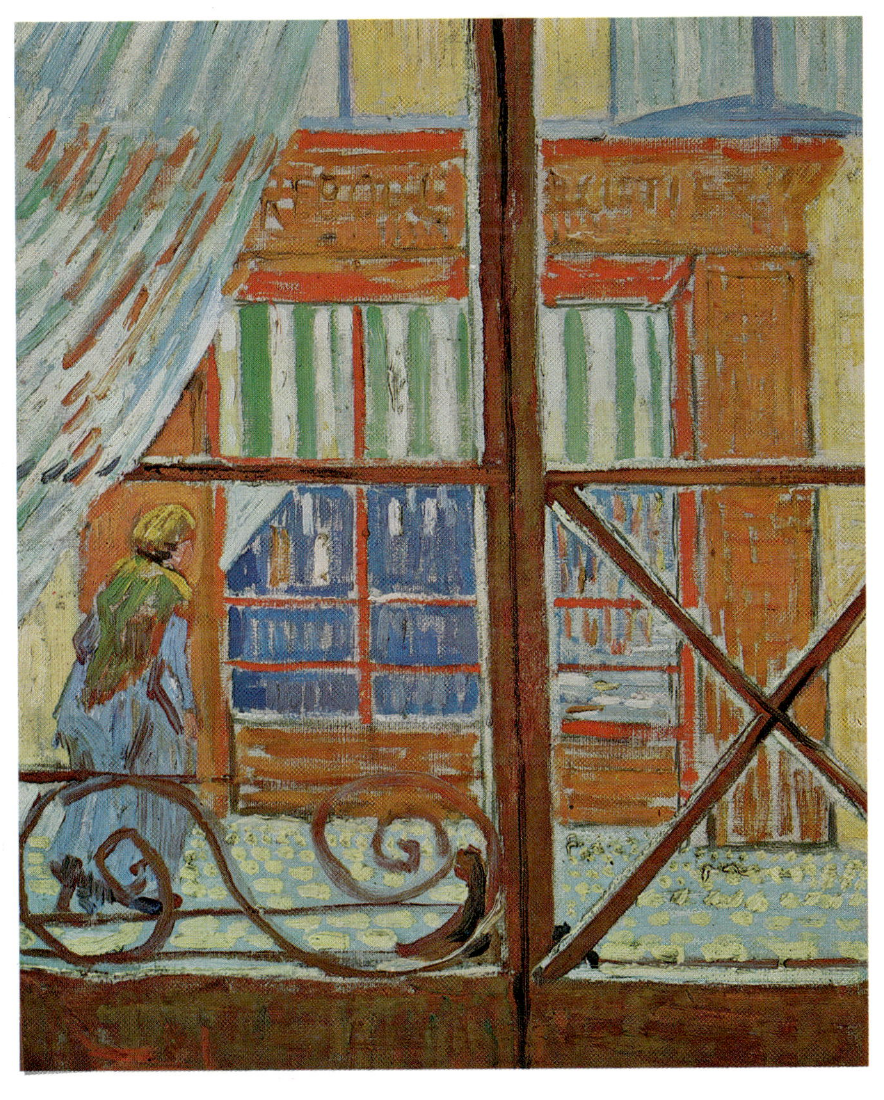

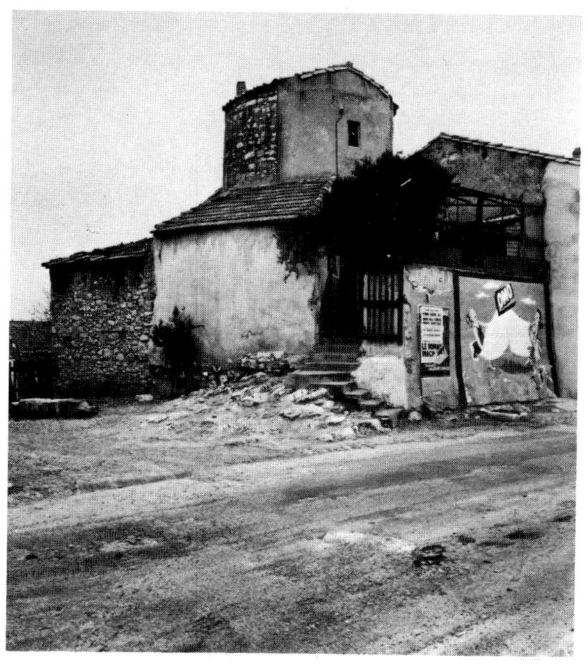

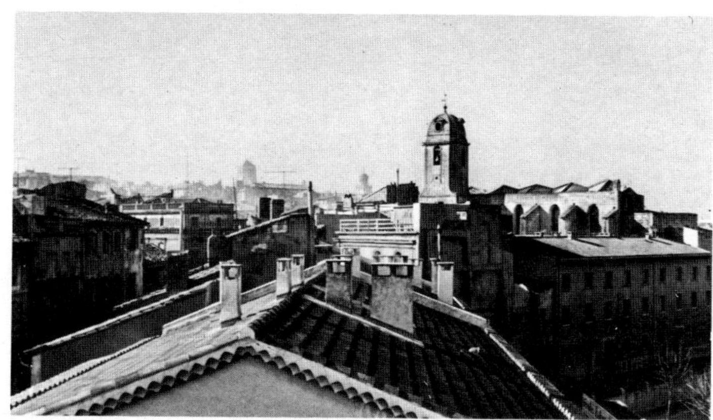

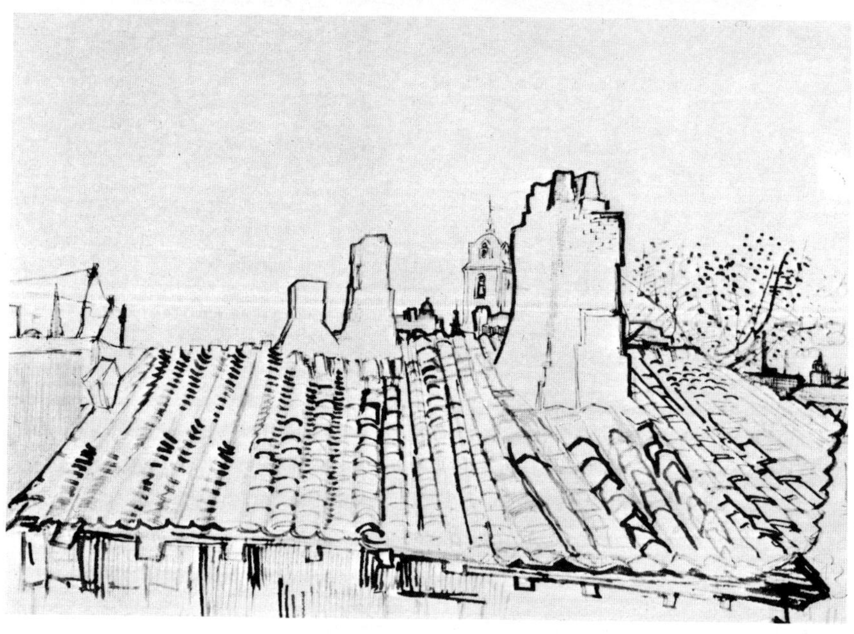

Photograph of the old mill once called "la Tour de Jonquet"

Photograph. From his window, Vincent saw Arles as he showed it in the previous drawing

Rooftops

February 1888 - pen - 25 x 34 cm
Private collection

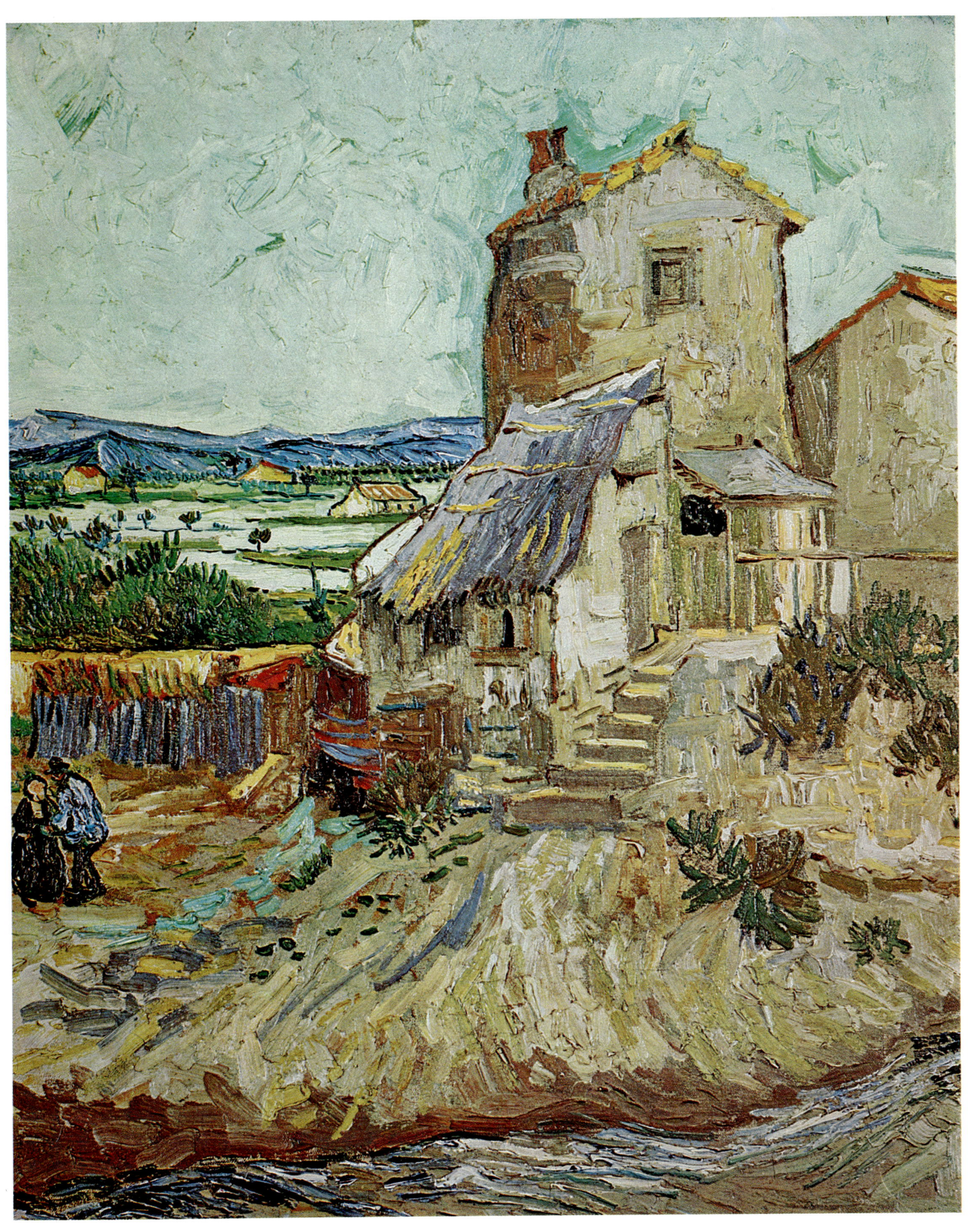

The Old Mill

September 1888 - oil on canvas - 64.5 x 54 cm -
Albright Knox gallery, Buffalo, New York

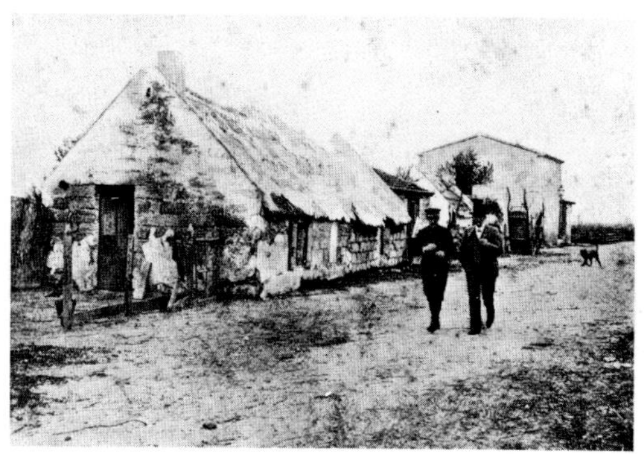

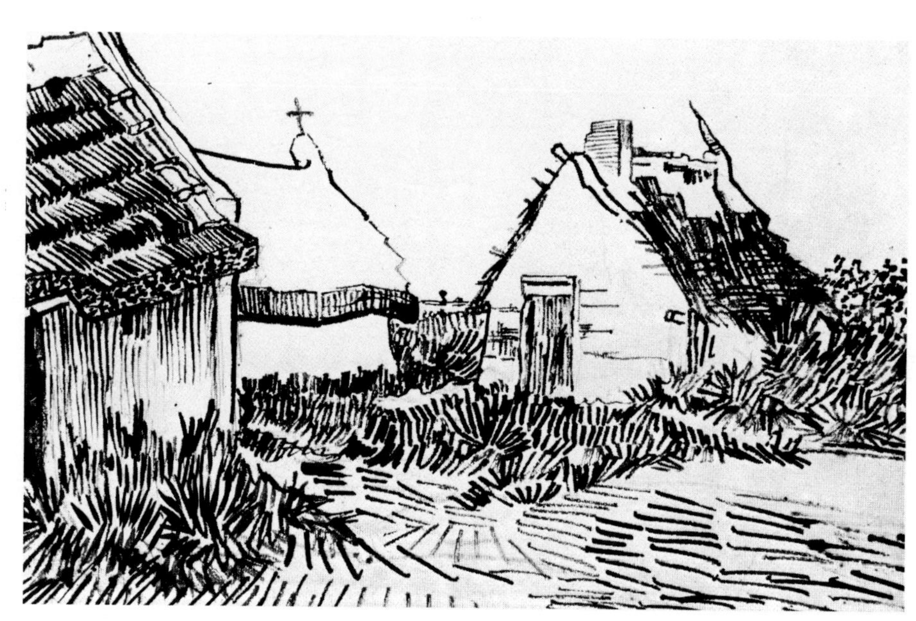

Photograph of the guardians' cabins as they were in Vincent's time

Cabins of the Guardians of Saintes-Maries-de-la-Mer

June 1888 - indian ink - 30 x 47 cm -
Vincent van Gogh Foundation, Amsterdam

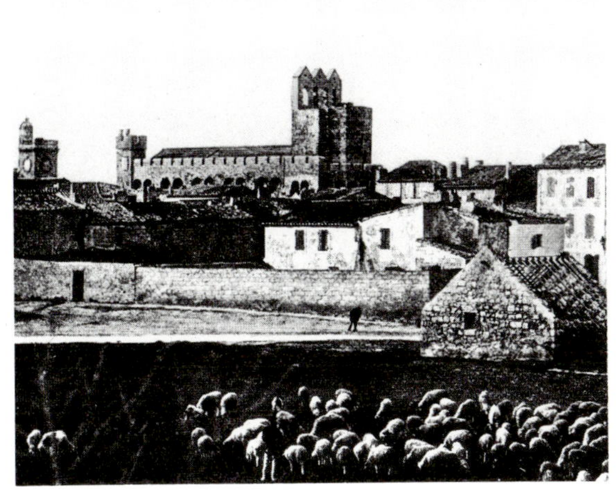

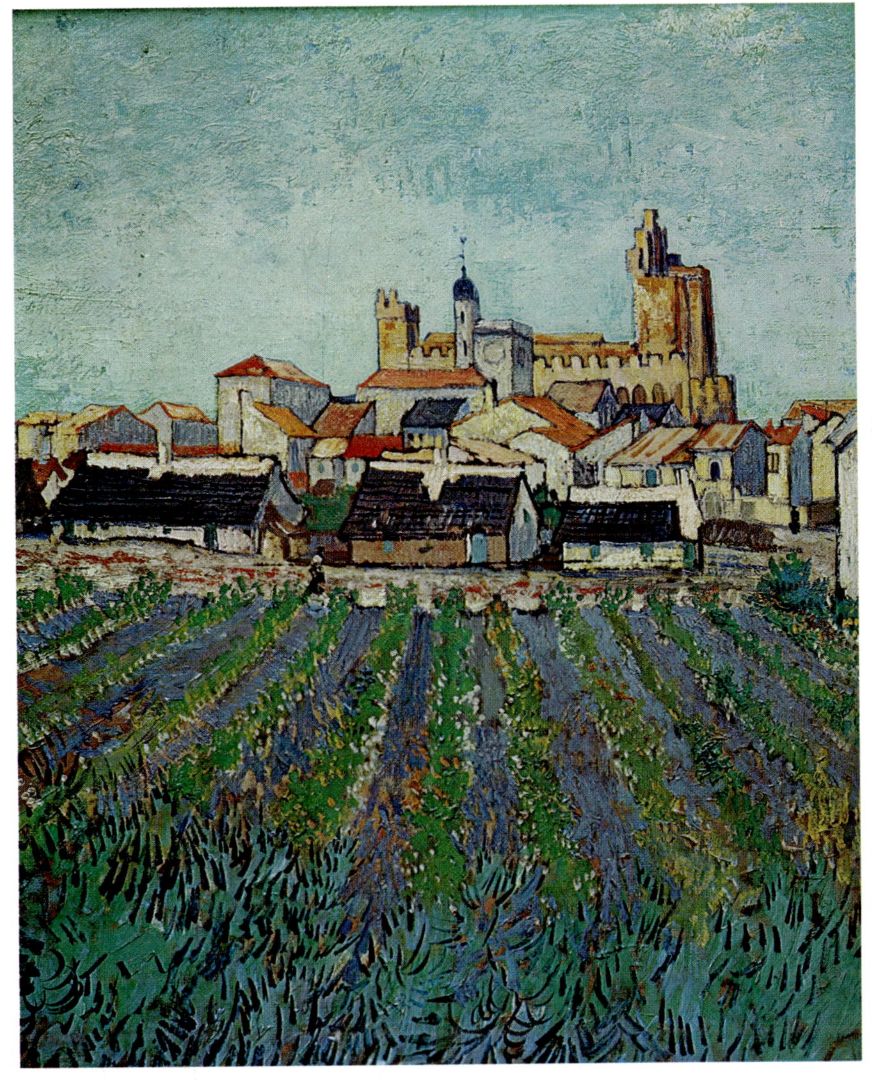

Photograph of Saintes- Maries-de-la-Mer

View of Saintes-Maries-de- la-Mer

June 1888 - oil on canvas - 64 x 53 cm -
Rijksmuseum Kröller- Müller, Otterlo

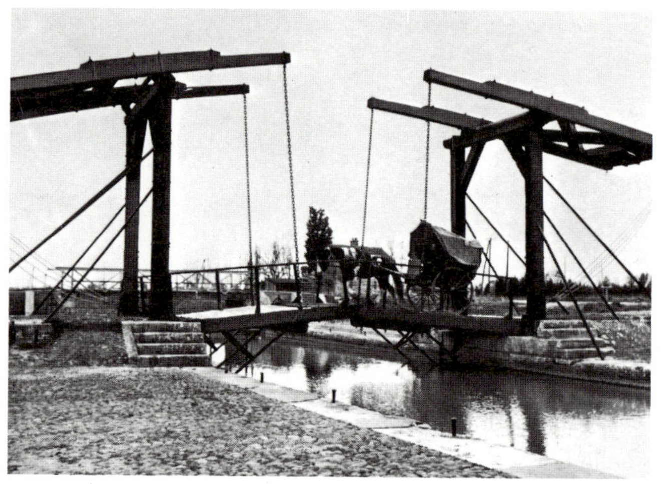

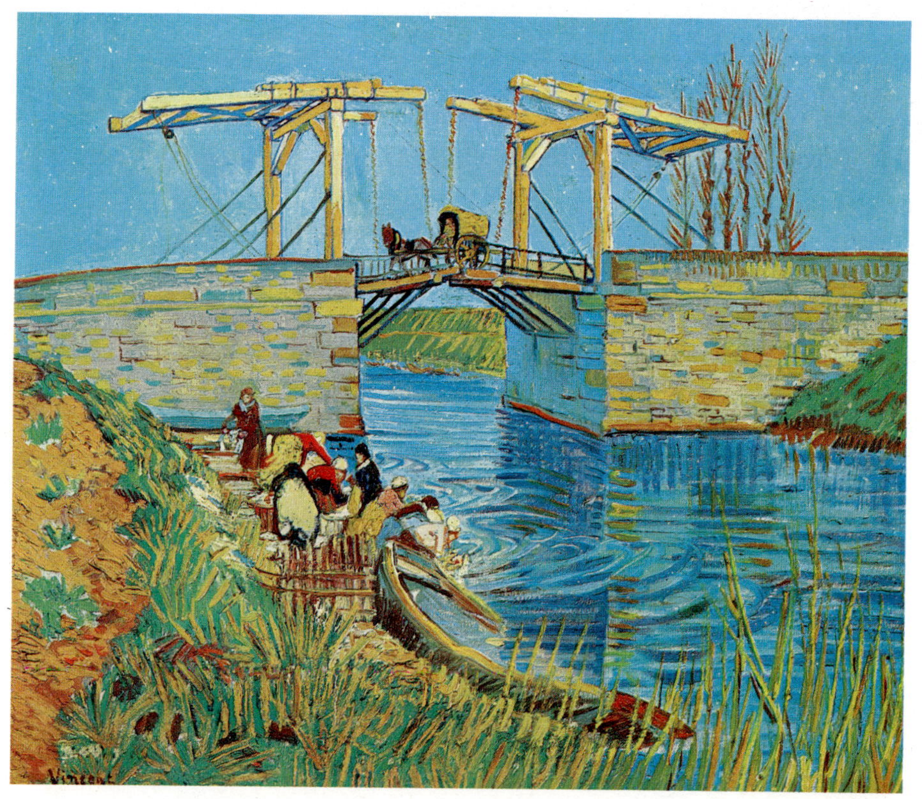

Photograph of the small lifting bridge rebuilt after the war in a different place

The Langlois Bridge

March 1888 - oil on canvas - 54 x 65 cm - Rijksmuseum Kröller- Müller, Otterlo

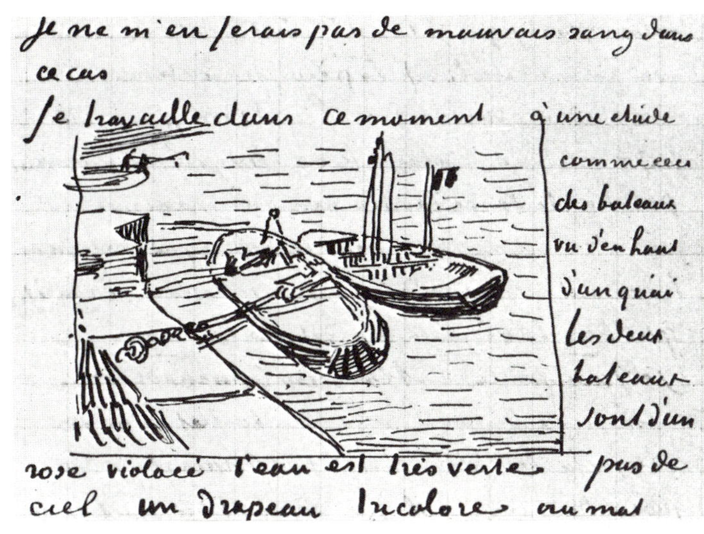

Je ne m'en ferais pas de mauvais sang dans
ce cas
Je travaille dans ce moment à une étude
comme ceci
des bateaux
vu d'en haut
d'un quai
les deux
bateaux
sont d'un
rose violacé l'eau est très verte pas de
ciel un drapeau tricolore au mat

Pen sketch - 7 x 10 cm -
Vincent van Gogh Foundation, Amsterdam

Quay with Men Unloading Sand Barges

August 1888 - oil on canvas - 55 x 66 cm -
Folkwang Museum, Essen

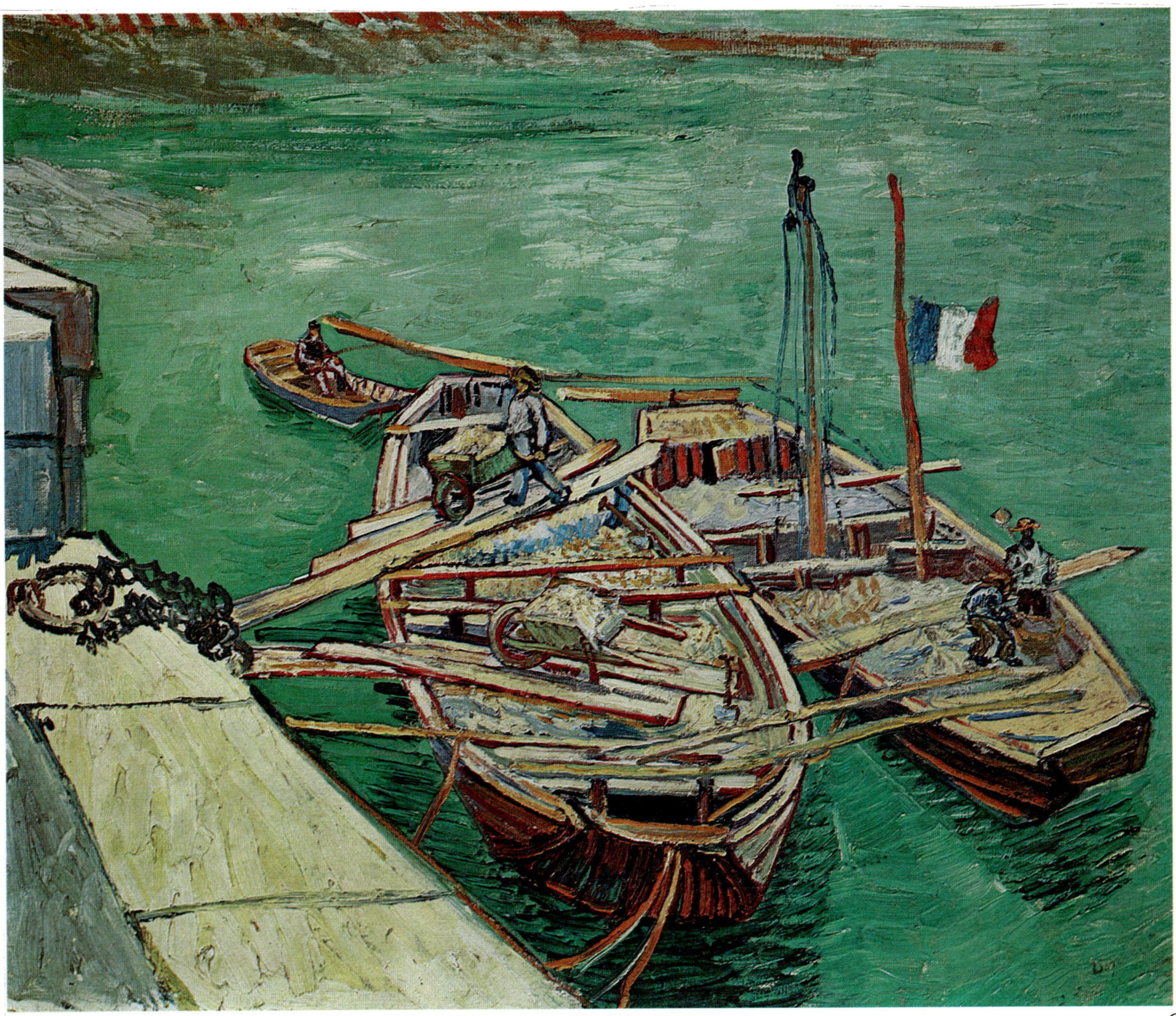

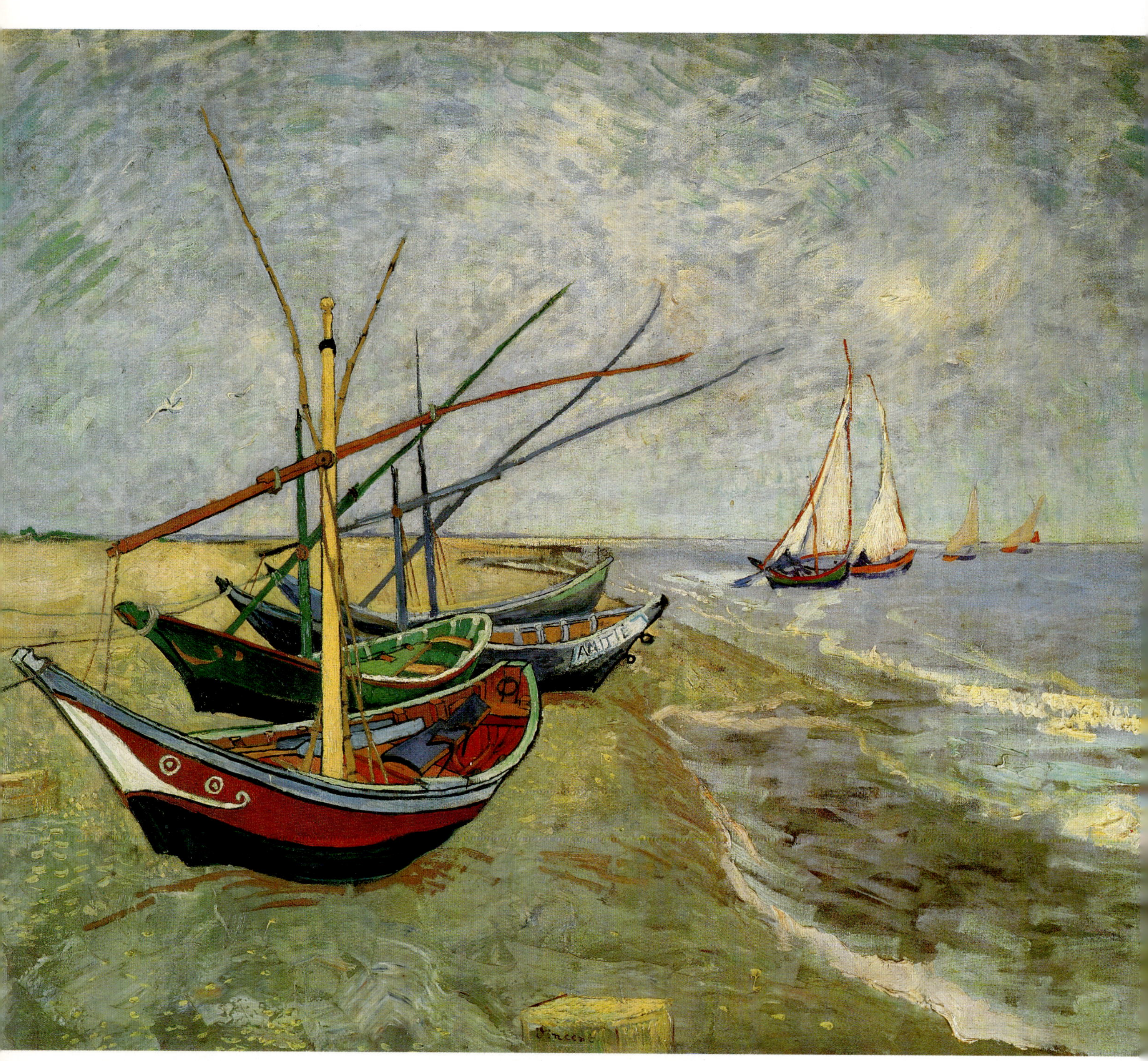

Boats on the Beach at Saintes-Maries

June 1888 - oil on canvas - 64 x 81 cm -
Vincent van Gogh Foundation, Amsterdam

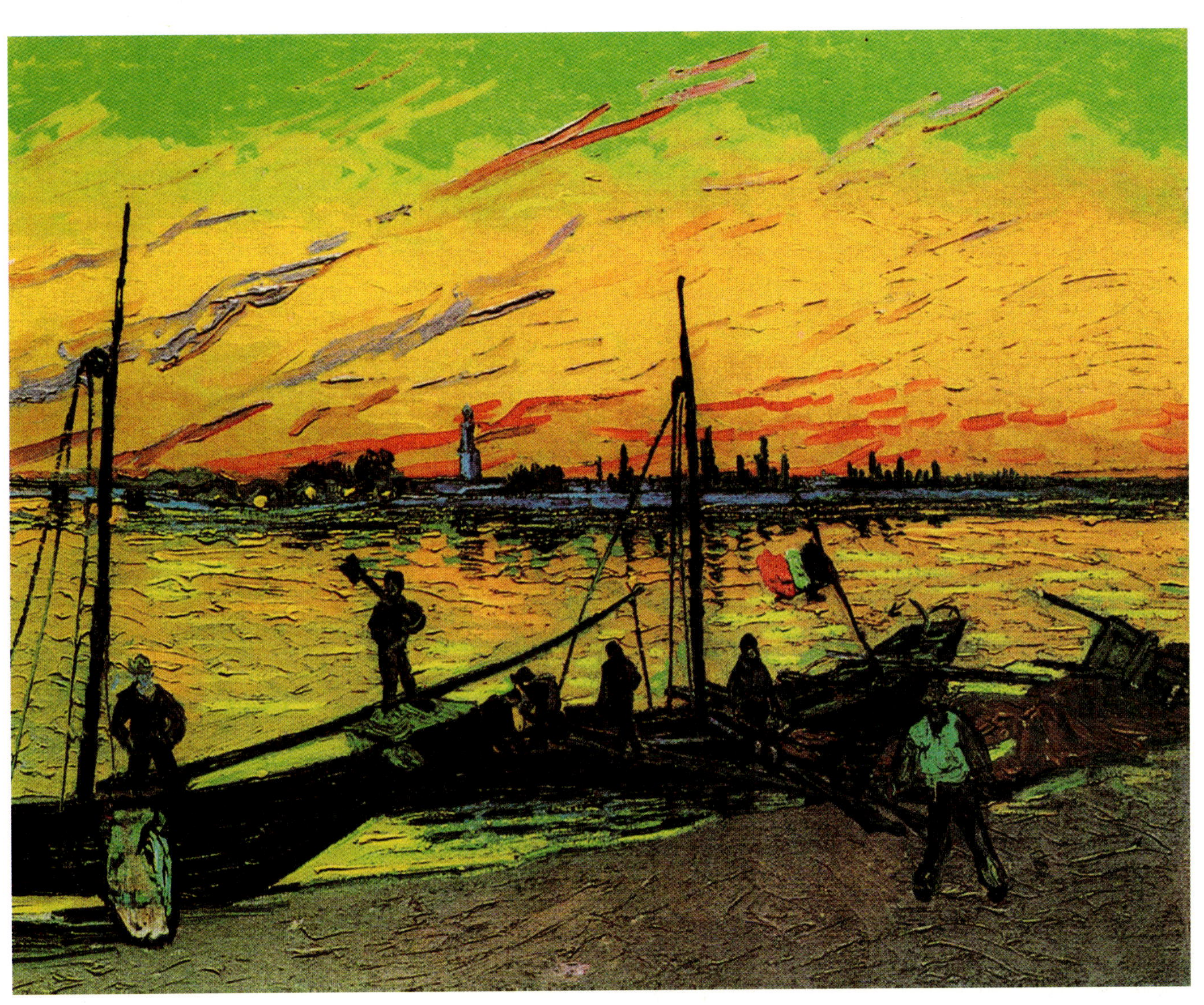

Coal Barges

August 1888 - oil on canvas - 64 x 81 cm - Carleton Mitchell Collection, Annapolis, Md.

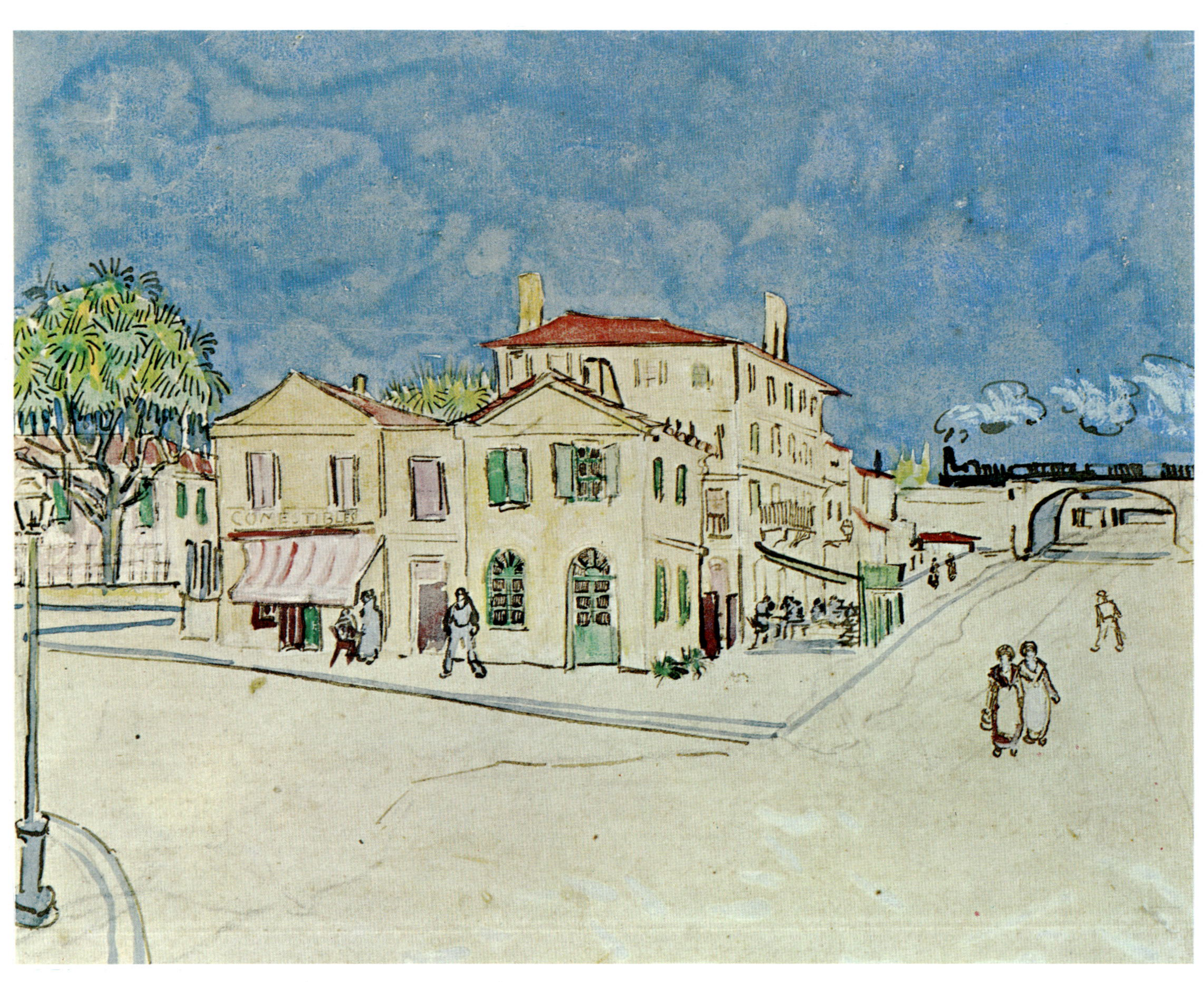

Vincent's House in Arles

May 1888 - watercolour - 24.5 x 30.5 cm -
Vincent van Gogh Foundation, Amsterdam

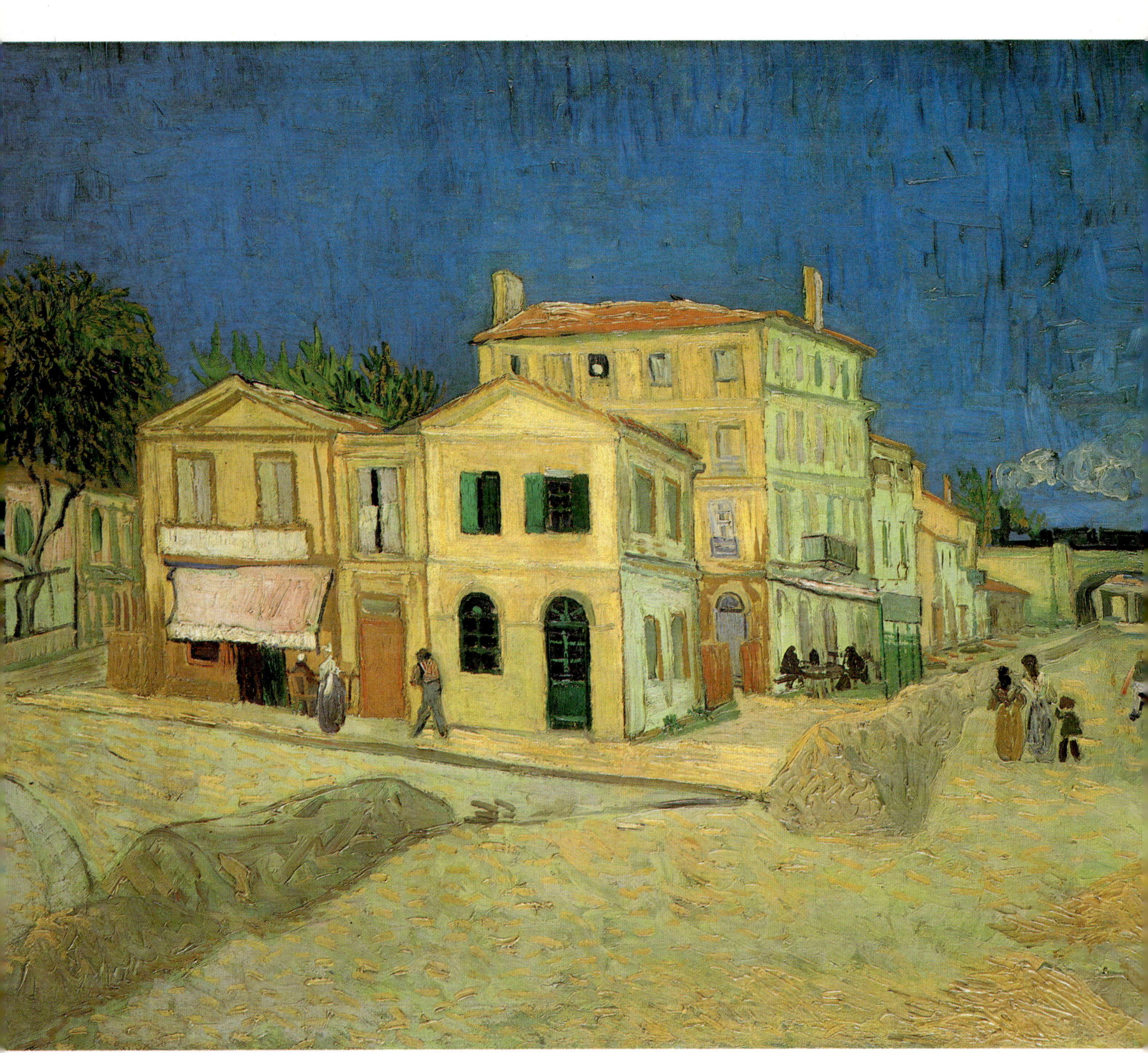

The Yellow House

September 1888 - oil on canvas - 76 x 94 cm - Vincent van Gogh Foundation, Amsterdam

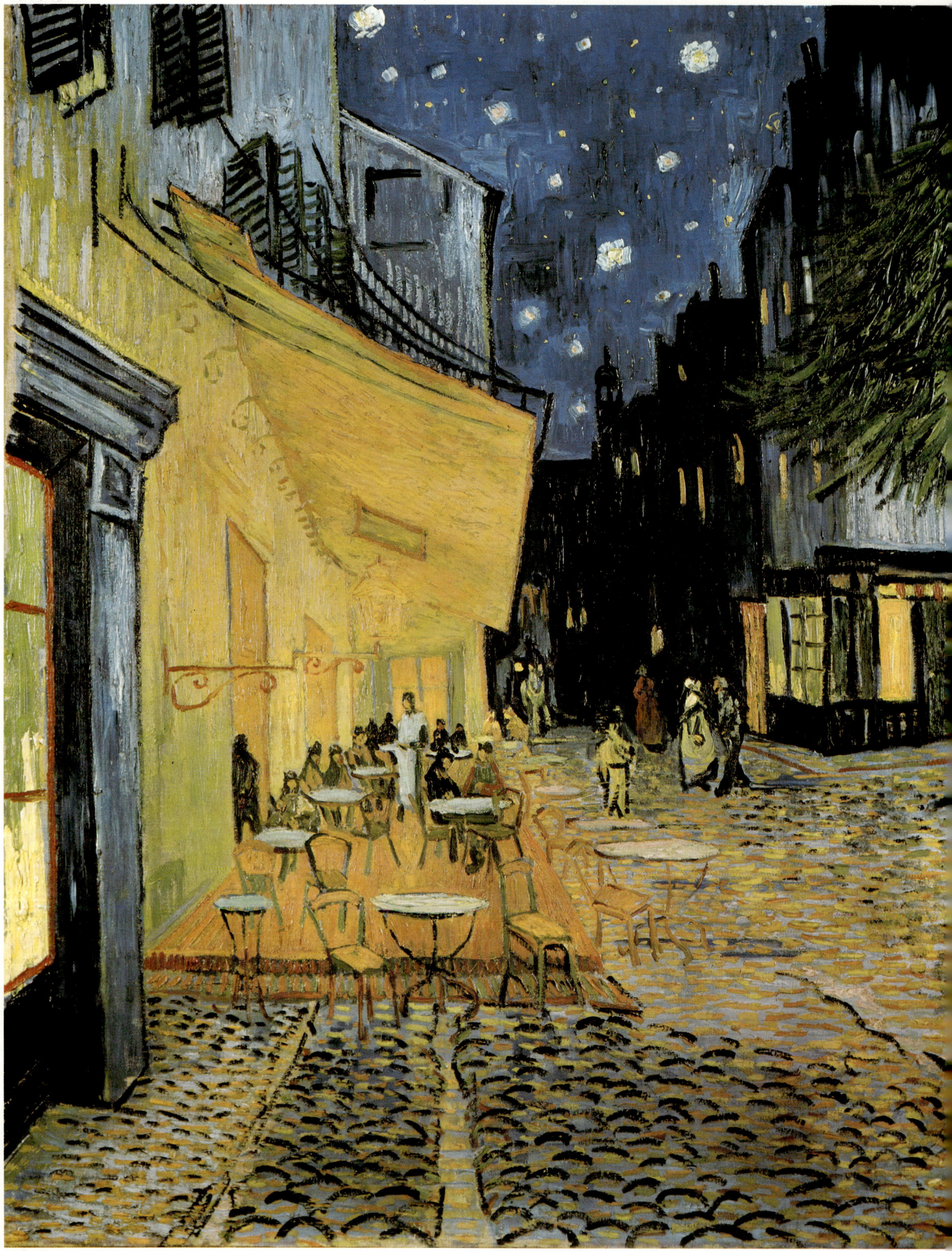

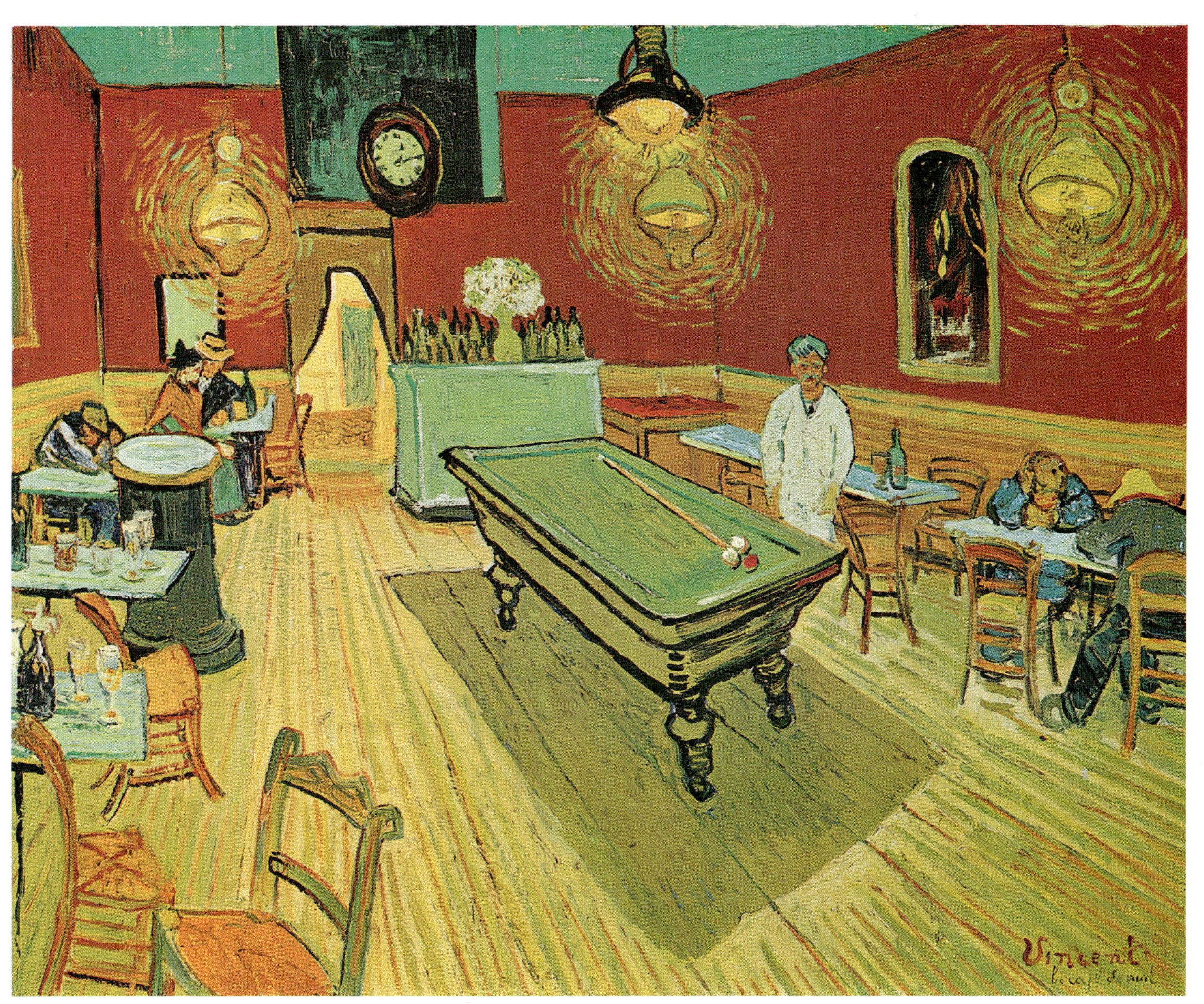

Night Café

September 1888 - oil on canvas - 70 x 89 cm -
Yale University Art Gallery, New Haven

Terrace of the Café at Night

September 1888 - oil on canvas - 681 x 65.5 cm -
Rijksmuseum Kröller- Müller, Otterlo

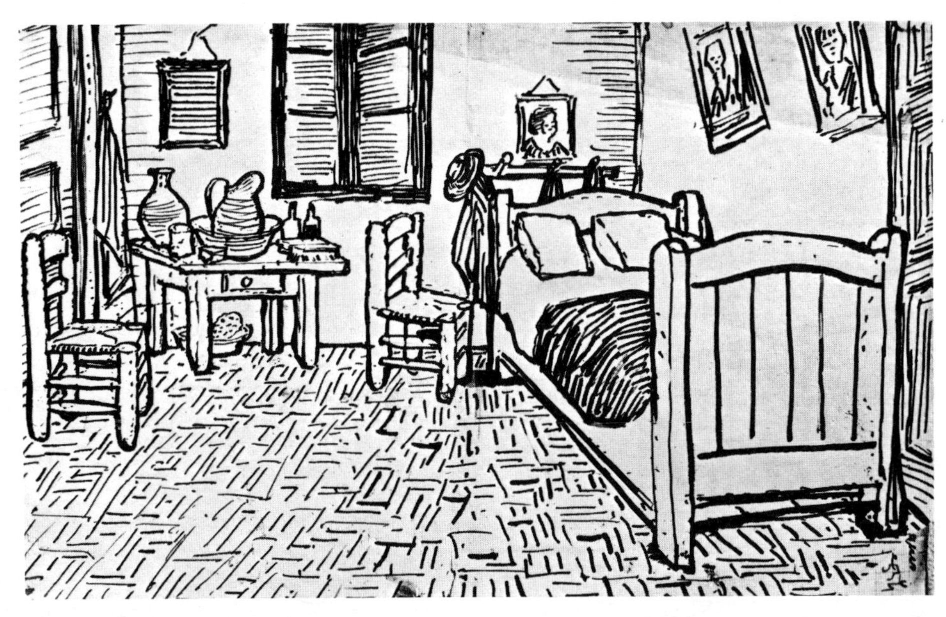

Vincent's Bedroom in Arles

1888 - pen - 13.2 x 20.5 cm -
Vincent van Gogh Foundation, Amsterdam

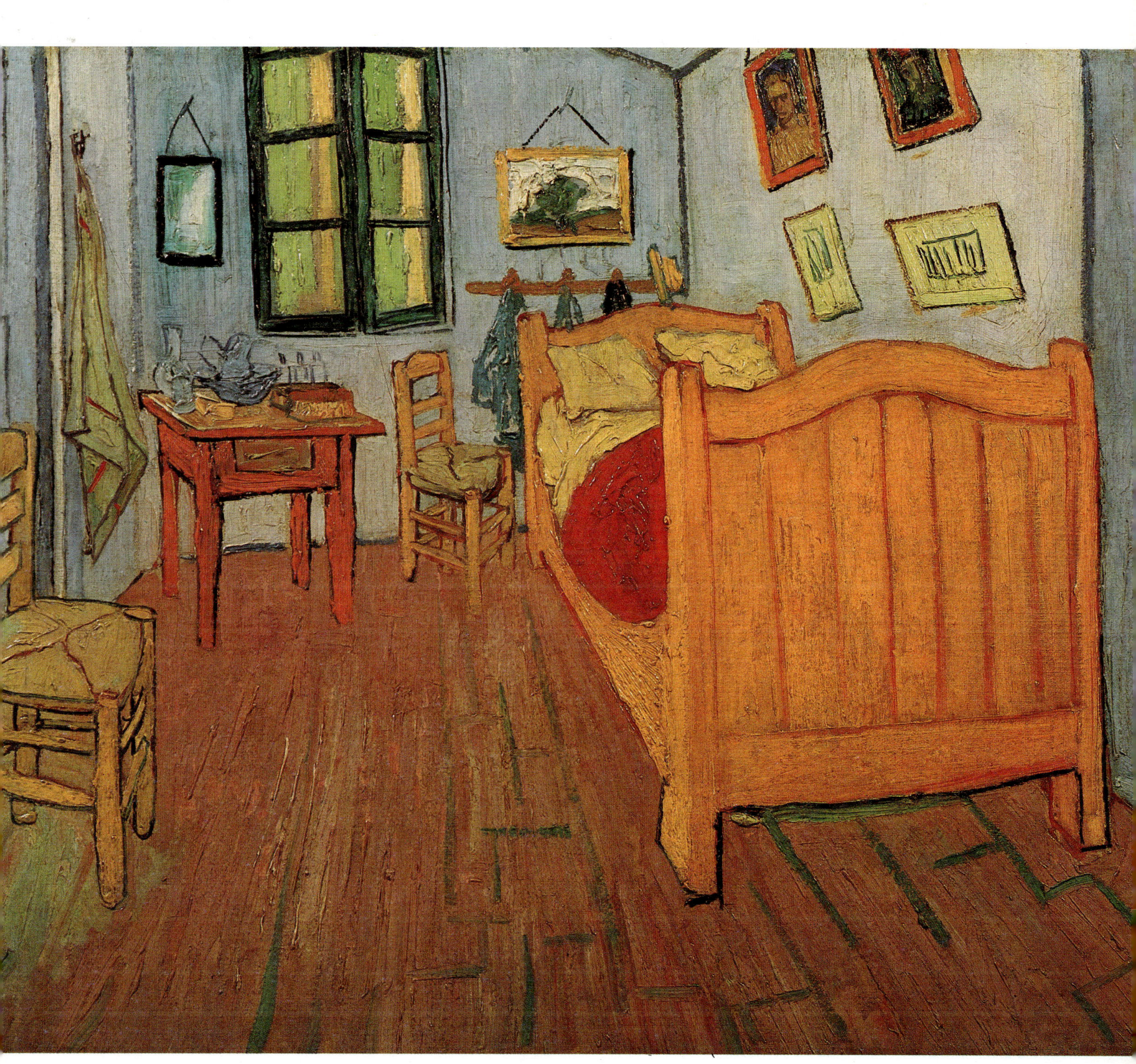

Vincent's Bedroom in Arles

October 1888 - oil on canvas - 72 x 90 cm -
Vincent van Gogh Foundation, Amsterdam

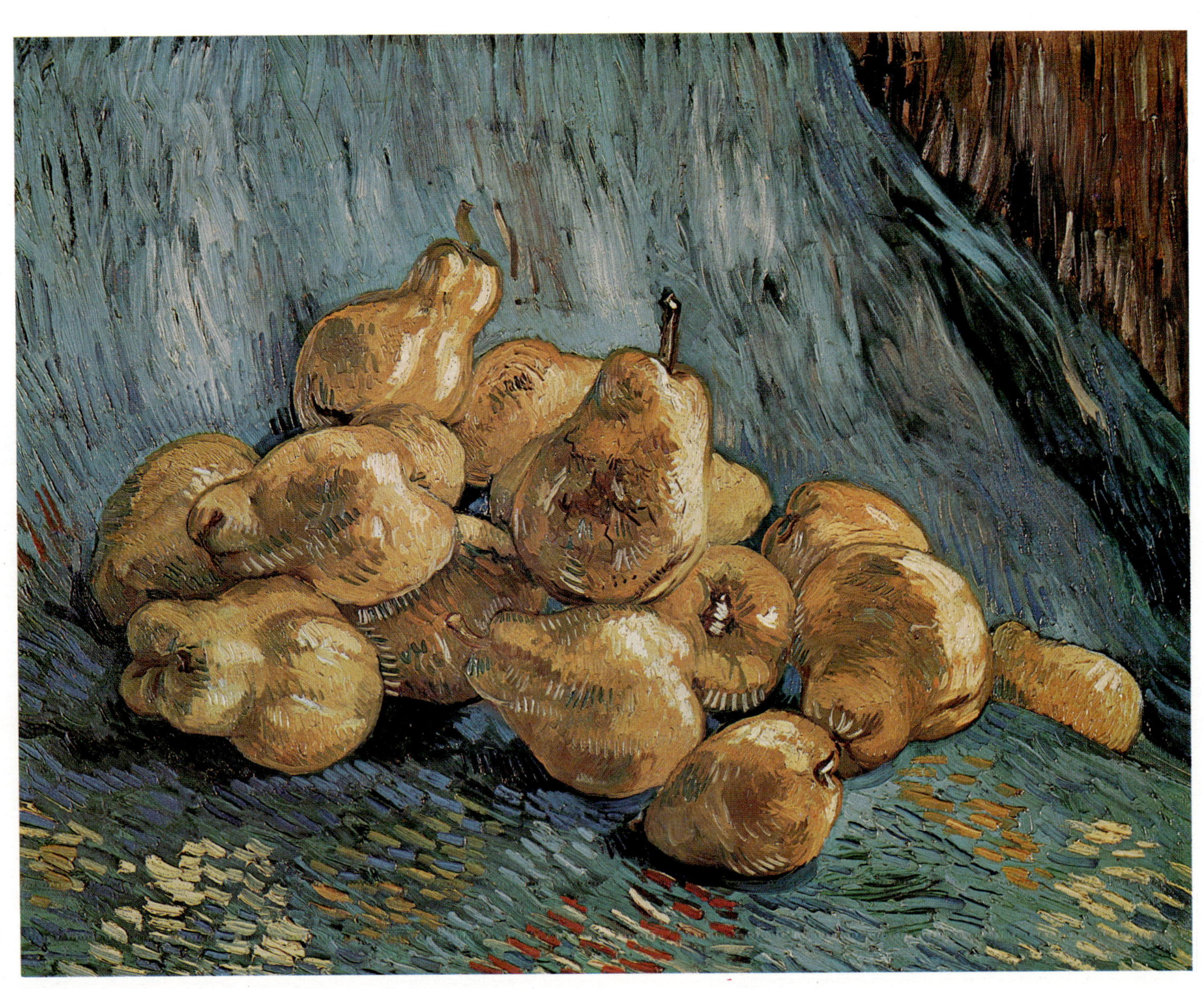

Still Life with Pears

1888 - oil on canvas - 46 x 59.5 cm -
Gemaldegalerie, Dresden

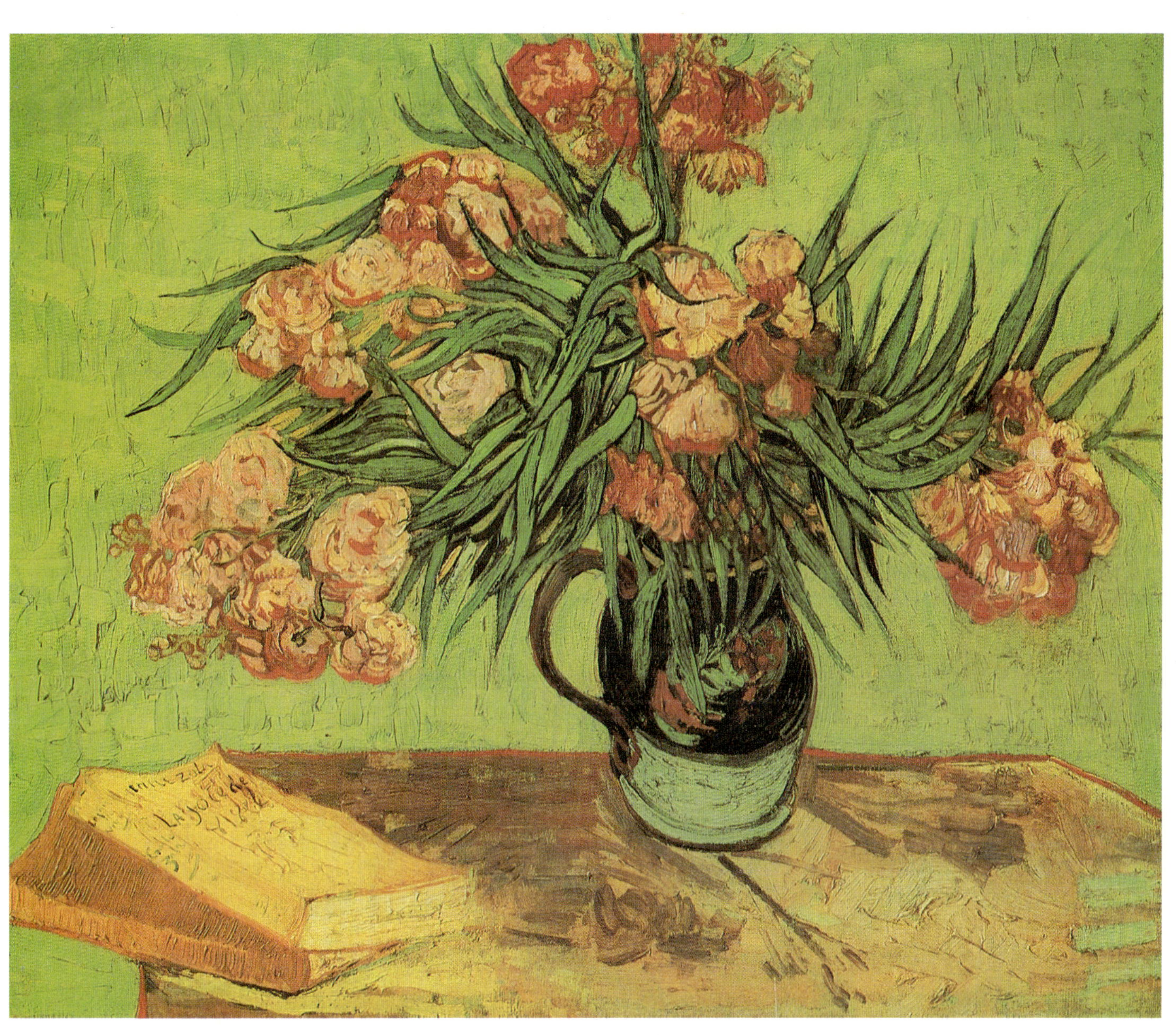

Still Life with Oleander and Books

August 1888 - oil on canvas - 60.3 x 73.6 cm - Museum of Modern Art, New York

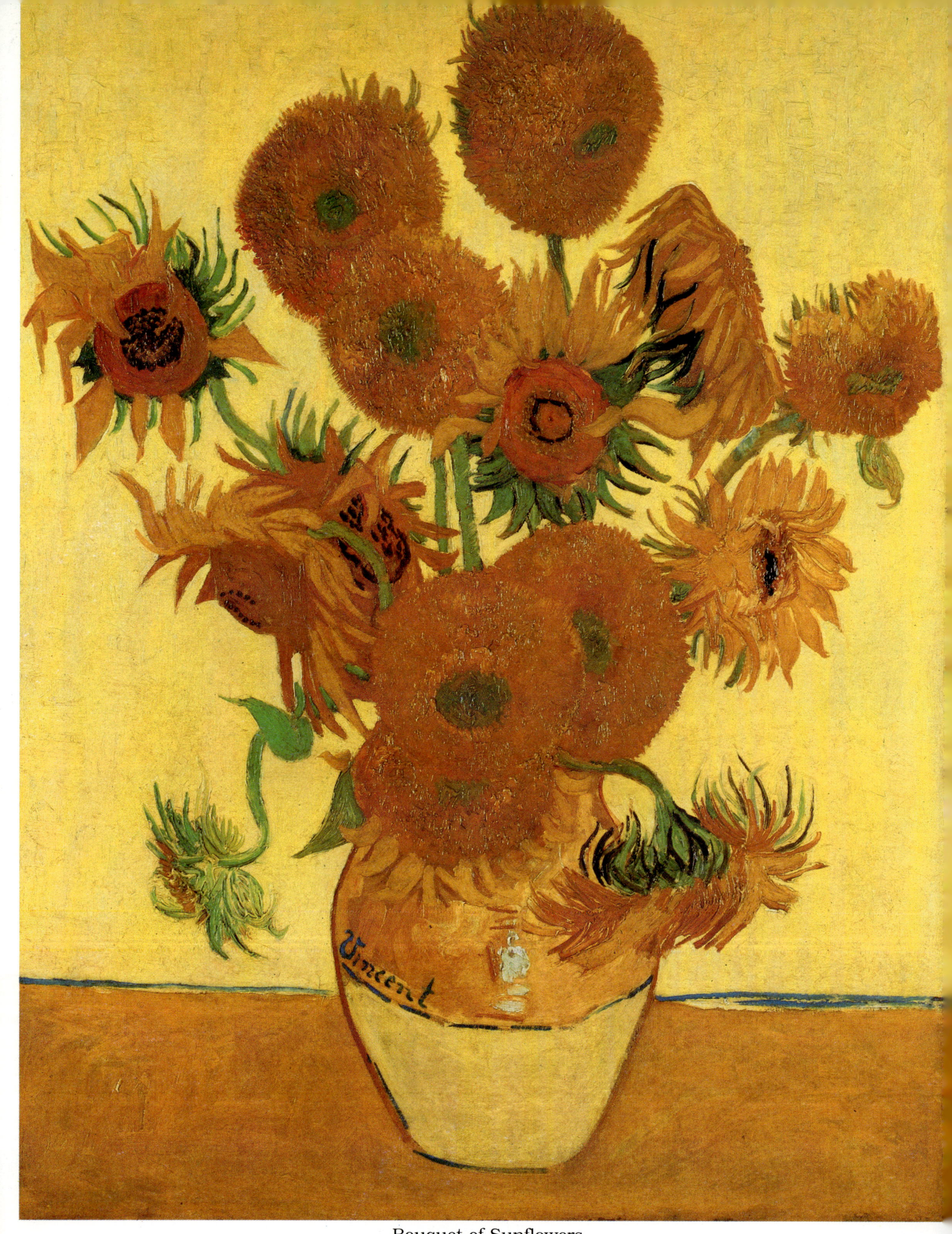

Bouquet of Sunflowers

August 1888 - oil on canvas - 93 x 73 cm -
National Gallery, London

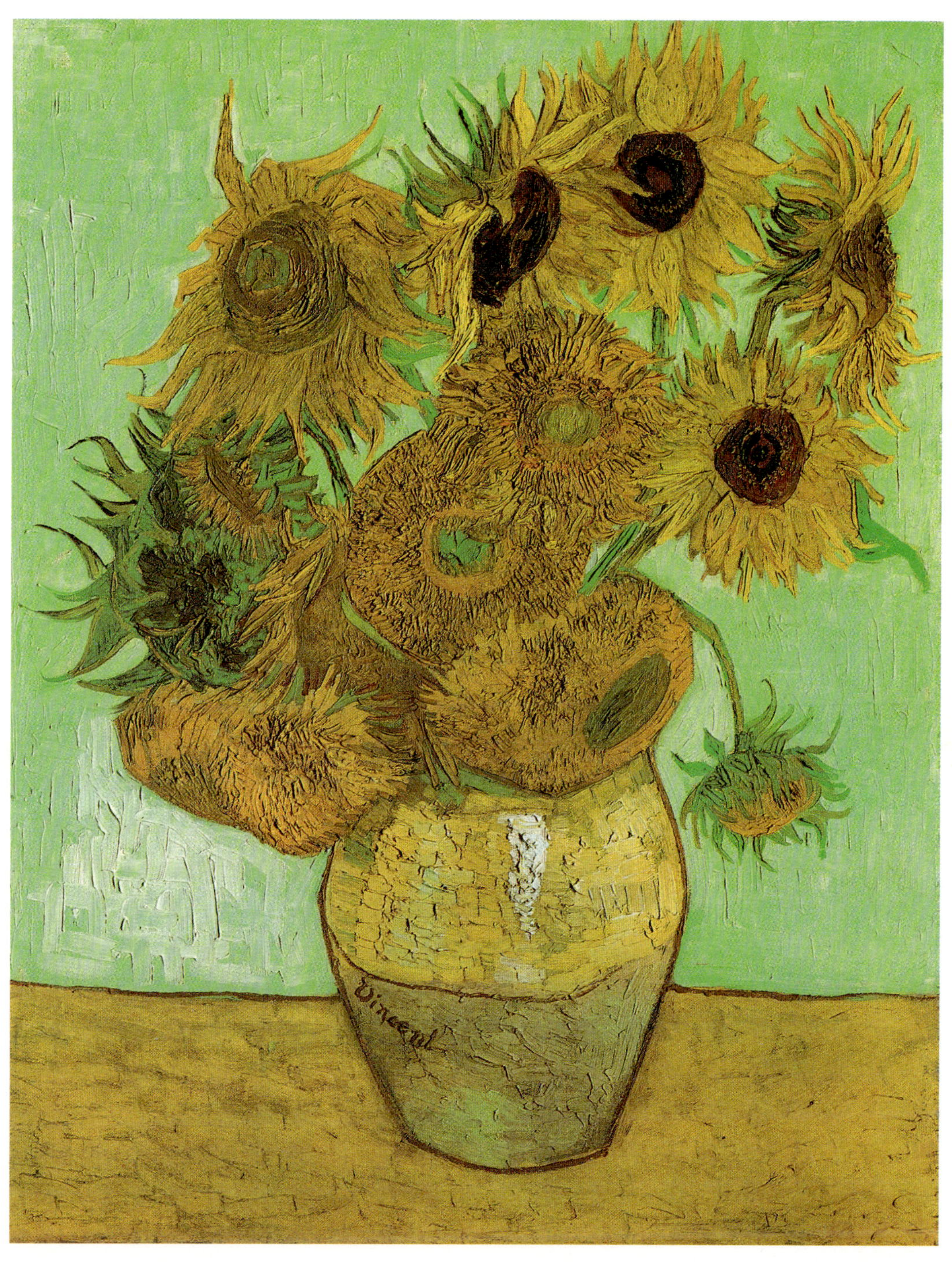

Twelve Sunflowers in a Vase

August 1888, - oil on canvas - 91 x 72 cm -
Neue Pinakothek, Munich

1888

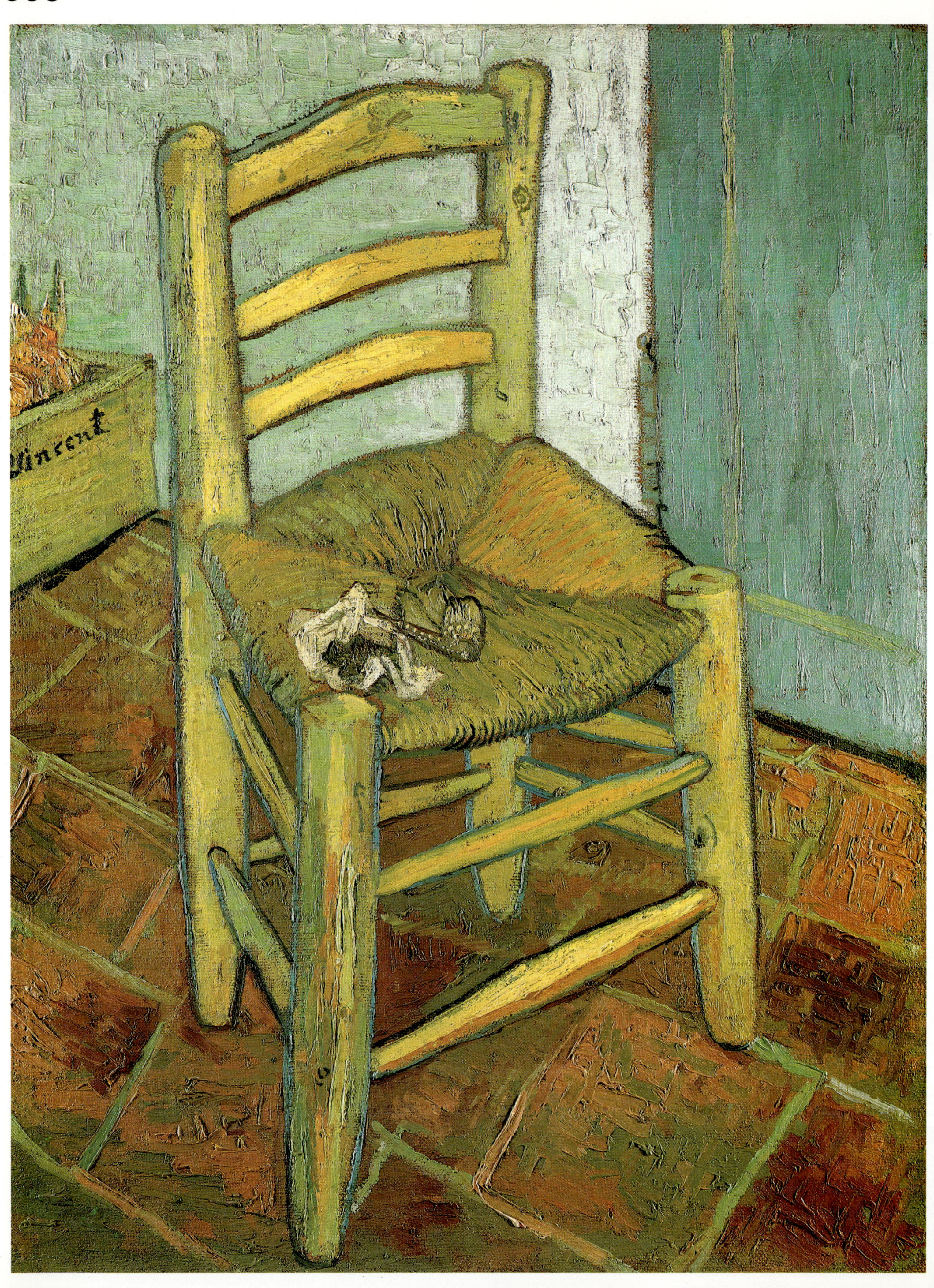

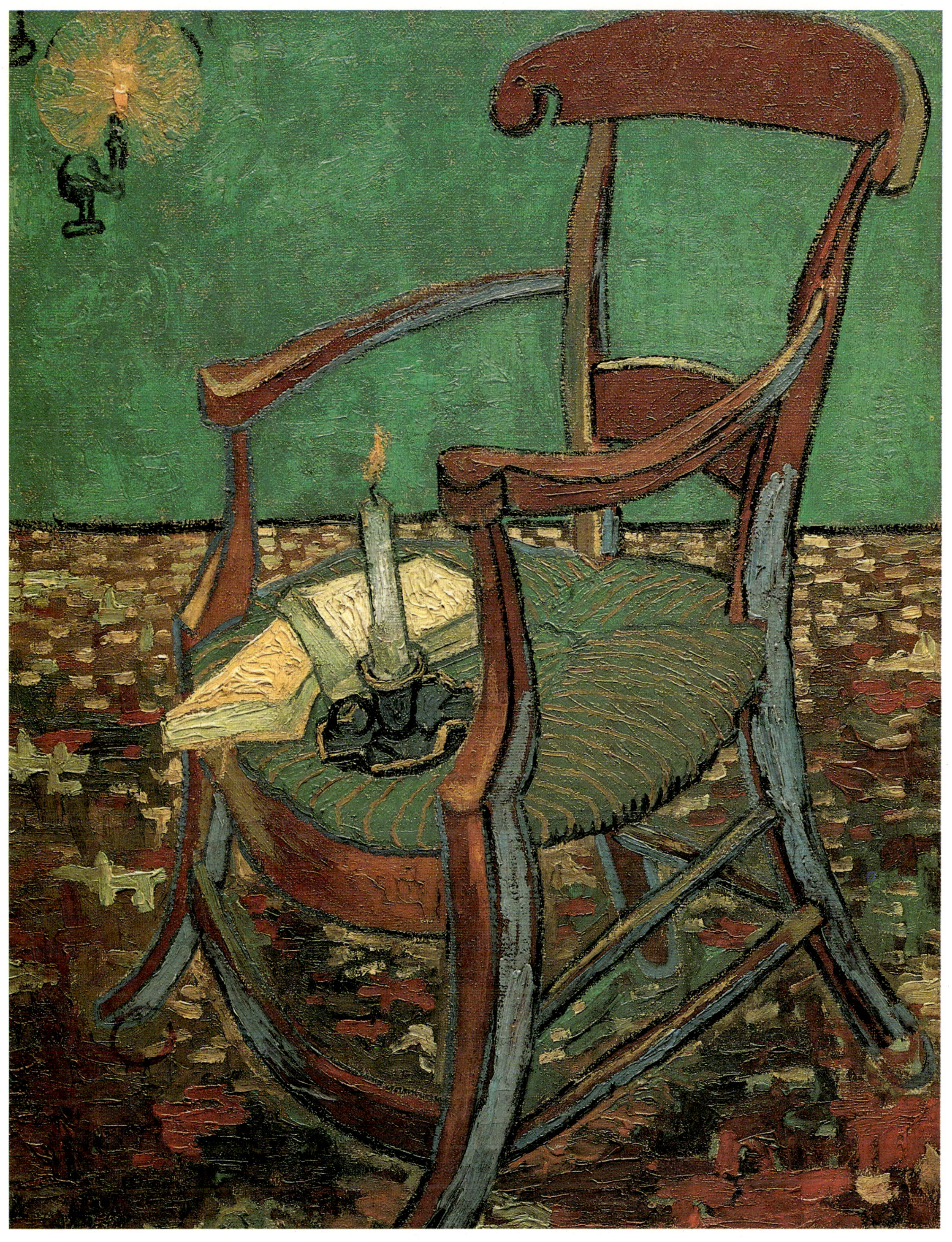

Vincent's Chair with His Pipe

December 1888 - oil on canvas - 93 x 73.5 cm - National Gallery, London

Gauguin's Armchair

December 1888 - oil on canvas - 90.5 x 72 cm - Vincent van Gogh Foundation, Amsterdam

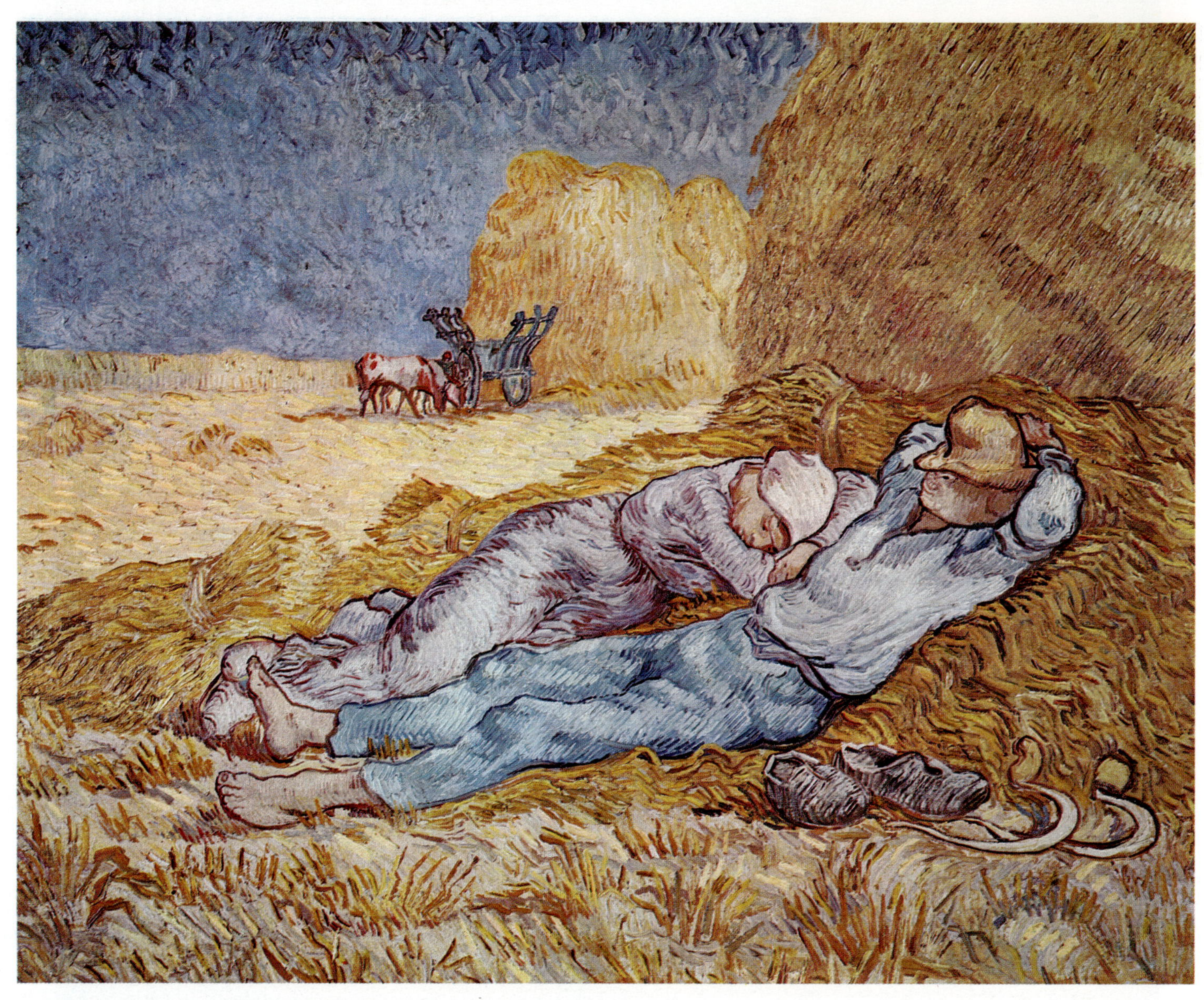

The Siesta

December 1889 - oil on canvas - 979 x 91 cm -
Musée d'Orsay, Paris

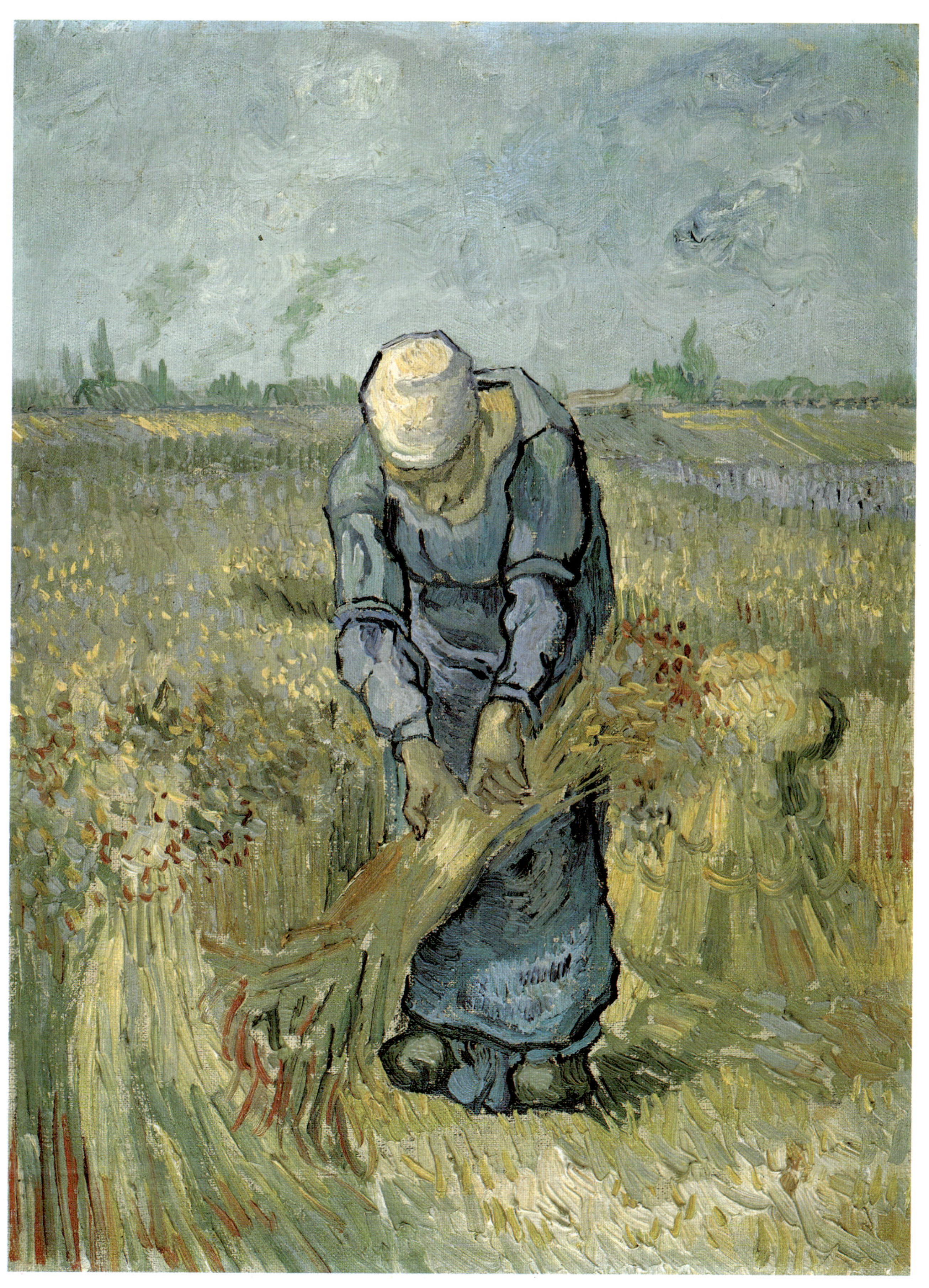

Peasant Woman Binding Sheaves (after Millet)

September 1889 - oil on canvas - 43.5 x 33.5 cm -
Vincent van Gogh Foundation, Amsterdam

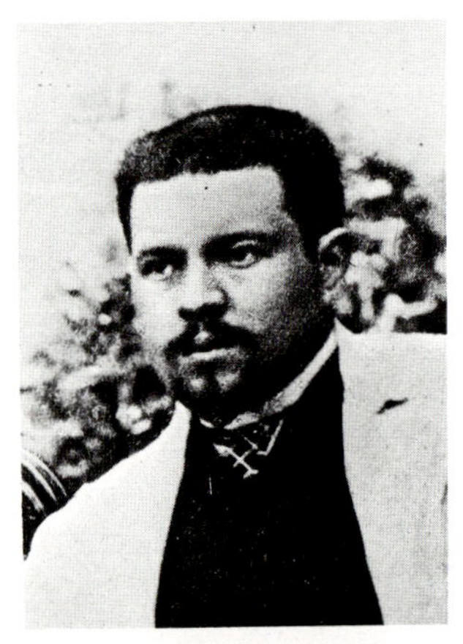

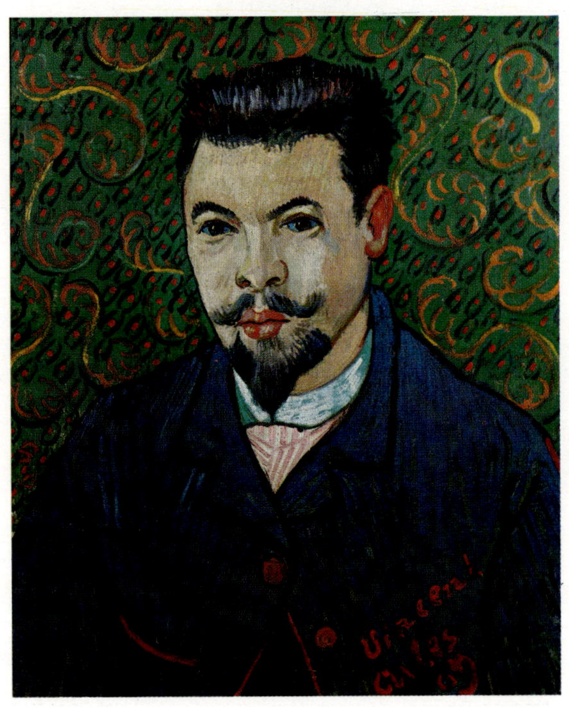

Photograph of Dr Rey

Portrait of Docteur Rey

January 1889 - oil on canvas - 64 x 53 cm -
Pushkin museum, Moscow

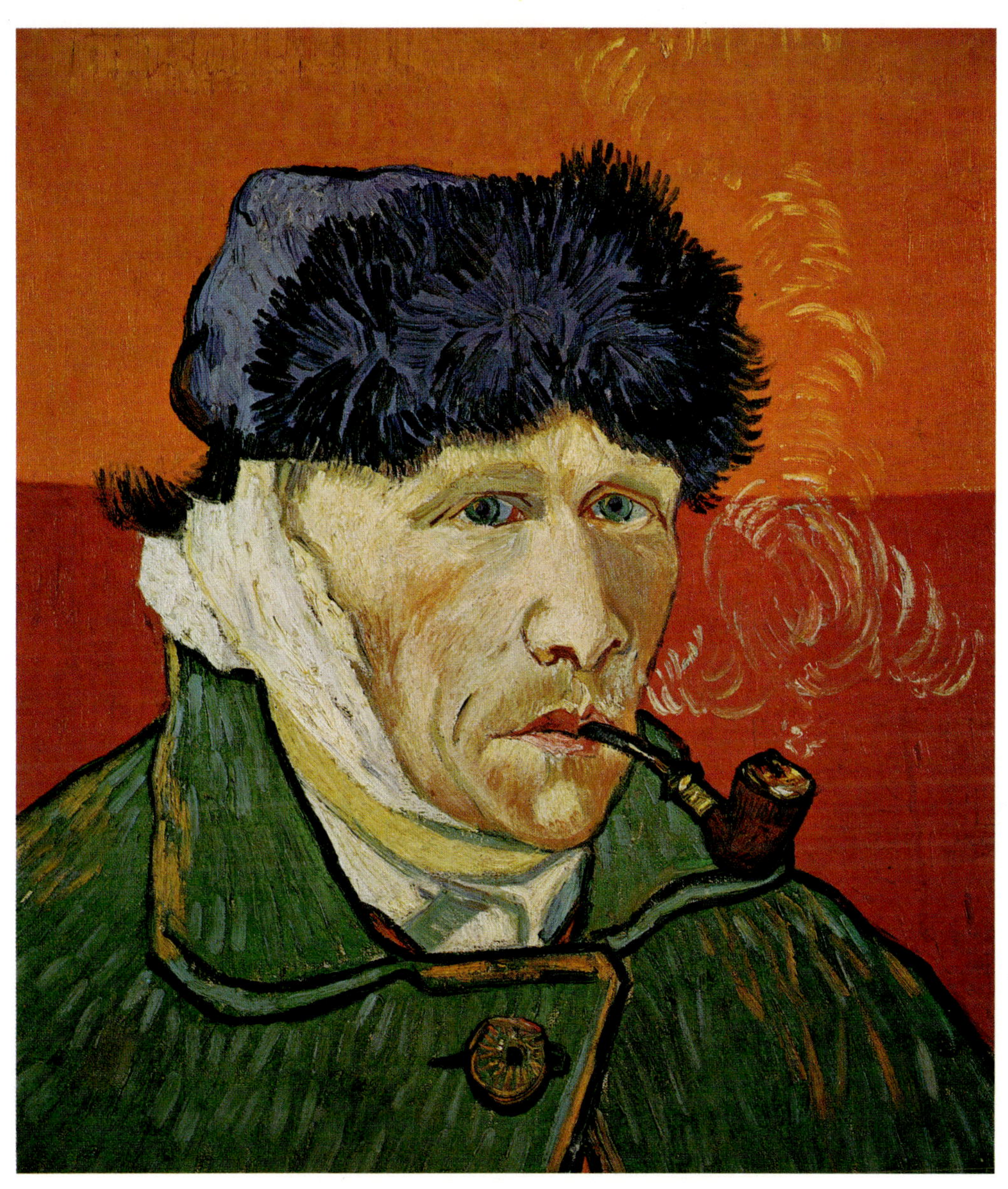

Self-Portrait with Bandaged Ear and Pipe

January-February 1889 - oil on canvas - 51 x 45 cm - Leigh B. Block Collection, Chicago

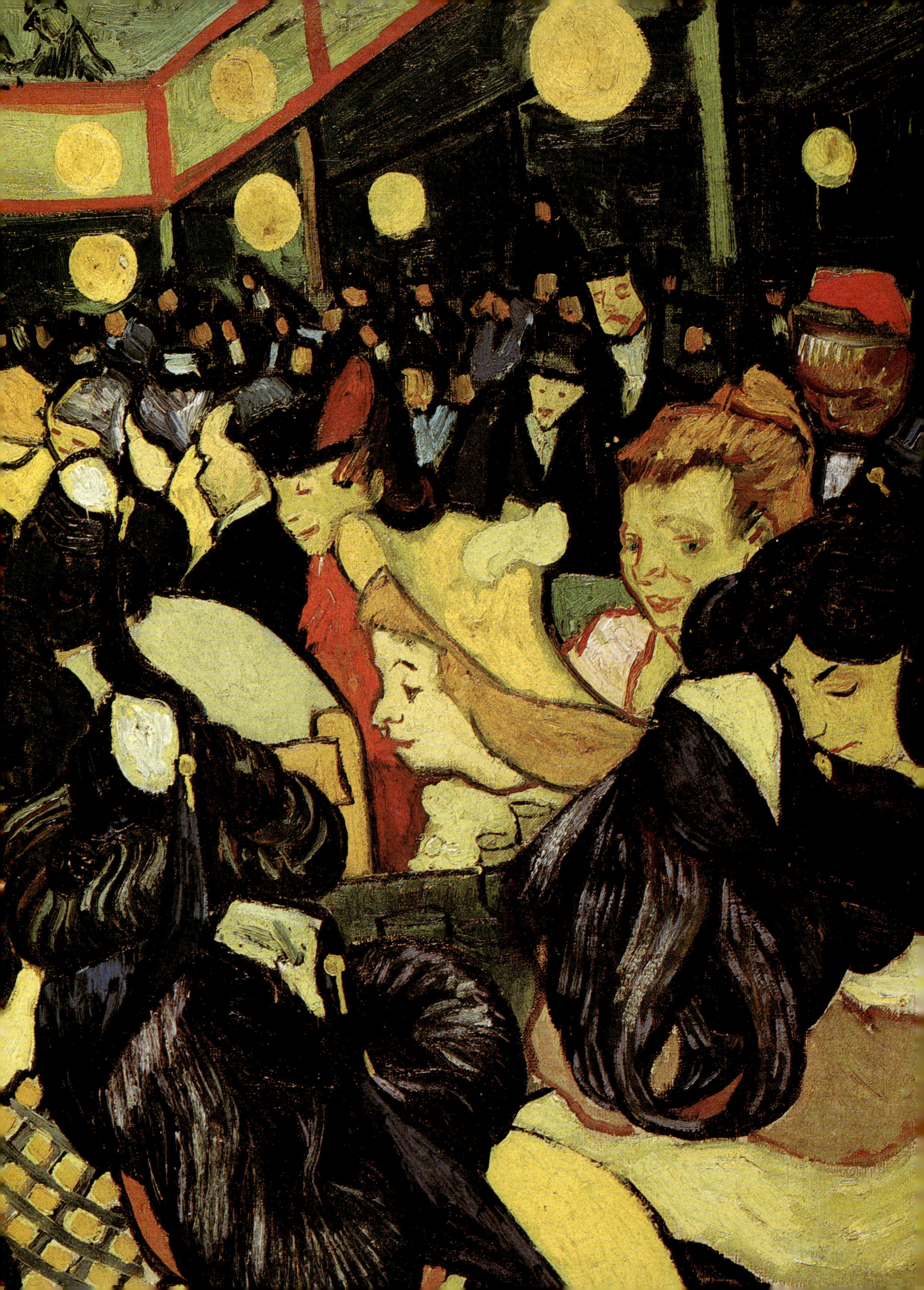

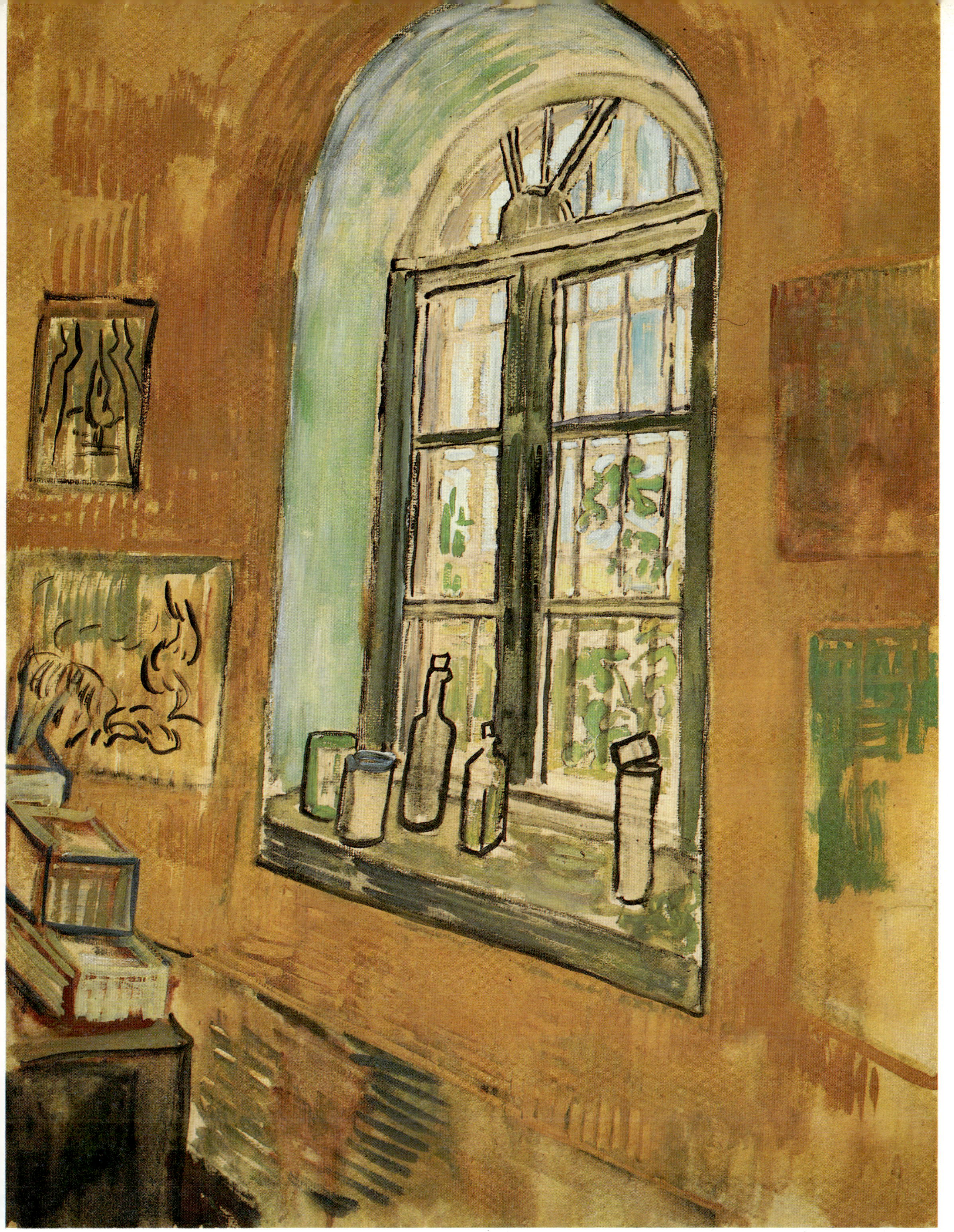

Dance Hall at Arles

December 1888 - oil on canvas - 65 x 81 cm - Vincent van Gogh Foundation, Amsterdam

Vincent's Room at the Hospital

October 1889 - gouache - 61.5 x 47 cm - Vincent van Gogh Foundation, Amsterdam

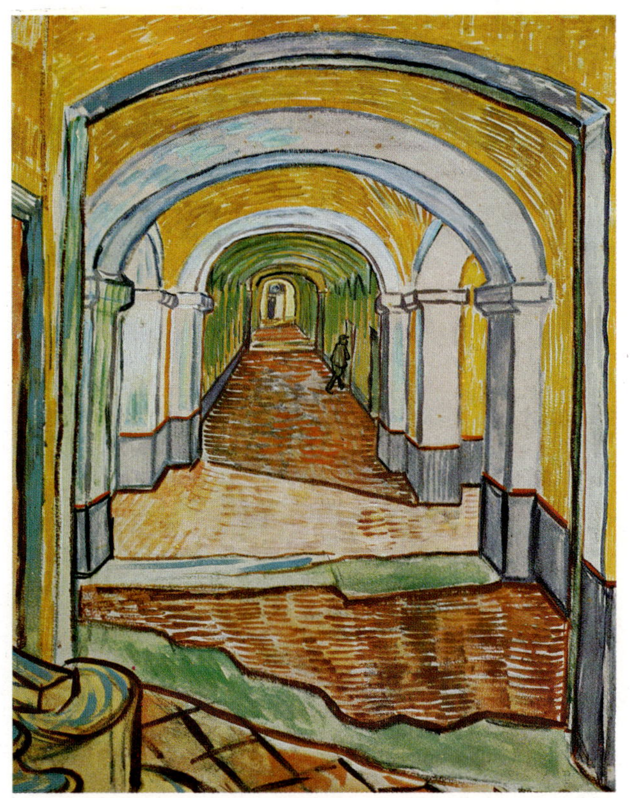

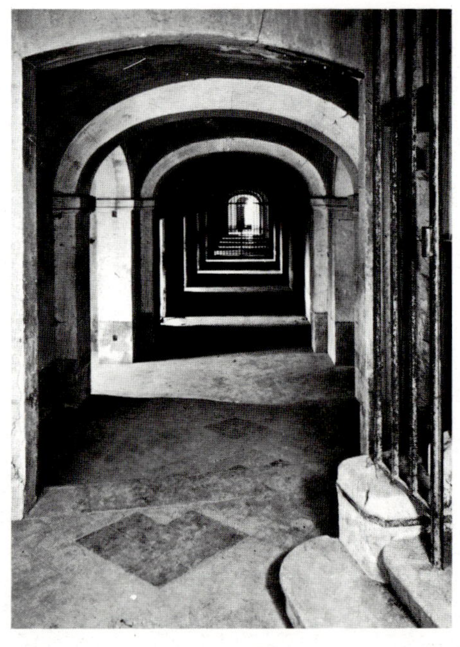

Corridor in the asylum

1889 - gouache and watercolour - 65 x 49 cm -
Museum of Modern Art, New York

Photograph of a corridor in the asylum

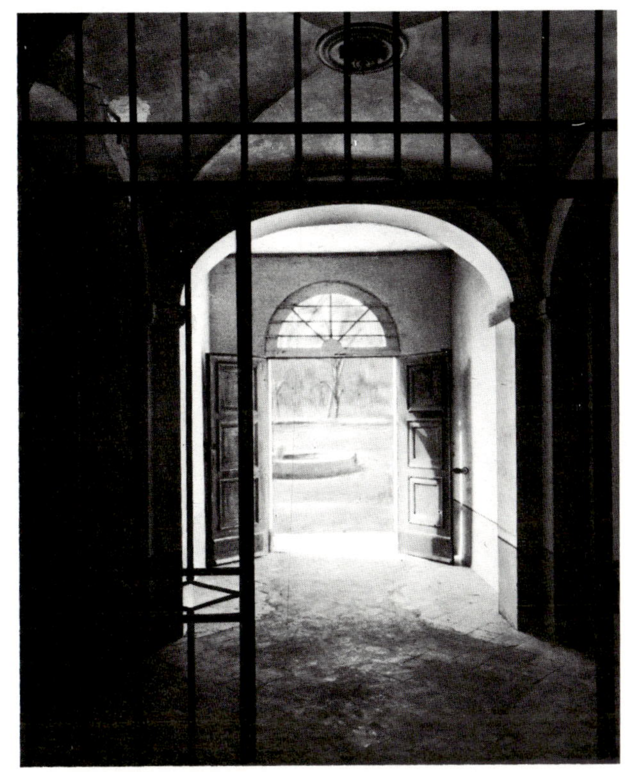

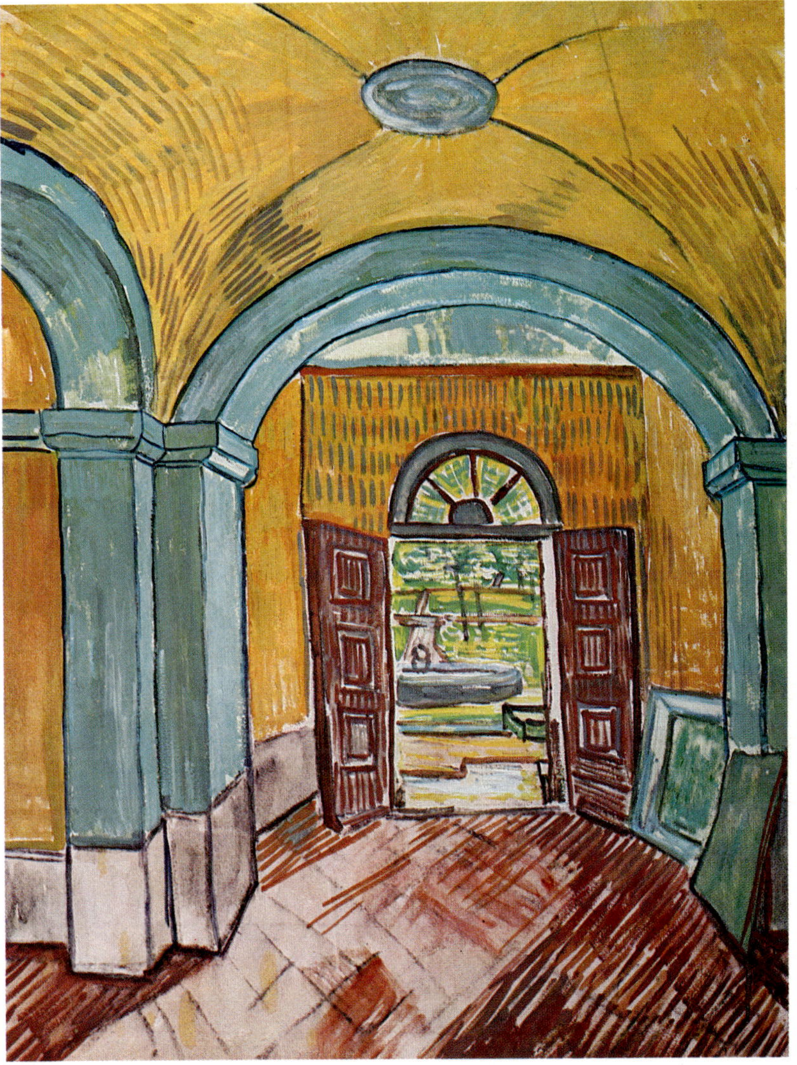

Photograph of the asylum hall

Entrance Hall to the Asylum

1889 - watercolour and gouache on pink Ingres paper - 61 x 47 cm -
Vincent van Gogh Foundation, Amsterdam

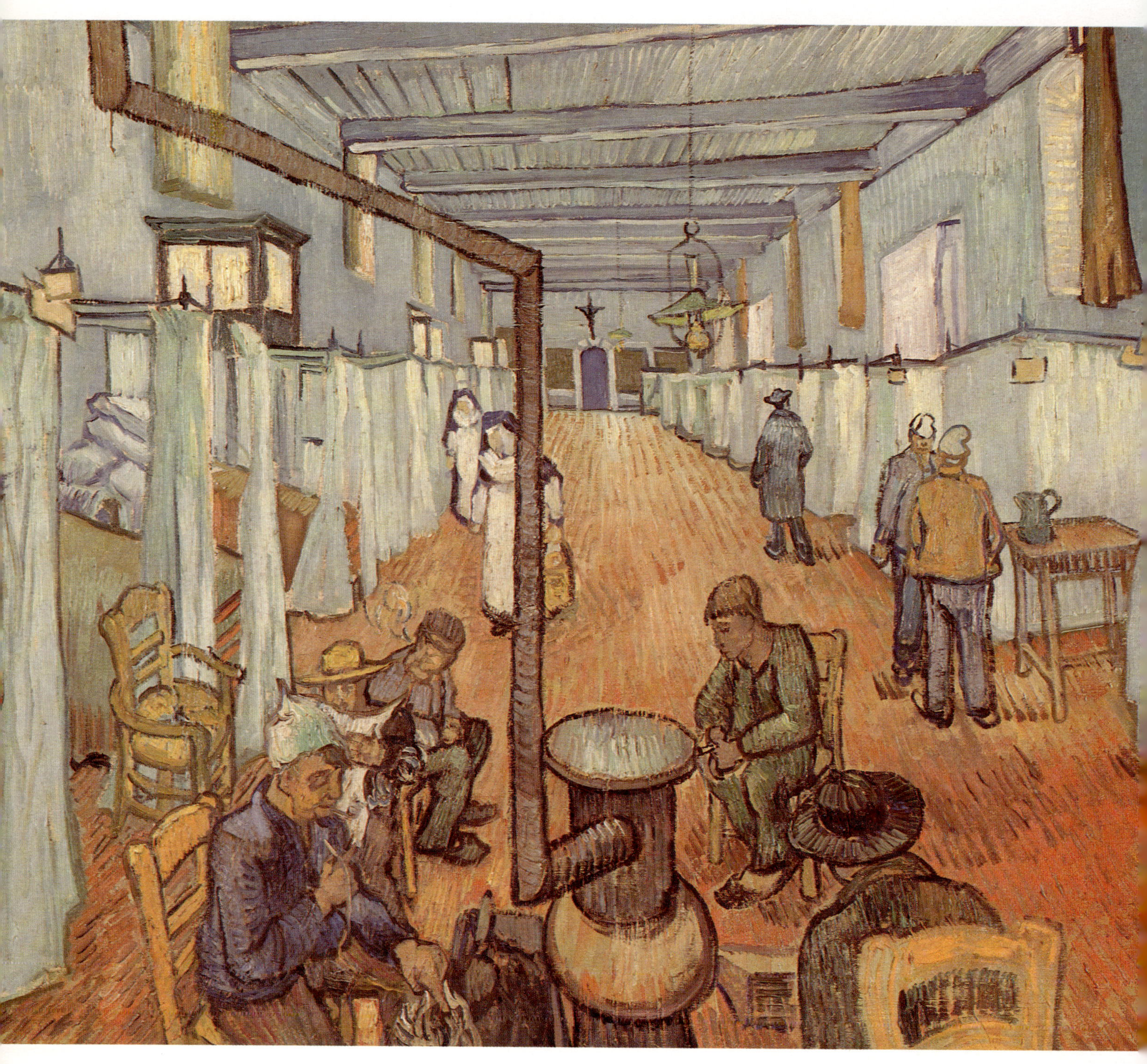

Dormitory in the Asylum

April 1889 - oil on canvas - 74 x 92 cm -
Oskar Reinhart Collection, Winterthur, Switzerland

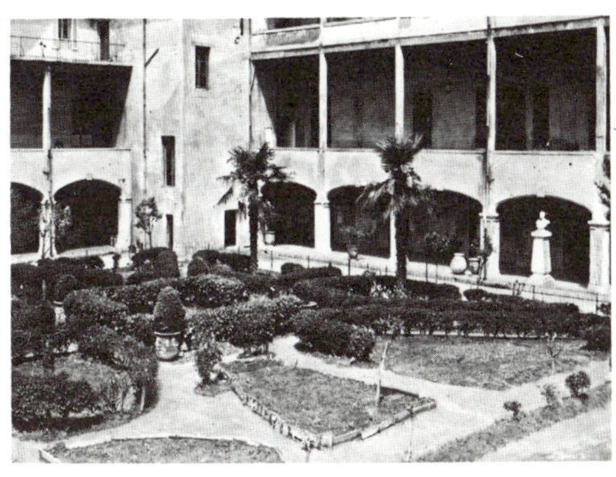

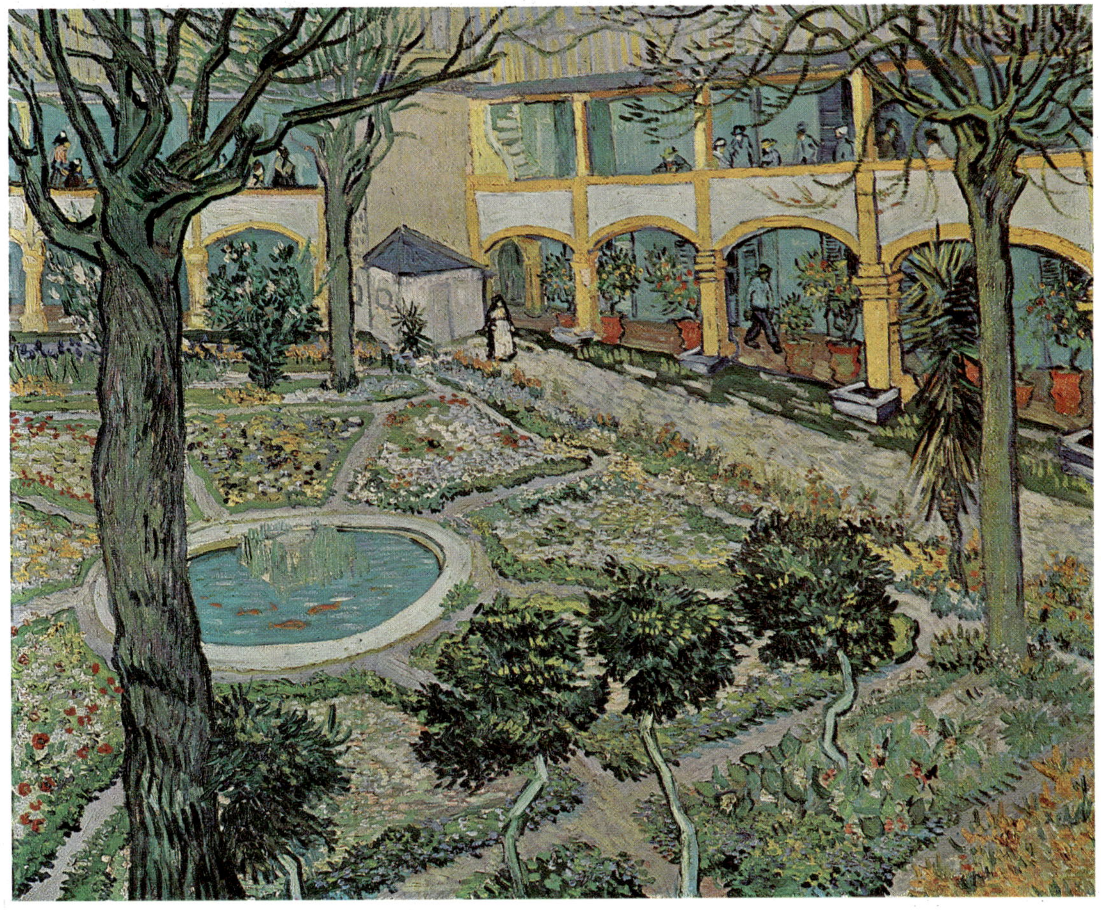

Photograph of the hospital where Vincent went after the incident with Gauguin

Garden in the Asylum

May 1889 - oil on canvas - 73 x 92 cm - Oskar Reinhart collection, Winterthur, Switzerland

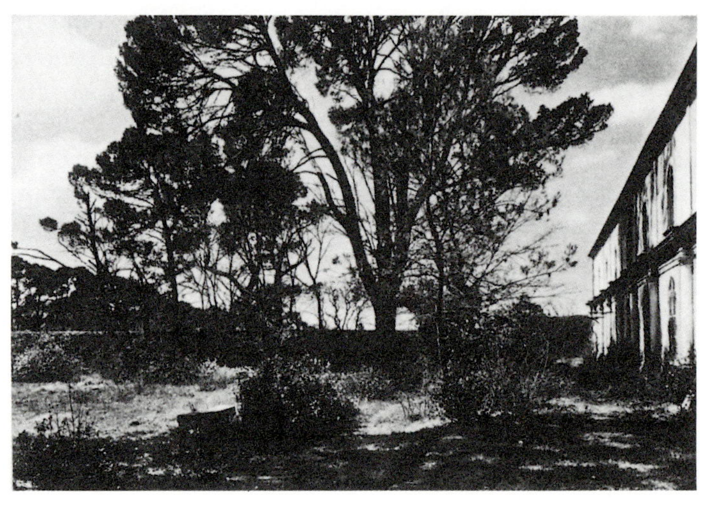

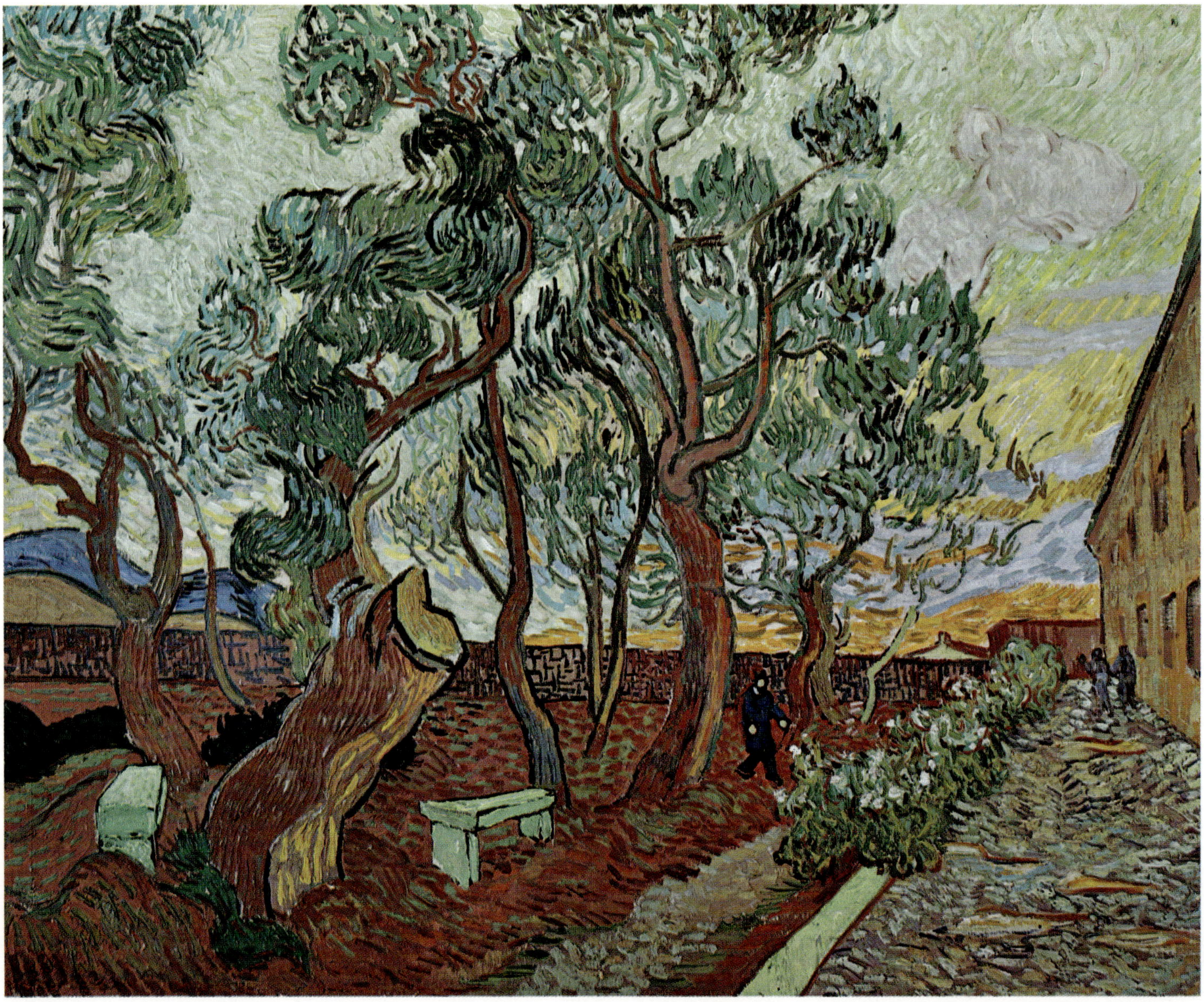

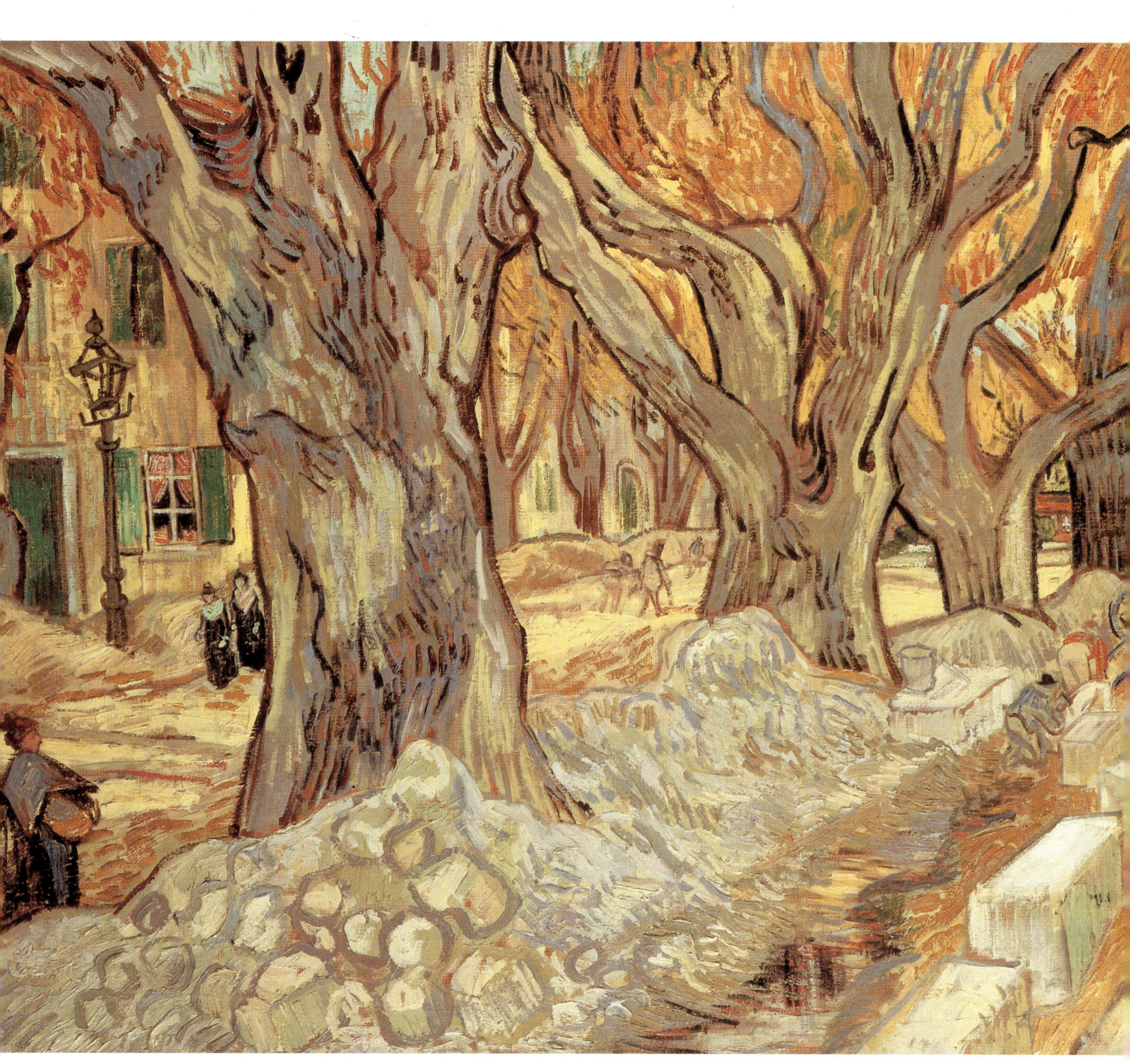

Photograph that shows the same view as the painter's

The Park in the Asylum

October 1889 - oil on canvas 73 x 92 cm -
Folkwang museum, Essen

The Pavers

December 1889 - oil on canvas - 74 x 93 cm -
Cleveland Museum of Art, Cleveland

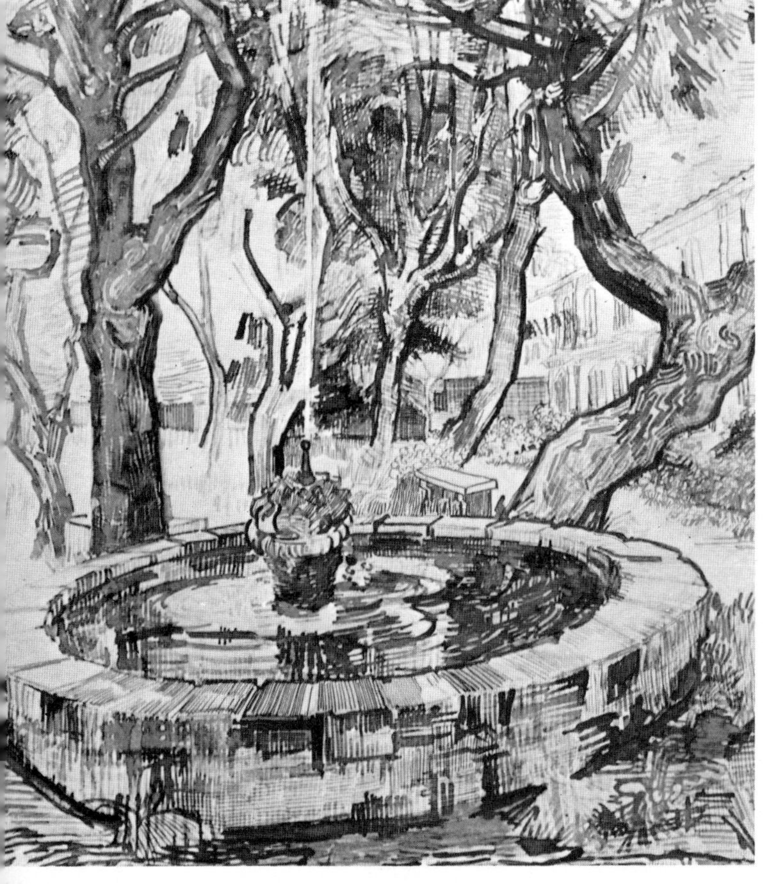

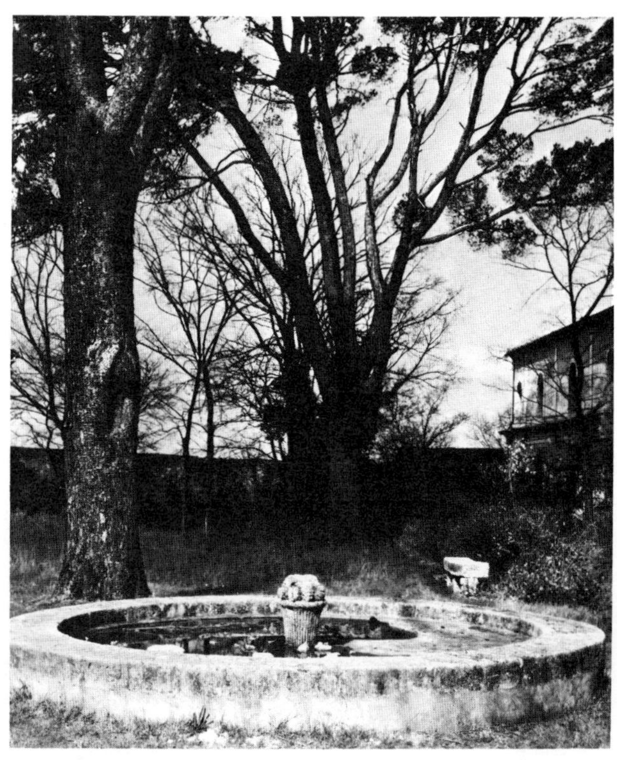

Fountain in the Garden of the Asylum

1889 - indian ink -45 x 48 cm -
Vincent van Gogh Foundation, Amsterdam

Photograph of the fountain on the asylum grounds

Orchard in Blossom with View of Arles

April 1889 - oil on canvas - 50.5 x 65 cm -
Vincent van Gogh Foundation, Amsterdam

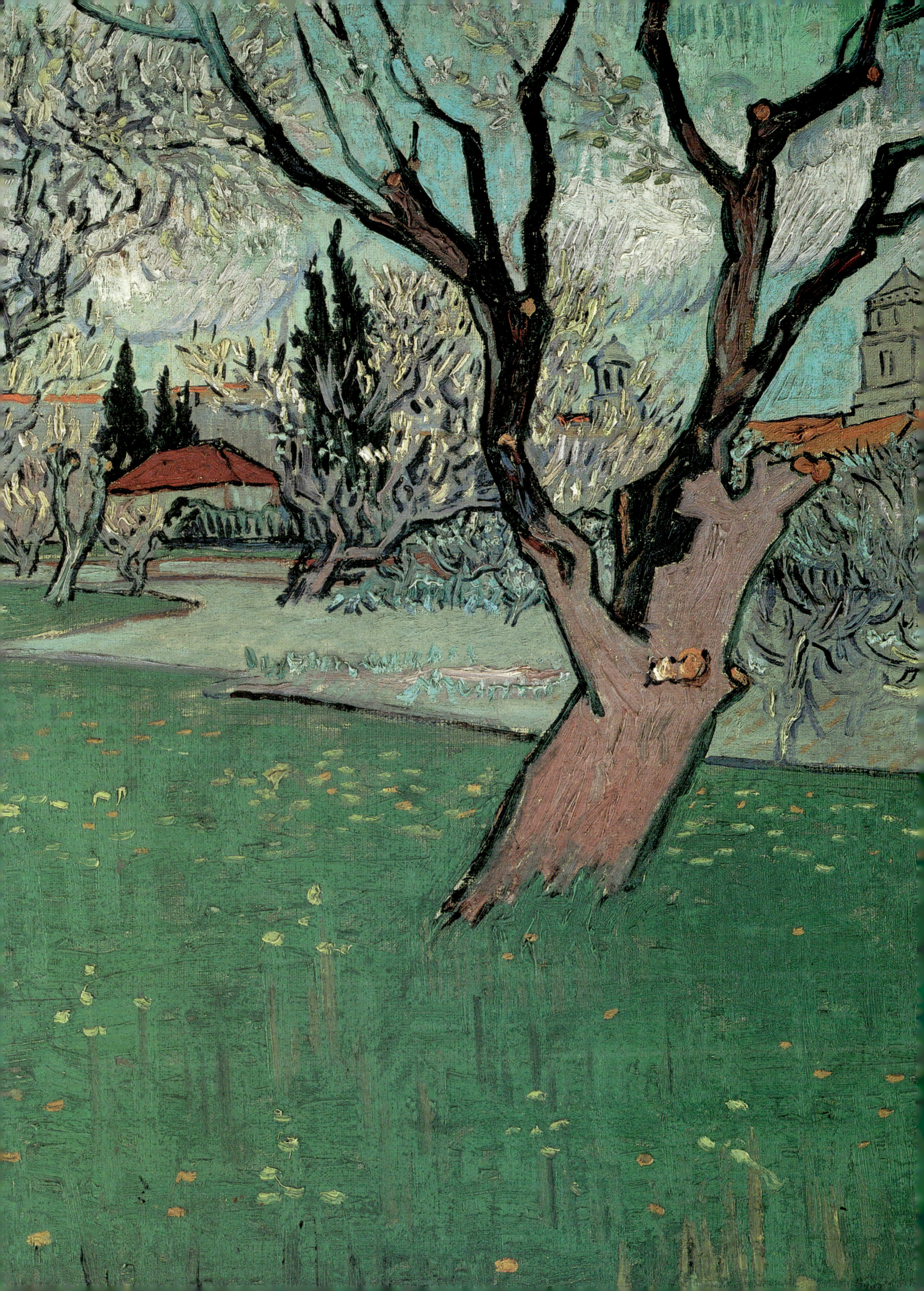

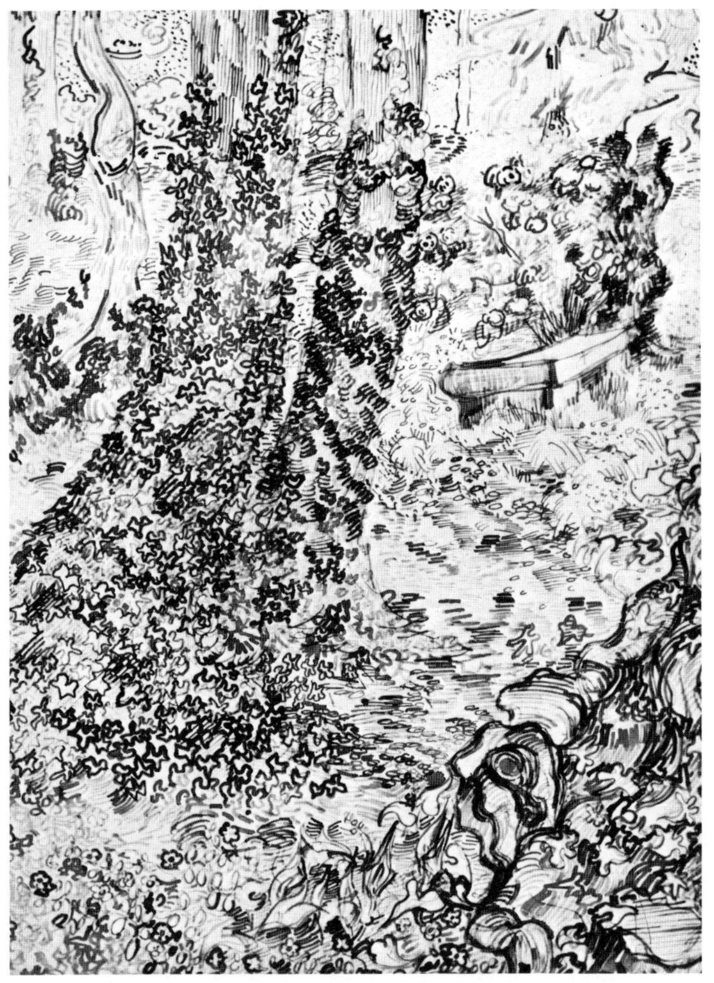

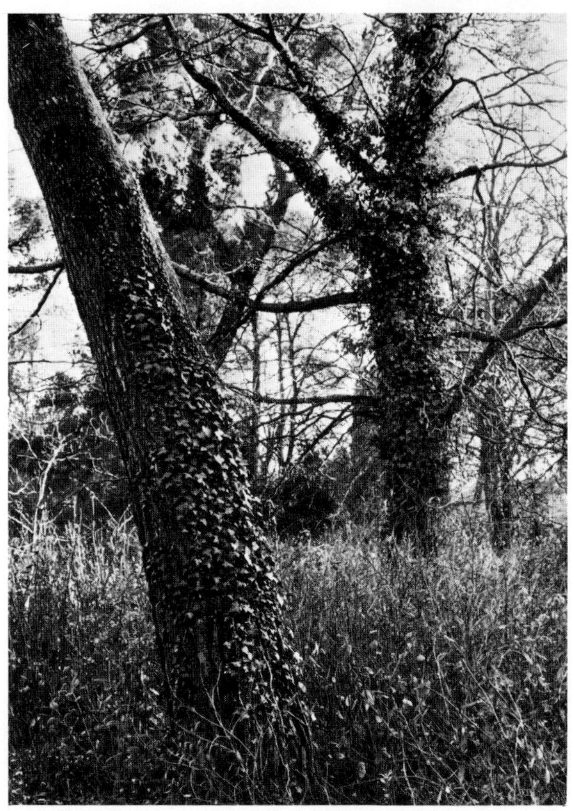

Tree Trunks with Ivy

1889 - indian ink - 62.5 x 47 cm -
Vincent van Gogh Foundation, Amsterdam

Photograph of ivy-covered trees

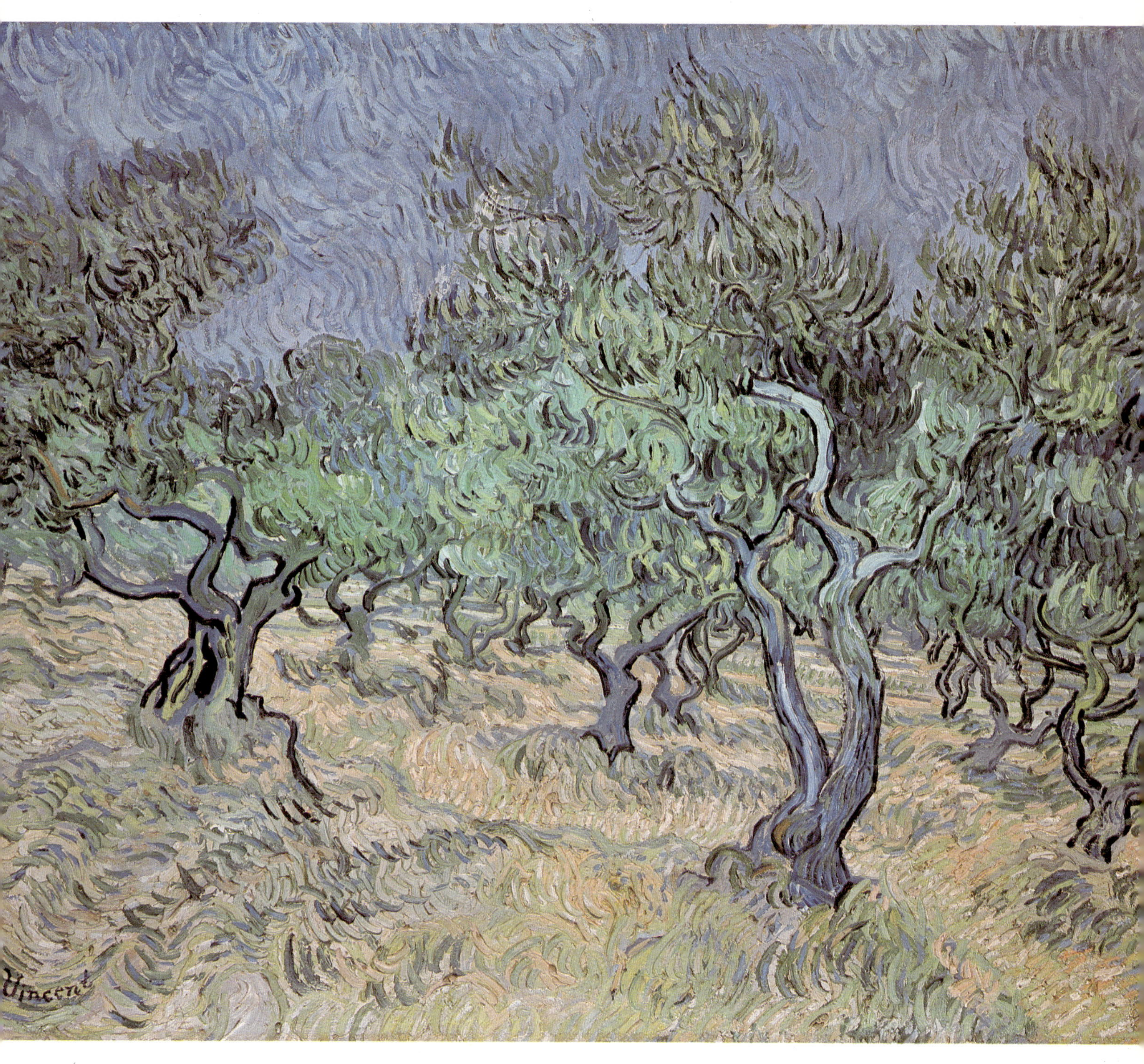

Olive Grove

June 1889 - oil on canvas - 72 x 65 cm -
Rijksmuseum Kröller- Müller, Otterlo

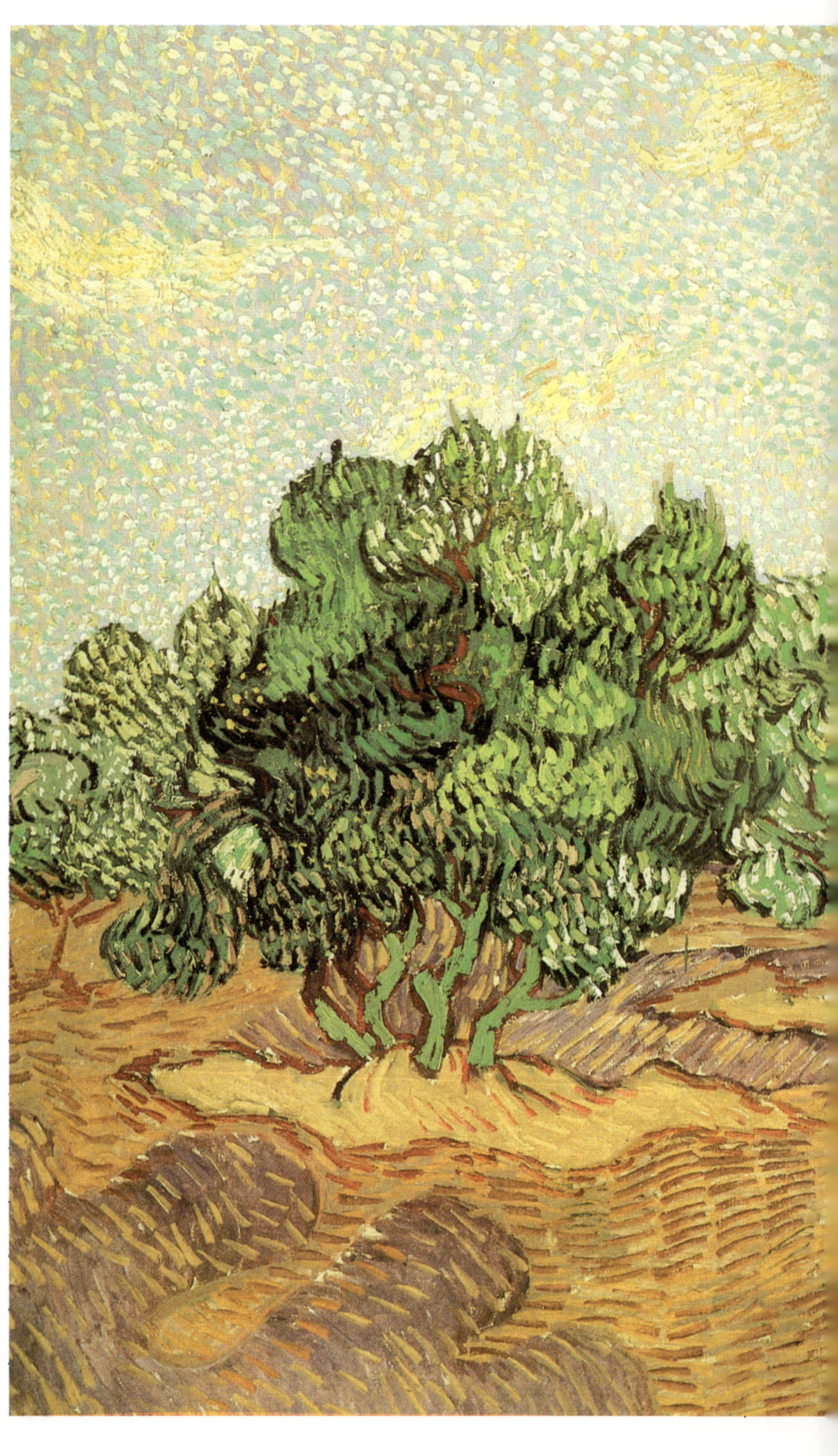

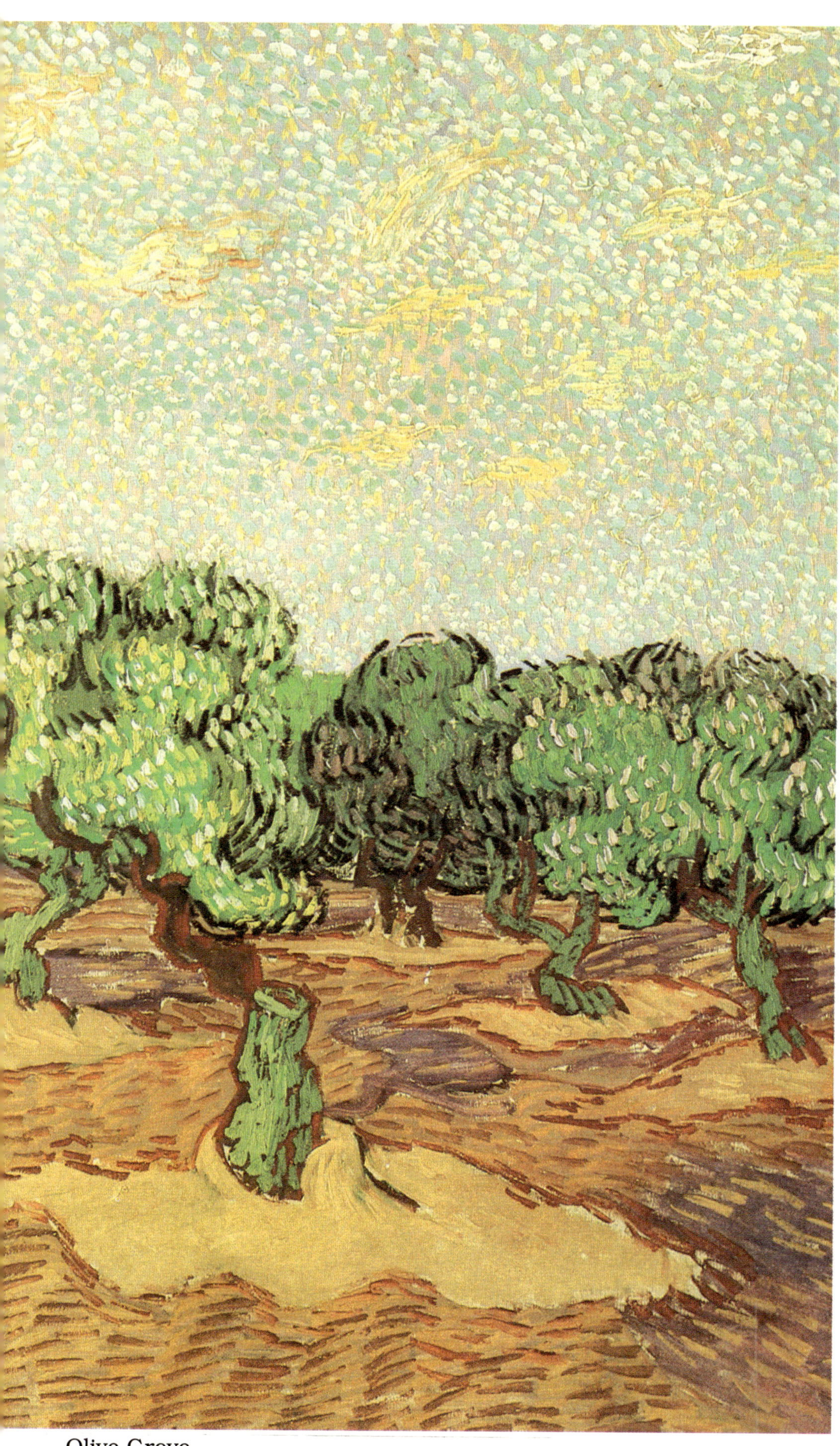

Olive Grove

November 1889 - oil on canvas - 72.5 x 92.1 cm - Walter H. Annenberg Collection, Rancho Mirage, Cal.

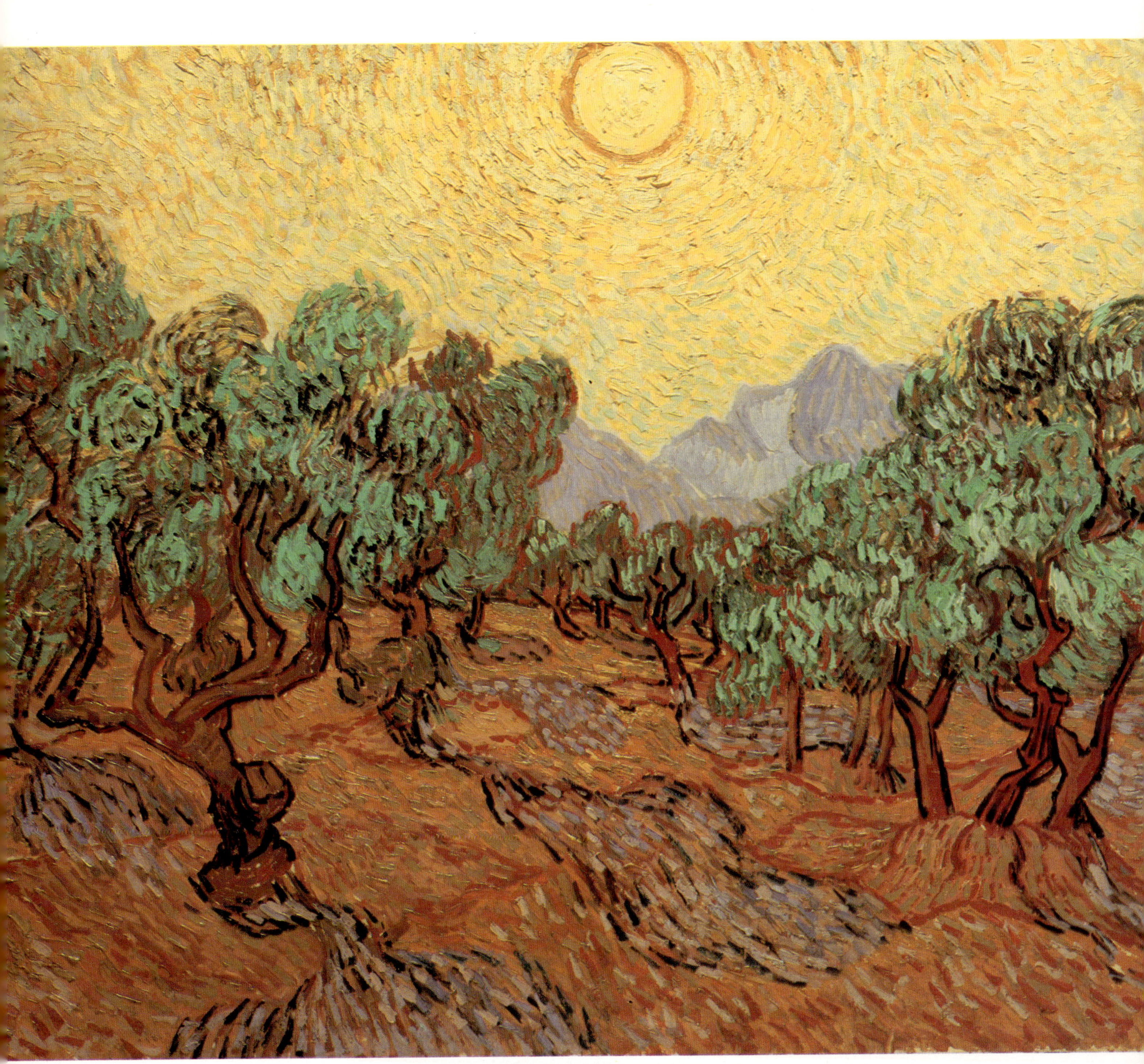

Olive Grove

November 1889 - oil on canvas - 74 x 93 cm -
Minneapolis Institue of Art, Minneapolis

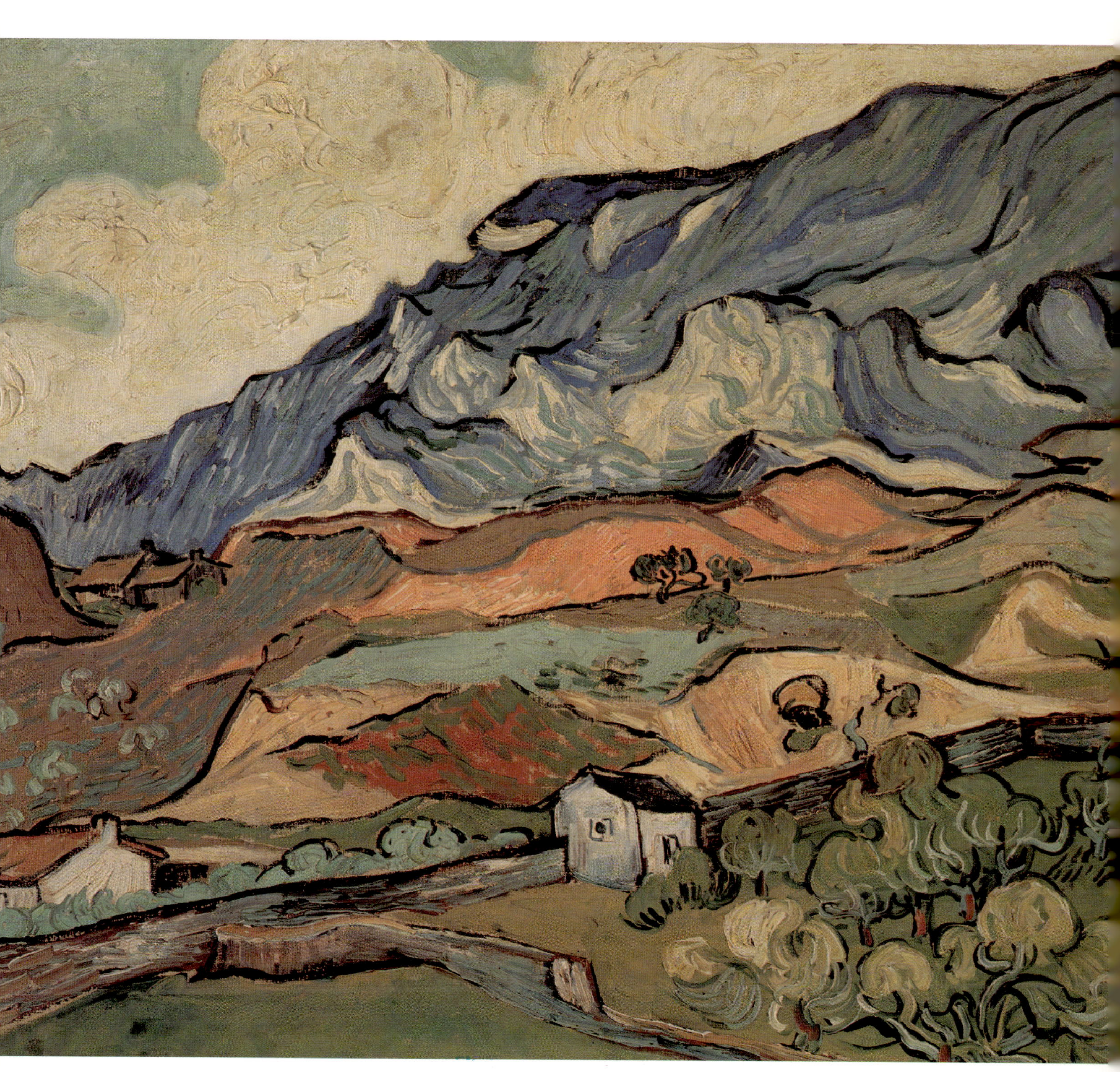

View of the Apilles

June 1889 - oil on canvas - 59 x 72 cm - Rijksmusuem Kröller- Müller, Otterlo

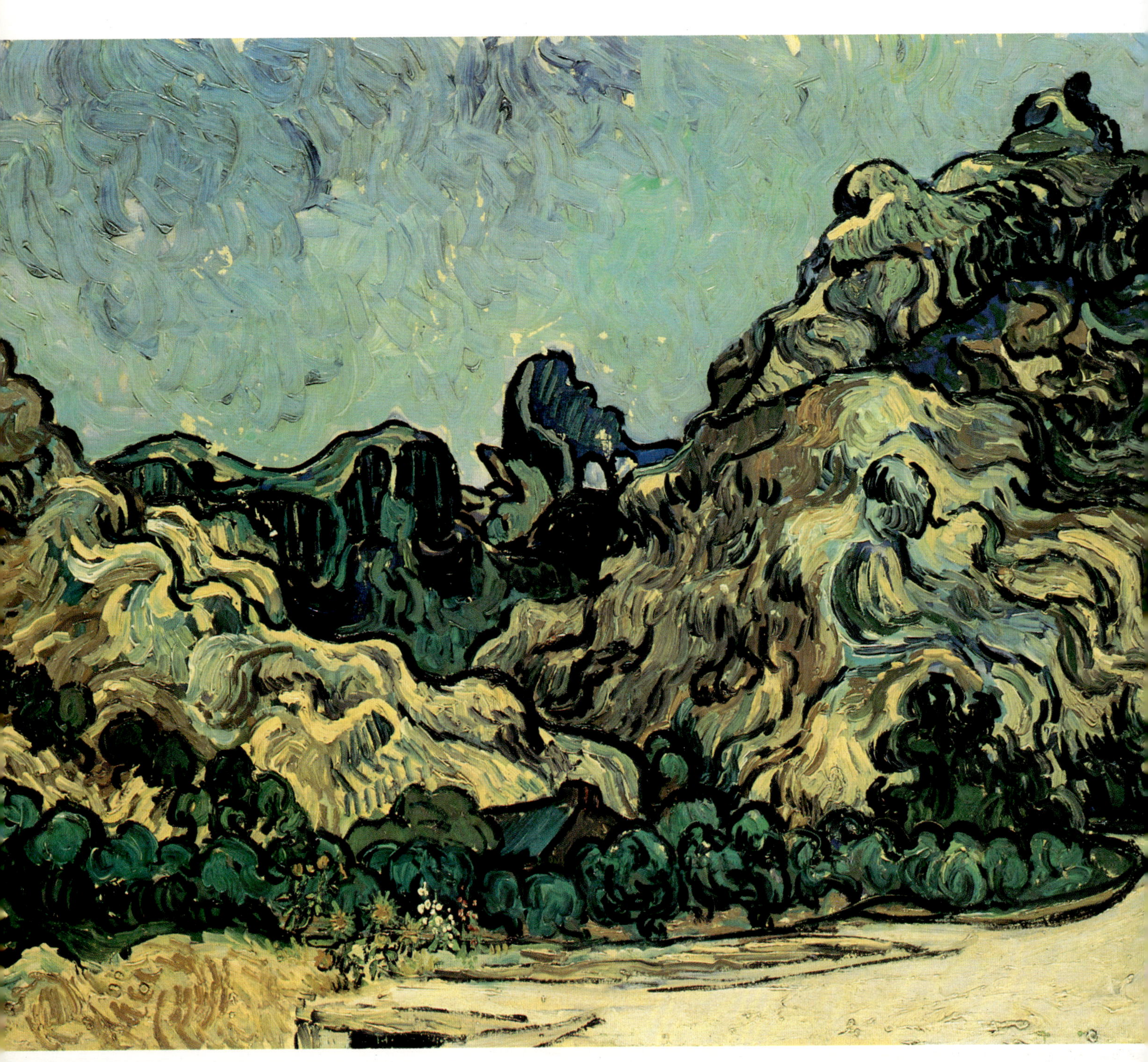

Mountains at Saint-Rémy

July 1889 - oil on canvas - 73 x 93 cm -
Justin Thannhauser collection, Solomon R. Guggenheim Museum,
New York

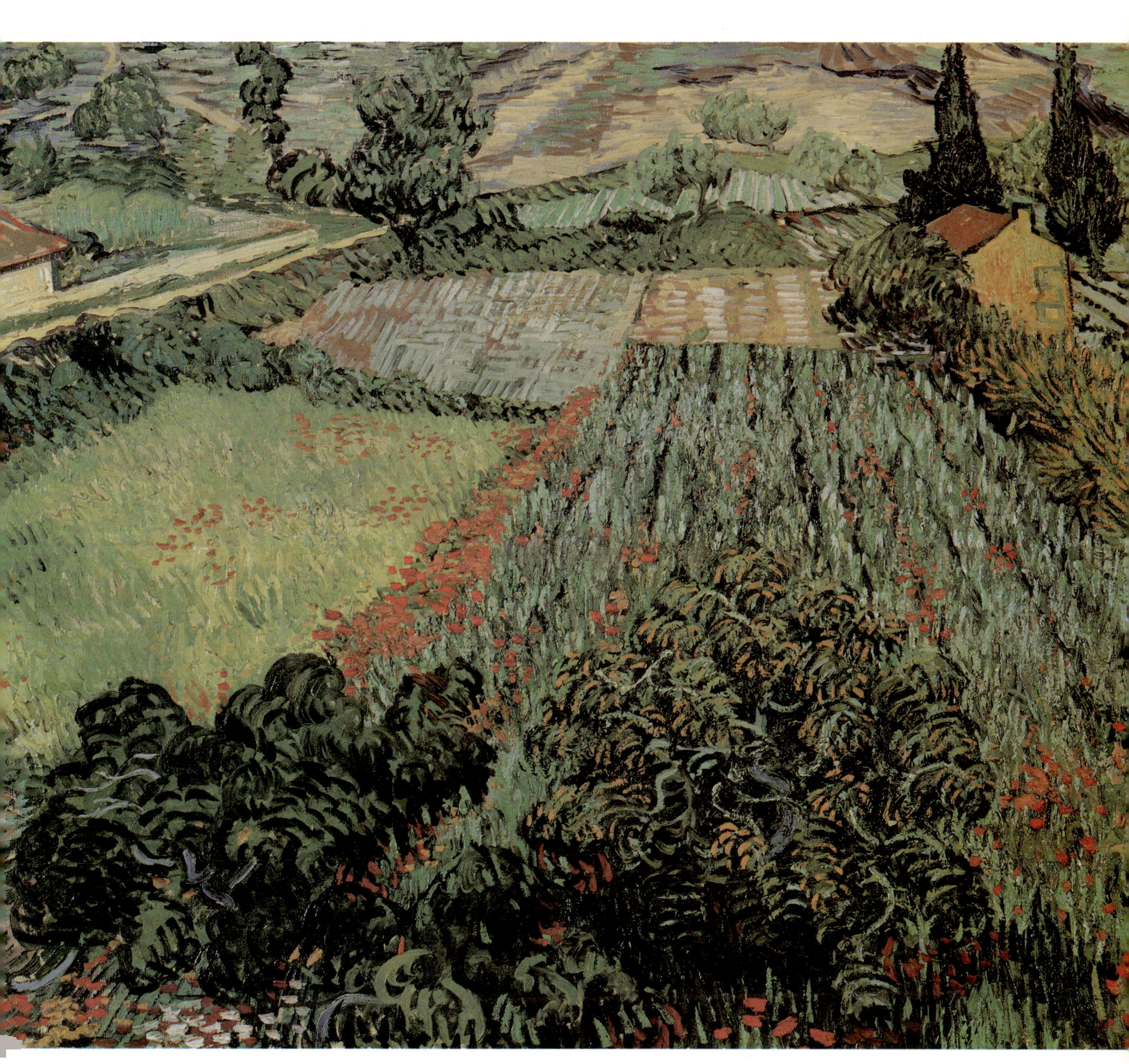

Field with Poppies

June 1889 - oil on canvas - 71 x 91 cm - Kunsthalle, Bremen

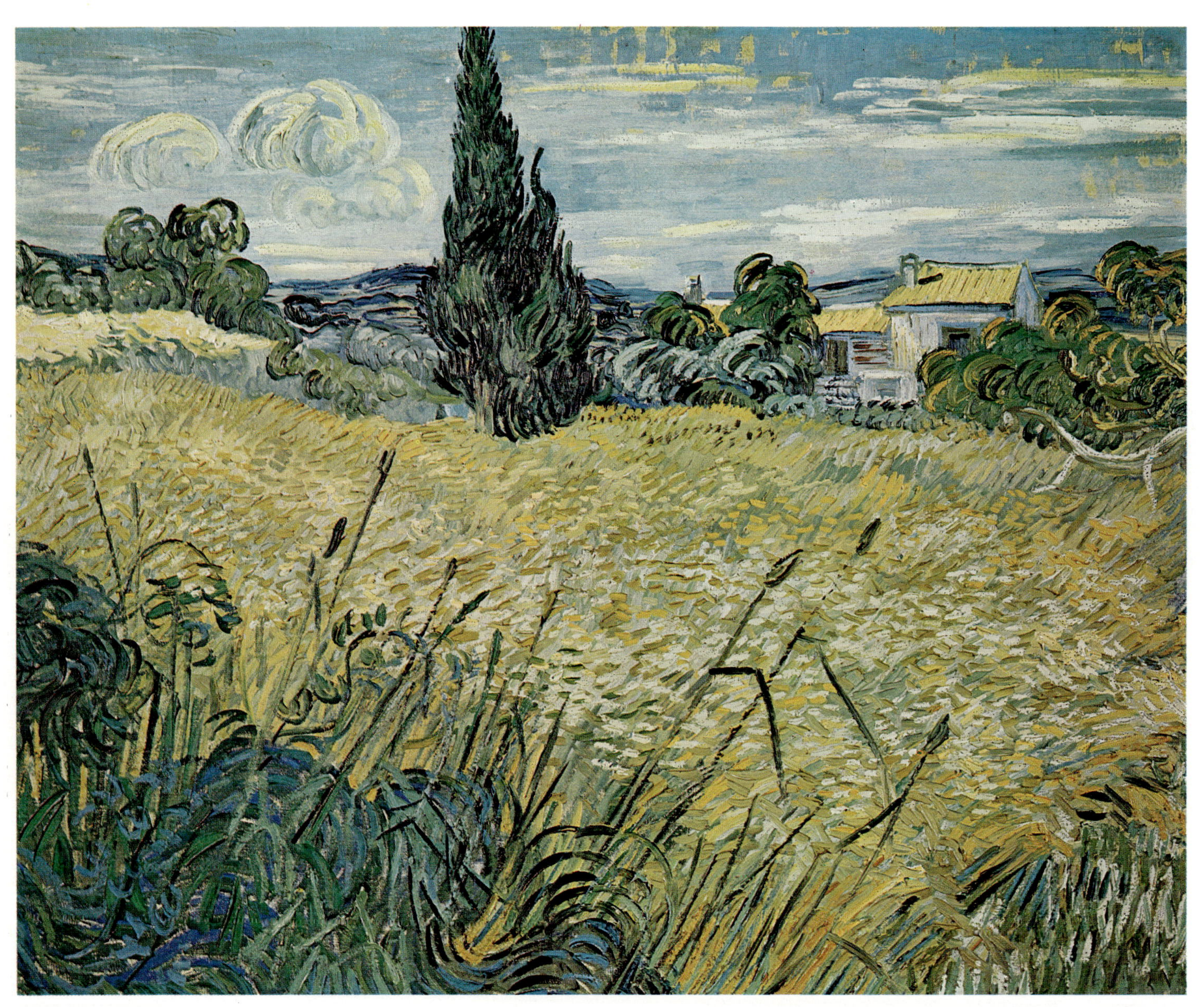

Green Wheat Field with Cypress

June 1889 - oil on canvas - 73 x 92 cm -
Narodni Gallery, Prague

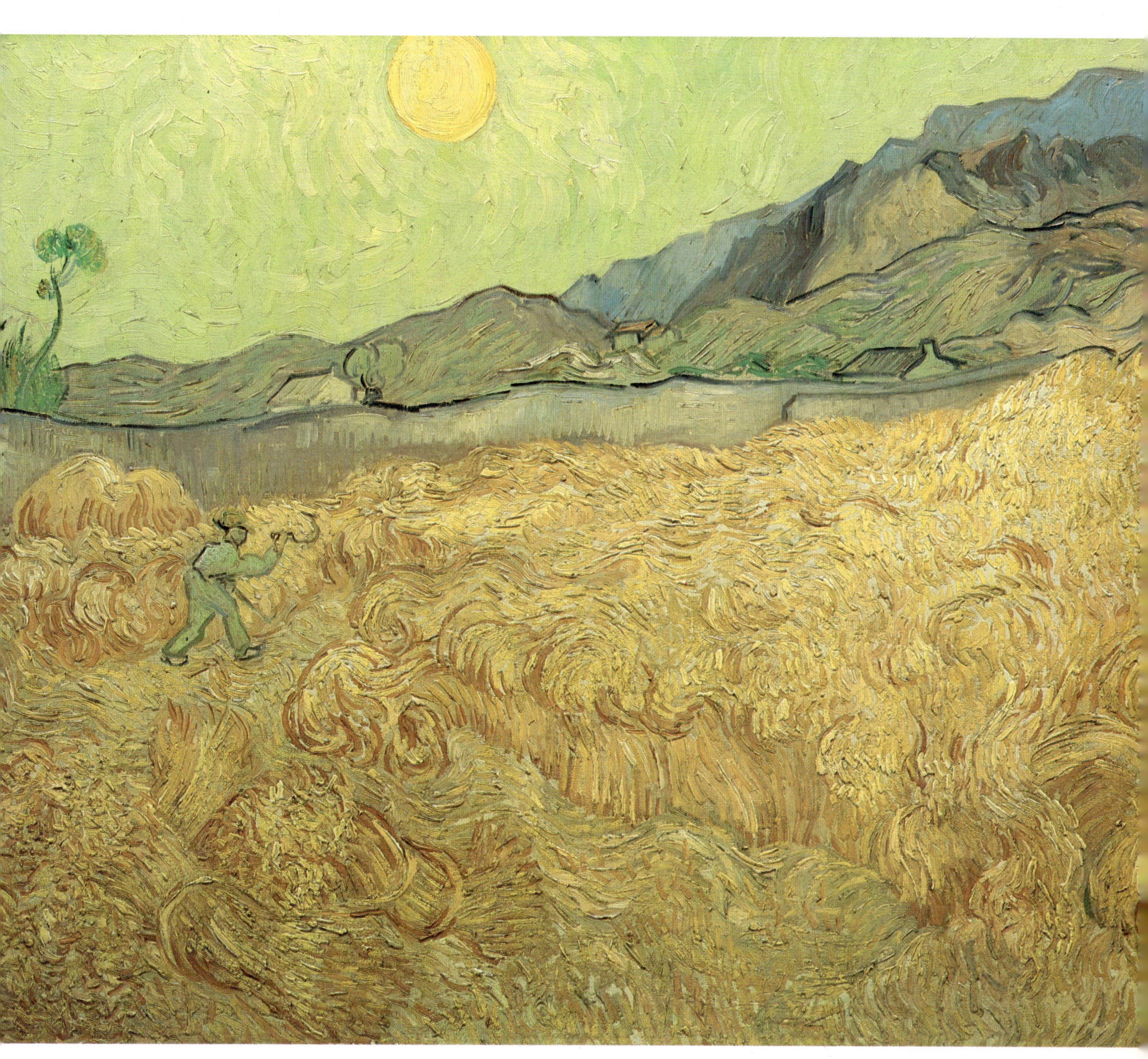

Wheat Field with Reaper

September 1889 - oil on canvas - 74 x 92 cm -
Vincent van Gogh Foundation, Amsterdam

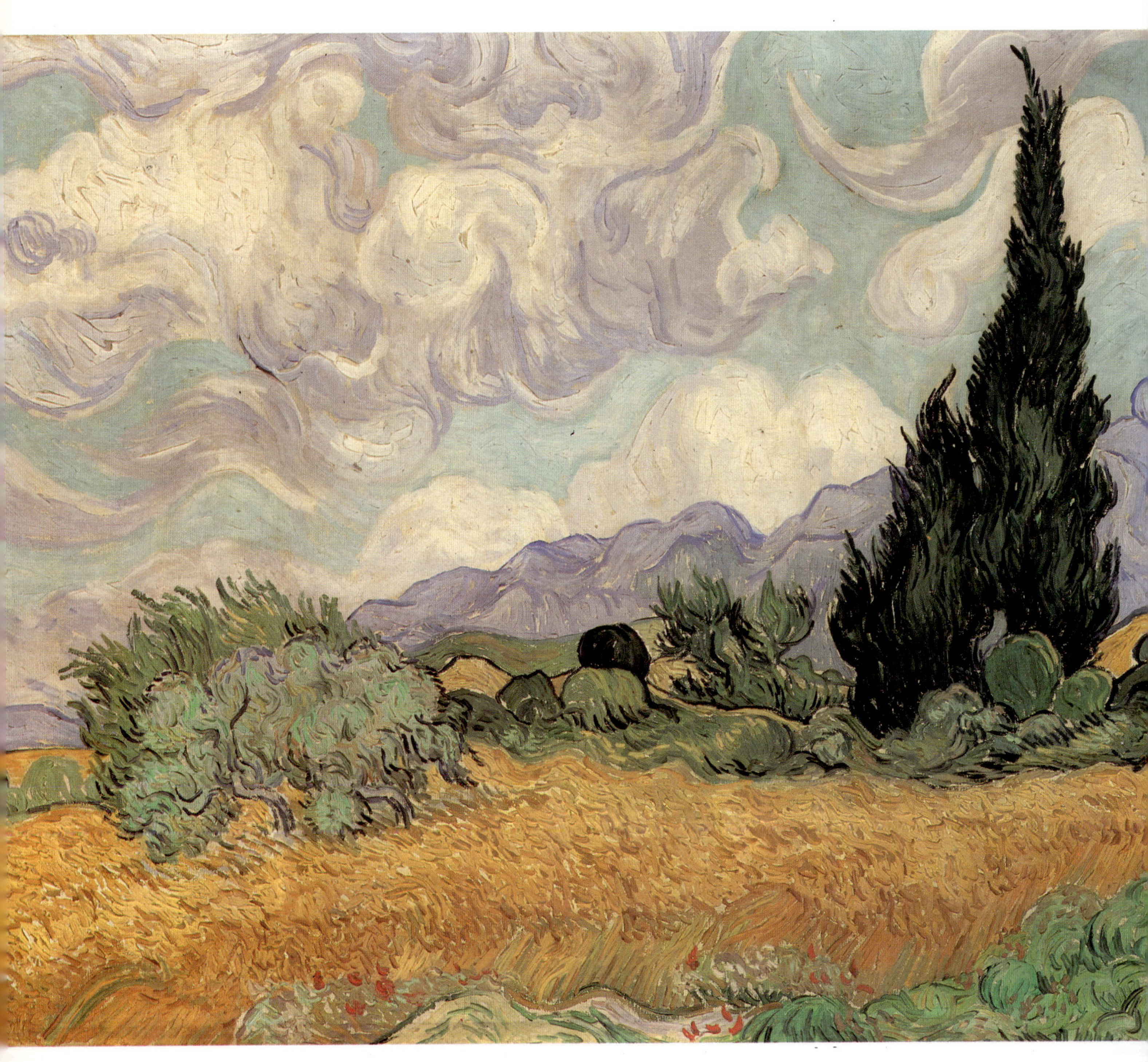

Wheat Field with Cypresses

June 1889 - oil on canvas - 73 x 92 cm - National Gallery, London

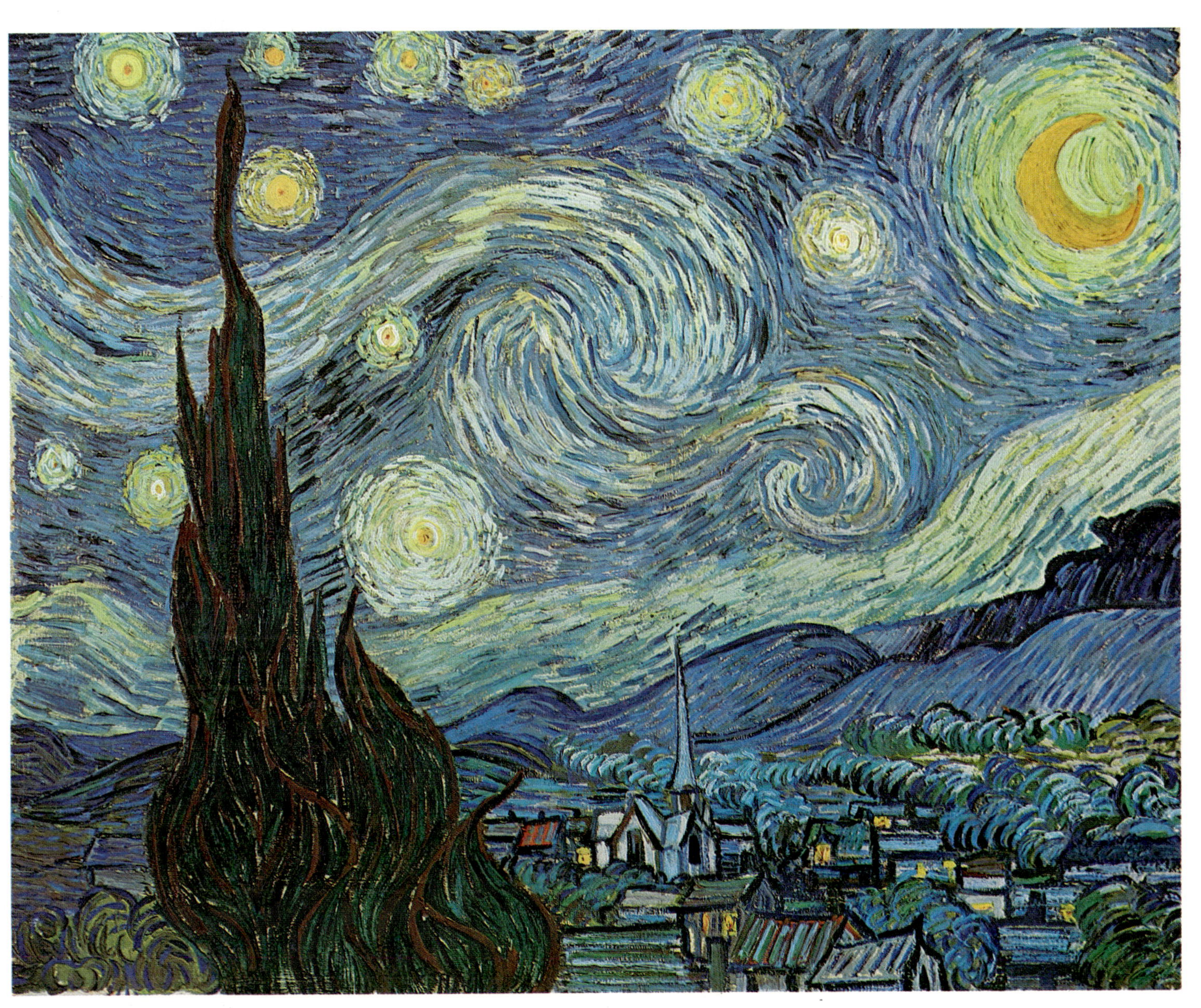

Starry Night

June 1889 - oil on canvas - 732 x 92 cm -
Museum of Modern Art, New York

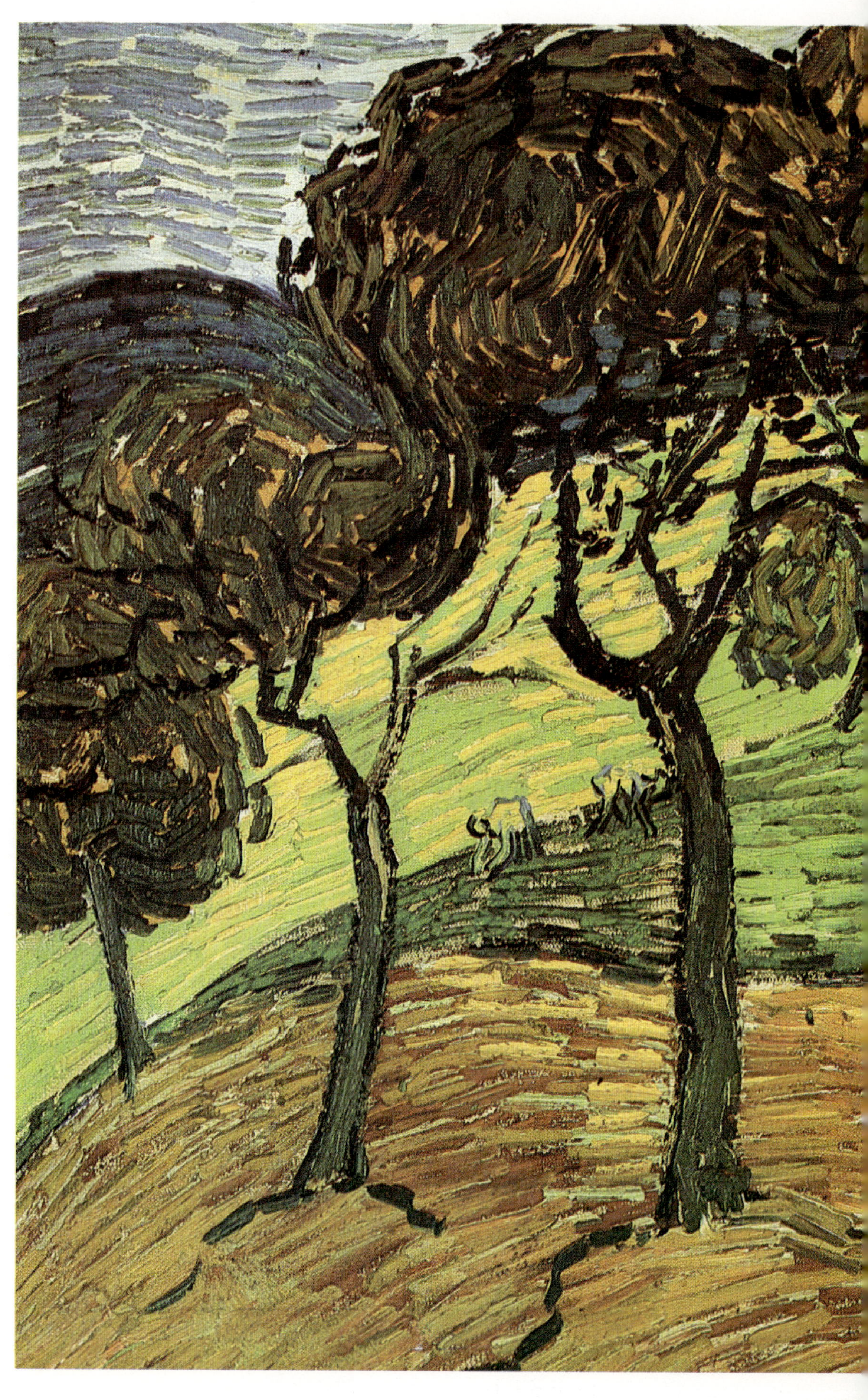

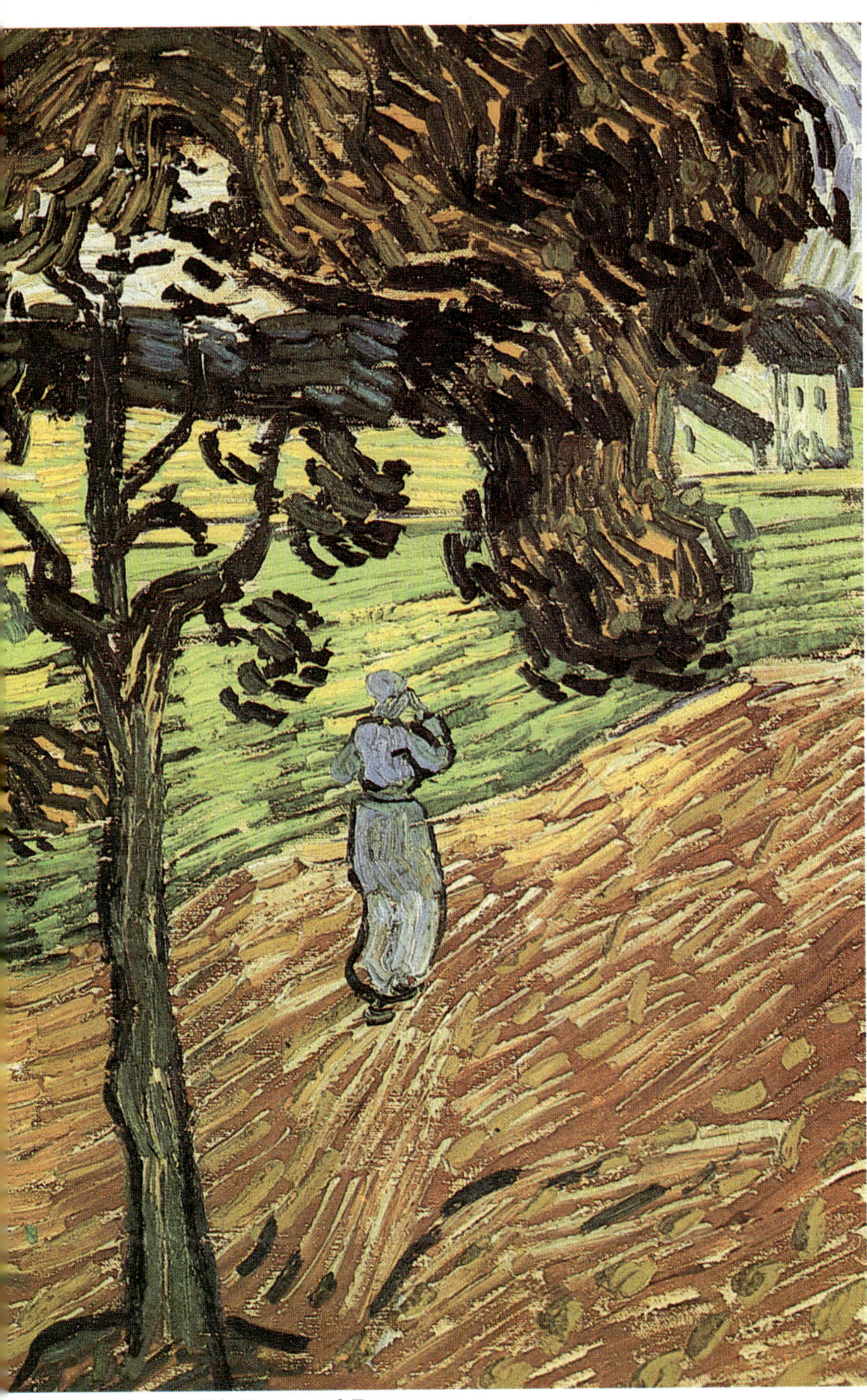

Landscape with Trees and Figures

November 1889 - oil on canvas - 49.9 x 65.4 cm -
Cone collection, Baltimore Museum of Art, Baltimore

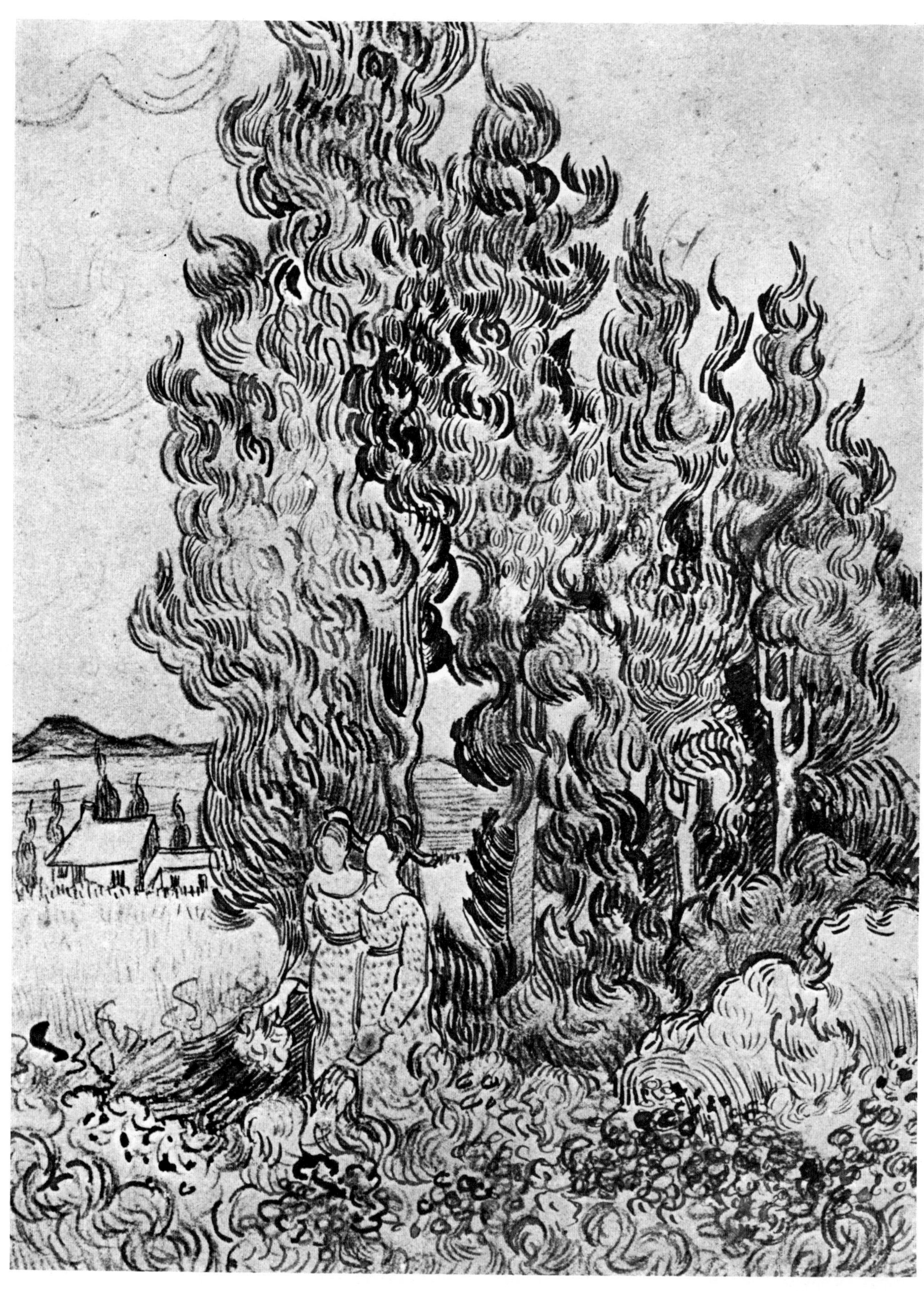

The Cypresses

June 1889 - ink, red and black chalk - 91 x 23 cm
Rijkmuseum Kröller- Müller, Otterlo

The Cypress

June 1889 - oil on canvas - 92 x 73 cm -
Rijksmuseum Kröller-Müller, Otterlo

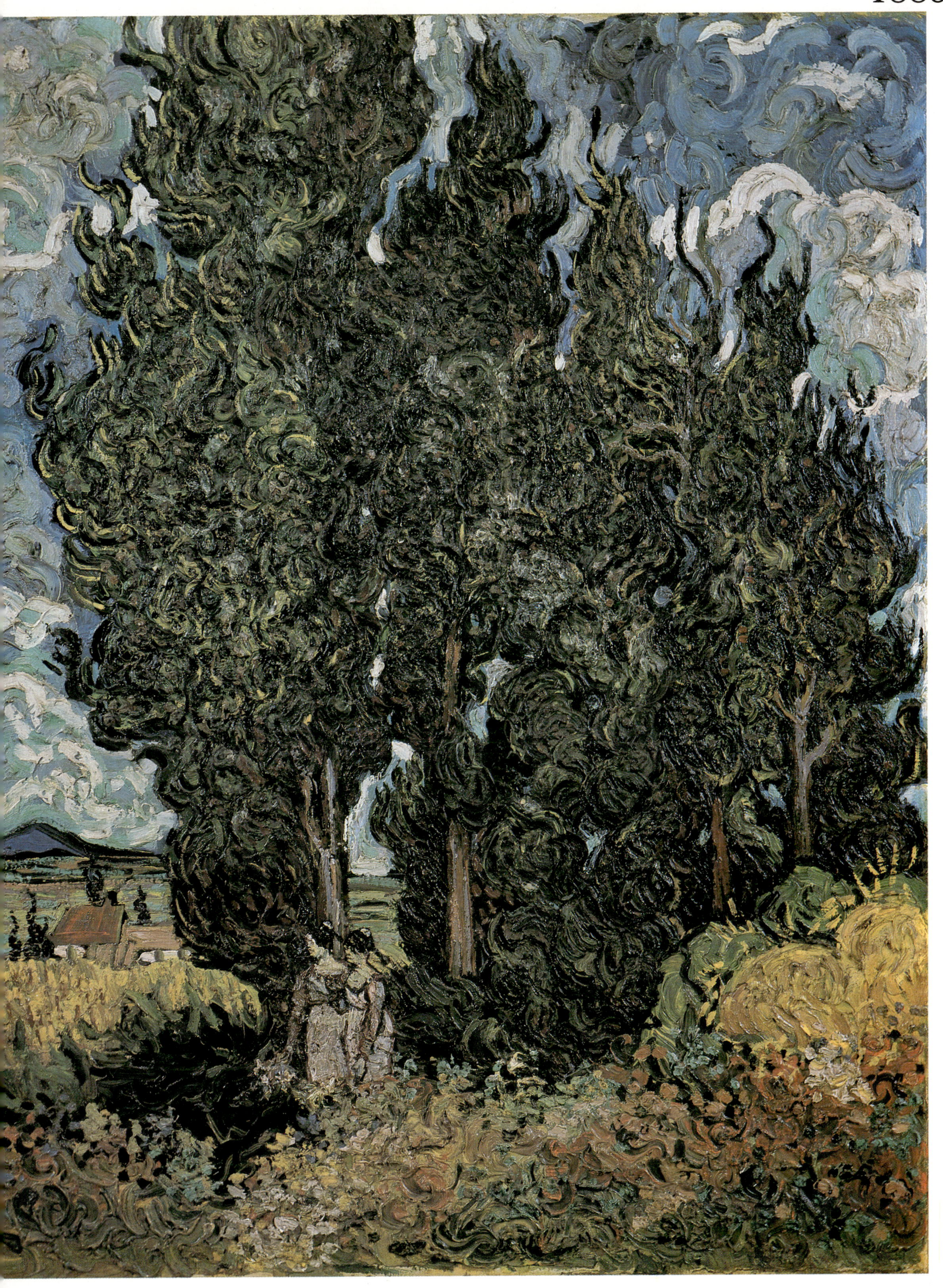

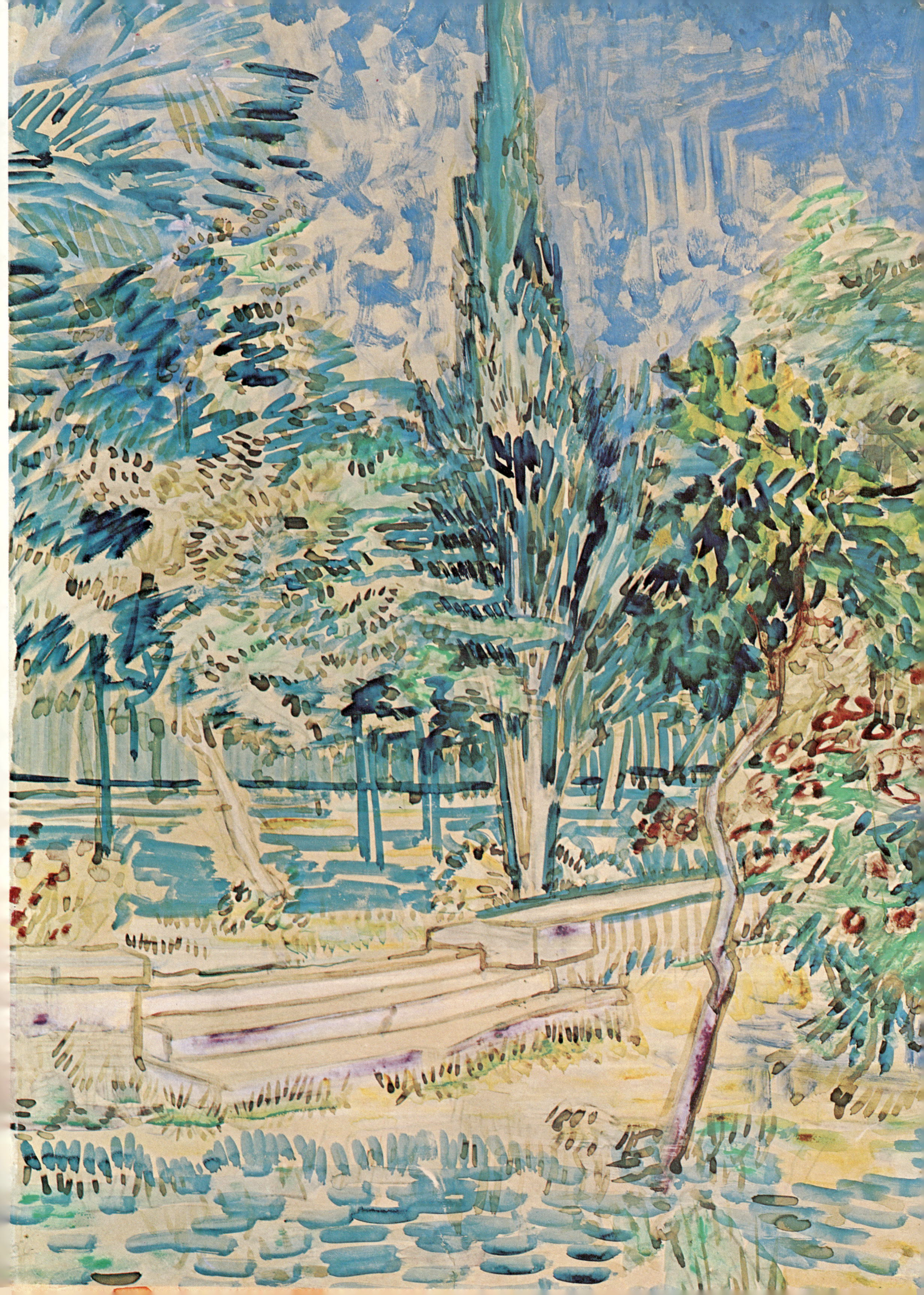

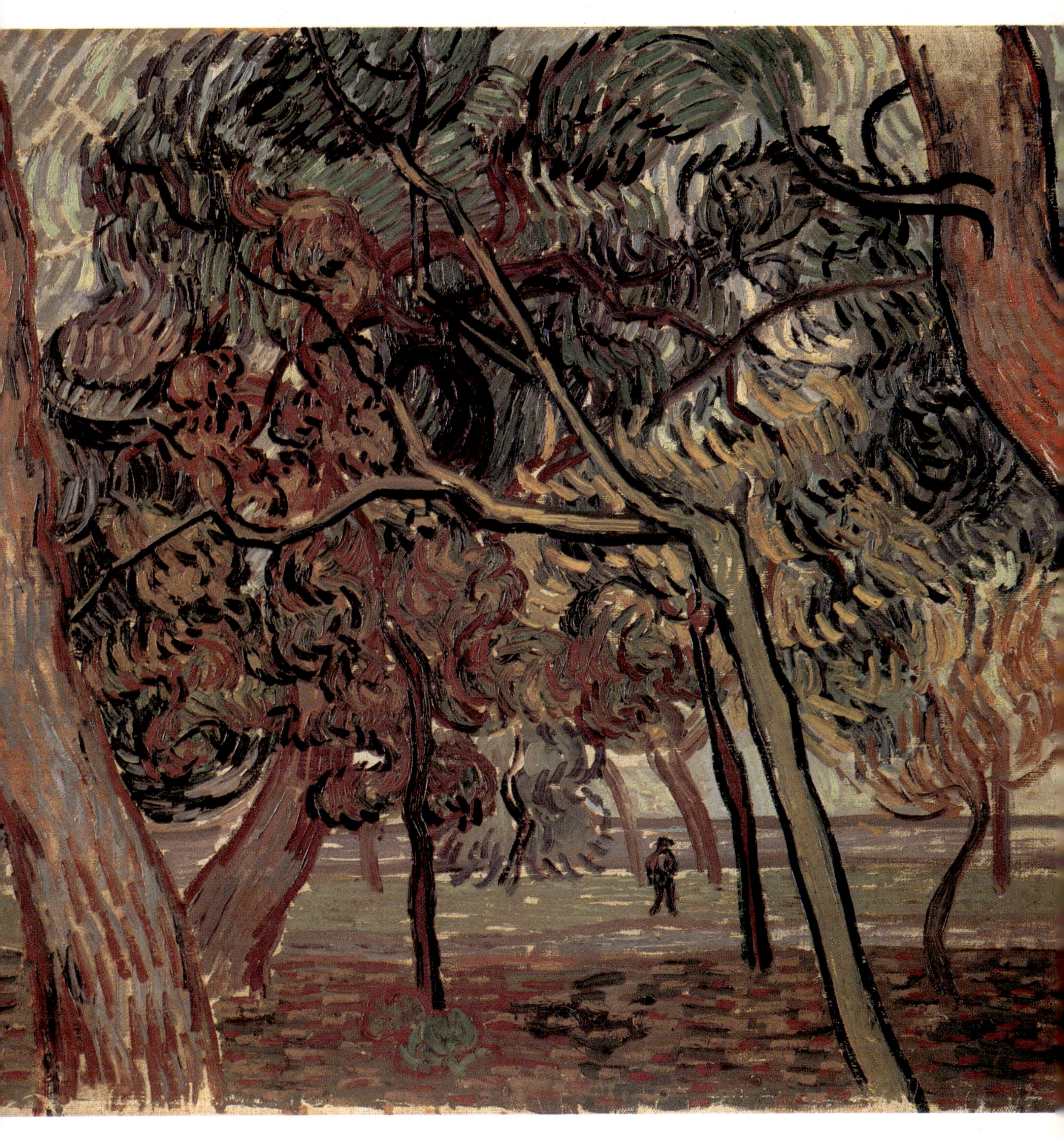

Garden in the Asylum of St. Paul-de-Mausole

1889 - watercolour - 62 x 44.5 cm -
Vincent van Gogh Foundation, Amsterdam

Man Walking in a Grove of Trees

November 1889 - oil on canvas - 46 x 51 cm -
Rijksmuseum Kröller-Müller, Otterlo

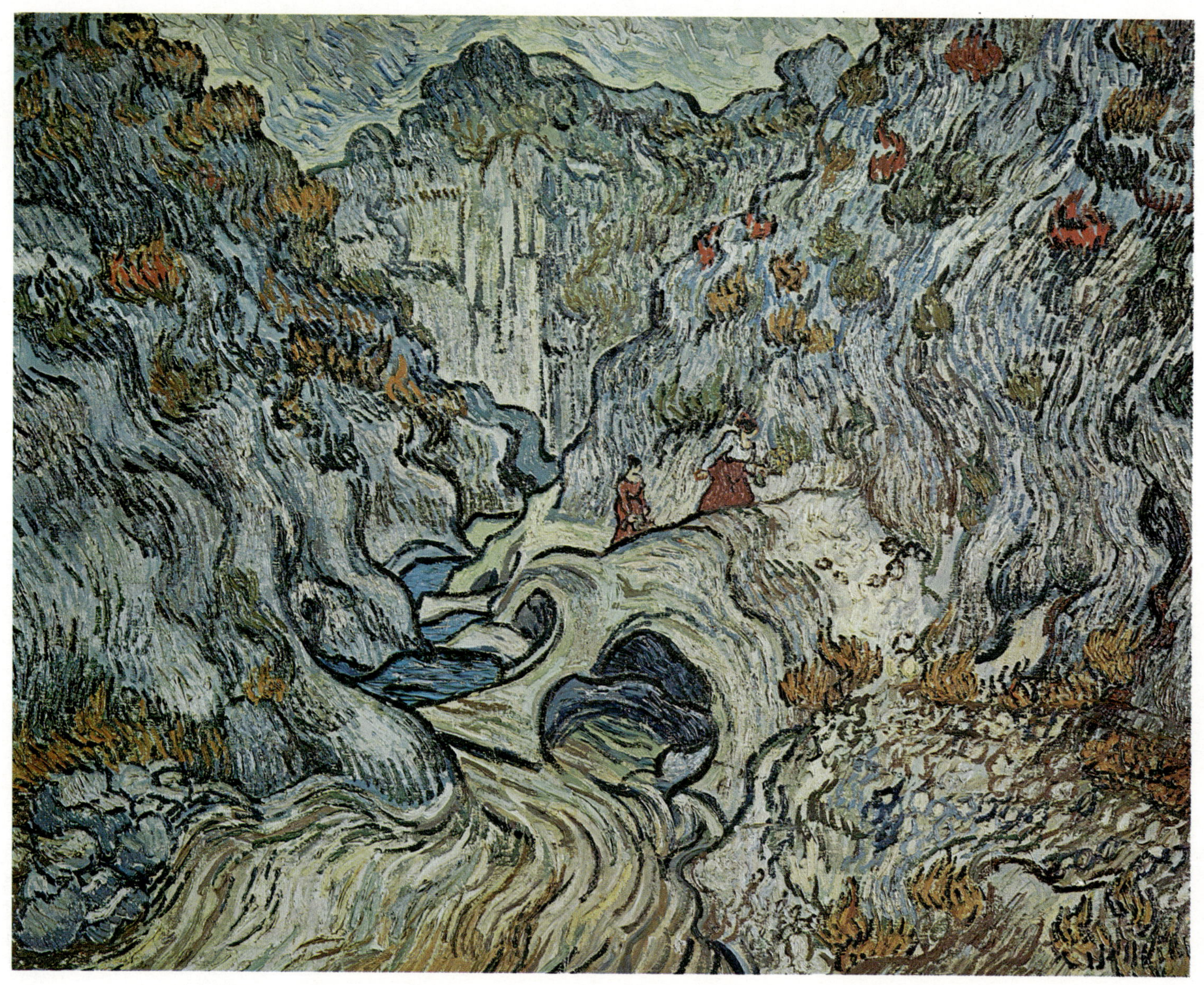

Les Peyroulets Ravine

December 1889 - oil on canvas - 72 x 92 cm - Rijksmuseum Kröller-Müller, Otterlo

Pine Trees with Setting Sun

November 1889 - oil on canvas - 92 x 73 cm - Rijksmuseum Kröller-Müller, Otterlo

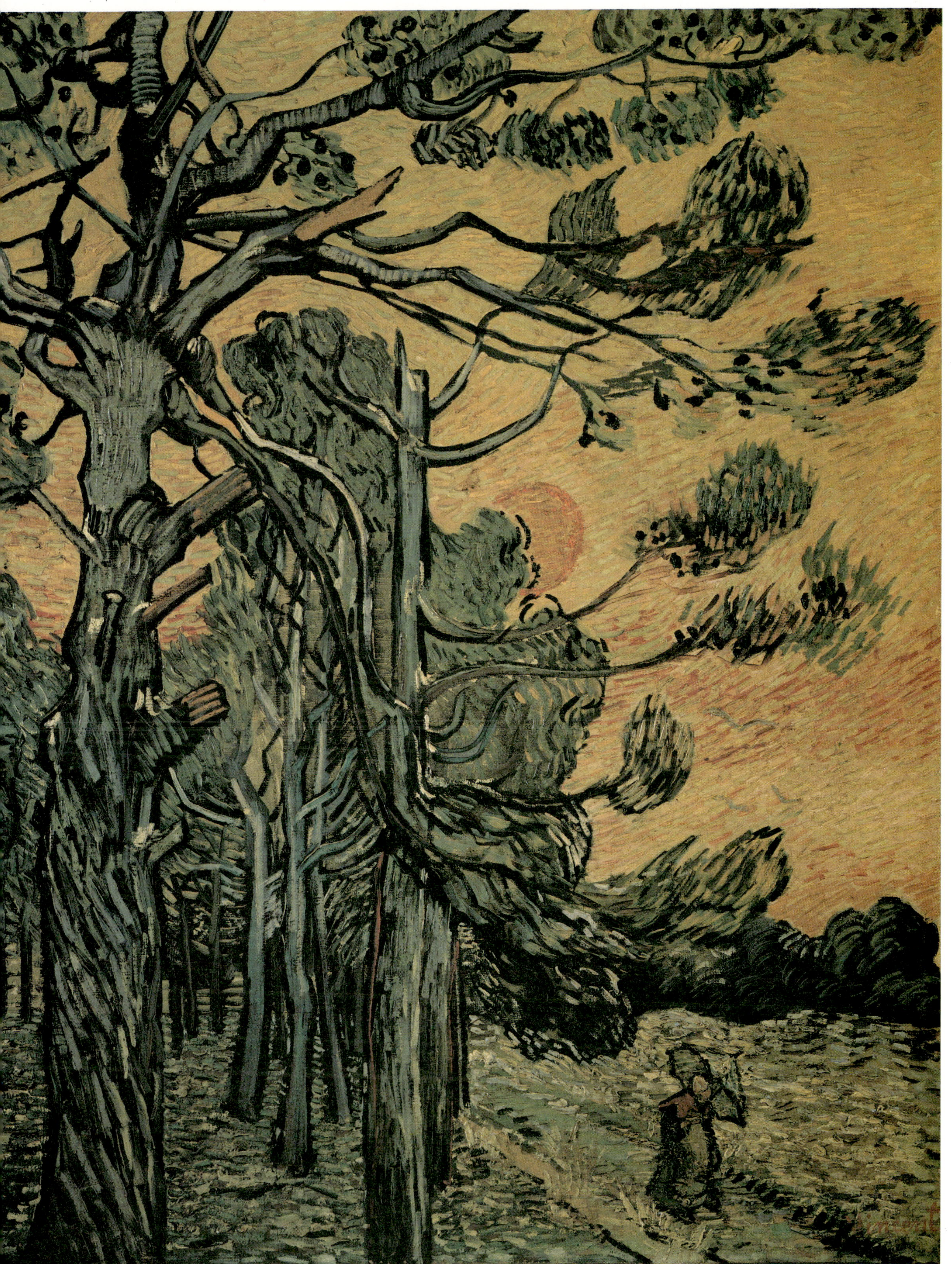

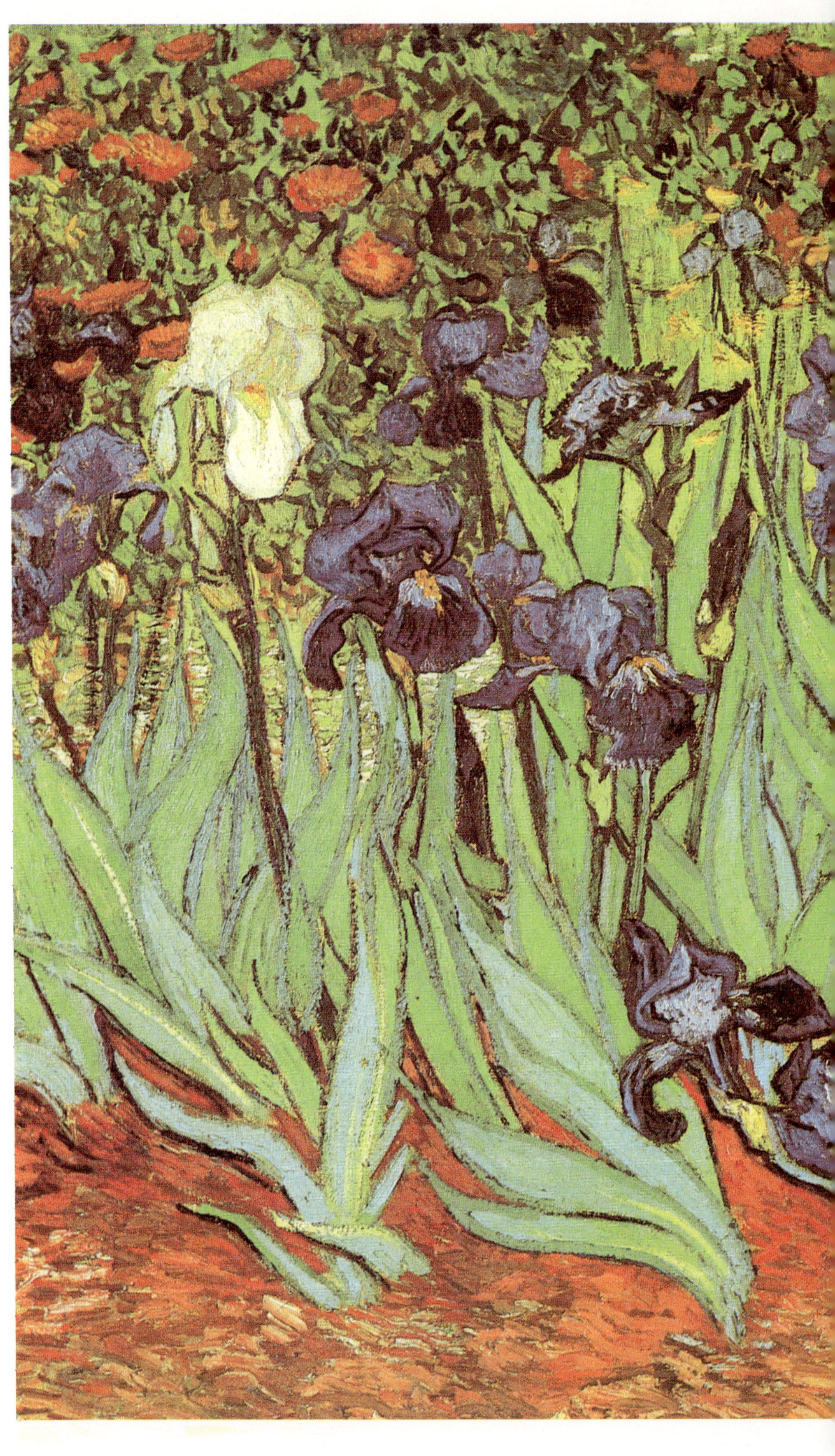

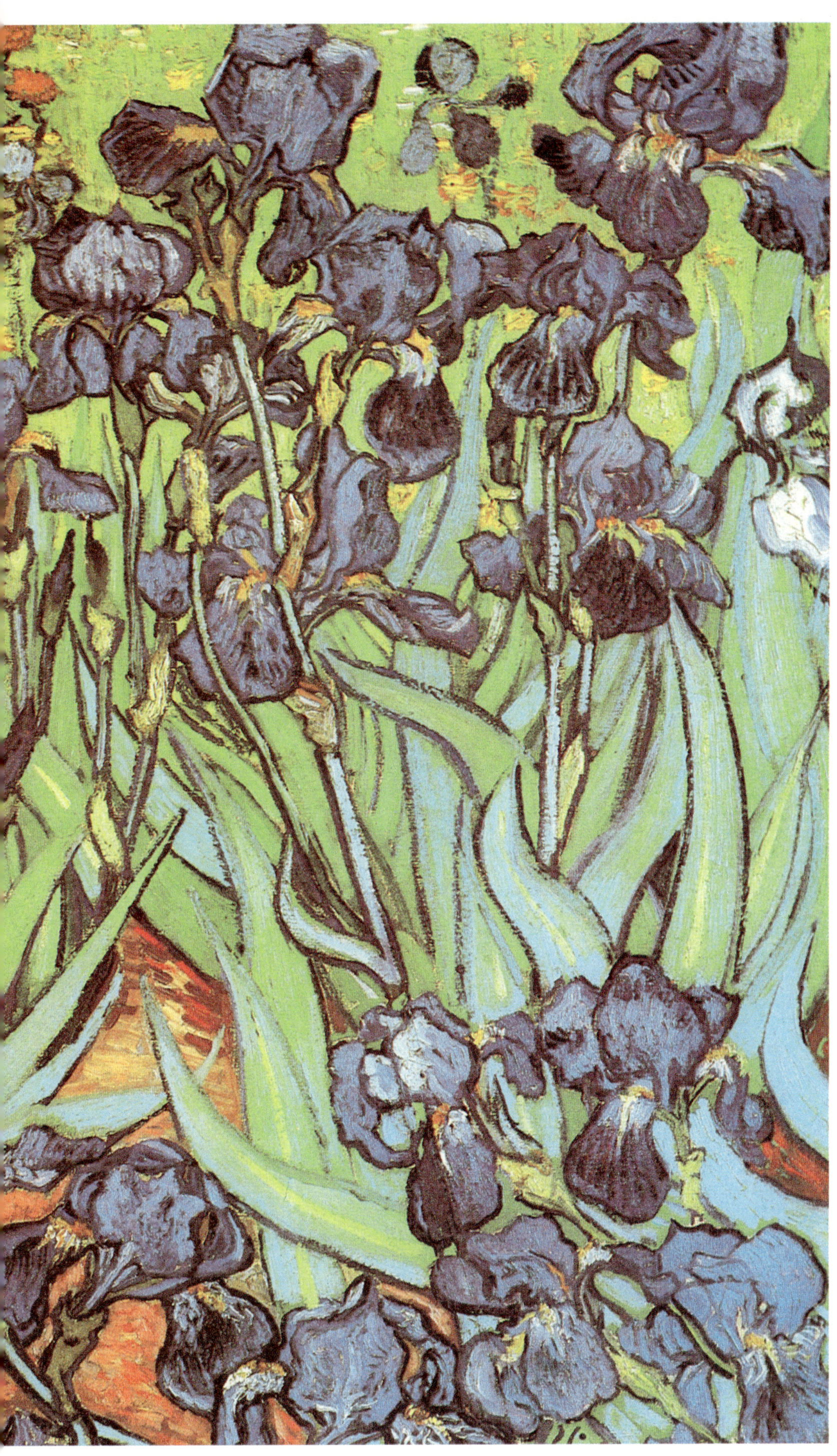

Irises

May 1889 - oil on canvas - 71 x 93 cm - Getty Museum, Malibu, Cal.

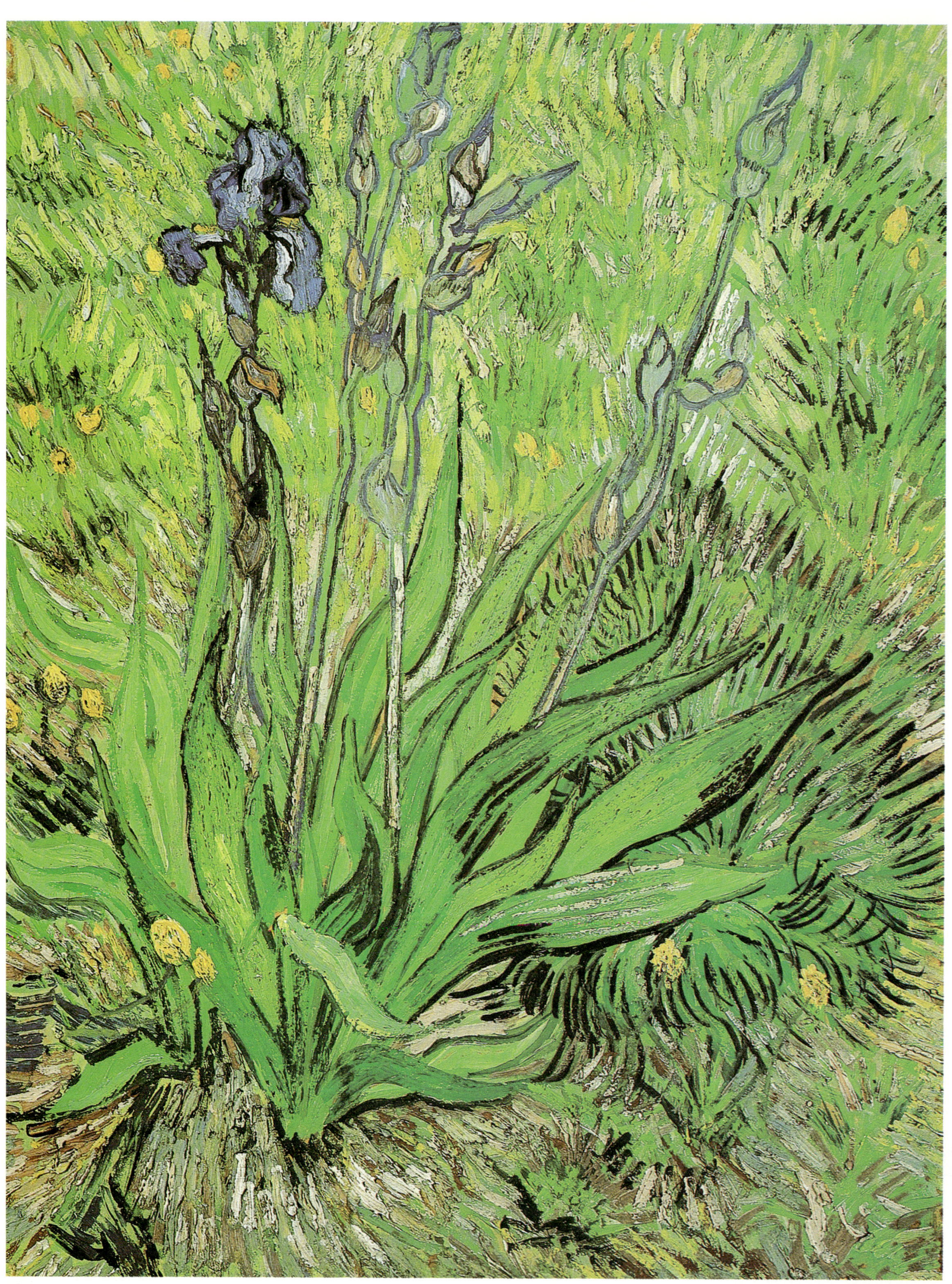

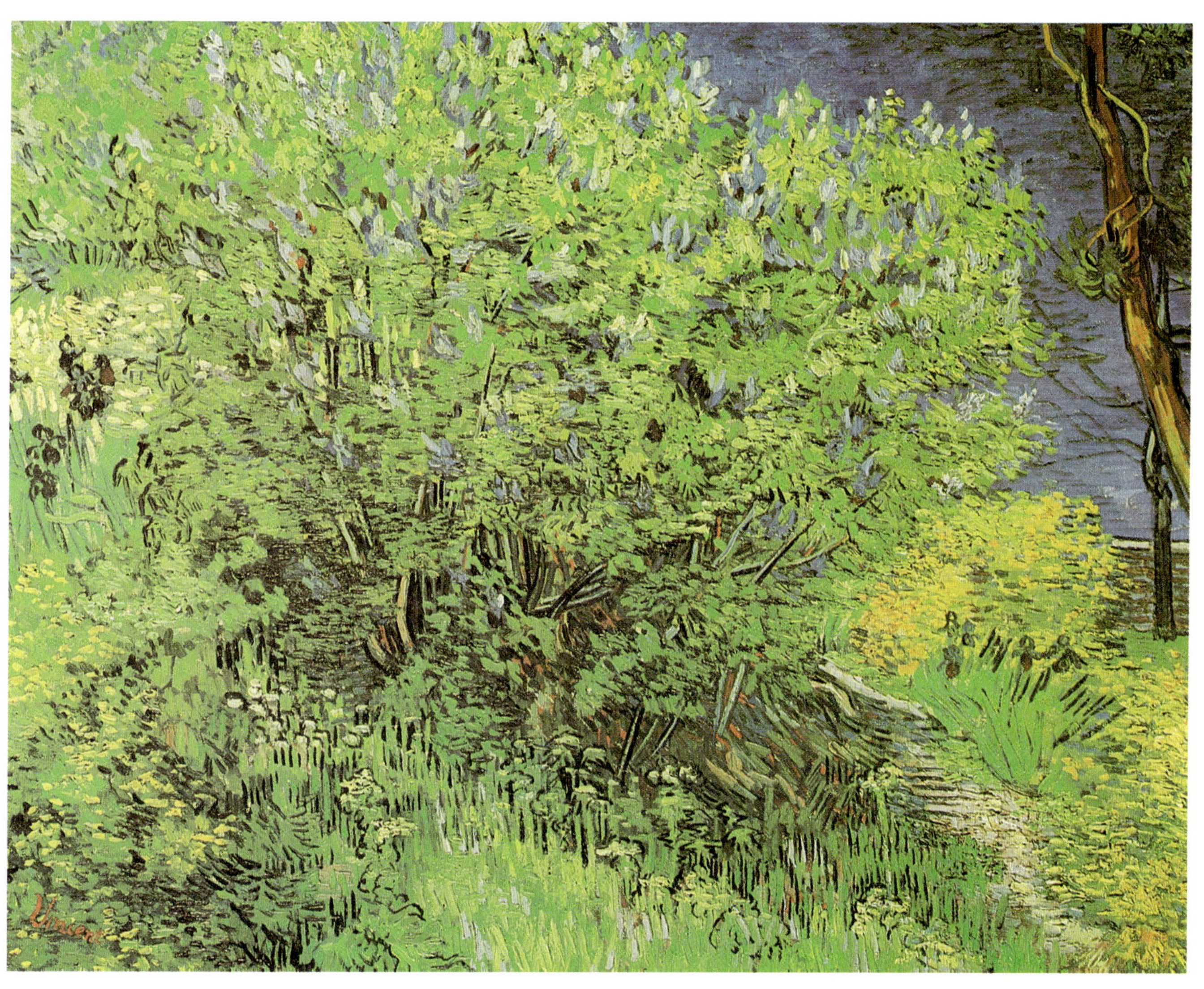

Lilac Trees

May 1889 - oil on canvas - 73 x 92 cm -
Hermitage, St. Petersburg

Irises

May 1889 - oil on canvas - 73 x 92 cm -
Hermitage, St Petersburg

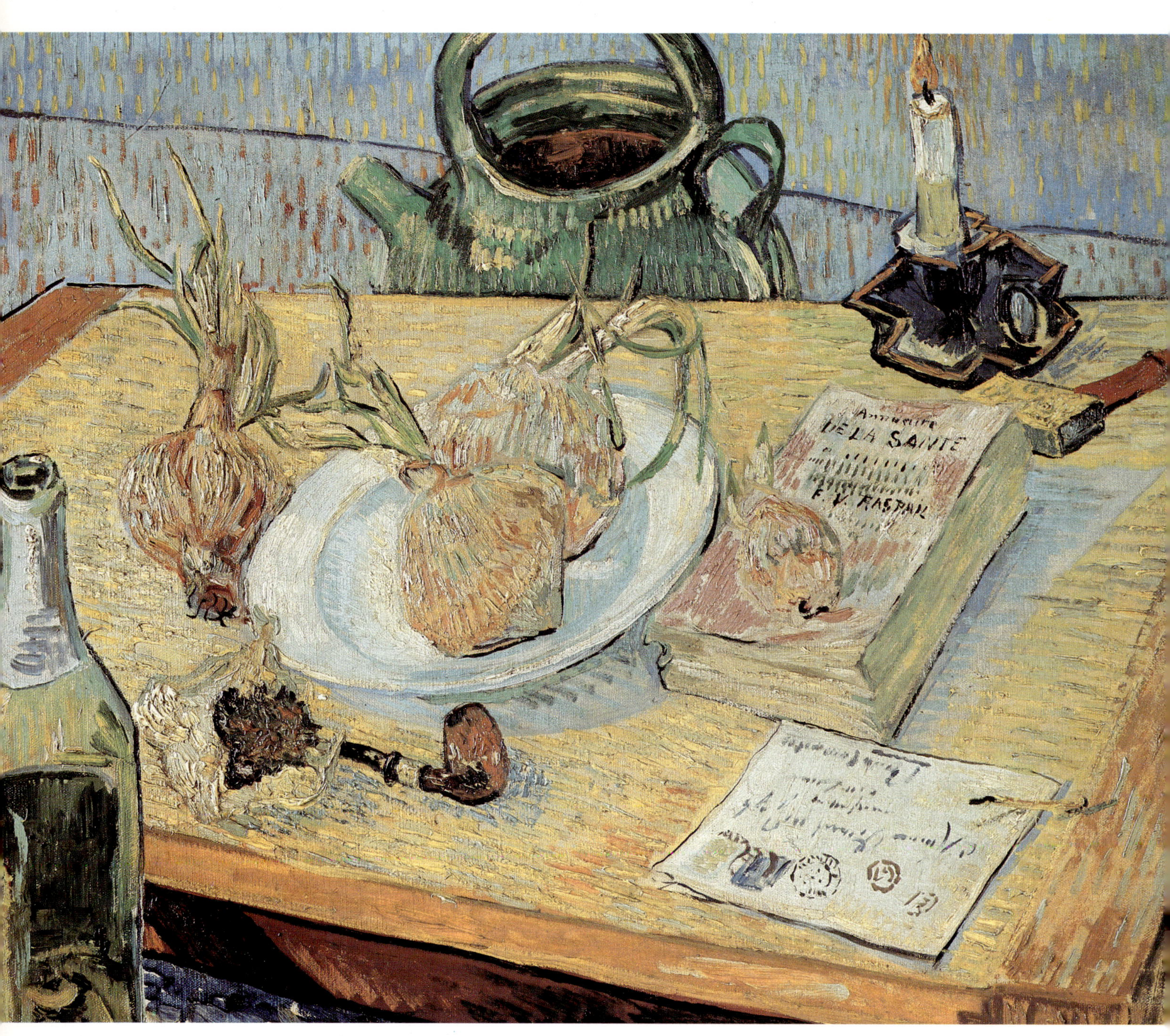

Still Life: Drawing Board, Pipe, Onions and Sealing Wax

January 1889 - oil on canvas - 38 x 46.5 cm -
Vincent van Gogh Foundation, Amsterdam

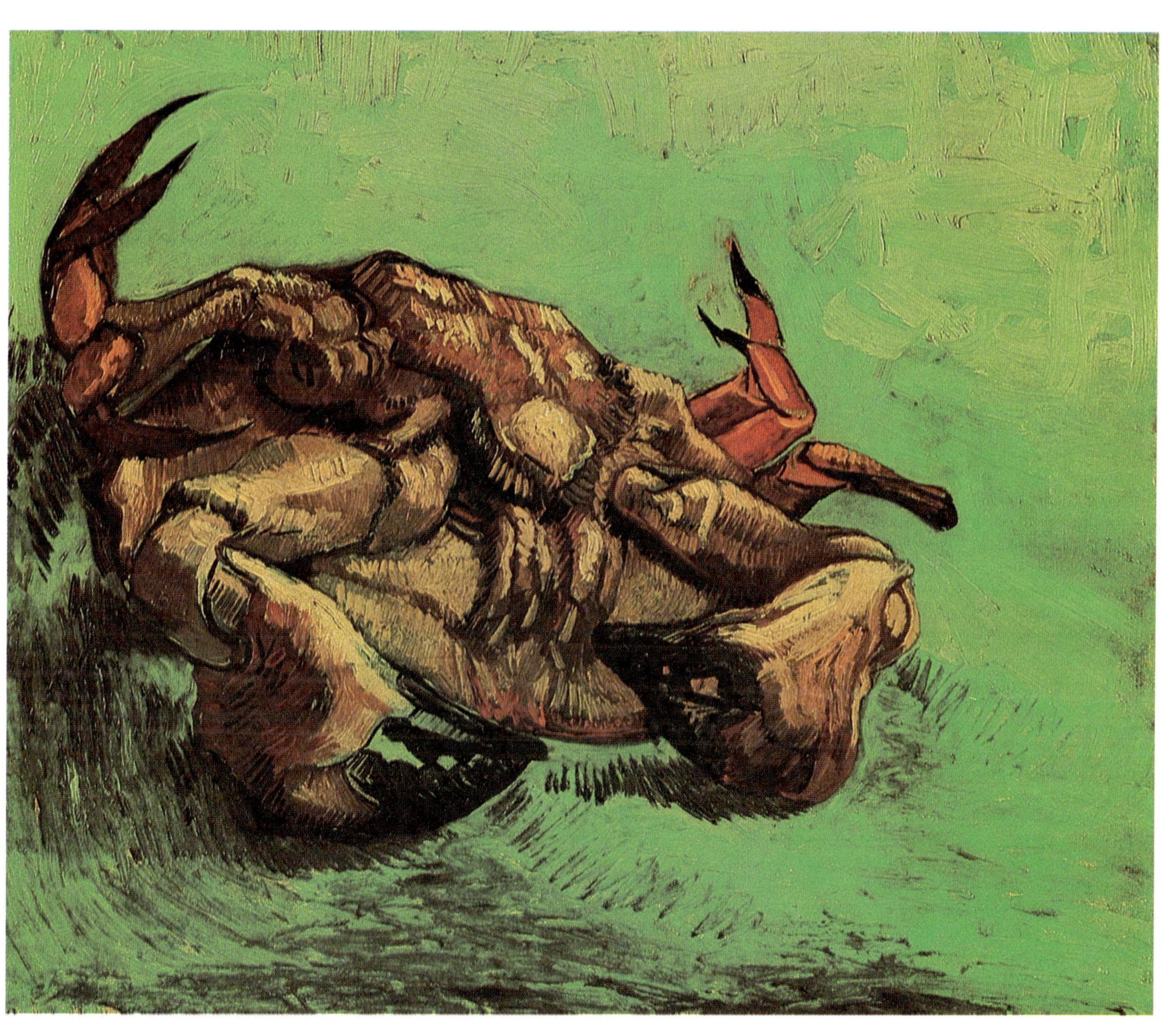

Two Crabs

January 1889 - oil on canvas - 38 x 46.5 cm -
Foundation Vincent Van Gogh, Amsterdam

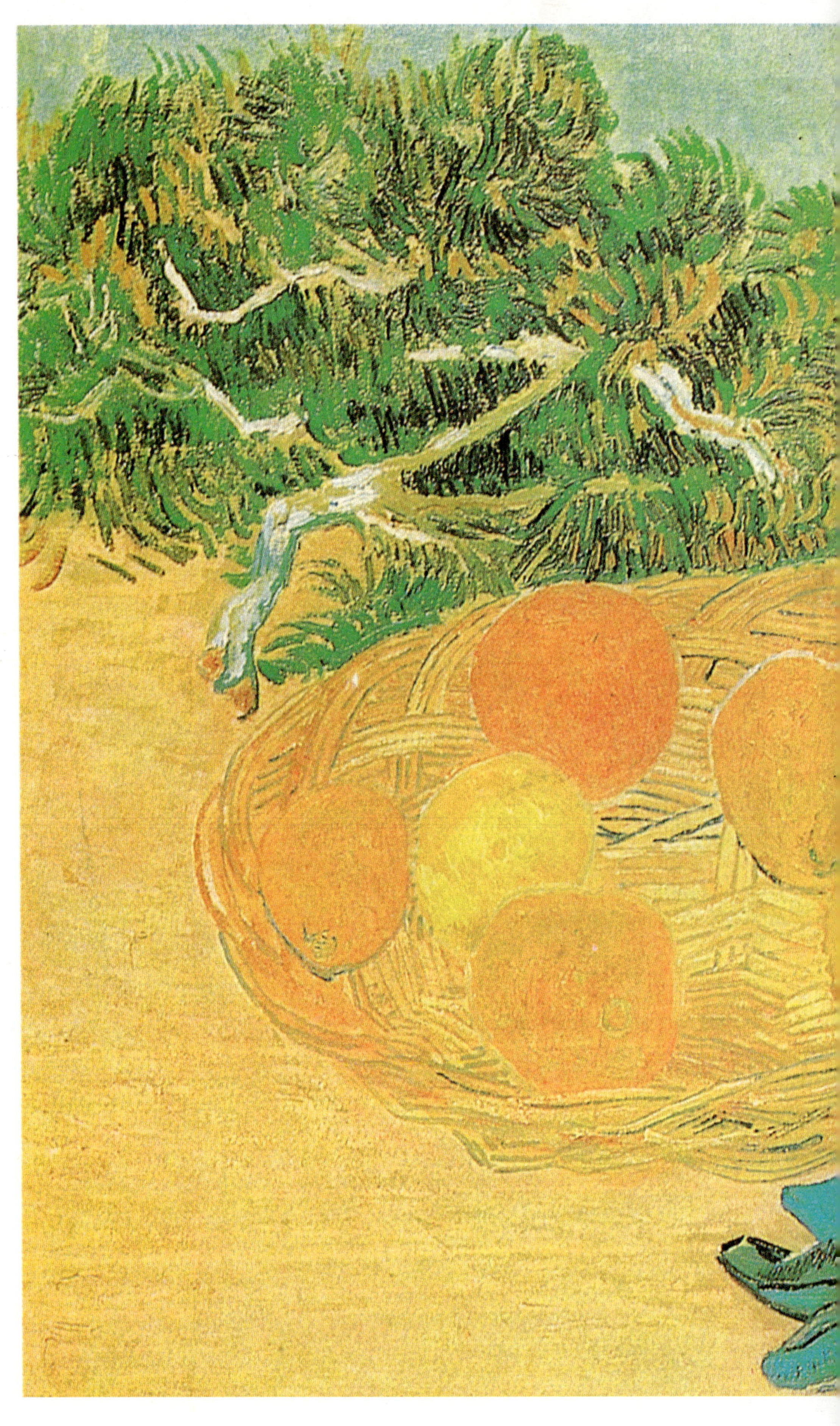

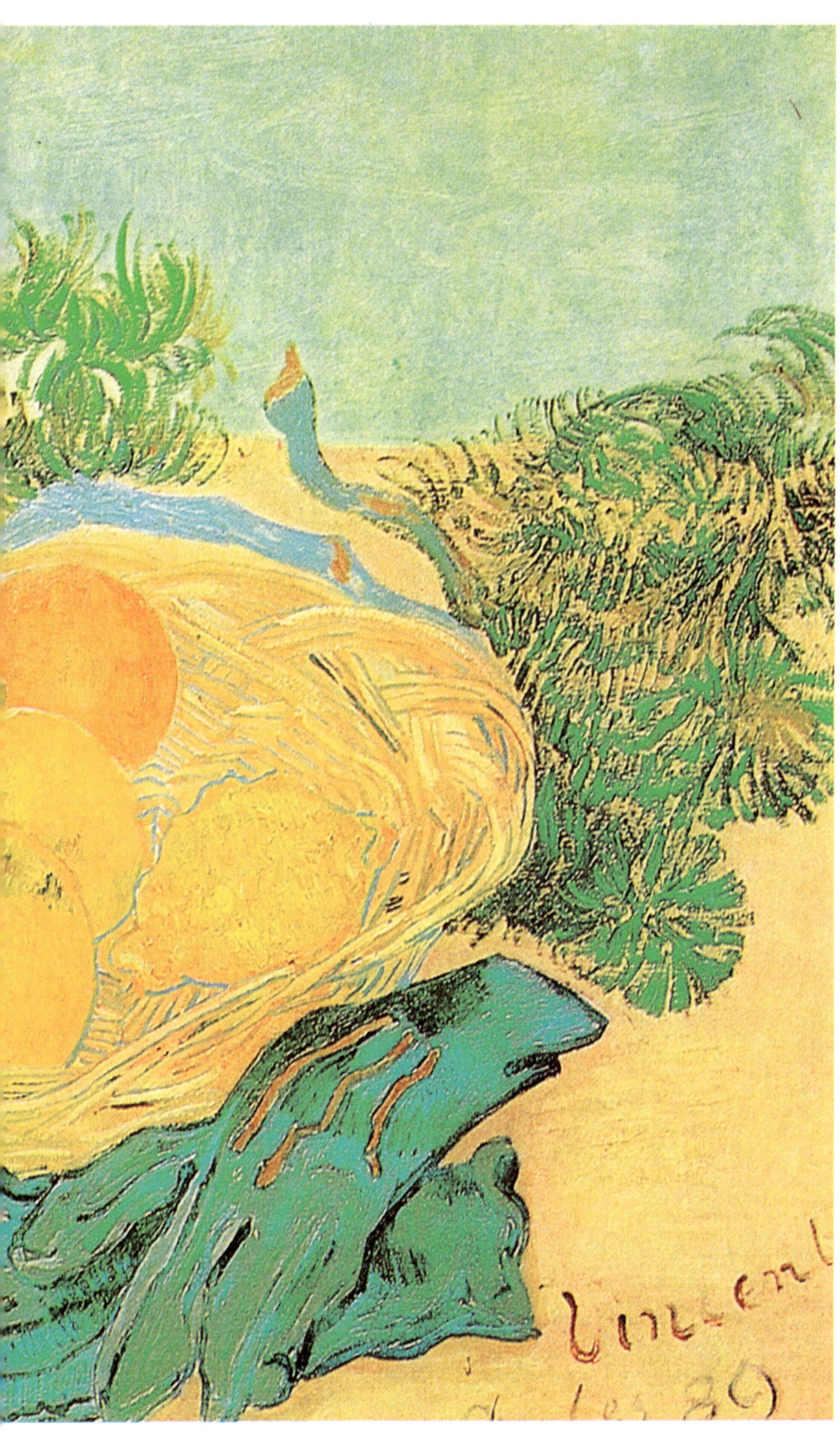

Still Life with Lemons, Oranges and Blue Gloves

January 1889 - oil on canvas - 47.3 x 64.3 cm -
Mr. & Mrs. Paul Mellon collection, Upperville, Va.

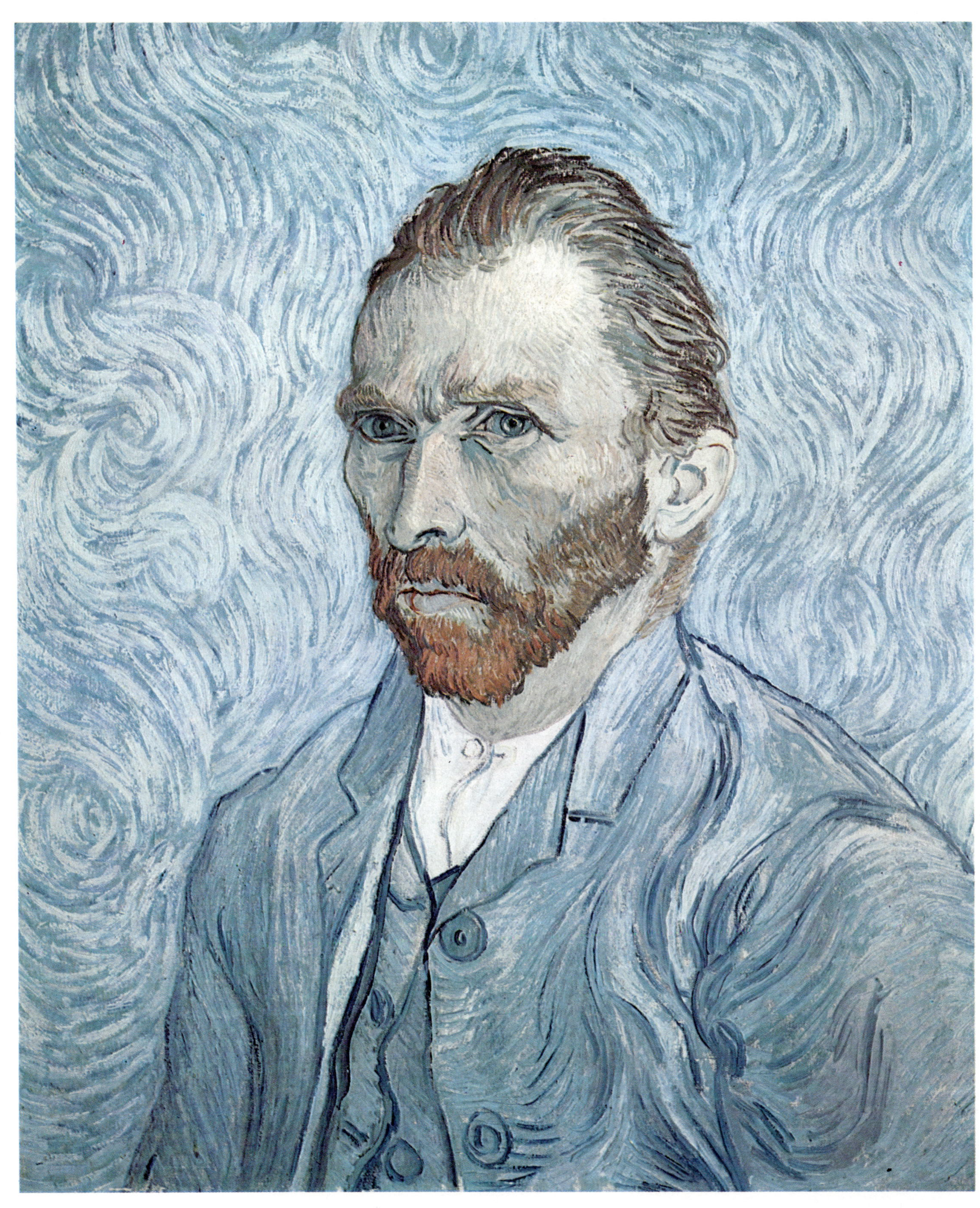

Self-Portrait

May 1890 - oil on canvas - 65 x 54 cm -
Musée d'Orsay, Paris

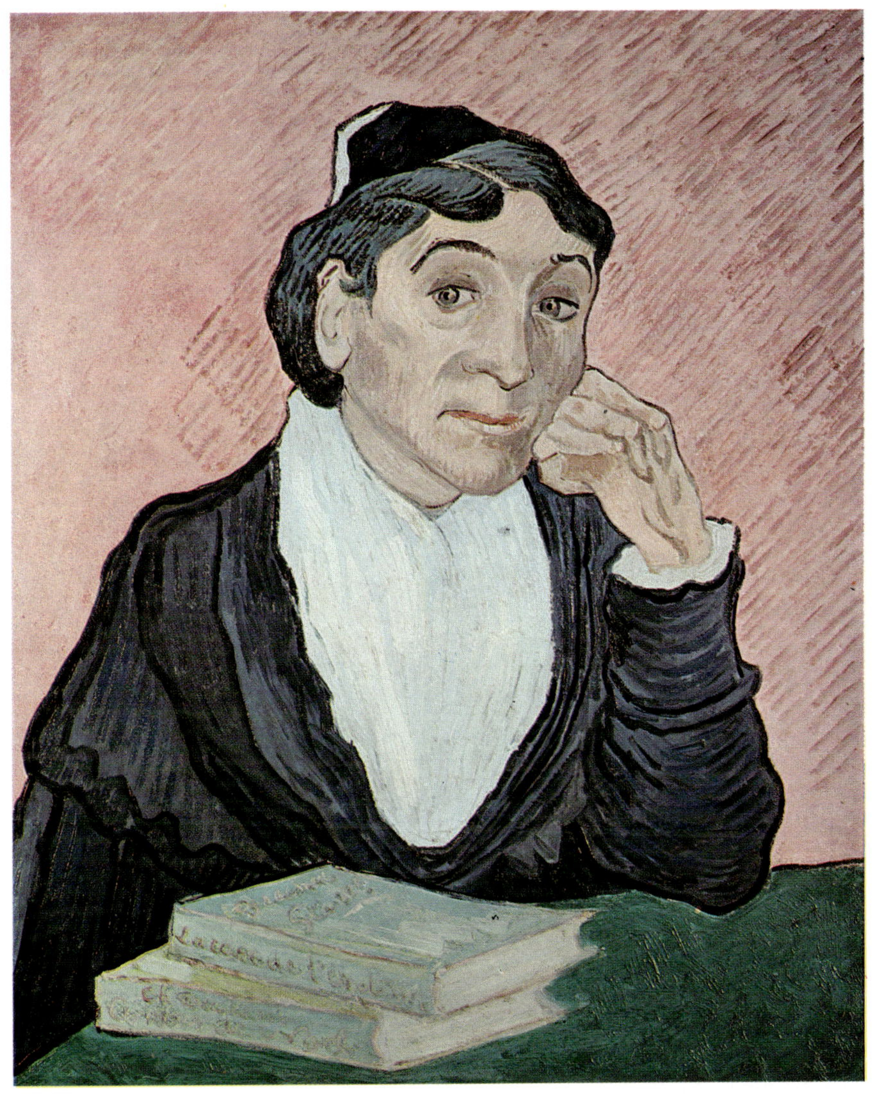

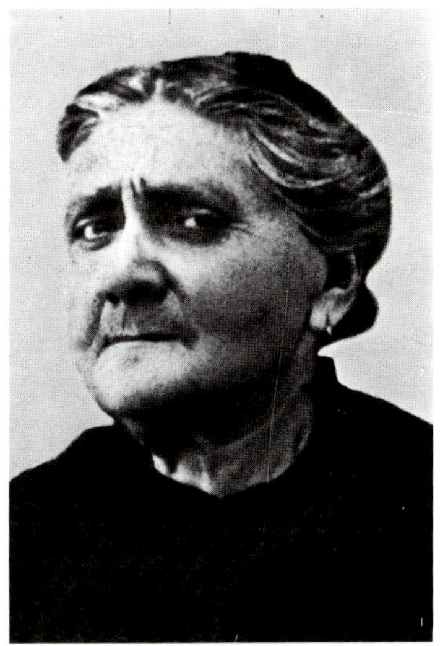

L'Arlésienne

January-February 1890 - oil on canvas - 65 x 49 cm - Museu de arte de Sao Paolo, Brazil

Photograph of Mme Ginoux who was the model for l'Arlésienne

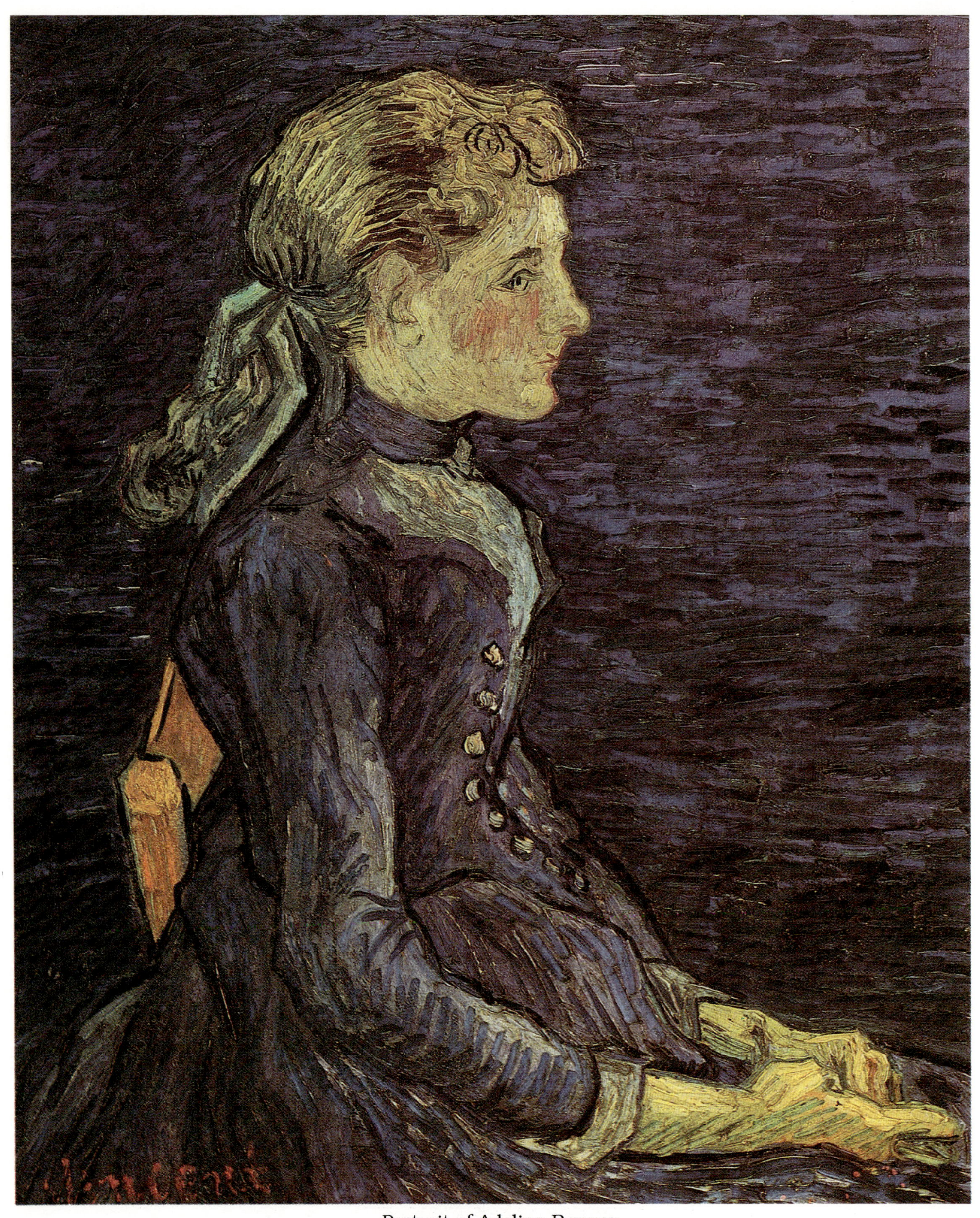

Portrait of Adeline Ravoux

June 1890 - oil on canvas - 73.7 x 54.7 cm - Private collection

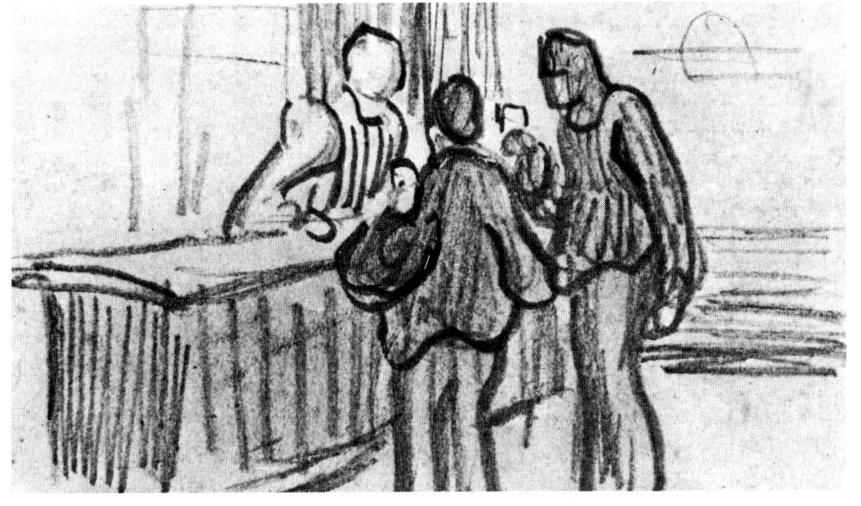

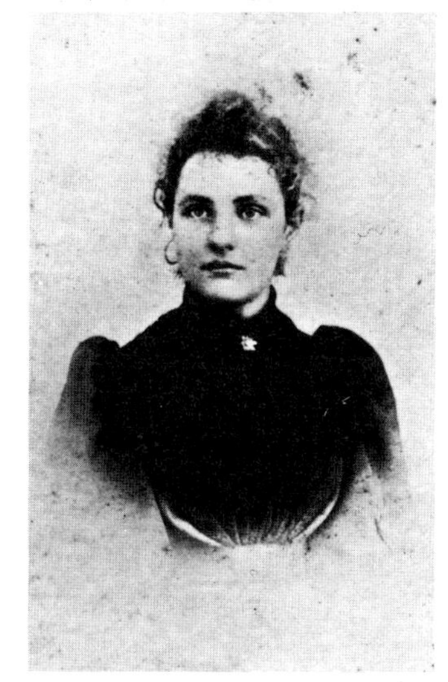

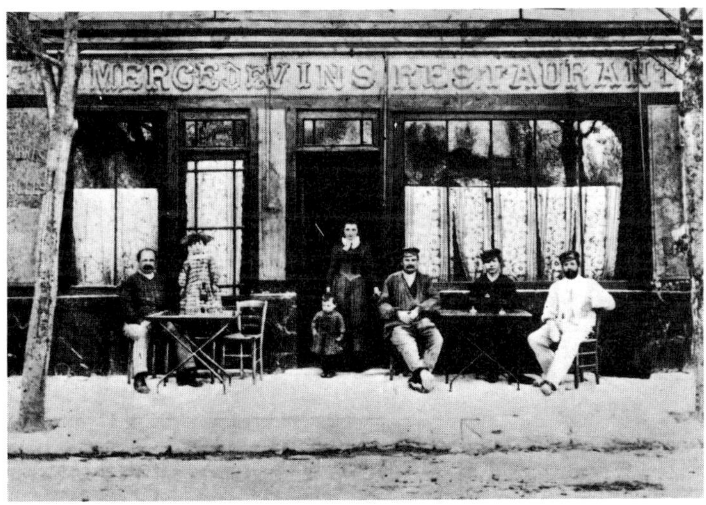

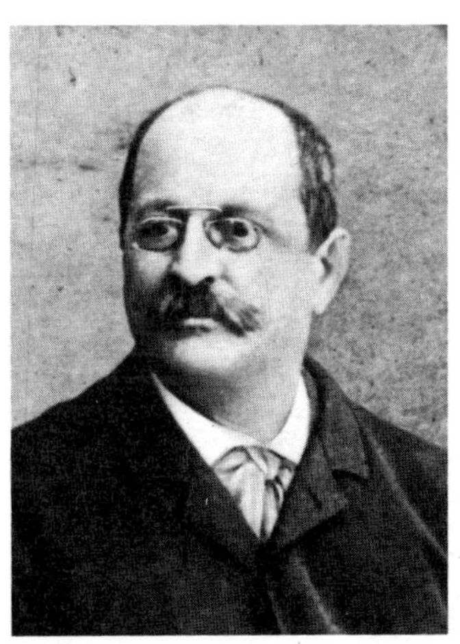

Photograph of Adeline Ravoux

Photograph of Arthur Gustave Ravoux

At the Bar

June 1890 - pencil -
Ed Buckman collection, Richmond,Va.

Photograph of the Ravoux auberge taken in 1890,
at the time Vincent lodged there

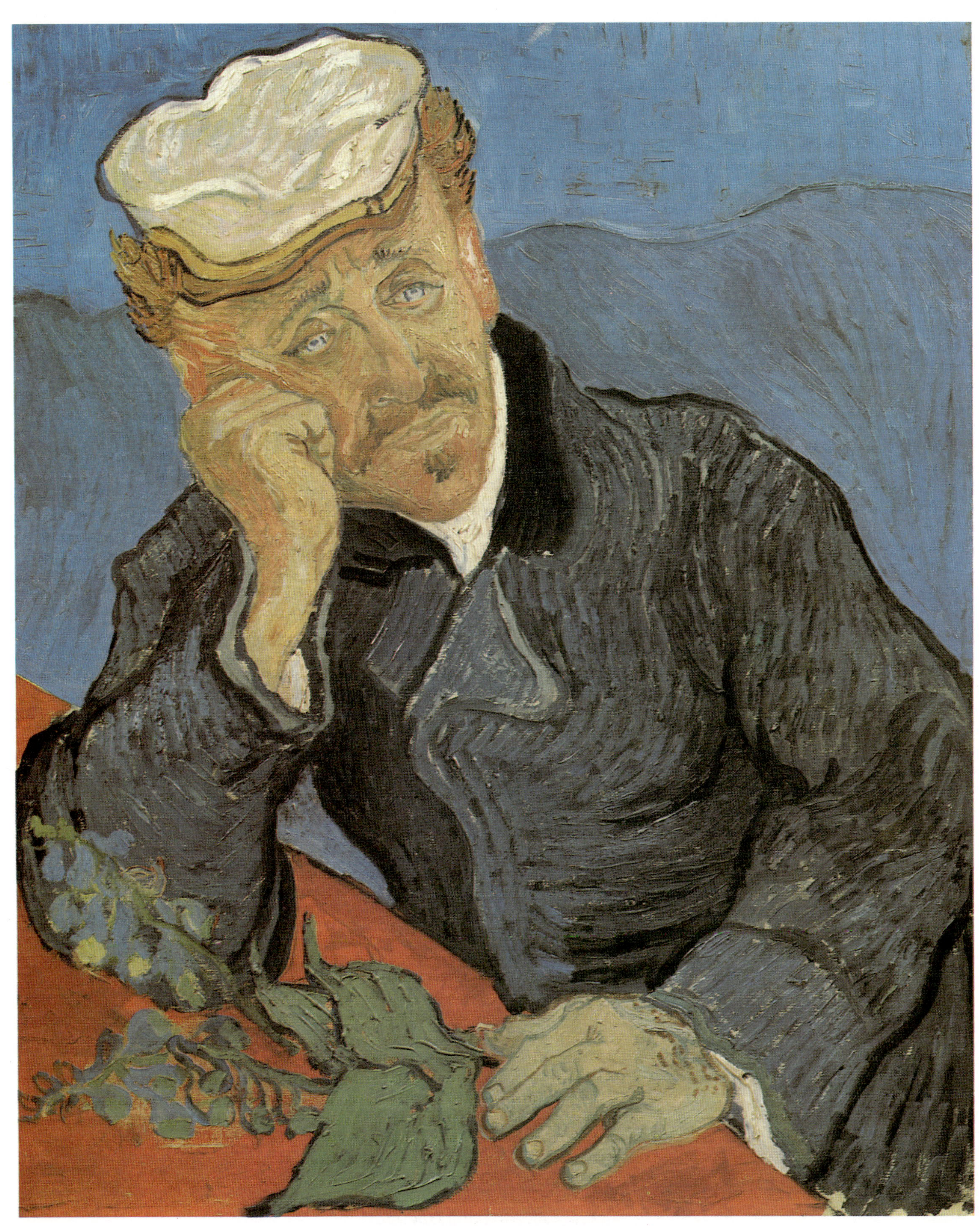

Portrait of Doctor Gachet

*June 1890 - oil on canvas - 68 x 57 cm -
Musée d'Orsay, Paris*

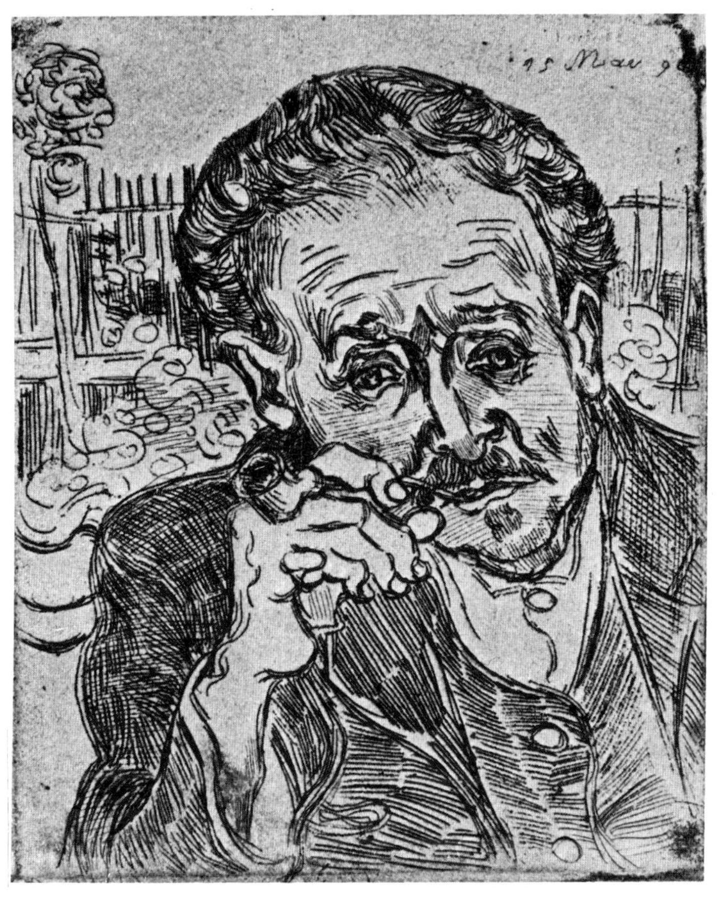

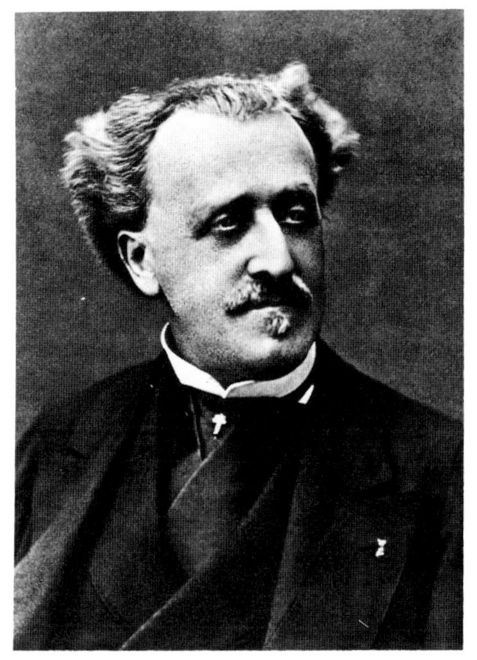

The Doctor Paul Gachet

May 1890 - etching - 17.5 x 14.5 cm

Photograph of Dr Gachet

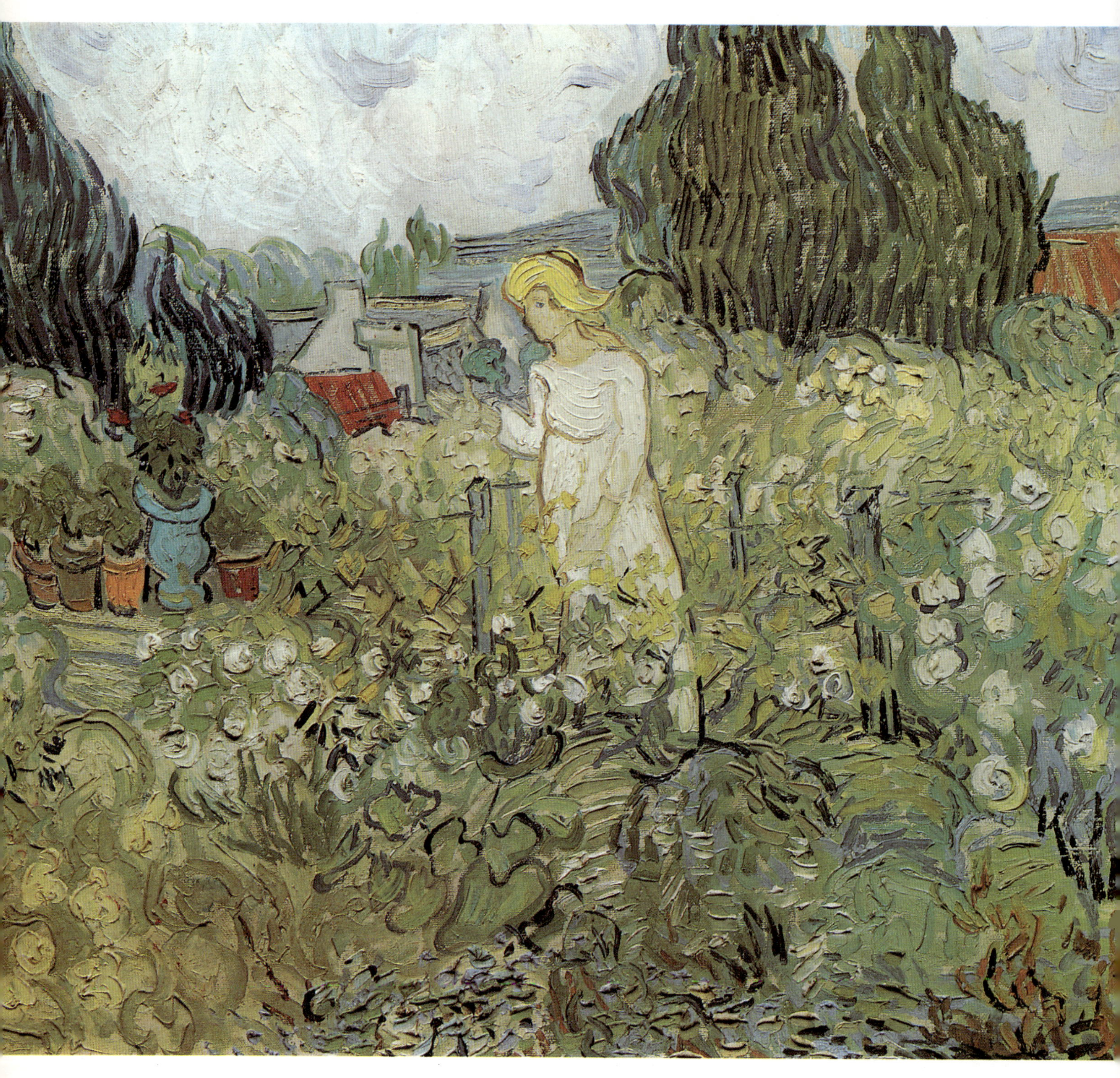

Mademoiselle Gachet in Her Garden

June 1890 - oil on canvas - 46 x 55 cm -
Musée d'Orsay, Paris

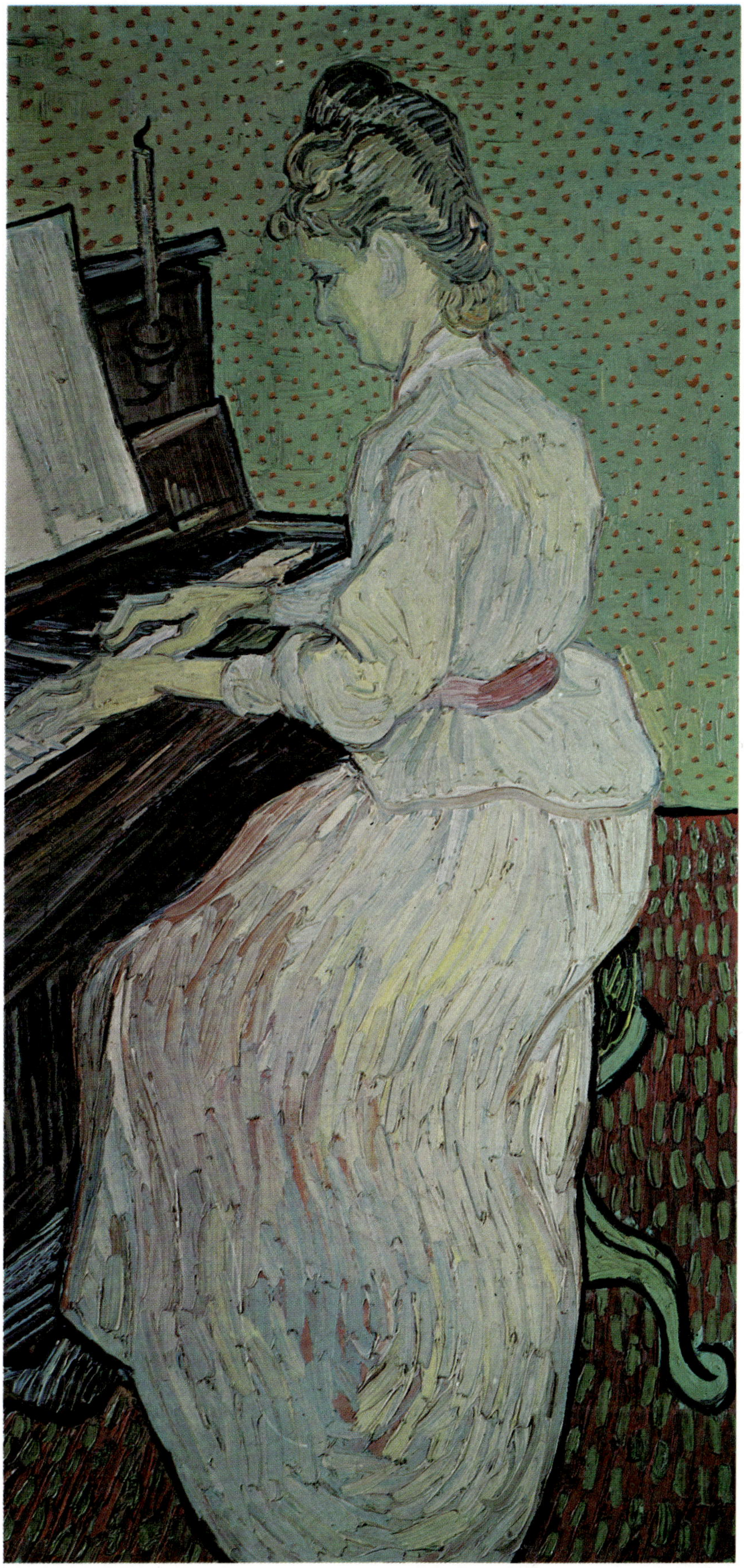

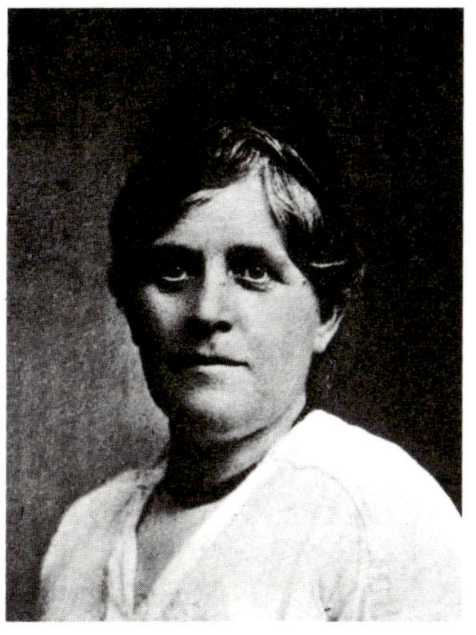

Photograph of Marguerite Gachet

Mademoiselle Gachet at the Piano

June 1890 - oil on canvas - 102 x 50 cm - Basle Museum, Switzerland

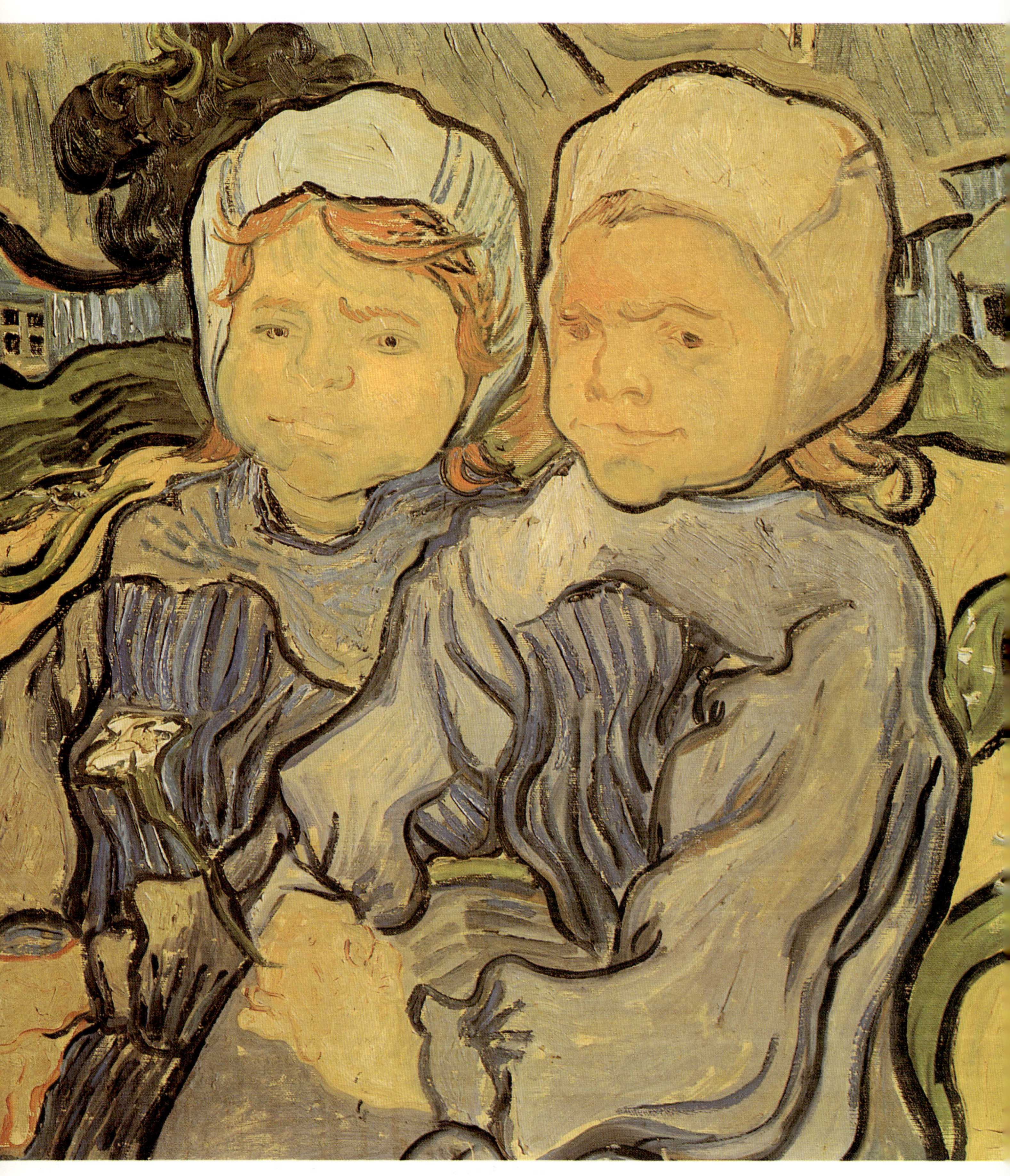

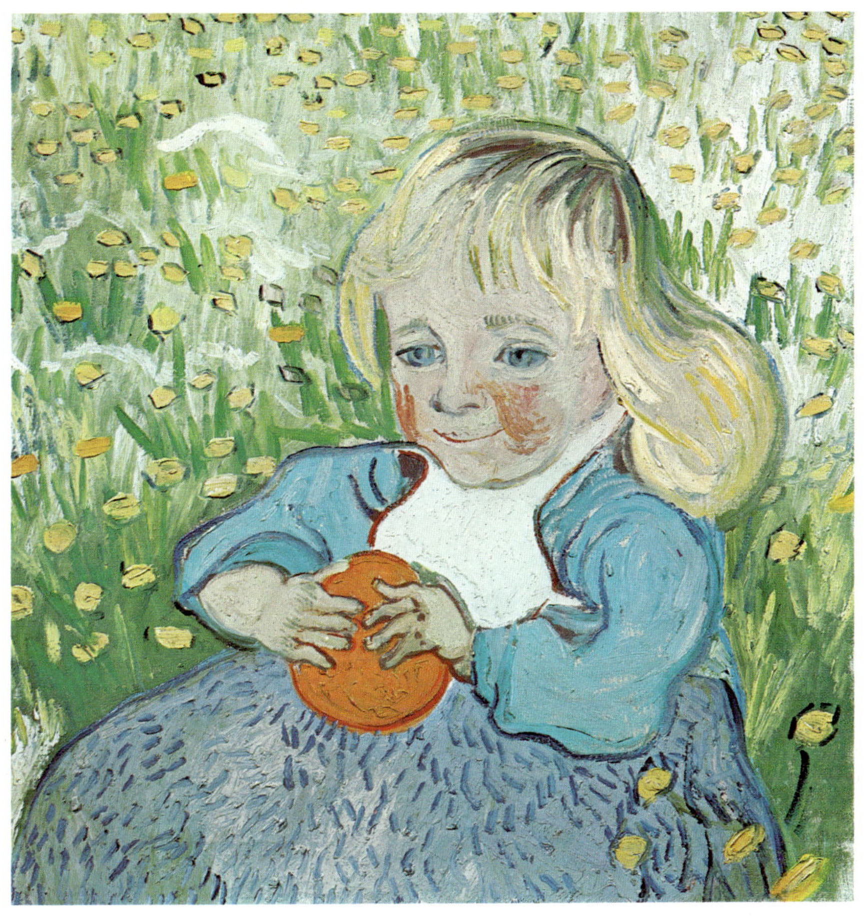

Child with Orange

1890 - oil on canvas - 50 x 51 cm -
L. Jaeggli- Hahnloser Collection, Winterthur, Switzerland

Two Children

June 1890 - oil on canvas - 51.5 x 51.5 cm -
Musée d'Orsay, Paris

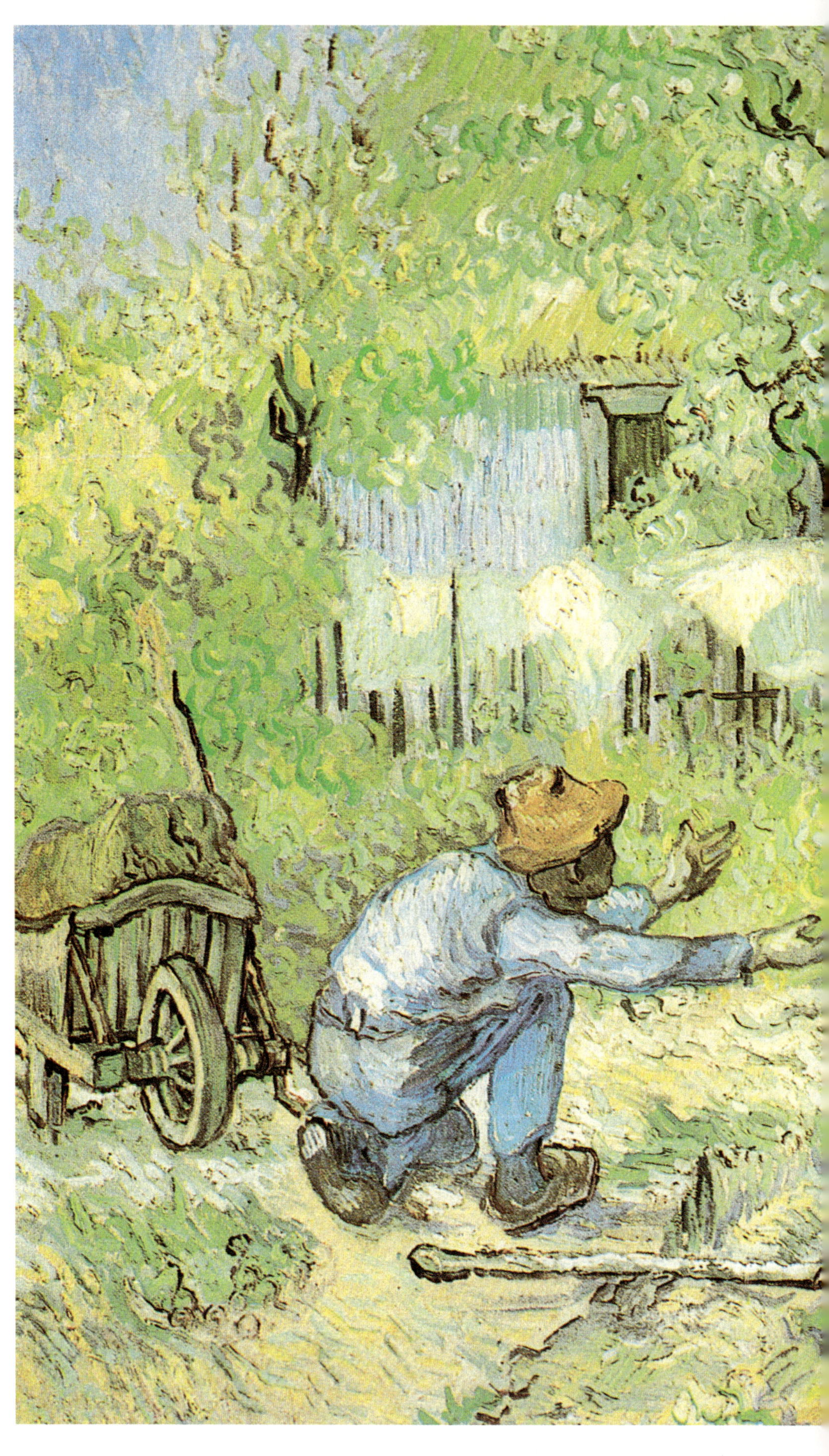

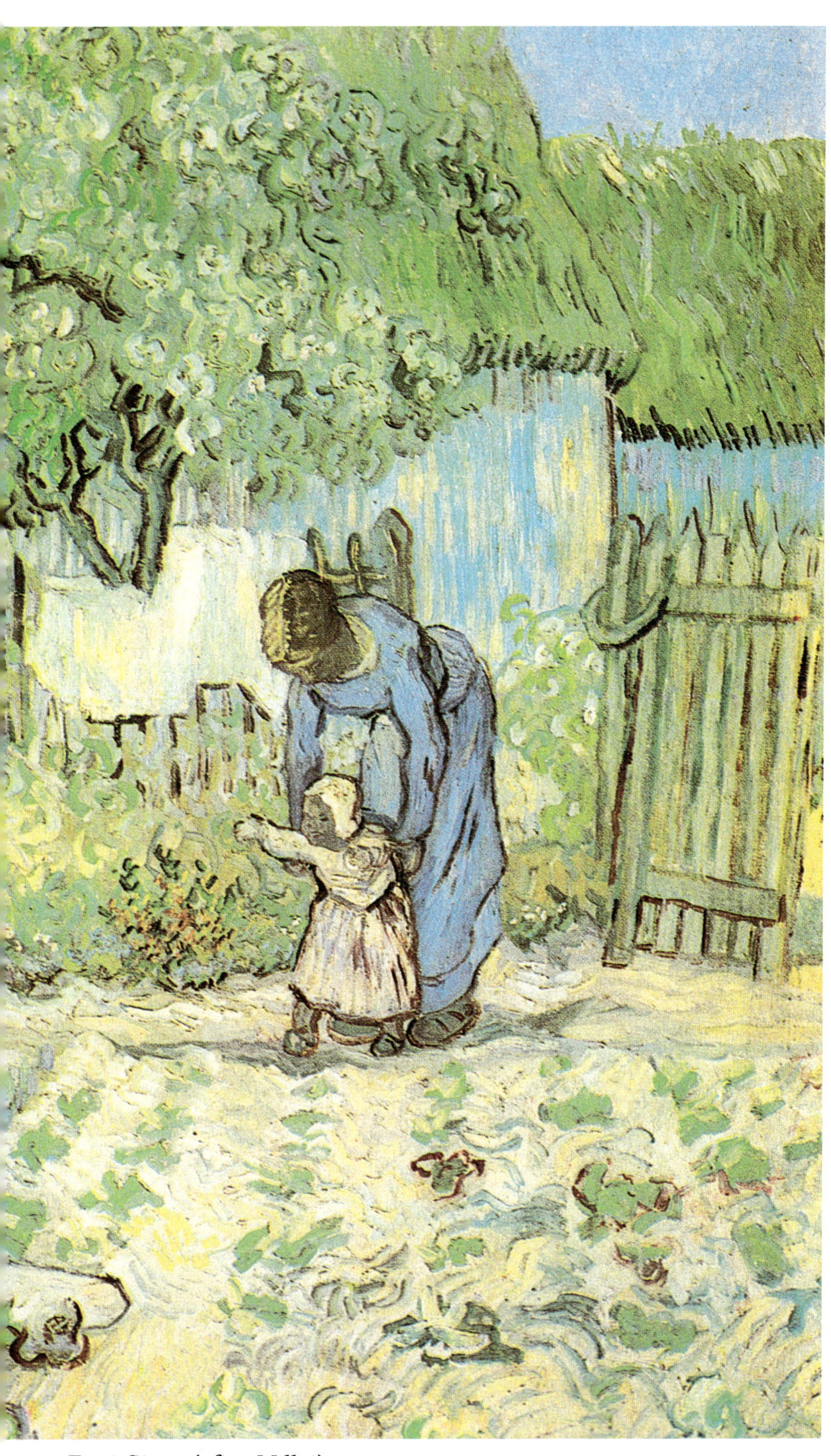

First Steps (after Millet)

January 1890 - oil on canvas - 72.4 x 91.2 cm - Museum of Modern Art, New York

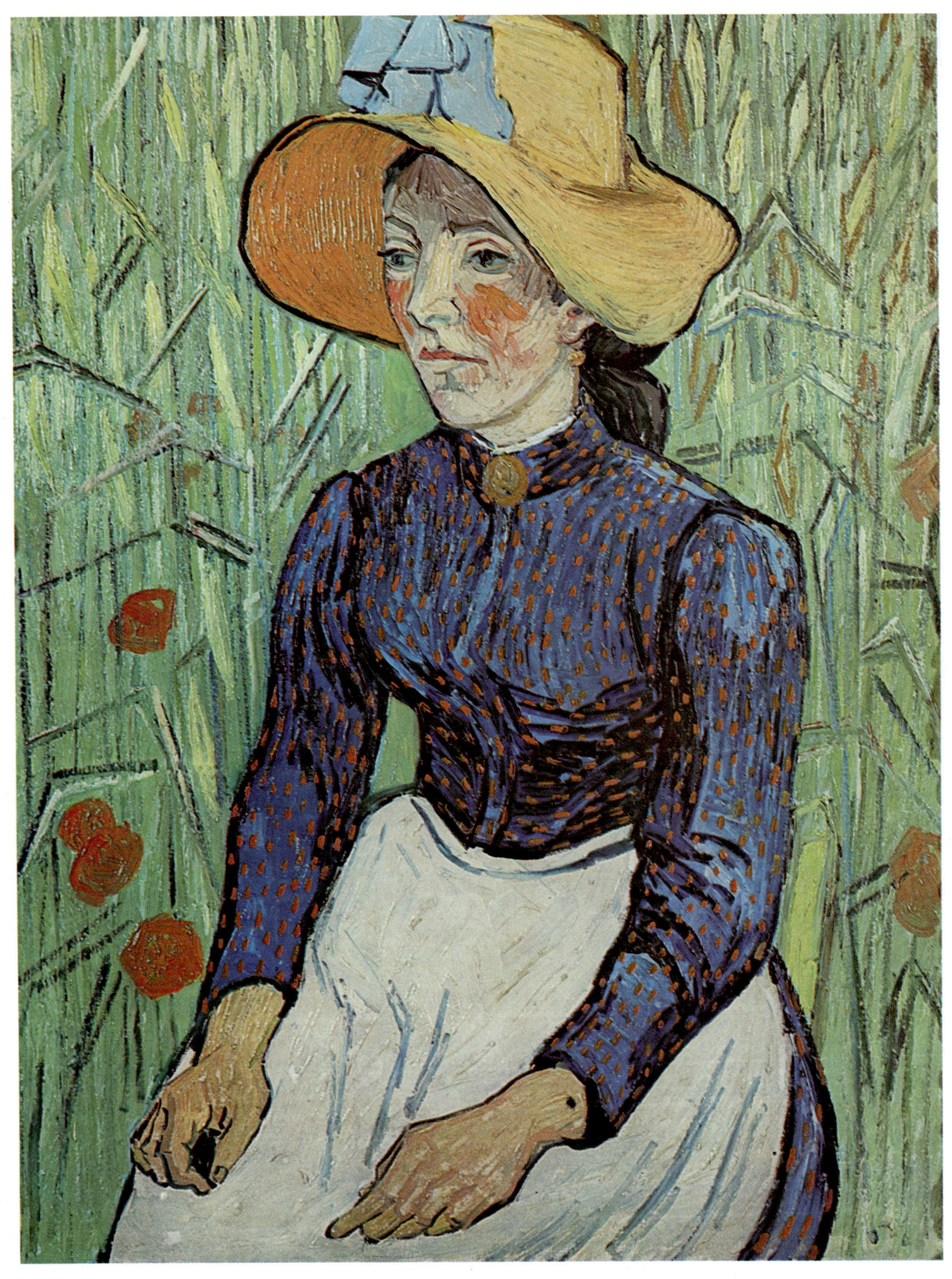

Young Peasant Woman

June 1890 - oil on canvas - 92 x 73 cm -
Musée d'Orsay, Paris

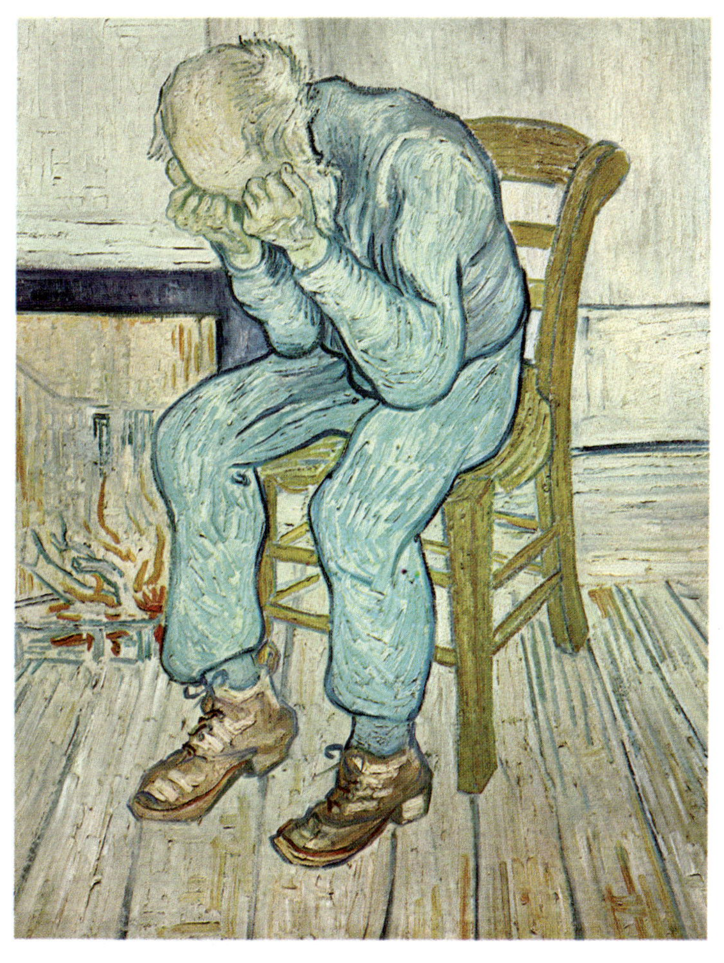

On the Threshold of Eternity

May 1890 - oil on canvas - 81 x 65 cm - Rijksmuseum Kröller- Müller, Otterlo

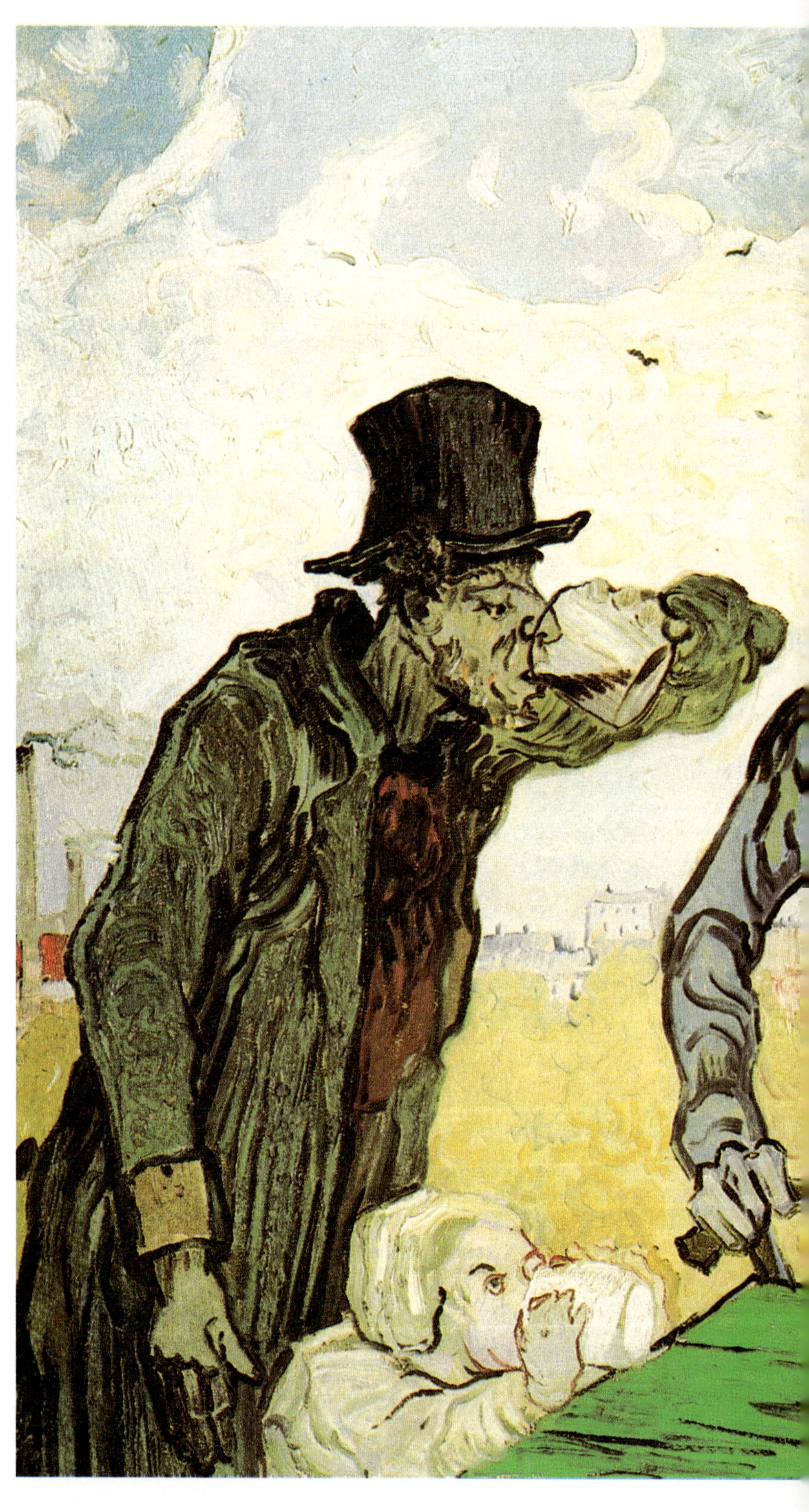

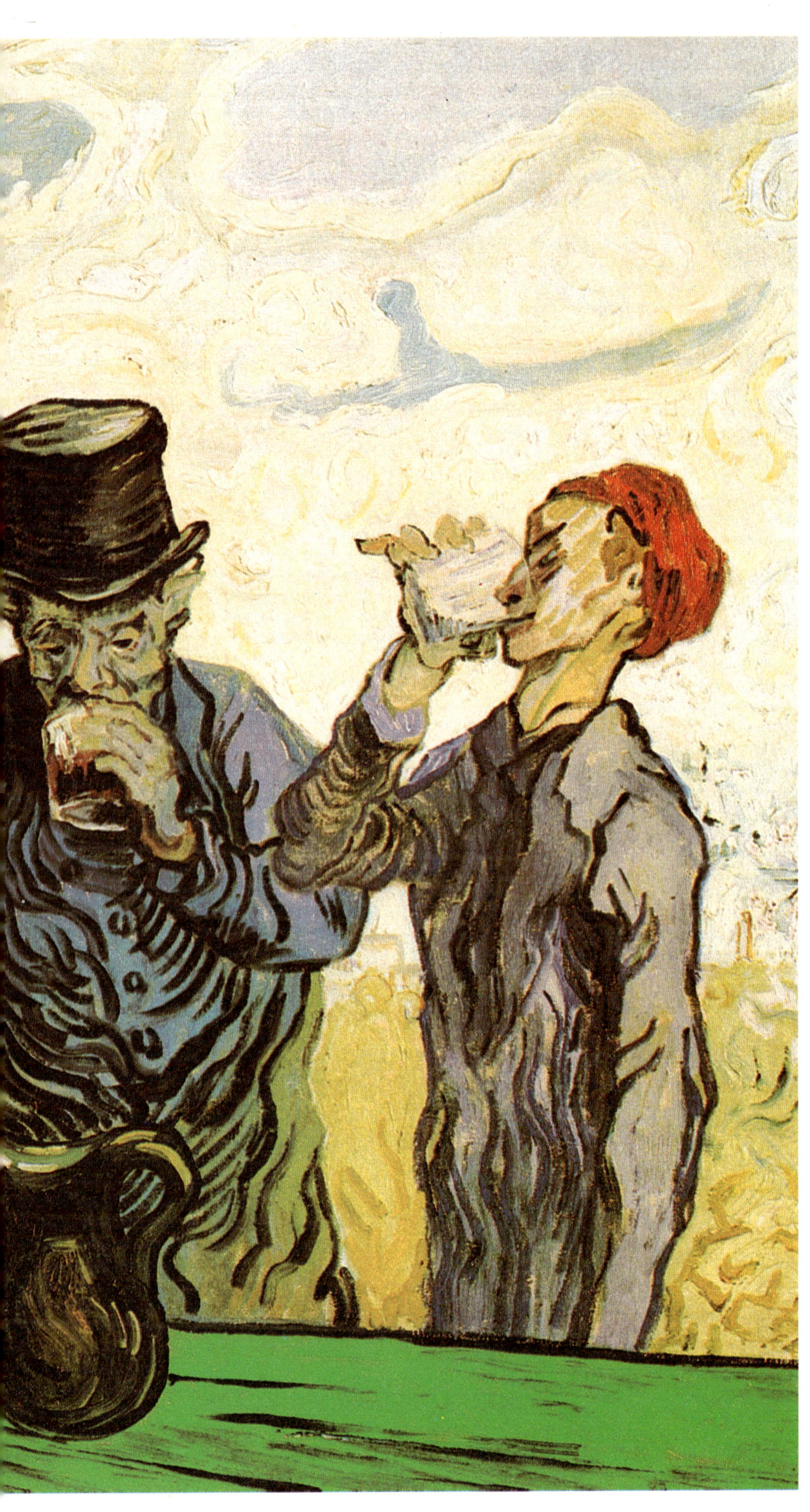

The Drinkers (after Daumier)

February 1890 - oil on canvas - 59.4 x 73.4 cm - Art Institute, Chicago

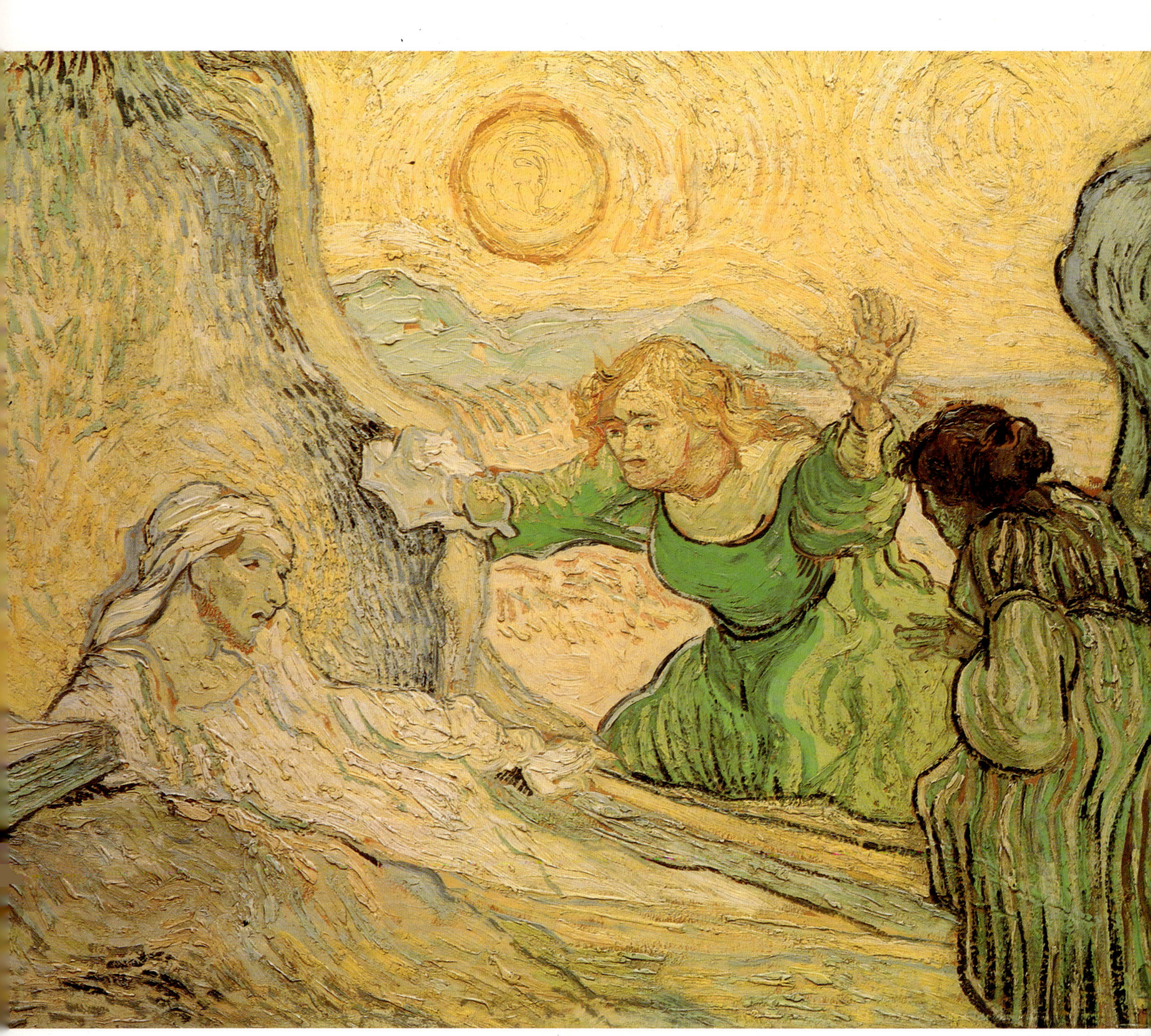

The Raising of Lazarus

*May 1890 - oil on canvas - 48.5 x 63 cm -
Vincent van Gogh Foundation, Amsterdam*

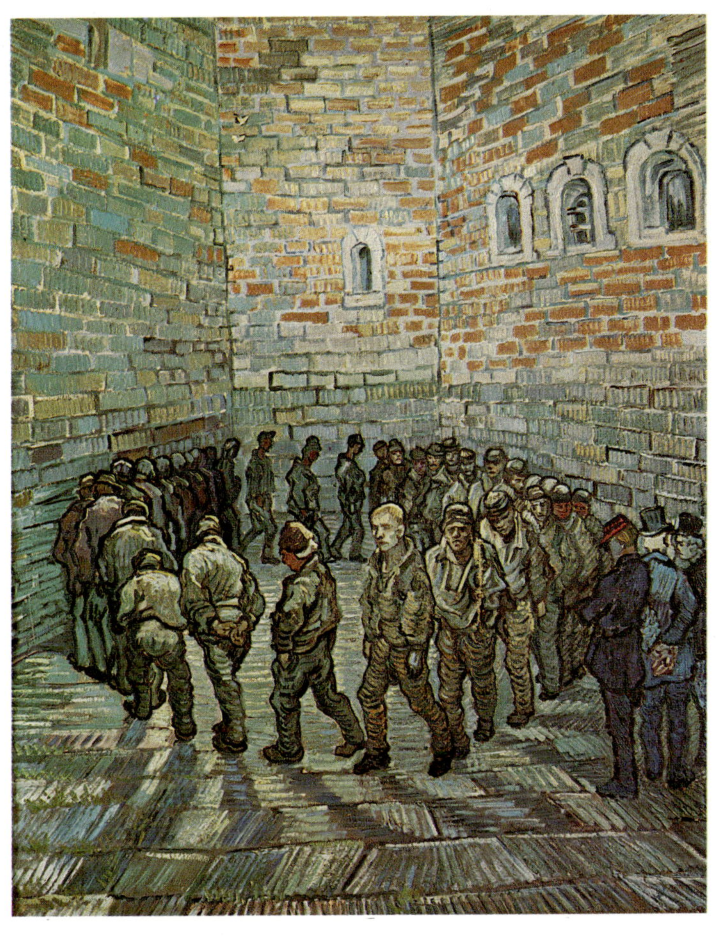

Prisoners Exercising (after Doré)

February 1890 - oil on canvas - 80 x 64 cm -
Pushkin Museum, Moscow

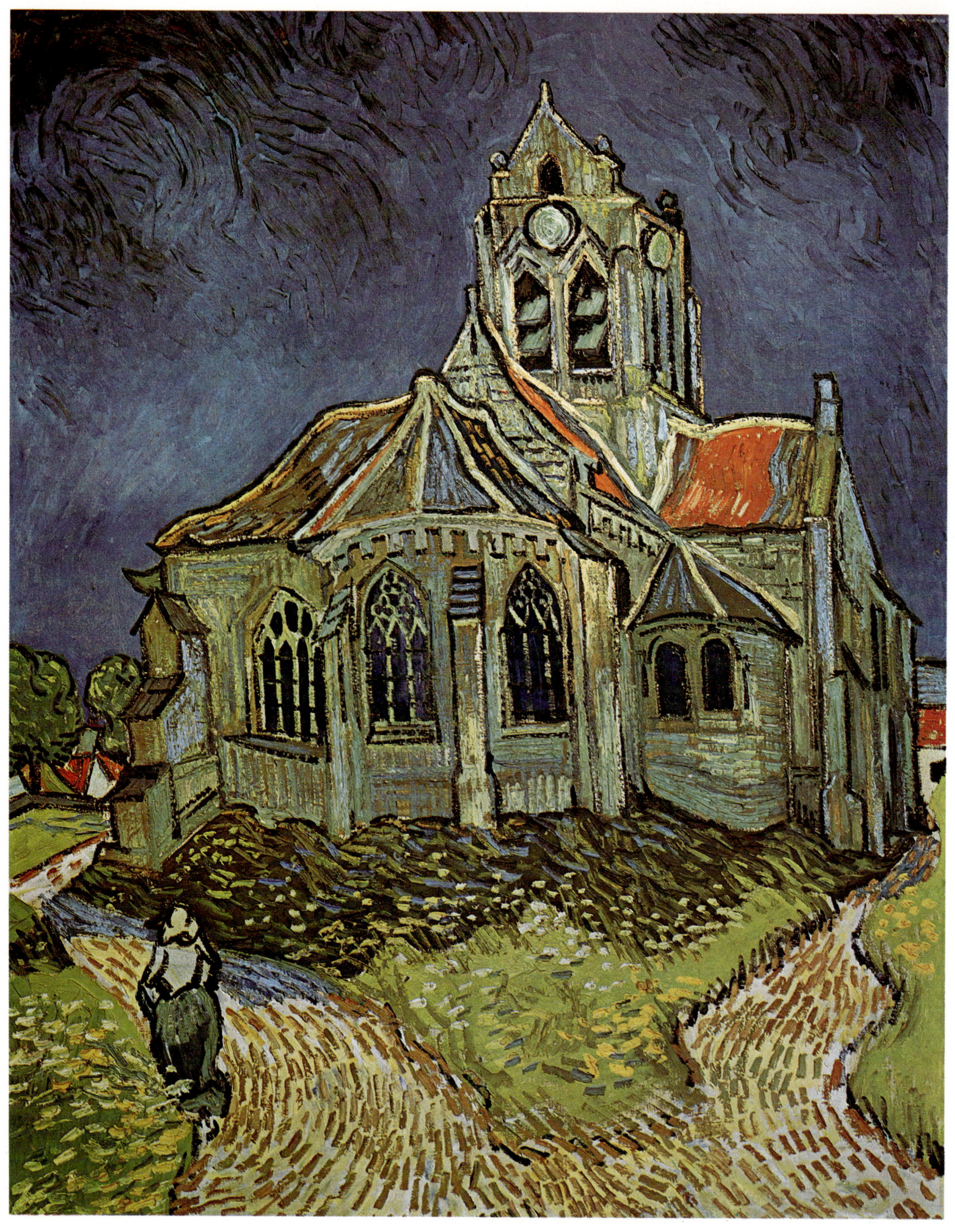

The Church at Auvers

June 1890 - oil on canvas -
Musée d'Orsay, Paris

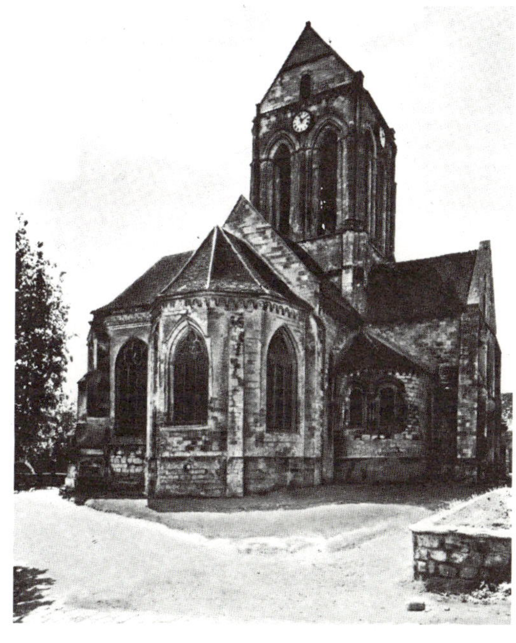

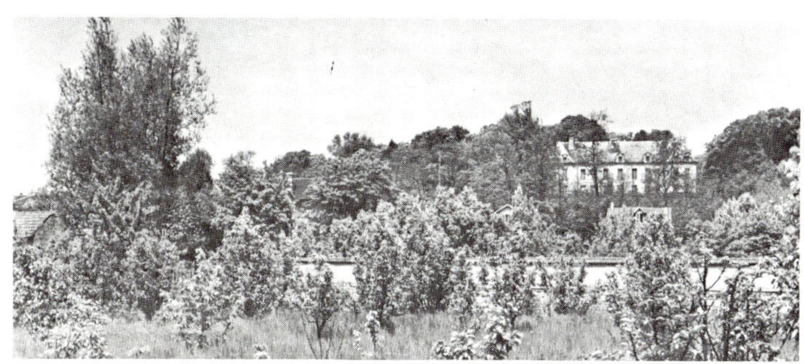

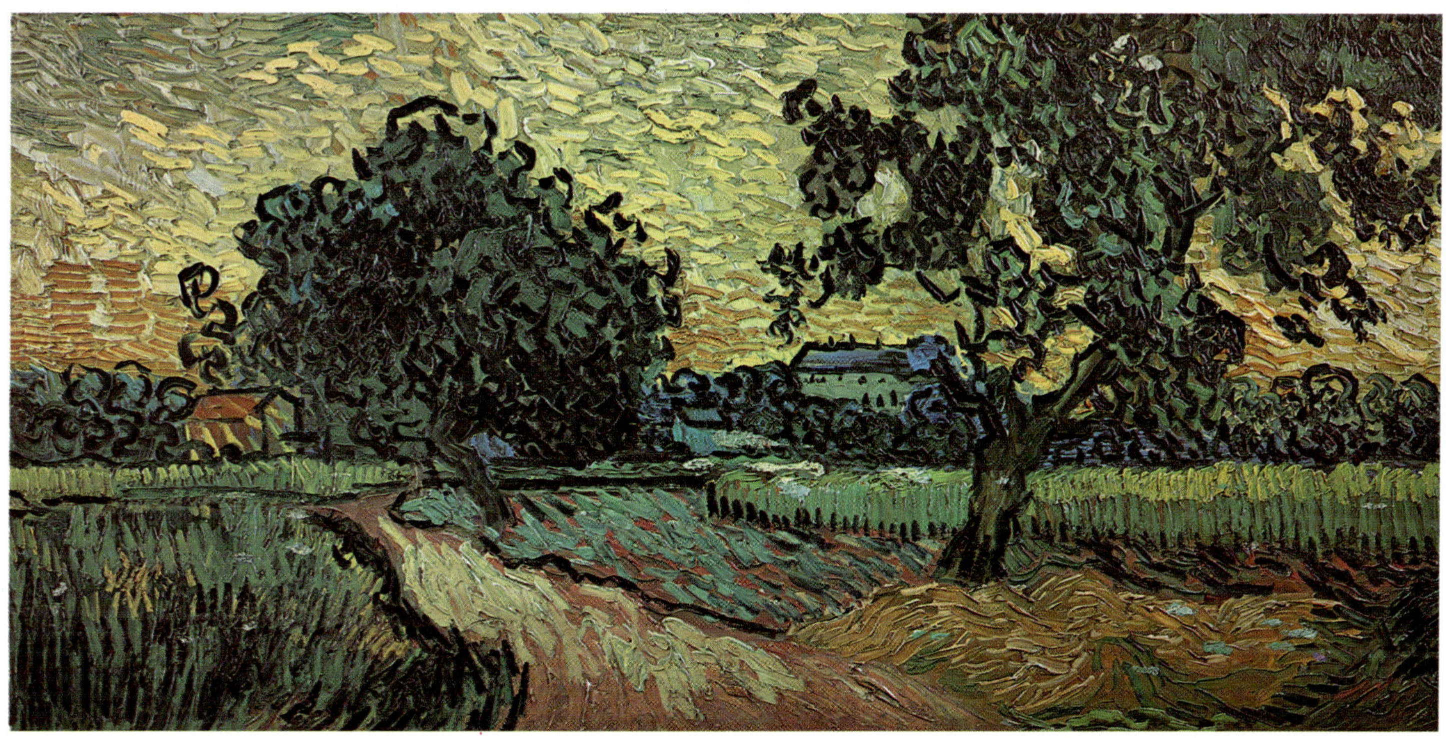

The Château of Auvers

June 1890 -oil on canvas - 50 x 100 cm - Vincent van Gogh Foundation, Amsterdam

Photograph of Auvers church

Photograph of the Château of Auvers

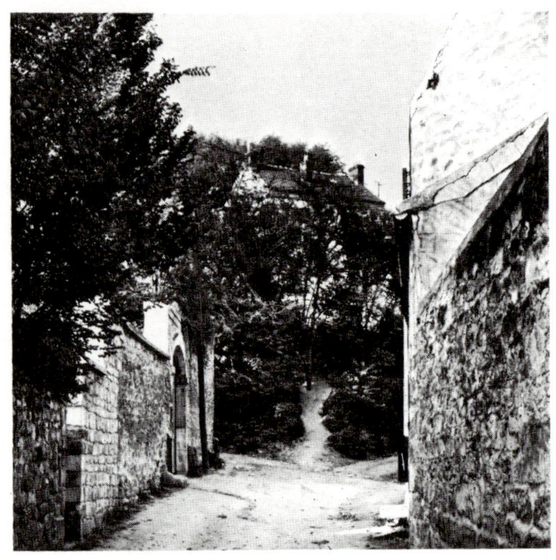

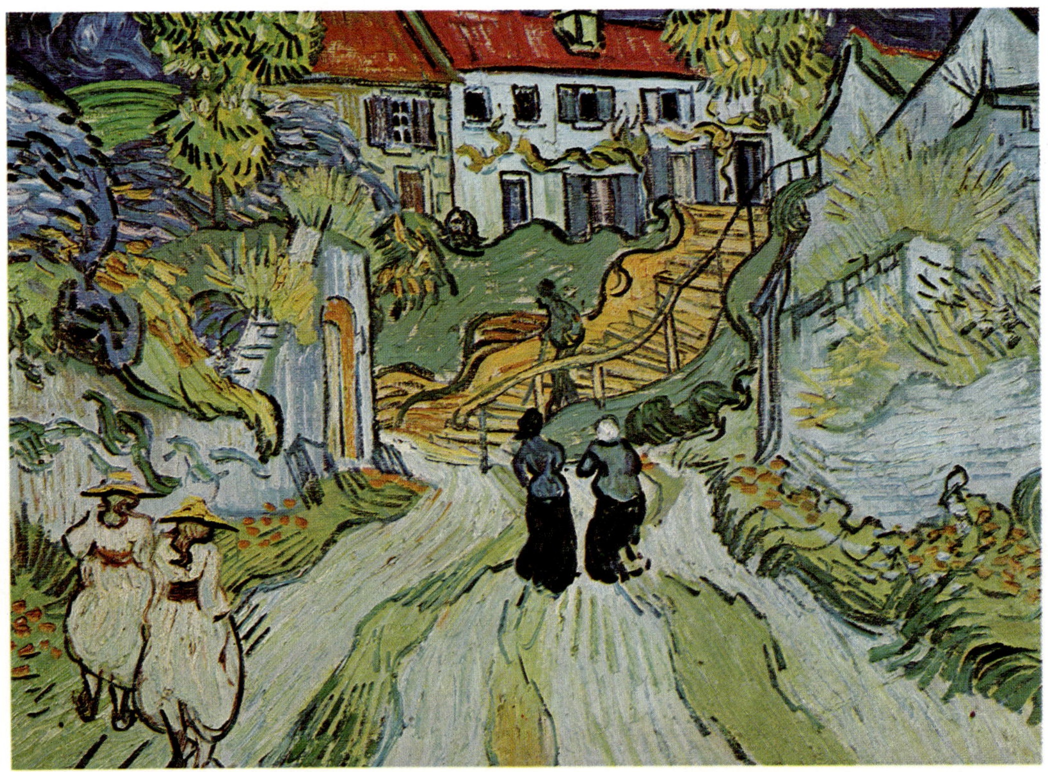

Photograph showing still existing buildings on each side of the road, however the ramp and the stairs have disappeared

Stairway in Auvers

June 1890 - oil on canvas - 48 x 78 cm - St. Louis Art Museum, St Louis

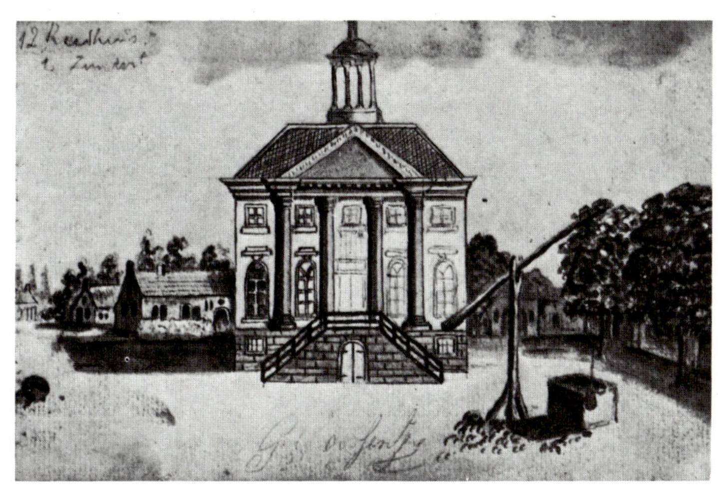

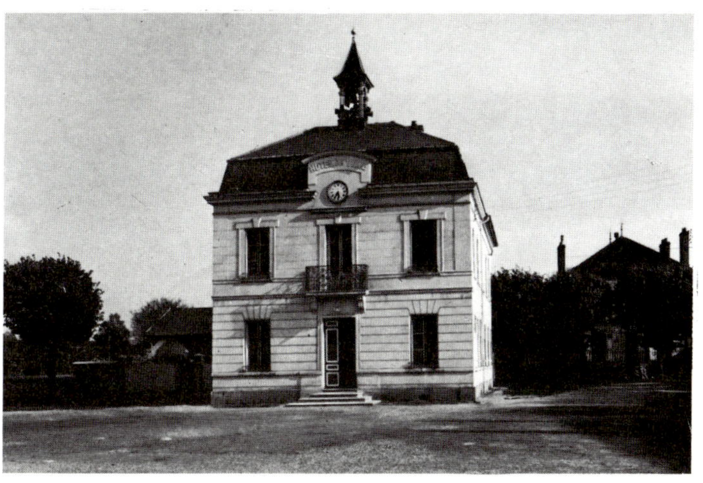

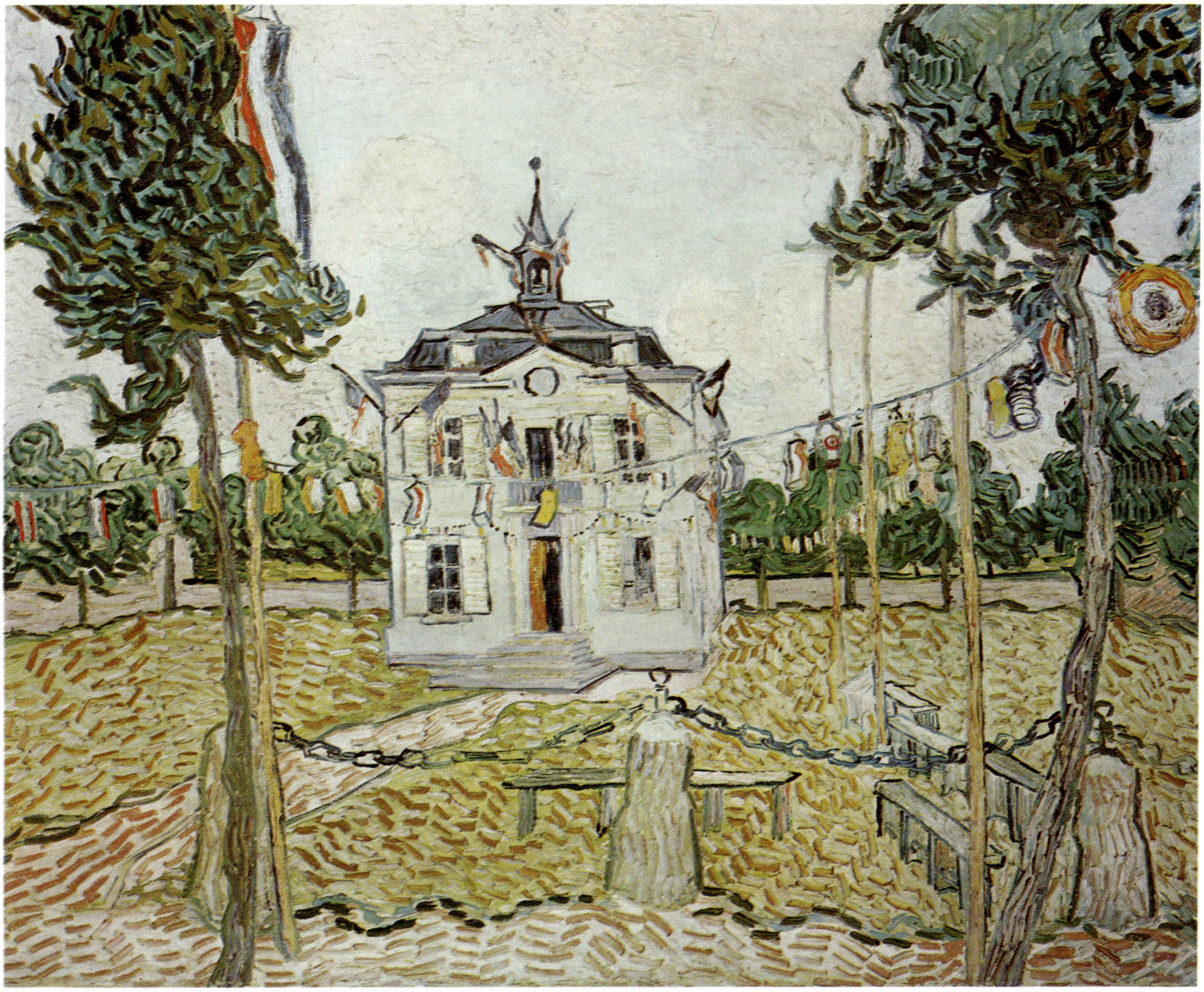

Auvers Town Hall

Black chalk - 21 x 31 cm

Photograph of Auvers town hall taken in 1956

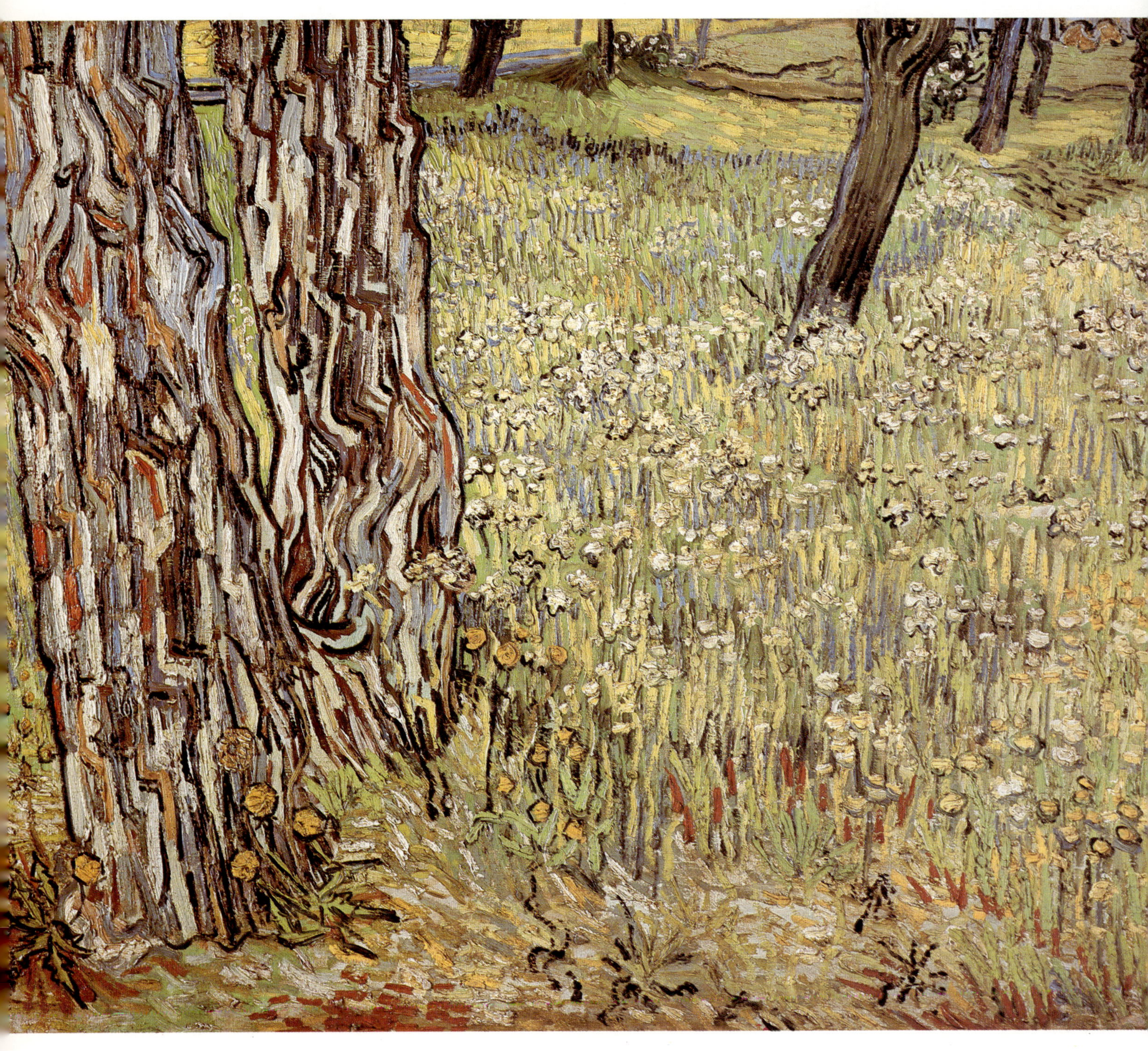

Field of Dandelions

May 1890 - oil on canvas - 472 x 90 cm - Rijksmuseum Kröller- Müller, Otterlo

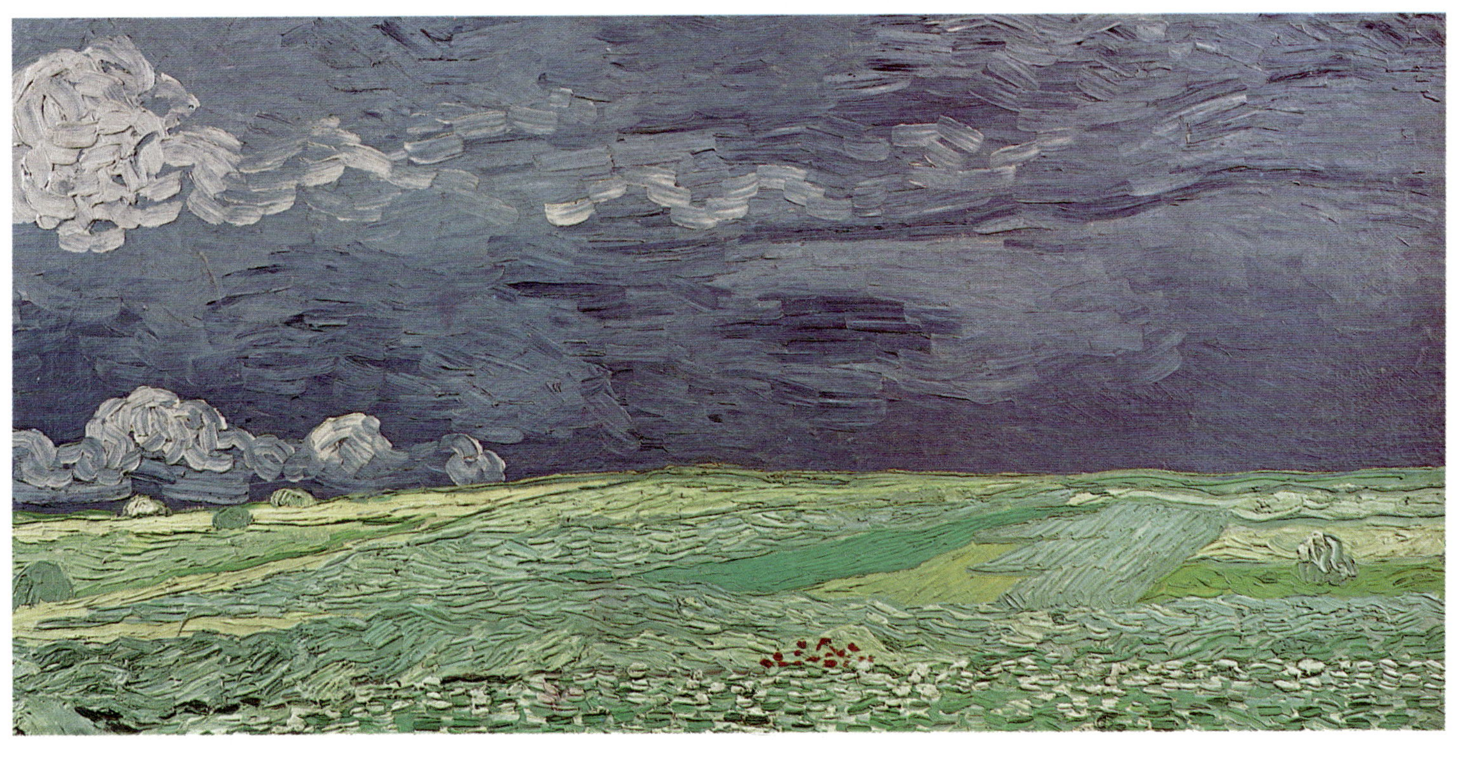

Fields under a Stormy Sky

July 1890 - oil on canvas - 50 x 100 cm -
Vincent van Gogh Foundation, Amsterdam

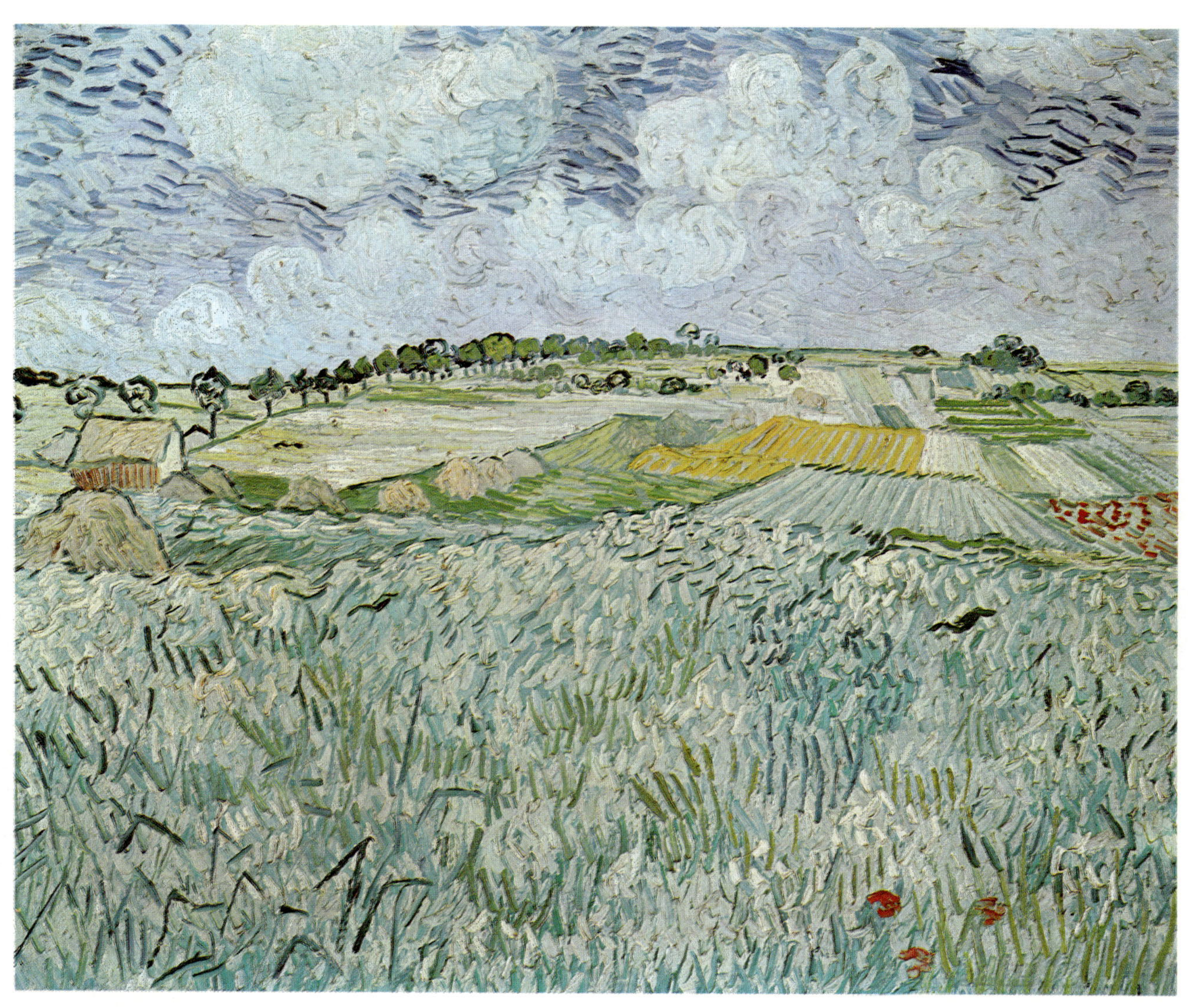

Plain near Auvers

July 1890 - oil on canvas - 73.5 x 92 cm -
Neue Pinakothek, Munich

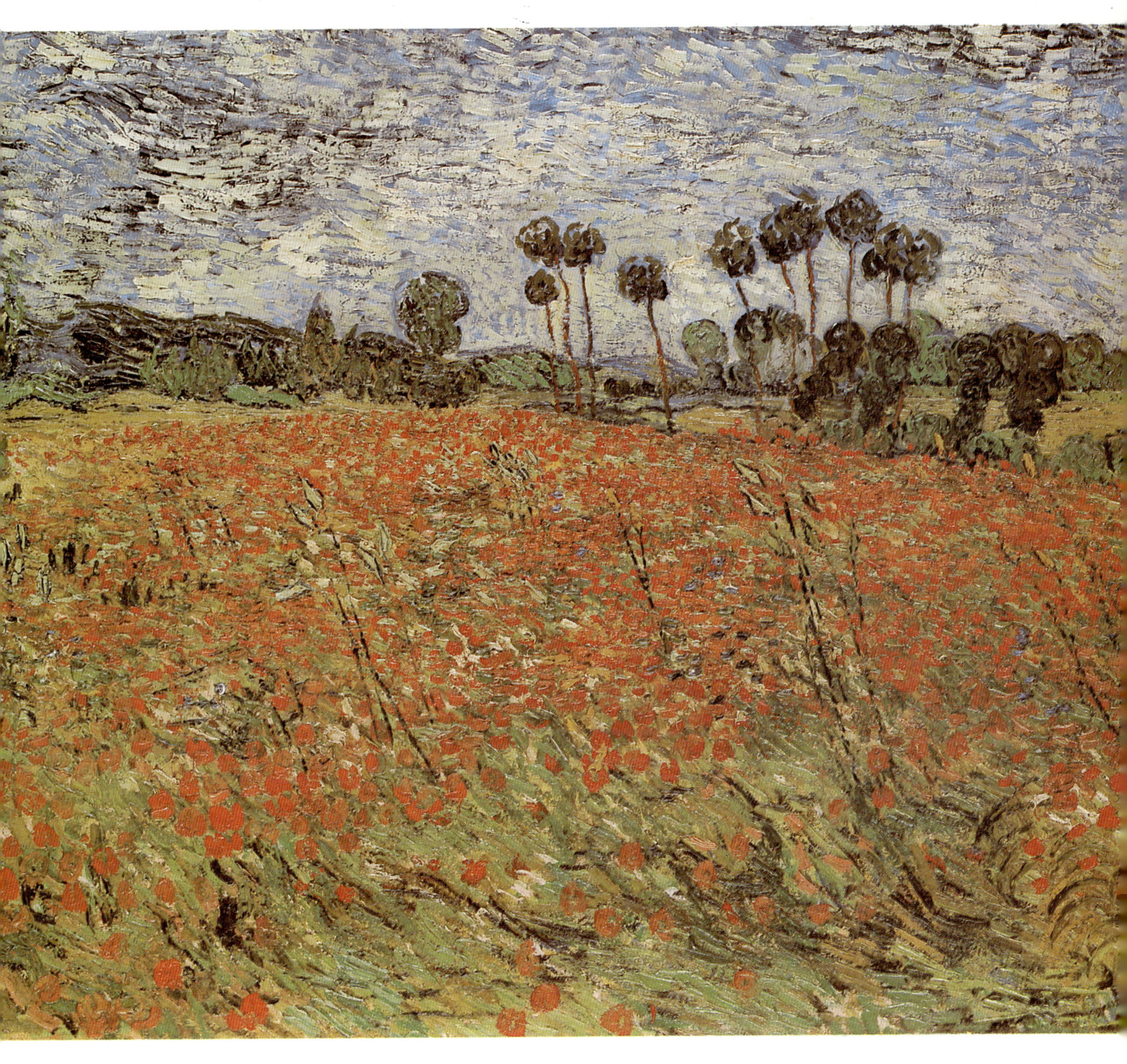

Poppy Field

June 1890 -oil on canvas - 473 x 91.5 cm - Gemeentemuseum, The Hague

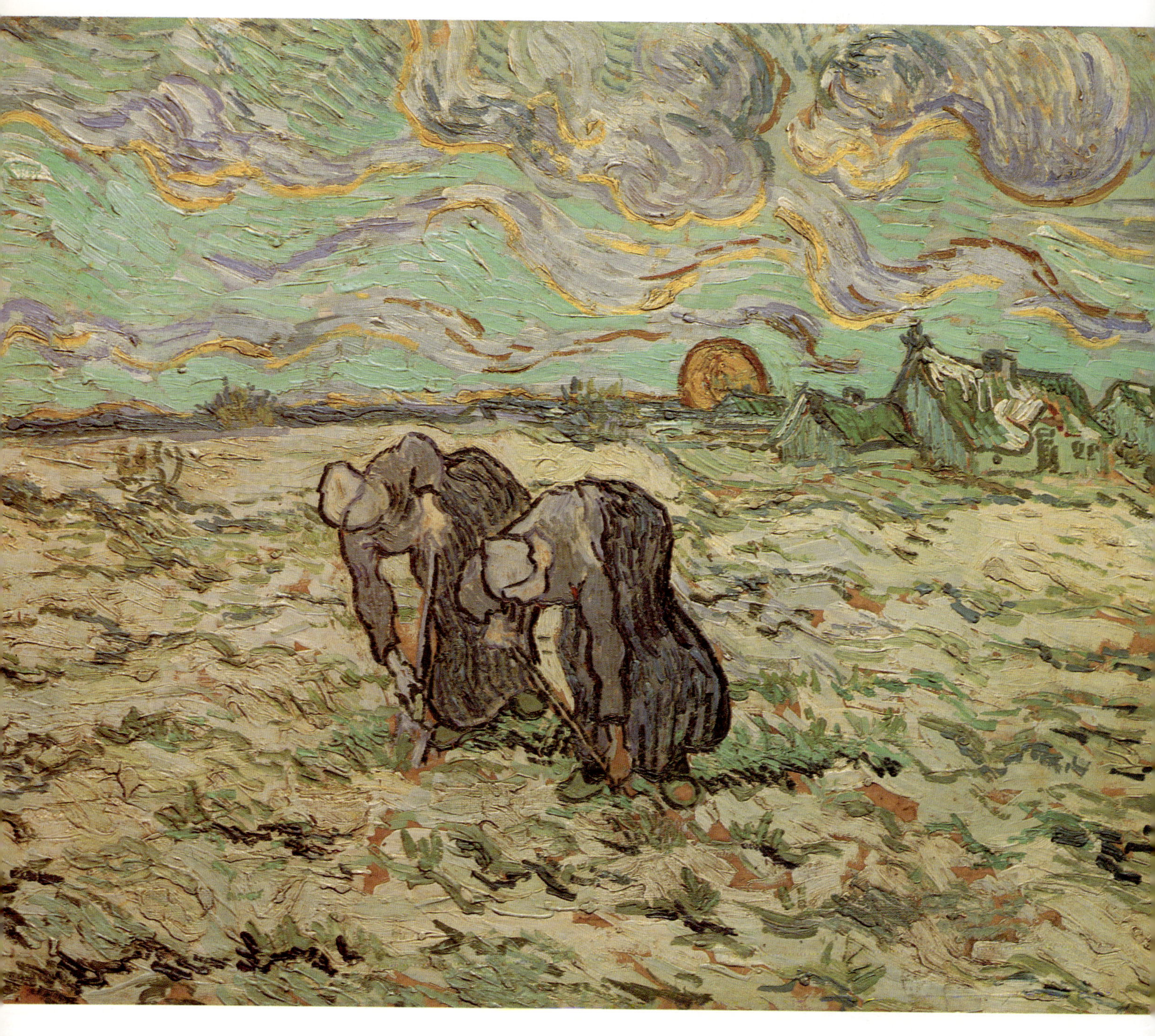

Two Peasant Women Digging in the Snow

March-April 1890 - oil on canvas - 50 x 64 cm -
E.G. Bührle collection, Zurich

Enclosed Garden

1889 - indian ink - 47.5 x 56 cm -
Art Museum, Middelburg, Holland

Photograph of the walled garden with the Alpilles
and Mont Gaussier in the background

Wheat Field at Sunrise

March-April 1890 - oil on canvas - 72 x 92 cm -
Rijksmuseum Kröller- Müller, Otterlo

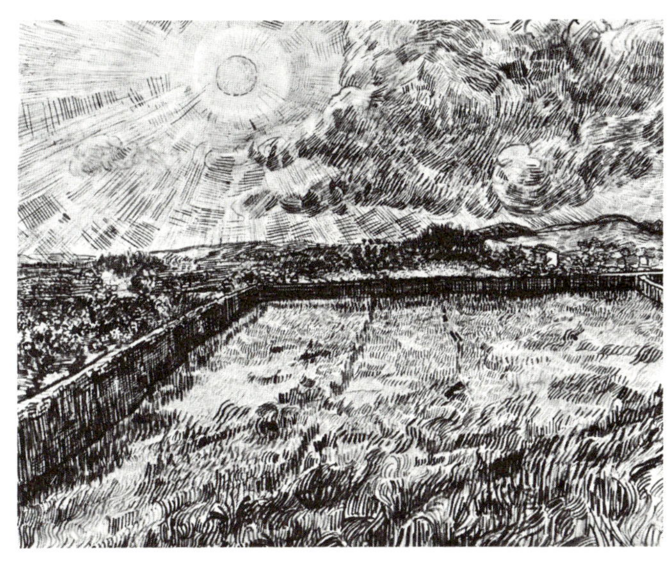

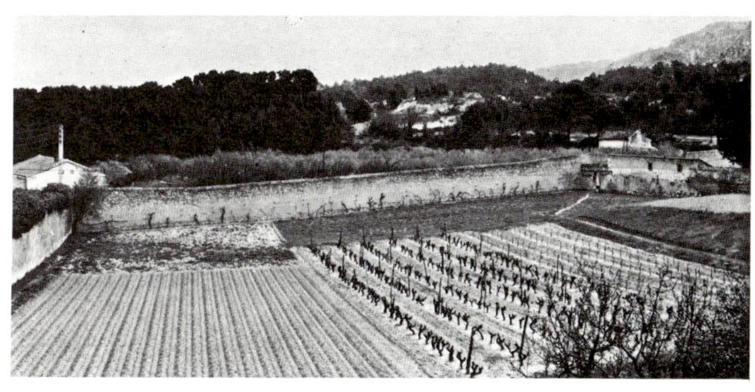

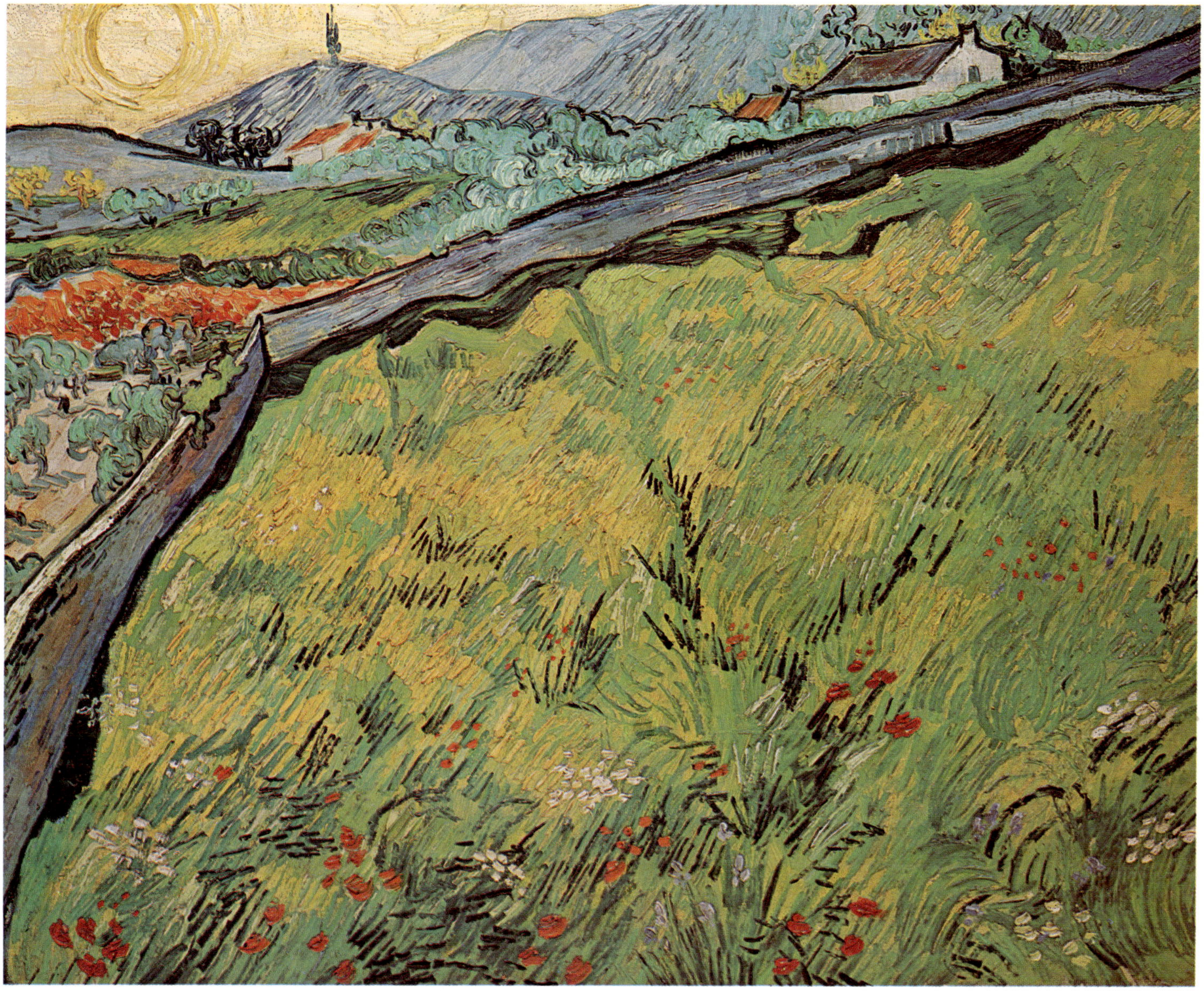

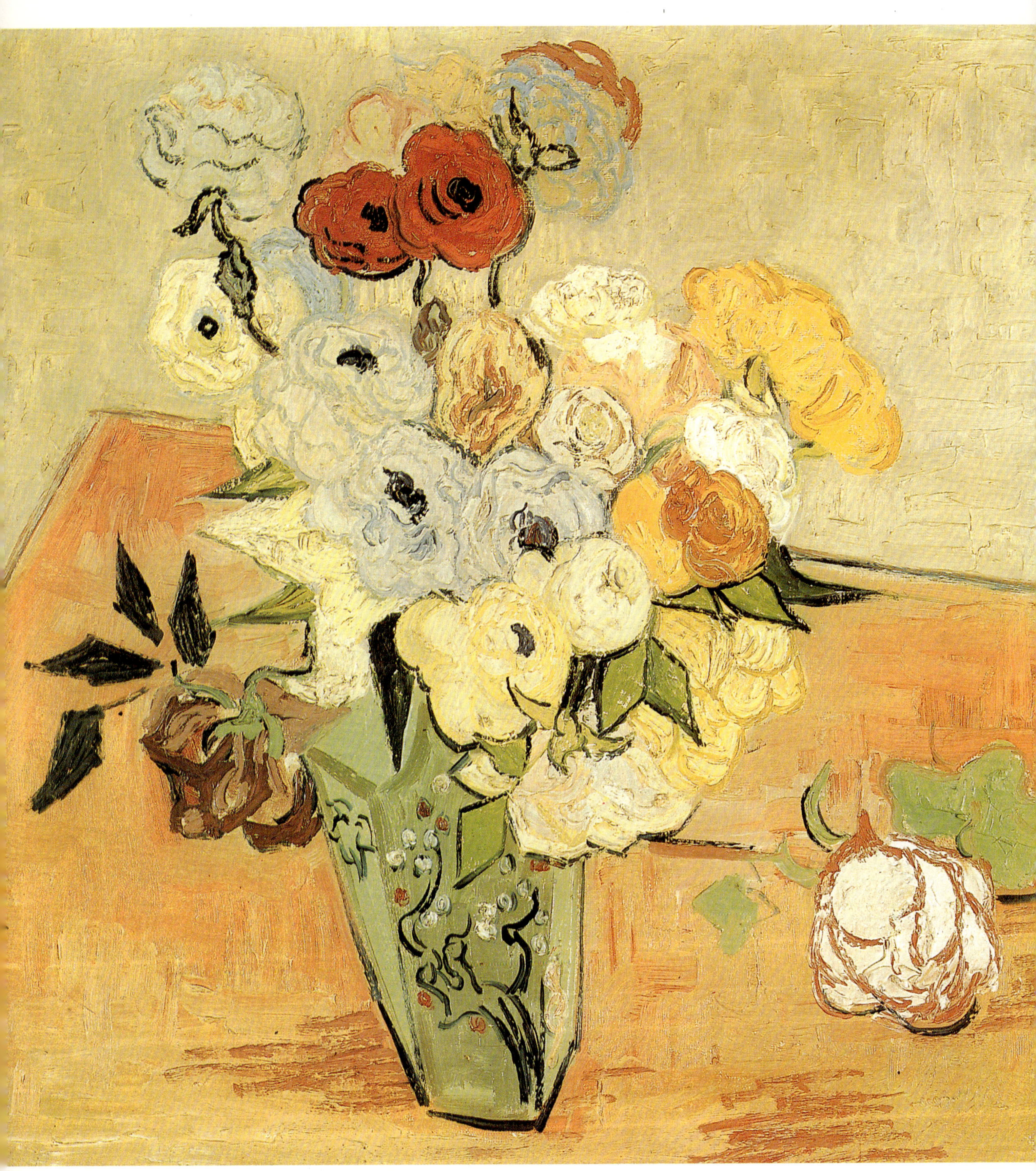

Roses and anemones

June 1890 - oil on canvas - 51 x 51 cm -
Musée d'Orsay, Paris

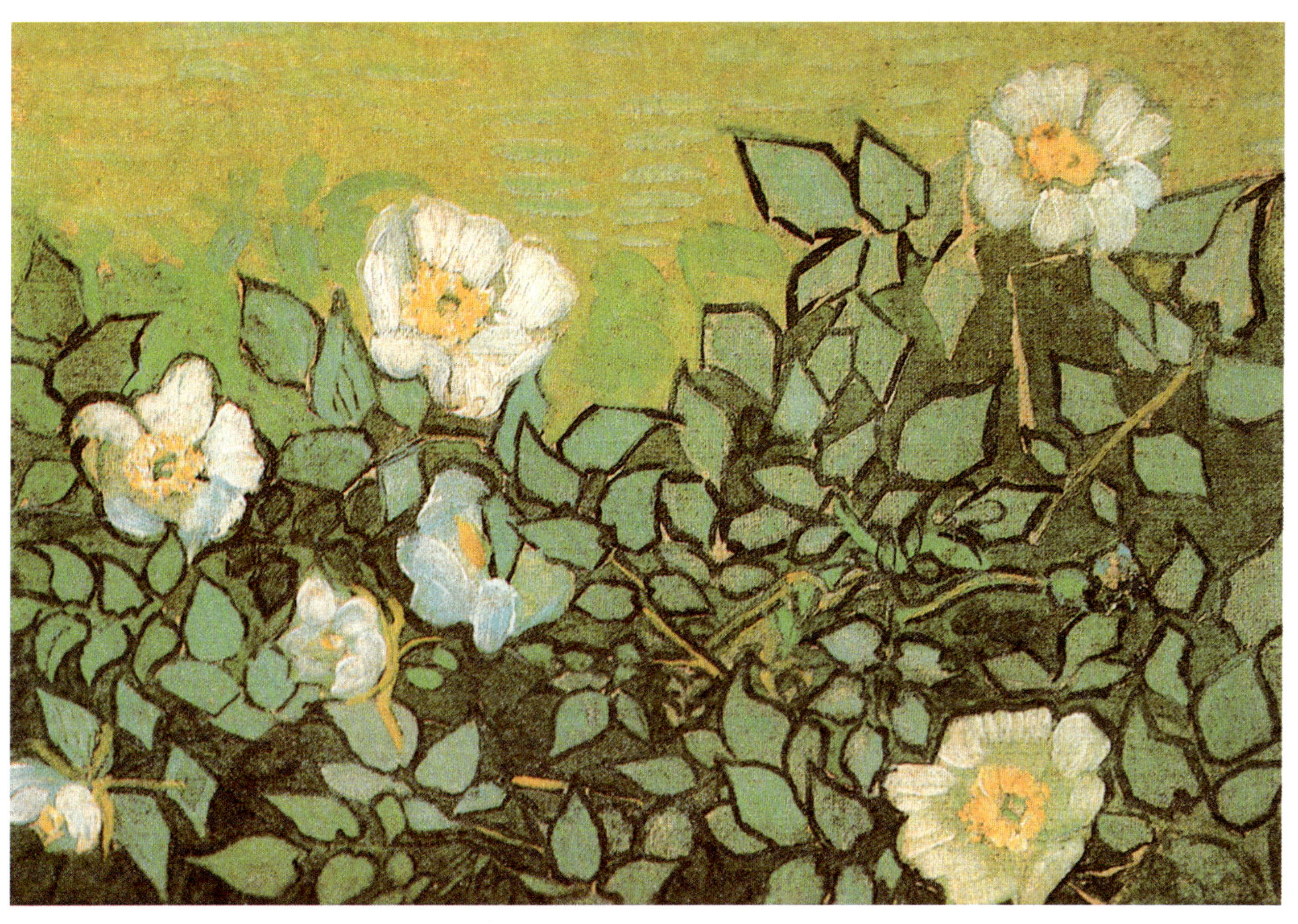

Wild Roses

April-May 1890 - oil on canvas - 24.5 x 33 cm -
Vincent van Gogh Foundation, Amsterdam

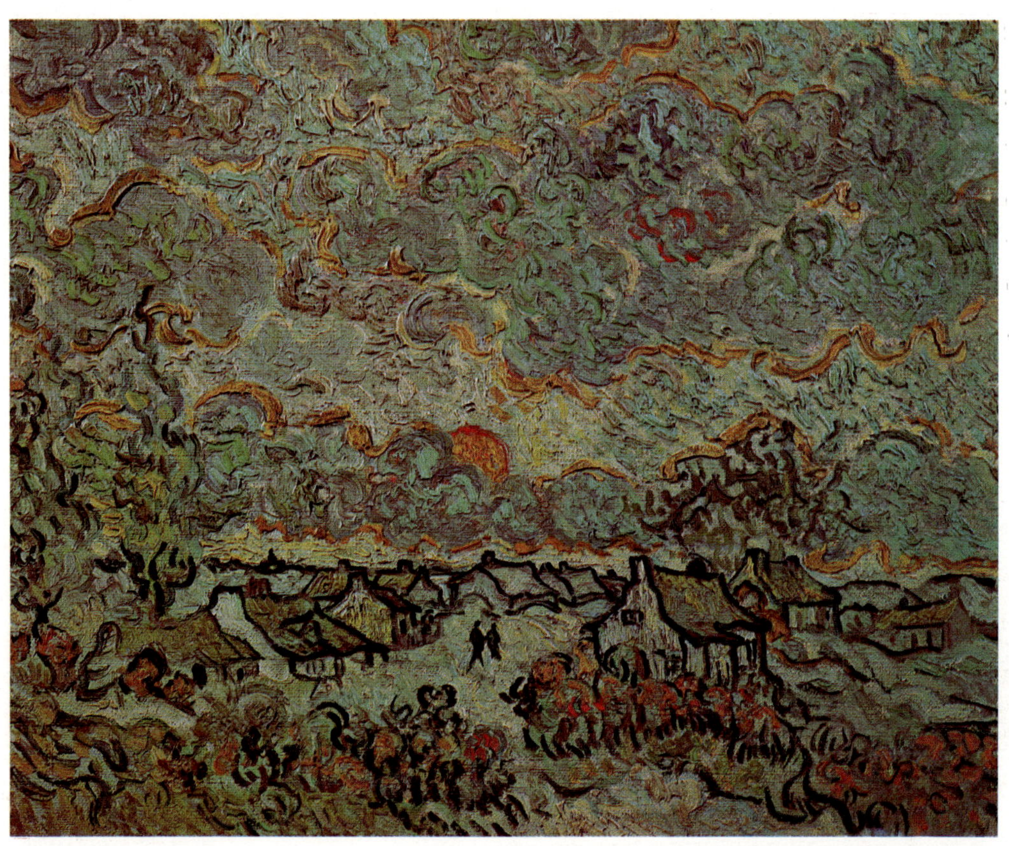

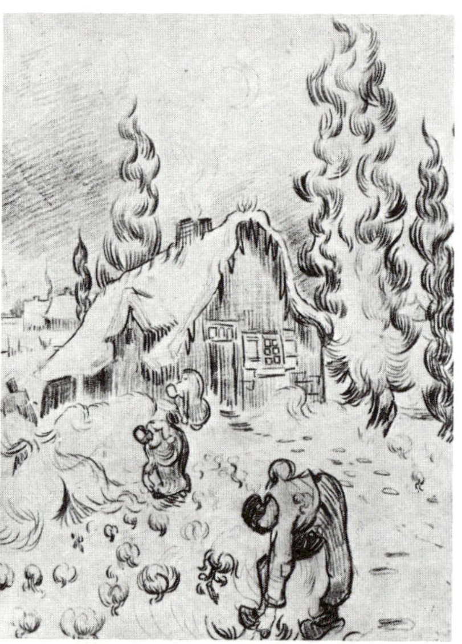

Memories of the North

April 1890 - oil on canvas - 29 x 36.5 cm - Vincent van Gogh Foundation, Amsterdam

Countryside at Saint-Rémy

1890 - black crayon drawing - 31.5 x 24 cm - Vincent van Gogh Foundation, Amsterdam

Road with Cypress

May 1890 - oil on canvas - 72 x 73 cm - Rijksmuseum Kröller- Müller, Otterlo

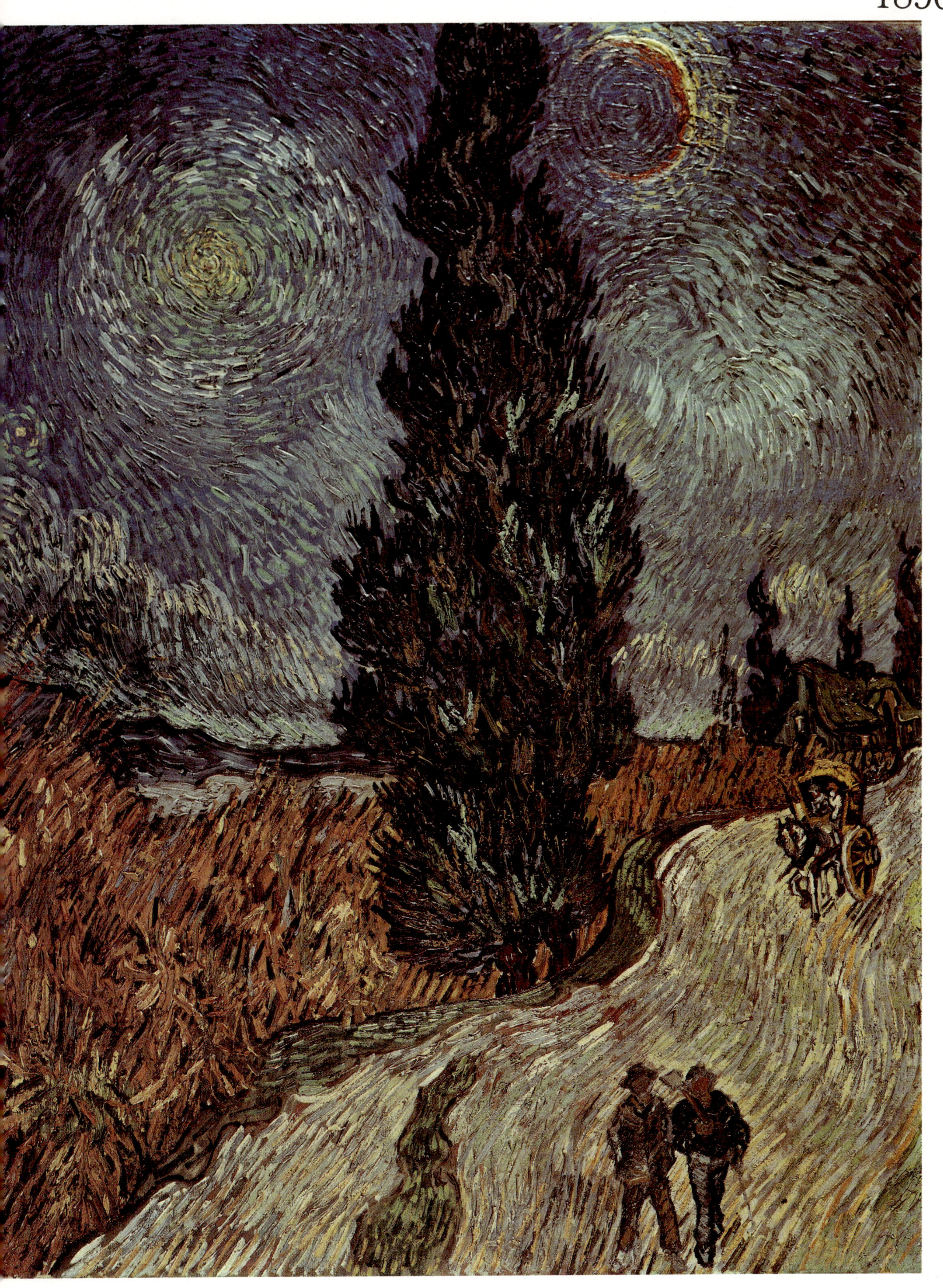

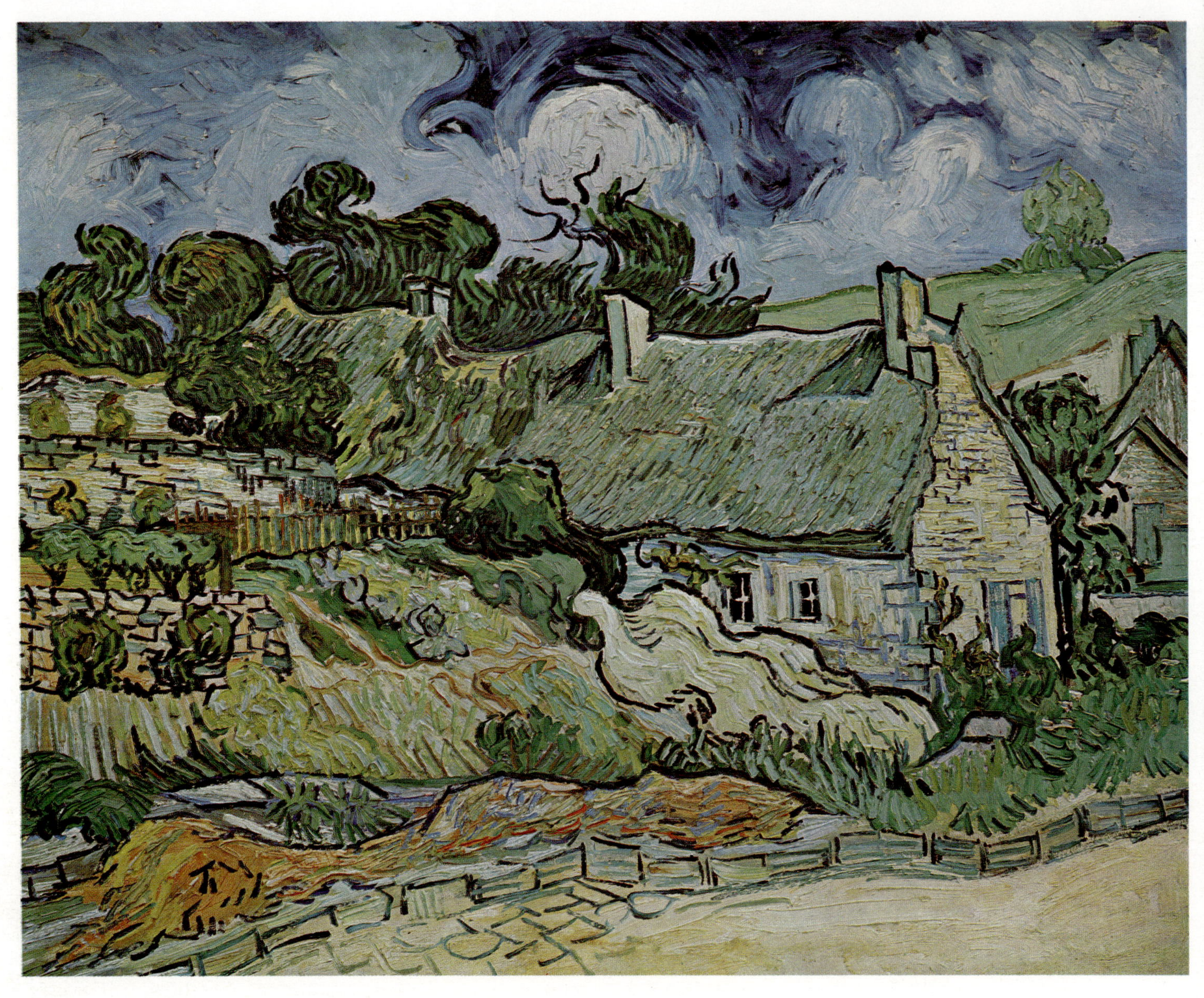

Thatched Cottages

June 1890 - oil on canvas - 72 x 90 cm - Musée d'Orsay, Paris

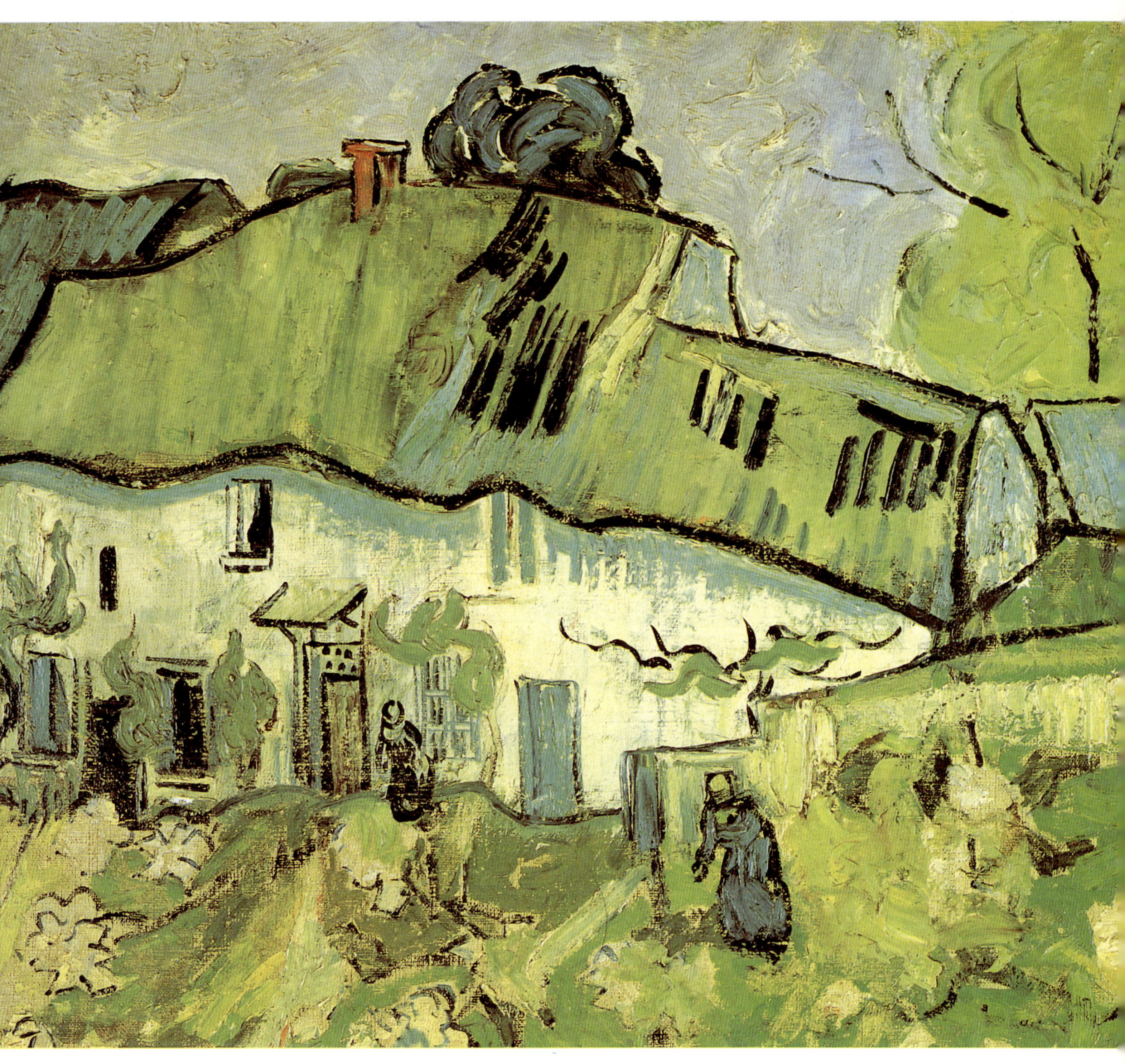

Farmhouse with Two Figures

June 1890 - oil on canvas - 38 x 45 cm -
Vincent van Gogh Foundation, Amsterdam

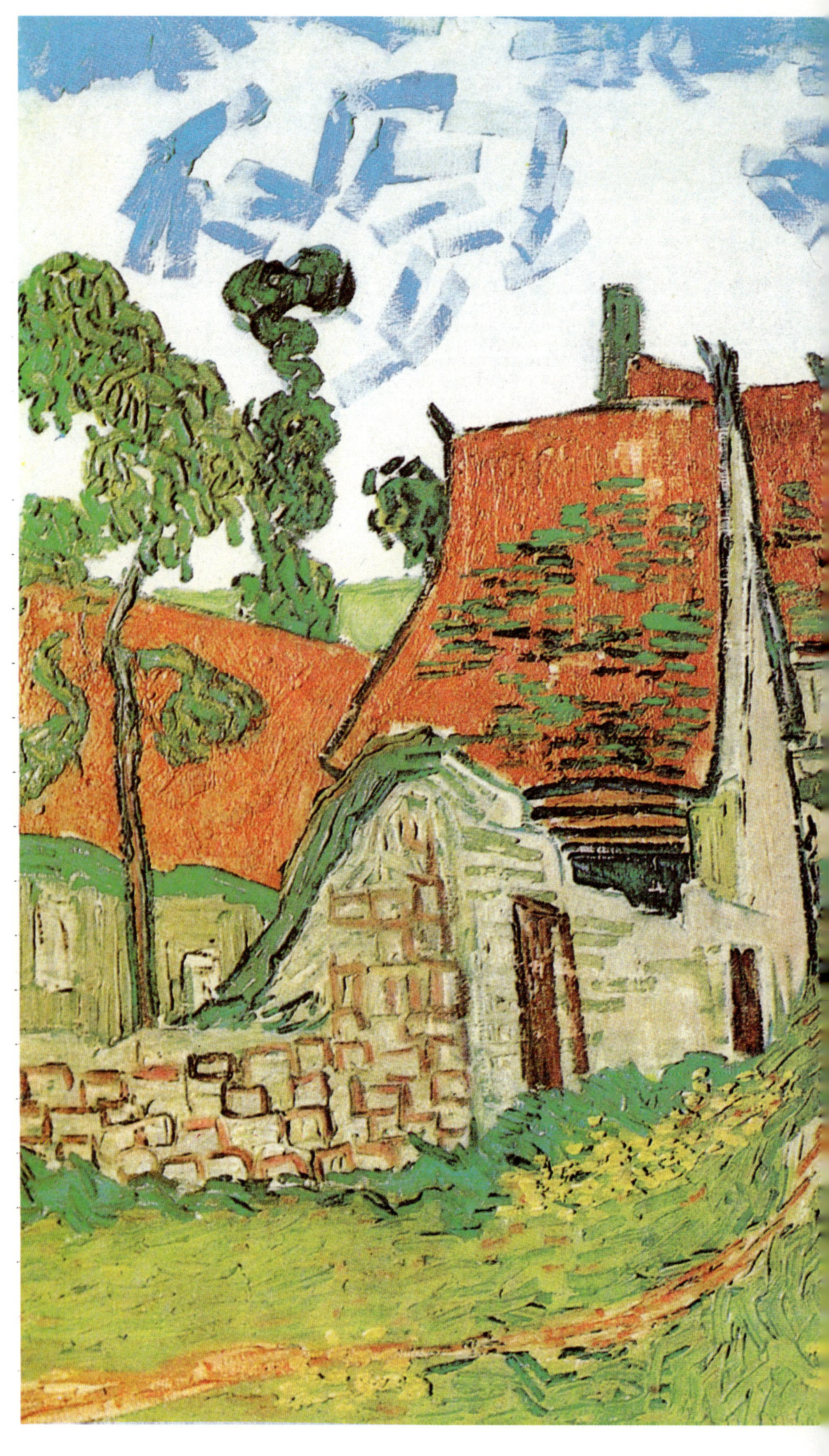

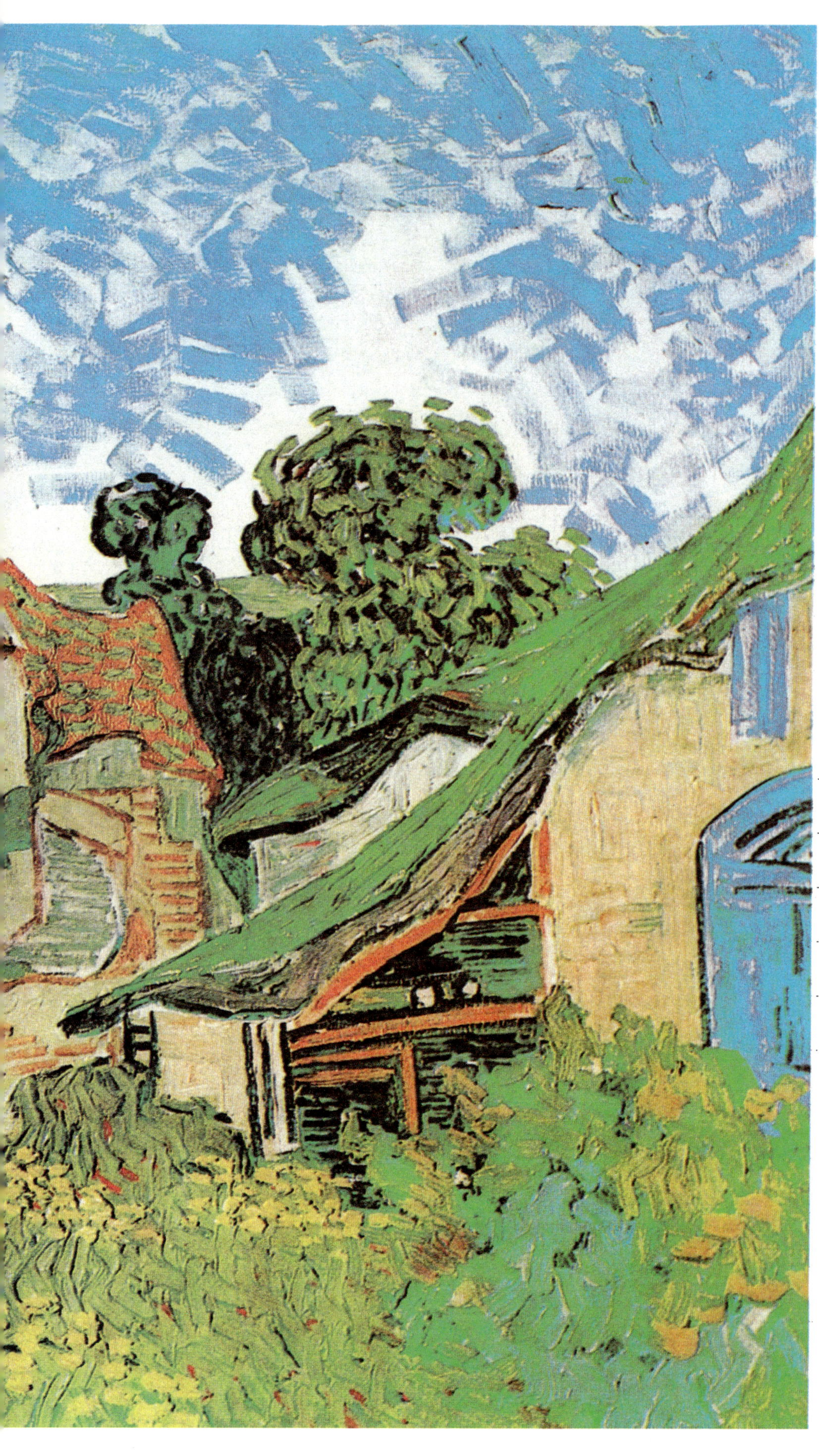

Street in Auvers

May 1890 - oil on canvas - 73 x 92 cm -
Atheneumin Taidemuseo, Helsinki

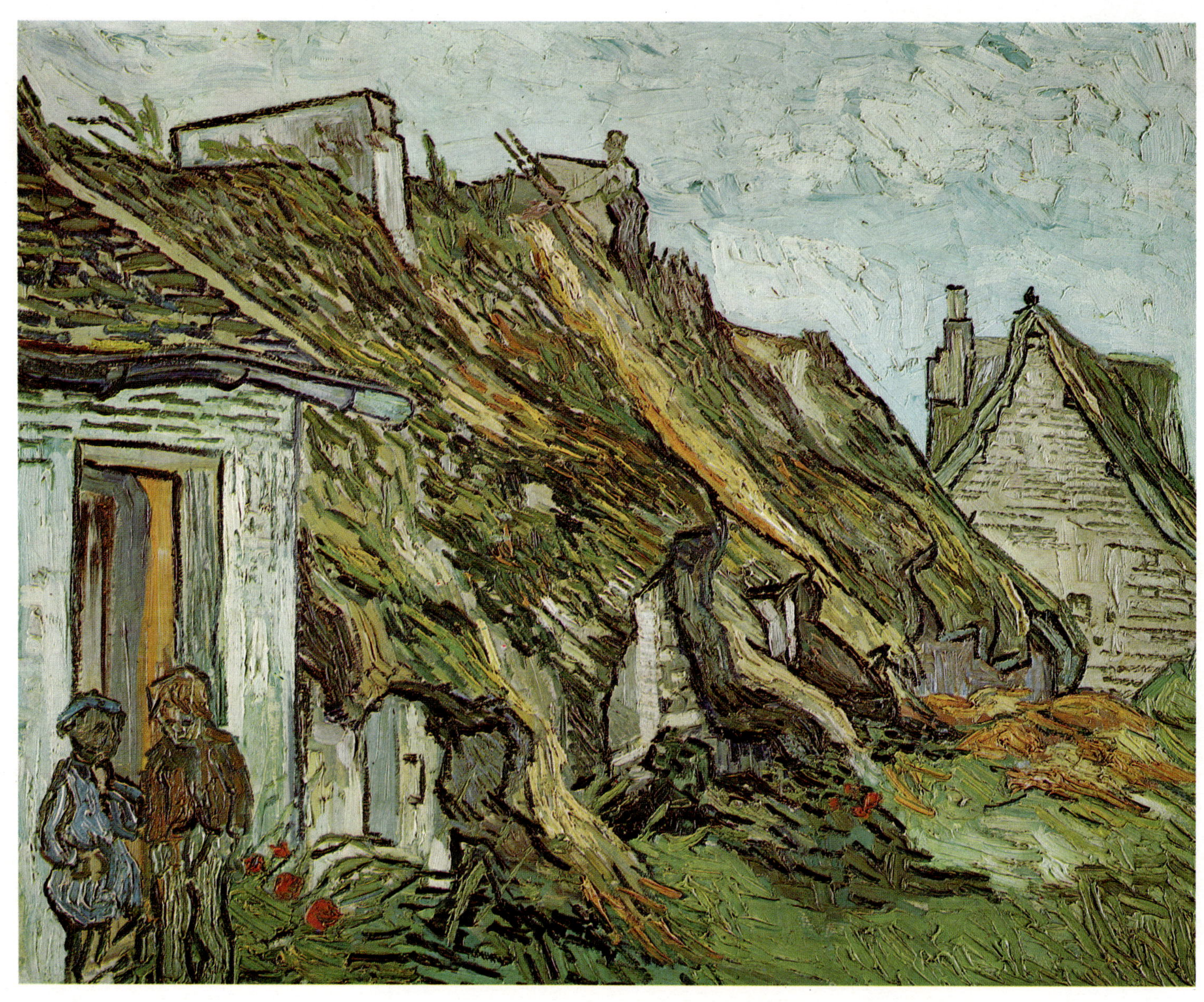

Thatched Cottages in Chaponval

July 1890 - oil on canvas - 65 x 81 cm -
Kunsthaus, Zurich

Promenade under the Moon in an Olive Grove

May 1890 - oil on canvas - 49.5 x 45.5 cm -
Museu de arte de Sao Paolo, Brazil

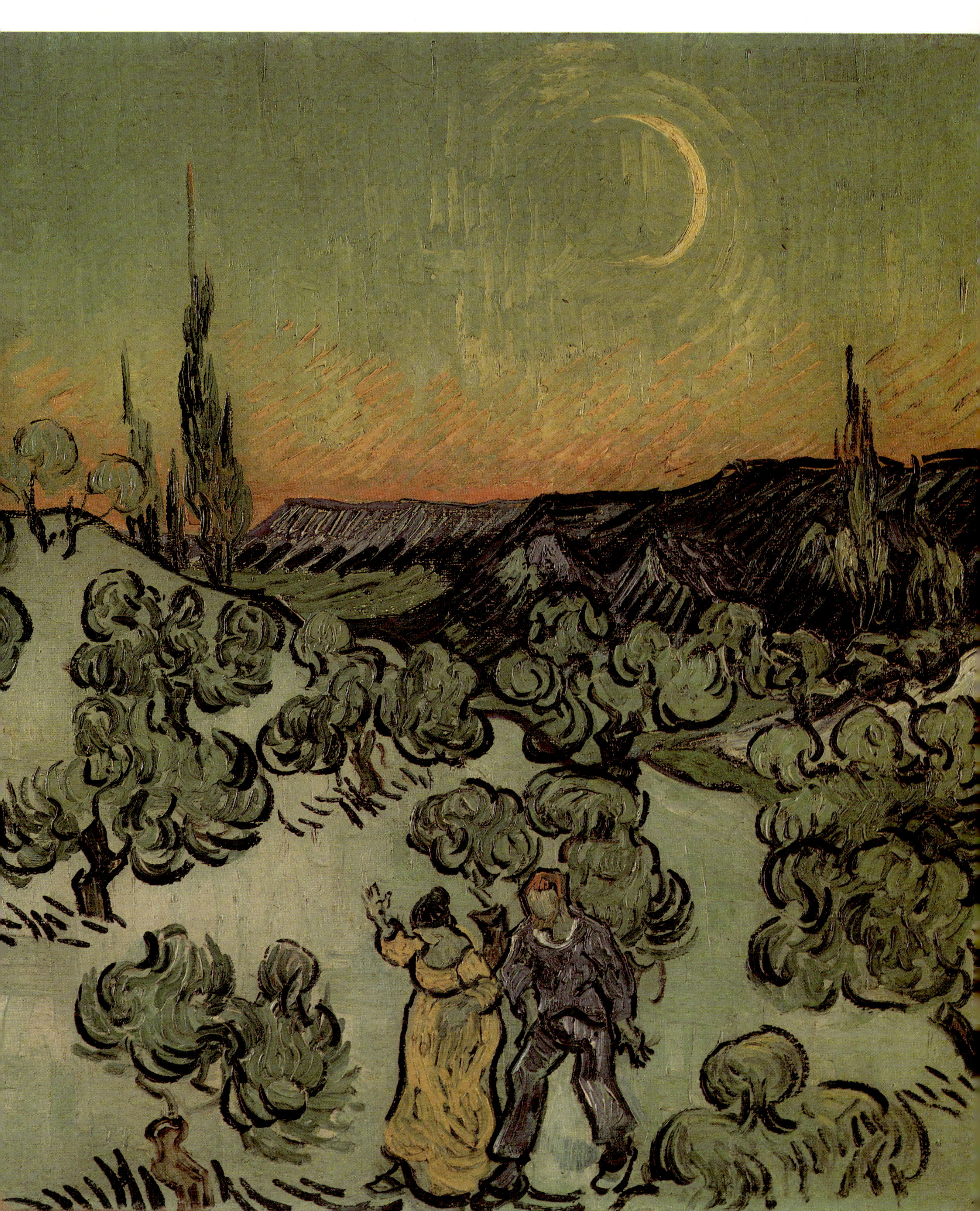

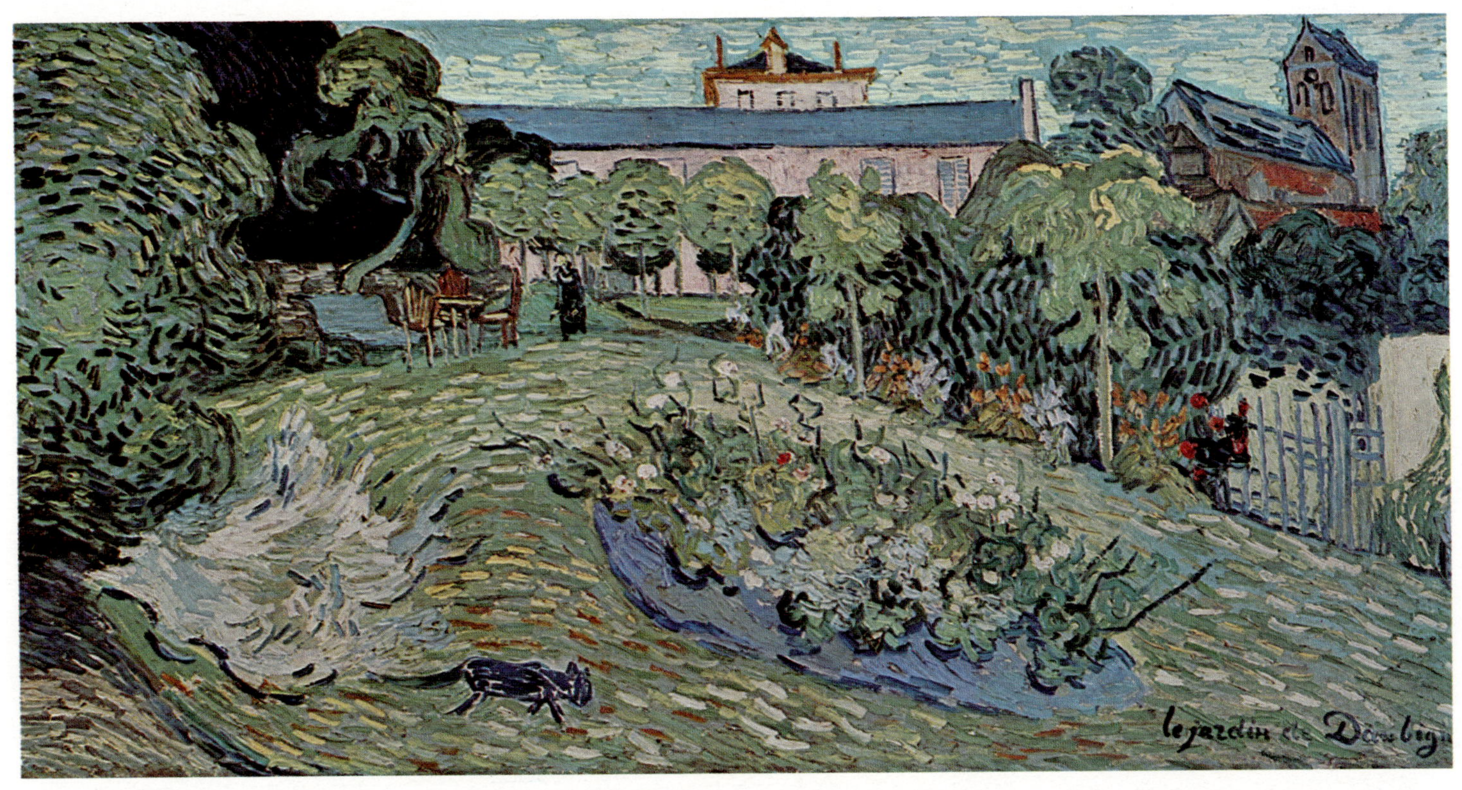

Daubigny's Garden

July 1890 - oil on canvas - 55 x 100 cm -
Staechelin collection, Basle

The Garden of Doctor Gachet

May 1890 - oil on canvas - 73 x 51.5 cm -
Musée d'Orsay, Paris

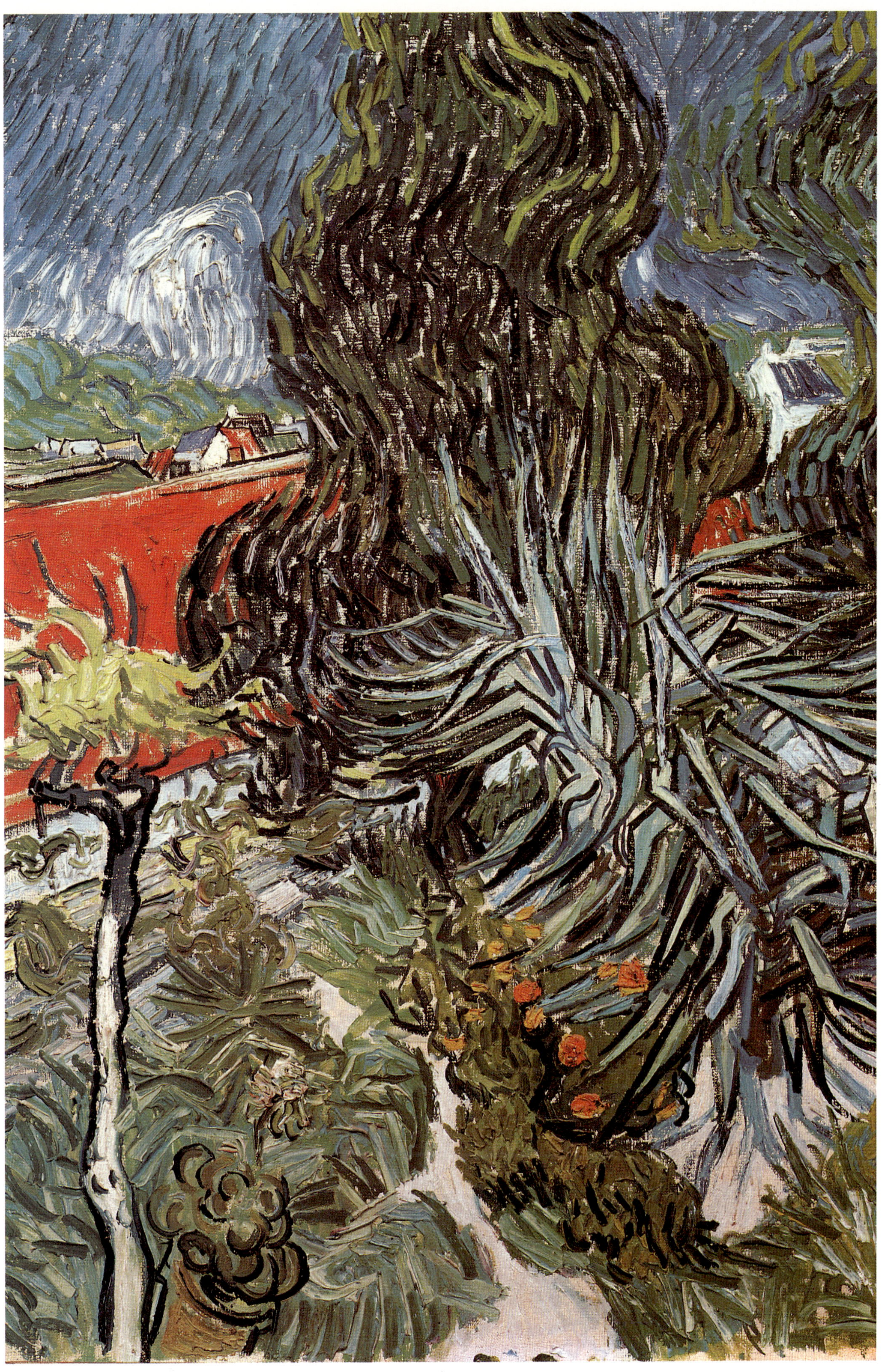

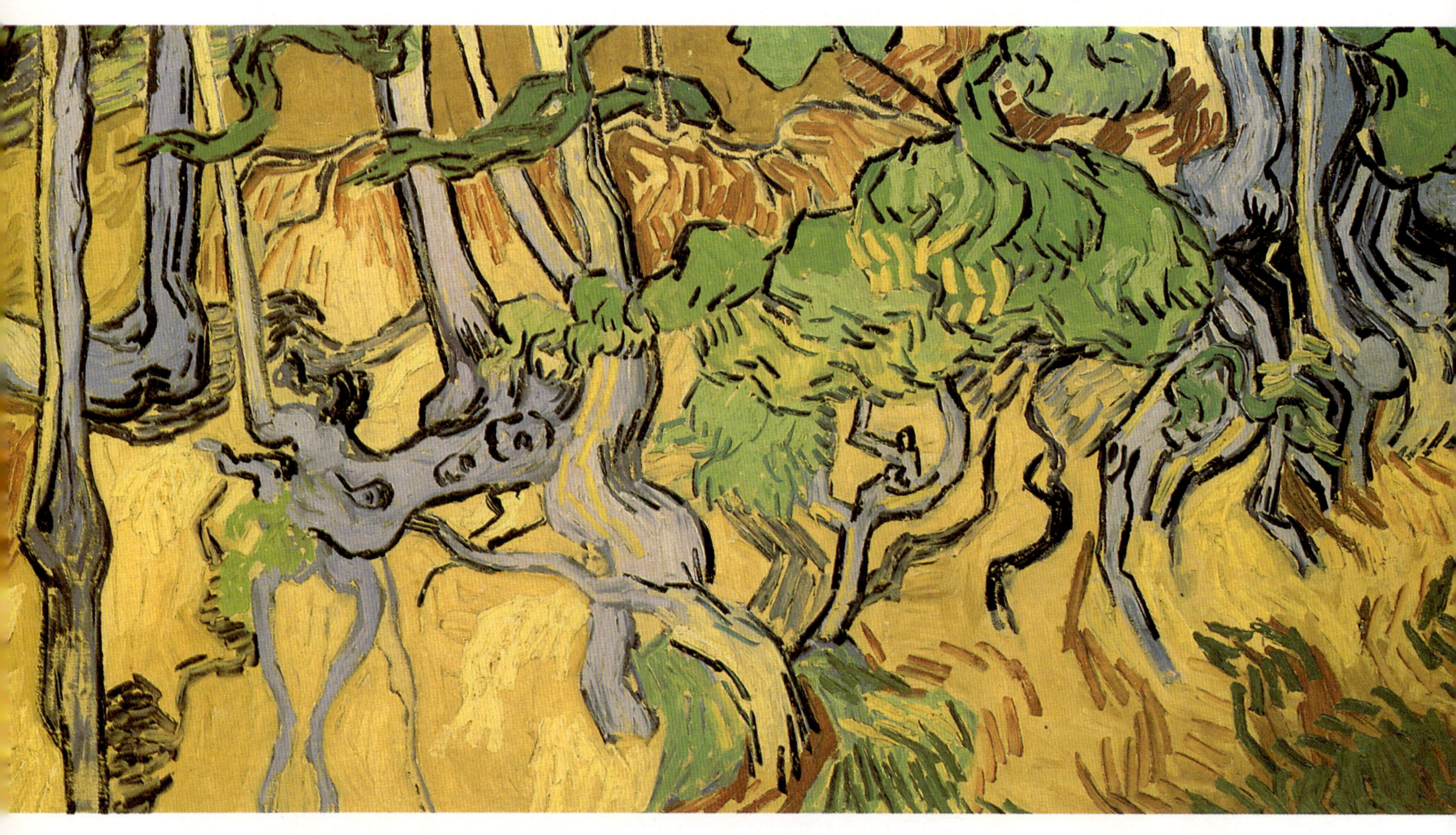

Roots and Tree Trunks

July 1890 - oil on canvas - 50.5 x 100.5 cm - Vincent van Gogh Foundation, Amsterdam

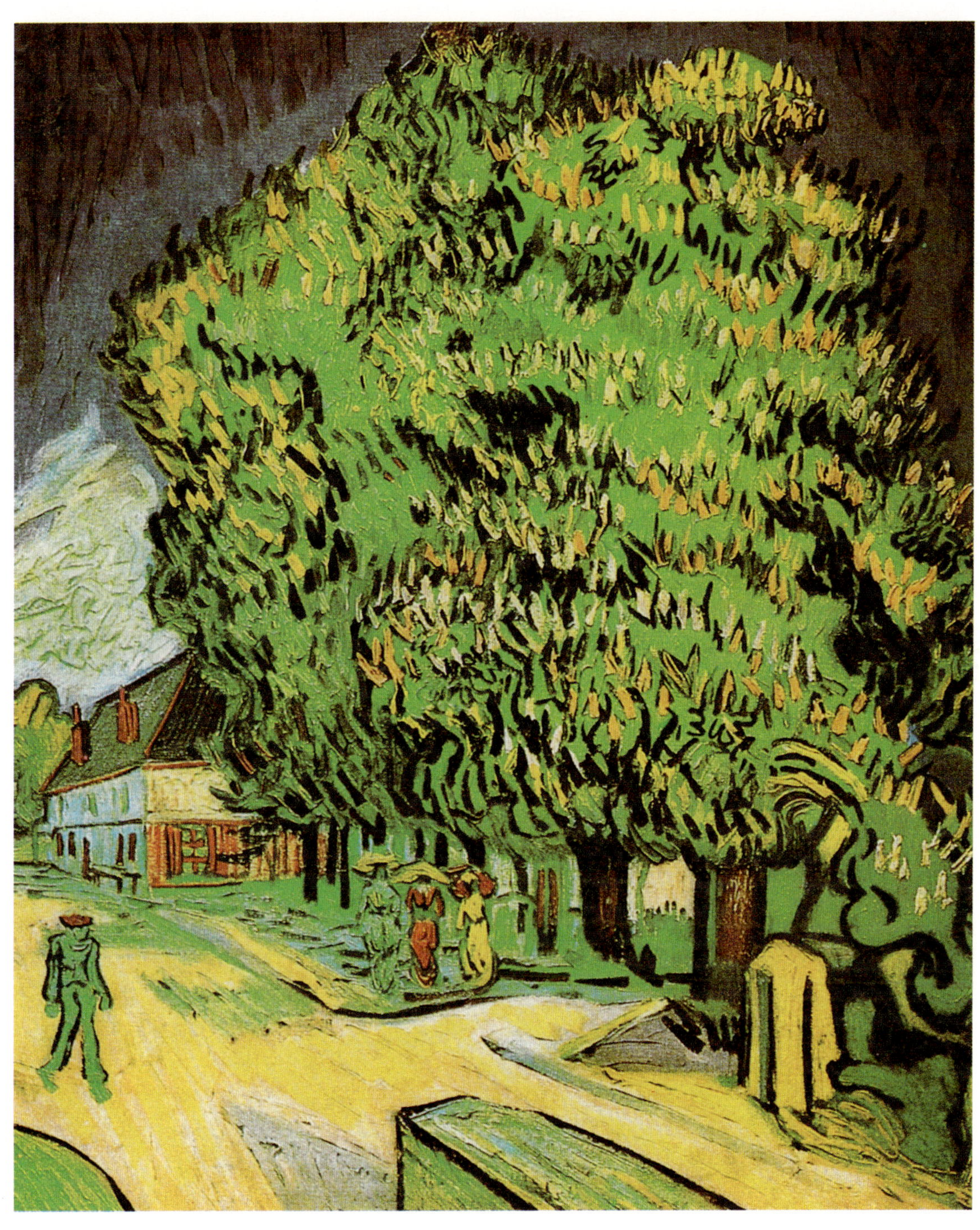

Chestnut Treees in Bloom

May 1890 - oil on canvas - 70 x 58 cm -
Private collection, South America

1890

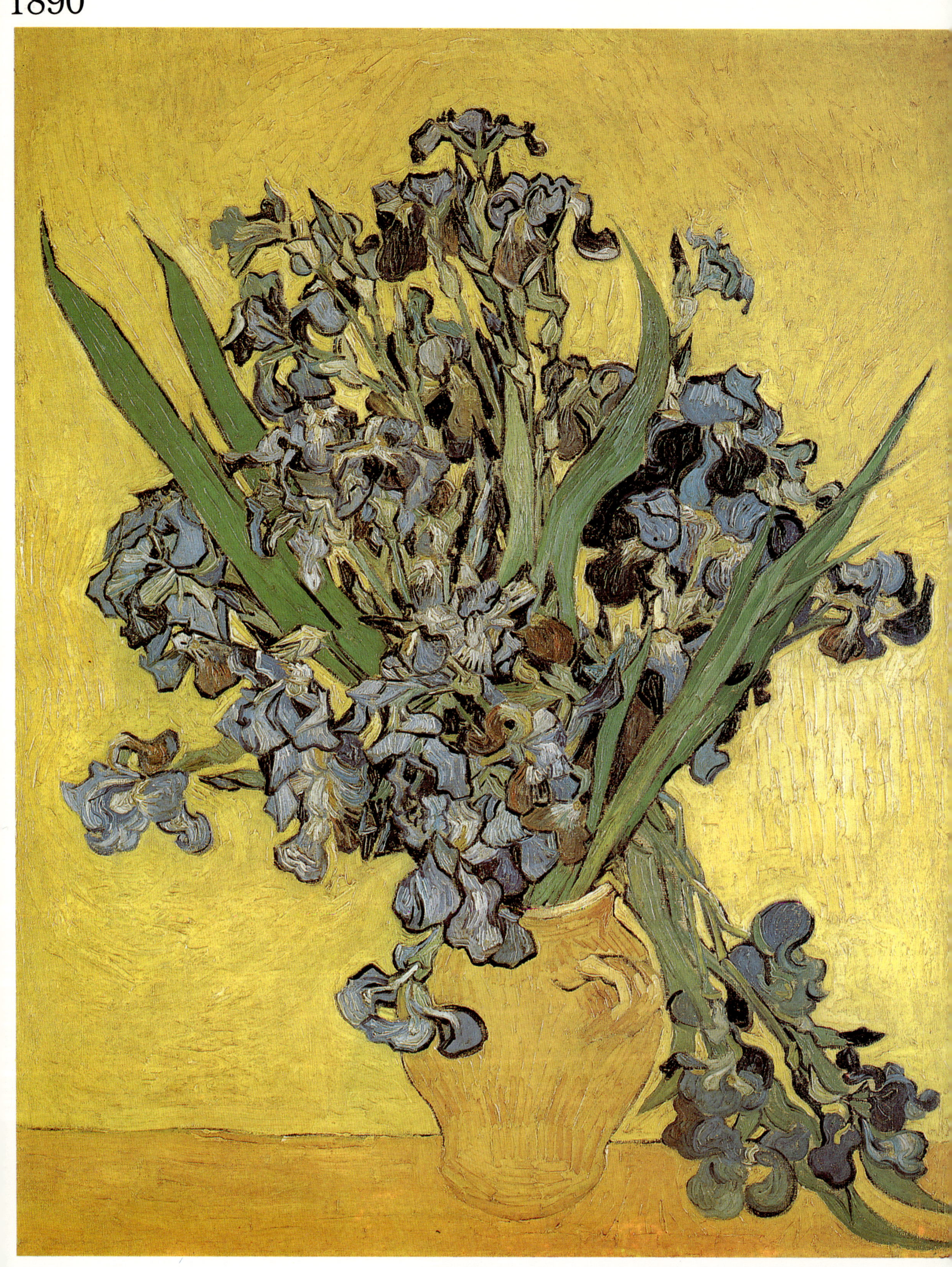

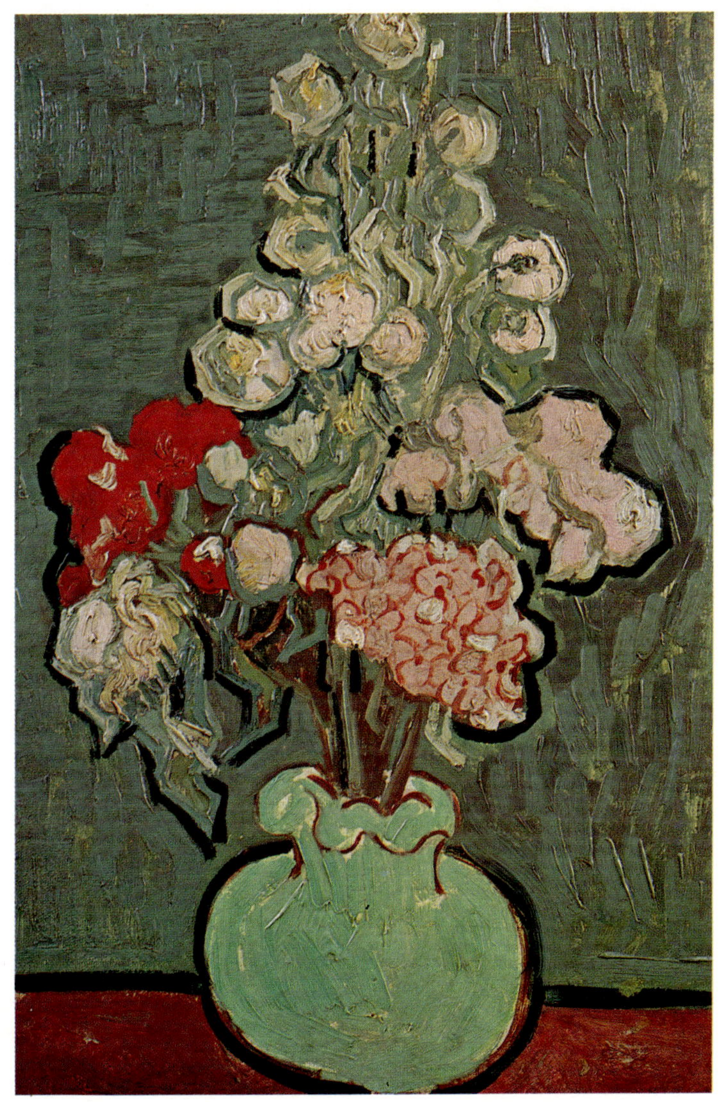

Small Vase with Flowers

May-July 1890 - oil on canvas - 41 x 28 cm - Vincent van Gogh Foundation, Amsterdam

Still Life: Irises

May 1890 - oil on canvas - 92 x 73.5 cm - Vincent van Gogh Foundation, Amsterdam

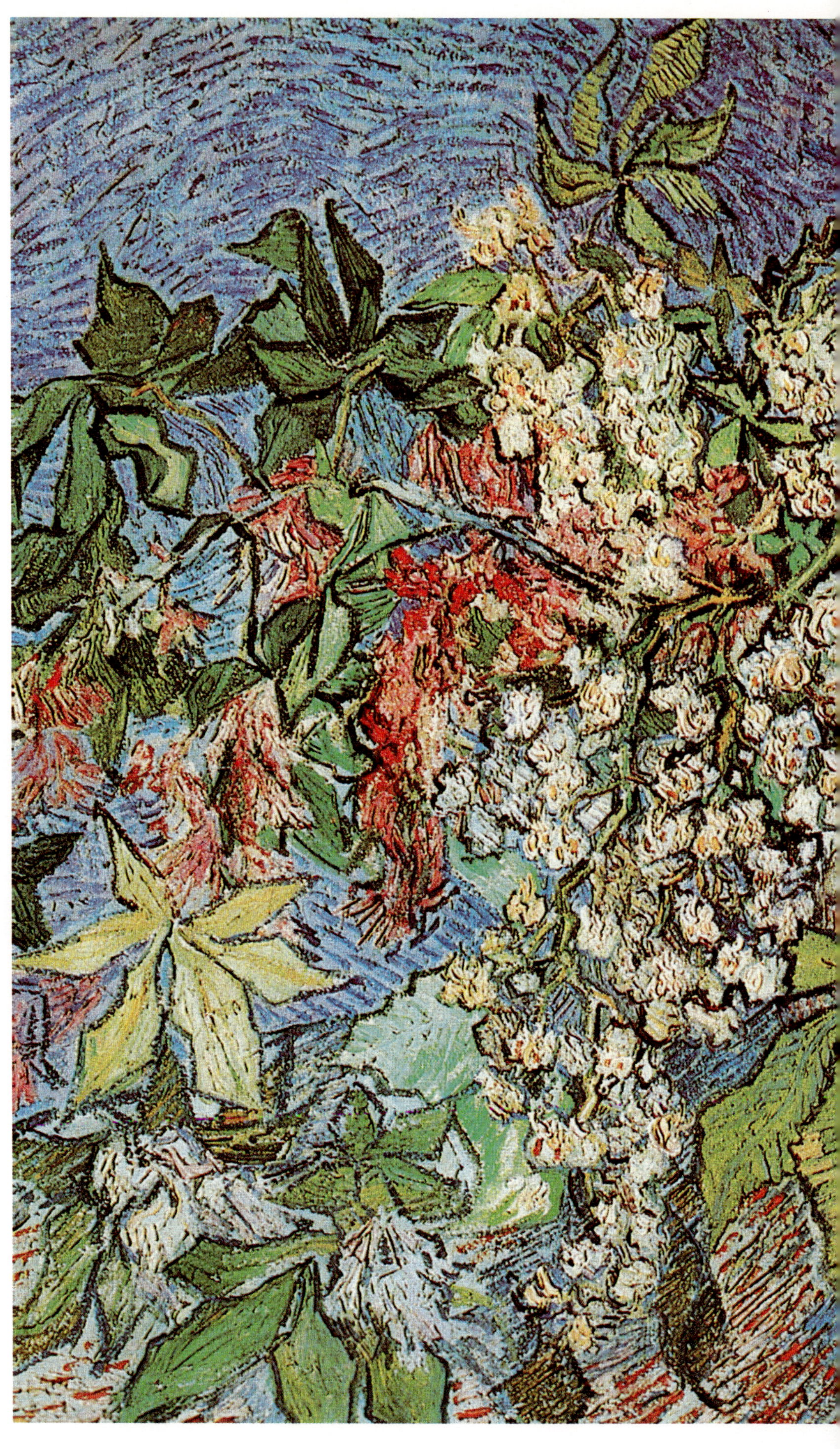

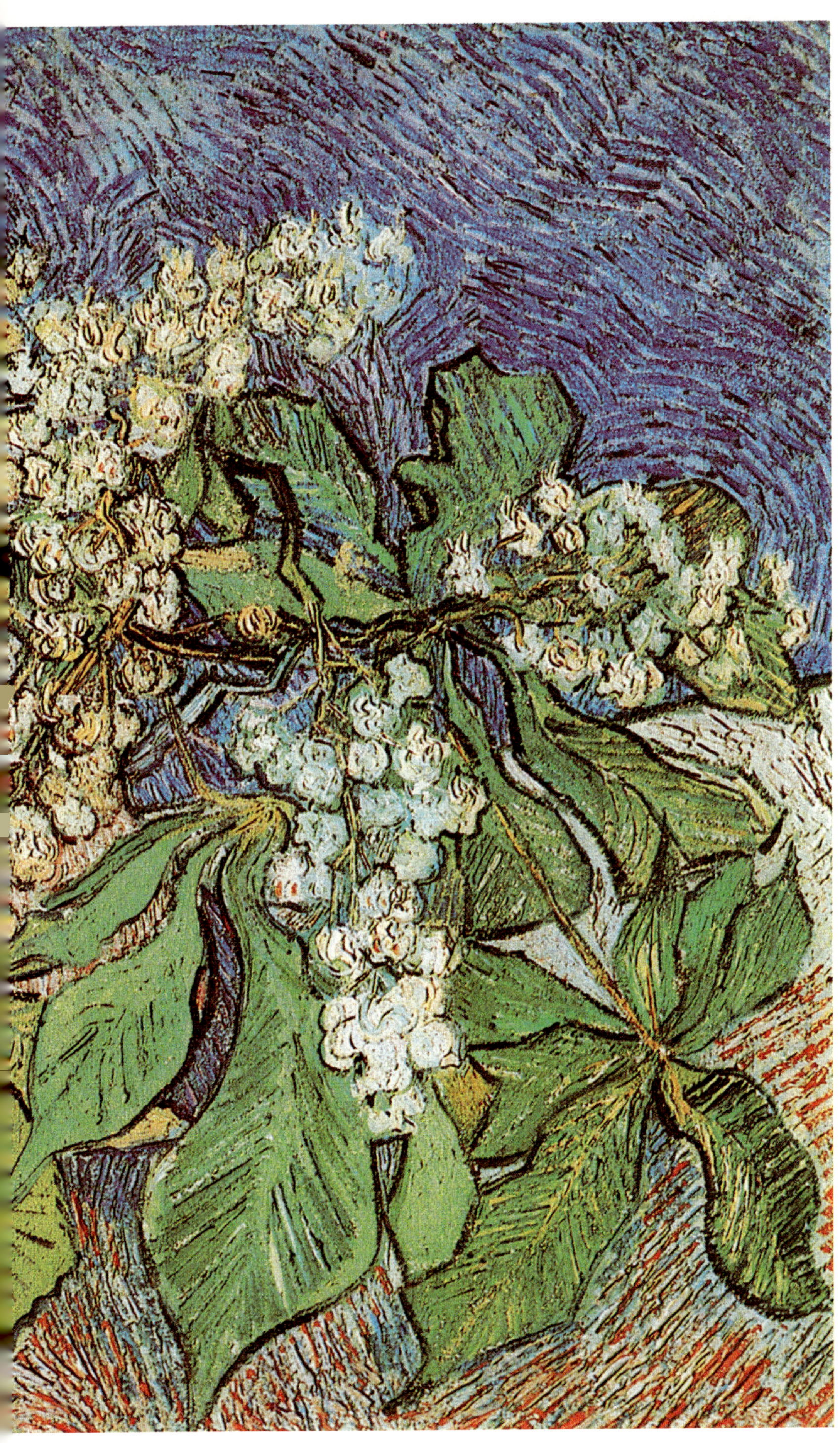

Blossoming Chestnut Branches

May 1890 - oil on canvas - 72 x 91 cm -
E.G. Bührle collection, Zurich

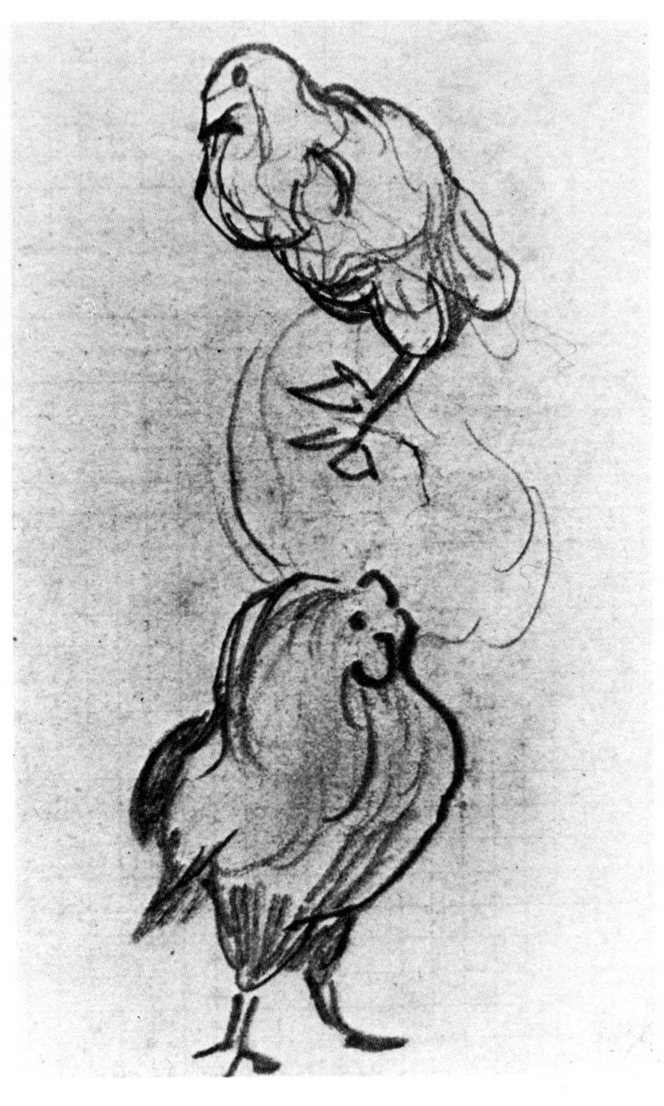

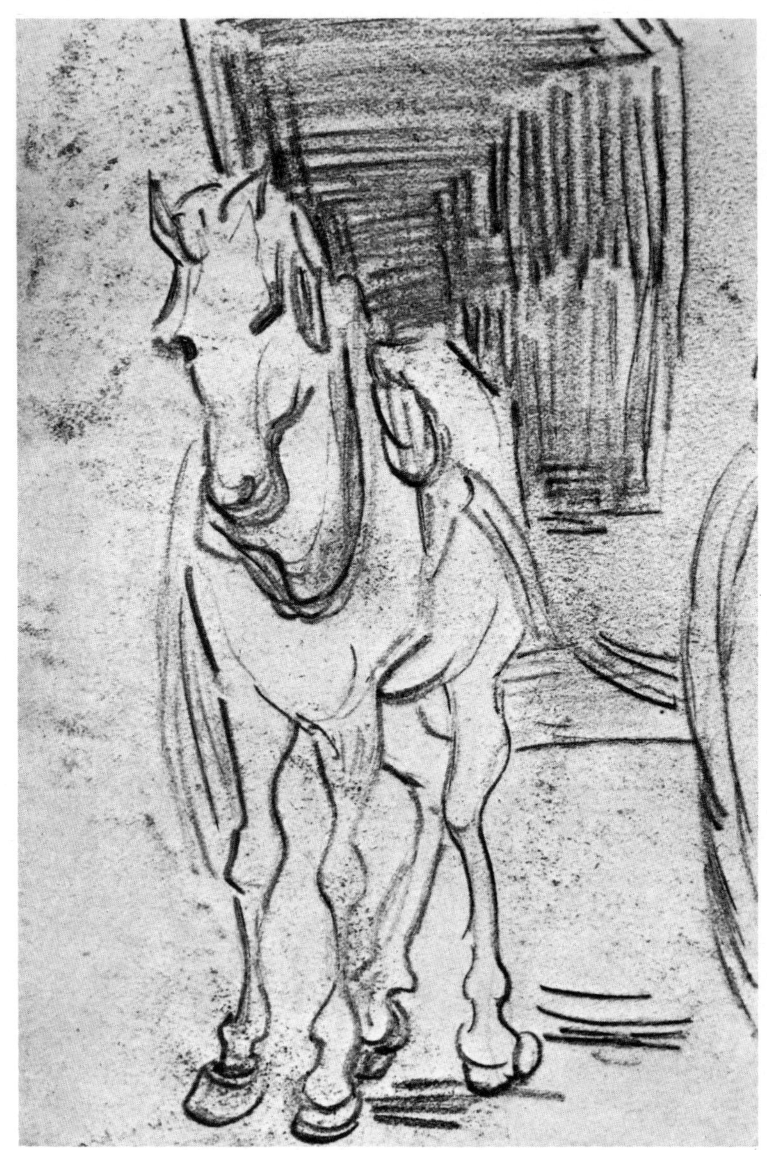

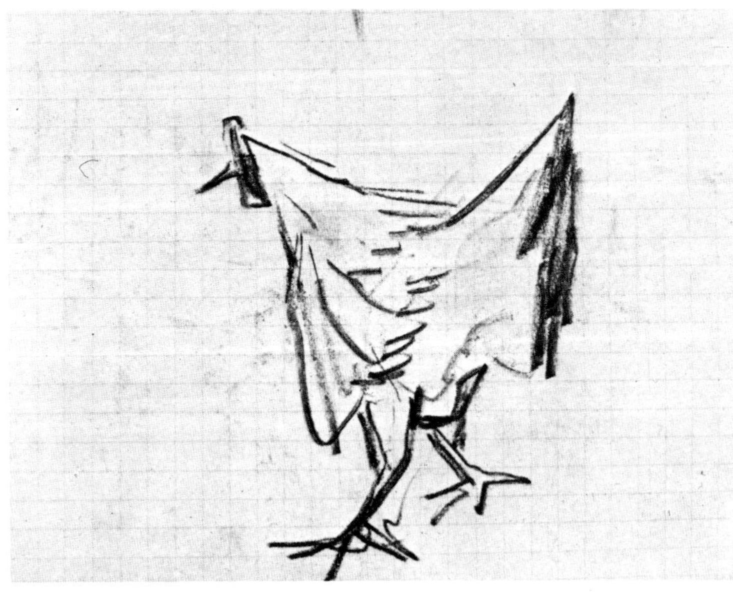

A Cock and a Hen

June 1890 - pencil - 33 x 13.3 cm -
Ed Buckman Collection, Richmond, Va.

Horse

June 1890 - pencil -13.3 x 33 cm -
Vincent van Gogh Foundation, Amsterdam

Hen

June 1890 - pencil - 34.5 x 25.5 cm -
Vincent van Gogh Foundation, Amsterdam

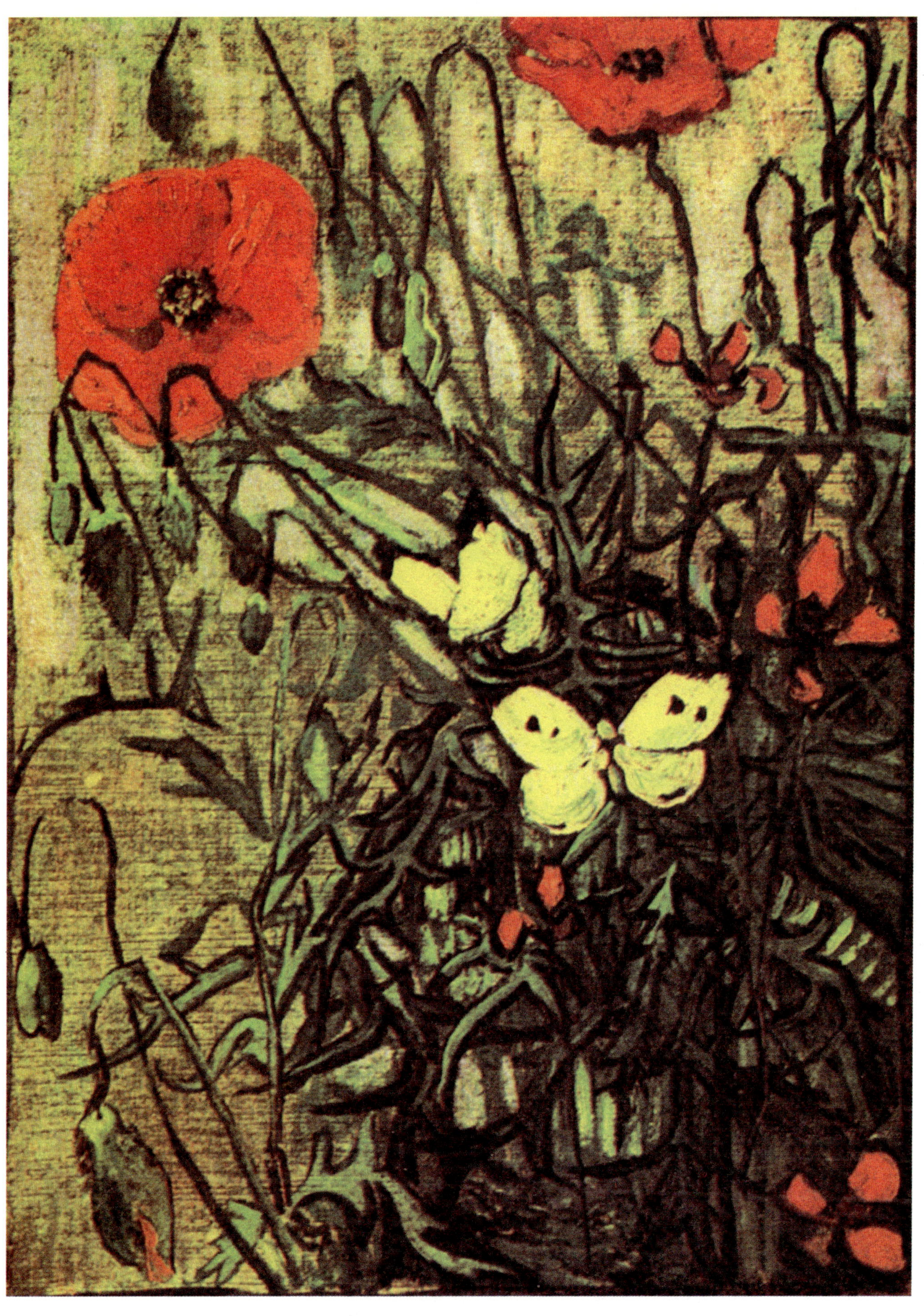

Poppies and Butterflies

April-May 1890 - oil on canvas -
Vincent van Gogh Foundation, Amsterdam

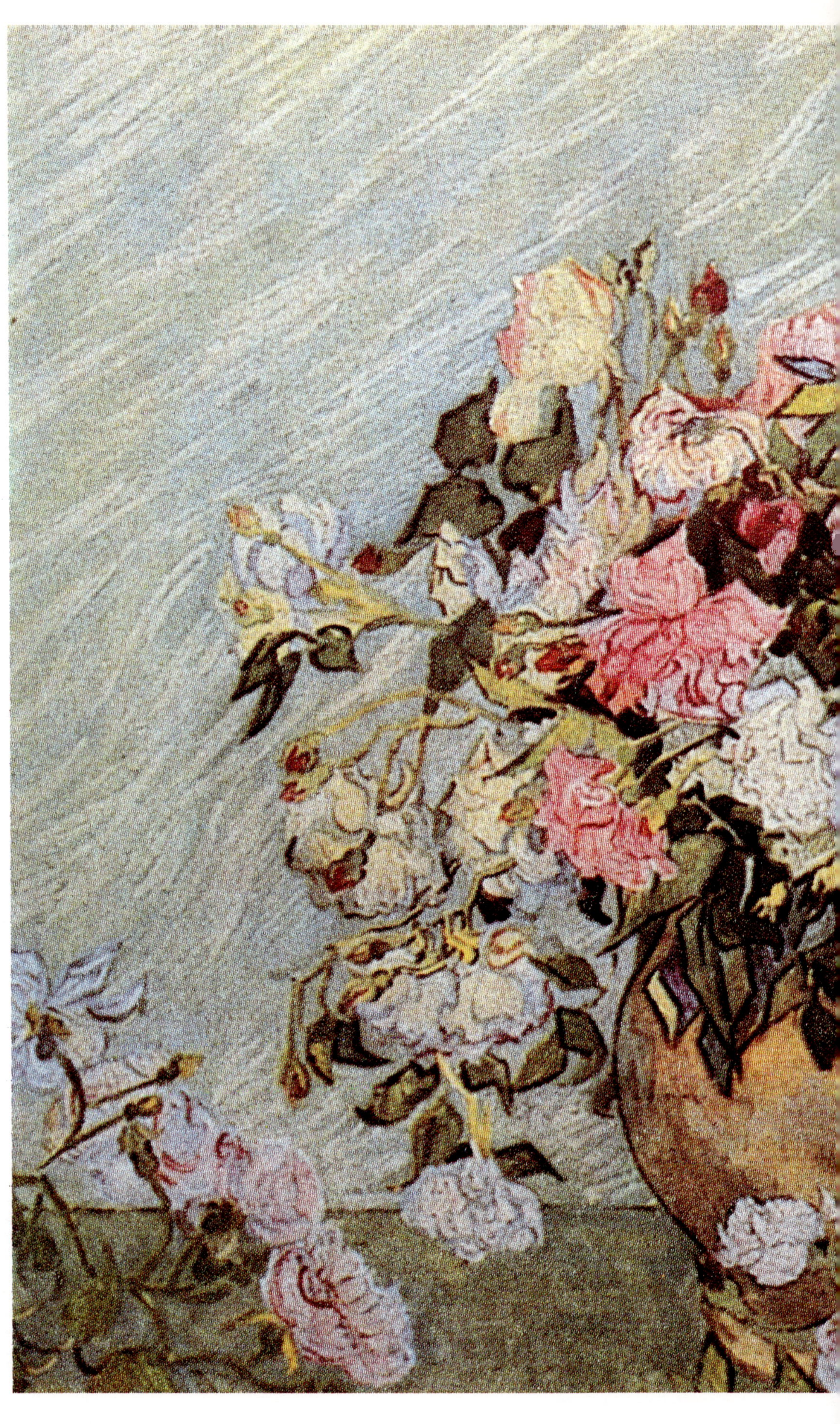

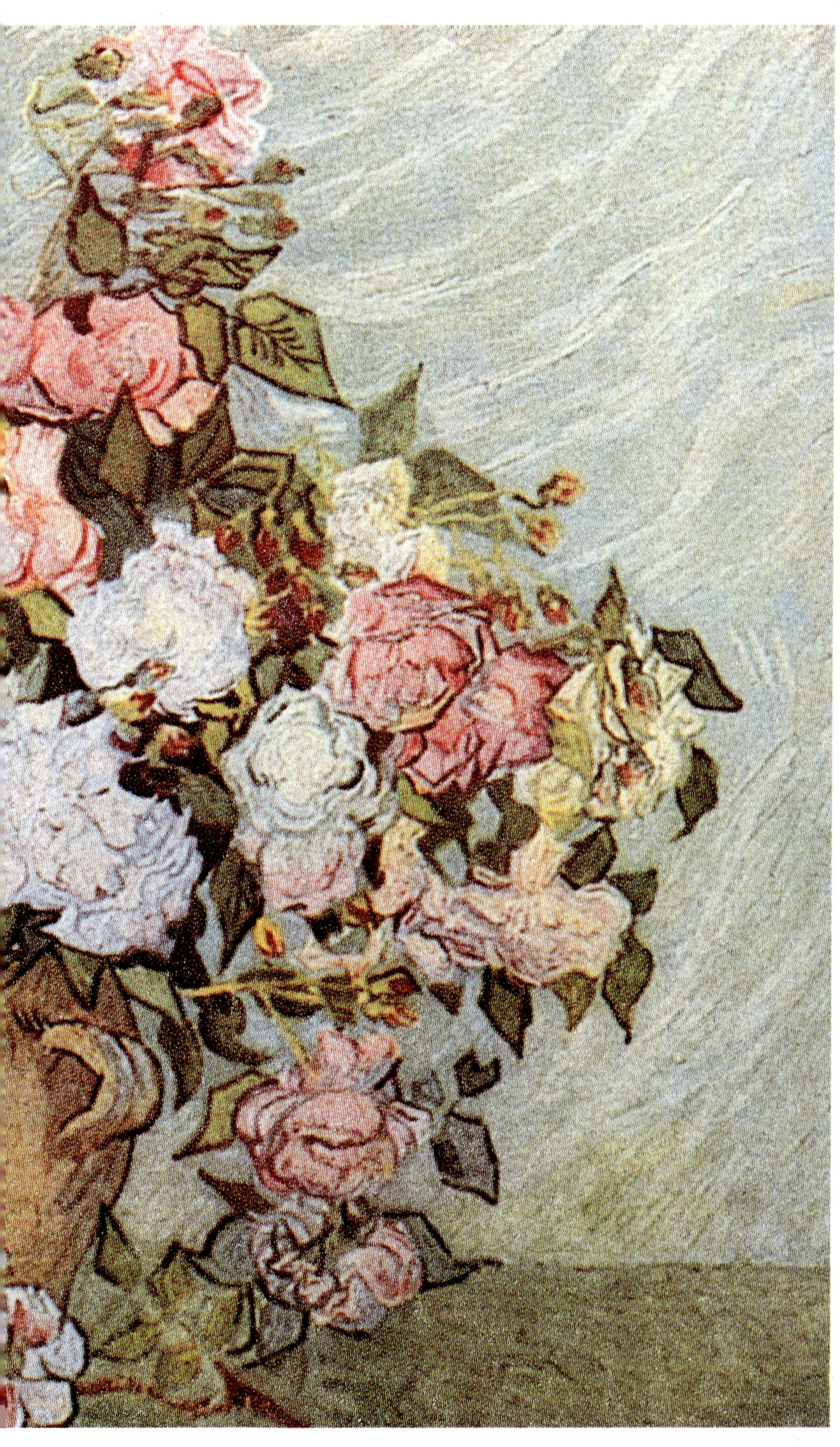

Vase with Roses

May 1890 - oil on canvas - 71 x 90 cm -
Pamela C. Averell Collection, New York

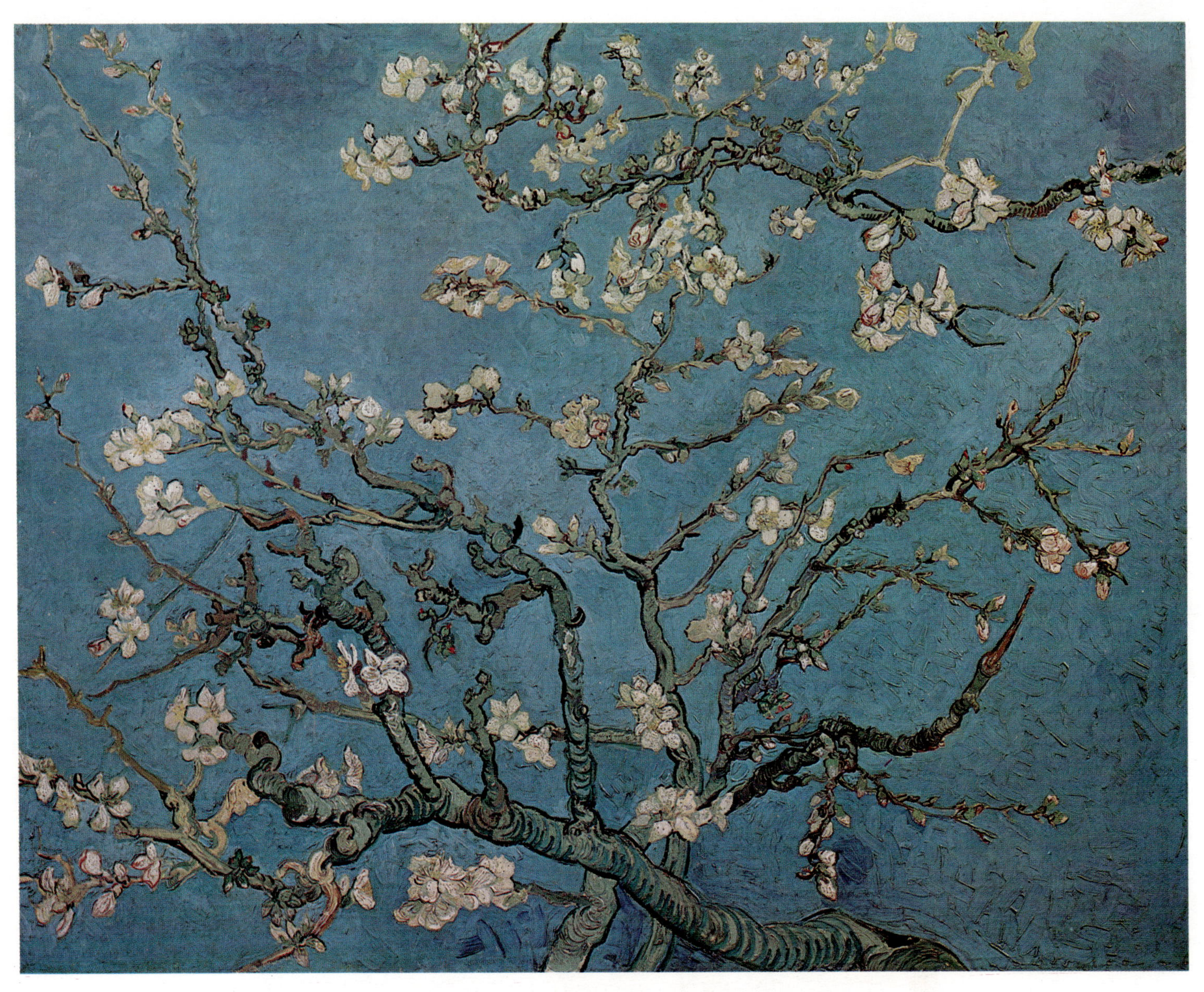

Blossoming Almond Tree

February 1890 - oil on canvas -73 x 92 cm -
Vincent van Gogh Foundation, Amsterdam

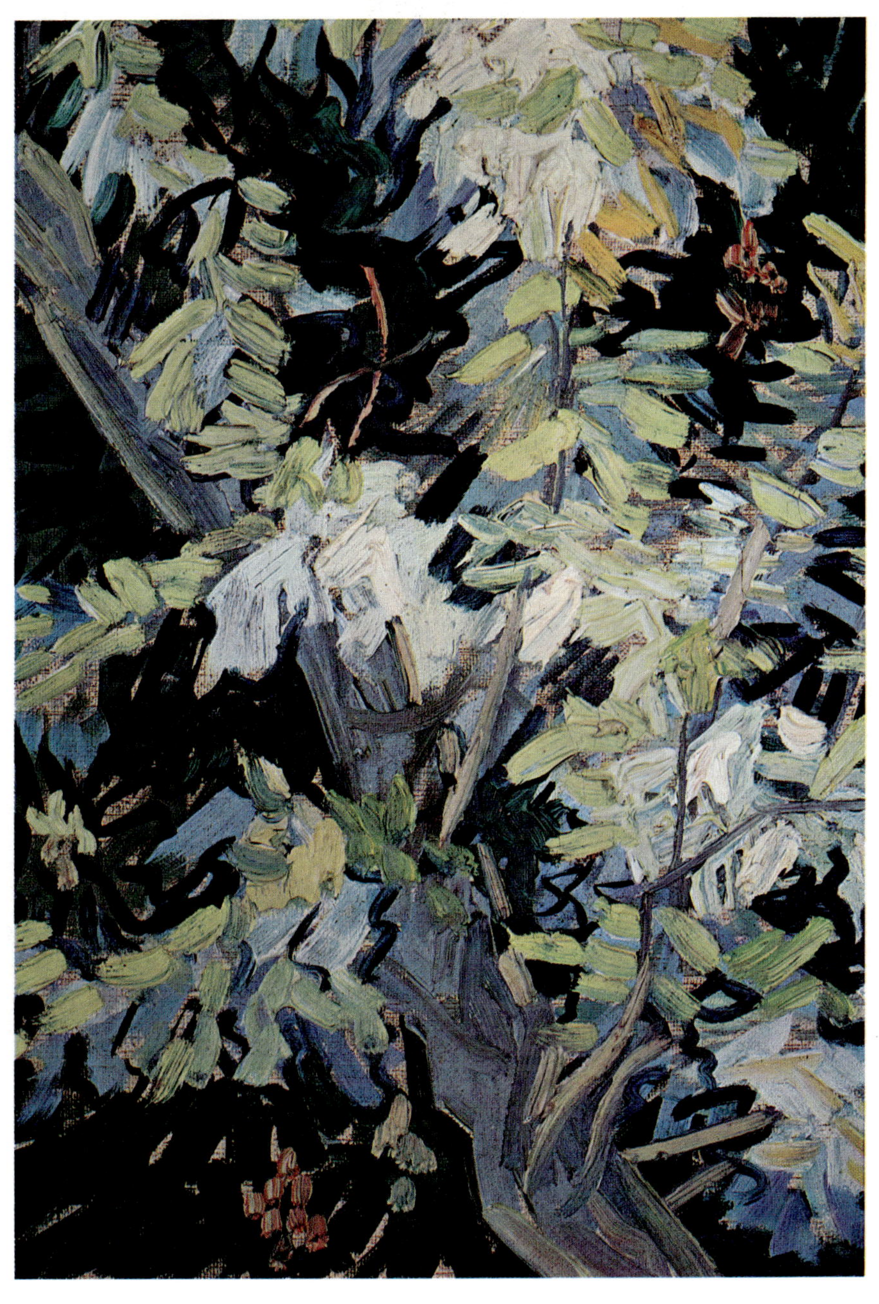

Flowers and Foliage

June 1890 - oil on canvas - 433.5 x 24.5 cm -
National Museum, Stockholm

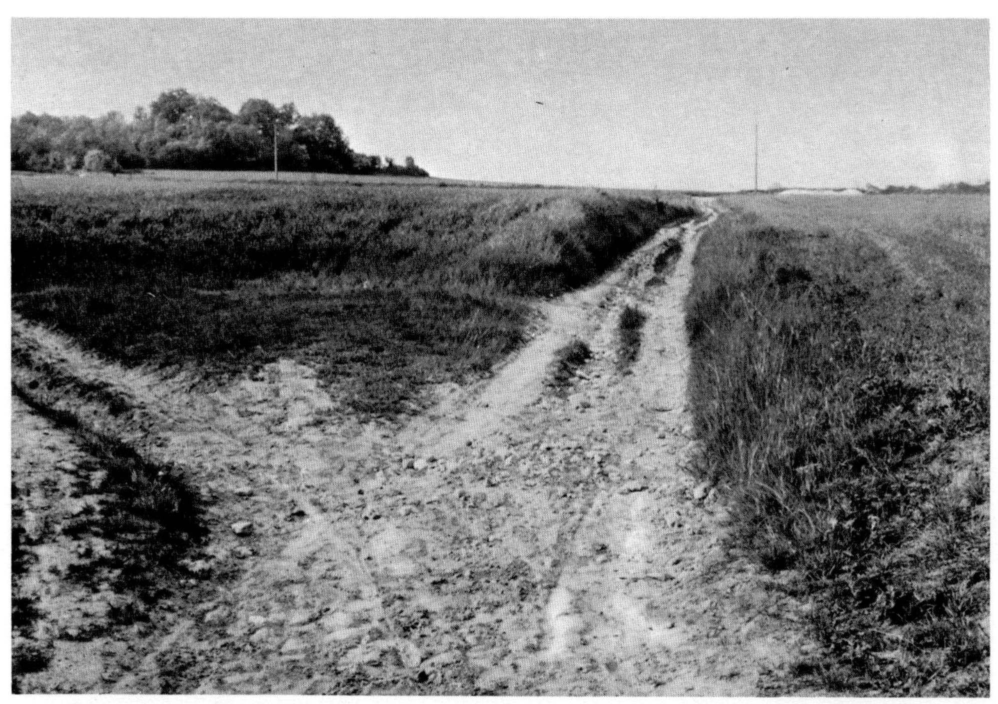

Photograph of the place where Vincent set up his easel to paint the wheat fields

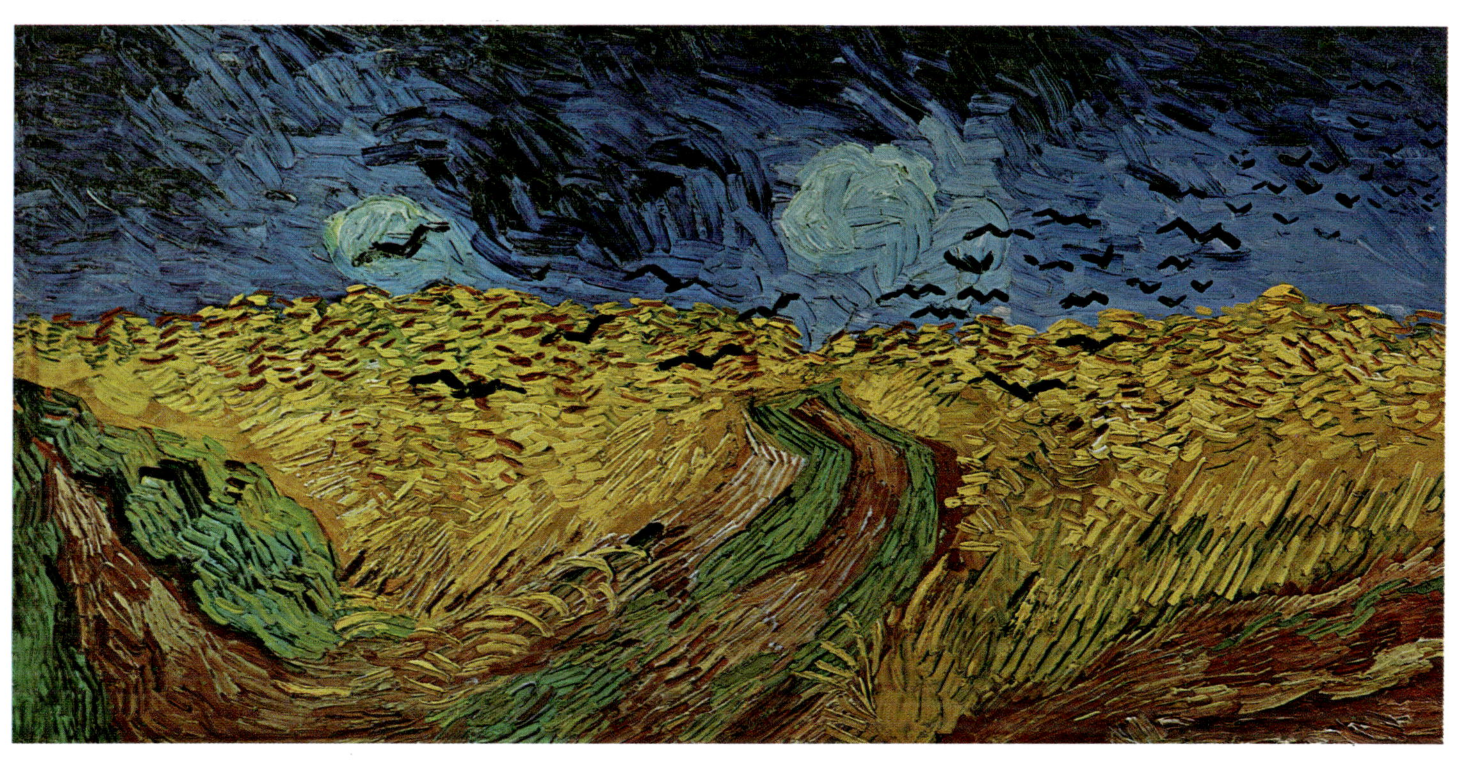

Wheat Field with Crows

July 1890 - oil on canvas - 50.5 x 100.5 cm -
Vincent van Gogh Foundation, Amsterdam

Typesetting : Perrissin-Fabert, Annecy
Separations : AAA Concept, Vernon
Manufacturing : P.P.O., Pantin, France